Patrick Boucheron is a French historian and broadcaster. He previously taught medieval history at the École normale supérieure and the University of Paris-Sorbonne, and is currently a professor of history at the Collège de France. He is the author of twelve books, including *Machiavelli: The Art of Teaching People What to Fear* (Pushkin, 2020), and the editor of five, including *France in the World*, which became a bestseller in France.

Stéphane Gerson is a cultural historian and a professor of French Studies at New York University. He has won several awards, including the Jacques Barzun Prize in Cultural History and the Laurence Wylie Prize in French Cultural Studies. He currently directs NYU's Institute of French Studies.

France
in the
World

GALLIC

EDITED BY

Patrick Boucheron

WITH
Nicolas Delalande
Florian Mazel
Yann Potin
Pierre Singaravélou

ENGLISH-LANGUAGE EDITION
EDITED BY

Stéphane Gerson

TRANSLATED FROM THE FRENCH BY
Teresa Lavender Fagan
Jane Kuntz
Alexis Pernsteiner
Anthony Roberts
Willard Wood

France in the World

A New Global

History

Gallic Books
London

A Gallic Book

Copyright © Éditions du Seuil, 2017
English translation copyright © Other Press, 2019
Originally published in 2017 as *Histoire mondiale de la France*
by Éditions du Seuil, Paris

This edition first published in 2021 by Gallic Books
12 Eccleston St, London SW1W 9LT

ISBN 9781913547011

Typeset in Fournier by Gallic Books
Printed in the UK by CPI (CR0 4YY)

EARLY STIRRINGS IN ONE CORNER
OF THE WORLD

FROM ONE EMPIRE TO ANOTHER

THE FEUDAL ORDER TRIUMPHS

FRANCE EXPANDS

THE GREAT MONARCHY OF THE WEST

ABSOLUTE POWER

ENLIGHTENMENT NATION

A HOMELAND FOR A UNIVERSAL REVOLUTION

GLOBALIZATION IN THE FRENCH STYLE

MODERNIZING IN TROUBLED TIMES

LEAVING THE COLONIAL EMPIRE, ENTERING EUROPE

TODAY IN FRANCE

PREFACE

TO THE ENGLISH-LANGUAGE EDITION
Stéphane Gerson

This is an urgent book.

The world in which we live is saturated with history — in reenactments, themed video games, cable shows, books about our national history (or at least some aspects of it). And yet, this public appetite is often fed by media-savvy journalists or politicians and ideologues whose fast-paced, anecdote-rich sentimental sagas meld fact and fiction while appealing to the emotions. Rarely do they engage with the past in a serious, critical manner. For this, for guidance on how to situate ourselves in an unstable world, we need historians — not only in our universities, but in the public realm as well.

In 1931, the president of the American Historical Association, Carl Becker, reminded his colleagues that their "proper function is not to repeat the past but to make use of it, to correct and rationalize for common use Mr. Everyman's mythological adaptation of what actually happened." In a more recent *History Manifesto* (2014), Jo

Guldi and David Armitage urged their fellow historians to explain large historical processes and small events in terms all of us can understand. This task, they said, should not be farmed out to economists and journalists. History has "a power to liberate" — from, for example, false notions about climate change or national destiny.

While some historians concur, others are reticent, or else too timid to write in a new key. Current attacks on truth and expert knowledge make this a pressing matter — and not just in the US. Consider France. For a long time, French historians were public intellectuals, making their voices heard in books, magazines, newspapers, and later on TV and radio. From Jules Michelet in the nineteenth century to Jacques Le Goff and Emmanuel Le Roy Ladurie after World War II, and later Michelle Perrot, historians rendered their craft topical and enthralling for a wide readership.

But things have changed in recent decades. Book sales have declined; the mass media have grown less welcoming; academic historians have been accused of writing a convoluted history, neglecting chronology, and in some cases not loving their country enough. Journalists, essayists, and even film actors have filled this void in recent years, appointing themselves curators of the *roman national*, a national narrative with which French citizens can identify. The mournful, nostalgic story they typically tell is one of loss and decline, in which national identity must battle immigration, multiculturalism, Islam, feminism, and "declining" school standards. Salvation rests upon a return to imagined origins.

In 2017, a collective of French historians responded to these developments by publishing a non-nationalist history of the nation. *Histoire mondiale de la France*, or *France in the World: A New Global History*, makes a deceptively strong statement: historians have a distinctive contribution to make to our public debates and collective self-understanding. The book was an instant success, "the literary phenomenon of the year" (in the words of one newsmagazine), with more than 110,000 copies sold. In newspapers and magazines, on TV and radio, commentators celebrated a work that, as one of them put it, "is good news for those among us who yearn for new pathways into the past of our dear old country." Fellow historians agreed, lauding an "immense collection of knowledge and analysis" whose wide-ranging curiosity made it, they said, an "enemy of the tragic." In other countries, *France in the World* provided a blueprint for histories that, while investigating the past, unravel contemporary notions we deem self-evident. Similar global histories of Italy, the Netherlands, Catalonia, Flanders, and Spain quickly followed — or will in the near future.

The book's lead editor, Patrick Boucheron, is a specialist in late-medieval Italian history, a professor at the prestigious Collège de France, and the editor of, among other books,

Histoire du monde au XVe siècle (History of the World in the Fifteenth Century). He also belongs to a generation of French historians who seek to recover the public role, the civic engagement of their predecessors — not as grand intellectuals who, like Jean-Paul Sartre, share their views on all issues, but rather as measured commentators who bring their expertise to bear on specific questions. In order to reach a broader readership, these historians are consulting on historical TV shows, participating in theater festivals, and writing threads about history on Twitter. They are also experimenting with graphic novels, memoirs, and other unconventional forms of historical writing.

France in the World is one such experiment, bold in its scope and its commitment to scholarship coupled with freedom and formal creativity. Patrick Boucheron and his four coeditors made several key decisions at the outset. They organized the book as a series of essays about 146 dates in the history of France, each one distilling the latest scholarship while avoiding jargon and footnotes. Ranging from 34,000 BCE to 2015, these essays either explore turning points, such as Charlemagne's coronation in 800 or the May 1968 civil unrest, or else delve into less momentous yet still telling events, such as the draining of a Languedoc pond in 1247. "Some rare events are like glimmers of light in the darkness," Antony Hostein writes in his essay on Gauls in the Roman Senate (48 CE). "Illuminated by a few extraordinary accounts telling of singular lives and exploits, they reveal truly significant historical occurrences."

The editors invited dozens of historians to write these essays, and few turned them down. The members of this collective represent a multitude of historical specialties, from the Middle Ages to the contemporary era, archaeology to technology, law to finance, gender to cinema. The book thus invites readers to learn about states, wars, expeditions, and peace treaties, as we would expect, but also about diseases and penal colonies, canals and promenades, fashion and perfume, museums and best sellers, swindles and engineering feats. Generals and politicians, aristocrats and bureaucrats comingle with cave dwellers and textile traders, novelists and feminists, soccer players and philosophers, vagrants and immigrants, all of them protagonists in a variegated history.

The editors provided the contributors with considerable latitude, inviting them to select their own points of departure. History does not correspond to a single outlook, an all-knowing stance, pinpointing truth from its lofty heights. Instead, these multiple perspectives make it clear that the past becomes history through the questions we pose and the methods we fashion. "[I]t is not historical material that shapes interpretations," Pierre Monnet writes in his essay on the 1214 Battle of Bouvines, "but rather the historian's questions that shape historical material. And these questions are far from exhausted." *France in the World* opens up the historian's workshop, drawing attention to craft and sources, to doubts and choices and the debates that advance knowledge.

The editors also urged the contributors to embrace a free, welcoming language, to avail themselves of "all the resources of storytelling, of analysis, contextualization, exemplification." Patrick Boucheron has long pushed his fellow historians toward "audacity and creativity and perhaps also greater confidence in the powers of language." Literary, even poetic historical writing opens up common language by unsettling what seems familiar and breathing life into "the textures of the past." And so, the essays in *France in the World* take different forms: narrative descriptions, direct addresses to the reader, slightly ironic glosses, political asides on the past and the present.

I want to emphasize the plural — resources, powers, contours of language — for the editors grant us — the readers — as much freedom and, therefore, as much trust and responsibility as they do the contributors. They encourage us to trace our own itineraries across the past, to read diagonally through time and the conventional periods that govern our vision of history. Begin at the beginning, or in the middle if you prefer, and see where you end up. By neglecting key dates (say, the 1916 Battle of Verdun) and adding others that may seem inconsequential, by

PREFACE

granting the same number of words to Coco Chanel as to
Charlemagne, they are telling us that all planes of history
are equally revealing, that all historical actors deserve
attention. Hierarchies exist, of course, but do not expect
to find one ready-made in this book. It falls upon us, as
attentive readers and critical thinkers, to create meaning out
of the apparent chaos of history.

France in the World is thus a political book if one
understands politics not as the partisan reading of evidence
or the explicit embrace of party positions, but instead as
the deployment of reason against despair. The book is also
political in its central question: What does it mean to belong
to a nation in our globalized yet nationalistic world?

This question carried particular resonance during the
book's gestation in 2015 and 2016 — so much so that *France
in the World* may already be read as a historical artifact, a
trace of the contemporary past, a source for future histories
of our troubled times. France's annus horribilis of 2015
began with terrorist attacks in several Parisian locations,
including the offices of the satirical weekly *Charlie Hebdo*
and a kosher grocery store, and ended with yet bloodier
assaults on the Bataclan concert hall and other targets. On
January 11, dozens of heads of state traveled to Paris to
reaffirm their commitment to political values — the rights
of man, freedom of expression — that have long been linked
to France. This gathering raised a new set of questions:

Does France still live up to these ideals? What exactly does the country represent nowadays? What do the French want it to represent at this complicated juncture in the country's history?

After all, the former global power has seen its stature and its political ambitions wither over the past century. France and its allies won World War I thanks to a US military intervention that forever altered the transatlantic balance of power. In 1940, the French Army's debacle cost the country more than its honor and its republic: an authoritarian regime in Vichy collaborated with Hitler and persecuted Jews and others. A second US rescue followed in 1944, ushering in a bipolar world that, combined with anticolonial insurrections and military defeats in Indochina and Algeria, shrank France's global presence. In the 1950s and 1960s, the construction of a unified Europe on a French model and new technologies such as the Concorde jet would reassure the French that they still mattered in the world. But the economic crisis that began in the 1970s deepened doubts about something more elemental: the French welfare state's ability to ensure social justice in an increasingly neocapitalist world. As growth slowed, high unemployment became an enduring reality, especially for women, young people, and immigrants. The labor market turned increasingly toward part-time, temporary, and unskilled employment with scant prospects for job security or social benefits. Growing segments of the population felt less secure in their positions in society. A 2006 poll found that half of the population feared losing their home one day. Sociologist Robert Castel gave a name to these feelings of uncertainty, fear, and isolation: "disaffiliation."

Should we be surprised, then, that so much of the recent public debate in France has revolved around national history, as if the past could renew collective *filiation*? To fully understand this latest nation-talk, we should return to the early nineteenth-century view of national history as "a kind of common property . . . for all the inhabitants of the same country" (Romantic historian Augustin Thierry). We should examine the national school curriculum that, from the 1880s on, turned the likes of Gaul chieftain Vercingetorix into heroic actors of the national narrative. We should also listen to the critical voices that, in the second half of the twentieth century, requested a less parochial approach to national history — with mixed success if one considers the curriculum's longtime neglect of immigration, its renewed emphasis on assimilation in the 1970s, and its difficulties reckoning with French colonial violence. When it comes to slavery and its demise in the French Caribbean, pupils have learned more about French abolitionists such as Victor Schœlcher than about their country's brutality or the ways in which colonized subjects fought for their own emancipation.

To understand the current nation-talk, we must finally recall that, since the 1980s, the French right, the extreme right National Front, and some die-hard *républicains* have promulgated a closed notion of national identity. The presidency of Nicolas Sarkozy (2007–2012) looms large, with its embrace of a history rooted in an immemorial past, a history in which the Gauls constitute the sole ancestors of all French citizens, regardless of their geographic origins. The title of Sarkozy's new Ministry of Immigration, Integration, National Identity, and Co-Development left little to the imagination. During the past decade, the aftereffects of the Great Recession, the arrival of migrants and refugees, the circulation of workers across the EU, and the radicalization of certain Muslim Europeans have galvanized nostalgia for an eternal, exceptional spirit — true France.

Convinced that neglect of this spirit is accelerating their nation's undoing, some French ideologues insist that the only way to reconcile the French with one another is to defend their vision of the country's history. Right-wing and extreme-right candidates sang the same tune during the 2017 French presidential campaign. "To be French is to feel at home in an epic in which everything flows together," declared Sarkozy's former prime minister François Fillon. "With our homeland desperately thirsting for meaning, with the threat of internal division looming, shouldn't our schools impart the story of the nation?" And with the British choosing Brexit in June 2016, Trump's victory months later, and Marine Le Pen leading many polls in 2017, France's own political future seemed as uncertain, potentially, as those of its allies.

The editorial collective behind *France in the World* deemed it imperative to tell a story about the nation that refuted this panicked recourse to ethnic categories, this rush to enclose, separate, contain, and delimit what properly belongs within French history. Following the January 2015 attacks, Patrick Boucheron and writer Mathieu Riboulet spelled out the specific interventions historians could make in the current climate: puncture slogans and symbols (such as the "Marseillaise"), define the principles worth defending, stimulate understanding by describing people and historical situations with precision and beauty, and write an open, generous, inclusive history.

The book's focus on the nation thus owed much to tactical considerations and political conviction. On the one hand, it enabled historians (and certain segments of the left) to regain their public voice, to intervene in a debate that had sidelined them. On the other hand, it tapped into and bolstered history's ability to weaken habits of obedience and belonging, inviting readers to imagine alternative horizons. In dialogue with Nietzsche and Michel Foucault, Boucheron has insisted that the historian's primary responsibility is to institute *discontinuity*. "Even in the historical realm, to know is not to 'recover' and especially not to 'find oneself.' History is 'effective' to the extent that it introduces *discontinuity* within our very being."

Accordingly, *France in the World* disrupts the seemingly natural, exhaustive order of chronology. By inviting us to slow down as we read, to take a step sideways or even a detour in order to *see* something else, it draws us into the accidental and sometimes imperceptible movement of historical time. By unmooring political myths that have taken shape over the centuries, most notably in the works of nineteenth-century historians, this critical book also opens dialogues between historical eras. Contrary to the national narrative, the 843 Treaty of Verdun did not distinguish what would become Romance-speaking "France" from German-speaking lands; this is a "projection onto the past" of modern nationalism. Countless other myths are laid bare in *France in the World*: among them, Marseille founded by Greeks who civilized "savages" in 600 BCE; Charles Martel stopping the "Arabs" at the Battle of Poitiers in 732; and the Gaullist Resistance to Hitler emerging in London alone (rather than in France's African colonies). All have been fashioned at specific historical moments, following procedures that require elucidation — *demythification*.

Discontinuity also shapes *France in the World*'s relationship to space. This decentered history moves between the city and the region, the nation and the continent, or rather the various nations and continents of our planet. The familiar expanses of mainland France are visible in the essays: mountains and rivers, coastlines and

30

vineyards, Paris and Versailles, Flanders and the Riviera. But France as it is rendered here remains open to the world, its borders permeable. The contributors connect the country and its residents to Carthage and Siam, Scandinavia and the Middle East, Algiers and New Caledonia, Rome and New York City.

In this regard, *France in the World* recognizes, along with a growing number of historians, that nation-states are embedded within networks, connections, interdependencies that range far and wide. Global history has come into its own these past two decades, in a world that, given the fall of the Berlin Wall, shared environmental challenges, and the acceleration of technological innovation and capitalist exchanges, is increasingly interrelated. Scholars have examined the circulations and power dynamics that have shaped the Atlantic world across several continents. Drawing from postcolonial criticism, they have rejected the assumption that European ideas and processes are necessarily embraced or replicated elsewhere. Seeking out the visible or hidden threads that connect peoples and regions across national borders, they have followed flows of people and goods, of cultural horizons and political designs.

France in the World hence displays affinities with transnational or "connected" history. We detect in this volume the same attention to minute yet meaningful interactions and relationships; the same curiosity for both non-Western and Western perspectives; and the same comingling of temporalities and geographical scales. There is the same desire to understand, not just abstract economic or social forces, but the ways that individuals of various social stations have understood, experienced, and shaped their "lived world."

In this domain as in others, the editors refrain from imposing a single framework, thereby freeing the contributors to write this history of France in the world as they see fit. Some essays explore French relationships to globalization, from technological embrace (the Suez Canal in 1869) to economic doubts (the 1992 referendum on European unification). Others juxtapose developments taking place in different lands, or else follow the circulation in and out of "France" of legal codes, consumer products, texts (the Quran), political programs (feminism), and architectural styles. Yet others scrutinize French notions of universalism and national genius. France's imperial and colonial presence surfaces in numerous essays. Embracing an increasingly prevalent view of the country as a longtime empire-state, *France in the World* pays as much attention to the colonizers' governance and their violence as it does to the culture and politics of formerly enslaved people, subjects, and independence fighters.

This book stands out, moreover, because, despite recent advances, France has relatively few journals, academic chairs, programs, and research centers devoted to global history. Is it because of French distrust of intellectual frameworks that seem to originate in the English-speaking world and might thus represent a form of US soft power, spreading neoliberalism? Is it because new historical labels such as "world" or "global" history have seemed superfluous in a country where eminent French scholars have long looked beyond national borders (Fernand Braudel, Pierre Chaunu) while colonized or postcolonial writers penned penetrating analyses of racial politics (Aimé Césaire, Leïla Sebbar, Abdelmalek Sayad)? Patrick Boucheron has suggested that the complex ideological legacy of Braudel's "grammar of civilizations," which gives little consideration to change or contacts between world cultures, prevented French scholars from fully embracing global history. Institutional factors may have come into play as well. Small, selective centers of research and higher learning such as the National Center for Scientific Research (CNRS) and the École des Hautes Études en Sciences Sociales have the means and flexibility to put disciplines into conversation with one another while training faculty in new methodologies and languages. The situation is more complicated, however, in most public universities, with their threadbare budgets, operating deficits, heavy bureaucracy, overflowing classrooms, and high faculty workloads.

We must, finally, consider the impact of a French

republican ideology that defines citizenship in purely political terms, entertaining the legal fiction that citizens and the nation are abstractions, divorced from race, ethnicity, or sexuality. Since the French Revolution, one has in theory been French before being Protestant, Jewish, an Italian immigrant, homosexual, a black woman. The Vichy regime's racial and ethnic record-keeping exacerbated the taboo surrounding the political uses of such categories. While subnational identities are not completely suppressed in France today, their public expression remains problematic. As the political philosopher Elsa Dorlin recently explained, French scholars still must justify their attention to race or ethnicity as contributing factors behind social inequality. They must make it clear that they are not contesting their republic's understanding of citizenship and color blindness. How then, asks legal scholar Mathilde Cohen, "can one study and make sense of what appears to be largely unspoken and unspeakable?"

Debates over the pertinence and even the legality of racial or ethnic categories in law, official statistics, scholarship, and public discourse are far from exhausted in the French Republic. And yet, there are signs of change within nation-talk. A growing number of scholars reject the notion that racial or ethnic inequalities result from socioeconomic domination alone; they also insist that shunning notions like *race* stymies efforts to contain racism. Theatrical troupes like We Will Never Give Up Hope (NAJE, in the Parisian suburb of Antony) dramatize pressing questions like migration in order to generate "social transformation." The National Museum on the History of Immigration (founded in 2007) tells visitors that "adaptation, borrowings, and mixings" are central to France's national heritage. In 2018, the television channel Arte aired *Le rêve français* (The French Dream), a miniseries about residents of Guadeloupe and Réunion Island who were brought to metropolitan France from the 1960s on and pushed toward low-wage jobs. Seldom has this story been told. "This is a movie about national identity," explained one of its producers. "We have sought to free up language in order to enable people to recapture their history."

France in the World thus represents one of many forces that, within French civil society, seek to free up language (about the nation and the world, the present and the past) in order to enable people to recapture meaningful yet sometimes silenced histories. More resolutely than others, perhaps, this collection marries critical clarity with hope. Annie Jourdan sets the tone in her essay on 1789, speaking of an "internal conflict . . . between the resolve to emancipate people across Europe and the temptation to turn inward." Read the essays on 1790, 1927, or 1974 to watch French institutional and cultural forces stymie hospitality. At the same time, recall that the Hungarian-born Saint

Martin (397), the foreign corsairs and privateers of Dunkirk (1662), the Kanaks who fought either for or against France in 1917, and many other "foreigners" all shaped a national space in which, as Alain de Libera puts it in his essay on the medieval University of Paris, "different origins and identities gathered, clashed, and fused" (1215). One can be French and also Spanish or Tunisian. One can espouse several identities at once. This has happened before; new forms of diversity do not threaten France; the country is not waging an internal battle against new barbarians. There are other stories worth telling besides national decline. In France today, this needs to be said.

Others concurred at the time of publication: The newsweekly *L'Obs* praised *France in the World* as an "antidote to all national pseudo-identities"; the daily *Libération* applauded it for "refuting the idea of a rigid, solemn, teleological history that leads to nationalism alone"; the magazine *Témoignage chrétien* commended it for showing that French history "is before all the history of the French in their plurality and mobility." Emmanuel Macron confessed to reading the collection with pleasure and rejected, during his presidential campaign, the notion of a fixed national identity: "The French national project has never been sealed off from the world," he declared.

It must be said, however, that Macron the candidate also paid homage to the mythic Joan of Arc and advocated the teaching of "a national narrative," and also that, in the midst of the Yellow Vest protests in the winter of 2018–2019, Macron the president called for a national agreement on France's "deep-seated identity," a question he linked to immigration. Beyond such rhetorical contradictions, the more reactionary champions of this national narrative have denounced *France in the World* in pointed language. In its narrowest terms, the polemics revolved around what the book leaves out or minimizes, from the building of cathedrals to radical French revolutionaries. The editors' decision to begin with prehistoric times rather than mythical moments (such as the baptism of Clovis I) did not go unnoticed, either. More broadly, these critics decried an "intellectual act of war" that sought to "assassinate France" by denying its true genius.

How could one include Frantz Fanon, the Martinique revolutionary and philosopher, and Zinédine Zidane, the soccer player whose parents were born in Algeria, but not writer Germaine de Staël or composer Claude Debussy? Every historical work rests on editorial decisions, and the ones that lay behind *France in the World* are naturally open to discussion, but, for these critics, these choices represented a crime of *lèse-nation*. "How can one go so far in the deconstruction of French identity?" asked essayist Alain Finkielkraut, the forlorn defender of the French Republic, mourning "a wounded [national] identity."

Should we assume that "anything that comes from abroad is good?" asked the nationalist provocateur Éric Zemmour, whose anguished ruminations on national decline yielded a best seller in 2014, *Le suicide français*. Historian Patrice Gueniffey — author most recently of *Napoléon et de Gaulle: Deux héros français* (2017) — warned that the editors' perceived disregard for the country's heritage was bound to feed what he called "disaffiliation." The term brings to mind Robert Castel even if, in Gueniffey's prose, recent transformations of labor matter less than, once again, the disintegration of an idealized nation. The threat posed by *France in the World* justified the most furious indictments (Gueniffey accused the book's editors of being "heirs of Vichy France").

While this language was surprisingly violent, one might have expected this kind of objection from such quarters. After all, the editors were convinced from the start that intellectual energy alone could counter retrograde visions of the nation. To this end, they invited contributors from multiple generations and disciplines. There is a preponderance of younger scholars, and essays by not only historians, but also political scientists, literary scholars, art historians, archaeologists, journalists, economists, and half a dozen archivists. *France in the World* opens a conversation among scholars who do not always speak to one another within France's specialized and hierarchical academic circles.

In this respect as in others, the French situation can prove befuddling to outsiders. The centralization of higher education, with seventeen universities and hundreds of thousands of students in or around Paris, creates a concentration of historians without parallel in, say, the US, where scholars are located in numerous centers of comparable importance (Washington, DC, to be sure, but also Boston, New York, Chicago, Los Angeles, the San Francisco Bay Area, and others). Universities in the French provinces and overseas territories such as Martinique or Guadeloupe often lack the intellectual density and institutional resources of their Parisian counterparts (even if many of the latter have equally tight budgets). Moreover, women face considerable obstacles in the French academic world. While they make up roughly half of the junior faculty in the humanities, their number drops precipitously once one moves up the ladder. The same is of course true in the US, but calls for equity and diversity are much more vigorous on American shores, where attempts to rectify such inequalities are connected to longstanding political movements, academic departments, and intellectual currents (gender studies, critical race theory, intersectionality) that, like affirmative action and efforts to limit implicit bias, have acquired on most campuses a legitimacy that remains fragile in France.

These factors help explain why just under a third of the contributors are women; why the majority were trained and work in France and especially in Paris; and why none are based in Martinique or Guadeloupe or former French colonies such as Algeria. While the US is no paragon, an equivalent American book would no doubt have conceptualized diversity in different ways. We can presume that its initial premise would have been that different scholars write different global histories, that they ask different questions and notice different things depending on their physical, institutional, and cultural locations.

It must be said, however, that some things are changing in France in this regard as well. Regional centers of academic excellence are gaining stature. Prestigious journals such as *Annales. Histoire, Sciences Sociales* (whose editors are well represented among the contributors to *France in the World*) have recently reexamined their editorial procedures to include more women in their editorial committee and within the ranks of the scholars they publish. Furthermore, in the fall of 2018 more than five hundred female historians signed a petition protesting "masculine domination" in their profession. The signatories included more than fifteen contributors to *France in the World*. Might we cautiously speculate that, alongside other factors (including in this case the #MeToo movement), this editorial venture, this forceful public intervention energized certain historians? The book's aftereffects may well play out in unpredictable ways in the years to come.

As this translation goes to press, wistful accounts of national history keep landing in French bookstores. In 2018, the right-wing writer Jean-Christian Petitfils penned his own history of France on the grounds that his divided country needs a unifying narrative to "once again instill pride in national cohesion." Predictably, Petitfils subtitled his book "The True National Narrative" (*Le vrai roman national*). No surprise here. But surely there are other ways of exploring the past (or rather our multiple pasts), other reasons why in France as elsewhere we need historians. Beyond what it teaches us about the French past and present, *France in the World* raises fundamental questions about the place of history and the kind of history we want in our public space. It also intervenes in one of the central political battles now being waged on several continents, when closed, populist visions of national identity target looser, pluralistic understandings of cultural identification.

It is impossible to tell which camp will prevail, even in the US. In an age of disquiet in the face of global mobility, an age when national myths of continuity and rootedness retain such a strong hold, nothing guarantees that open-ended histories of diversity and flux will win the day, even if they show how some people and institutions draw lines that define and separate, and how some people cross these very lines. At the same time, there are costs to refusing to counter rigid national narratives with freer, more precise alternatives that are grounded in research. Let us then believe, along with the contributors to this bracing collection, that historians have something distinctive to tell us about the world we inhabit.

Let us expect historians to play a vocal role in our public debates — sometimes to clarify and sometimes to make our world more complicated, more open to ambiguity, more *discontinuous*.

And let us pay close attention to the literary experiments of historians who are also writers, historians who believe, with audacity and necessity and — yes — urgency, that knowledge and language have the power to liberate us.

A note on the translation: This edition is both slightly slimmer and slightly heftier than the original. We have translated 90 percent of the French-language essays, asked the editors to flesh out the twelve section introductions, and invited the contributors to update some of the references that follow each essay, and where pertinent add English-language sources. Otherwise, the book is the same.

OVERTURE

Patrick Boucheron

"It would take a history of the world to explain France."
— Jules Michelet, *Introduction to World History* (1831)

An *introduction* to the history of France?

Most readers, I know, would rather do without. You'll skip it. You'll want to embark directly on this fresh ocean of history, full of events, hopes, and memories; you'll expect plain sailing as well as sudden squalls of things remembered and associations of ideas, buffeting you from one shore to the next. Who needs an introduction to that? Who needs ponderous preliminaries? The introduction to French history can prove wearisome, if not intimidating, with its accumulation of centuries, its solemn and eminent scholars, and its controversies. Historians are after all expected to express, practically on their own, the anxieties of their era.

The very thought of an introduction induces lethargy. I know all this, and will thus confine myself to explaining as briefly as possible the astonishing speed with which this book brought a number of us together, and why this collective endeavor sparked so great a sense of urgency in us all.

So this is more an *overture* (whatever is morally or politically meant by this) than an *introduction*; and even then, it bears comparison less to a musical composition's majestic prelude than to a camera's aperture (*ouverture*), which a photographer adjusts to change the depth of field. In sum, the authors of this volume shared a common ambition to write a history of France that would reconcile the storyteller's art with absolute critical rigor. This new history would be open and accessible to the widest possible readership, while remaining within the familiar framework of dates.

The result is political inasmuch as it seeks to mobilize a pluralist concept of history against the general shrinkage of national identity that is such a central component of the public debate in France today. As a matter of principle, the history we set forth refuses to surrender the "History of France" to knee-jerk reactionaries or to concede them any narrative monopoly. By approaching the subject from the open sea (so to speak), by catching the élan of a historiography driven by strong, fresh winds, it seeks to recover the diversity of France. This is why this venture has taken the form of a collective editorial project. *France in the World* gives voice to a group of historians, male and female, working in concert toward a history that is both committed (*engagée*) and scholarly. This book is a joyous polyphony, not by happenstance (how could anybody today presume to write a full history of France single-handed?), but by choice.

We have traveled light. Embarking on this adventure, the 113 authors who put their trust in the initial project agreed to shed the theoretical apparatus that typically accompanies academic writing. They would no longer accept the increasingly prevalent apportioning of roles that places historians at a disadvantage: meaning, to journalists and essayists, the easy narrative option of a story invidiously discounting evidence, and to historians, the awkward exercise of aligning a good story with the cold requirements of a rigorous method. "It's more complicated than that" is the constant objection to straightforward history. Certainly — but hiding behind complexity cannot be the last resort of historians, unless they want to be professional purveyors of disenchantment. Responsible critical work is not systematically dry and dreary; in fact, it can be absolutely enthralling. Using the investigative approach, a historian can show how the past is forever made and unmade by the changing frames of history. History does not speak for itself, in the clear light of the evidence; we can only view it through the prism of our knowledge.

Consequently, our general guidelines have been to write history without footnotes and without compunction — a history that is living because it is constantly renewed by research, a history for those with whom we enjoy sharing it — in the hope that some of the pleasure of the sharing would relieve some of the desolation of our present times. Writing without notes and without compunction does not mean that we compromised the requirements of our profession, for at the end of each chapter the author has listed the key scholarly references on which it was based.

Every contributor was given complete freedom to construct an essay coinciding with a given date in the history of France — whether that date was already part of the chronological frieze of the national legend or had to be imported from another compartment of the world's memory. Focusing on dates was clearly the most effective way of unraveling the fictitious continuities of the traditional narrative: for dates make it possible to point out connections, or readjust them, or even resolve apparent incongruities. Indeed it is this dual action — displacing and unmooring feelings of belonging while welcoming the strange familiarity of what is distant — that the chronicle, with its cheerful sequence of events, tends to put to the test.

We didn't have to systematically seek out counterintuitive or untraditional positions; the canonical dates in French history are present in this book, although they are sometimes a bit off-kilter, shaken by the will to see in them the local expression of wider movements. From the ashes of a pseudo-nostalgic tale we were taught in school, there might arise the phoenix of a broader, revivified, and more diverse history.

Our contributors had something else to go on: a line by the historian Jules Michelet, chosen as our book's epigraph: "It would take a history of the world to explain France." These enigmatic words convey a certain longing — and a certain unease. In truth, longing and unease have turned out to be among the driving forces behind our project, forcing each of us to write with complete freedom.

When he wrote the line above in 1831, Michelet was thirty-two years old. As a lecturer at the École normale, he was teaching people younger than himself a history that had much in common with philosophy: in fact, it was, strictly speaking, a philosophy of history. The 1830 Revolution, which toppled the Bourbon dynasty for good, had brought the hope of political freedom. This hope awakened the people of France, a humanity within which, unlike most historians of his time, Michelet detected sufficient strength to resist the fatal destiny of what contemporaries called race. A true son of the Revolution, he championed an open, energetic, vital history that could not be shackled by theories of immutable origin, identity, or destiny. "That which is the least simple, the least natural, and the most

47

artificial, meaning the least predestined, most human, and freest entity in the world, is Europe; and the most European country of all is the land of my birth, which is France." Thus the arrow of time flew onward, and this is why, for Michelet, an *Introduction to World History* could only be an introduction to his history of France.

But we should be wary of facile parallels. Although Michelet appeared out of place in his own time, he is by no means squarely in line with our own. We can no longer agree with him that France is "the glorious fatherland [that] will henceforth steer the ship of humanity." Today, Michelet's patriotism is fatally compromised by a history — for which he was of course not responsible — in which France's "civilizing mission" excused blatant colonial aggression. Was this a terminal surrender of principles? Many since Michelet's time have believed that the reinvention of a universalist "constitutional patriotism" open to the diversity of the world could provide the best defense against a dangerously narrow-minded nationalism and its constricted understanding of national identity. But this is not our subject here. It is enough to acknowledge the extent to which Michelet's dream of a France that one can only explain in global terms has been a source of comfort and inspiration.

Lecturing at the Collège de France from 1943 to 1944, the brilliant historian Lucien Febvre reflected at length on Michelet's little-known text. He did so to cast light on the much more celebrated *Tableau de la France* that opens the second volume of Michelet's *History of France* (1834). As far as Febvre was concerned, Michelet's idea was to loosen this geographical entity, to undo "the idea of a necessary, predestined, preordained France, ready made by Frenchmen, by describing as 'France' all the formations and human groupings that existed before Gaul on what is today our territory" (lecture 25, 1 March 1944). Living in Nazi-occupied Paris, receiving from his disciple Fernand Braudel, then a prisoner in Mainz, chapter after chapter of the latter's *The Mediterranean*, Febvre evoked the historical moments when, as in the time of Joan of Arc, France "came close to vanishing." He also spoke of historians who, like Michelet, had "erased the French race from our history."

Once and for all? Let's not be naive. After the war, Lucien Febvre reentered the fray against what he had earlier called the "prejudice of predestination," the idea that a country's history can only be guided by a national destiny (*A Geographical Introduction to History*, 1949). Answering a 1950 appeal by UNESCO, which wanted to make history an auxiliary science in the search for universal peace, Febvre and historian François Crouzet developed a project for a textbook describing the development of French civilization as a fraternal growth of mixed cultures (this book was finally published in 2012 as *Nous sommes des sang-mêlés* [We Are of Mixed Blood]). What Febvre called civilization was the capacity to overflow: "French civilization, to speak only of that, has always gone beyond the political borders of France and the French state. Knowledge of this fact does not belittle France; on the contrary it makes the country greater. It is a source of hope for her future."

Whence comes the strange notion that opening to the world would diminish France? By what paradox have we come to view the history of our country as an endless struggle to protect its sovereignty from outside influences that somehow denature and hence endanger its very essence? In the last thirty years, the travails of French society confronted by the challenges of globalization have focused public debate on the question of national identity. In terms of historical writing, the tipping point came somewhere between the publication of the first volume of Pierre Nora's *Les lieux de mémoire* (*Realms of Memory*) in 1984 and that of Fernand Braudel's *The Identity of France* in 1986. The demand for a specific French identity, which found early supporters among the left (then in power), led to the defense of a French culture defined by a right to be different. Thereafter it fed a critique of cultural diversity wherein hostility to the supposedly destructive effects of immigration became more and more clearly defined.

On October 16, 1985, Braudel presented his lycée pupils in Toulon with a fascinating analysis of a siege of the city that took place in 1707. This world-history story was designed to show not only that "France's second name was diversity," but also that France's political and territorial unity had been forged slowly, "through connections made more recently by the railways" rather than at the time of Joan of Arc, as Braudel's students might still have been taught. Braudel's death a month later ended the writing of what he had begun to call his "History of France," which he predicted would be "misunderstood." And so it was: his unfinished *Identity of France*, published posthumously, was read as the political testament of a historian who dealt with long-term historical structures (the *longue durée*). In reality, the book was no more than a provisional time halt for history on the move. We cannot relaunch this history without drawing — as Braudel did — on Lucien Febvre, who himself explained Michelet's *Tableau de la France* through his scintillating *Introduction to World History*.

Many young French researchers are already moving in this direction. Some draw inspiration from Thomas Bender's striking book *A Nation among Nations: America's Place in World History* (2006), which proposes a global history of the US as no more than "a nation among others." To approach the American Civil War as just one among numerous independence struggles which, in Europe and in the wider world, articulated the issue of nationality and the ideal of liberty, inflicted a narcissistic wound on a country that sees its national story as something unique and exceptional.

Other historiographical experiments in the same vein have been attempted; for example, a transnational history of Germany, and an account of the Italian Renaissance in terms of the Mediterranean. But while historians of the French Revolution and of France's colonial empire have begun to adopt a global approach, a global history of France herself is yet to come. *France in the World* certainly isn't that: it merely formulates the premise — perhaps the promise — of such an approach in future.

What do we mean by the global history of France?

First of all, a history of France that forsakes neither the great places nor the great figures of our history. It is not so much a case of embracing another history entirely as of writing the same history in a different way. Instead of embracing knee-jerk counterhistories or losing ourselves in the labyrinths of deconstruction, we have tried to come to grips with the questions that the traditional history of an immutable France falsely claims to resolve. We hence offer a global history of France, not a history of global France: we have no intention of following the long-term expansion of a globalized France in order to exalt the glorious rise of a nation devoted to universalism. Nor do we wish to sing the praises of self-satisfied ethnic diversity and migratory cross-pollination. Believe us when we say that we are not trying to celebrate or denounce anything. The fact that history has for so long been a critical science and not an art of acclamation or detestation is an issue that we hoped had long been settled. And yet, it faces such vehement enemies nowadays that it is perhaps a good idea to once again say something in its defense.

To explain France by the world, to write the history of a France that is explainable with the world, that engages with the world: such a venture is bound to undermine the false idea that France and the world are somehow symmetrical. France does not exist separately from the rest of the world; likewise, the world's consistency in France changes over time. The world of Roman Gaul and the world of the Franks looked to the Mediterranean. The kingdom of Saint Louis looked to Eurasia. But at different points in the long history of globalization, of the changing relationships between what took the name of "France" and that which was understood as "the world," there kept arising other social configurations, multiple affiliations, unexpected bifurcations, and geographical shifts. In short, history was on the move. Rather than calling our own book a global history, we might have defined it as a "long" history of France, starting eons before the brief period during which the country has come into its own as a political entity, as a nation. The old notion of "general history" may also be applicable inasmuch as our approach aspires to nothing more than the honest analysis of a given space in all its geographical breadth and historical depth.

Such then is our project. It is neither linear nor aimed at a particular target, and it has no beginning, no end. Our earliest dates explore the most shadowy periods of human occupation of the territory today identified as French, precisely to circumvent the question of national origins. The dates draw closer together when the connections between them grow more numerous (in the years 1450–1550, for example) or when France attempted (as in the seventeenth century, with the growing power of its absolute monarchy) to fan out across the world or even to contain the world by embracing a universalistic outlook within which French constituted our planet's language of revolutionary hope. At other times, this history opens onto missed opportunities, withdrawals, and retractions — for instance, in the wake of the globalization à la française that begins in the late nineteenth century

In all honesty, none of this adds up to a coherent history, at least not yet. If the 131 dates we have chosen in this edition of the book do not exactly form an articulated chronology, it is because they cannot on their own support the exhaustive recital of a global history of France. By drawing attention to certain events, they naturally add weight to political and cultural readings, neglecting longer-term economic and environmental changes. We have knowingly left open yawning gaps that readers will certainly notice: while some were perhaps unavoidable, for others we will be held responsible, and rightly so. Let me add that the sequences or sections these dates define are not supposed to represent definite periods: they are only there to guide the reader, who may also wish to escape the beaten path by way of the index, the list of pertinent dates that close each chapter, or the journeys across time that, at the end of this book, suggest thematic routes and unexpected juxtapositions.

Finally we have to confess that, more than anything, it was the principle of pleasure that guided us as we put this book together. Not that we ever meant to write a happy history: *France in the World* is neither lighter nor darker than any other book (though its gravity is hardly despondent). Still, there is something to be said today on behalf of the joyous energy of a collective intelligence. We hope that a little of the delight we experienced while perpetually surprising ourselves, while joining forces in this collective enterprise, while trusting one another and working hard to avoid disappointing one another, will prove contagious. To those who ask why this history of France is a global one, we simply respond: "Because this makes it so much more interesting!"

EARLY STIRRINGS IN ONE CORNER OF THE WORLD

To start a global history of France by reaching back to the dimly lit strata of prehistoric societies might seem an unlikely gambit. It is even slightly perverse to suggest that France already existed at the dawn of humanity. It is precisely because the world had neither design nor foreordained destiny at that time that we may consider the area that would become France in the same way we would any other patch of earth. The forty thousand years of man's history covered in this section at breakneck speed are more than a preliminary: they constitute, in many ways, the methodological boundary and the bulwark of any global history, preserving us from the misguided notion that intellectual structures remain static in space over the long term.

This "France prior to France," as the historian Jean Guilaine calls it, shades off into the earliest history of a human population that, from the start, was necessarily mixed-race and migratory. The societies that, for tens of thousands of years, traversed the future territory of France were nomadic. How can we not measure the few millennia of mankind's recent, sedentary history against the thirty thousand years of the Upper Paleolithic, with its complex and hierarchical societies, very likely structured by religious forces whose existence we can infer from cave paintings? Although the first villages of the Neolithic period are sometimes buried under densely populated centers, artifacts from Bronze

Age graves sketch an economic geography that is European and Mediterranean in scope. Only with the city-states that cropped up in the Iron Age do we start to see political and regional entities assume a durable form that could persist through the centuries. As early as the fourth or third century BCE, these came under the influence of Rome.

There is no escaping the fact that this area on the western end of the European continent was a laboratory for societies whose social, cultural, and even biological identities were no different from those of societies in other parts of the world. Like the famed carved ivory Venus of Brassempouy, these "French" predecessors lack identifiable faces and yet we find them familiar. In fact, everything seems to have come originally from elsewhere, starting of course with groups of early people, and then agriculture, which arrived from the Middle East as a conquering technology. But would we be right to conclude that the developments in Paleolithic cave art from 35,000 to 12,000 BCE correspond to these different migrations, following one another in time? It is very uncertain. Regardless, the preservation of material remains from the Stone Age depends heavily on long-term variations in the physical environment. The temperate conditions that prevailed in the space that would become France, from the warming period at the end of the Paleolithic onward, better preserved evidence of human activity.

This corner of the world, a cul-de-sac at one end of Eurasia, was also adjacent to an isthmus for the passage to Africa. It seems therefore to have promoted the meeting and mixing of peoples. Its southern coastline provided a stopping-off point for the early Greek seafaring kingdoms in the seventh century BCE, and as the Romans expanded their influence, it also provided them with territory and a trade route to northern Europe. The rows of megaliths at Carnac, in Brittany, dating from the fifth millennium BCE, and the giant Vix Krater, dating from the first millennium BCE, suggest a movement toward societies that were structured around social, political, and symbolic dominance, although the real or imaginary meaning of this symbolism is beyond our grasp.

Since their accurate identification in the nineteenth century, the traces of human activity recovered from the earth and discovered on rock walls have allowed us to imagine the complex genealogy of the region in an entirely new way. They have also enabled us to rethink the even more complex notions of a "people" and a "nation." Prehistoric archaeology is one of the more radical ways of claiming an indigenous or aboriginal identity. But while the illusion of an unbroken ancestry may hold on the local level, it would be extremely difficult to make the same retroactive claim for France's national territory. No entity approaching the scale of France existed until the Romans expanded their territory into the region, a few decades prior to the start of the first century CE — and even then Gaul needed the external perspective of a proto-imperial power and the writings of Julius Caesar, building on those of Posidonius of Apamea, to convey the idea of its unity down to our own time.

From another perspective, the written memoirs of societies that existed in historical (as opposed to prehistorical) times seem a paltry appendix to the great chain of human existence, which is known to us only through the fragile records of archaeology. In a vertigo-inducing twist, the discovery of early human remains can, retroactively, become an act of founding. We cannot think of prehistoric times outside the history of their scientific and political invention during the second half of the nineteenth century, a program that quickly turned into a race between nations to see which could claim the earliest humans. From the discovery of Cro-Magnon Man (1868) to the Chauvet Cave (1994), France has been a leading participant in this competition, with the obsessive quest for racial identity progressing in parallel. Priding itself on being "the country of man," contemporary France has managed to unearth a prominent share of the world's prehistoric remains by combing its territory for archaeological sites. It should be said that, in something of a snub to the productive and industrial north, most of these remains have turned up in the south. This glorious gallery of fossils and sites, imbued with the aura of early man, has gradually helped relegate the notion of France's Gallic origins to the attic of ideas.

Is this foundation story not the exact reverse of that earlier one, which took a defeat at the hands of the Roman invaders as the start of France's history?

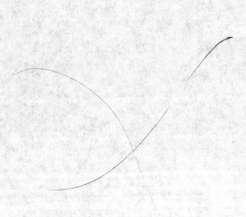

34,000 BCE

Creating the World Deep inside the Earth

Today, as in the distant past, visitors to the Chauvet Cave
in southern France share a "Cro-Magnon" lineage. Almost
forty thousand years after it was created, can this cave
art really be considered a universal shared memory? The
path traveled by that resolutely modern *Homo sapiens*
establishes the unutterable depth of his origins as well as
his irreducible hybridization.

It is an early spring day, thirty-six thousand years ago. The
men are walking toward the cave, a young boy following
close behind them. He is relishing his good fortune, because
the year before they had stayed only briefly in the region;
everything was still frozen then, battered by the winds, and
there was not enough game for them to remain any longer.
Now, spring is returning more quickly, the herds of horses
and bison promise to be larger, and so they have decided to
settle down for the season, setting up their tents in the shelter
of trees on the banks of the river, below the path they are
walking on now. The boy is going with them.

When they arrive at the entrance to the cave, the one who knows it best goes in first, without a sound, then comes back some time later to report that he has not sensed the presence of bears. In fact, there was only the dried-out remains of a bear that died while hibernating a long time ago. The party enters, the boy still in the back. The walls of the cave dance in the light of the torches and then disappear. After walking for some time, they stop. The boy is told to close his eyes. When he reopens them, he sees ochre-colored rhinoceroses painted on the walls, and also lions and a mammoth; and then, not far from where he is standing, red handprints. Pointing to one in particular, they tell him that the print was left there by the mother of his mother. He places his own hand on top of it and feels the cool, damp limestone.

They move on and after a while lower their torches and begin walking faster; the boy thinks he sees some deer in the distance, drawn in black, and, beyond them, even deeper in the cave, horses, aurochs, and more rhinoceroses. But he is not sure, and in any case his eyes are drawn to a large fire at the entrance to a gallery. Who lit it? As they walk by, the smoke burns his eyes. He grabs the tunic of the man in front of him while they slowly descend into the gallery where, when given permission to look, he sees the secret of a world born of incredible violence. He senses, even if he isn't allowed to tell anyone, that the story told here has already transformed the way he will see the world. The adults tell him that these images are very ancient, that they date from the very origin of the world. And this strikes him as obvious.

In 2016, in the middle of summer, a large crowd gathered in the Gorges de l'Ardèche to visit the reproduction of this famed cave. Whether or not the facsimiles of those frescoes astounded them, visitors at least encountered a simple fact: we were not born yesterday. I speak of "we" because the intrinsic force of these images — unless it is our own gaze that conveys this force — invariably summons something universal. Because these images come out of nowhere, they seem available to all of us, beyond our particular origins and identities. And yet, these images also exist within a specific historical trajectory whose significance we must assess to understand the feelings of universality they bring to life.

What do we know about the creators of those frescoes and of their motivations? We don't know what language they spoke, or why they invented that pictorial language, or why they expressed it at that particular site. We know nothing about what they said to one another standing before those works. All we can do is recognize the animals in amazement, and describe how they were created. The story that opened this chapter is fictional; the boy who might have discovered those paintings never existed. It is an imagined picture superimposed upon images from another time, images that are forever mute even though they seem to shout out to us. As for dates, all we know is that the first frescoes in the Chauvet Cave were painted between thirty-seven thousand and thirty-four thousand years ago.

That said, the boy has a real place in the story. He speaks to us of the construction of a new world brought to life by the strokes of a brush, or rather of charcoal, a world he could believe existed throughout eternity.

This was the world of the Cro-Magnons. Like us, the Cro-Magnons were the product of a complex biological journey during which some of our distant ancestors (*Homo erectus*) left Africa while others remained. Once they reached Europe, those who left gradually became Neanderthals, while those who stayed transformed into *Homo sapiens*. About 100,000 years ago, *Homo sapiens* in turn left Africa for the Middle East and then, still later, for Eurasia, where they then met up with the Neanderthals. This genetic mix produced the Cro-Magnons, our direct ancestors, a mixed-race people if ever there was one. These population movements and exchanges took place a few millennia before the frescoes were painted. Between sixty thousand and forty thousand years ago, *sapiens* spread across the world, beyond their earlier borders, all the way to Australia and, according to some models, the Americas soon after.

And so here they are, around 45,000 BCE, in Europe. In a world that was still far from overcrowded, demographic growth alone cannot explain these population movements. Powerful social forces were no doubt involved as well.

What made the world go round? Does a human society first find an explanation for itself in a form of "biological-economic rationality" (technical and economic mutations linked to demographic growth and environmental variations)? Or does it derive its essence from ideals that govern relationships of gender, generation, power, and the like? The Chauvet frescoes provide answers to those questions. They tell us that the societies of the Upper Paleolithic were founded on political and religious values, and that that is perhaps the reason for both the frescoes' modernity and their universality. These works brim with spirituality, and they define humanity's place within the universe and animal world. The Cro-Magnons invented themselves as social beings by organizing a system of values, through the probable codification of the relationship between the sexes, or even the link between generations.

And that is probably why generations of Aurignacians — the name prehistorians use for the first human beings who entered the cave — went there to paint in strings of chambers and galleries, passing by alcoves and hidden diverticula. We know that they came from far away, traveling over vast regions covering the southern part of what is now France, from Aquitaine to the Mediterranean. They moved from natural shelters to open-air camp sites, depending on the circumstances and the seasons. Brilliant hunters and skilled artisans who could work with bone, wood, and animal skins, they ornamented their bodies with necklaces made of teeth or beads or ivory pendants, and thus once again codified the place of individuals within groups and the identity of groups vis-à-vis others.

They were brilliant artists, too. This cave, which contains more images than any other we have uncovered from the Aurignacian world, is their masterpiece. There are close to five hundred animal figures. In addition to the species our imaginary boy may have seen, let us add bison, ibexes, and megaloceroses, as well as bears and owls. The frescoes also include one of the most ancient representations of a woman, reduced essentially to her vulva. As such, the Chauvet Cave and its works encompass the main themes of that great cave art to which generations of artists would dedicate themselves for more than twenty thousand years.

The distribution of the paintings in the gigantic space of that cave seems to follow a true logic, perhaps even an initiatory path. The first sections, principally decorated with red paintings, alternate easily accessible panels with others hidden in cave diverticula. The most complex and richest frescoes, in black paint, reside in the back. This is where we find the "panel of horses" and that of "lions" — powerful scenes that provoked such strong feelings in our imagined boy. There are countless animals and geometrical motifs as well, most often simple finger paintings on the wall. This artwork must have been the work of many people over several centuries, although a few artists or even a single "master" may be responsible for the spectacular black panels in the back. The quality of these works alone allows us to speak here of artists. It was through art and no other activity that the notion of the "specialist" emerged at that time.

By inventing such a pictorial language, those artists indeed contributed to founding a new world, a world entering into history not through texts but through the legacy that a generation intended to leave behind by dissociating body and mind and giving material consistency to ideas that would endure on the wall of a cave. A collective memory was thus fashioned, and then reinvented again and again over the centuries. We are in some ways its last avatar. Indeed, we know that for several centuries after the first frescoes were created, the cave continued to welcome other visitors. The paintings, in other words, continued to be seen. After having been abandoned for a time, the cave was rediscovered a few millennia later by Gravettians (who followed the Aurignacians). What did they feel upon discovering these frescoes? We have no way of telling, but do know that the cave was forgotten again and buried until its latest discovery, in 1994.

We may yearn for an "original" rendering of the cave, but it is equally important to reflect on its significance and its transformations over the centuries. Any effort to decode the exact meaning of those works is bound to fail, not only because that meaning has been forgotten, but also because that meaning has a history of its own. We can, however, attempt to grasp the political, religious, and social dimensions of this crucial stage in the mutation of human societies, accompanying the early days of *Homo sapiens* in Europe. Standing before the frescoes, we feel as if we are contemplating the source of our history. As much as those paintings, it is this very feeling that warrants attention.

François Bon

REFERENCES

Bon, François. *Préhistoire: La fabrique de l'homme*. Paris: Seuil, 2009.

Clottes, Jean, ed. *Chauvet Cave: The Art of Earliest Times*. Salt Lake City: University of Utah Press, 2003.

—, ed. *La France préhistorique: Un essai d'histoire*. Paris: Gallimard, 2010.

Jaubert, Jacques. *Préhistoires de France*. Bordeaux: Confluences, 2011.

Leroi-Gourhan, André. *Gesture and Speech*. Cambridge, MA: MIT Press, 1993. (First French edition: 1964–1965.)

Stringer, Chris. *Lone Survivors: How We Came to Be the Only Humans on Earth*. London: Times Books, 2012.

Valentin, Boris. *Le Paléolithique. Que sais-je?* Paris: Presses Universitaires de France, 2011.

RELATED ARTICLES

23,000 BCE, 12,000 BCE, 1907, 1940

23,000 BCE

Man Gives Himself the Face of a Woman

The world's oldest preserved representation of a sculpted human face is twenty-five thousand years old. The features of the Venus of Brassempouy now seem destined to eternally symbolize prehistory. But has that always been the case? Let us review the tribulations of an icon, from the Atlantic to the Ural Mountains.

We humans need icons — which is why, in order to think about prehistoric times, we have given them a face. In fact, several faces come to mind when we think of that period, each embodying one of the contradictory feelings prehistory summons in our collective imagination. Some frankly grimace — such as the toothless skull of the Cro-Magnon "old man" — while others are peaceful and reassuring. It is one of those serene faces, among the most famous and beautiful, that we will consider here.

Truth be told, this little head is tiny, just a little over an inch tall. It is sculpted out of beautiful mammoth ivory with soft hues, seemingly very fragile, with a large, desiccated crack across its cheek. What this enigmatic face expresses

73

is left entirely to our imagination: the eyes are neither open nor closed (we can only guess at them, hidden as they are under the eyebrows); the mouth is nonexistent; the ears are hidden under her hood. The figure seems to be turned inward, all her senses at rest. And yet, the less she displays emotion, the more she grows in meaning. The message she seems to deliver, conveyed only by her grace, appears all the more profound and universal. This is why this little "Lady with the Hood" from Brassempouy is so often used as a frontispiece in works on prehistory throughout the world, as if her ineffable charm were the ideal emblem of a period that is at once foundational and impossible to narrate.

It hasn't been long since this figure entered our collective imagination, because it wasn't so long ago that prehistory itself was invented. The first step, one made not without difficulty, was to admit that humans are far more ancient than the written traces of their history; that step was taken around 1860, following in particular archaeological work and writings by Jacques Boucher de Perthes in Abbeville and others in surrounding locations in the Somme valley. Second step: a vociferous debate on the nature and evolution of that prehistoric human, which lasted until the beginning of the twentieth century and continues to this day, even if biological evolution has been proven and accepted for at least the past hundred years. And the third step — overlapping with the second — was to attempt to write this history without any written records and to describe the evolution not only of humans, but of their societies. This is what Édouard Piette, among others, sought to do in the nineteenth century. A magistrate from the Ardennes who settled near the Pyrenees, and one of the prehistorians who built upon the foundational work of the archaeologist Boucher de Perthes and the paleontologist Édouard Lartet, Piette sought to extract the buried archives that would buttress the new science of prehistoric archaeology. One finds him at work in the village of Lortet in the Neste Valley in 1873, then in the town of Mas-d'Azil in the department of Ariège in 1887, and finally, a few years after that, in Brassempouy.

Located in the heart of the Chalosse, a wine-growing region in southwestern France, the caves of Brassempouy were not entirely unknown when Piette began his work there, but he was the one who made them famous. Piette's remarkable stratigraphic sequence would play an important role in the establishment of Paleolithic chronicles. Still, the caves would not have attained such fame were it not for this figurine, whose renown would shine brightest. When Piette first extracted it from the ground in the summer of 1894, no doubt as hot and stormy a season as summers in the Landes region tend to be, he hesitated. The figure was too beautiful, too familiar; it did not fit nineteenth-century preconceptions about prehistoric artists, these wandering hunter-gatherers.

Piette wondered whether he was the victim of a hoax. But when his discovery was published, the "Venus of Brassempouy" quickly became, in the popular imagination, one of the most emblematic objects of the Paleolithic period and its peoples.

Today, this tiny figure represents prehistory to people in France and around the world. But does it truly embody the culture of the man or woman who, we believe, fashioned it out of ivory some twenty-five thousand years ago? Yes and no — and this is indeed one of the paradoxes of this little sculpted face. Piette did not know he had put his hands on one of the first examples of an emblematic theme in the art of the European Upper Paleolithic: the representation of woman. We tend to think of art from this time and place as centered on the portrayal of animals. But representations of female bodies, which portray women not as social beings, but womankind as symbolic values, are no less central. They are expressed in many ways, notably in the ivory, stone, and terra-cotta statuary that the artisans of the Gravettian people, who lived in Europe between twenty-nine thousand and twenty-two thousand years ago, created and dispersed from the shores of the Atlantic to the banks of the Don River, in what is now Russia. One might say that artistic use of the abstracted female body constituted one of the most palpable catalysts of the cultural unity of these populations. Rather than categorize prehistoric peoples based on their technological abilities alone, archaeologists used it to sketch for the first time the contours of a tradition on the basis of a shared ideology. Humans of the Paleolithic, in short, invented the first icons. This was a turning point in the history of humanity.

And yet, the "Venus of Brassempouy" remains an exceptional and even eccentric object in this context. Though we are aware of several dozen female representations, she is one of the few to exhibit a face. In most cases, the artist focused on what we might discreetly call the "attributes" of womankind — breasts, vulva, stomach, hips — with little or no attention to the head. Even when the latter is represented, it is often "coiffed," showing as in Brassempouy the care given to head ornamentation (plaited hair or a true hairstyle, for example). But facial features are nowhere to be found. All of this to say that our exceptional object reversed common values: a face rather than a head, a face without the body to which most contemporaneous representations limited themselves.

Is that why the figurine was discarded along with other artisanal rejects? It's impossible to know, but this marvelous object was indeed abandoned at the entrance to the Grotte du Pape in Brassempouy. It was not alone: alongside it, amidst fragments of tusks and ivory shavings, we find other figurines of various shapes, both whole and incomplete, all of them reduced to the profiles of voluptuous or svelte bodies and, of course, devoid of faces. Perhaps the cave was an artisanal workshop and perhaps this piece, which was never anything but a face detached from the body, was the equivalent of an early draft or, at least, a representation that took liberties with the norms and canons of that time. In short, if the Venus of Brassempouy expresses a major theme in Paleolithic iconography — female representation — it nonetheless remains a subversive icon in its own culture.

Was it, then, a caveman's fancy that became an emblem for the prehistorian? Perhaps. But above all, it is a beautiful lesson: the grace of the figure's features calmly sweeps away every possible assumption concerning the presumed unsophistication of those cavemen and cavewomen who, at a distance of twenty-five thousand years, emerge before our eyes out of the shadowy mystery of their culture. It is a perfect object, full of surprise, whose slight distance from what appear to be the norms of its own culture might just enable it to incarnate others.

Whatever the truth, its profile, like that of a Paleolithic Marianne, an unknown soldier of the "eternal feminine," constitutes the crown jewel of the French National Archaeology Museum. Perhaps it is only right that this face, unique in its prehistoric context given its aesthetic, allegorical, and even — looking backward — political dimensions, finds its place in this history of France.

François Bon

REFERENCES

Bon, François, Yann Potin, Dominique Henry-Gambier, et al. "Préhistoires parallèles. Henri Delporte, Édouard Piette et les grottes de Brassempouy." In *Arts et cultures de la préhistoire: Hommages à Henri Delporte*, edited by René Desbrosse and André Thévenin, 185–96. Paris: Éditions du CTHS, 2007.

Delporte, Henri. *Édouard Piette: Histoire de l'art primitif, preceded by Piette, pionnier de la préhistoire*. Paris: Picard, 1987.

———. *L'Image de la femme dans l'art préhistorique*. 2nd ed. Paris: Picard, 1993.

Guy, Emmanuel. *Préhistoire du sentiment artistique: L'invention du style il y a 20,000 ans*. Paris: Presses du Réel, 2011.

Simonet, Aurélien. *Brassempouy (Landes, France) ou la matrice gravettienne de l'Europe*. Liège: Études et recherches archéologiques de l'Université de Liège, 2012.

Stavrinaki, Maria, and Stefanos Geroulanos, eds. "Writing Prehistory." *RES: Anthropology and Aesthetics* (Spring/Autumn 2018): 69–70.

White, Randall. "The Women of Brassempouy: A Century of Research and Interpretation." *Journal of Archaeological Method and Theory* 13, no. 4 (December 2006): 251–304.

RELATED ARTICLES
34,000 BCE, 397, 1815, 1858, 1949

12,000 BCE

Climate Unhinged and Art Regenerated

About twelve thousand years before our own era, well
before its nomadic populations became settled, humanity
underwent a slow but profound transformation coinciding
with a period of global warming. By providing a fine-
grained scan of this era, archaeology enables us to clear
away the myths surrounding prehistory. Do the mysterious
decorated pebbles of the Mas-d'Azil reveal, then, an
ideological revolution in the farthest reaches of the Eurasian
world?

Two hundred centuries separate the underworld artworks of
the Chauvet cave, in today's Ardèche, from those of Niaux
in the Ariège. After Niaux, the representation of animals in
caves came to a halt, along with the ritual decorations of
caves in southwestern Europe with geometrical symbols
and beasts, real or imagined. The title of this chapter
appears to offer a precise date for the discontinuation of
this cave art, but in reality its abundant symbols are just as
likely to have lapsed in use between 12,026 and 12,015 BCE

as between 12,198 and 11,874 BCE; or indeed at any two-hundred-year interval around 12,000 BCE, our approximate chronological reference. This is because the margin of error in radiocarbon dating for this era is about two hundred years, a vast improvement on the millennia of imprecision that surrounds — for example — the more distant Chauvet cave drawings of the Upper Paleolithic. Still, the endpoint of this cave art remains elusive; we have not identified an event that might have precipitated it. At a time when many historians are equally interested in archaeology and in the study of ancient history that goes farthest into the past, I plead for the rigor of a paleo-historical approach that can subvert prehistory's imprecise methods of dating.

The approach I propose rejects both monolithic understandings of prehistory as a single entity and mocking clichés, like the ones that surround the Middle Ages. These clichés reduce prehistory to stock images of dinosaurs (a patent anachronism, given the sixty-million-year disconnect), mammoths (a little better but still problematic: there were some mammoths but not everywhere, and the last ones vanished from Europe in the thirteenth millennium BCE), bludgeons (none have ever been found), or women dragged about by their matted hair (clearly a projection of more recent power dynamics!). All these stereotypes demonstrate our supreme arrogance before these distant Others, whom we turn into dusty wax figures that bring to mind the nineteenth-century "human zoos" in which Europeans displayed colonized subjects. The title of this chapter pokes fun at the idea of "degeneration" and the total blindness to history from which it proceeds; as we know, the fantasy of "decline" periodically gains traction. For example, here is a 1995 passage by an archaeologist that is contained in *Histoire de la France* by famed historian Georges Duby: "Short, not particularly robust physically, with a head disproportionately large, one of these would cut a sorry figure beside a proud Cro-Magnon male." This expert was referring to the people who lived through the period that concerns us here. Even some of the founders of the young science of prehistoric archaeology have been taken in by (oft racialized) myths, be it of a supposedly static prehistory, a linear ascent of humanity toward the light of progress, or a fluctuation between moments of so-called triumph and regression.

The paleo-historic approach is more promising, but, to succeed, practitioners must first acknowledge the imprecision of their timelines and the limitations of their sources, which are exclusively archaeological. For example, take the pebbles (*galets*) scored or ochred with dots and lines found at the Mas-d'Azil (in present-day Ariège), created several centuries after the disappearance of cave paintings. To call them "art" seems borderline ethnocentric. These river pebbles, which have been found all the way from

Cantabria to the east of France, nevertheless carry symbols of a sort: this is a certainty, even though we have no idea what the symbols signify. We only know that they were marked all at once and therefore have nothing to do with any calendar. Moreover these "Azilian pebbles" — the term "Azilian" covers both a historic phase and a broad cultural trend — are obviously not vehicles of writing, contrary to what earlier Western scholars had insisted while seeking to disprove the Latin adage *ex oriente lux* ("all light comes from the East"). The so-called evidence of inscribed stones found at Glozel (Allier department) and theories about Indo-European inscriptions and early European agriculture display the same reluctance to concede that French soil has for very long periods been a mere tributary of the Middle East. (Although the latter was of course dependent on what happened in the West at certain points in history.) Seen on this vast scale, the globalization of ordinary practices is a far more ancient phenomenon than historians ever imagined. The same goes for incessant human migrations.

As for the discreet pebbles of the Mas-d'Azil, they have nothing to do either with the cave of Niaux, its older zoomorphic images, and its cathedral-like "salon noir." The contrast between these pebbles and the art of Niaux gave rise to the now obsolete theory of a "degeneration of symbolic expression" between the two, around 12,000 BCE. There are parallels between this ideological revolution and a sudden climate change at the end of the last ice age, which led to a profound modification in the types of quarry available to hunters. Moreover, clear changes have been pinpointed in the subsistence activities and even the techniques used at that juncture by nomad hunter-gatherers. The global warming event also brought to an end over two hundred centuries of a reindeer civilization in France, in other words of a narrow adaptation by human beings to the (then steppe-like) French landscape and its emblematic animal. Reindeers reacted to this drastic change by migrating north to regions they still inhabit today, whilst in lower latitudes hunters turned to forest game for survival.

It is by no means certain, however, that these events were truly concomitant given that they can only be dated with a margin of error of several centuries. This, of course, encapsulates the great (and stimulating) challenge of the paleo-historic approach: How can we comprehend the complex links of causality between these ideological, economic, and environmental changes? Doubtless there were major demographic changes too, since paleo-genetic studies have recently turned up evidence of important human migrations taking place in the same bracket of time. The innovative perspective of Alain Testart, one of the few French anthropologists who has closely studied the thirteenth millennium BCE, and his colleagues suggests that this era witnessed a major sociological mutation (at least in Europe), namely, dwindling interdependence amongst nomad communities. This hypothesis, which relies on regressive reasoning based on more recent hunter-gatherers, is very difficult to test archaeologically, for sociology rarely leaves fossil traces, especially when there is a dearth of tombs.

Yet from around 9000 BCE, the number of tombs vastly increased, in parallel with other technological and economic changes. A second powerful global warming took place in Europe, setting off what is conventionally known as the Mesolithic era. The term covers a variety of ways whereby people adapted to a suddenly temperate environment. One option was to settle permanently in one place. Neighbors were now buried close to one another in cemeteries. This was the case in Brittany and other parts of the Atlantic seaboard toward 6000 BCE. Elsewhere, various types of nomadic economy continued to prevail.

Similar settlements — without agriculture or stock rearing — can be observed in hunter-gatherer societies in other parts of the world: around 12,000 BCE in Japan and in the Middle East, around 4000 BCE in Peru, or even on the Pacific coast of North America just a century ago. But the most ancient sedentarization of hunter-gatherers was probably accompanied by another major sociopolitical change, namely the advent of wealth in the form of a buildup of stores and reserves. Alain Testart considers this change even more revolutionary than the arrival of agro-pastoral economies in the Neolithic era.

As far as France is concerned, we have yet to identify explicit signs of social differentiation in settled communities of the Breton Mesolithic era. As we have said before, paleo-sociology is tricky. Nor does archaeology offer any serious evidence of great wealth in the villages of those who, in the sixth and fifth millennia BCE, introduced the culture of cereals and stock-rearing from the Middle East by way of the Balkans. From there, it took the best part of a thousand years before Neolithic economies were able to spread, through two routes, as far as France, and another thousand before they covered the whole of today's French territory. Within this timeframe, the history of the last hunter-gatherers veered into new directions, with some converting or even proselytizing on behalf of new methods and others who, without giving up their traditional way of life, either took advantage of new forms of exchange with farmers or were forced to compete with these farmers — perhaps violently. The historic trajectories of these people were no doubt many and various. In Lapland, for example, nomad hunter-gatherers were still present in the seventeenth century. If we think that societies in other parts of the world have failed to "enter history," we must acknowledge that the same is true of Europeans.

It is easy to exploit or politicize the yawning divide between prehistory — a concept that historian Lucien

Febvre thought comical — and history. Definitions of when this transition occurred vary: sometimes it is seen to coincide with the arrival of agriculture, and sometimes with the advent of writing, or even of contact with people who knew how to write. This uncertain matter surfaced recently when the Upper Paleolithic and Mesolithic eras — encompassing more than 99 percent of universal history — were withdrawn from the French middle-school history syllabus, followed by the early history of agriculture. Luckily, revised syllabi have reintegrated them both into the curriculum. This is good news because the ice age — and the millennia that followed it — belong to a vast, little-known body of history that was by no means as cold as we have been led to believe. We all deserve to know what the frozen myths conceal.

Boris Valentin

REFERENCES

Guilaine, Jean. *De la vague à la tombe: La conquête néolithique de la Méditerranée*. Paris: Le Seuil, 2003.

Marchand, Grégor. *Préhistoire atlantique: Fonctionnement et évolution des sociétés du Paléolithique au Néolithique*. Paris: Errance, 2014.

Testart, Alain. *Avant l'histoire: L'évolution des sociétés, de Lascaux à Carnac*. Paris: Gallimard, 2012.

Valentin, Boris. *Jalons pour une paléohistoire des derniers chasseurs (XIVe–VIe millénaire avant J.-C.)*. Paris: Publications de la Sorbonne, 2008.

———. *Le Paléolithique*. *Que sais-je?* Paris: Presses Universitaires de France, 2011.

———. "Magdalenian and Azilian Lithic Productions in the Paris Basin: Disappearance of a Programmed Economy." *The Arkeotek Journal* 2, no. 3 (2008): 2–54.

RELATED ARTICLES
5800 BCE, 1610, 1816, 1940

5800 BCE

From the Plenitude of Eastern Wheat Fields

The Neolithic revolution clearly represents the greatest rupture in the global history of humanity. It was necessarily universal: a complex connection between a mastery of agriculture, animal domestication, and the sedentarization of societies reached Europe three thousand years after it began in the Middle East.

Let's face it: agriculture was not invented in France. It was not even invented in Europe. For ten thousand years before our era, Europe was covered by a thick temperate forest: oaks, lindens, beech trees, and also hazelnuts, alders, and elms. There were also many fruit trees, wild by definition: apple, plum, and others. And there were grape vines, various berry bushes, and at least six hundred species of edible plants. That forest was inhabited by abundant game: aurochs (the last ones disappeared in the seventeenth century), deer, and wild boar. Groups of indigenous hunter-gatherers of the Mesolithic wandered peacefully, and some even domesticated the dog from the wolf. Regions with rich aquatic resources (fish, shellfish, marine mammals) encouraged people to settle along the banks of the large rivers and in the coastal or marshy regions, something that seems to have occurred at least in Brittany.

But, at the same time, groups of hunter-gatherers from the Middle East, between the Negev and south of what is present-day Turkey, had begun to settle down and domesticate local species: wheat and barley, sheep, goats, cows, and pigs. In a semi-arid environment, such domestication assured abundant food. In fact, the invention of agriculture and animal farming (in the Neolithic period) occurred in only a very small number of regions in the world, independent from one another, and with different animal and plant species: the Yellow River Basin, the Yangzi Jiang Basin, the Andes, Mexico, New Guinea, and perhaps North Africa. The success of domestication required a subtle mix of ecological conditions (abundant species did not have to be domesticated), technical mastery (stockpiling, for instance), and cultural attitudes (notably toward nature).

Once agriculture had been firmly established, the quality and dependability of the food supply improved. The population exploded. If hunter-gatherers had on average one child every three years, women on farms gave birth every year, although half the newborns died within months of their birth. This demographic boom in the seventh millennium BCE incited a portion of the new peasants of the Middle East to gradually push farther into neighboring regions: northeast Africa, central Asia, and finally Europe, beginning in 6500 BCE.

Within a few centuries, the Balkan peninsula was occupied by those Neolithic pioneers. This colonization movement was sometimes contested by later Balkan historians, in part for nationalist reasons: the Neolithics came from Turkey, home of the former Ottoman masters. That same desire for autochthony could be found just about everywhere, including in France. Nevertheless, successive archaeological discoveries make such early movement irrefutable, especially since many domestic species that did not previously exist in Europe (wheat and barley, sheep and goat) came from the Middle East, as confirmed by genetic research. Similarly, one finds striking resemblances in material and cultural artifacts found in Europe and the Middle East, from the shapes of pottery and tools to figurines and ornamentation.

Two currents of Neolithization came out of the Balkans. One, with the mastery of navigation, followed the coasts of the Mediterranean from the Adriatic, as proven by the occupation of most islands and the discovery of dug-out pirogues. That culture's pottery was decorated with shell impressions on soft clay, primarily cockles (*Cardium edule*), leading to the name "Cardial culture." It reached the present-day French territory around 5800 BCE, gradually penetrated the interior (as far as Auvergne), but also reached the Atlantic by way of the Garonne Valley. At the same time, it traveled toward the Spanish coasts, as far as Portugal. The various settlements were nonetheless small, and dwellings have still not been fully identified.

By contrast, the colonization of the interior of the Balkans, where many villages have been excavated, is much more obvious. Settlements are characterized by houses measuring around five square meters, painted pottery, and various forms of plastic art, principally female figurines in terra-cotta or marble. For around a thousand years, the Balkan farmers scarcely went beyond the Danube, remaining in a relatively Mediterranean climate. But beginning in 5500 BCE, when settlers had fully adapted to their environment, a new current of colonization began to form, which moved into all of temperate Europe, from the Black Sea to the Atlantic, and from the Alps to the Baltic Sea. This current is described as the "Linear Pottery" or "Linear Band" culture, terms derived from the continuous geometric designs engraved on their pottery. It was once called the "Danubian" culture. Villages contained groups of rectangular houses, up to 45 meters (150 feet) long, which probably housed several families. The houses show a remarkable uniformity of construction from one end of Europe to the other.

The dead were buried in a fetal position with a few

material objects, and exhibited no obvious social distinction, though their gender and age were apparent. However, the quality of the pottery diminished as they traveled from east to west, and the plastic arts all but vanished. Scholars believe that around 5000 BCE this culture had a population of close to two million people at any one time.

The Linear Pottery culture crossed the Rhine around 5300 BCE and reached the Paris Basin around 5100 BCE. Painstaking excavations, notably in the Aisne, Oise, Marne, and Yonne Valleys, have highlighted the systematic grid pattern found in the layouts of these villages throughout the territory. Villages had on average between a half-dozen and a dozen houses, each lasting about as long as a generation. Settling first at the bottom of a valley, those farmers soon occupied the plateaus, filled in any gaps, and reached the Atlantic around 4800 BCE. The two colonization movements thus met up in the middle of the French territory.

From that time, essentially all available European space was occupied by farmers, who could not go further west in "forward flight," which had until then enabled them to maintain small communities and avoid the disadvantages of an unmanageably large population. In that defined space, France being the westernmost peninsula of Eurasia, and the population continuing to grow, it became necessary to make "gains in efficiency." In time, this led to technological inventions: animal traction, the wheel, the swing plow, and copper metallurgy. Flint and hard rocks used for axes were now extracted on a large scale from mines containing thousands of shafts. Regions that did not lend themselves to extensive farming or mining — mountains, swamps, lakes — were nevertheless occupied. This explains the "houses on stilts" that have been excavated in the Chalain and Clairvaux Lakes (in the Jura Mountains). Once emblematic of the Neolithic way of life, they are in fact evidence of people adapting to regions that provide safe havens.

The invention of copper metallurgy in Europe between 4500 and 2200 BCE led to the terms "Copper Age" and "Chalcolithic," even if that technological innovation had only a marginal impact, copper being too soft on its own for making tools and weapons. Copper was above all a marker for power and prestige, which is why it gave its name to this era. Gold was also mined, but primarily in Eastern Europe.

Continuous demographic growth resulted in tensions, both external (between communities) and internal (increasingly visible social inequalities in what we now call "chiefdom" societies). Megalithic monuments are testimonies to those two types of tension. They are both markers of a territory concentrated on the edge of the continent, from which one could not go any farther, and expressions of the power of the elite who were buried there. Villages sprang up on the hills and surrounded themselves with moats and fortifications. Traces of wounds on skeletons, even evidence of massacres, become more numerous. Social hierarchies were not consistent: the great megalithic monuments reserved for a small number in 3500 BCE were followed by "covered walkways," i.e., modest stone mausoleums some twenty meters long where up to several hundred bodies were placed along with a small number of objects. Figurines began to depict armed warriors rather than women.

During the third millennium BCE, the French territory was one of the theaters of two vast pan-European movements, which we still struggle to comprehend. One, in around 2900 BCE, involved the "Corded Ware" culture, whose pottery is decorated with cord-like impressions and whose "chiefs" were buried under little tumulus mounds with battle axes. Because these tombs are found from Russia to the Paris Basin, some scholars have linked them to supposed Indo-European migrations that would have brought the languages of the same name to Western Europe. The other emerging culture is called "Bell Beaker," as its pottery adopts a reversed bell-shape (*campana* in Latin), and is decorated with engraved strips of geometrical motifs. Though it appears to be of Iberian origin, it has been found sporadically from Spain to Denmark and from Great Britain to Hungary. It is not yet known if it reveals a migration, albeit discontinuous, or points toward the exchange of goods, or both.

Around 2200 BCE, this complex landscape yielded the Bronze Age. Bronze was but a kind of technological progress, made by adding a small quantity of tin (about 10 percent) to copper. From a historical and social point of view, this "age" was in truth but a continuation of the Chalcolithic. It would take the arrival of the Iron Age for state-level societies to begin taking form on French territory.

Jean-Paul Demoule

REFERENCES

Bellwood, Peter. *First Farmers: The Origins of Agricultural Societies*. Oxford: Blackwell, 2005.

Coudart, Annick. *Architecture et société néolithique*. Paris: Éditions de la Maison des sciences de l'homme, 1999.

Demoule, Jean-Paul, ed. *La Révolution néolithique en France*. Paris: Inrap and La Découverte, 2007.

———, ed. *La Révolution néolithique dans le monde*. Paris: CNRS Éditions, 2010.

———, *Mais où sont passés les Indo-Européens? Le mythe d'origine de l'Occident*. Paris: Le Seuil, 2014.

Shennan, Stephen J. *The First Farmers of Europe: An Evolutionary Perspective*. Cambridge: Cambridge University Press, 2018.

Tarrête, Jacques, and Charles-Tanguy Le Roux, eds. *Le Néolithique.*
Archéologie de la France. Paris: Ministère de la Culture et de la
Communication and Picard, 2008.

RELATED ARTICLES

1247, 1962

600 BCE

Marseille: A Greek Outpost in Gaul?

The fairy-tale version of the Greek colonial enterprise has broad appeal, but Marseille's founding in 600 BCE needs to be seen within the broader history of an interconnected and conflict-ridden Mediterranean region. Far from wanting to spread Hellenic influence to Gaul, the Greek colonists were trying to establish a relay point in a preexisting network of maritime routes.

Around 600 BCE, a Phocaean ship landed not far from the mouth of the Rhône, returning from a long journey that took it from its home waters on the Ionian Coast, in what is now western Turkey, to eastern Spain and Andalusia. The Greek seamen and their two leaders, Simos and Protis, went to find the king of the Segobrigii, Nannus, to ask if they could build a city on his territory. The Roman historian Justin, writing at the end of the second century CE, describes the Segobrigii as welcoming the Greeks warmly:

> It so happened that on that particular day, the king was busy with arrangements for the wedding of his

daughter Gyptis; in accordance with the tradition of his people, he was preparing to give her in marriage to a son-in-law who would be chosen at the wedding-feast. All Gyptis's suitors had been invited to the ceremony, and the Greek visitors were also summoned to the banquet. The girl was then brought in and told by her father to hand some water to whomsoever she chose as her husband. Passing by everyone else, she turned to the Greeks and handed the water to Protis who, becoming a son-in-law instead of a visitor, was given by his father-in-law a site on which to build his city.

It makes a nice story: Greek adventurers settle peaceably, with the willing consent of the native population, on soil that will become France. The indigenous Celts, still living in a savage state, sit at the knees of the Phocaeans and thus improve their lot:

It was from these Greeks that the Gauls learned to live in a more civilized manner, abandoning or modifying their barbarous ways; they learned to practice agriculture and encircle their cities with walls. They became used to a life governed by law rather than armed might, to cultivating the vine and planting the olive tree; and so brilliantly successful was the society and its affairs that, instead of Greece emigrating to Gaul, it looked as if Gaul had been moved to Greece." (*Epitome of the Philippic History of Pompeius Trogus*, XLIII, 3)

According to this tale, France, before France existed, received the spark of civilization from Greek colonists, who introduced the half-savage natives to life in a city-state, from town planning (ramparts) to political organization (laws), while bringing the Mediterranean triad (cereals, grapes, and olives) to a land never broken by the plow.

In the nineteenth century, the marriage of Gyptis and Protis was a much-used allegory for representing the implantation of Hellenic culture on Gallic soil. The wedding scene appeared in a prominent mural painted at the Marseille Stock Exchange around 1860; it figured on a poster celebrating the 2,500th anniversary of the founding of the city at the turn of the last century; and it was even engraved on an official medal struck in 1943. In 1987, a table with a dedication to the two lovers was erected on the city's Quai Marcel Pagnol, carved in marble that had been quarried in Greece. This new commemorative site was sponsored by the Office of Tourism.

To be sure, the bride is a little too perfect in this telling. Let's raise a tiny corner of her veil to examine her more closely. Justin's account is based on a lost history by Pompeius Trogus, a Celt by ancestry, from the town of Vaison-la-Romaine in southern Gaul, who wrote in Greek at the end of the first century BCE. The narrative structure accordingly reflects the author's straddling of two worlds and his double allegiance to Greek and Celtic cultures. It is therefore hard to give the story any credence, particularly as it abounds in factual errors, both chronological and geographical. It also follows the stereotypical arc of many Greek founding myths, in which welcoming natives voluntarily cede their territory to newly arrived Hellenes, in Cyrene, Libya, for instance, and also in Megara Hyblaea, Sicily.

Counter to this fairy-tale version of the Greek colonial adventure, the founding of Marseille deserves to be analyzed in a broader historical perspective, in which the Mediterranean region is seen as interconnected and strife-ridden. At the time Marseille was founded, Phocaean ships were not alone in crisscrossing the Mediterranean. By 600 BCE, the Rhône delta had long been visited by other Greeks, most likely from Cyprus and Rhodes, as well as by Etruscans and Phoenicians — there is even a late tradition ascribing the founding of Marseille to the inhabitants of Tyre. The city's founding in no way eradicated these competing trade networks: for almost a century, Marseille hosted numerous cross-pollinating exchanges, with Greeks and non-Greeks alike selling their goods there. In the wrecks excavated on the nearby sea floor — notably off the island of Porquerolles — the cargoes are composed equally of pottery from Greece (Corinth, Ionia, and Laconia), Etruria, and Phoenicia. It seems likely that for several decades at least, Marseille was a vast *emporion*, a market port and trading post open to all, rather than a proper Greek city.

If there was coexistence, however, there was also conflict. The Phocaeans, sailing in war ships propelled by fifty oarsmen and not in the rounded ships used to transport merchandise, had a tendency to consider piracy as the continuation of trade by other means. In the mid-sixth century BCE, the situation degenerated into a naval war, after the Phocaeans founded Alalia, in Corsica, in their flight from the Persian advance across Asia Minor. Although the sea battle finally turned in favor of the Greeks and against the coalition of Carthaginians and Etruscans, losses were heavy on both sides. On land, the colonists in Marseille were finding their relations with the local population anything but peaceful. Bordered by steep cliffs, the city was further encircled by a fortified wall to protect the Greeks from external assault. The Greek historian Strabo, writing in the first century BCE, makes it clear that the Marseille colonists faced considerable aggression from the Iberians, Salyes, and Ligurians. Conflict was one of the structuring elements in the early life of the colony.

Despite Justin's account, the Hellenic graft did not flourish for a long time, and the arrival of the Greeks at first had little impact beyond the walls of their city. Facing threats on all sides, the inhabitants of Marseille were largely cut off from their own territory, which was unappealing because of its rocky soil: "Consequently, they trust more to the resources of the sea than to the land, and avail themselves in preference of their excellent position for commerce" (Strabo, *Geography*, Book IV, Chapter 1, section 6). The disconnect between the town and its surrounding countryside lasted into the middle of the Hellenistic period: the ridge of L'Estaque, though just north of Marseille, only became part of the city in 150 BCE, while the *oppidum* or fortified stronghold of La Cloche, though only a few miles from the city center, retained its indigenous character for a further hundred years. Similarly, it would take nearly a century for inland trade to develop and engender any real degree of hybridization. Only at the end of the sixth century did the Rhône River become an important axis of trade, bringing the Greeks and Celts into close contact.

The reason is that the Phocaeans did not found Marseille to engage in trade with the local populations — or to civilize them — but to create a support base along an already well-established trans-Mediterranean route. The evidence suggests that the Phocaeans had several trading posts in Spain by the time they founded Marseille. Far from being the Greeks' advanced outpost in the Western Mediterranean, Marseille was no more than a link in a preexisting trade network, whose purpose was to help transport pewter from Cornwall and silver from the Sierra Nevada of southern Spain toward Asia Minor.

These intense commercial exchanges were accompanied by major institutional and religious transfers. As Strabo tells us, the Phocaean colonists built a temple on the model of the great temple of Artemis in Ephesus, the Ephesium, where they had made a stopover on their sail westward. Near the Ephesium, they built a temple to Delphian Apollo, in imitation of a cult from Miletus that was common to many Ionians. The new city was regulated by Ionian laws, which were posted in public as in the Ionian capital, contributing to the propagation of a common political culture across the Mediterranean region. Thus we start to see, through the instance of Marseille, the outlines of a powerful Ionian network, which was in competition with long-established Etruscan and Phoenicio-Carthaginian networks. Far from being the first stage in the Hellenization of Gaul, the founding of Marseille marked the strengthening of a complex of maritime routes in the midst of a strongly but unevenly connected Mediterranean.

Vincent Azoulay

REFERENCES

Bats, Michel. "Les Phocéens, Marseille et la Gaule (VIIe–IIIe siècle av. J.-C.)." *Pallas 89* (2012): 145–156.

———, Guy Bertucchi, Gaëtan Conges, et al., eds. "Marseille grecque et la Gaule." In *Actes du colloque de Marseille, 18–23 novembre 1990.* Aix-en-Provence: Publications de l'Université de Provence, 1992.

Bouiron, Marc, and Henri Tréziny, eds. "Marseille: Trames et paysages urbains de Gyptis au roi René." In *Actes du colloque de Marseille, 3–5 novembre 1999*. Aix-en-Provence: Édisud, 2001.

Collin Bouffier, Sophie. "Marseille et la Gaule méditerranéenne avant la conquête romaine." *Pallas 80* (2009): 35–60.

Malkin, Irad. *A Small Greek World: Networks in the Ancient Mediterranean*. Oxford: Oxford University Press, 2011.

RELATED ARTICLES

52 BCE, 719, 1347, 1446, 1923

500 BCE

The Last of the Celts

The grave discovered in Vix more than a half century
ago confirms the complexity of the political and economic
structures of a now vanished Mediterranean world in the sixth
century BCE. The large krater found with the body of what was
probably the equivalent of a queen suggests an extraordinary
circulation of luxury goods of Greco-Etruscan origin.

The Vix Grave discovered in January 1953 around the Mont
Lassois, at the foot of a fortified settlement, dating from
the Early Iron Age, was part of a peripheral funerary zone
established on a plateau on the right bank of the Seine. The
first funerary monuments erected there during the second
half of the ninth century BCE — burial mounds — were
clearly intended for individuals in the upper ranks of society.
The Vix Grave is one of the very last funerary mounds built
at the beginning of the fifth century BCE. With a diameter of
130 feet, the mound covered a central funerary chamber of
around a hundred square feet, dug into the ground and lined
with wood.

In the middle of the funerary chamber was a box from a four-wheeled wagon, inside of which were found the remains of a woman aged between thirty and thirty-five. It must have been a light vehicle, constructed mainly of wood, decorated with delicate bronze appliques. The wagon's wheels had been removed, wrapped in fabric, and lined up along one of the sides. On the floor of the funerary chamber archaeologists discovered what J. R. Maréchal described as "a thin layer of lovely blue pigment dotted here and there with brilliant red pigment." The red pigment has been identified as cinnabar; it may have been part of the decoration of a sort of "tarp" whose organic material, since disintegrated, might have covered the funerary objects.

The dead woman was lying on her back, in the direction in which the vehicle would have been moving. Next to the skull was an extraordinary gold torc, or rigid neck ring. Its ends are decorated with winged horses on intricate filigree pedestals and lions' paws. Remnants of a necklace with three large amber beads and four rings of polished slate were also found, as well as seven brooches known as fibulae alongside the woman's chest. One of them is made of iron with two rings, ornamented with two gold cabochons. These brooches must have been used to hold a garment together. On the forearms there are a pair of armlets made of slate and a bracelet of amber beads strung on bronze wire. A pair of bronze ankle rings has been placed at the base of the tibias. Finally, on the stomach rests a large ring-shaped bronze object with markings suggesting that a leather strap had been wound around it.

The household objects buried with her include an impressive number of metal and pottery drinking vessels. An enormous bronze krater, with a capacity of three hundred gallons, was placed next to the dead woman, along with a shallow silver and gold-plated umbilicate phiale. There are also two Attic cups, one of solid black varnish, the other decorated with a motif of black figures. Near the krater, three bronze basins have been placed vertically at the base of one of the walls of the chamber. At the foot of the large receptacle, a bronze *oenochoe* (wine pitcher) must also have been placed on the lid: it seems to have fallen on the ground when the ceiling of the funerary chamber collapsed due to the decomposition of the wooden support beams, which had given way under the weight of the earth that had accumulated on top of the mound.

Since the end of the nineteenth century, archaeologists have been aware of the existence of such monumental sepulchers, containing wagons and rich gold ornamental objects. Dating from the end of the Early Iron Age, they have been discovered mostly in eastern France and southwestern Germany. The Vix Grave is a spectacular example, showing how elite tombs reflected a robust trade in luxury goods of Greco-Etruscan origin. Its discovery has also enabled archaeologists to situate this phenomenon more precisely within the history of the ancient Celtic world's relationships with classical Mediterranean civilizations.

Recent research carried out on the objects found in the Vix Grave has revealed that they can in fact be grouped into two distinct chronological periods, separated by about the equivalent of a generation. The oldest group mainly includes the exceptional banquet objects, such as the giant krater, made in a specialized workshop in Magna Graecia around 540–520 BCE. One of the drinking cups of Attic pottery was produced in an Athenian workshop in 530–520 BCE; whereas one of the large bronze basins placed at the foot of the krater seems to be of Etruscan origin dating from the third quarter of the sixth century BCE.

The more recent objects form part of the dead woman's personal belongings. The bronze ankle rings and bracelets, the slate rings, and the collection of seven fibulae, as well as the large ring placed on her body, were produced in the eastern French region and date from a period between 500 and 450 BCE. The four-wheeled wagon belongs in this second grouping, as does the bronze wine pitcher and two of the basins, which were made in Etruria, in the Vulci region, between the end of the sixth century and the first half of the fifth century BCE. One of the two Attic cups, of black varnish, was made around 500 BCE. It is the most recent piece among the tomb objects, buried with the woman in the first decades of the fifth century BCE.

And so the "Lady of Vix" was buried with ornamental objects and clothing that reflected her life as an adult; she was also buried with foreign luxury items that arrived in Vix at the latest during her childhood, and which likely date from her parents' generation. The key point here is that those two sets of objects belong to different worlds. The more recent ones, essentially personal items, were common for a class of women from a local privileged social stratum, buried with wagons between the end of the sixth and the beginning of the fifth century BCE. The older objects — which mainly belonged to the "funerary accoutrements" of the deceased — were by contrast imported luxury goods explicitly associated with the banquets and libation practices that have been known to exist in urban Mediterranean cultures.

The "Lady of Vix" had obviously inherited her status from a preceding generation, which left her a series of objects emblematic of the power and prestige of the dominant social class to which she belonged. But what was the origin of this opulence, which clearly resulted from trade with the Mediterranean world? According to René Joffroy, the man who discovered the grave, the region of Vix, to the northwest of present-day Burgundy, constituted a point of "intermediate reloading" at the intersection of the "routes" by which Atlantic tin was imported to the European continent and the great route by which Mediterranean trade traveled up the Rhône Valley. It is believed that the Celtic chiefs who controlled the region would have exacted a "toll" from Greco-Etruscan merchants who were importing tin through the pre-Roman Gallic territory.

It is difficult to prove this hypothesis, which, moreover, seems at odds with what anthropology has enabled us to reconstruct of the economy of pre-monetary Celtic societies. The luxury items from the Mediterranean region that were placed in graves of the Vix type indeed seem to have been prestigious "gifts" geared to a barbarous Celtic clientele rather than mere commercial products. Thus the oversized Vix Krater clearly appears to have been an attempt to reproduce a classic Greek object — in this case a receptacle in which wine and water were mixed — and to adapt it to a foreign milieu in which larger and larger quantities of drink were collected to be distributed by the dominant Celtic classes as a sign of their social prestige and political power. This deliberate transformation of valuable objects that denoted social status suggests that trade relations between the Mediterranean elite and their Celtic equivalents were not entirely equal.

Following the Etruscans, the Greeks exploited the extraordinary profits offered to them by a type of barbarian economy based on gifts and indebtedness, in which the wealthiest individuals concentrated wealth in order to distribute it to allies, vassals, and dependents.

The Celtic "upper class" siphoned off for itself local resources — metals, to be sure, and possibly slaves — that Mediterraneans came to collect within the barbarian confines. In exchange, the Celts obtained goods — notably Greek wine and ostentatious vessels — that were inaccessible to most of their countrymen, thereby reinforcing their prestige and power. Celtic aristocrats were thus drawn into a system in which relationships of dependence destabilized the social order by causing the emergence of powerful if ephemeral actors who accumulated hitherto unseen levels of wealth. The opulence of the Vix Grave is one of the last visible signs of this Celtic elite's fortune. Its downfall a short time later marked the end of the civilization of the Early Iron Age.

Laurent Olivier

REFERENCES

Egg, Markus, and Albert France-Lanord. *Le Char de Vix*. Mainz: Römisch-Germanisches Zentralmuseum, 1987.

Joffroy, René. "La tombe de Vix (Côte-d'Or)." *Monuments et mémoires de la Fondation Eugène Piot* 48, no. 1 (1954): 1–68.

Maréchal, Jean R. "Quelques considérations sur les objets trouvés dans la sépultures hallstattienne de Vix (Côte-d'Or)." *Techniques et Civilisations* 4, no. 1 (1955): 1–27.

Olivier, Laurent. "Early Iron Age Gold Jewellery: 150 Years of

Discoveries in France." *In Early Iron Age Gold in Celtic Europe: Society, Technology and Archaeometry*, edited by Roland Schwab, Pierre-Yves Milcent, Barbara Armbruster, and Ernst Pernicka, 11–42. Rahden: Verlag Marie Leidorf, 2018.

———. "The Hochdorf Princely Grave and the Question of the Nature of Archaeological Funerary Assemblages." In *Time and Archaeology*, edited by Tim Murray, 109–38. London and New York: Routledge, 1999.

———. "Tombes princières et principautés celtiques. La place du site de Vix dans la recherche européenne sur les centres de pouvoir du premier âge du Fer." In *Autour de la Dame de Vix, Celtes, Grecs et Étrusques*, 11–25. Châtillon-sur-Seine: Musée du Châtillonnais, 2003.

Rolley, Claude, ed. *La Tombe princière de Vix*. 2 vols. Paris: Picard, 2003.

RELATED ARTICLES

23,000 BCE, 600 BCE, 52 BCE, 719, 1825, 1949

52 BCE

Alésia: The Meaning of Defeat

Caesar's account of the surrender of Vercingetorix after the Battle of Alésia in 52 BCE drew an abrupt though artificial line between "Gallic" and "Roman" Gaul, one evanescent and the other permanent. The truth was that the economic and cultural Romanization of Gaul was a long and laborious process that took centuries. How did the Gauls' "providential defeat" described in Caesar's *Commentaries* acquire such a mythic status, and why does the idea behind it persist to this day?

"On the flanks of Mont Auxois, now so arid, the fate of the world was decided. In these fertile plains, on these hilltops which are now so quiet, nearly 400,000 men met in battle.... The entire cause of civilization was at stake that day." With florid emphasis, Napoleon III (Emperor of the French between 1852 and 1870, but also a historian of Julius Caesar) magnified the universal consequence of the Gauls' glorious debacle at Alésia.

Glorious...but entirely improbable, given the unequal

resources of the two sides. How on earth had sixty thousand Roman legionaries, bottled up in the Laumes plain at the foot of the *oppidum* of Alésia, contrived to overwhelm eighty thousand warriors led by Vercingetorix and backed by an army of two hundred thousand fellow Gauls? Ever skeptical, Napoleon I had been one of the few military strategists who bothered to expose the obfuscation that Caesar or his Gallic allies or both had carried out in their rendering of Alésia. The destiny of his nephew, the future Napoleon III, would give this obfuscation the aura of myth.

It was the ambition of Napoleon III to make himself the "Divine Julius" of the French nation, but in September 1870 — barely five years after the publication of his *History of Julius Caesar* — he found himself a latter-day Vercingetorix, trapped in the fortress of Sedan by an army of Prussians. Sedan was a sublime irony of fate as well as a tragic turning point in the history of Europe. Its direct consequence, a reversal of the roles of victor and vanquished, launched a cycle of imaginary transpositions whereby the antagonism smoldering between the French and the Germans found justification right through to the collapse of France in 1940.

The myth of Alésia, underscored by the romantic theme of the Gallic origin of France, has been a French fantasy for the last 150 years. In the early years of Napoleon III's reign, the hilltop village of Alise-Sainte-Reine at the northern end of the Massif Central was consecrated as the site of Year I of

115

French history. Despite extensive excavations begun by the emperor at Alise in 1861 and continued by a Franco-German archaeological dig in the 1990s, the location of the battlefield remains strongly disputed. Indeed yet another "Battle of Alésia," apparently interminable, continues to be fought today. As recently as 2014, the French TV historian Franck Ferrand rekindled the dispute by denouncing Caesar's story as a deception, and the hill of Alésia as an ill-inspired venue for an impossible story about France's origin.

How, then, could a military defeat — any military defeat — acquire such valence as a foundational moment? Why was nineteenth-century France so determined to date the origin of the nation from its lock, stock, and barrel absorption into a global Roman empire? Is there any way to cross-check the jealous word of the Roman general, who grafted a conqueror's vision onto his classic *Commentaries*, with the conclusions of modern archaeology? Can we ever escape the trap of Alésia's narrative?

To do so we must return to the kernel and the function of the myth, an absurd scene involving Caesar and Vercingetorix. The latter was only famous up to a point: before the historian Amédée Thierry rescued him from oblivion in 1828, the very name of the man who Jules Michelet would call the "hero of Gaul" was no more than a military title, roughly equivalent to Generalissimo in today's parlance. As the historian Jean-Paul Demoule mischievously suggests, Vercingetorix's military capitulation is no more believable than the idea of Saddam Hussein in an army vehicle surrendering to George Bush in person. Six years after his capture, in 46 BCE, a chained Vercingetorix was reportedly exhibited in Rome as a trophy of Caesar's triumph. Whether that is true or not, he must have perished later in hideous conditions, just like the Iraqi dictator. Nineteenth-century sculptors (such as Aimé Millet, whose statue was given by Napoleon III to the commune of Alise in 1865) and historical painters (such as Lionel Royer in 1899) later imagined the edifying scene of Vercingetorix laying his weapons at Caesar's feet. This gave symbolic expression to the "providential man" who, by giving his life for his compatriots, sacrificed himself to a greater destiny.

This symbolism has always been the principal driving force of the Alésia myth.

Like his fellow archaeologist Christian Goudineau, Jean-Louis Brunaux — a specialist in Celtic history — has pointed out that stories featuring the surrender scene had been relayed by Plutarch, Diodorus of Sicily, and Cassius Dio. All of them postdated Caesar's *Commentaries*. Whether or not Caesar himself wanted to paint Vercingetorix as a brilliant tactician and a serious threat, the surrender is conspicuously absent from his lapidary account. Indeed, his use of the impersonal, passive verb in the phrase *Vercingetorix deditur* (literally, "Vercingetorix was handed over") allowed him to remain vague about the event. History does not tell who handed Vercingetorix over.

Given our necessary reliance on Caesar's text, anything is conceivable, including the possibility that Vercingetorix, a former hostage and friend of Caesar's, could have been the ally and even the indirect agent of his enemies in Rome. Vercingetorix's rebellion of 53 BCE, which suddenly appears in Book VII of Caesar's *Gallic Wars*, could have been linked to the political crisis that took place in Rome that year. Following the death of Crassus in Syria, the Senate had made Pompey a kind of dictator, directly threatening Caesar's own ambitions. Thus the campaign that led to Alésia could have been a move in the overall crisis shaking the institutions of the Republic, echoing the geopolitics of an evolving Roman Mediterranean. Basically the "permanent conspiracy" of the 59 BCE triumvirate of Crassus, Caesar, and Pompey had become a struggle to the death between Caesar and Pompey, both seeking control of what was an empire in all but name.

But this is not the story that tradition has preserved. Perhaps to mask the evidence that coalesces in the first seven books of the *Gallic Wars*, Caesar in 58 BCE answered the request of the Aedui tribe's assembly at Bibracte to establish a Roman protectorate against their hereditary enemies, the Sequani (who a year earlier had themselves been "friends of Rome"). Alliance with Rome was something that these people wanted and for which they competed, for conquest by Rome meant pacification and effective policing in a territory whose institutions and commerce were already Roman-controlled. The Bibracte assembly — by which Vercingetorix was briefly semi-legitimized — may itself have been an instrument of indirect Roman power.

So the roughly sixty city-states that made up the "Gallic" territory (i.e., the plural Gauls rather than a unique Gaul) were not conquered by Rome after a fierce struggle to defend their liberty. They submitted freely, of their own volition.

Yet with the scene of Vercingetorix's surrender after the battle at Alésia, the national idea of France endowed itself with a matrix, at once retroactive and prospective, whereby a gloriously "necessary" defeat justified French history and gave it meaning. The fervor invested in the cult of Alésia was transformed into what can best be described as a "glorious defeat" syndrome. Indeed it forms the first link in a chain of lost battles that exercise a curious fascination on French national memory, from Poitiers to Agincourt, Pavia, Waterloo, Trafalgar, and Dien Bien Phu. Hence the glorious loser, Vercingetorix, the Christ-figure of a secular republic, whose role was to predate the Merovingian baptism of France and even anticipate the collaboration of Vichy, even if that meant reminding the French that he was also (occasionally) on the winning side.

On August 30, 1942, it was at Gergovia, on the occasion of the second birthday of Vichy's French Legion of Combatants and Volunteers of the National Revolution, that soil samples dug up from every *commune* of France and its empire were brought together in a single marble cenotaph. For the occasion, the sacrifice of Vercingetorix was eulogized by a senator, the uncle of the future president Giscard d'Estaing, in identical terms to those used by General de Gaulle six years earlier, in his book *France and Her Army*. Both agreed that in French history defeat was superior to victory — because defeat lay at the root of the nation's unity.

Alésia amounts to a historical myth in reserve, curiously reversible in its uses and moral and chronological significance. It is hard to pinpoint a genuinely "historic" moment in the story, which resonated so much deeper in the second half of the nineteenth century than it did in antiquity. The Alésia syndrome highlights a certain relationship between France and the outside world, beginning with the moment when signs of France's growing international power began to compete with those of its "decline." Interestingly, Napoleon III interpreted the embryonic Alésia myth and the "meaning" of this defeat by way of a curious factual contortion. "The defeat of Caesar," he wrote,

> would have stalled the advance of Roman domination for a long time.... The Gauls, delirious

with their success, would have called to their aid all those other tribes streaming southward in hopes of creating a fatherland for themselves, and their combined force would have been hurled upon Italy; and that vessel of light which was destined in the future to enlighten all peoples, would have been utterly destroyed....Thus, though we honor the memory of Vercingetorix, we may not regret his defeat....Let us not forget that we owe our civilization to the triumphant armies of Rome: our institutions, traditions, and language all derive from the Roman conquest.

Nothing could be less certain. Had Vercingetorix been victorious, he would most likely have gone straight to Rome to seek consecration as what he probably already was: a Romanized military leader, perhaps even a Roman one.

This then is the deeper meaning of the cult of defeat: it sacrificed a prehistoric history of Gaul (which was impossible to write because there were no sources) to the notion of a brutal but providential Gallo-Roman merger. And this served to exorcise the aristocratic, Germanic origin of the Franks.

Romanization was synonymous with what we call globalization today. The Alésia syndrome simply masked the fact that, for Gaul, incorporation into this larger phenomenon was voluntary — part of a slow, centuries-long process underway around the Mediterranean, from

121

Tunisia to Spain. Alésia depicted the Roman "colonization" of Gaul as the equivalent of nineteenth-century seaborne empires rather than the drawn-out process it really was. The Gauls' full integration into the sphere of Roman influence had actually come about at the end of the fourth century, with the legendary sack of Rome by the "hordes" of the Senone chieftain Brennus.

From the Po to the Rhine, three hundred years of connections and interactions between Cisalpine Gaul and Rome's Transalpine province produced a Romanization that was at first social and then cultural and religious. Alésia, a sanctuary that was dedicated to Hercules well before 52 BCE, was in theory an ideal location for a showdown between two competing military leaders. On the other hand, the most striking archaeological discovery at the modern site of Alise has been that of six Greco-Roman coins, struck with the effigy of a beardless Vercingetorix, resembling Apollo, in a style dating from the reign of Philip II of Macedonia. This, unsurprisingly, has had no more effect on the popular representation of Gauls as pigtailed, heavily bearded figures, as seen in the beloved French comic book character Obélix.

Yann Potin

REFERENCES

Brunaux, Jean-Louis. *Alésia: Le tombeau de l'indépendance gauloise*. Paris: Gallimard, 2012.

Buchsenschutz, Olivier. "Les Celtes et la formation de l'Empire romain." *Annales. Histoire, sciences sociales* 59, no. 2 (2004): 337–61.

Goudineau, Christian. *Le dossier Vercingétorix*. Arles: Actes Sud, 2001.

Simon, André. *Vercingétorix et l'idéologie française*. Paris: Imago, 1989.

Thébert, Yvon. "Romanisation et déromanisation en Afrique: histoire décolonisée ou histoire inversée?" *Annales. Économies, sociétés, civilisations* 33, no. 1 (1978): 64–82.

RELATED ARTICLES

48, 212, 1357, 1420, 1763, 1815, 1871, 1940, 1965

FROM ONE EMPIRE
TO ANOTHER

I n the spring of the year 800, a new emperor was crowned in Rome by the Pope: Charles, King of the Franks, soon to be known as Charlemagne, or Charles the Great. By the close of his reign in 814, Charlemagne's writ extended across most of Western Europe, from the Marca Hispanica (present-day Catalonia) to the frontiers of Poland, from northern Italy to Friesland (present-day Holland) and the North Sea, from Austria to Armorica (present-day Brittany). Only the British Isles escaped the emperor's control, but even there his prestige was strong, attracting to his court scholars from York and Ireland. More than three hundred years after the death of the last Roman emperor, in 476, a new empire had emerged in the West: a Frankish empire, named Carolingian after its first sovereign.

"Carolus Magnus," as his biographer Einhard called him, "Karl der Grosse," as he was called in Germany, "Charlemagne," as he was called in France, long remained the mythical emperor "à la barbe fleurie" (with the flowing beard) in the French national imagination. For centuries, the French remembered him — anachronistically — as a brilliant king of France even if he was often taken to task for "inventing the school" and for encouraging classical Latin and a broad cultural renaissance, spanning from poetry, exegesis, music, and law to illuminated manuscripts and architecture in a hitherto "barbaric" Europe.

In point of fact, it was highly unlikely that Charlemagne

had a beard at all, let alone a flowing one. Moreover, he could barely read Latin and was absolutely not French — or even German. Charlemagne was Frankish; he belonged to a warlike Germanic people, the Franks, who had maintained close links with the Romans from the third century onward and eventually established themselves in Gaul, annexing its entire territory in the early sixth century. The Franks were not very numerous; the aces they held were military superiority and a shrewd, consistent alliance with Gaul's established Catholic bishops and Gallo-Roman aristocracy. They consolidated their power at the expense of other Germanic peoples who were striving to win a foothold at roughly the same time: the Visigoths in the southwest, the Ostrogoths in the southeast, and the Burgundians in the east and in the Alps. Clovis, the first king of the Franks, was baptized a Christian at the turn of the fifth and sixth centuries by Remi, bishop of Reims. By becoming Catholic, his successors, the kings of the Merovingian dynasty, won reluctant recognition of their power by the emperors of Byzantium. The latter claimed to be the heirs of ancient Rome even though their capital was Constantinople, their language Greek, and their authority almost nonexistent in the western Mediterranean.

In the middle of the eighth century, Charlemagne's father, the head of a powerful Frankish aristocratic family, dislodged the last descendant of Clovis and, with the support of the Roman papacy, founded a new Carolingian dynasty. Power was concentrated in the hands of the Franks, but with the extension of their domination to Italy, northern Spain, and eastern Europe, their kings became emperors of a realm that was both Frankish and Roman. Although he was crowned in Rome, Charlemagne made the significant choice to build his capital at Aachen, at the heart of his ancestral domain in the hills of the Ardennes, a region that now straddles France, Belgium, Germany, and Luxembourg. Charlemagne was implicitly recognizing the slow upheaval that had shifted the center of gravity away from the Mediterranean and turned the Frankish regions into what they have remained ever since: the heartlands of Western Europe.

The old Roman culture was not forgotten by Charlemagne. He had set his heart on Aachen (in Latin *Aquae*), the site of ancient hot springs, for a reason: while a Frankish warrior, he loved steaming Roman baths. The park adjoining his palace contained a white elephant, a gift of the caliph of Baghdad, Hārūn al-Rashīd: naturally the Frankish emperor, like his Byzantine counterpart, was in close diplomatic touch with the "Prince of the Muslims," who reigned from Persia to Andalusia. The chapel where Charlemagne worshipped was a mirror image of the Church of the Holy Sepulcher in Jerusalem, decorated with porphyry columns brought from Ravenna, the former Byzantine capital of the sixth century. The emperor's wholesale removal of his center of power from the shores of the Mediterranean to northern Europe was already a powerful statement to his Byzantine neighbor, but he still felt obliged to ape Byzantium's magnificence and appropriate its symbols (imperial purple, religious pomp, tall columns, and gorgeous mosaics) along with its ideology. The Frankish emperor saw himself as at least the equal of the Eastern emperor, who had no choice but to accept this reality.

The same notion of empire had been ever-present throughout the eight centuries separating the reign of the Lyon-born Claudius (41–54 CE), the first Roman emperor of Gallic origin, and the coronation of Charlemagne in 800. The Gauls, who were only ever united in the eyes of Caesar, had been thoroughly absorbed into the Roman Empire. Southern regions, like the province of Gallia Narbonensis bordering the Mediterranean eastward from Nice to Toulouse and northward to Lake Geneva, succumbed to the Romans early (between 125 and 121 BCE); they were soon covered by a dense fabric of cities and vast private estates (*villae*). The northernmost territories were absorbed later on, during the period that began with the Lyon Tablet of 48 CE, an extraordinary stone fragment recording the speech whereby Claudius opened the Roman

Senate to the elites of Gallia Comata (long-haired Gaul, as the Romans called it), and ended with the edict of Emperor Caracalla in 212 CE, whereby Roman citizenship was automatically given to every free inhabitant of the Empire.

Thereafter the Gauls were Romans just like everybody else, gradually absorbing new Germanic, Frankish, Gothic, and Burgundian populations from the third century on. This was achieved in a number of ways, ranging from the individual settlement of families of auxiliaries of the Roman military to the collective integration of whole populations following the conclusion of a treaty. The result was always the same: the newcomers merged with the local inhabitants. This was most pronounced in the northern and eastern regions of the empire, close to the outer frontiers (the *limes*), where Frankish expansion commenced at the end of the fifth century.

In the sixth century, with the consent of local elites, the kingdom founded by Clovis and his sons began to creep southward and eastward, tracing the contours of an entirely new political entity: a "Kingdom of the Franks." This kingdom acquired a unity of its own despite being regularly carved into sub-kingdoms (Neustria, Austrasia, Burgundia) to accommodate brothers or cousins in the Merovingian royal family, within which every male had an equal right to the crown. The Kingdom of the Franks in no way coincided with present-day France. In the north and east, it began with present-day Belgium and expanded, along with its conquests, into Friesland, Franconia, and Bavaria (the latter two in present-day Germany). In the south, it had yet to annex Gascony, Septimania (present-day Lower Languedoc), or Provence. Nor did the kingdom of the Franks correspond to the later kingdom of West Francia (*Francia occidentalis*), which emerged from the division of Charlemagne's empire between the sons of Louis the Pious by the Treaty of Verdun in 843. *Francia occidentalis* is sometimes described as the territorial matrix of the French ancien régime. Apportioned to the youngest son of Louis the Pious, Charles the Bald, it included Flanders in the north and Catalonia to the south, but was bounded to the east by four rivers (the Scheldt, the Meuse, the Saône, and the Rhône), leaving the eastern half of present-day France within the realm of Middle Francia (*Francia media*). This region was inherited by Lothair, Charles the Bald's elder brother.

So the kingdom of the Franks was very much cobbled together. Several tongues were spoken: a form of Latin which evolved into a Romance language, various Germanic dialects including Frankish, the Breton language of the Armorican peninsula, and perhaps Basque on the Pyrenean frontier. Its people were a mix of Gallo-Roman and Germanic, whose customs and usages were a blend of Frankish, Burgundian, and Gothic influences, tempered by a strong dose of Roman law. Its material culture was highly varied (with radically differing house designs, clothing, and tableware) having been exposed to a host of cultures: Anglo-Saxon and Irish along the Atlantic coast; Iberian, Gothic, and Arab-Berber in Aquitaine and around the Mediterranean fringe. At the heart of the Western Empire recast by Charlemagne in 800, the Kingdom of the Franks melted into his empire as part of a Babel of peoples and realms extending throughout Europe: Frankish by name and Christian by faith.

From the Germanic migrations between the third and sixth centuries to the Viking and Arab expeditions of the ninth and tenth centuries (the last Muslim foothold on the territory of what was formerly Gaul, at La Garde-Freinet near Saint-Tropez, disappeared in 972), these were years of shifting populations, political accommodation, and reciprocal acculturation. But over and above population movement and cultural diversification, one shared element made for real unity within these motley societies. This was the fact that all had embraced an Eastern religion, Christianity, and carried it to the western edge of the known world.

Quietly injected into society by merchants, missionaries, and monks from beyond the Mediterranean, Christianity was proclaimed unique and universal by the West's all-powerful sovereigns — Frankish kings and

133

Carolingian emperors, the immaculate successors of the emperors of Rome and Byzantium. More than half the earliest Christians recorded in Lyon in 177 were natives of the Roman province of Asia. After the conversion of Constantine in 312 and the suppression of paganism in 392, Gallo-Roman elites made a massive commitment to the episcopal function, which emerged, once the Roman Empire had vanished, as the best hope for preserving not only the Christian religion but also the entire ancient culture of Rome. Beginning in the fourth and fifth centuries, monasticism — which had also originated in the East — constituted one of the most powerful factors in the Christianization of ordinary people, especially in the countryside, where beliefs, landscapes, and social practices underwent significant transformation.

Thus it was a political alliance between the church and the Franks — initiated by Clovis and the Gallo-Roman Bishops and then renewed, deepened, and extended onto the Roman papacy by the Carolingians — that allowed the Frankish monarchy to achieve its imperial destiny.

48

Gauls in the Roman Senate

In 48 CE, notables from the "long-haired" Gallic provinces demanded, with the support of Emperor Claudius, the right to join the Roman Senate. Only the Aedui were successful, but the negotiations show the early integration of the Gallic elite into the Roman Empire and its Mediterranean culture.

Some rare events are like glimmers of light in the darkness. Illuminated by a few extraordinary accounts telling of singular lives and exploits, they reveal truly significant historical occurrences. What unfolded in the Roman Senate in the autumn of the year 48, in the presence of Emperor Tiberius Claudius Germanicus, more commonly known as Claudius, counts among these significant moments with wide-ranging stakes.

The facts have been well established thanks to two relevant sources. The first comes from the Latin historian Tacitus, who in Book XI of his *Annals* describes in detail the historical context of the year 48 CE and the voyage to Rome of a delegation of notables from three Gallic provinces

(Aquitania, Lugdunensis, and Belgica), all of them demanding the right to sit in the Senate. That right — *ius adipiscendorum in Vrbe honorum* in Latin — was denied to them even though they were officially Roman citizens. Tacitus describes the arrival of those delegates, the audience they were granted, and the speech that Claudius delivered on their behalf. He then relates the assembly's decision to concede the right to senatorial honors to only those from Lugdunensis, known as the Aedui, who were deemed brothers (*fratres*) on account of their ancient connections to the Romans.

The second text, exceptional in more than one way, was discovered by chance in 1528 on the hill of La Croix-Rousse in Lyon, on the very spot where in antiquity the Sanctuary of the Three Gauls dedicated to the cult of Rome and its emperors had been established. It is a Latin inscription carefully engraved on a gilded bronze plaque weighing close to five hundred pounds. The surviving fragments transcribe half the speech delivered by Claudius in the Senate on behalf of the Gauls, the same speech that Tacitus reported in detail. This inscription, which became known as the Lyon Tablet, had been placed near the sanctuary in an area where the high priests and their families customarily erected statues and built monuments to their own glory. Although it was revised before being monumentalized, the text is the only one of its kind. A source of local pride and a component of France's national heritage, the tablet fragments were exhibited in the town hall of Lyon before finding a home in the city's Museum of Gallo-Roman Civilization.

But let's return to the affair of 48 CE. It is one of a chain of events that had begun to unfold a century earlier, in 52 BCE, when Caesar annexed Gaul following the surrender of Vercingetorix in Alésia. To understand the upheavals that occurred between those two dates, the concept of generations provides a useful tool for analysis.

The Gauls who presented their petition to the Senate were older men, notables with acknowledged authority in their cities, born at the turn of their era. Grandsons and great-grandsons of fighters from Alésia, they participated in the transformation of the Gallic space into a territory that was juridically and culturally Romanized, as witnessed by the cities and monuments, the temples, forums, and theaters constructed in the Mediterranean and Roman styles. There are other, no less significant, elements that reflect the Roman imprint on Gallic spaces. New or reestablished cities often took the name of the Roman leader, such as *Juliobona/* Lillebonne, *Caesarodunum/* Tours, *Augustodunum/* Autun, and so forth. Members of the most loyal elite likewise adopted the same onomastic sequence from the names of Caesar and Augustus before 27 BCE — *Caius Julius* — to which they added a personal family name. This *tria nomina* was a badge for those who had obtained Roman citizenship

137

in return for loyalty and merit. One of many such examples was the Aedui priest who dedicated the Sanctuary of the Three Gauls: *Caius Julius Vercondaridubnus*. When Claudius in turn carried out a policy of individual or collective attribution of citizenship, the provinces of the Empire were filled with individuals named *Tiberius Claudius*. The bonds of loyalty thereby created between new citizens and their benefactors ran deep.

Standing before the petitioning Gauls was the legitimate emperor, heir to the Julio-Claudian dynasty. In power for seven years, acclaimed by the Praetorians even though he hadn't been destined to wear the imperial purple since his own nephew, Caligula, had been chosen over him upon the death of Tiberius in 37 CE, Claudius undertook a broad census in 47 CE. He thus reactivated the office of the censor, an old republican jurisdiction that had been dormant since Augustus. Claudius' decision is explained by his desire to inventory the inhabited world following the Empire's recent western expansion into Brittany in 43 CE. If Seneca sarcastically called him Claudius "the Gaul," it was due to the personal connections he had with those regions, but also because he had been born in Lyon in 10 BCE at the very moment when his father, Drusus, son-in-law of Augustus and brother of the future emperor Tiberius, consecrated the Sanctuary of the Three Gauls.

Let us not misunderstand this prince, who was so often

derided by ancient authors. In truth, Claudius was a cultured man and an astute administrator, worthy of his position. It was he who, for example, created an efficient government organized into specialized bureaus. His openness of mind can be seen in his speech to the Senate when, using many edifying examples, he recalled that Rome remained an open city because, since its origins, it had been governed by foreign kings, whether Sabine or Etruscan. Had Romulus not shown infinite wisdom when on the same day he considered his adversaries as enemies and then citizens? By defending the cause of the petitioners, Claudius was not just fulfilling his role as emperor or foremost senator (*princeps*), but above all positioning himself as the patron of the Gauls.

Let us now consider the senators who were members of the curia. By 48 CE, a clear majority of the six hundred *patres* came from Italian families that had been naturalized a century and a half earlier, the upheavals of civil wars having led to the extinction of the most ancient plebeian and patrician families. Several senators came from influential groups originating in the well-integrated Roman provinces, such as Baetica (southern Spain) or Gallia Narbonensis (southern France). Close collaborators of the emperor and endowed with strong class consciousness, these senators formed a conservative group. In order to block access to newcomers who were likely to threaten their interests, in 48 CE they invoked an ancestral fear anchored in the psyches of the Romans, the famous *metus Gallicus* (fear of the Gauls) that harked back to the sacking of Rome by Brennus's Celts in 390 BCE.

The 48 CE event raises important questions about fluctuating relationships within a Roman space that, while now perceived as French, saw itself as an entire world close to 2,000 years ago. There are two ways of viewing this delegation, either emphasizing the fact that Gauls traveled to the Roman Senate or else focusing upon their request for admission into this august assembly. Behind the confrontation between these provincials and the senators, triggered by that petition, we discover the complex mechanisms involved in integrating the peoples and territories that made up the Roman Empire. We also apprehend, in a more subtle fashion, the very functioning of this unique political system.

Through this specific example we can measure the strength of law and of the personal connections involved in the process of integration into the Empire. A century after the conquest, the emperor relied on a network of loyal allies who were rewarded with a Roman citizenship that provided many political and civil rights and secured their preeminence in their city. On a higher level, imperial unity was guaranteed by the common worship of Rome and its rulers at the Sanctuary of the Three Gauls. Each year, on the first day of August, delegates from the Gallic peoples elected a high priest who presided over religious ceremonies and games, and was also charged with submitting to the emperor decrees that had been voted on — petitions, honors, or accusations relating to imperial administrators. By dint of its status as privileged interlocutor with the Senate and the emperor, the assembly thus played an eminently political role. If the delegation's request was apparently rejected in 48 CE, the petition did enable several Gallic notables, the most famous being the Aquitanian Julius Vindex (one of the principal participants in the revolt of 68 CE against Nero), to secure admission into the Senate.

Finally, the event provides insights into the functioning of the *Imperium romanum*, which is still not completely understood even though we now have abundant studies focusing on other periods in the Roman Empire's history. The affair of 48 CE shows that the Empire's government relied on "internal diplomacy," a term that denotes the particular nature of the relations between local powers and Rome. These relations were neither simple administrative ties between governors and the governed nor diplomatic and bilateral relations (in the contemporary sense of the word) between two sovereign states. The ancients had no knowledge of these modern concepts. Sometimes decisions were made from on high, sometimes they followed dialogues that came about because provincials had requested them.

Contemporary historians, often prisoners of the nation-state model, may struggle to characterize this type of governing. But it was indeed an amalgam of administration and diplomacy that explains, first, this singular moment during which, within the confines of the Senate, an emperor stood up for the Gauls against the advice of the senators and, second, the reason why the Aedui alone, on the grounds that they bore the title of brothers of the Romans before the conquest, obtained the requested honor.

Antony Hostein

REFERENCES

Briquel, Dominique. "Claude, érudit et empereur." *Comptes rendus de l'Académie des inscriptions et belles-lettres* 132, no. 11 (1988): 217–32.

Burnand, Yves, et al., eds. *Claude de Lyon, empereur romain*. Paris: Presses de l'université Paris-Sorbonne, 1998.

Corpus inscriptionum Latinarum, vol. XIII, inscription no. 1668. Berlin, 1899.

Fabia, Philippe. *La table claudienne de Lyon*. Lyon: Audin, 1929.

Levick, Barbara. *Claudius* (2nd edition). London/New York: Routledge, 2015.

Tacitus. *Annals: Books 11–12*. Translated by John Jackson. Loeb Classical Library. Cambridge, MA: Harvard University Press, 1937.

RELATED ARTICLES

52 BCE, 212, 882, 1960

177

Eastern Christianity's Eldest Daughter?

The first Western Christians to face martyrdom outside of
Rome were killed in Lyon in 177. Because they represented
a multiethnic society, mostly originating in Asia Minor
and loyal to Eastern Christianity, they were put to death
after rejecting the imperial cult — in a town that otherwise
favored integration into the Roman Empire.

"May the steadfastness of our Eastern brothers awaken the
faith of Western Christians, as it did in the first hours of
Christianity in Gaul." These were the words of Cardinal
Philippe Barbarin, Archbishop of Lyon, alluding to the
violence of jihadis in his preface to a recent book about
the martyrs of 177 — the first known Christians not
only in Gaul, but anywhere in the West outside of Rome.
Some of these martyrs originated in Asia Minor, but
Cardinal Barbarin seems to have been referring to a theory
first advanced by the nineteenth-century historian and
philosopher Ernest Renan, who called the early church of
Lyon a "missionary daughter" of the strong, long-standing

Christian communities founded by St. Paul in Asia.

The events of 177 became known through a letter from the churches of Lyon and Vienna to the churches of Asia and Phrygia. This document, written in Greek, was included (and perhaps rewritten) by Eusebius of Caesarea, one of the fathers of the Eastern church, in his *Ecclesiastical History* at the beginning of the fourth century. This work, the first description of the Christian concept of humanity's salvation, reveals, among other things, that Greek was spoken by the first Christians of Lyon. To this day, the archbishop of Lyon bears the title "Primate of the Gauls," and Monseigneur Louis Duchesne, the great nineteenth-century historian of the ancient church, recognized that the See of Lyon was predominant in Gaul as early as the second century.

But how do we explain the presence and martyrdom of a small Christian community in Lyon in 177?

As the principal crossroads of Gaul at the time, both on rivers and over land, Lyon attracted large numbers of merchants from the East. Eastern trade was also a feature of Marseille, Narbonne, and Arles, towns located in the Roman province Gallia Narbonensis, along the Mediterranean coast. Pliny the Elder had assimilated this region into Italy in the first century because of its advanced state of Romanization. The sprawling, pioneer town of Lyon, however, did not belong to this territory, which had been submissive to Rome for a very long time. The original

Lugdunum colony — the Lyon of antiquity — was founded on the western hill of Fourvière in 43 BCE to house Roman legionaries. As a natural communications hub and the only Gallic territory whose citizens were entitled to Roman citizenship outside Gallia Narbonensis, it became the capital of Gallia Lugdunensis. To the south, toward the junction of the Rhône and the Saône Rivers, was the huge commercial and labor quarter of the *canabae* (warehouses). To the east, on the slopes of the Croix-Rousse, was Condate, the site of the federal Sanctuary of the Three Gauls. Every year, delegates from the sixty cities of the provinces of Gallia Lugdunensis, Gallia Aquitania, and Gallia Belgica gathered around its altar to Rome and Augustus, to the imperial cult.

The presence of a Christian community in the region derives from the existence of this new township, open to the outside and primed to expand across the rest of Gaul. The early church was already part of the geography of the Roman world, but not yet controlled by the rigorous administrative organization that would characterize the Christian empire of the fourth and fifth centuries.

The Christian community of Lyon in 177 is known only through its martyrs, who were its most obstinate and courageous members. As a supplement to his main story, Eusebius of Caesarea included a list of forty-eight martyrs, whose names were corroborated in later Latin texts and eventually carved into the crypt of Saint Pothinus in Lyon in the nineteenth century. But these names are very questionable; in all likelihood, Eusebius devised the list to denounce as heretical Asian Christian currents that had surfaced more than a century earlier. We can surmise that the ten martyrs quoted in the famous letter are genuine, and that half of these originated in the Roman province of Asia. They include Attalus of Pergamum, a Roman citizen who supported the community with his fortune, and Alexander, a doctor from Phrygia who had been living in Gaul for several years. Three Greek names also show up: two men, Alcibiades and Pothinus, and one woman, Biblis. There was also Vettius Epagathus, a Roman citizen and notable descended from a freed slave from the east. The remaining four martyrs were Gauls, including Maturus, the Deacon of Vienna; Sanctus; and most famously two slaves, Blandina and her fifteen-year-old brother Ponticus. While Blandina is in some accounts thought to be an "Oriental" from the city of Blandos in farthest Armenia, her name is perfectly well represented in Gallic inscriptions. In art, she is traditionally depicted as a young girl, though she was actually an adult woman.

Let us return to Pothinus, described by Eusebius as a bishop in his nineties, and also as a clerk of the local Christian community at a time when officials in the church hierarchy were thin on the ground. Beyond his name, which suggests origins in Asia, we can retrace his career by way of his successor Irenaeus, author of a treatise entitled *Against*

Heresies. Irenaeus hailed from the province of Asia, where he had been trained by Polycarp of Smyrna, before spending time in Rome and then moving to Lyon. He was not among the martyrs (contrary to legend), but did carry the letter by the Christians of Lyon to Eleutherius, the bishop of Rome. The eastern origins of some of the martyrs explain why, without maintaining close links with the Asian church, the Lyon community kept them informed of their activities. In fact, the Christians of Lyon largely followed customs, like the date of Easter, that were established in Rome rather than in the East.

Why was this socially and ethnically diverse group suddenly attacked in 177? Certainly not because of the general imperial edict that was only issued by Emperor Decius in the middle of the third century. The first persecutions of Christians in the Roman Empire took place within a dual context. First, they were prompted by catastrophes such as the burning of Nero's Rome in 64 CE. Christians were tortured as presumed culprits and also because they refused to take part in expiatory pagan ceremonies. Second, they were denounced for purely religious reasons, such as their reticence vis-à-vis the imperial cult. Toward 112, Emperor Trajan told Pliny the Younger, who at the time governed Bithynia in Asia Minor, that Christians should only be arrested if they were formally and openly denounced according to the judicial procedures of Rome; anonymous accusations would not suffice. In 177, the emperor and Stoic philosopher Marcus Aurelius condemned in his *Meditations* the "theatrical stubbornness" shown by the Christians in their search for martyrdom. Still, he was no more responsible than other emperors for any kind of systematic persecution. Eusebius nevertheless claims that during the reign of Marcus Aurelius "persecution resumed against us with great violence in certain regions of the earth…following popular attacks in city after city." A number of examples, notably in Asia, show that there were serious anti-Christian pogroms. We need only point out that people were apt to blame religious scapegoats for the misfortunes of the times, such as invasions from beyond the Danube frontier and smallpox epidemics.

The Lyon persecution began as a pogrom. Christians were first banned from public places — the forum and the baths — after which their houses were ransacked, while they were insulted, beaten, and stoned by the mob, and eventually interrogated in the forum of Lugdunum by the tribune of the military garrison and civil magistrates. Lyon's society was unusual for the diversity of its origins and for its rigid conformity to the imperial cult. The Christians were indeed diverse, but their rejection of the cult made them unwelcome. They were locked up until they could appear before the region's governor, who alone had the right to hand down death sentences.

Vettius Epagathus confessed his faith, but was not executed, probably on account of his social rank. According to Eusebius, ten of Vettius's fellow Christians then forsook their faith. Afterward, there was a widespread hunt for Christians across the city. This contradicted the laws of Trajan, but must have reflected an official concern for the maintenance of public order. Lyon was thus moving toward the kind of persecutions, overseen by a governor, that had taken place under Nero in 64 CE.

Christians were then tortured. Strips of white-hot bronze were applied to Sanctus's body, although he continued to answer every question with the statement "I am a Christian!" Biblis, who had earlier retracted, returned to the faith under torture, while the other apostates were held in prison without trial — again contrary to the laws of Rome. The venerable Bishop Pothinus died in his cell after surviving a determined attempt to lynch him. This first phase of imprisonment and torture was aimed at forcing recantations from as many individuals as possible; the second saw the most intransigent among them thrown to wild beasts (a fate that was by no means confined to Christians).

This horror took place in the amphitheater of Lugdunum during the August games, beside the altar dedicated to Rome and Augustus. Sanctus, Maturus, Alexander, Blandina, and Ponticus were whipped, mauled by animals, and forced to sit on burning chairs; afterward, their heads were cut off (with the exception of Ponticus, who died under torture). Blandina is always portrayed facing a lion; according to Eusebius she was wrapped in a net and subject to assault by a bull, which she resisted. The case of the Roman citizen Attalus was submitted by the governor to the emperor's officials, who confirmed his sentence of death, along with the others who had refused to renounce their Christian faith. Attalus was again delivered to the wild beasts, while those Roman citizens who continued to confess their faith were beheaded on the spot. Finally, the corpses of the martyrs were exhibited in public for six days, after which they were thrown to packs of dogs, then burned and dumped in the Rhône. In Roman law, death without burial was reserved for the worst criminals.

The cult that would form around these martyrs cemented France's position as the "eldest daughter of the church," not only because the martyrs were linked with primitive Eastern Christianity, but also — quite simply — because they were the first of their kind in the West.

Vincent Puech

REFERENCES

Bowersock, Glen Warren. *Martyrdom and Rome*. Cambridge: Cambridge University Press, 1995.

Les Martyrs de Lyon (177). Paris: CNRS Éditions, 1978.

Maraval, Pierre. *Les Persécutions des chrétiens durant les quatre premiers siècles*. Paris: Desclée, 1992.

Musurillo, Herbert. *The Acts of the Christian Martyrs*. Oxford: Clarendon Press, 1982.

Pietri, Luce, et al., eds. *Histoire du christianisme, vol. 1, Le Nouveau Peuple (des origines à 250)*. Paris: Desclée, 2000.

RELATED ARTICLES

212

Romans Like the Rest

Emperor Caracalla extended Roman citizenship to all
inhabitants of the Roman Empire in 212. All of the
"Gauls," and not just the more privileged among them,
became full-fledged Romans. No longer a political
privilege, citizenship indirectly structured the great
"barbarian migration" into the heart of the empire.

Histories of the Roman Empire put Gaul on a special footing
in at least one respect: they refer to its people as "Gallo-
Romans," a usage not followed with any other province.
Were the Gauls more Roman than the Pannonians, the
Syrians, or the Britons? The term describes the inhabitants,
but it also applies to their art, their culture, and their
religions. Was Gaul truly the "eldest daughter" of Rome,
as sometimes claimed? Other provinces in Africa and
Asia had more Roman citizens than Gaul, as many nobles
in the Roman Senate (in Spain) or captains in the army
(in Thrace). Does the usage reflect a historical reality, or
is it just puffery, given that definitions of "Gallo-Roman"

suggest nothing that is not also applicable to other peoples forming Roman provinces? By chance, the only surviving speech by an emperor that clearly advocates integrating the privileged classes of subject peoples into the Roman citizenry was given by Claudius and preserved on bronze tablets found in Lyon in the sixteenth century. This may have been history's way of giving the Gauls an edge over other, more anonymous subject peoples.

In fact, nothing justifies a special nomenclature for the Gauls. The term "Gallo-Roman" first appears in a French dictionary of historical terms in 1833, but was used as early as 1830 by the polymath Arcisse de Caumont. It seems designed to cover the bases: by itself, the term "Gaul" suggests barbarity and lumps the ancestors of the present-day French with the other *peregrini*, or provincial subjects of the empire; but calling those who had achieved citizenship "Roman" erases their ethnic origins and any pride they might have taken in them. "Gallo-Roman," though, evokes the Gauls' glorious traditions (for instance, the valorous leader Vercingetorix) while inserting them into the new world order symbolized by Rome.

Yet, whether they lived in northern Britain, on the fringes of the Sahara, or on the banks of the Tigris, the Gauls were Romans like the rest. But an event occurred in 212 CE that rocked the Empire. That year, Emperor Caracalla granted equal citizenship to all residents of the Roman Empire, with the exception of the *dediticii* (those who became subjects through surrender in war). This revolutionary measure is hardly mentioned by classical authors. The historian Cassius Dio, who was alive at the time, raises it only to impute base motives to the emperor: "He made all the people of his empire Roman citizens; nominally, he was honoring them, but his real purpose was to increase his revenues by this means, as noncitizens did not have to pay most of these taxes" (*Roman History*, Book 78, Chapter 9). Most other writers did no more than refer to it in passing.

By chance, a papyrus from Egypt preserves the text of the imperial edict, though in highly mutilated form. Though vague, the motivations it suggests go beyond greed: "To render grace unto the immortal gods," meaning the gods of Rome, by increasing the number of the faithful; farther on there is a reference to "the multitude responsible… for the financial burden weighing on us all," with the intent of "enfolding that multitude in Victory." The text is interrupted, but not before the emperor suggests that "[the present edict] will augment the majesty of the Roman [people]: [it is in keeping with that majesty] that others be admitted to the same [dignity that Romans have always enjoyed], whereas exclusion has always been the lot of…" Coalescing all who lived within the Roman Empire around its gods and its army went well beyond a simple concern about taxes.

In the end, Caracalla's true motivations matter little, whether informed by piety, zeal for Rome's glory, or a desire to fill the state's coffers — factors that are not mutually exclusive. It is more interesting to analyze the effects of Caracalla's action and to gauge how it affected its beneficiaries' view of themselves, on intellectual as well as ideological planes.

By way of quick review, freeborn men in the Roman Empire before 212 fell into two groups: Roman citizens and *peregrini* (leaving the small number of *dediticii* aside). Since the Social War (90–88 BCE), all the inhabitants of Italy and their descendants had citizenship, on a par with the citizens of the Roman Republic proper. Then there were the provincials who had acquired citizenship by other means, and their descendants. After Augustus, either the emperor or the Senate could grant citizenship to an individual — to the king of a client state, for example, as was the case with Herod (Caius Julius Herodes). This rarest, most prestigious way of receiving citizenship was reserved for the most prominent provincials. With the passage of time, almost all the civil magistrates in the cities of Greece, Asia Minor, Africa, and Spain appear to have become citizens in this way.

But the privileged were not the only ones to become citizens. Inhabitants of the "Roman colonies" were also citizens. In the beginning, colonists were Romans who had been given land confiscated from the natives, but by the second century CE, the "colonies" were for the most part indigenous cities that had been promoted to the rank of colony; their freeborn inhabitants thereby became Roman citizens. Former slaves also became citizens on being freed, and their children were citizens as well. In addition, soldiers who had served in auxiliary units of the Roman army became full citizens on their demobilization, and many such soldiers had been recruited from the least Romanized peoples of the empire: Thracians, Germans, or Hispanics from Northwest Iberia. The number of Roman citizens therefore increased rapidly, but their percentage within the population as a whole varied greatly from province to province. It was distinctly higher in Gaul (particularly in the south, or Gallia Narbonensis), Spain, Africa, and the Aegean Basin than it was in Syria, Arabia, and Egypt. The non-citizens or *peregrini* generally had citizenship in a local community — a *civitas* in the West, or a *polis* in Greek-speaking lands. They came under the laws of their own community and did not have to pay certain taxes required of Roman citizens, such as the five-percent tax on inheritances.

The edict of 212 existed within the context of a long-standing policy of integration. Rome's strength lay in its ability to integrate the peoples it had vanquished, as Tacitus reports Emperor Claudius to have said in his famous speech at Lyon: "What caused the ruin of Sparta and Athens unless it was that, mighty as they were in war, they dismissed as aliens those whom they had conquered?" (Tacitus, *Annals*, Book 11, Chapters 23–25). In fact, this sentence does not appear in the official transcript of the speech, though it is entirely consonant with its spirit. Rome is seen as generous in matters of citizenship, whereas Greece is miserly. But the parallel is somewhat misleading, because citizenship in Athens and Sparta came with real political rights (electing magistrates, voting for or against laws, taking part in trials), whereas by the end of the Roman Republic the rights of citizens were largely illusory, and none remained under the Roman Empire. That there had long been an open door to citizenship for subject peoples no doubt explains Caracalla's decree, and also the little notice taken of it within the Roman Empire. It was not unusual, all things considered, for large numbers of people to be made new citizens on short notice. And the increase did not deprive anyone else of the slightest benefit: the distribution of wheat at low rates, for instance, applied only in Rome and Italy, where everyone had been a citizen since the end of the Social War.

Yet the Antonine Edict seems in retrospect an extraordinary step for an empire to take. It goes counter to the practice followed by other empires, which assume the coexistence of multiple communities, each living by its own laws, but with the leadership in the hands of an ethnic or religious minority that, alone of the empire's constituencies, holds the full range of citizens' rights, notably the right to vote. An empire, then, is nothing more than an amalgam of "nations" (e.g., the Ottoman Empire) that enjoy a relative degree of autonomy, but only so long as the empire's ruler consents to it. The Roman Empire mostly skipped this stage, since its provinces were not defined by nations or peoples. Although there might exist within Gaul, as within many other provinces, a common language and common gods, the identification with a broader community was a stronger basis for patriotism than the sense of forming a culturally united people. Conversely, on the scale of the empire as a whole, Roman citizens — meaning the minority in possession of the full range of citizens' rights — were not recruited from any particular ethnic or religious group but belonged to all and any of the Empire's peoples. Integration was therefore occurring at every level of the population, and in every ethnic community.

The edict of 212 allowed every freeborn inhabitant of the Empire to call himself a Roman, whether in Latin (*Romanus*) or in Greek (*Rhomaios*). Like other provincials, the Gauls therefore became full-fledged Romans, if they weren't already, and nothing distinguished them in the eyes of the law from the Romans of other provinces. When the Germanic tribes invaded and new masters from the north took control in Gaul, Spain, and Italy, two aristocracies came into play against each other: the new, which was Germanic, and the old, whose culture might be Gallic, Hispanic, or

Italian according to location, but which could still claim to be "Roman." The powerful integrating mechanism that characterized the Roman Empire worked just as well in Gaul as elsewhere, despite attempts by later historians to give Gaul a special place within a whole whose judicial system was uniform while its culture was diverse.

In promulgating the edict of 212, Caracalla was laying the basis — perhaps unwittingly — for a novel type of empire. With most residents of the Empire sharing a common citizenship, a patrician from the Aventine Hill in Rome was on an equal legal footing with a merchant from Gaul, a peasant from Fayum, a Thracian soldier, an Athenian professor of rhetoric, a caravan driver from Palmyra, and a shepherd from the mountainous Rif. There had already been a move toward linguistic uniformity, with all the administration's business conducted either in Latin or Greek. Now all could claim equality under Roman law and a common civic membership. Gaul hence settled more fully into this global empire founded around the Mediterranean. Caracalla came that much closer to bringing the *populus Romanus* into alignment with the boundaries of his territory, even if a Roman nation-state never materialized. Today's historian cannot help but notice the modernity of Caracalla's act.

Maurice Sartre

REFERENCES

Beard, Mary. *SPQR: A History of Ancient Rome*. New York: Liveright, 2015.

Coriat, Jean-Pierre. *Le Prince législateur. La technique législative des Sévères et les méthodes de création du droit impérial à la fin du Principat*. Rome: École Française de Rome, 1997.

Inglebert, Hervé, ed. *Idéologies et valeurs civiques dans le monde romain: Hommage à Claude Lepelley*. Paris: Picard, 2002.

Johnson, Allan Chester, Paul Robinson Coleman-Norton, and Frank Card Bourne. *Ancient Roman Statutes: A Translation with Introduction, Commentary, Glossary, and Index*. Clark, NJ: Lawbook Exchange, 2003 [1961].

Woolf, Greg. *Becoming Roman: The Origins of Provincial Civilization in Gaul*. Cambridge: Cambridge University Press, 1998.

RELATED ARTICLES

48, 800, 1804, 1927, 1965, 1974

397

St. Martin: Gaul's Hungarian Patron Saint

Within a few decades of his death in 397, Martin, bishop of
Tours, a Hungarian-born ascetic who converted the Poitou
and Touraine countrysides, was canonized as the patron
saint of Gaul. As such he became a lasting symbol of the
alliance between the church and the Frankish royal line,
from the Merovingians to the Capetians.

The fourth century was a crucial era in the definition of
Christian doctrine and the ideal of sainthood. Freedom of
worship, made possible by religious peace in 313, and the 380
edict of Theodosius, which sealed the triumph of the Nicene
church over the Arian (a rival Christological doctrine that
had been labeled heretical in 325), laid the era of martyrdom
to rest. In Gaul, sainthood began to be characterized by
concern for the community, charismatic pastoral care, and
purity of heart. The time of confessors, ascetics, pilgrims,
and hagiographers had come.

And so around 380, a young woman named Egeria
traveled from Galicia in northwest Spain to Mesopotamia,

crossing the known world of that time. The origins of Egeria — also called Aetheria — have been disputed, and it is thought today that she was probably born in Galicia though she was described as a "young woman of Gaul." It doesn't really matter. The *Itinerarium* of Egeria — remnants of which were found in a library in Arezzo at the end of the nineteenth century — is first and foremost a story of the discovery of Eastern monasticism and the Holy Land. Written in ordinary Vulgar Latin, it was made possible by the hospitality of ascetics encountered along the way. The first part is devoted to the different stages of the pilgrimage. From Constantinople, Egeria traveled through Galilee, Samaria, Jerusalem, and the Thebaid, and went on to climb the slopes of Mount Sinai, the mountain of God, where hermits showed her a horizon dotted with holy places and, further to the north, the edges of Palestine, the promised land. Egeria then returned to Jerusalem, where she discovered the liturgical practices of the Eastern Church, before continuing on to Mesopotamia. Finally, she reached the sanctuaries of Edessa, the city of Abraham, today's Urfa in southeast Turkey, which is now populated largely by Kurds and Sunni Arabs.

Egeria finished her tour at Harran before returning westward via Antioch and Constantinople. The second part of her text, which concentrates on the liturgical and sacramental practices of Jerusalem, teaches us nothing more about her or the people for whom this story was intended: her *sorores* (sisters), who may have been nuns or merely relatives. The attribution of this anonymous text to Egeria is in itself hypothetical. It rests on a letter written by Valerius, a seventh-century hermit, telling his brothers in the mountains of Bierzo (Visigoth northern Spain) about a virgin whose voyage to the east corresponds exactly to the stages of the *Itinerarium*. In biblical memory and Judeo-Christian geography, Egeria's wanderings share little with those of St. Martin, a patron saint of Christian Gaul and a leading protector of the Frankish Royal family, whose name was still omnipresent in 2016 (the 1700th anniversary of his birth) in the names, the topography, and the holy places of France's religion.

And yet, Martin himself was a foreigner. Originally from Pannonia, or more precisely Sabaria, the present Hungarian town of Szombathely, he seems to have been an exception in the gallery of Gallic bishops, nearly all of whom were members of the senatorial aristocracy who saw in the priesthood a means of preserving their dominant position in society. These bishops had no confidence in Martin, a "new man" whose origins and coarseness they disliked. Martin was obsessed with asceticism, however. The son of a pagan military tribune, he had been forced to join the army at age fifteen; according to Sulpicius Severus, he was quickly distinguished for his humility and charity. In midwinter, he shared his soldier's cloak with a poor man he found begging at the gates of Amiens, in northern France. He subsequently had a vision of Christ wearing half a cloak, and this persuaded him, at the age of eighteen, to request baptism. Two years later, he left the Imperial Roman army to become a soldier of Christ, joining Hilary of Poitiers, whose teachings were renowned across Gaul at the time.

But Martin had not forgotten his origins. With Hilary's assent, he returned to his parents, who had remained pagan. His hagiographers explain that, during his long journey to Illyria, Martin had to confront bands of brigands in the Alps as well as diabolical apparitions. Back home, he converted his mother and a few close relatives, but found himself powerless in the face of his homeland's Arianism. Beaten and forced to return to Italy, he set himself up in a Milan hermitage, where he was again persecuted and evicted. After a short stop in Rome, he returned to Gaul, where he was welcomed "in the most gracious manner" and, it is said, founded the first monastic community in Gaul, at Ligugé, not far from Poitiers, and then created a new hermitage for himself at Marmoutier, outside Tours. He remained attached to this hermitage for the rest of his life, despite his accession to the bishopric of Tours in 371 as the popular choice of local Christians.

Celebrated as one of the pioneers of monastic life in the West and a timeless incarnation of Christian charity,

St. Martin also symbolizes the evangelization of the pagan countryside as well as the early work of monk-bishops in Gallic cities. Such images, which are ubiquitous in Western hagiography and iconography, owe much to fifth- and sixth-century Latin texts: the *Life of St. Martin* by his disciple Sulpicius Severus, the first Christian biography produced in Gaul and the founding text of Frankish hagiography; the two verse *Lives of St. Martin* composed by Paulinus of Périgueux and Venantius Fortunatus; and the *Histories* of Gregory of Tours, who claimed to have been miraculously cured by St. Martin and was one of his successors as bishop of Tours (in 573). Gregory's historiographical work made a fundamental contribution to the glorification of St. Martin as the first bishop to have founded a church by his actions and, after his burial on November 11, 397, by the spread of his cult, by the donations he inspired, and by the protection he offered in equal measure to the weak and the strong. St. Martin inaugurated a new era in the construction of Christian societies and cities within Gaul. By the sixth century, the rise of his cult and the spiritual vigor of his suburban basilica on the road to Poitiers had overshadowed the secular *castrum* of the old town of Tours.

Gregory's "Martinocentric" approach, his personal connections to members of the reigning family in Austrasia, and the antiquity of the cult of St. Martin explain its importance to the Merovingian dynasty. The memory of

Martin came hand in hand with the Christianization of the Frankish monarchs that followed the Battle of Vouillé in 507, during which Clovis had the saint's "cloak" displayed to his troops before defeating the Visigoth king Alaric. This took place just before the Council of Orléans in 511 made the Tours pilgrimage the official pilgrimage of Gaul. The understanding that existed between the powers of church and the king were made clear to all by the veneration of St. Martin's cloak (which was probably the blanket that had covered his tomb). In time this became the most precious relic in the treasury of the Merovingian kings.

In the seventh and eighth centuries, a series of Frankish sovereigns redoubled their devotion to St. Martin. In the oratory of the Merovingian kings, a circle of ecclesiastics known as the "chaplains" (*capellani*) guarded the famous cloak on which oaths were now sworn. Churches dedicated to St. Martin proliferated across Europe. According to a letter written by St. Boniface to Pope Stephen II in 753, the Franks made the cult of the Bishop of Tours one of the principal emblems of their authority in Utrecht after seizing the city in the middle of the eighth century.

Later, Carolingian spirituality consolidated the political imprint of Martin's sainthood. Charlemagne himself built a private chapel in honor of St. Martin's cloak at Aix-la-Chapelle, in today's German region of North Rhine-Westphalia. The political spirituality of Martin's memory was clearly not confined to France, at least not until his cult was adopted by the Capetian heirs of Robert the Strong, who would rule over France in direct or collateral lines from 987 to 1848.

The name of Capet is linked to the founder of the dynasty, Hugh Capet, who had been the lay abbot of the Saint-Martin-de-Tours collegiate church. While Adémar de Chabannes appears to have been the first to describe Hugh as the *Roi à la Chape* (the king of the cloak) around 1030, it was not until the English chronicler Ralph de Diceto in the twelfth century that the word *Capetian* was applied to the kings of France. His "Capetian Franks" were named in reference to (what else?) the *cappa* of St. Martin, who remains famous the world over (he is also the patron saint of Buenos Aires, among other cities). Forged in the crucible of piety and Frankish royalty, St. Martin's legacy spread along with the expanding frontiers of Charlemagne's empire, from Flanders to the kingdom of Croatia. Even now, it remains part of a dream of cultural and political unity in which memories of contemporary Europe reflect the literatures, beliefs, and territories of medieval France.

Stéphane Gioanni

REFERENCES

Burton, Philip, ed. *Sulpicus Severus'* Vita Martini. Oxford: Oxford University Press, 2017.

Maurey, Yossi. *Medieval Music, Legend, and the Cult of St Martin: The Local Foundations of a Universal Saint*. Cambridge: Cambridge University Press, 2014.

McKitterick, Rosamond. *History and Memory in the Carolingian World*. Cambridge: Cambridge University Press, 2004.

Pernoud, Régine. *Martin of Tours: Soldier, Bishop, and Saint*. San Francisco: Ignatius Press, 2006.

Stancliffe, Clare. *St. Martin and His Hagiographer: History and Miracle in Sulpicius Severus*. Oxford: Clarendon Press, 1983.

Wilkinson, John. *Egeria's Travels*. Liverpool: Liverpool University Press, 1999.

RELATED ARTICLES

177, 910, 1137, 1534

511

The Franks Choose Paris as Their Capital

The council summoned by the barbarian Clovis in Orléans
in 511 marks the alliance between the "king of the Franks"
and the civilian powers vested in the assembled bishops.
The alliance was accompanied by many developments,
notably the carving out of a new political space and the
adoption of Paris as its capital.

"For me, the history of France starts with Clovis, chosen
to be King of France by the tribe of the Franks, who gave
France its name. Before Clovis, there was Gallo-Roman
and Gaulish prehistory. The decisive element for me is that
Clovis was the first king to be baptized a Christian." Thus
spoke Charles de Gaulle, heir to the French republican
tradition of a history of France he would bind to his own
Christian convictions. De Gaulle would likely have been
surprised to learn that his understanding of the Franks as a
separate "tribe," possessing their own political system and
capable of freely choosing a king from their ranks, thereby
giving birth to the French nation, was a construct largely

based on research by nineteenth-century German scholars. Because the Franks spoke a Germanic language, they were considered by these scholars the ancestors of a German nation that, though not yet built, was destined to exist given the Germanic traditions stretching back to pagan times.

Yet tracing the discrete existence of the Franks as a "tribe," with its own past and political traditions, has proved difficult. The name "Franks" is first mentioned by Latin authors in the second half of the third century. In the following century, the Franks were in league with the Saxons and carried out a number of naval raids along the coast of the English Channel. In comparison with the Goths and the Burgundians, however, the Franks were insignificant enough that their arrival in Gaul, probably during the crossing of the Rhine by a band of barbarians in the winter of 406 to 407, was not even mentioned by chroniclers of the time. Frankish kings subsequently served as mercenary captains, troublesome and rarely loyal, for claimants to the Roman Empire.

It was in the Roman province of Belgica Secunda, between the Scheldt and the Somme Rivers, that the Franks and their kings first drew notice. The funeral of Childeric, Clovis's father, in Tournai in 481, was an occasion for extravagant display. When Childeric's tomb was discovered accidentally in 1653, it contained a hoard of sumptuous objects and coins. Recent excavations show that the funeral ceremony was itself impressive: twenty horses were sacrificed, and a tumulus twenty meters in diameter was built over the tomb. These practices can be traced to barbarian traditions dating back no more than half a century before Childeric's death. Starting in the 430s, rulers were buried with precious funerary objects, including a great number of weapons, suggesting the evolution of a group that specialized in warfare and developed distinct funerary customs that set them apart socially. Elaborate burials and valuable funerary goods were not known beforehand, either in the Roman or the Germanic traditions. Funerals such as Childeric's represent an amplified version of these practices, whose scope was no longer local but regional; the point here was to demonstrate an authority beyond that of the warrior caste and to assert an unbridgeable dominance.

These superior nobles, who had recently appeared and were in effect kings, invented rituals to show their dominance. And though these rituals may have been presented as ancestral, they were in fact new and still uncertainly established. For instance, the distribution of royal power between a Merovingian king's sons at his death is presented by Gregory of Tours as a Frankish custom (in *History of the Franks*, written 573 to 594). Yet this custom was unknown before the death of Clovis, who was his father's sole heir. The fact that, throughout his reign, Clovis systematically eliminated other Frankish kings suggests that his family's hold on paramount authority was not unchallenged. Neither Clovis's royal dominance over the Franks nor the partition of his power between his sons came from the application of ancestral customs. The evidence suggests instead that social norms were in a period of rapid and creative transformation.

Similarly, the rituals invented for Childeric's funeral were not repeated for his son's, thirty years later. So long tumulus and horse sacrifice! Clovis was buried in the Church of the Holy Apostles, which he had built in Paris on what is today the Montagne Sainte-Geneviève. The model this time was the burial of Constantine, who had erected a church in Constantinople also dedicated to the apostles Peter and Paul, where he was buried along with his successors. Clovis's tomb, which has still not been found, was perhaps furnished with sumptuous goods, but his prestige resided mainly in having built the church, following the imperial model, and being buried near the tomb of St. Geneviève.

The power that Childeric amassed is confirmed by a letter that Remi, bishop of Reims, sent to Clovis not long after 481. In this letter, Remi congratulates Clovis on inheriting dominion over lands that extended to Belgica Secunda. Clovis comes across as a territorial ruler, to the point of replacing the Western Roman emperor Romulus Augustulus, whose reign ended in 476. Clovis and his warriors, after defeating the Roman general Syagrius in

486, enjoyed a considerable string of victories, expanding their control to the Loire and the kingdoms bordering the Visigoths and the Burgundians. Despite these military conquests, the cities remained under the stewardship of Gallo-Roman aristocrats. Ever since the Council of Nicaea (in 325), bishops, as direct successors of the apostles, had been the leaders of the Christian community, theoretically elected by the clergy and the people. In practice, bishoprics were passed down within aristocratic families, whose ties to the central authority were weakening because the emperors' reigns were so short, and entailed municipal governance.

In their dealings with Clovis and his Frankish warriors, the bishops represented the civilian nobility. The lack of a common religion between the two sides was not an obstacle: Remi's letter of congratulations, written when Clovis was still a pagan, shows that conversion to Christianity was not a requirement for cooperation. Still, the pull of Catholicism proved inexorable for many barbarian kings. Paganism, which had no textual sources, and Arian Christianity, based on an older doctrine of the Trinity, could not stand up to Catholic Christianity and its brilliant theologians. Clovis's conversion to Catholicism was a major political event largely because of its early date, but also because the resulting alliance proved so enduring. Whatever the exact date of Clovis's baptism, somewhere between 496 and 508, he joined the Catholic Church about a century before the Visigoth kings converted, in 589. This gave Clovis an advantage in conquering the Visigoth kingdom, a campaign punctuated by his victory at the Battle of Vouillé in 507. Clovis convoked a council at Orléans in 511, and the attendance of thirty-two bishops, some of them from recently conquered Aquitaine, speaks to the breadth of Clovis's alliance. But it could easily have fallen apart.

Conversion to Catholicism, it turned out, was not in itself enough to earn the support of the bishops. Sigismund, son of the Burgundian king, converted from Arian Christianity to Catholicism before 508 and became ruler of the Burgundian kingdom in 516. Yet the council of bishops in Epaone did not include Sigismund the following year, and the prelates even excommunicated him a few years later for failing to enforce the prohibition against incest. This occasioned internal turmoil, which Clovis's sons exploited in conquering the Burgundian kingdom between 523 and 534.

The importance of Clovis's conversion, therefore, did not play out at his baptism, nor at the Council of Orléans, but in the years following, when his sons were able to keep their alliance with the bishops active, as evidenced by the fact that councils continued to be held in Orléans — the fifth council taking place in 549. The various elites were now becoming more closely knit. The civil wars that ravaged the Frankish kingdoms starting in 572 grew out of other differences.

Clovis, then, was the first monarch to base his rule on an alliance between the Frankish military nobles and the Gallo-Roman civilian elite. Though his neighbors soon followed suit, the entity he created was unusually stable, and this stability, accompanied by military victories, allowed his sons to weather the turbulence Emperor Justinian caused when he tried to reconquer areas around the western Mediterranean from 533 to 554 and install a mechanism for dynastic succession.

Another novel aspect of Clovis's reign was the political space carved out by his conquests. Unprecedented, it extended from Belgium to the Loire River and to the Pyrenees beyond. This Atlantic-facing territory — it would only gain access to the Mediterranean with the recapture of Provence in 537 — did not correspond to the old Roman administrative framework, and had no obvious center. Clovis decided in 508 to establish his capital in Paris, bypassing more prestigious cities such as Trèves (now Trier) and Tours. The decision had little concrete effect, as the monarchy remained an itinerant one, and no central administration existed beyond the king's immediate entourage. Nevertheless, by having himself interred in Paris, Clovis gave the city added symbolic weight. St. Geneviève seems to have played a role in his choice. Coming from a family of the highest Gallo-Roman aristocracy, she had emerged from her pious retreat in 451 to protect the city during its clash with the Huns, and again ten years later when it confronted the Franks. She was buried around 502, and Clovis chose a spot beside her for his eternal rest.

When Clovis's grandchildren divided royal power between them fifty years after his death, Paris was kept as joint property and a symbol of the dynasty. Subsequently, Paris came to seem a central city, ready to be chosen as capital for any territorial configuration that again featured this long exposure to the Atlantic, whether that territory was known as Neustria, West Francia, or France.

Magali Coumert

REFERENCES

Bührer-Thierry, Geneviève, and Charles Mériaux. *La France avant la France (481–888)*. Paris: Belin, 2010.

Dumézil, Bruno. *Les Racines chrétiennes de l'Europe. Conversion et liberté dans les royaumes barbares (Ve–VIIIe siècle)*. Paris: Fayard, 2005.

Isaïa, Marie-Céline. *Remi de Reims: Mémoire d'un saint, histoire d'une Église*. Paris: Cerf, 2010.

Rouche, Michel, ed. *Clovis: Histoire et mémoire*. 2 vols. Paris: Presses de l'université Paris-Sorbonne, 1997.

Wood, Ian. *The Merovingian Kingdoms (450–751)*. London/New York: Longman, 1994.

RELATED ARTICLES

1215, 1357, 1682, 1900

719

Africa Knocks on the Franks' Door

In 719, shortly after pillaging Narbonne, a band of
Muslims divided their spoils in Ruscino, near present-day
Perpignan. From Iberians to Arabs, Celts, Romans, and
Visigoths, the region from the Pyrenees to the Rhône
was traversed by peoples, cultures, and religions. They
coexisted and merged there — until the Franks made the
region their own.

Imagine yourself there. We must speak of an Islamic threat
since it is so close now. Ever since Muhammad had begun
preaching in the East, his saber held high, calling for an
attack on the world, the sound of approaching horses could
be heard. Can you hear them? The Islamic wave would soon
wash over a wide expanse, causing death and destruction.
From where you are posted, standing guard, you can already
see the dusty clouds of the sinister stampede. The place
you are standing is called Ruscino. It's on a hill, a two-hour
walk to the sea, in the Roussillon, a region whose name is a
deformation of Ruscino. You live there amid familiar ruins.

As soon as the alert is sounded, you hide your tools because iron is rare and if the enemy spares your life, life will resume. Neither historians nor archaeologists know who you are nor what you did there. You are waiting, like a solitary sentinel watching for the barbarians behind the wall of a guard post in the far reaches of the world. Are you afraid, or resigned? If waiting is a poison, what is the antidote?

In Ruscino, coins struck by rulers with strange names such as Wittiza or Akhila have been found. But there was no longer a king in Toledo, the capital of the region. All the kings had been defeated or killed by the Saracens. You're living in the provinces, but in a province that is no longer the province of anything. You are living in the outskirts of Perpignan, but you don't know that because Perpignan does not yet exist. It's 719, the conventional date, the one on the Gregorian calendar (because there needs to be a fixed point in a history that was as fluid as borders at that time). The land belongs to the Visigoths, at least the elite among them. And it looks like you have Northern European–style weapons and furnishings. If those objects belong to you, if you didn't steal them from a merchant on the Via Domitia, whose paving stones were pulled up and whose ruts are very deep, then it's likely you speak the Germanic dialect of your great-great-grandparents, or a Low Latin patois with a heavy German accent, something that sounds like French or Catalan. You're probably Christian (though there is no material evidence of that), that is, a good Trinitarian (what would later be called a Catholic). In settling in Gaul and Hispania, in becoming a reformed invader and a Romanized barbarian, you have purged the old Arian heresy (you have become "mainstream"). And, you've learned to hate the Jews, who, according to rumor, helped the Saracens conquer Africa.

And now, Africa is here. Africa, swollen with the religious zeal of the Arab East, Berber Africa, dark-skinned Africa had passed through the Pillars of Hercules seven years before, seized Toledo from the last of the Visigoth kings, carried off Pamplona and Saragossa, and filled Hispania like a waterskin. From your vantage point on the promontory you have seen the African army pass by on their way to pillaging Narbonne. If you weren't trembling with rage or fear, you would appreciate their success, for you were the former terror of the local population, you who split the Roman Empire like the trunk of a tree to make a place for yourself within it. You would appreciate the irony of hearing yourself curse the barbarians du jour, of depicting them as ferocious enemies, especially of depicting *yourself* as the guardian of peace in the world.

The antiquarians and archaeologists who have excavated the Ruscino site have revealed a sequence of occupations. Our understanding of these events is still a work in progress, like a manuscript that is missing pages without our knowing how many or which ones exactly. It begins in the Late

Bronze Age and continues to the Iron Age. Let's describe the establishment on this *oppidum* as a good old Gallic village — although "Gallic" isn't exactly correct since, judging from the inscriptions on amphorae and texts written on lead tablets, the inhabitants were Iberian. They engaged in trade (hundreds of surviving coins of all origins attest to this), and so they gradually became Latinized. They were so successful that under Augustus their town was endowed with a forum, an attribute of Roman colonies. Marble plaques with dedications to members of the Julio-Claudian dynasty have been found.

Its good fortune began to wane before the end of the first century. Then the site was abandoned for centuries (in any case, by anyone who might have dropped their coins out of their purses, thereby providing evidence for later scholars), and dismantled. No one has found evidence of dwellings on this site prior to the coming of the Muslims in the early eighth century, evidence hidden, perhaps, by erosion or a leveling of the ground. True, however, silos that were used as silos, and later as dumpsites or hiding places, have been found, as have gold coins struck with the names of Visigoth rulers dating from the very end of the seventh century or the very beginning of the eighth. And it is from that time, the era of our anxious vigil on the rocky ledge of the promontory, that several dozen small, lead seals have been found, on which "*Maghnûm tayyib / qusima bi-Arbûnah*," or

"Lawful booty divided in Narbonne" is stamped in Arabic script. Having carried out its plans, the group would have taken a break on the hill of Ruscino to divide up their spoils, leaving only hastily created lead stampings as the single and fleeting vestige of their brief passage. This is but a theory, but probably not too far from historical fact.

What became of you, oh lonely look-out? No one knows. A century later, after another occupation, Ruscino was made a Carolingian comtal seat and acquired a castle. There would be no more barbarian incursions tearing and stitching the wounds of the world; no more murky middle space of Languedoc. Henceforth, the boundary between the empire of the Franks and the empire of the Saracens, between the Christians and the Muslims, and, metaphorically speaking, between France and Africa would pass over the mountain peaks of the Pyrenees. The tenuous lead vestiges of the Ruscino stopover point toward an intermediary state that predated the geographical order later imposed upon the region. The traces of its existence mix together in the archaeological site, just like the movements that crossed one another on its surface. The terms and outcomes of the encounters between the Africans and the Franks remain essentially unclear.

Of course, we could have chosen other dates and other places to evoke this encounter. Perhaps we should have looked at another incursion, the one that collective

French memory has preserved like a precious relic because it ended in French victory: the Battle of Tours (known as Battle de Poitiers in French) in which the troops of Charles Martel battled an army of the Umayyad Caliphate led by Abdul Rahman Al Ghafiqi. Nevertheless, let's agree that "Poitiers," fourteen years after "Ruscino," partakes in the factual precision of the national narrative, the one French boys and girls learn in school, only to become an illusory event. This battle took place somewhere between Poitiers and Tours (in fact we really don't know much about it). This battle resembles dozens of others that were waged at this time, all either won or lost. And I'm very sorry to say that what gives the Battle of Poitiers its epic proportions is not the bravery of a mayor of the palace who wasn't even crowned amidst barons riding gigantic stallions. Rather, it is the mark left on that skirmish by the saga of the Other, that of the adversary, reconstructed and described as a wave that conquered Syria, Persia, Egypt, Byzantine Africa, and Visigoth Hispania, only to have been courageously stopped in the Poitou.

Armed with a much more substantial body of facts we might instead have looked at the tenth-century Muslim fortress Fraxinetum, which is opportunely located in the Massif des Maures ("Mountain of the Moors"), overlooking the Gulf of Saint-Tropez. At one time, we pictured a band of land-based pirates perched on an eagle's nest, living off rapine and pillaging throughout Provence, as far as the Alps and the upper Rhine valley. But when the pirates hold on for eighty years and obey the Caliph of Córdoba, are they still mere adventurers, greedy for immediate gain? Should we not rather see their redoubt as an inhabited and governed territory, a trading post or a colony, even a small state established on the edge of the ocean in the land of the Franks, like so many others that existed on other *sahels* in Islamic civilization?

In fact, the French national narrative might want to revise its account of the encounter, which was not truly nor univocally a confrontation between two foreign camps. In the eyes of our imaginary witness in Ruscino, the Arab-Berber detachment first pillaged and then settled in Narbonne. For close to fifty years (until another enemy, this time Frankish, took the town), an emir, an Arab administration, Berber soldiers of the garrison, and their families were Narbonnais. And other Narbonnais who were born Christian or Jewish attended Friday prayers. Even in Nîmes, caught in the movement that enveloped Narbonne, but Islamic for only a generation, Muslims were given an Islamic burial, as was the custom throughout al-Andalus; a Christian mother would bury her Muslim husband or son in the communal cemetery.

In nurturing their national genealogies, the French have repressed the memory of that grave. If we acknowledge it today, it is only as a precursory, unusual, and ultimately insignificant sign of our goodwill toward our neighbors. But we have failed to uncover that place in the common cemetery, or to recognize it within ourselves.

François-Xavier Fauvelle

REFERENCES

Ballan, Mohammad. "Fraxinetum: An Islamic Frontier State in Tenth-Century Provence." *Comitatus: A Journal of Medieval and Renaissance Studies* 41 (2010): 23–76.

Blanc, William, and Christophe Naudin. *Charles Martel et la bataille de Poitiers. De l'histoire au mythe identitaire.* Montreuil: Libertalia, 2015.

Gleize, Yves, Fanny Mendisco, Marie-Hélène Pemonge, Christophe Hubert, Alexis Groppi, Bertrand Houix, Marie-France Deguilloux, and Jean-Yves Breuil. "Early Medieval Muslim Graves in France: First Archaeological, Anthropological and Palaeogenomic Evidence." *Plos One* 11, no. 2 (2016).

Gutiérrez-Loret, Sonia. "Early al-Andalus: An Archaeological Approach to the Process of Islamization in the Iberian Peninsula (7th to 10th century)." In *New Directions in Early Medieval European Archaeology: Spain and Italy Compared. Essays for Riccardo Francovich*, edited by Sauro Gelichi and Richard Hodges, 43–86. Turnhout: Brepols, 2015.

Rébé, Isabelle, Claude Raynaud, and Philippe Sénac. *Le premier Moyen Âge à Ruscino (Château-Roussillon, Perpignan, Pyrénées-Orientales) entre Septimanie et al-Andalus (VIIe–IXe s.).* Lattes: Association pour le Développement de l'Archéologie en Languedoc-Roussillon, 2004.

Wolf, Kenneth Baxter, ed. *Conquerors and Chroniclers of Early Medieval Spain* (3rd edition). Liverpool: Liverpool University Press, 2011.

RELATED ARTICLES

212, 1143, 1270, 1446, 1863, 1931, 1940

800

Charlemagne, the Empire, and the World

In 800, Charlemagne was crowned Emperor by the pope in Rome. Behind the tangled web of ambitions and scheming that spread over the world, from Byzantium and Baghdad to Córdoba and the land of the Avars, this event captures the emergence of Papal States in the shadow of the Franks as well as the irreparable break between two forms of Christianity.

"The Romans had grievously outraged Pope Leo, had torn out his eyes and cut off his tongue, and thus forced him to throw himself upon the protection of the King. [Charlemagne] therefore came to Rome to restore the condition of the church, which was terribly disturbed, and spent the whole of the winter [800–801] there. It was then that he received the title of Emperor and Augustus…" Einhard, Charlemagne's biographer, described his imperial coronation as the apotheosis of a reign devoted to the defense of the faith. In its aftermath, and for several centuries, the coronation of the emperor by the pope served to establish their collaborative government of the *ecclesia*. But the meaning assigned to *ecclesia* evolved more quickly than did the immutable imperial ritual. Did it mean the "Christian people," whose vocation it was to populate the earth? Did it refer to the Latin Church that recognized Rome as its center? Did the Emperor Charlemagne govern a Frankish empire, or the entire world?

At the outset, the matter was of local interest alone. The Franks, rulers of the Lombard kingdom (which encompassed most of northern and central Italy), since 774 had the reputation in Rome of acting like conquerors of a foreign land. Gluttons for relics (which they exported), they had exacted from Pope Hadrian the promise that a Frankish monastery would be built next to the Basilica of Saint Paul Outside the Walls. A Frankish enclave on Church land? Inalienable property ceded to Barbarians? Romans protested; on April 25, 799, they interrupted a procession led by Leo III, Hadrian's successor, and roughed him up. The pope escaped the riot thanks to Winiges, Duke of Spoleto and representative of the Carolingian ruler. From Paderborn, he was now forced to request military support from Charlemagne in order to return to Rome. The coronation at Christmas would thus have been, at least in part, a form of payment for services rendered. Pope Leo III placed a crown on the head of the praying king, whom the crowd cheered: "Long live Charles, most serene Augustus crowned by God, the great, peaceful emperor ruling the Roman Empire!"

The interpretation of events within the Roman context did not convince the court historian who, in 807, continued the first *Royal Frankish Annals* (*Annales regni Francorum*) to the glory of the Carolingians. In his opinion, the coronation was the result of Frankish territorial hegemony rather than the Roman riot. He wrote:

> The Lord King set out for Saxony, crossed the Rhine at Lippeham, and stopped at Paderborn, where he pitched camp. After splitting up his army he sent his son Charles with one part into the Bardengau to negotiate with the Slavs....In the same place he received Pope Leo with highest honors....The pope at once proceeded to Rome and the king returned to his palace at Aachen....On the same campaign an envoy of Michael, governor of Sicily, by the name of Daniel came to the Lord King and was dismissed again from there with great honors. In the same year the tribe of the Avars broke the faith which it had promised, and Eric, duke of Friuli...fell a victim to an ambush of its inhabitants near the city of Tarsatika in Liburnia [present-day Croatia]. Count Gerold, commander of Bavaria, perished in a battle against the Avars. The Balearic Islands, which had been plundered the year before by Moors and Saracens and had sought and received aid from us, submitted to us and with God's help and ours were defended

against the raids of the pirates. Military insignia of the Moors were carried away in battle and presented to the Lord King. Count Wido...entered Brittany, traversed the whole land and conquered it. On the king's return from Saxony Wido presented to him the weapons of the leaders who had surrendered with their names inscribed on them...the whole province of Brittany was subjugated by the Franks. In the same year a monk arrived from Jerusalem and brought blessings and relics of the Lord's Sepulcher, which the patriarch of Jerusalem sent to the Lord King. Hassan, governor of the city of Huesca, by his envoy sent the keys of the city with presents....[The king] left the palace of Aachen in the middle of March and traversed the shore of the Gallic Sea...and celebrated Easter at St.-Riquier in Centulum. From Centulum he marched again along the shore of the ocean to Rouen, crossed the River Seine at this point, and arrived at Tours in order to pray at St. Martin's....From here he returned to Aachen by way of Paris and Orléans....At the beginning of August he came to Mainz. Announcing an expedition into Italy, he left Mainz and went with his army to Ravenna. There he arranged a campaign against the Beneventans...[then] headed for Rome.

This amazing portrayal participates in the most optimistic of disinformation. Brittany was far from integrated into the Frankish kingdom. Southern Italy, like al-Andalus and even Saxony, put up tenacious resistance to the conquest. But the annalist justified through political geography the imperial coronation that would follow. He presented it to the pro-Carolingian elites as the church's recognition of the supremacy of the Frankish monarchy over the European continent.

The *Royal Annals* thus provide the official version of the coronation that prevailed around 807 — the same one as in the *Annales Mettenses* (Annals of Metz). They purposefully render abstract the true context of the years 790–800, and notably the major threat that the existence of an emperor in Byzantium posed to the coronation. This wasn't true, however, of the *Annales laureshamenses* (Annals of Lorsch). In this version, Charlemagne acceded to the imperial throne because it was vacant: "And because the title of emperor had expired on the side of the Greeks, and they had a woman who was ruling over them, then it seemed to Pope Leo…as to all of the Christian people, that they should name that Charles Emperor, King of the Franks." The Annals of Lorsch in fact echo the justificatory narrative developed by the Frankish court in 801–802. They repeat the assertion that the reign of a woman — Irene — in Byzantium had left the empire without a true ruler. Except that once Irene was overthrown in 802 by Nikephoros I, who immediately seized the reins as emperor, the justification through a vacancy became less effective, and the *Royal Annals* became mute on the Byzantine situation.

Charlemagne's coronation did indeed consummate an irreversible rupture with Byzantium, where the Roman Empire alone had ruled since 324. In the eighth century, the empire was ruled by the Isaurian dynasty, which owed its ascent to power to the expansion of Islam. Leo III the Isaurian saved the empire from annihilation during the Siege of Constantinople by the Umayyads in 717. Since then, they counted on Frankish power to open a second front in the West against the caliphs. The *Chronicle* of the Greek monk Theophanes, written around 814, mentions their continuous efforts to win over the Carolingians. It tells of the admiration the Byzantines exhibited for the Frankish ruler Charles Martel, conqueror of the Arabs, and how the Empress Irene herself proposed to Charlemagne so that the Christian East and West would be united by their marriage (798).

How, then, can we explain Charlemagne's decision to break with Byzantine imperial power, which viewed him so favorably? Papal diplomacy played a role. After the reconquest of Italy by Justinian (d. 565), the pope's political and military independence had been guaranteed by the local presence of the exarch of Ravenna, a representative of the Byzantine emperor. But it was threatened by Lombard invaders of the Arian religion. This balance shifted during the eighth century. The Lombards embraced the Catholic faith and maintained an acceptable *modus vivendi* with the popes, whereas the Byzantines adopted a divergent interpretation of the orthodoxy regarding the intercession of the saints, images of devotion, and the consecrated life — positions that Rome called heretical in 737 and that were labeled "iconoclastic." The popes immediately sought among the new Frankish rulers protectors of the church capable of replacing the impious Byzantines.

The creation of the Papal States was the first concrete outcome of their plan. In 756, twenty-two cities that the Franks had taken from the Lombards formed the core of a territory endowed perpetually "to Saint Peter" — an endowment that Charlemagne, the new king of the Lombards, confirmed to Pope Hadrian in 774. The popes' correspondence with the Carolingians, which the Frankish king had copied in 791 in the *Codex Carolinus*, contains multiple traces of this papal plan for an alliance, including a stand against Byzantium. One sees popes supporting the rise of the new dynasty against the weakening Merovingians and crowning Pepin the Short (754), celebrating the perfect orthodoxy of the Franks, and preventing any marriage the Isaurians might have sought with the Carolingians. From this point of view, the ceremony of December 25, 800, consecrated the success of the pope more than it did Charlemagne's. This might have been the origin of the Frankish king's bitterness (Eginhard says he "was so opposed to [that imperial coronation] that he said he would never have entered into the church [Saint Peter] that day, although it was a feast day of highest importance, if he had known in advance the decision of the pontiff ").

For the Carolingians, the advantage of a papal alliance seems *a posteriori* obvious. Their choice, which ended up making the Roman Church the standard for the entire Catholic Church, had not been made in advance, however. It was most likely inspired by their own understanding of the political situation of Islam. Seen from the Isaurian side, the Islamic threat was represented by the Abbassid caliphs from Syria and Egypt, which the Umayyad resistance, established in al-Andalus in 751, might weaken. From the Carolingian side, on the contrary, the caliphate of Hārūn al-Rashīd was a distant alliance that was to be maintained so that the Holy Land would remain accessible. Meanwhile, the conflicts of legitimacy internal to Muslim Spain allowed for the hope of a renaissance of a Christian Spain. Charlemagne's choice was unequivocal. He exchanged embassies and gifts with the Abbassids, especially in 801 and 802, but continued to exploit the weaknesses of the Umayyad world in al-Andalus and, the Battle of Roncevaux notwithstanding, went as far as to create a buffer zone against the Umayyads, the Marca Hispanica. In truth, the coronation of December 25, 800, conceived as the return of the single Christian Empire from Constantinople to Rome, sanctified a territorialization of power and solidified the separation between East and West.

Marie-Céline Isaïa

REFERENCES

Collins, Roger. "Charlemagne's Imperial Coronation and the *Annals of Lorsch*." In *Charlemagne: Empire and Society*, edited by Joanna Story, 52–69. Manchester/New York: Manchester University Press, 2005.

Costambeys, Marios. "Alcuin, Rome and Charlemagne's Imperial Coronation." In *England and Rome in the Early Middle Ages: Pilgrimage, Art and Politics*, edited by Francesca Tinti, 255–89. Turnhout: Brepols, 2014.

Fried, Johannes. *Charlemagne*. Translated by Peter Lewis. Cambridge, MA: Harvard University Press, 2016.

Nelson, Janet L. "Why Are There so Many Different Accounts of Charlemagne's Imperial Coronation?" In *Courts, Elites and Gendered Power in the Early Middle Ages: Charlemagne and Others* by Janet L. Nelson. Aldershot: Ashgate, 2007.

RELATED ARTICLES

842–843, 882, 987, 1515, 1804, 1863

THE FEUDAL
ORDER
TRIUMPHS

When considered in the long view of history, the period between the tenth and twelfth centuries emerges as the time when the kingdom of France took shape. These centuries also saw the emergence of an actual "French" identity that, while embodying earlier Frankish traditions, would from now on distinguish itself from them. This identity was forged by an extraordinarily dynamic feudal aristocracy, the true crucible of French identity, as its members confronted and negotiated with varieties of otherness. Interestingly, France's neighbor, the kingdom of Germania, could equally define its national identity using the same Frankish legacy; in other words, both French and German national identities were paradoxically declaring their differences by claiming the same cultural background.

It was in the early twelfth century that the expression "kingdom of France" (*regnum Franciae*) began to compete with the earlier designation "kingdom of the Franks" (*regnum Francorum*). And yet, for nearly three centuries, this kingdom's territory was based on the part of the Carolingian Empire granted to Charles the Bald (d. 877) at the Treaty of Verdun in 843. In keeping with Frankish inheritance customs, the empire was divided among the three sons of Louis the Pious (d. 840). The youngest of the brothers, Charles, received the western third — "West Francia" (*Francia occidentalis*) — which stretched from

Flanders in the north to Catalonia in the south. Its eastern border followed the course of the "four rivers," from the Scheldt to the Rhône by way of the Meuse and the Saône. This partition left half of today's France, from Lorraine to Provence, in the hands of Lothair, already king of Italy. Louis, the second son, was given "East Francia," soon to be renamed Germania.

Political upheaval swept aside Charles the Bald's descendants on three separate occasions (in 888, 922, and 923) before they were finally ousted altogether in 987 by an aristocratic lineage that historians would call the Capetians. Nevertheless, the boundaries of this new "kingdom of the West" would not shift for a long time to come. This was largely due to a change in inheritance practices, under the influence of Germanic sovereigns during the tenth century. The custom of dividing a kingdom among brothers was abandoned in favor of passing the throne to the eldest son. In 987, the newly elected King Hugh Capet set a new precedent by having his son Robert crowned while he was still alive. This practice was taken up by all his descendants until Philip Augustus (1180–1223), thereby delegitimizing any attempt by a younger brother to seize power.

The medieval and modern tradition of the French monarchy, not unlike a certain national mythology at work today, has framed Hugh Capet's 987 election by a handful of grand secular and ecclesiastic aristocrats of northern France as a major political break: nothing less than the founding event of a French history that has been conflated with that of the Capetian kings. A case in point: the commemoration of the "Capetian millennium" in 1987 seemed at times to celebrate national origins in distinction or even opposition to the upcoming bicentennial commemoration of the French Revolution of 1789.

In truth, this royal election took place thanks to the decisive and self-serving support of the powerful neighbor to the east, the emperor and king of Germania, Otto II. It also went practically unnoticed in the din of world events. At the very most, it is remembered for founding a new dynasty, the Capetians, which at the time showed few signs of enduring for eight centuries. The Capetian royal line would long bear the mark of its Frankish heritage: its kings continued to call themselves "kings of the Franks" and issued decrees and currency as Carolingians. At the end of the century, they once again named their sons after the first Frankish king to be baptized Catholic. "Louis" referred to "[C]lovis."

Ultimately, the early Capetians' only innovation was to cease any expansion into the old heartland of the Frankish empire, a region still at the center of today's European Union, straddling what is now Luxembourg, Lorraine, Belgium, and the Rhineland. Home to Charlemagne's palace at Aix-la-Chapelle/Aachen, given over to Germanic rulers for many centuries, this region would also be the repository of Carolingian memory. Throughout the eleventh and twelfth centuries, the Capetian king stayed mainly in his own corner, rarely venturing beyond the central regions of the Île-de-France, Picardy, and Orléans. Reduced to prestige alliances (with the likes of the princes of Kiev), the monarch would either be upstaged by conqueror princes — for instance, William, Duke of Normandy, who would become King of England after the 1066 conquest — or forced into inglorious retrenchment, notably by Henry II Plantagenet, Count of Anjou, who would rise to become Duke of Normandy, Duke of Aquitaine, and eventually King of England from 1152 to 1189.

The leadership and momentum that was missing among the kings was evolving elsewhere: sustained demographic and economic growth, driven and contained by a rigorous feudal order. Between the tenth and twelfth centuries, feudalism expanded throughout France — more vigorously than elsewhere in Europe. The feudal system structured the secular aristocracy around martial activities and, more precisely, a system of dependence and service that bound lords and vassals (all of them knights) through a series of rites (loyalty oath, tribute, hunting, tournaments), social relations (military assistance, counsel, matrimonial alliances), and transfers of wealth and privileges (prestige gifts, fiefdoms, pensions).

Feudalism also regulated the means of accessing and transmitting land — the principal source of wealth at the time — and consolidated the aristocracy's dominion over peasants through a system of manorial estates. This increasingly dense network of landed castles subjugated peasants, be they free laborers or serfs, by imposing levies on a share of their resources, which were then allotted to the lords, be they clerics, monks, or laymen. Indeed, the church was a major stakeholder in this system — it was the principal landholder in Europe. The church made feudalism legitimate by promoting the ideology of "the three orders." According to this Carolingian theory that was taken up by the episcopal entourage of the Capetian king in the early eleventh century, society was broken into three groups, both hierarchical and interdependent: those who prayed (clerics and monks), those who fought (knights), and those who worked (everyone else). All fell under the higher authority of the anointed king. Each order needed the others, and each was to remain in its place, in accordance with the will of God as conveyed through the church and the king.

The feudal order was thus an ecclesial order, marked by the influence of monasticism on society and by church reforms promulgated by the papacy around the mid-eleventh century. For three centuries, France was the most active center of Benedictine monasticism. By the early twelfth century, Cluny Abbey, founded in Burgundy in 910, was branching out across Christendom. Several popes emerged from its ranks; its church was the largest in Europe and would remain so until the construction of Saint Peter's Basilica at the Vatican during the Renaissance. France also witnessed a flourishing of other orders that renewed the Benedictine tradition, such as the Cistercians, whose astounding popularity spread throughout Christendom, or the soldierly monks who emerged with the overseas crusades. Down through the ages, the Knights Templar or Hospitaller have stood as the embodiment of the ideal Christian knights.

Originating with Popes Leo IX (1049–1054) and Gregory VII (1073–1085), church reform had powerful channels in France, particularly at Cluny, within the Order of Cistercians, and among episcopal circles in the west of the kingdom. For a time, these reforms weakened the power of the king and the secular princes. But they also fostered the emergence of a society intent upon purging itself of its internal enemies: Jews (this was the time of the first pogroms) and heretics, i.e., anyone opposed to the mediation of the clergy or the power of the church. This purge made it possible to contend with the external enemy: Islam. It was after all from France that in 1095 Pope Urban II, a nobleman from the Champagne region and former prior of the Cluny community, preached the First

Crusade, "to deliver the Holy Places." Despite the waning reign of the king (about to face excommunication), France sent most of the crusaders, who would capture Jerusalem in 1099 and then found in the Levant new feudal states that Byzantines and Muslims would deem "Frankish."

Although this feudal order was apt to present itself as custom-based, deep-rooted, and legitimized by tradition, it was hardly static or immovable. By encouraging population growth and enrichment of the elites, by promoting war and adventure, and by exalting faith and defense of religion, it propelled countless noblemen and knights out of French lands and into far-flung military expeditions to England or Sicily, onto pilgrimage routes that led to Rome and Santiago de Compostela, or into holy wars against the Muslims — in Spain during the 1060s and 1070s and then in the Levant between the late eleventh and late thirteenth centuries. For two centuries, inhabitants of the Capetian kingdom made their voices resound and their weapons clang on the shores of the English Channel, the Atlantic, and the eastern Mediterranean. Their wars sometimes ended in genuine conquests. In Spain, French forces were able to push the border with Islam further south by 1064. Elsewhere, their battles gave rise to new feudal states, such as the Latin kingdom of Jerusalem in the early twelfth century or the Norman kingdom of Sicily in 1130. In some cases, these battles led to veritable colonial undertakings. Thus, the new French elites, whether ecclesiastic or secular, settled in England in large numbers after the 1066 conquest, so much so that French became the language of the court and the aristocracy until the close of the Middle Ages.

From Great Britain to the Levant, these conquests expanded the horizons of those who, though still called "Franks," were now increasingly perceived as "French," whether they hailed from that land or were simply assumed, correctly or not, to originate from those few northern regions where people spoke "the gentle language" (*"la douce langue de France,"* as coined by the poet Chrétien de Troyes). The first *chanson de geste* — *The Song of Roland*, which was also the first large-scale literary text in French — was written around 1100, and the first courtly narratives (notably the Arthurian romances of Chrétien de Troyes, written between 1160 and 1170) were starting to ensure the renown of the French language.

Still, this France of the north did not fully control the kingdom or even the territory that corresponds to the country's present-day borders. Its entire southern region, from Aquitaine to Provence, had its own language, the langue d'oc, as well as multiple dialects and a cultural and social organization that differed from the north's, with a dense urban fabric, a relatively weak ecclesiastical power, the early development of a legal scholarship influenced by a renewal (initiated in Italy) of Roman law, and the troubadours' lyric poetry, which flourished by the late eleventh century. As they sharpened in the eleventh and twelfth centuries, these differences fed the stereotypes that the "French" (residents of the north) maintained toward the "Provençals" from the south. The church's suspicions of heresy further reinforced such stigma in the mid-twelfth century.

If the kingdom of France was indeed born in a specific place between the mid-ninth and early twelfth centuries, it ultimately owes its exceptional vitality to the social forces of feudalism and the church more than to its kings. And while a "French" identity began to take shape toward the end of the eleventh century, through interactions with others in Norman England, the Crusader East, or even the southern reaches of the kingdom, this identity remained limited to the aristocratic elites of northwestern France.

842–843

When Languages Did Not Make Kingdoms

The Oaths of Strasbourg, when two grandsons of
Charlemagne pledged their allegiance to each other in
842, one using a "Romance" and the other a "Teutonic"
language, have long been seen as the starting point of the
French and German nations. A year later, the Treaty of
Verdun would crudely carve out their eventual territories
from the ruins of the Carolingian Empire. But in the
multilingual lands of the Franks, language did not yet
define a kingdom.

Both the Oaths of Strasbourg and the Treaty of Verdun
belong to the "national" heritage of France and Germany
and have been studied, interpreted, and taught as such since
the nineteenth century. They are thought to define those
countries' national identities, based on a binary opposition
between a supposed Romance-speaking "nation" (France)
and a supposed German-speaking one (Germany). In fact,
nothing justifies this view, which reflects a projection onto
the past of much more recent nationalism, ignoring the

reality and outlooks of the actors, witnesses, and narrators of these two events. These dates are important in other ways. The Oaths are a minor historical incident that owes its fame to its narrator and participant, Charlemagne's grandson, the historian Nithard, who gives us the exact language of the spoken oaths, a practice counter to the usual Latinization of such official documents. For its part, the Treaty of Verdun, while retaining the memory of the unified Carolingian Empire, is the first sign of a geographical division that would eventually crystallize into a difference in language.

As the sole surviving son of Charlemagne, Louis the Pious inherited his father's empire, but his own sons revived the inveterate Frankish tradition of engaging in war with one's siblings, just as their distant Merovingian ancestors had done. Each wanted to increase his share of the territories known as *regna*, or kingdoms, which were more or less fictitiously parts of Charlemagne's vast Christian *imperium*. This overarching entity sewed together a patchwork of regions, peoples, and languages: Celtic dialects, Germanic dialects (Old English, Rhine-Franconian, Central-Franconian, Saxon, Alemannic, Thuringian, Lombard), French Romance dialects (Picard, Champenois, Norman), Occitan dialects (Limousin, Gascon, Languedocien, Provençal, Catalan); Basque-speaking areas; pockets where Greek (in Italy) and Arabic (in the Marca Hispanica) were spoken. The repeated partitioning of territories and the rulers' constant travel from palace to palace seldom corresponded to the sustained creation of predominantly Romance or Germanic entities. The symbolic basis of power was successional legitimacy within the Carolingian line; what made it real was military force, associated with a coherent, writing-based administration and religious unity. These last two elements depended entirely on the mastery of Latin, which was crucial in implementing the system.

During the repeated clashes that brought Louis the Pious into conflict with his sons and his sons into conflict with each other — sometimes resulting in bloody engagements (e.g., the Battle of Fontenoy-en-Puisaye in 841) — the narratives and the evidence confirm that the protagonists were constantly negotiating, often under the direction of bishops, abbots, and even popes. In other words, they fought, they argued, and they committed to truces and treaties that were easily broken, but that required an effective spoken word, something readily understandable by at least the foremost ranks of the participants.

It was in this context that the two brothers spoke their oaths in Strasbourg on February 14, 842 — on the one hand Charles, the youngest of Louis the Pious's sons, later nicknamed *Calvus*, the Bald, and on the other Louis, later nicknamed *Theotiscus*, the Germanic. They swore a mutual alliance against their eldest brother, Lothair, the theoretical ruler of the empire (Pepin II, a nephew, had withdrawn to his home in Aquitaine). By chance, Nithard, himself a member of the imperial family and a brilliant man of letters, was deeply involved in the whole business. In fact, he probably wrote the treaties himself. More notably, he left us a detailed account of the ceremony and a verbatim transcript of the words spoken by the two rulers and their men.

We do not know what edifice was used for the assembly, nor exactly who participated. It seems that the two sovereigns were surrounded by the inner circle of their followers, perhaps involving a few dozen (or maybe even a few hundred?) direct participants. At that point in the struggle, whose geographic configuration was constantly evolving, it happened that one of the brothers, the weaker, Louis, ruled a political space that was primarily Germanic-speaking, while the slightly stronger Charles ruled a political space that was primarily Romance-speaking. Nithard first presents the two preliminary speeches that the brothers addressed to the assembly before swearing their oaths. They are brief (probably taking less than five minutes to deliver), and they confirm both the bilingualism of the brothers and the care taken in interleaving the two languages.

Louis spoke in *theudisca lingua* and Charles in *romana lingua*. At this stage, they both sought to explain themselves to their own nobles. When making their promise to the nobles of the opposing camp, who spoke another language, they reversed their linguistic choice: Louis swore in *romana* and Charles in *theudisca*. Finally, each of the opposing groups of men took the oath in *propria lingua*, their own language. The sense of the adjectives in Carolingian Latin is clear: *theudisca* means "of the people," therefore of the Frankish speakers, and *romana* means "of Rome," and therefore of the Latin speakers. These names are followed by a transcription of the two languages. The writing, seemingly designed to minimize dialectical excesses, has been recognized by experts in the Germanic languages as Rhine-Franconian on the one hand, and by Romance linguists as Romance (and not Latin) on the other, though the specific dialect has not been identified. Although many have wrestled with the question of which version, Romance or Germanic, was the original, the jury is still out.

What follows is the portion of the oath spoken by the followers, first those in Charles's camp, then those in Louis's. The text was almost certainly read aloud, phrase by phrase, from a script prepared by a herald (Nithard himself perhaps?), and repeated in chorus by the followers (vassals):

*Si Lodhuuigs sagrament, que son fradre Karlo iurat,
conservat, et Karlus meos sendra de suo part non los
tanit, si io returnar non l'int pois, ne io ne neuls, cui
eo returnar int pois, in nulla aiudha contra Lodhuuig
non li iu er.*
*Obar Karl then eid, then er sinemo bruodher
Ludhuuuige gesuor, geleistit, indi Ludhuuig min*

*herro, then er imo gesuor, forbrichit, ob ih inan es
irruenden ne mag, noh ih noh thero nohhein, then ih es
iruenden mag, widar Karle immo ce follusti ne uuirdhit.*
If Louis keeps the oath that he has sworn to his
brother Charles, and Charles, my lord, on his side
breaks his oath, and if I cannot dissuade him, and
neither I nor any other can dissuade him, I will give
him no help against Louis.
[The Franconian text is virtually identical to the
Romance text, translated above, with the proper
names reversed.]

The two oaths had been modeled and adapted in
their entirety from formulas long since written into the
Carolingian book of ordinances, notably in 802 during a
loyalty campaign when oaths were publicly spoken by all the
men of standing in the four corners of the empire, as dictated
by jurists. In fact, the phrasing of those short documents
is Latin in appearance only: the written form reproduces
with little distortion the real structure of the natural spoken
language but obscures its pronunciation — they are fake-
Latin oaths. That is not the case here: Nithard, the guiding
spirit behind this deposition, wanted to treat both languages
identically, setting down in writing the spoken Germanic
and the spoken Romance, meaning that in the latter instance
he wanted to replicate how the ordinary Latin of the
Carolingian administration was pronounced. At this stage

in the evolution of the common language, it was certainly Romance, most likely one of the langues d'oïl, and it was not unique — the written language had for a long time been more fake-Latin than Latin — but exceptional because it gives us a window onto the oral character of the *lingua romana rustica*, the "Latin spoken by illiterates." Naturally, the transcription of formal oaths in these two native spoken languages elevated them to the rank of high-level literacy.

At the stage in which we find them, it would be premature to call these languages "the French of France" or "the German of Germany." Louis is wrongly called "Louis the German": he was born and raised in Aquitaine, before receiving a domain (an *honor* or *feod*) that, by the hazards of war, lay largely within German-speaking territory. His adversary, Charles, was born in Frankfurt and raised in Strasbourg. When documents of the time mention Francia, the reference was to a small Romance-speaking territory with enclaves of German speakers. In any case, when the Carolingian rulers and their dignitaries, whether lay or ecclesiastic, made their plays for power, they did so without regard for linguistic, or even geographic, boundaries. The highest ranking among them, especially the Carolingian kings, were at least bilingual: they spoke a form of Franconian (a dialect) and had mastered several levels of "Latin," most often a compromise between the common speech and the standard ancient language. In brief, neither "France" nor "Germany" existed; contemporaries defined themselves according to cultural concepts that do not correspond to our own national divisions.

The Treaty of Verdun, which ended the Carolingian War in 843, may provide the first counterexample to the conventional view. Having no witness like the perspicacious Nithard on hand, we must look closely at the outline of the three main kingdoms. The partition created an entity for Louis to the east that was overwhelmingly German-speaking, one to the west for Charles that was Romance-speaking, and an enormous vertical swath between the two, extending from Frisia to Lombardy, for Lothair. This last parcel illustrates the indifference to language in the politics of that time, since the budding "Lotharingia" spoke Frisian, a Germanic dialect, in its northern portion and the Romance of Italy in its southern. The division of Europe into distinct and competing linguistic areas would come about much later as a result of divisions based on other criteria (and on the hazards of history).

Michel Banniard

REFERENCES

Auzépy, Marie-France, and Guillaume Saint-Guillain, eds. *Oralité et lien social au Moyen Âge (Occident, Byzance, Islam)*. Paris: Association des amis du Centre d'histoire et civilisation de Byzance, 2008.

Geuenich, Dieter. "Sprach Ludwig der Deutsche deutsch?" In *Spoken and Written Language: Relations Between Latin and the Vernacular Languages in the Earlier Middle Ages*, edited by Mary Garrison, Árpád P. Orban and Marco Mostert. Turnhout: Brepols, 2013.

Haug, Walter. *Vernacular Literary Theory in the Middle Ages. The German Tradition, 800–1300, in Its European Context*. Cambridge: Cambridge University Press, 1997.

Maiden, Martin, John Charles Smith, and Adam Ledgeway, eds. *The Cambridge History of the Romance Languages*, vol. 1, *Structures*, and vol. 2, *Contexts*. Cambridge: Cambridge University Press, 2011 and 2013.

Pohl, Walter, and Bernhard Zeller, eds. *Sprache und Identität im Frühen Mittelalter*. Vienna: Verlag der Österreichischen Akademie der Wissenschaften, 2012.

Schneider, Jens. *Auf der Suche nach dem verlorenen Reich: Lotharingien im 9. und 10. Jahrhundert*. Cologne/Weimar/Vienna: Böhlau Verlag, 2010.

Scholz, Bernard Walter, and Barbara Rogers, trans. *Carolingian Chronicles: Royal Frankish Annals and Nithard's Histories*. Ann Arbor: University of Michigan Press, 1970.

RELATED ARTICLES

511, 800, 1105, 1539, 1883, 1919, 1992

882

A Viking in the Carolingian Family?

A few decades before Rollo's reign in Normandy, another
Viking leader, Godfrid, took Christian baptism, received
grants of land, and, in 882, was offered the hand of a
Carolingian princess. Relations with the northern raiders
never flared into war again, following instead pathways of
accommodation.

In July 882, Carolingian Emperor Charles the Fat laid siege
to the Viking settlement in Ascloha (probably Asselt, near
Roermond, in what is now the Netherlands). The emperor's
campaign came in response to a renewed wave of Viking
raids on the Frankish world, starting in 879, when a portion
of the Great Heathen Army that had been in England came
to the continent. After several days of unavailing siege,
Charles negotiated terms with his opponents. One of the
Norse chiefs, Godfrid (though another source calls him
"Sigfrid"), agreed to be baptized and received territories
in Frisia that had formerly been ruled by the Viking Rorik.
A large sum of money, which some sources called a tribute

and others a baptism gift, was presented to the Vikings. A short time later, Godfrid married Gisela, sister of Hugh, the illegitimate son of King Lothair II, thus entering into a marriage alliance with the Carolingian family, either as part of the peace agreement or, more probably, in the interest of forging an alliance with Hugh. In point of fact, Godfrid soon began to meddle in the intrigues of the Carolingian family, supporting Hugh in his revolt against Charles the Fat and demanding a greater share of the tax revenues in return for his continued loyalty. He quickly met his death in an ambush laid by the emperor's commander-in-chief, Henry, in 885 at Herespich, at the confluence of the Waal and the Rhine. Shortly after, Henry also captured Hugh, who was blinded and shut away in a monastery. Godfrid, who had elevated himself to the top stratum of the Frankish world, paid dearly for his cupidity, his role in the dynastic intrigues, and the animosity his rapid rise provoked.

In point of fact, the available historical sources (the *Annals of Fulda*, the *Annals of Saint Bertin*, the *Annals of Saint Vaast*, and the *Chronicon of Regino of Prüm*) give contradictory accounts, making it hard to narrow the incident down to a single story. The *Annals of Fulda* alone contain two versions that differ completely in their assessment of Charles the Fat. In one, he is characterized as pragmatic, bringing the Norsemen to an agreement while in a position of strength. In the other, he appears as a "new

Ahab," badly advised by his treacherous counselors, and entering into a hateful compromise with the Norse attackers even though his army was still unbeaten.

Charles the Fat is better known for another compromise, which was just as controversial. At a time when Paris was stoutly defending itself against another Viking attack, he offered to pay the aggressors a tribute to lift the siege (a bargain, at seven hundred livres) and authorized them to spend the winter farther up the Seine, in Burgundy. This episode would paint Charles the Fat in dark colors, and contemporary sources were already picking up on the trend. French historians of the nineteenth century, using these same accounts, were even more critical. Charles became the antihero par excellence, in contrast to Odo (sometimes known as Eudes), Count of Paris, who defended the city valiantly — until Charles undercut him. Paris's heroic resistance earned the city the right to be considered a capital, as Henri Martin explained in his mid-nineteenth-century *History of France*: "Paris was acclaimed the capital of those who had newly been made conscious of their power by repelling the enemy and would soon confirm it by choosing a national leader. Paris had embarked on its glorious destiny! Henceforth, the city would be the head and heart of France." A painting by Jean-Victor Schnetz, *Count Eudes Defends Paris Against the Normans* (1837), was hanging in the newly established Gallery of Battles in the palace at Versailles, which may explain this somewhat fulsome account. No other battle, from the reign of Charlemagne to the Battle of Bouvines more than three hundred years later, had made the cut.

The Siege of Asselt is an episode in what are commonly known as the "Viking invasions." The expression, which gained currency among historians of the nineteenth and twentieth centuries, gives a reductive view of the Viking phenomenon, not least by foregrounding its destructive, military aspect. To be sure, we should not minimize the terror these pillagers sowed, their ravages, and the impact they had on the church's disorganization and political developments in the territories they overran. The Viking raid on the Seine Valley in 841 is the likely explanation for the traces of fire found in Jumièges Abbey and in the area of Rouen Cathedral; the Normans are also believed to have razed a portion of Zutphen, in the Netherlands, possibly in 882, and Landévennec Abbey, sacked in 913. The ports of the Frankish Empire that had most profited from the rise of the North Sea countries were more than once targeted for attack, though this cannot be held entirely responsible for their decline.

It's not clear, however, that framing the situation as the "Viking invasions" gives us a better understanding of the growth and expansion of the Scandinavian peoples. A recent change in perspective, marked by the increasingly frequent use of such terms as "Viking world" and (more controversially) "Viking diaspora," invites us to take a more global approach, even if we don't allow it to color our view entirely. It is worth keeping a few points in mind. In the first place, the spread of the Vikings prolonged, reflected, and helped bring about a profound transformation in Scandinavian societies. Economic activities diversified; new trading posts appeared and later grew into urban centers; central authorities, the nuclei of later Scandinavian kingdoms, increased in power; and Christianity began to filter into the region. In the second place, the spread of the Vikings was part of a broader expansion of the known world. New areas were coming into relation with each other, and peoples and cultures were mixing in new ways. Finally, the Viking presence met with very different outcomes according to the societies involved and the ways the newcomers were accommodated. Accordingly, the Frankish world's contacts with the Vikings should be seen as but one facet of a complex Viking world.

To get back to Godfrid, it wasn't the first time — nor the last — that the Frankish authorities came to a settlement with a Viking chieftain. The practice may date back to the later years of Charlemagne's reign (768 to 814), if we are to believe one later source, or more certainly to the reign of Louis the Pious (814 to 840), when the Franks were becoming deeply involved in Danish affairs, and Ebbo, archbishop of

Reims, followed by Ansgar, later archbishop of Hamburg-Bremen, began sending missions to convert northern peoples. Although King Harald Klak came to the Frankish imperial court in 826, was baptized with Emperor Louis as his godfather, and received the county of Rüstringen in East Frisia as a gift, it did not lead to the wholesale conversion of Denmark, though it paved the way for further missionary efforts. In 837, a certain Hemming, son of Halfdan, died while defending Walcheren from Viking pirates. In several instances, the Frankish authorities installed Scandinavian rulers — Danes in particular — in Frisia: thus Rorik, who was active from 840 to 870, controlled part of the country, most notably the Dorestad emporium, on behalf of the Frankish kings, maintaining relations with Lothair I, Charles the Bald, Louis the German, and Lothair II.

On occasion, the Carolingian kings and other magnates of the realm would turn to Scandinavian chiefs to help them against their adversaries, even when it was a question of driving off other Vikings: from 860 to 861, for instance, Charles the Bald paid a large sum of money to the Viking chieftain Weland's fleet, which was based in the Somme Valley, to oust pirates ensconced in Oscellum (now Oissel) on the Seine River above Rouen. Others are known to have been intermediaries in negotiations between the Franks and the Vikings. A certain Ansleicus (known in modern Scandinavian as Aslak), a Dane in service to the Frankish king and a "companion of the palace," conducted the bargaining between Weland and Charles; and a man named Sigfrid, scion of a royal Danish clan, a Christian and a follower of the young Carloman II, was picked to negotiate a tribute with the Vikings in Amiens in 884. Clearly, Scandinavians became sufficiently integrated into Frankish society over the course of the ninth century to serve as intermediaries between the two worlds.

The alliance with Godfrid led nowhere, but it is significant for showing how, at the end of the ninth century, a Scandinavian chief could rise to the highest ranks of Frankish society. It also shows the resistance that the rapid promotion of these newcomers could provoke. In 897, the archbishop of Reims, Fulk, railed against his protégé, Charles the Simple, for having joined forces with a leader named Hundeus, though the young Carolingian king had managed to obtain the Norseman's conversion. A few years later, the compromise between Rollo, Charles the Simple, and the leading nobles of his kingdom (most importantly Robert, Marquis of Neustria, who would one day depose Charles and become king himself) proved more successful. It granted the Norman chieftain a territory near the mouth of the Seine in return for his baptism as a Christian and the *tutela regni* (protection of the realm). This land would form the nucleus of what became Normandy. Records indicate that Rollo may have become Robert of Neustria's godson and married another Gisela, daughter of Charles the Simple, though the historians are still in some doubt about the latter event. The Treaty of Saint-Clair-sur-Epte in 911 not only marked the start of the only durable bulwark the Scandinavians would have in the Frankish kingdom, but it also integrated the new rulers of Rouen into the elites of the realm. In a sense, Rollo succeeded where Godfrid had failed a generation earlier.

Pierre Bauduin

REFERENCES

Bauduin, Pierre. *Le Monde franc et les Vikings (VIIIe–Xe siècle)*. Paris: Albin Michel, 2009.

Brink, Stefan, and Neil Price, eds. *The Viking World*. London/New York: Routledge, 2008.

Coupland, Simon. "From Poachers to Gamekeepers: Scandinavian Warlords and Carolingian Kings." *Early Medieval Europe 7* (1998): 85–114.

Ridel, Élisabeth, ed. *Les Vikings dans l'Empire franc: Impact, héritage, imaginaire*. Bayeux: OREP, 2014.

Simek, Rudolf, and Ulrike Engel, eds. *Vikings on the Rhine: Recent Research on Early Medieval Relations Between the Rhinelands and Scandinavia*. Vienna: Fassbaender, 2004.

RELATED ARTICLES

800, 1051, 1066, 1550

910

Who would have predicted that, in the centuries following its foundation on the periphery of the Carolingian realm in 909 or 910, the Cluny Abbey would extend its influence far beyond its original feudal structures and become the center of the Benedictine order in Latin Europe?

Cluny Abbey was founded in 909 or 910, in the Mâconnais district of east-central France, to house a few Benedictine monks. Within two centuries, this modest establishment had acquired an international presence. Its network of daughter houses counted two hundred monasteries scattered across every part of Europe, and its main basilica, built at the end of the ninth century, was the biggest church in Christendom until the end of the Middle Ages, bigger even than the papal basilica in Rome. Only ruins of the medieval structures are left, however, as they were sold off during the French Revolution as assets of the state, then turned into a quarry and later a stud farm. The founding of the abbey is an event that is almost totally forgotten today, and even its date is not accurately known.

It was on September 11, presumably in 910, that the powerful Duke of Aquitaine, William the Pious (d. 918), together with his wife Engelberge, sister of the king of Provence, founded the abbey. That day, the couple traveled to Bourges, one of William's principal cities, for the drafting of a long and solemn charter describing a new monastic establishment to be created in the county of Mâcon. William and Engelberge set their decision down in writing, as witnessed by forty-three members of their court, including several bishops and numerous lay vassals. Also presumed to be there was Berno, the first abbot of Cluny, a Burgundian who was already in charge of four monasteries and had ties with Engelberge's family going back twenty years. The charter was written by Odo, a great intellectual and a protégé of William, who became a monk in service to Berno and later the second abbot of Cluny.

William and Engelberge sited the new community of monks in the little town of Cluny, on one of the duke's holdings, which they deeded to the apostles Peter and Paul, tutelary saints whose relics the future abbey would eventually house. The monks were to follow the Rule of Saint Benedict, care for the poor, and pray for the eternal salvation of the founders, their families, and their vassals. Finally, William and Engelberge asked that the abbey be independent of all local authority, whether lay or episcopal, and asked the apostles Peter and Paul and the pope, the apostles' representative, to defend the abbey and put a curse on any who might interfere with it.

The founding of Cluny Abbey was similar to the founding of many Carolingian institutions, but it marked the start of a new equilibrium that would see a profound alteration in the social structure and the exercise of power in the region. Starting in 888, the Carolingian Empire was divided into several kingdoms, each of which included coherent territories known as principalities, which were governed by powerful aristocratic families. In 890, the principality belonging to Engelberge's family became a kingdom in its own right in the southeast quarter of present-day France: the kingdom of Provence, with territorial ambitions turned toward Italy. William the Pious, for his part, governed a vast collection of territories that were mostly in the kingdom of the West Franks, including the provinces of Aquitaine, Berry, Septimania (present-day France's western Mediterranean shoreline), Auvergne, as well as the Mâconnais and the Lyonnais. By marrying Engelberge, around 890 to 893, he forged an important alliance between two great families with contiguous principalities.

The founding of Cluny Abbey would appear in several respects to be a symbol of this alliance. In the first place, the witnesses who would benefit from the monks' prayers were vassals not of one family but of both, thus expressly sealing the union. And the location of the new monastery would seem designed to promote peace between the families, as the Mâconnais was a county on the border between the kingdom of Provence and William's principality, one that had once belonged to Boso, Engelberge's father, before the family turned it over to the Duke of Aquitaine's family. Placing Cluny Abbey there put a definitive stamp on William's presence in the heart of this strategic area, with an endorsement from the kings of Provence.

The great princely families began to assert themselves during the early feudal period, and William and Engelberge's founding of Cluny was in line with that tendency. In the second half of the ninth century, these families grew decidedly more powerful, with the king granting them an increasing number of counties. As they came to control vaster areas, they were able to make more claims on the king and consistently assumed an intermediary role between the royal faction and a lesser, regional nobility. In order to distinguish themselves from the latter, and to legitimize the increase in their power, these princes modeled their behavior on the king's. So it was that William assumed more and more prestigious titles that had previously belonged only to sovereigns, gathered vassals around him to form a court, and married a princess who, through her mother, was a Carolingian, associating her closely with the majority of his decisions.

Finally, he founded a monastery, Cluny. Gaining the protection of the church and the monastic orders was a central element in the ideology of the Carolingian royals. Like all princes, William took hold of this ideology by posing as a defender of the church. He also wanted to share in the legitimacy that surrounded the saintly relics in the monks' keeping, and he wanted the monks' prayers on his behalf. Founding the abbey also involved a large circle of his relations and friends, not least because the holdings deeded to Cluny had belonged to his family for a very long time and had possibly served as a burial place for many of his ancestors.

One of the most unusual aspects of the agreement signed by William and Engelberge is that, from the start, and very much against the custom of the times, they recused themselves from subsequent intervention in the life of the community. This choice was likely prompted by Odo, who drafted the founding charter, and whose strong convictions led him, once he became abbot, to enact reforms in a number of monasteries in different kingdoms. The unusual statute governing Cluny reflects a new form of monasticism that was then coming into prominence, in which the monastery's autonomy and independence from the lay aristocracy were strongly safeguarded. By explicitly denying themselves or

227

their descendants the right to any authority over Cluny's assets, William and Engelberge turned them over entirely to the monks, who were then free to increase their seigneurial power. For Cluny to be protected by the apostles and the pope also seems to be an unusual aspect of the charter, at a time when the papacy enjoyed a certain moral prestige but had no real means of action. By choosing a protector at too great a distance to keep the abbey under close watch, and by supplementing that protection with a spiritual curse, the monks had found a novel and effective way to preserve Cluny's property from potential enemies.

In deeding their property directly to the apostles Peter and Paul, the princely couple also changed its nature: any and all assets of the abbey, belonging as they did to saints of the church, became sacred, and to take them was to commit sacrilege. The atypical nature of Cluny's founding charter seems to be the expression of a radical monastic ideal, providing for the possession and protection of a sacralized endowment, with the support of a distant papacy.

Before long, Cluny began to receive bequests, at first relating only to the newly formed abbey. However, it soon received a very large number of grants scattered over a wide geographic area — from the Holy Roman Empire to the Spanish kingdoms, and from southern England to Italy. By the early eleventh century, Cluny had become a powerful monastic congregation that held a network of monasteries and priories together under the authority of the central abbey. The phenomenon was a new one, and it led monks to recast their origin story and plot out a path toward their future power.

It was only much later, at the turn of the twentieth century, that the founding of Cluny came to serve a commemorative purpose. By that time, the network of monasteries under the abbot at Cluny had been dissolved during the French Revolution, and an attempt to resurrect it between 1888 and 1896 came to nothing. But the 1910 celebration of the thousand-year anniversary of the founding of Cluny made the abbey a symbol of a certain Catholic, monarchical, and even anti-Semitic France (as witnessed during the Dreyfus Affair). The commemoration came on the heels of other highly charged debates: the suppression of most French religious orders (1901), new laws on the separation of church and state (1905), and protests over state audits of church property (1906). This anniversary celebration, which focused on the alliance of religion and politics, expressed a pugnacious nostalgia for a Catholic France that had been martyred at the hands of the secular movement, just as Cluny had fallen victim (so it was believed) to revolutionary chaos.

Isabelle Rosé

REFERENCES

Bouchard, Constance Brittain. *Sword, Miter, and Cloister. Nobility and the Church in Burgundy, 980–1198*. Ithaca, NY: Cornell University Press, 1987.

Iogna-Prat, Dominique. *Études clunisiennes*. Paris: Picard, 2002.

———, Michel Lauwers, Florian Mazel, and Isabelle Rosé, eds. *Cluny: Les moines et la société au premier âge féodal*. Rennes: Presses Universitaires de Rennes, 2013.

Méhu, Didier, ed. *Cluny après Cluny: Constructions et commémorations 1790–2010*. Rennes: Presses Universitaires de Rennes, 2013.

Rosé, Isabelle. *Construire une société seigneuriale: Itinéraire et ecclésiologie de l'abbé Odon de Cluny (fin du IXe – milieu du Xe siècle)*. Turnhout: Brepols, 2008.

Rosenwein, Barbara H. *Rhinoceros Bound: Cluny in the Tenth Century*. Philadelphia: University of Pennsylvania Press, 1982.

RELATED ARTICLES

177, 397, 1287, 1534, 1789, 1954

987

The Election of the King Who Did Not Make France

Thanks to a fortunate combination of events and the discreet but powerful support of the Germanic emperor, the crown of Western Francia was bestowed upon Hugh Capet, the most powerful of Frankish princes, in 987. Although he founded a new dynasty, there was still a huge difference between the kingdom he stabilized and the nation it would one day become.

On May 21 or 22, 987, Louis V, king of West Francia, died in Senlis following a hunting accident. Only nineteen years old, he left behind no heirs. Upon his death, the Carolingian dynasty that had reigned over the Frankish kingdom for more than two centuries also died. Three days before Louis's death, Hugh Capet, the Duke of the Franks, had gathered the nobles of the kingdom in Compiègne to render a judgment in the trial for treason against the archbishop of Reims, Adalbero. After burying the young king and deciding a mistrial in favor of Adalbero, the group traveled to the estate of the Duke of the Franks in Senlis to debate the choice of a new king. On June 1, upon Adalbero's initiative, the nobles rejected the last Carolingian survivor, Charles, Duke of Lower Lotharingia, the uncle of the dead king, and instead elected Hugh, Duke of the Franks, who was crowned a month later in Noyon or perhaps Reims. A few months later, on Christmas Day 987, Hugh named as successor to the throne his eldest son, Robert, who had just reached majority at the age of sixteen, having him crowned by Adalbero in the church Sainte-Croix in Orléans.

And so the principle of heredity was restored.

Having become king, Hugh was not done with the Carolingians, however. Charles of Lower Lotharingia wasn't giving up quietly, seizing Laon in May 988 and gaining the city of Reims from the new archbishop, Arnulf, in January 989. The kingdom was divided. But on March 31, 991, just after Palm Sunday, the bishop of Laon set a trap for Charles and delivered him to the king. Imprisoned, he died a few months later.

An account of these events by Richer (circa 940–998), a monk from the Abbey of Saint-Remi in Reims, enables us — despite its rhetorical flourishes — to situate the matter in its historical context and to grasp Adalbero's arguments on behalf of Hugh. The lone survivor of the Carolingian dynasty, Charles was a pretender to the crown, but his behavior was unworthy of a candidate for the monarchy. He had misallied himself by marrying the daughter of a simple knight and had chosen to serve a foreign ruler: removed from the royal succession in 954, he became Duke of Lower Lotharingia, vassal of the Germanic emperor. Hugh, Duke of the Franks, however, was attuned to the public good. He had king-like qualities, and readily assumed the role. He also benefited from the support of those who wished to maintain peaceful relations with the neighboring empire and also of the church, which he was in the process of reforming. His piousness earned him the nickname Capet, from *cappa*, the half-mantle of Saint Martin, preserved in the Tours chapter of which he was the lay abbot.

Hugh Capet's accession to the throne has been elevated to a founding event in French history. Historians describe it as a major break, a rupture, a coup d'état, a usurpation, a *mutatio regni*, a pivotal date, or, even more often, a revolution. The nineteenth-century historian and politician François Guizot depicted 987 as the date of the "birth of French civilization." The nation begins at that moment, Guizot wrote. "Henceforth it is no longer the Gauls, the Franks, or the Romans, but the French, but ourselves who are on the historical stage." Later, in the nineteenth century, this view became ubiquitous within the school curriculum. Textbooks make 987 the point of departure of a process of nation-formation that concluded with the French Revolution. The date's nationalist credentials were strengthened by its proximity to the year 1000. According to historian Jules Michelet, this date marked the start, in the aftermath of harrowing times, of a period of hope and creativity that included the birth of France. More recently, the Capetian tale has been integrated into the period of expansion that, it is said, ranged from the eleventh to the thirteenth century. This type of teleological appreciation has for a long time hindered historical analysis.

At the current moment, however, historians see in the election of Hugh Capet a prime example of a nonevent, of an epiphenomenon. If anything, they place it within a broader evolution, a mere stage in the irremediable decline of the Carolingian dynasty.

The election of Hugh Capet was not a revolution. Two of his ancestors, his great-uncle Odo (r. 888–898) and his grandfather Robert (r. 922–923), had been kings before him. In 888, the breakup of the Carolingian Empire had already inspired the nobles of the kingdom to select as king whoever appeared most capable of defending the land. They ruled out the Carolingian Charles the Simple and elected Odo, Marquis of Neustria, who had distinguished himself in the defense of Paris against the Normans. In 922, Odo's brother Robert was elected following the dethronement of Charles the Simple. Those alternative elections indicate the existence of two legitimate dynasties: the family that was heir to the Carolingian Empire and the Robertians (future Capetians). In 936, the latter preferred to become makers of kings. Hugh the Great, father of Hugh Capet, would seek out Louis IV, son of Charles the Simple, who was exiled in England, and install him on the throne. The new king bestowed the title of Duke of the Franks upon Hugh the Great, making him the second-ranking figure in the kingdom. In 960, upon the death of his father, Hugh Capet inherited that position.

Life in the kingdom remained strongly influenced by its relations with Germania, its powerful neighbor to the east. In fact, the last Carolingians cultivated an imperial yearning that became fixed on Lotharingia, cradle of their dynasty, seat of the former empire, and source of recurrent conflicts between Francia and Germania, especially after the Saxon Dynasty ascended in Germania, following the refounding of the empire by Otto I in 962. The weakness of the kingdom of Francia and its lack of influence contrasted with the prestige of the empire and Germanic supremacy. A relationship of dependency took form, which historians have likened to guardianship. Concerned with maintaining a balance that would guarantee peace and inspired by an imperial mission, the Germanic emperor readily intervened as mediator in internal conflicts in the kingdom to the west, where ongoing competition led the Carolingians and the Robertians to seek out imperial protection and advantageous marriages.

The Carolingians didn't give up on Lotharingia, however. In 978, the well-named Lothair launched an attack on Aix-la-Chapelle, but came up against a victorious imperial counteroffensive. In 984, he undertook a new offensive that also failed. Adalbero, the archbishop of Reims, was from a Lotharingian family, and sought to maintain peace between the two neighboring lands; he supported the imperial cause and was accused of treason. If he backed the election of Hugh Capet, it was because his accession would end the conflicts created by the Lotharingian obsession of the last Carolingians. But the reign of Hugh Capet also concluded the Germanic emperor's dominion over the Frankish kingdom. Henceforth, two fully sovereign states would coexist, sharing the task of leading the Christian people onto the path to salvation.

Historians emphasize the territorial weakness of the new king. He only had true authority over his domain, which encompassed a disparate collection of land holdings, cities, rights, and prerogatives, with boundaries close to those of the former Neustria, which was beginning to be called Francia. Around a Senlis–Paris–Orléans axis, we find a cluster of royal lands inherited from the Carolingian crown as well as some twenty bishoprics in the north and the east, and a few prestigious abbeys of which the king was the lay abbot (Saint-Denis, Saint-Benoît-sur-Loire, Saint-Martin de Tours). The sovereign no longer intervened south of the Loire River; there were no southern seigneuries or monasteries among the recipients of royal rights or titles. Some southern territories even broke away from the kingdom. The county of Barcelona, a south-Pyrenean principality predating Catalonia, acquired full sovereignty. In the aftermath of the sacking of Barcelona by Abbasid caliph al-Mansur in July 985, Count Borrell appealed to King Lothair and later Hugh Capet for help. In his response, the king proposed a possible intervention, but under specific conditions. That was the end of the matter. The episode put an end to any political relationship between the Catalan counties and the Frankish monarchy.

However, the king's subjects did not equate his power with territories. The events of 987 thus brought no change to contemporary understandings of monarchy. The king was never fought or contested. He could not pay tribute to a lord, and remained outside the feudal pyramid. Even the insolence of the Count of Périgord ("Who made you king?") suggested that, regardless of the conditions of his accession, the figure who had become king would remain so. His anointment during the coronation conferred upon his reign a supernatural and quasi-magical aura, illustrated by his thaumaturgical power. The king carried out a ministry, the coronation made him a figure of the church. It was from the church that he received his mission as a Christian sovereign: to ensure the reign of justice, to maintain peace and public order, to lead the people in his care to salvation.

Although the election of 987 may have been a nonevent, its historical significance is paradoxical since the election of the king resulted a few months later in the establishment of a new dynasty. A mere function, born from an election, became a dignity that was transferred by blood. The first Capetians did, in fact, manage to stabilize the institution of the monarchy by defining the rules necessary to ensure its duration. These were primogeniture (which sheltered the dynasty from successional conflicts), the link to the throne, and the coronation of the heir (to avoid elections). Having renounced the former home of the Carolingian Empire, they definitively removed their kingdom from the self-interested protection of the Germanic sovereign.

In the longer term, the Capetians' success appears exceptional. They founded a dynasty that lasted eight centuries and continued in a direct line for more than three hundred years. Earlier than elsewhere in Europe, the French monarchy thus had chronological continuity and territorial stability. But while this internal history accompanied the slow construction of a state, it would be wrong to view it as the wellspring of the French nation. In 987, Hugh Capet was made king, but he did not make France.

Michel Zimmermann

REFERENCES

Guillot, Olivier. *Hugues Capet et les premiers Capétiens (987–1180)*. Paris: Tallandier, 2002.

Mazel, Florian. *Féodalités (888–1180)*. Paris: Belin, 2010.

Parisse, Michel, and Xavier Barral i Altet, eds. *Le Roi de France et son royaume autour de l'an mil*. Paris: Picard, 1992.

Sassier, Yves. *Hugues Capet: Naissance d'une dynastie*. Paris: Fayard, 1987.

Theis, Laurent. *L'avènement d'Hugues Capet (3 juillet 987)*. Paris: Gallimard, 1984.

RELATED ARTICLES

800, 842–843, 1137, 1214

1051

An Early Franco-Russian Alliance

The marriage of Henry I of France to Anne of Kiev in 1051 allowed the House of Capet to enter the broader European marriage market for royals. And yet, Henry's choice of bride seems to have been motivated by a desire for prestige more than by political strategy.

On May 19, 1051, Pentecost Sunday, the Reims Cathedral hosted the coronation of Anna Yaroslavna (b. circa 1030), daughter of Yaroslav the Wise, Grand Prince of Kiev, and her wedding to King Henry I of France (crowned in 1027), the grandson of Hugh Capet, founder of the Capetian dynasty. The king was in his twentieth year of full royal power and the seventh year of his widowhood; Anne became his third wife.

Communications were neither frequent nor easy between the kingdom of West Francia — increasingly known as the "kingdom of France" or more precisely "kingdom of the Franks" — and the principality of Kiev, whose dynamism and stability came from its Swedish merchants (the so-called Varangians) and their enterprising, settled compatriots. These last had initially marshaled the local Slavic peoples — who were ruled by or paid tribute to the Rus' (slavicized Swedes) — into a nation. Extending over a vast area from Lake Ladoga in northwestern Russia to the Black Sea and covering the present lands of Belarus, Ukraine, and western Russia, this territory was repeatedly divided and reassembled.

Like their neighbors, the Kiev rulers looked with a mixture of fascination and hatred at the Byzantines, whom they protected and envied, imitated and pillaged. The Byzantines, for their part, felt no great kindness toward "the surly and honorless tribes to the north," but they were quick to appreciate and pay for their military prowess. Again like many of their neighbors, the Slavo-Varangian princes of the mid-eleventh century were caught in the complex transition to Christianity, which was supported by and directed from Byzantium. Vladimir the Great, who ruled Kievan Rus' from 980 to 1015, was baptized in 988, but his religion spread slowly among the common people. The way was smoothed for Yaroslav, who ruled from approximately 1020 to 1054; he was the son of Vladimir and Rogneda, daughter of the prince of Polotsk (Belarus), and he came to power after eliminating his elder brother. Yaroslav's consolidation of the Kievan territory and its religion remained fragile and called for a succession of alliances, negotiations, and marriages, at which Yaroslav was a consummate artist, marrying off sons and daughters to shore up his alliance with the Byzantines and lining up a block of alliances with the West (Poland, Hungary, the Lower Elbe region, Norway). Through his daughter Anne, he even made a stealth advance on the Latin empire.

Our window onto the reign and powers of the King of France is, paradoxically, more limited. The historical sources consist of a handful of skeletal annals and flowery hagiographies. While his father, Robert the Pious, had made full use of his ties with Fleury Abbey in the north-central commune of Saint-Benoît-sur-Loire, Henry I was not significantly associated with any particular place, if we except the Abbey of Saint-Denis, whose scriptorium (the room where scribes copied, wrote, and illuminated manuscripts) was not yet flourishing. This was probably a consequence of the king having redirected his ambitions and the power of his state toward the north, as confirmed by the trust he placed in his brother-in-law, Baldwin V, Count of Flanders, who was present at the king's death in 1060 and acted as regent for the underage Philip I until 1067.

The marriage of the King of France was a major event. The first Capetians had received critical help from their Ottonian relatives and protectors. Otto I, king of Germany and Italy, who became emperor in 962, had married his sister Hedwig to Hugh the Great, father of Hugh Capet. Henry I quickly set his sights on marrying into the emperor's family, becoming betrothed in 1033 to the young princess Matilda, who died within the year. He then married another Matilda, the daughter of the Margrave of Frisia, who was in turn a half brother of Emperor Henry III. The second Matilda was also under the age of ten; she died in 1044, after giving birth to a daughter who died in infancy. Hampered by papal laws against marrying one's relatives, the king was unable to find a suitable bride among the princesses in his own kingdom or in neighboring ones.

And he was taking his time. This slackness on the part of a king who was known both as a hunter and a warrior (at Fleury Abbey, he was nicknamed *municeps*, "castle taker") has led to much speculation. Those who believe that the royal power declined over the course of the century suspect Henry of misogyny or effeminacy; those who see him as a king constrained by lack of choice interpret his delay as poise and self-assurance. As we now know, he would eventually prove capable of contributing to the "Capetian miracle," the unbroken succession of Capetian heirs from father to son, from 987 to 1328. When necessary, Henry could summon the great to his side, weave complex alliances, and hold his ground in a confrontation with a weakened emperor, Henry III. The Capetian king was in his actions and in the exercise of his authority "an emperor within his own kingdom," whereas the emperor himself had a hard struggle both in

Germany and in Italy. Word went out at this time that the ruler of Kiev had put his daughter Anne on the marriage block and been refused by Emperor Henry III. King Henry I's advisers no doubt saw an opportunity, even if no action was taken for several years.

There was nothing imperial about the French king's marriage to Anne of Kiev, which replicated in a minor key the union of Emperor Otto II (cousin of Hugh Capet) to the Byzantine princess Theophanu. It did offer the king and his descendants a promise of prestige, as can be seen in the Capetians' naming practices. Until Robert the Pious, an overwhelming number of names were drawn from the great Robertian forefathers (Hugh, Robert, Odo), with a sprinkling of Ottonians (Otto and Henry — Hedwig's two brothers had the same names as Hugh Capet's). The family's naming tradition was shattered with Philip I (r. 1060 to 1108), the son of Henry I and Anne of Kiev, and further abandoned with their grandsons, Philip and Louis. "Philip" was Greek and possibly contained an allusion to the apostle Philip, who is said to have converted the Scythians and the Sicambri, foreshadowing the Rus' and the Franks. "Louis" reached back to Charlemagne's son, Louis the Pious, but also to Clovis, *Hludovicus*, or "*Chlodoweg*."

A first delegation set out for Kiev in 1049. The agreement was concluded on its return, and a second delegation was sent out to escort the princess back, the girl being about twenty years old. The glory of her father, Yaroslav, was at its apogee: Saint Sophia's Cathedral in Kiev had recently been completed. As the historian Andrew Lewis has aptly said, "The king's marriages were considered and purposeful."

After the coronation, there followed nine years of quiet and largely undocumented rule. Anne rolled up her sleeves and set about the business of being a queen. Within a year, in 1052, she presented the Capetian dynasty with a male heir, Philip. Following the Capetian custom, he would be crowned during his father's lifetime. This would happen later, when he was seven, on the Feast of Pentecost, May 23, 1059. Once again, King Henry had taken his time, and his strength was starting to fail. Meanwhile, the queen had brought two more sons into the world, Robert and Hugh. The latter would soon receive the counties of Valois and Vermandois through marriage.

For the rest, outside of her duty to produce male heirs, we should imagine a queen serving various duties, setting an example that would pass down through the centuries: she was sacred and wore a crown, worked to perpetuate the dynasty, but was held at a distance from the seat of power. On a daily level, modeling herself on the wives of Hugh Capet and Robert the Pious, the queen may have managed the affairs of the palace or worked at her loom. She would have had the service of a seneschal, who no doubt raised revenues for her and guarded her coffers; and other servants besides, including the "pedagogue" whom she provided for her son. Anne entered her marriage with a dowry (including a gem that would later find its way to the reliquary of Saint-Denis), and disposed of a dower, whose revenue she received.

The extent to which Anne took part in royal "politics" is impossible to know. A brief account of Philip's accession to the throne in 1059 does not even mention her name; but the real purpose of the document, which was to reconfirm the prerogatives of the archbishop of Reims, may explain the omission. In fact, the queen came center stage only after her husband's death, when she was informally associated with the regency of Baldwin V of Flanders. Passion was not lacking, and she took Count Ralph IV of Valois (a devotee of the late king) to her bed, marrying him in 1061. Historians may have exaggerated the gravity of their transgression, as only Ralph seems to have been excommunicated, on charges of bigamy, and he returned to the court of Philip I before long. Anne seems never to have left her son's side, or never for long, up to her last known appearance in 1075. In both periods of her public life, before and after King Henry's death, she usually appears alongside one or another of her sons, corroborating one of the many royal pronouncements, consenting to decrees, witnessing their signing, in many cases signing it jointly, on at least two occasions by making a cross. She was also present during legal arguments held before her husband in 1055. While her son was still a minor, from 1060 to 1067, her name appeared on twenty-three royal decrees. It was only in 1061 or 1062, in a document relating to the abbey of Saint-Crépin de Soissons, that she first affixed her name and title, in a firm hand, in Latin transcribed into Cyrillic characters: "Anna re[g]ina ." A facsimile of her signature would be presented to Czar Nicholas II when he made an official visit to France in 1896. This brief autograph contrasts with the more Byzantine terms and conditions she set forth in the document rededicating Saint Vincent Abbey in Senlis.

Like other women of the high aristocracy in France and Germania, and like princesses in the Byzantine Empire, Anne could read and write, and she had acquired enough elements of theology and liturgy to suggest themes and associations inspired by the Byzantines for incorporation into the abbey's charter. Still, all of this is mere speculation, and it may simply prove that Anne had a chaplain at her side. Nor do we know how she managed during the schism between Byzantium and Rome, provoked in 1054 by a spate of mutual excommunications. Officially, in any case, she was the wife and subsequently the widow of the king of the Franks, never violating the moral standards meant to govern her behavior.

Alone among French queens who claimed Russian descent, the memory of Anne of Kiev was conscripted in

1825 to celebrate relations between France and Russia, a practice that started again in czarist times and continued into the Soviet era. More recently, Ukraine has stepped in to reclaim what was, after all, a dialogue between the royal city of Senlis and Kiev. This relationship has been officially sanctioned by an exchange of statues, a sister-city bond, and official support for a French lycée in Kiev.

Olivier Guyotjeannin

REFERENCES

Bautier, Robert-Henri. "Anne de Kiev, reine de France, et la politique royale au XIe siècle: Étude critique de la documentation." *Revue des études slaves* 57, no. 4 (1985): 539–64.

Dunbabin, Jean. "What's in a Name? Philip, King of France." *Speculum* 68, no. 4 (1993): 949–68.

Lewis, Andrew W. *Royal Succession in Capetian France: Studies on Familial Order and the State.* Cambridge, MA: Harvard University Press, 1981.

Vodoff, Vladimir. *Naissance de la chrétienté russe: La conversion du prince Vladimir de Kiev (988) et ses conséquences (XIe–XIIIe siècle).* Paris: Fayard, 1988.

Zajac, Talia. "*Gloriosa Regina* or 'Alien Queen'? Some Reconsiderations on Anna Yaroslavna's Queenship (r. 1050–1075)." *Royal Studies Journal* 3, no. 1 (2016): 28–70.

RELATED ARTICLES
882, 987, 1137, 1420, 1659

1066

Normans in the Four Corners of the World

In the mid-eleventh century, the Normans were the
spearhead of Frankish knighthood. Their taste for war
and adventure, their avidity for gain, but also their feudal
discipline and the ambition of their princes drove them to
the four corners of the world, from the hills of England to
the shores of the Mediterranean.

On October 14, 1066, on the battlefield near Hastings
in the south of England, William, Duke of Normandy,
crushed the army of King Harold, who died on the field.
William earned himself the kingship of England and the
epithet "Conqueror." England has never been successfully
invaded since his exploit. The story is well known thanks
to numerous chronicles, most of them favorable to
William, and thanks also to the famous graphic depiction
(much embroidered) on the Bayeux Tapestry, probably
commissioned by William's half-brother Odo, bishop of
Bayeux. These developments had important repercussions
in Europe and led to the formation of an unusual entity that

straddled the English Channel: what historians have taken to calling the "Anglo-Norman world." In the following century, the Plantagenets would be its heirs, and from the mid-eleventh century to the early thirteenth, it served as a powerful vector for advancing the ends of France's Capetian dynasty.

William of Normandy's accession to the throne of England was not in any way foreordained. According to Norman chronicles, the sonless Edward the Confessor named William as his successor early on, largely because his mother, Emma, was William's great-aunt, and Edward had sought refuge in Normandy during the crisis of 1051 to 1052, when conflict between Edward and powerful aristocrats threatened to turn into civil war. When Harold Godwinson, the most powerful of England's princes, landed in Normandy around 1064 to 1065, he apparently swore an oath to uphold Edward's choice of successor. But Harold was the king's brother-in-law and, cresting a wave after his victories over the Welsh, he had the support of the aristocracy. On January 5, 1066, while Edward lay on his deathbed, he apparently switched his choice to Harold. Whatever the truth of this, the assembly of nobles that convened at Westminster Abbey proclaimed Harold king. If he was to assert his rights, William would have to fight for them. These two were not the only claimants to the throne. Harald Hardrada, king of Norway, based his own claim on the rights of King Cnut, who had ruled England, Denmark, and Norway at the beginning of the eleventh century. A fourth, Edgar Aetheling, Edward's nephew, who had newly returned from a distant exile in Hungary, also claimed to be the rightful heir. The succession to the English throne was a matter that riveted the attention of all of northern Europe: England was the wealthiest kingdom in the West and the one whose king held the securest seat.

Convinced that his claim was legitimate, William mobilized all his forces: the Norman aristocracy, first and foremost, but also his allies and an army of mercenaries imported from Flanders, Brittany, and the province of Maine. Thanks to the intercession, probably, of Norman clerics of Italian descent, William received the support of Pope Alexander II, who sent him the Standard of Saint Peter. The pope was already allied with the Normans of southern Italy and wanted further support from powerful princes to enact his reforms of the church. The Norman fleet, long delayed by adverse winds, finally crossed the English Channel on September 28, 1066. Harold learned the news a few days later, having defeated and killed Harald Hardrada at the Battle of Stamford Bridge, on September 25, near York. Harold marched posthaste toward William's army and engaged him in battle. The fighting, which was unusually violent, lasted a full day. A large number of Anglo-Saxon nobles lost their lives, to the horror of the chroniclers, whose experience of local warring and knightly combats had left them unprepared for such bloodshed.

William's supporters interpreted his victory as God's judgment in his favor, a notion perpetuated by the founding on the very spot of Battle Abbey, whose monks were charged with praying for the souls of those who had died in combat. The abbey helped to install a new ecclesiastical order in England, as the first monks were from the powerful Marmoutier Abbey, near Tours. The victory at Hastings allowed William to advance on London, where, after dealing with minor opposition, he was crowned king on December 25, 1066. Edgar Aetheling himself bowed down to William and recognized his sovereignty. The conquest was not final, however, and rebellions simmered across England for many years, leading to increasingly drastic measures of repression, eventually eliminating most of the old aristocracy.

Beyond the outcome of the succession, the Norman conquest of England had considerable consequences for Europe at large. It showed that the feudal aristocracy need not confine its political horizons or matrimonial strategies to the boundaries of its own kingdom. The English Channel, in this instance, was not an obstacle: trade, as well as men and ideas, had been moving readily between Brittany, Normandy, Flanders, and the south of England since the early Middle Ages. With William's victory, a French prince had become a king in his own right, and his power posed a serious challenge to France's Capetian king: the Anglo-Norman Empire stretched from the province of Maine in eastern France to the Scottish border, and though it was for a time divided between William's two eldest sons, the actions of the youngest, Henry Beauclerc, who was at first excluded from the inheritance, unified it again in 1106.

Newcomers, most of them from Normandy, but also from Brittany, Flanders, Île-de-France, Champagne, and Picardy, continued to arrive in England in the years following William's accession, as though the island were under colonization. These families owned seigneuries and made alliances on both sides of the Channel. Their sons embarked on careers in the church and in civil administration that straddled England and Normandy. Though British historians continue to debate it, this colonization was remarkable in extent. Did it not encompass the replacement of the Anglo-Saxon aristocracy and high clergy by imports from the continent, the extension of feudal customs, the transfer of bishoprics, the acquisition of seigneuries in England by abbeys in Normandy, Brittany, and the Loire Valley, the diffusion of the French language, and the appearance throughout England of royal churches and castles?

The conflict with England also contributed to defining a "French" identity, which was still often spoken of as "Frankish," but which increasingly referred to the northern half of the French kingdom, whose regional divisions it papered over without erasing them altogether. Significantly, where the Bayeux Tapestry names the adversaries of the "English," it calls them "Franks," not "Normans." Similarly, the oldest manuscript of *The Song of Roland*, the epic poem that is considered the first "French" literary work and contains the first celebration of *douce France* ("lovely France"), was written in Anglo-Norman, the langue d'oïl dialect spoken by the Anglo-Norman aristocracy. It was on the banks of the Thames, therefore, that "French" literature blossomed.

The conquest of England, however, represents only one facet of the powerful expansionist dynamic of the "French" aristocracy of the eleventh century, which also took part in the *Reconquista* of the Iberian Peninsula, the First Crusade, and the conquest of southern Italy and Sicily. Before 1066, other groups of Normans had assumed control of Apulia, Calabria, and eastern Sicily, which was finally subjugated in 1091. Normans and other "Franks" had arrived in this region as far back as the 1020s, and their presence lasted into the early twelfth century. Their arrival was not brought about by an ambitious prince or by marriage and succession, but by the rise of mercenary knights in service to the Byzantines, to Lombard nobles from Capua and Salerno, and to the pope. These mercenaries managed to emancipate themselves from their masters and, in a region torn by deep political rifts, effect a conquest of their own. A number of rivals competed for the leadership until an obscure seigneurial family from Lower Normandy, the Hautevilles, managed to impose unity.

Among their chief figures were Roger I of Sicily and Robert Guiscard — whose son, Bohemond, would travel to the Levant and, during the First Crusade, found the Principality of Antioch. The unification, completed by Roger II in 1139, was the result of gathering the assembled lands — with the pope's support — into a new kingdom, the Norman kingdom of Sicily, which chose Palermo as its capital and acknowledged vassalage to the pope. As in England, the royal dynasty and the secular aristocracy retained an attachment to their Norman identity and to a "French" feudal and knightly culture. But unlike in England, the families that settled in South Italy and Sicily did not generally maintain direct ties with Normandy. And they melded more deeply and diversely into the surrounding cultures, with the dominant Normans drawing heavily on the legacies of the Byzantines, Arabs, Jews, and Lombards.

In the eleventh century, knightly adventure, conquest, and colonization contributed to shaping the identity of the "French" nobles, at the same time reflecting their demographic, military, and political dynamism. The important role the Normans played in this period offers a surprising reversal. These "men from the North" had been disparaged as barbarians and pagans only a century or two before, but now that they were directing their energy outward at the world, they were considered admirable Franks and heroes of Latin Catholicism.

Florian Mazel

REFERENCES

Bates, David. *William the Conqueror*. New Haven/London: Yale University Press, 2016.

Bouet, Pierre. *Hastings (14 octobre 1066)*. Paris: Tallandier, 2014.

Canosa, Rosa. *Etnogenesi normanne e identità variabili: Il retroterra culturale dei Normanni d'Italia fra Scandinavia e Normandia*. Turin: Silvio Zamorani, 2009.

d'Onofrio, Mario, ed. *Les Normands, peuple d'Europe (1030–1200)*. Paris: Flammarion, 1994.

Martin, Jean-Marie. *Italies normandes (XIe–XIIe siècle)*. Paris: Hachette, 1994.

RELATED ARTICLES
600 BCE, 882, 1282, 1550

1095

The Frankish East

When Pope Urban II called for a crusade in 1095, the knights and princes of France responded in greater numbers than those of any other country. Out of the crusaders' violent confrontation with the "complicated Orient," as de Gaulle later called the Middle East, arose a first colonization of the Levant and, beyond their feudal rivalries, a growing sense of their identity as "Franks" and as Latins — in other words, as Catholics.

On November 17, 1095, on the last day of the council he had convened in the French city of Clermont, Pope Urban II called on Western Christians to come to the defense of the Christians in the Middle East who had come under Muslim oppression and to free Christ's tomb from infidel control. He promised to remit the sins of every warrior who took the road to Jerusalem and place any property left behind under the special protection of the Holy See. Repeated in Nîmes on November 28, this call to arms created a great stir and set in motion a large number of pilgrims in the spring of 1096, most of them common people, followed in the summer by armies of princes and knights, all of them wearing the sign of the cross on their chests as a symbol of their allegiance to the cause and their status as crusaders. What we know as the First Crusade was under way. It ended in 1099, after three years of trials and tribulations, with the capture of Jerusalem and the founding of new feudal states in the Holy Land. The venture showed the extent to which the pope's power had increased as a result of his reforms to the church. It also expanded "Frankish" control of the Mediterranean and hardened the Latin Christians' sense of identity vis-à-vis Muslims, Jews, and Greeks. There would be more crusades during the next two centuries. While they ultimately led to failure — the surrender of Acre in 1291 marked the end of the Frankish presence in the Levant — they also fed long-term bitterness among Eastern Christians and a desire for revenge among Muslim peoples.

Before Urban II gave his sermon at the Council of Clermont, no pope had set foot outside of Italy since the Carolingian period. He traveled in the company of his curia, the clerics in his administration, all through the former territories of Gaul, notably in the southern, central, and western portions of France, holding gatherings along the way, confirming appointments, settling lawsuits, and consecrating churches and burial grounds. Urban was himself a Frenchman, from a noble family in the northeastern town of Châtillon-sur-Marne, and a former grand prior of Cluny Abbey. Although his relations with the Germanic emperor were strained, he made a point while in France, and particularly while among the Capetians, of displaying his full authority as pope over the church. He was concerned with having his authority accepted, along with the new social norms promoted by the Gregorian Reform.

Designating an enemy, the Muslims, and setting a goal on the distant horizon, Jerusalem and the Holy Land, were the first steps in a vast program of ecclesiastical control over warfare and the chivalric ideal. An earlier pope had sanctioned a war against Islam in the 1060s, during the *Reconquista* of the Iberian Peninsula, and the tradition of legitimizing violence can be traced back even further, to Saint Augustine. In 1095, however, it reached a new level. At Clermont, the pope extended the Peace and Truce of God, which limited the use of warfare within Christian lands, to all of Christendom, the better to direct chivalric violence outward. A new ideal was offered to Western knights: they could achieve salvation by fighting infidels. Jews were the initial victims of the campaign against the "enemies of God." The first crusaders, led by Peter the Hermit and Walter Sans Avoir, conducted violent pogroms in the Rhineland, wreaking severe damage on Ashkenazi Jewry. When the crusaders encountered Byzantine Greeks on their passage through Constantinople, they accused them of weakness and complicity with the Muslims.

The literature traditionally distinguishes a "People's Crusade," which in fact incorporated German knights, from a "Princes' Crusade," captained by French and Lotharingian nobles (Hugh, Count of Vermandois, the king's brother; Robert, Duke of Normandy; Stephen, Count of Blois; Robert II, Count of Flanders; Baldwin II, Count of Hainaut; Raymond of Saint-Gilles, Count of Toulouse; Godfrey of Bouillon, Duke of Lower Lotharingia; and Baldwin of Boulogne, Godfrey's brother) and commanded, at least in theory, by the pope's legate, Adhémar of Monteil, Bishop of Le Puy. Neither the German emperor nor any European monarch took part, not even the king of France; they were all, in consequence, on delicate ground with the pope. The voyage proved extremely long and arduous. The first crusaders, led by Peter the Hermit, were poorly prepared and committed many atrocities along the way. They ended up massacred by the Hungarians and the Turks, after being steered away from Constantinople by the Emperor (*basileus*) Alexios I Komnenos.

The French nobles, who traveled separately, reached the Byzantine capital one after another, and were joined there by two Norman princes from southern Italy, Bohemond of Taranto and his nephew, Tancred. All of them (with the exception of Raymond of Saint-Gilles) begrudgingly consented to pay homage to Emperor Alexios before continuing on to Jerusalem. The march across Anatolia and the Siege of Antioch proved especially difficult because of heat, illness, short rations, harassment from the Turks, and internal squabbling among the Frankish leaders. The shock force of the mounted knights had its effect nonetheless, and the crusaders prevailed in their encounters with the Muslim warriors. The armies that finally arrived at the gates of Jerusalem were depleted and exhausted, but managed all the same to take the city on July 15, 1099, and then plunder it.

Empowered by their victory, the "Frankish" nobles broke their oaths of fealty to the Byzantine emperor and established new and independent principalities on the model of Western feudalism. Baldwin of Boulogne led the way by creating the County of Edessa in February–March 1098. In Jerusalem, the clergy managed to forestall the crowning of a king, on the grounds that the title would be offensive to the memory of Christ: Godfrey of Bouillon was named "Defender of the Holy Sepulchre." But on his death in 1100, his brother Baldwin assumed the title of King of Jerusalem and claimed rulership over the other Frankish principalities: the County of Tripoli, governed by a lesser branch of the Counts of Toulouse; the Principality of Antioch, governed by the Normans from Italy; the County of Edessa, governed by the house of Boulogne. Many crusaders returned to the West in 1099 and 1100, believing that they had accomplished their vows. Those who stayed, along with various latecomers, took control of the territory, spreading the seigneurial system of land ownership and feudal bondage, building castles that drew on Muslim techniques (and would in turn inform the art of fortification in the West), and awarding trading privileges to the Italian merchants who had transported and revictualed them on numerous occasions. Catholic bishoprics and monasteries were founded: a Latin Christianity became established. Despite the Franks' small numbers, which remained so during the new expeditions of 1100–1101, 1107–1108, 1120–1124, and 1129, a true process of colonization gradually occurred.

Despite the quarrels and factions that regularly divided their camp, the crusaders were clearly seen by the Muslims and Byzantine Greeks as a coherent group, defined less by its religion — the Greeks and non-Orthodox minorities of the Middle East were also Christians — than by its "Frankish" identity. The use of this term makes the crusaders lineal descendants of the Franks of the Carolingian period, defines them as Roman Catholics, and links them to the language and country of origin of the greater number of them: the kingdom of France, particularly its northern half, and the proto-French langue d'oïl. There were many tensions and disagreements between the northern French, the French from Provence and the south, Italians (mostly Ligurians and Lombards), Normans (from France and Italy), and Germans. But in the crucible of the East, the common

"Frankish" identity assigned to the crusaders by the natives, both Christian and Muslim, tended to blur any regional or dynastic affiliation they carried with them from the West.

When the crusaders were later mythologized as worthy descendants of an earlier race of heroes both real and fictional (Charlemagne, Roland, Olivier de Vienne, etc.), this same Frankish identity came to the fore. The exploits of the Christian warriors against the "Saracens" and the "Moors" in Spain were, after all, being sung in epic poems, the *chansons de geste*. Within this developing mythology was an ideal of Christian chivalry that the church was quick to seize on, accentuating the Christian aspect of the knighting ceremony and supporting the creation of new religious-military orders. Founded in Jerusalem and operating under the pope's authority, the Knights Templar and the Knights Hospitaller would protect pilgrims and ensure the safety of the Frankish states. They played a growing role in the defense of the Holy Land, while the ongoing recruitment to their numbers, essentially from France, created close ties between the West and the Levant throughout the twelfth and thirteenth centuries.

It is hardly surprising, therefore, that the Second Crusade, prompted by the fall of the County of Edessa in 1144, also started in France, or that Pope Eugene III entrusted its preaching to Bernard of Clairvaux, abbot of Cîteaux and most celebrated figure of his day. Bernard preached for the first time on Easter Day 1146 at Vézelay Abbey, which held the relics of Mary Magdalene, who had purportedly left the Holy Land to end her days in ancient Gaul. This time around, King Louis VII decided to join the crusade, and France began to assert itself as the eldest daughter of the church, to the great benefit of its monarchs.

Florian Mazel

REFERENCES

Balard, Michel. *Les Latins en Orient (XIe–XVe siècle)*. Paris: Presses Universitaires de France, 2006.

Demurger, Alain. *Moines et guerriers: Les ordres religieux-militaires au Moyen Âge*. Paris: Le Seuil, 2010.

Flori, Jean. *La Première Croisade: L'Occident chrétien contre l'Islam*. Paris: Complexe, 1992.

Le Concile de Clermont de 1095 et l'appel à la croisade. Rome: École Française de Rome, 1997.

Riley-Smith, Jonathan. *The First Crusaders (1095–1131)*. Cambridge: Cambridge University Press, 1997.

RELATED ARTICLES

177, 1143, 1202, 1270, 1572, 1685, 1863, 1962

1105

Troyes, a Talmudic Capital

At the beginning of the twelfth century, the city of
Troyes in Champagne was home to an exceptional figure,
Rashi. This rabbi and commentator of the Bible and the
Talmud invigorated not only Jewish tradition throughout
the world, but also Christian exegesis. He also provided
an invaluable account of the beginnings of the French
language.

On July 13, 1105, Rabbi Shlomo Yitzchaki (aka, Solomon,
son of Isaac), known throughout the world by his acronym,
Rashi, died at the age of sixty-five or so in his native city
of Troyes, where he had spent most of his life. For more
than nine hundred years, he was considered the greatest
Jewish Talmudic and biblical commentator of all time, and
his texts and ideas crossed geographical as well as religious
borders. Circulating beyond the network of Jewish schools
(*yeshivot*) and their birthplace in Champagne, they inspired
the greatest Christian scholars, both at the time and later.
In 1109, the abbot of Cîteaux, Stephen Harding, produced

a more reliable Christian version of the scripture thanks to his collaboration with the rabbis of France — perhaps including Rashi himself — following a methodology that would be developed in the twelfth century among Christian theologians. In the north of France rabbinical schools were taking form around renowned rabbis — for instance, Rashi's school in Troyes. Cathedral schools followed a similar design, solidified in the first universities of the following century. They summarized bodies of knowledge that would serve as a basis for a renewed teaching.

The new version of the Christian Bible created in 1109 is only one piece of evidence of the immense influence of the "master of Israel," as Rashi was also called in Hebrew. His lifelong work on the Talmud was huge in scope. Not only did Rashi subject Talmudic treatises to critical study, but he did the same with his own text, which went through three versions, the final one unfinished. Rashi's commentaries were integrated into the Babylonian Talmud, whose authority reigned widely in the Jewish world. There are no parallels in the Middle Ages.

The legacy of Rashi's resolutely pedagogical approach to the Torah has endured until the present day. In Talmud-Torah centers and synagogues in large American cities and hamlets in Yemen, from Birobidzhan, Russia, to Canberra to Johannesburg to the mellahs of Morocco, Jews continue to ask themselves, while reading the Torah, how the "Master of Masters" (*More Morenu*) understood a given passage. Rashi's Bible can be described as anthropocentric: it teaches a knowledge and practical love of humanity, which God made free.

Rashi's influence was immense. His sons-in-law (the husbands of his three daughters) and his grandsons added glosses to those of the master, and medieval scholars called Tosafists later offered commentaries on the commentaries. Rashi's texts were found in medieval Jewish libraries throughout the West, including the Mediterranean Basin. They were referred to directly by Christian Hebrew scholars, such as Herbert of Bosham, secretary to the Archbishop of Canterbury, and Thomas Becket (both of them exiled to Champagne in 1164). The great Franciscan thinker from the early fourteenth century Nicholas of Lyra cited him in Latin on so many occasions that he was sometimes dubbed "a Rashi impersonator." Later, Protestants and early modern translators of the Bible such as Martin Luther included Rashi's glosses. In the late Middle Ages, the master's ideas gained a second wind: his great commentary on the Torah (1475) remains the foremost work in Hebrew whose date of printing is known.

Although they are written entirely in Hebrew, the language of the liturgy and of educated Jews, his glosses contain thousands of words taken from French, which Rashi called "our language." Thanks to the almost phonetic properties of Hebrew characters, they not only reveal a nearly forgotten composite repertoire of words, but also allow us to grasp the way in which these words were pronounced in Champagne in the second half of the eleventh century. To make these texts accessible through the ages, Rachi strove to express the realities of the Bible and the Talmud in the language spoken in his time. We may thus consider him one of the first great French authors, before even Chrétien de Troyes. No other eleventh-century work — not *The Song of Roland* or *La Vie de saint Léger* or *La Vie de saint Alexis* or even the *Roman d'Alexandre* — provides such a lexicon of French terms (*le'azim* in Hebrew) in the realm of daily life. There are words relating to all manner of domestic objects and activities, including articles of clothing, furniture, weapons, names of animals and plants, food, illnesses, weaving, viticulture, tanning, inland shipping, hunting, and fishing. The best present-day dictionaries of the French language in fact refer frequently to Rashi's glosses as containing the first known occurrence of numerous words and even onomatopoeia. As if this were not enough, Rashi also displayed a true curiosity for Arabic, Slavic, and other languages he did not know.

If he can be considered one of the first great French authors, it is also because he lived almost his entire life in Champagne. We know little about his biography, though. Born around 1040, he only left the city of his birth to study in the greatest Talmudic centers, in the Rhine Valley cities of Worms and Mainz. He returned to Troyes around 1067. Though he may have earned a living as a winemaker, he devoted most of his time to teaching in his school, which quickly became famous throughout Western Europe. He also became known for having imported from the Rhineland the institution of the rabbinate, which had existed in the Talmudic era before apparently disappearing in the first half of the Middle Ages. Legends and popular traditions tell us that Rashi undertook distant voyages. In fact, he only made one other working trip to Worms, at the beginning of the 1070s. Though he was alive at the time of the massacres of Rhine Valley and Bohemian Jews by bands of crusaders in May and June of 1096, Rashi's pen surprisingly didn't make the slightest mention of those terrible events, traditionally seen as the beginning of the decline of the Jewish population in the West.

Rashi was also a community leader who, through his *responsa* (*techuvot* in Hebrew) or acts of rabbinical jurisprudence, oversaw the application of the laws of the kingdom. These laws were primarily those of the Capetian king, a monarch who was not deemed transcendent at the time and thus had to reckon with the rival powers of lay and ecclesiastical rulers — counts and ranking members of the clergy. In Rashi's time, the Capetian kingdom was familiar with Jews, whose presence was ancient though interrupted. Although it is impossible to identify them with certainty, many Jews lived in the towns and villages of the royal realm and in the principalities that made up the *regnum*: Paris, Saint-Denis, Lyon, Mâcon, Nîmes, and more. It was only in the twelfth century that monarchs sought to assert their prepotency through wide-reaching decrees. The first one, promulgated in 1144 by Louis VII, specifically ordered the expulsion from the kingdom of relapsed Jews — those who had converted to Christianity, then returned to Judaism. The order wasn't followed up on, and for a long time afterward the privileges and undertakings of the Jews were regularly negotiated with local authorities.

The laws of the kingdom were thus also, and above all, those of the country's leading counts, a number of whom sought to "secure" the Jews in their principalities against jurisdictional incursions by the Capetians. Among them was the Count of Champagne, whose policies can be seen in the *responsa* of the learned and decision-making rabbi. As in all of the Latin West, Jews flourished in Troyes by operating as a community whose leaders saw to it that everyone paid the tax exacted by the count.

Rashi's *responsa* provide precious information on the life of Jews in Troyes and on their relationships with Christians. For instance, he records that "according to custom in France," a Christian had given him some eggs and cakes during Passover (*Pessach*). We also learn that the Jews of Troyes engaged in agriculture and trade and provided interest-bearing loans. They owned houses, vineyards, fields, and tools. Allowed to live following the commandments of Judaism, they had their own synagogue.

Today, nothing remains of the synagogue in which Rashi read and prayed. But by devoting a room to his life and work in the recently renovated sixteenth-century edifice, the Rashi Cultural Center helps visitors understand all that Judaism owes to him and grasp what his writings have provided Western Christendom. Rashi's legacy and that of the Tosafists constitute an important element of Troyes's tourism industry and cultural development. The Rashi European University Institute, a center for higher education and Hebrew research established in 1989, continues to contribute to the intellectual and academic influence of the city and the region. And beyond such questions of local and regional heritage, 1105, the year of Rashi's death, now finds its place within French national commemorations.

Juliette Sibon

REFERENCES

Catane, Moshé. *La vie en France au XIe siècle d'après les écrits de Rachi*. Jerusalem: Gallia, 1994.

Darmesteter, Arsène. *Les gloses françaises de Raschi dans la Bible*. Paris: Durlacher, 1909.

Ginsberg, Harold Louis, ed. *Rashi Anniversary Volume*. Texts and
   Studies. New York: American Academy for Jewish Research, 1941.
Schwarzfuchs, Simon. *Rachi de Troyes*. Paris: Albin Michel, 2005 [1991].
Sirat, René-Samuel, ed. *Héritages de Rachi*. Paris/Tel-Aviv: Éditions de
   l'Éclat, 2006.

RELATED ARTICLES
842–843, 1539, 1894

1137

A Capetian Crosses the Loire

The 1137 marriage of Louis VII and Eleanor of Aquitaine
almost allowed a Capetian to extend his power south of
the Loire for the first time. But the marital difficulties
of the royal couple, and the clever politics of Henry II
Plantagenet, a French prince as well as King of England,
made the marriage a failure that was quickly forgotten.

On that day, July 25, 1137, Geoffrey du Loroux, archbishop
of Bordeaux, was getting ready to celebrate one of the most
important events of the time: the marriage of the duchess
of Aquitaine and the son of the King of France. In a time
when the game of dynastic alliances had the power to create
new political spaces, what could be more strategic than the
marriage of the offspring of the greatest lineages in Europe?
In the shadows of the new archway, under the sculpted,
brilliantly colored covings of the portal of the Cathedral of
Saint Andrew of Bordeaux, Geoffrey received the couple's
vows and blessed the union of the kingdom of France and

the Duchy of Aquitaine through the marriage of their young descendants.

A few weeks earlier, in Paris, the news of the death of William X of Aquitaine on the Way of Saint James, upset the plans of the old king, Louis VI, also known as Louis the Fat. He dispatched an escort made up of hundreds of clerics and knights led by three men: his dear Suger, abbot of Saint-Denis; the palatine count Theobald II of Champagne; and his relative, Count Ralph of Vermandois. They would accompany his son, the young, seventeen-year-old Louis, to take as his wife the young and beautiful heir to the duchy, who at the time was only thirteen.

Before taking his last breath, William X recalled the oath he had sworn before setting off on his journey, recommending his daughter to the King of France and assigning him responsibility for arranging the marriage of Eleanor, who had become in a few days the most coveted heiress in Europe. That request was not only a godsend for the Capetian Louis VI, who could find no better match than his own son, but also a victory that crowned his efforts to impose the ideology of royal sovereignty and the juridical principle of *ligesse*, by which the great barons of the kingdom swore allegiance to their lord. By choosing the French king to be guardian of his daughter, William of Aquitaine in fact granted the Capetian what the King of England already rightfully possessed over his vassals: the guardianship of minors and heirs to the great fiefs of the kingdom, which constituted enormous leverage in feudal power. In this instance, it enabled Louis VI to fulfill an old dream: the reunification of the *regnum Francorum* and the *regnum Aquitanorum*, the territories that, with Burgundy, had initially formed the heart of the Carolingian empire. This dream was made all the more real by the celebration of Eleanor's Carolingian ascendancy. Louis VI himself had been named in the Merovingian fashion (Louis / Clovis) to embody the aspirations of his father, Philip I, to the glory of the first kings of the Franks.

And so, everything in this union was conducive to strengthening Louis's resolve to achieve dynastic and imperial legitimation, since the rise of territorial principalities had for more than a century weakened the political power of the kings of France. They suffered numerous military humiliations, notably at the hands of the dukes of Normandy who had seized the throne of England in 1066. The Duke of Normandy's coronation in Westminster had granted them the status of sacred kings and placed them on an equal footing with the kings of France. As equals, they opposed the sovereign claims of the Capetians, developing their own imperial and sovereign ideology and maneuvering to keep the feudal status of Normandy ambiguous. However, upon the death of Henry Beauclerc in 1135, the power of the new king of England, Stephen of Blois, was contested by Matilda, the daughter and only heir of the dead king, who claimed the throne for her son, Henry Plantagenet. The chasm created by the civil war that lasted until 1153 opened a space that facilitated the Capetian revival. Though not as loud as the clashing of armor, the Capetian strategies involved the scratching of pens on parchment and the imperialist activities of the chancellery. Royal charters gave a new reality to Capetian supremacy, which soon encompassed a concept that would undergird its expansion: the sphere of influence of the crown.

In the Ombrière Palace, adjoining the old Roman fortress in Bordeaux, the wedding feast was lively. Wine from the Garonne valley — already a commercial success at that time — flowed freely. Eleanor chose to serve it in a magnificent rock crystal vase, engraved entirely in a honeycomb pattern in the Sassanid style. Having chosen it from her grandfather's treasures, she offered it to her new husband as a wedding gift. He in turn gave it a few years later to the abbot Suger, who had it plated in gold and silver filigree, with an engraving of its epic origins: "As a bride, Eleanor gave this vase to King Louis, Mitadolus to her grandfather, the King to me, and Suger to the saints." William IX had, in fact, received it in 1120 from Imad al-Dwal abd al-Malik, sultan of the *taifa* of Zaragoza, known by the Latin name Mitadolus, when he had come, along with Alfonso of Aragon, to help William IX fight against the Almoravids. This gift from the East, a symbol of the cultural wealth of a pluralistic Aquitaine that was in contact with southern societies — it comprised numerous seigneuries from the Berry and the Pyrenees to Aunis and the Massif Central — was in many ways the emblem of Eleanor's immaterial dowry. It displayed the contribution of the lively and dynamic culture of the langue d'oc, infused by many influences and celebrated by troubadours, to the austere culture of the people of the langue d'oïl. In fact, when Eleanor arrived at the staid French court, she created quite a scandal with her liberated ways and her love of life.

Brought back to political reality by the death of Louis VI on August 1, 1137, the young couple hastily left Aquitaine for Paris "to avoid the disorder that usually occurred upon the death of kings," as chroniclers of that time described it. On the return journey, the formalities for the ducal coronation took place in Poitiers on August 8. This ritualized the ascension of the new king, although he had been crowned six years earlier while his father was still alive — as had all his predecessors since Hugh Capet. It was no doubt a repetition of the coronation ceremony, but this time in the presence of new Aquitaine subjects, and in a place where no king of France had entered for close to three centuries. The king's body suddenly became visible to more of his subjects. The many voyages that Louis VII subsequently undertook, from the North to the South as far as Aragon, transformed the reality of royal mobility. The contrast with his father, whose obesity had made journeys on horseback improbable or extremely short, even within the royal domain, was stark. The years that followed the 1137 marriage thus established the foundations of a new mode of government turned toward territorial expansion.

Still, this horizon did not materialize exactly as the 1137 union had promised.

From the point of view of the Capetians, that event could have been a turning point in the history of the dynasty if it had not ended in 1151 in divorce, granted by the Council of Beaugency. But the repudiation of the queen turned out to be a huge political mistake for King Louis, who was henceforth called "the Pious." Eleanor did not remain alone for long. In the weeks that followed her departure from Paris, she found refuge with, and quickly married, the young Duke of Normandy and Count of Anjou, Henry Plantagenet, pretender to the throne of England. This turn of events explains the muted attention late twelfth-century chroniclers gave to her first union. It amounted to a nonevent for Western authors, and *a fortiori* for Greek and Arab historians, who, from a universal perspective, described the great deeds of the Franks they had encountered during the Crusades. In fact, traces of that unhappy union of the King of France have remained very faint since that time.

Historians working for the French court attempted to

justify the political folly of Louis VII by blaming Eleanor: at best they stressed the incompatibility between the puritan values of the Capetian and the emancipated exuberance of his wife; at worst they accused her of incestuous adultery. But what already appeared to contemporaries as a dishonorable tale could not make up for the political impotence to which it relegated the Capetians. That impotence endured until Philippe II managed at last (in other ways) to unite the northern and southern regions of the kingdom of the Franks. It was, in fact, because he was able to enlarge his kingdom, just as Caesar had expanded the *res publica*, that his biographer called him Augustus. But nothing was accomplished before 1202. Eleanor's death at Fontevraud seems to have removed the final psychological and political barriers that were blocking Capetian expansion. Two years later, Philip Augustus conquered Normandy, and in 1206 Anjou. His conquest of the Languedoc between 1209 and 1216 opened the doors to the Mediterranean Basin, and provided access to the largest zone of trade of that time. He also enjoyed revenge by crushing the Anglo-Imperial coalition in the Battle of Bouvines in 1214.

But Aquitaine continued to elude French kings for another two centuries. Whereas it could have belonged to the royal domain as early as 1137, it wasn't until the recapture of Bordeaux by the armies of Charles VII in 1453, at the end of the Hundred Years' War, that it became definitively connected to France. While the unification of the kingdom of the Franks was too ephemeral to mark a historic turning point in 1137, the precedent it created haunted the final centuries of the Middle Ages. If Aquitaine may have been "French" before being "English," it nevertheless constituted an essential point of connection between the English and a continental empire. They only abandoned it in the sixteenth century to pursue archipelagic interests that both compensated for and accentuated their isolation from Europe.

Fanny Madeline

REFERENCES

Brown, Elizabeth A. R. *"Franks, Burgundians and Aquitanians" and the Royal Coronation Ceremony in France*. Philadelphia: American Philosophical Society, 1992.

Dunbabin, Jean. *France in the Making (843–1180)*. 2nd ed. Oxford: Oxford University Press, 2000.

Evans, Michael R. *Inventing Eleanor: The Medieval and Post-Medieval Image of Eleanor of Aquitaine*. London: Bloomsbury, 2014.

Flori, Jean. *Aliénor, la reine insoumise*. Paris: Payot, 2004.

Sassier, Yves. *Louis VII*. Paris: Fayard, 1991.

RELATED ARTICLES
397, 987, 1051, 1420, 1949

1143

"The Execrable Muhammad"

To mark his voyage to Spain in 1143, Peter the Venerable, Abbot of Cluny, commissioned the first translation into Latin of the Quran. He was by no means motivated by enlightened curiosity. On the contrary, his intention was to find out everything possible about Islam, the better to twist its meaning and wage war upon it.

In the spring of 1142, Peter of Montboissier traveled to Spain. This scion of an aristocratic Burgundian family was not headed for Compostela, in the farthest reaches of the west, to honor St. James as so many other thousands of pilgrims had done since the year 1000. Montboissier, known to posterity as Peter the Venerable, was the head of the great monastic order of Cluny, whose network now extended to the four corners of Christendom, from Spain to Palestine and from southern Italy to England. Peter was compelled by the administrative needs of the Cluniac order to visit his brothers on the front line of the struggle against Islam, in a country with an ancient Gothic tradition that the Roman

Papacy, with the help of the sovereigns of Navarre, Asturias, and Castile, was struggling to hold for the church.

As the head of the Cluniac order, Peter was also a herald of Christendom, which as a geopolitical entity had been confronting Islam in a struggle between the Christian and Muslim faiths ever since the second half of the ninth century. While the envoys of Popes Nicholas I (858–867) and Adrian II (867–872) were working on the eastern front (especially in Pannonia and in Bulgaria) to win a religious market share from Byzantium — the other end of Christianity, drifting ever so far from Rome — the Latin world had also to defend itself against serious inroads by Islam in the western Mediterranean. It was this confrontation that led Latinity to reinvent itself as "Christendom," in the territorial sense of the word.

At the beginning, in the fourth century, *christianitas* encompassed anything that related to the community of the disciples of Christ (rituals, dogma, and all other aspects of belonging to that community). By the early twelfth century — say, the pontificate of Innocent III (1198–1216) — Christendom with a capital C had become a full-fledged organic entity made up of a series of Christian kingdoms whose apostolic head claimed temporal as well as spiritual overlordship. Two turning points of unequal importance had contributed to the evolution of the term: the ninth century in general and then the monarchist political approach of the reforming popes after 1050. The high point of this drama — when Christendom with a small c became Christendom with a big one — occurred during the pontificate of John VIII (872–882). Like his predecessors, this pope had to defend Rome against the attacks of Saracen marauders. The building of walls, the construction of a fleet, repeated calls for help: his letters leave no doubt about the urgency with which, as the disintegration of the Carolingian Empire accelerated, Pope John was forced to act. In his view, Christendom was a duty; indeed it was the task of all Christians to protect the community of the disciples of Christ against the growing menace of Islam. The "defense of all Christendom" was assimilated to the "defense of the land of St. Peter," as if one was synonymous with the other, brought together around a territory that distilled a Christian essence and whose destiny was to spread, from Rome, a worldwide unity that the spirit of crusade would endow with a sense of divine mission two centuries later.

Peter the Venerable's activity among the Christian outposts of the Iberian Peninsula lay at the heart of the new approach. His journey to Spain took place only a few years in advance of the call to the Second Crusade by his alter ego, the Cistercian Bernard of Clairvaux, in 1146. Peter's own crusade was carried out with words — lethal ones. When he arrived on the banks of the Douro, at Tarazona or Tudela, he commissioned the astronomer Robert of Ketton and his team of collaborators to undertake the first known Latin translation of the Quran, along with renderings of other texts relating to Muhammad and his doctrine. With these translations, Peter expected to supply the Christian world with a potent *armarium* (arsenal) to fight a war of ideas against Islam.

This handbook for Christian polemicists began with two texts by Peter the Venerable himself: a letter, and *Summa totius haeresis Saracenorum* (The Sum of the Saracens' Heresy), describing the content of the *armarium* and offering a basic justification for the struggle against Islam and Muhammad, who Peter called a "man of low extraction" and a "manipulator of simple Arabs." According to Peter, Muhammad led a "detestable life," providing "false" teachings about the Trinity and Christ (notably his rejection of the Incarnation) and Paradise, which he presented as a world of "perpetual luxury." Peter's little book of Christian combat sought to prove that Islam represented a combination of all the heresies known to date while posing the paradoxical question: Were Muslims truly heretics, or just ordinary pagans because they did not sacrifice as Christians did? This introduction set the tone by making clear the bias running through the endeavor. Ketton's translation of the Quran itself was tendentious, not only due to its highly approximate translations, but in the very organization of the text, whose surahs (or chapters) were now given "original" titles in Latin.

Peter expected to supply the rhetorical ammunition required for an attack on the founding tenets of Islam, even as the knights of Christendom were preparing to embark on a second crusade. The correspondence between the Abbot of Cluny and Bernard of Clairvaux shows that Peter expected a Cistercian initiative in this regard. But for lack of any other contributors in the Christian camp, Peter himself did the heavy lifting in what was to be his final treatise: *Contra sectam Saracenorum* (Against the Saracen Sect), which represents the first challenge by a Western Christian to Islam on the basis of a corpus of authorities. Book I attempts to establish a framework for the quarrel by naming Islam's authorities and presenting the scriptural sources which Christians and Muslims shared. However, Peter also attempted to lock his opponents into a zero-sum logic by forcing Muslims to accept as authorities all the books in the Jewish and Christian canons. According to this logic (a principle of all or nothing), Islam was obliged to embrace the entire heritage of the two older religions of the Book, without the possibility of freely selecting certain elements.

Thus Peter shifted the debate onto the terrain of his own authorities as a Christian polemicist, which he compared most favorably with the Islamic authorities compiled in the collection translated in Spain. On this basis, Book II of his *Contra sectam Saracenorum* tackled the two fundamental questions that taxed Christians in the age of the Crusades:

What was prophecy? And was Muhammad a true prophet, or, worse, the ultimate prophet, an authentic transmitter of revelation and the messenger of God? Peter offers a broad definition of prophecy that gives pride of place to extraordinary manifestations of the divine: "The prophet is a man who reveals unknown realities from the past, present, and future to mortals — not because he is taught by any human knowledge, but because he is inspired by God." According to this narrow definition, Muhammad was no prophet inasmuch as the Quran reveals no miracle, no extraordinary signs. Attached as he was to the Christian idea of a connection between the miracles described in the scriptures and the extraordinary signs reported by hagiographic tradition, the Abbot of Cluny was unable to grasp the Islamic distinction between, on one hand, a Muhammadian prophecy that granted little import to miracles and, on the other, the hagiographic models that sprouted from the legends that surrounded the prophet.

The expected debate was abruptly cut short, for the conditions for a meaningful exchange were absent. The first problem was the mediocre and biased quality of the translation, beginning with the difficulty to put into Latin the term "Muslim" and its recourse to circumlocutions when it came to "believe"; as if Christians could not imagine that the "faithful" of Islam could "surrender" and "submit" to God. There was a second and deeper problem: a Christian inability to escape its specific system of authorities and grasp the logic of Islam's own arguments. This explains the Christian repudiation of the "diabolical" Muslim as well as the considerable space afforded to stereotypes of Muslims despite Peter's avowed desire to conduct a debate according to the principles of reason and scholarship.

In the end, this first apologia of the medieval West against Islam broadly functioned as a decoy. It was not so much a case of convincing Muslims of their error as of reassuring Christians that they were on the right track. Like the other polemicists who followed, among them Thomas Aquinas in his *Summa contra Gentiles* (Tractate against the Gentiles), Peter the Venerable failed to engage in a significant dialogue with Islam. However much he appealed to the natural reason shared by all men, he came up against the impossibility of discussing divine matters on the basis of reason. There remained only the terrain of proof, by way of miracles or extraordinary phenomena (*mirabilia*). This cleric, who wrote from the heart of the Christian sacramental miracle of the Eucharist, could not conceive that divine truths could be approached otherwise than through faith. To believe or not to believe was the only question as far as he was concerned.

The two other translations of the Quran undertaken later by Mark of Toledo (in 1210) and John of Segovia (in 1456) did not change matters, though their texts, in Latin and Castilian respectively, were of better quality relative to the original Arabic. Islam's written message having resisted the Christian system of authority, that system would duly open up at the beginning of the thirteenth century to authors belonging to non-Christian traditions. But under the circumstances, what religious leeway could be given to the thinkers of Islam, whose influence was spreading within the universities of the Latin West? This was a major problem in the development of philosophy, and the solution devised at the time consisted in labeling Islamic thinkers Christians who failed to understand their true religion. Islam having been declared irrational by such figures as Peter the Venerable, the argument went, free-thinking philosophers like Avicenna or Averroes had no option but to reject the "fabulations" of the Prophet Muhammad. These thinkers might have even have been crypto-Christians of the kind that Dante, in his *Divine Comedy*, placed in the First Circle of Hell. Muhammad, for the record, was placed in the Eighth Circle.

Dominique Iogna-Prat

REFERENCES

Gázquez, José Martínez."Trois traductions médiévales latines du Coran: Pierre le Vénérable-Robert de Ketton, Marc de Tolède et Jean de Segobia." *Revue des études latines* 80 (2003): 223–236.

Geelhaar, Tim. *Christianitas: Eine Wortgeschichte von der Spätantike bis zum Mittelalter*. Göttingen: Vandenhoeck & Ruprecht, 2015.

Iogna-Prat, Dominique. *Order and Exclusion: Cluny and Christendom Face Heresy, Judaism, and Islam (1000–1150)*. Translated by Graham Robert Edwards. Ithaca: Cornell University Press, 2003.

RELATED ARTICLES

1095, 1105, 1270, 1380, 1712, 1798, 1863

FRANCE EXPANDS

The long thirteenth century, which began with the reign of Philip Augustus (1180–1223) and ended with that of Philip the Fair (1285–1314), saw the first French hegemony in Europe. The Capetian dynasty became the most powerful monarchy on the continent, largely because its main rivals were weakened. The Plantagenet kings, driven from most of their French dominions (Normandy, Anjou, Maine, and Poitou) by the victories of Philip Augustus in 1204, retired to England and a reduced Aquitaine (soon to be renamed Guyenne) centered around Bordeaux. The Holy Roman Empire, which ruled Germany, central and northern Italy, and Sicily, had exhausted its resources in a bitter confrontation with the pope for the universal domination of Christianity, to the point that the imperial throne was vacant between 1250 and 1273.

The Capetians, meanwhile, expanded the sovereignty of their monarchs, "emperors in their kingdom," as Philip Augustus put it. They rejected all imperial or pontifical influence while steadily appropriating the symbolic and legal attributes of empire. Witness the propaganda that surrounded, in 1307–1312, their annexation of Lyon — a major ecclesiastical center, the former capital of Gaul, and until that time a city of the Holy Roman Empire. To justify this coup, Philip the Fair dryly informed Holy Roman Emperor Henry VII that by virtue of Christ's special favor no king of France had ever acknowledged any power greater than his own; therefore the kingdom, "being securely founded in the Christian faith," owed no fealty to any other prince on earth. The claims of Philip the Fair were all the more forceful because they were conveyed by a group of brilliant legal advisers, known as the "king's jurists," and rested on the authority of a royal government whose administrative power had been growing since the close of the thirteenth century.

Within the Capetian kingdom, the growth of this royal authority coincided with a vast extension of territory. Basically, the king imposed his own direct rule over lesser fiefdoms. After 1204, France grew at the expense of the Plantagenets in the west of the country. Between 1209 and 1271, after the crusade against the Albigensians, the monarchy acquired huge areas of the south (lower Languedoc, Toulousain) at the expense of the Viscount Trencavel and the counts of Toulouse. This latter expansion also prevented the kings of Aragon of the house of Barcelona from absorbing any more southern regions of France; thereafter, north of the Pyrenees, they held only Montpellier (annexed by France in 1349) and Cerdagne and Roussillon (both taken by Louis XIV in 1659). The Capetian monarchs thus acquired their first access to the Mediterranean in 1229, and by 1240 Louis IX (known as Saint Louis) was building a port on the Mediterranean seaboard, known today as Aigues-Mortes, from which his army later embarked on a crusade to the Holy Land.

Outside the kingdom of France, the spread of Capetian hegemony took a spectacular turn. At the Battle of Bouvines, in 1214, Philip Augustus defeated a coalition comprising an emperor (Otto IV), a king (John Lackland, king of England), and two princes (the Counts of Flanders and Boulogne, among the most powerful feudal lords in his kingdom). This victory gave birth to the first national myth exalting the superiority of the Capetians, a myth that would make its way into the school manuals of the Third Republic in the nineteenth century. In 1248–1250 and 1270, Louis IX led the last Crusades to Egypt and Tunisia, demonstrating a shrewd knowledge of the internal political organization of the Muslim world. The Crusades enabled the sovereign to acquire the status of sainthood; indeed, the lingering prestige of Saint Louis would assist France's overseas expansion.

Between 1266 and 1285, Louis's brother Charles I of Anjou undertook — with the backing of the papacy — the conquest of a vast Mediterranean empire extending from Provence to Constantinople by way of Piedmont, southern Italy, Sicily, Albania, and the North African coast. Ephemeral though it was in its more distant reaches, this "Angevin Empire" laid the groundwork for the French monarchy's obsession with the Italian Peninsula, and the kingdom of Naples in particular, as the priority of its expansionist dreams. Finally, at the turn of the fourteenth century, Philip the Fair confronted the papacy, whose theocratic ambitions he rejected, before facilitating its move from Rome to Avignon.

By that time France was growing in several different directions, maintaining its demographic and economic dynamism past the end of the century. The remaining wildernesses of the Capetian kingdom were broken to the plough; woods and forests began to be overexploited; and wetlands were drained with great technical ingenuity. This was exemplified by a major water control project at the lake of Montady, in lower Languedoc, using ancient methods adopted and transmitted by the Arabs of Andalusia. Above all, agricultural growth triggered commercial revolution and urban expansion. Many French towns built city walls that doubled or tripled the urban space, which was itself quickly surpassed by new suburbs. With this opulence came a demand for luxury fabrics (oriental silks, woven linens, high-quality bedsheets) and exotic products such as spices and ivory objects. Local fairs, notably in the Champagne region, became centers for material and monetary exchange between Italy and Flanders, the East and the West. A major European commercial highway took shape between the cities of Lombardy in Tuscany and those of Flanders, underwritten by merchant bankers and guaranteed by the protection of the Count of Champagne. Their activities continued year round, with fairs at Lagny, Provins, Troyes, and Bar-sur-Aube, not far from a rapidly growing Paris.

There was also international expansion in the domain of culture and the arts. The University of Paris, recognized by the king in 1200 and established under the aegis of the papacy in 1215, owed much of its growing success to its cosmopolitanism. Divided into four multilingual "nations," its teachers and students came from all over Europe: England, Flanders, Italy, Spain, Germany, the Slavic countries, and Scandinavia. The liberal arts — notably dialectics and theology — quickly became a specialty of Paris. Meanwhile, the teaching of Roman law retreated to Orléans, rejected by the king, who thought it overly favorable to the interests of the Holy Roman emperor. The left bank of the Seine, soon to be called the Latin Quarter because its teachings were propounded in that language, was transformed by a proliferation of new schools and colleges to accommodate the flood of students. All this reached a climax when the Sorbonne opened in 1257.

The influence of the language and literature of France grew, largely due to the success of Old French romances, or *chansons*, that drew from Carolingian and especially Arthurian traditions while granting them courtly and universal dimensions (as in the popular Lancelot-Grail prose cycle) or else a religious slant (as in the fourth section of that cycle, *The Quest for the Holy Grail*). Epic poets, trouvères, and troubadours spread the art of singing in French and Occitan throughout the courts and cities of Europe, along with the ideal of courtly love. Dante and Petrarch would write explicitly in a similar vein. Yet more popular genres appeared, such as the fabliaux and animal tales of Reynard the Fox. Gothic art, often described as quintessentially French, radiated outward with the students of Paris, the superb craftsmanship of the Île-de-France, and the fame of a single, emblematic monument: the cathedral of Notre-Dame, built on the Île de la Cité between 1163 and 1250. Only a few hundred yards away stood its smaller alter ego, the Sainte-Chapelle, which Saint Louis built within his palace as a monumental reliquary for Christ's crown of thorns, acquired in the Middle East in 1239.

All this richly served the prestige of the Capetian kings — and of their capital, which by the early fourteenth century was established as the greatest city in the Western world.

1202

Four Venetians at the Champagne Fairs

To finance their ventures overseas, the crusaders often had recourse to the services of Italian merchant-bankers. An exchange contract written in Venice in 1202 also points to the role of the Champagne fairs, which were central to continental European trade and the circulation of money between the West and the Levant.

The islet of Sant'Erasmo in the Venetian Lagoon was, in 1202, a prestigious and cosmopolitan place: several of the most powerful princes of the European aristocracy gathered there that year for the upcoming crusade. The venture would not be successful, as it ended in the capture and sacking of Zara and Constantinople and the excommunication of the crusaders, but it would prove to be a moment of financial innovation as payment came due for the transportation provided by the Republic of Venice to the crusaders. The sums in question appear to have been colossal: Venice was asking for 87,000 marks of silver — about fifteen or twenty tons of metal — of which the crusaders were able to gather about 50,000 marks. A sum of this magnitude was not payable in cash, at least not without unsettling the Venetian money market. It therefore required sophisticated financial instruments, which were only then coming into being.

According to a document preserved in the State Archives of Venice, one of the army's leaders, Baldwin, Count of Flanders and Hainaut (future Latin emperor of Byzantium, in 1204), made use of one of the newest instruments: an exchange letter payable at the Champagne fairs. By this contract, drawn up by a notary in the presence of a number of exceptional witnesses, including the doge of Venice, Enrico Dandolo, and the marshal of Champagne, Louis, Count of Blois and Clermont, Baldwin committed to a payment of 118 marks and 3 ounces of silver (about 65 pounds of silver in coins or ingots), which he would arrange to have remitted to four Venetian merchants, Marchesino Soranzo, Piero Zulian, Marino Gradenigo, and Luca Ardizon, or their representatives. The sum, which would be due at the next fair at Lagny, in January 1203, was presumably the exchange equivalent of an undisclosed amount in Venetian coin.

Rarely cited by historians, this document connects one of the major events in European and Mediterranean history, the Crusades, with one of the essential institutions of the European economy, the Champagne fairs. Since the middle of the twelfth century, an annual cycle of six fairs had been held in the counties of Champagne and Brie: two in the town of Provins, two in Troyes, and one each in the towns of Bar-sur-Aube and Lagny. The fair at Lagny began in January, followed by the one at Bar-sur-Aube, then the Saint-Quiriace fair in Provins in May, the "hot fair" of Saint John in Troyes, the Saint-Ayoul fair in Provins, and finally the "cold fair" of Saint Remi in Troyes. Lying on the outskirts of the Paris suburbs, the Lagny fair — where Baldwin's payment was to be made — was the January gathering place for Parisian merchants and moneylenders. Locally, it alternated with the other large commercial gathering in the Paris area, the fair at Lendit in the Saint-Denis plain, which occurred in June.

Unusual because of the prominence of its witnesses, the Venetian contract is also noteworthy for the precision of its language. The sum was to be paid in *esterlin*, or sterling silver, meaning silver that was 92.5 percent pure, at thirteen shillings and four pence per mark, the legal unit of weight. Sterling silver was often mentioned in monetary transactions at the Champagne fairs, until a common currency, the *denier* of Provins, was eventually agreed to. The use of silver reflects the gradual construction of a European market for goods and monetary values: a single metal whose weight and alloy were defined with increasing accuracy allowed for reliable exchanges to take place between commercial outposts in different parts of the continent. It also points to the role of fairs in the circulation of silver, which was extracted from German mines and constituted one of the main products for sale at the fairs. The agreement concluded by the Count of Flanders enabled his Venetian partners to have a large sum of money at their disposal in one of the central locations for European trade— a sum they could either spend on the spot or bring back to Venice.

To guarantee the contract, the count agreed to forfeit "as much property belonging to the men of my lands as is necessary to repay the sum in question." The language is clearly feudal, since the Count of Flanders is asserting his rights over his vassals' property. Yet it offers an early formulation of one of the fundamental principles of the fair system: members of a nation were jointly responsible for any outstanding debt owed by others of their nation. Accordingly, because the count was considered one of the active Flemish merchants at the fair, his debt — should he default — would be repaid by the seizure of property belonging to other merchants who had traveled from Flanders.

Since the nineteenth century, the Champagne fairs have been portrayed as the birthplace of European capitalism and one of the engines of European economic growth. A return to the sources prompts us to temper this view, which owes more to gauzy Eurocentric myth than to strict economic history. The fairs' success seems in reality to be the result of multiple factors, an important one being the political maneuvering of Henry the Liberal, Count of Champagne (1127–1181). One of the major figures of European aristocracy, Henry was lord of Reims, the city in which French kings were coronated, and also held fiefs on the borders of the Holy Roman Empire. He strengthened his principality by conducting a complex political strategy, melding loyalty to the Capetian sovereign with European diplomacy, of which the fairs were both an instrument and a product.

Two established practices guaranteed the fairs' success and made them, for at least a century, Europe's business center. The first was the *conduit*, or safe conduct, negotiated by the count with other princes and rulers across Europe, which provided for the local forces of order to protect merchants and their goods on their passage to and from the fairs. Built on agreements among nobles, this network created the first safe space for economic activity on a continental scale since the end of the Roman Empire. The second crucial element was the guarantee the Count of Champagne provided for every transaction made at the fairs and entered into the registers. This system relied on the simple and effective principle of solidarity among the members of the various groups of merchants, who were responsible for the debts of their brethren, on pain of being excluded from the fairs as an entire group. This threat, which affected the well-being of the entire enterprise, made the Champagne fairs obligations true monetary instruments. Their ready availability kept the fairs from having to depend on metallic coins, whose fluctuations in value were irregular and hard to predict. The threat also served as a powerful incentive for merchants to adhere to the common rules.

The success of the Champagne fairs is surprising enough that it has excited the interest of historians and economists for more than a century. Central as they were to the growth of the continent, the sites where they were held have little to show for it today. Provins is a sleepy medieval town, little changed since the fourteenth century; the fairgrounds at Lagny and Bar-sur-Aube have left no trace; and Troyes, a center for making cloth, paper, and clothing, stopped being a financial center long ago. The county of Champagne itself was dissolved in 1284 and absorbed into the royal holdings. The fairs' success has been linked, with good reason, to the growth of the textile industries, in Flanders especially. They were a place where wool and dyestuffs could be acquired, and where Italian merchants could buy or exchange cloth for resale on the Mediterranean markets. Contemporary sources also attest to the great diversity at the fairs, where many kinds of products — textiles, metals, spices, wines — were bought and sold, and where thousands of individuals with a high standard of living gathered. Their spending stimulated the local economy, particularly inns and suppliers of food. We should picture the towns that hosted the fairs as caravansaries, dependent for their prosperity on the number and nature of their visitors, rather than as true economic capitals.

These descriptions don't explain the economic success of the fairs, however. The Nobel-winning economist Douglass North has pointed to the system's efficiency, particularly singling out the fact that the "wards of the fair," a small group of officers, managed to ensure that the contracts in their books were carried out in every part of Europe without recourse to any state administration or court. The care that Capetian kings took not to extend their sovereignty to the fairs, but simply to confirm the rules set out by the previous counts of Champagne, illustrates this paradox. Although the counts' prestige and their alliances across Europe largely explain how the safe conduct network could be built, it was the merchants' ability to impose their own discipline on the business they conducted that was the main contribution of the fairs to the economic ascent of Christendom.

We still do not know how the agreement signed in Venice in 1202 was enforced or, more generally, the extent to which the Venetian merchants participated in the commercial exchanges conducted at the fairs. But it seems unlikely that the Count of Flanders would take the risk of defaulting on a financial obligation he incurred before such prestigious witnesses. The very existence of this contract shows that the Champagne fairs regulated financial transactions with enough legitimacy that they could be relied on even for agreements that concerned international politics, such as this one relating to the Fourth Crusade.

Mathieu Arnoux

REFERENCES

della Rocca, Raimondo Morozzo, and Antonino Lombardo. *Documenti del commercio veneziano nei secoli XI–XIII*. Turin: Libreria Italiana, 1940, t. 1, p. 452, n° 462.

Mueller, Reinhold. *The Venetian Money Market: Banks, Panics and the Public Debt, 1200–1500*. Baltimore: Johns Hopkins University Press, 1997.

North, Douglass C., and Robert Paul Thomas. *The Rise of the Western World: A New Economic History*. Cambridge: Cambridge University Press, 1973.

Pirenne, Henri. *Economic and Social History of Medieval Europe*. Translated by Ivy E. Clegg. London: Kegan Paul, 1936.

Spufford, Peter. *Money and Its Use in Medieval Europe*. Cambridge: Cambridge University Press, 1988.

RELATED ARTICLES
1066, 1282, 1456, 1720, 1860, 1973

1214

The Two Europes, and the France of Bouvines

Behind Philip Augustus's victory in Bouvines — stunning and widely celebrated in French national memory — one can see the contours of two Europes. To the east, a Europe of delicate balances maintained among princes and sovereigns; to the west, a Europe of more established monarchies. Among the latter, one claimed preeminence at the dawn of the thirteenth century: France.

"In the year 1214, July 27 fell on a Sunday," writes historian Georges Duby in the opening pages of *The Legend of Bouvines* (1990). The first lines of any book of history invariably set the scene, provide the tone, and introduce — or not — the unity of time, place, and action. Here, in what would quickly become a best seller and a classic in French historiography, the first page indeed sets the scene: a battle, kings, a confrontation of armies, the clash of bellicose rituals and codes of honor, stories of betrayals and vengeance, the myth of a victory. In short, Duby laid out a great national narrative, a long-lasting memory that had taken shape much earlier, first in the works of chroniclers and then in school textbooks. In short, July 27, 1214, was one of the days "that made France," according to the name of the series in which Duby's book appeared.

"Making France," "national narrative": these phrases have, like others, turned the Battle of Bouvines into a historical event and a national myth. On July 27, in the fields of Flanders, midway between the kingdom of France and the lands of the Holy Roman Empire, French King Philip II Augustus defeated a coalition formed by the Caesar of the Holy Empire, Otto IV, the Plantagenet king of England and Duke of Aquitaine John Lackland, and their allies at the time: Ferdinand, Count of Flanders, and Renaud, Count of Boulogne. How does an event that has garnered such national pride fit within a "global" history of France?

Let us begin with the action that unfolded that day, a brief fracas that, though initially undecided, lasted only a few hours. Less bloody than has been suggested, it was fought at a time when skirmishes were hand-to-hand, when strategy wasn't decided with the help of binoculars or from radio transmission posts behind the front lines. The objective was to capture high-ranking prisoners who would ensure large ransoms. Everything and everyone were thrown in pell-mell. At best, the combatants recognized each other, allies as well as enemies, by their weapons, shields, banners, and other displays. But, whether a fight ended in defeat or victory, the outcome was often a surprise, and it was up to chroniclers to put everything in good order and confirm that the end had been written in advance. Such military uncertainty lasted a long time in Europe. It would take a revolution in weaponry, communication, and military arts, in the technological and human composition of squadrons, around the eighteenth century, for the conclusion of battles to become, if not foretold, at least foreseeable. Georges Duby understood this perfectly. He made Bouvines a case study for a sociology of medieval warfare. July 27, 1214, was not "French," therefore: it represented the long pre-modernity of warfare.

There is a second answer to our question. This battle, which like all forms of medieval combat (trials, tournaments, *faidas*, cavalcades, duels, and crusades) took God as its witness to force His judgment, included a wide range of belligerents. This was a far cry from conflicts between "national" armies, with troops called up, regimented, and paid by a sole ruler or state. The fighters at Bouvines, as scholars have shown, were a mix of princes, barons, faithful, members of a king's inner circle, feudal lords, knights seeking glory and adventure, footmen, sergeants, urban merchants, mercenaries — all of them fighting side by side. In short, the battalions at Bouvines reflected the diversity of the states, orders, and loyalties or disloyalties that made up thirteenth-century society, a diversity that encompassed the kingdom of France and other Western principalities, territories, and cities.

A third answer: the kings and princes who quarreled and challenged each other were heads of broad networks, with wide-ranging territorial and dynastic connections that make it impossible to see the event as a national one alone. John Lackland (absent from the battle, but fully there in spirit) was the brother of Richard the Lionheart (himself Duke of Normandy, Duke of Aquitaine, Count of Poitiers, Count of Maine, and Count of Anjou) and heir of the Plantagenets, who had fashioned a true "empire" by amassing land in France and England, from the Pyrenees to Ireland. Otto IV, the other artisan of the coalition, himself the nephew of John Lackland, had spent much of his youth at the court of the Plantagenets. Descendant of the powerful House of Guelph, Count of Poitou, Duke of Swabia and of Saxony, King of the Romans and then Emperor of the Romans, he ruled a Holy Empire that extended over the kingdoms of Italy and Arles. He married a princess of Brabant and one of his daughters wedded Frederick II, the great Hohenstaufen emperor who, in 1214, was Otto's competitor. As for Philip Augustus, a "born and bred" Capetian, one of his wives was a daughter of the King of Denmark.

We see the same internationalism in the battle's two other protagonists, the unfortunate allies of Otto who were captured by the King of France: Ferdinand of Flanders, *infante* of Portugal, and Renaud, Count of Boulogne, one of whose daughters would marry a king of Portugal. In short, except for Spain and the kingdoms of what was not yet called central Europe, the great dynasties of the Christian West, encompassing Scotland, Ireland, England, Flanders, France, the Germanic Empire, Italy, and Portugal — as well as the papacy, always attentive to the balance of opposing powers — were all represented in Bouvines. Much has already been written about the battle's short- and long-term consequences for each protagonist. Let us simply add, first, that it undeniably strengthened the French crown around the Capetian Philip, henceforth called *Rex Francie* and no longer *Rex Francorum*. The monarchy now boasted an incipient bureaucracy, a capital, an army, consolidated territory, and forms of symbolic display that, while feudal in principle, announced the "great monarchy of France" and a practice of a state administration that would make the kingdom the most powerful on the continent.

As for the "unworthy losers," defeat at Bouvines accelerated preexisting trends. It further weakened the English hold over territories in France following the decline of John Plantagenet (who died two years after Bouvines). It solidified the leading vassals' control of royal power over a period that began with the Magna Carta of 1215 and ended with the successive wars among barons in England. It also exacerbated rivalries between the Guelph dynasty of Emperor Otto and that of the Ghibellines, their Hohenstaufen rivals, and between Otto and his successor,

Frederick II, neither of whom could stop the rise of the great principalities of the Empire.

What Bouvines fundamentally unveiled were the outlines of two Europes, or what we might call a "multi-speed Europe." The continent's territorial and political contours varied depending on the power the great feudal lords had over the kings. We find, on the one hand, political entities tightly controlled by kings who, in deed as in law, polarized governmental structures and loyalties and, on the other hand, a perpetual balancing act between princes and kings, a more horizontal distribution of authority. In this respect, 1214 has symbolic value: in the heart of a Christian West that was in theory controlled by the two universal powers of the pope and the emperor, these divergent political evolutions outlined a world in which, for centuries, sovereign entities would rule in widely varying capacities.

The fourth answer is closely related to the preceding one, for contemporaries grasped that something significant was happening that Sunday: the memory and the legend of Bouvines conferred on the event a greater and longer life. The battle was fortunate to have a great chronicler: William the Breton, whose *Gesta* of King Philip and his *Philippide*, composed under pressure, served as a great national narrative until the twentieth century, at the very least until its sad and deadly seven hundredth anniversary, in 1914, when its memory was summoned anew to repel the

THE TWO EUROPES, AND THE FRANCE OF BOUVINES

Germans. Following William's, eighteen other narratives, from Scandinavian countries, Sicily, and elsewhere, recounted the event during the century that followed the battle. In the thirteenth century, the story was set in the stone of the *Grandes Chroniques de France*, completing the long-lasting molding of the French king into an "august" monarch, a "king of war" (which he ultimately wasn't, given that 1214 proved to be Philip II's last battle). These stories would inspire Louis XIV and Napoleon, both of whom were "European" in their own (military) way.

The fifth answer is that Bouvines symbolizes a "moment," or rather a pivotal configuration. This may be its ultimate and most efficacious global "truth," for the outcome of the battle gave a hint of large-scale, profound structural changes at work in medieval Europe. Two years before that date, at the Battle of Las Navas de Tolosa (July 16, 1212), Iberian monarchies fended off Almohad armies and thereby signaled their ability to gradually put an end to the presence of Islam in Spain. A year before Bouvines, on September 23, 1213, allies of Philip II defeated Peter II of Aragon in Muret, near Toulouse, thereby stopping in a certain sense the Catalan expansion north of the Pyrenees and bringing the Toulousain, the Lower Languedoc, and Provence into the orbit of the Capetian monarchy. Finally, on the other side of the globe, the armies of Genghis Khan seized Beijing in May 1215, expelling the Jin dynasty and bringing northern China into the Mongol Empire. From west to east, in the three great constellations of the known world — the Christian West, Islam, and Asia — armed conflicts made visible deep-seated changes.

A sixth and final consideration: it is fundamentally appealing to think that the great figures of the twentieth-century *Annales* school, proponents of a history open to the contributions of internationalism, large-scale comparison, and interdisciplinarity, a history that today undergirds this global history of France, made their critical leaps starting from this classic Capetian ground. This is true, not only of Duby's *Bouvines*, but also of Marc Bloch's *The Royal Touch* (1924) and Jacques Le Goff's biography of Saint Louis (1996). Here is the broader lesson: it is not historical material that shapes interpretations, but rather the historian's questions that shape historical material. And these questions are far from exhausted: What can sovereign power accomplish? How is it imposed, or how does it persuade others of its legitimacy? Why choose war? How do social bonds take form within a process that brings together a dynasty (or a regime), a territory, and a population? As these questions make abundantly clear, the Middle Ages still speak to us today.

Pierre Monnet

REFERENCES

Baldwin, John. *The Government of Philip Augustus: Foundations of French Royal Power in the Middle Ages*. Berkeley: University of California Press, 1986.

Barthélemy, Dominique. *La bataille de Bouvines: Histoire et légendes*. Paris: Perrin, 2018.

Bradbury, Jim. *Philip Augustus, King of France*. London: Longman, 1998.

Church, Stephen D., ed. *King John: New Interpretations*. Woodbridge: Boydell Press, 1999.

Duby, Georges. *The Legend of Bouvines: War, Religion, and Culture in the Middle Ages*. Berkeley: University of California Press, 1990.

France, John. "The Battle of Bouvines 27 July 1214." In *The Medieval Way of War: Studies in Medieval Military History in Honor of Bernard S. Bachrach*, edited by Gregory J. Halfond, 251–71. London/New York: Routledge, 2015.

RELATED ARTICLES

1215

Universitas: The "French Model"

Between 1200 and 1231, the University of Paris
developed into an unusual and autonomous institution. A
cosmopolitan intellectual center with students divided into
linguistic groups or "nations" and independent professors
shielded from censorship, it created the model for a capital
of learning: Paris, new Athens of Europe and crucible for a
proliferation of identities.

1215. The University of Paris was fifteen years old when
Cardinal Robert of Courçon, legate of Pope Innocent
III, announced statutes that would make the *Universitas
magistrorum et scholarium Parisiensis* the leading scholarly
institution in the Christian world. This was the halfway
point of a longer process. On January 15, 1200, King Philip
II had granted the university's scholars the *privilegium
fori*, or the right to be judged by an ecclesiastical tribunal.
This protected them from the clutches of the civil courts
and confirmed their new status as "clerks" or clergy. And
on April 13, 1231, Pope Gregory IX issued a papal bull,

Parens scientiarum, that freed scholars from the oversight of the chancellor of Notre-Dame Cathedral and the bishop of Paris: they were now autonomous.

Or almost. Professors, students, officers, notaries, porters, watchmen, and staff all had the status of "suppots" of the university — an early term for civil servants. The institution had its own structure, its own organization, its own codes and rituals. Everything was regulated, from the rental of rooms to the assignment of graves. The university had sole decision on conferring degrees, and it recruited as it saw fit, admitted who it wanted, and went on strike at will, sometimes for as long as three years, as in the strike of 1229 to 1231. Composed of self-governing masters, the university was more than a "multitude," it was a "sworn community," held together by common intention and custom, where one made an oath of obedience each year to the statutes and officers, and undertook to be present without fail, following a calendar modeled on the liturgical year. Members of the university lived in a community of intellectuals. At the time, one became an intellectual by joining a guild. But were intellectuals as free as we conceive them? Were they fully independent?

We need to distinguish between the organization of this teaching from the definition of its contents. Papal authority protected the existence of the university and trade associations from the bishop, the king, and various civil and ecclesiastical bodies. It did not, however, defend the university's freedom of thought against the church or royal authorities. As an integral part of church power (its head, in fact), the papal authority monitored the substance of the curriculum. And it was not alone. Many others tried to meddle over the years.

Barely in existence, the university caught the censor's attention. As early as 1210, the provincial synod of the town of Sens, convened in Paris by the Archbishop Pierre de Corbeil in the presence of the bishop of Paris, Pierre de Nemours, and other bishops, prohibited "under pain of excommunication the teaching (*lectura*) in public or private of Aristotle's works on natural philosophy or the commentaries thereon" (*Chartularium Universitatis Parisiensis*, No. 11). From 1210 to 1277, prohibitions and interdicts rained down. In 1215, Robert of Courçon incorporated into his statutes the bishop of Paris's instructions to professors "not to read the works of Aristotle on metaphysics or natural history, nor the summaries of these works, nor the doctrines of David of Dinant, Amalric of Bena, or Mauritius of Spain" (*CUP*, No. 20). The *Parens scientiarum* bull of 1231 confirmed the prohibitions of 1210 "until such time as a commission shall have examined" Aristotle's works on natural history and "purged them of any taint of error" (*CUP*, No. 79). This was never to happen, for want of commissioners. On December 10, 1270, the bishop of Paris, Étienne Tempier, "condemn[ed] and excommunicate[d]" thirteen errors "as well as those who may have knowingly taught or affirmed them." On March 7, 1277, the same Tempier, on his own recognizance, based on information supplied to him by "great and powerful figures," and in response to a letter in which Pope John XXI instructed him to "open an inquiry" on the origin of "certain errors" recently propagated in Paris, relied on a commission of sixteen masters in theology to draw up a list of 219 theses whose teaching was proscribed. This ruling shows the importance of the University of Paris in European history: Tempier's syllabus would be brought back at the end of the fifteenth century for use against Giovanni Pico della Mirandola, at the start of the seventeenth against Copernicus and Galileo, and at the start of the eighteenth against the "new philosophy" of Descartes.

The reiteration of prohibitions is the tribute censorship pays to freedom: the sign that it wants for power. In the structure and organization of its colleges, in its polemical course of action, in its procedures for monitoring, censoring, and self-censoring, but also in its repeated transgressions, its adjustments, and its detours, the University of Paris lived out the conflict between faith and reason.

This institutional conflict distinguishes the Latin world from the Byzantine and Muslim worlds. Academics were not court scholars, subject to the goodwill of a sovereign whose protection they relied on. The philosopher and the theologian were peers. The one who was censored today would be censoring tomorrow. The secular and the religious thinker belonged to the same *communitas*. And most of them had exchanged roles over the years. One became a master of theology by studying the arts for ten years and Biblical theology and exegesis for fifteen. One gained access to theological knowledge — Peter Lombard's *Four Books of Sentences* — only after mastering the philosophical sciences — by studying Aristotle — just as the Neo-Platonists in the schools of Athens and Alexandria in the fifth and sixth centuries were given access to the "Greater Mysteries" of Platonism, Plato's dialogues, only after a thorough study of the "Lesser Mysteries," the Aristotelian writings on logic and natural history. By 1255, the university statutes prescribed studying Aristotelian texts that had been banned in 1210: prescription followed proscription. The latter had never prevented anything in the first place.

By dividing its professors and students into "nations," the University of Paris became the focal point of the medieval intellectual world. The "French nation" gathered Frenchmen from central and southern France, Italians, and natives of the Iberian Peninsula; the "Norman nation" was for Normans; the "English nation" included Britons, Scandinavians, and Germans; the "Picard nation" comprised Picards and scholars from eastern and northern France — the region that is today Belgium — and the Low Countries. Through its university, France entered the European era even though neither France nor Europe yet existed as such. A third of the masters who taught at the university between 1200 and 1231 were English. So were more than a third of the students at the Faculty of Arts (twenty-four of the sixty who are known). Robert of Courçon, who taught theology in Paris until he was appointed cardinal in 1212, was an Englishman from Derbyshire, close to the English royal family. He had met Lotario dei Conti di Segni, the future Pope Innocent III, in Paris as a student under Pierre, the cantor of Notre-Dame Cathedral, and after Robert was elevated to the cardinalship, the pope sent him back to France to lay the groundwork for the reforms and concepts of the Fourth Lateran Council in 1215.

From 1200 to 1400, Paris was the favored destination of the *peregrinatio academica*, the intellectual journeys of European students and sometimes masters. Among those drawn there were Albertus Magnus, Thomas Aquinas, Duns Scotus, Marsilius of Padua, Jean Buridan, and Meister Eckhart. It was in Paris that Averroism took root in the 1270s. It was from there also that the controversy between the *via antiqua* and the *via moderna* spread eastward, as the countries of Eastern Europe and the Holy Roman Empire gradually created universities, from Prague, with the first

"German" university in 1347, to Leipzig in 1409. During the Middle Ages, there existed a "French model" with proven success: the *universitas magistrorum et scholarium Parisiensis*.

With the university, France was creating its own myth as well. In 1180, Walter of Saint Victor, canon of St. Victor's Abbey in Paris and inventor of the term "nihilist" (*nihilianista*), wrote the *Contra quatuor labyrinthos Franciae*. He denounced the four "labyrinths" of France — Peter Lombard, Peter Abelard, Gilbert de la Porrée, and Peter of Poitiers — and the whole world of the "little schools" in which, on Paris's Left Bank, dialectics thrived. In the 1200s, the University of Paris absorbed the neighboring schools on the Montagne Sainte-Geneviève, the Rue du Fouarre, and the Rue du Petit-Pont. The four Paris faculties of arts, theology, canon law, and medicine were now depicted as the four branches of the river that irrigated the Garden of Eden, where the Book of Genesis situated the Tree of Knowledge (II, 9). Following the Fourth Lateran Council, Peter Lombard entered the syllabus. The Garden of Eden had replaced the Labyrinth.

France thus became the endpoint of every account devised since the Carolingian period to give cultural and political legitimacy to the transfer of power (*translatio imperii*) from the East to the West. The University of Paris, "fount of doctrine and wisdom," was the site of the *translatio studii*, the shift of arts and learning from Athens to Paris, by way of Rome, a city for which Dionysius the Areopagite, "Saint Denis," was thought to have been the primary architect. In his sermon *Vivat rex* in 1405, Jean Gerson, chancellor of the university, went even further. He took the Judeo-Hellenistic version of the transfer of power that Flavius Josephus had outlined in his *Antiquities of the Jews* and, going back to Adam, extended the story all the way to Paris. Gerson proclaimed that "the University of Paris [was] the first and principal intellectual endeavor that, in Eden at the dawn of the world, inspired the first man and subsequently was transmitted to the Hebrews in Egypt through Abraham, as Josephus has said, and from Egypt to Athens, from Athens to Rome, and from Rome to Paris."

There were not, strictly speaking, any great "French" philosophers in the Middle Ages. But there was something more important: the university, the physical and conceptual site where all the players in the world of knowledge mingled. Starting in the thirteenth century, Paris and its "nations" were truly — as the city still sometimes dreams of being — at the center of Europe. Let us retain the image that this *universitas* suggests: a vast crucible where for a time, as something of an unexpected prelude to modern France, different origins and identities gathered, clashed, and fused.

Alain de Libera

REFERENCES

Bianchi, Luca. *Censure et liberté intellectuelle à l'université de Paris (XIIIe–XIVe siècle)*. Paris: Les Belles Lettres, 1999.

de Libera, Alain. *La philosophie médiévale*. Paris: Presses Universitaires de France, 2014.

Gorochov, Nathalie. *Naissance de l'université: Les écoles de Paris, d'Innocent III à Thomas d'Aquin (v. 1200–v. 1245)*. Paris: Honoré Champion, 2016.

Lusignan, Serge. *"Vérité garde le Roy": La construction d'une identité universitaire en France (XIIIe–XVe siècle)*. Paris: Publications de la Sorbonne, 1999.

Verger, Jacques. *Les universités françaises au Moyen Âge*. Leiden: Brill, 1995.

RELATED ARTICLES

511, 1287, 1380, 1682, 1751, 1793, 1968

1247

The Science of Water Management in Thirteenth-Century France

The thirteenth-century draining of the Montady lake and its remarkable system of cadastral divisions bear witness to the vigor of agricultural growth in southern France. But behind the hydraulic and planning science of the people living in the lower Languedoc plain lay an ancient tradition of skillful water management, passed on by the Moors of al-Andalus.

It is a local and global story: the draining of the lake at Montady via a two-thousand-year-old technique: underground channels known as *qanats*, well-known to the Romans and Arabs. The drained lake basin has been a classified French heritage site since 1974; located between Béziers and Narbonne in Languedoc, a few miles from the Mediterranean seafront, it is remarkable for the perfect geometry of its fields, most of which are still used to grow cereal crops today. The bowl, or basin, of Montady is divided into narrow triangular parcels whose points converge at the center in a near-perfect wheel. The site as a whole is remarkable for its size, a thousand acres, with some straight lines up to a mile long. How did this extraordinary landscape come to be?

Its rational division is the fruit of advanced hydraulic engineering and a deliberate drainage plan. Here as elsewhere in the coastal plains of Languedoc and Roussillon, depressions hollowed out by eons of swirling winds had trapped rainwater and stream water flowing off the slopes of the hills, turning them into small lakes and marshes. Such pockets of humidity — in a dry climate where water was at a premium — were naturally prized, for they offered pasture for livestock, abundant fishing and hunting, and plants of many different kinds. Evidence of these riches is supplied by the pre-Roman *oppidum* of Ensérune, a fortified settlement that originally overlooked the lake of Montady, the agricultural estates of the Roman period, and finally the villages that sprang up around the basin's edges — Colombiers, Montady, and the now-vanished Tersan.

By the mid-thirteenth century, the marshy lake had been entirely replaced by an artificial stretch of fertile land. Ditches ran along the sides of its triangular parcels, channeling water into a circular trench, or *redondel*, at the heart of the depression, while three broad canals drained the various other streams of the lake basin. These different conduits emptied into a single main canal, *la grande maire*, which carried the water straight out of the lake. In another feat of engineering prowess, this canal departed the lake bed through a 4,500-feet tunnel beneath the hill of Ensérune, before joining the lake of Poilhès. Thereafter it flowed on for a further two and a half miles, eventually connecting with the Aude river and the Mediterranean.

When did this impressive enterprise, whose landscape is better known than its history, take shape? It began with a 1247 charter of the archbishop of Narbonne, who authorized the *comparsonniers* (co-owners) of the lake to build an underground aqueduct to drain its water. The line planned for this aqueduct crossed the lands of the village of Nissan, part of the archbishop's feudal domain. The beginning and end of the works have not been precisely dated, but we do know that everything was completed by 1268. The draining of the Montady lake hence coincided with the final decades of the agricultural expansion of the mid-Middle Ages across Western Europe. In the Languedoc, the extension of cultivated spaces was marked by the recovery of wet zones, banks of waterways, and marshy grounds. These lands were converted into cornfields to meet the needs of a growing population, providing income to the wealthy bourgeois who financed the works with the agreement of local overlords. In short, new parcels of land were created for farmers to cultivate, where none had been before.

Dozens of similar drainage projects were undertaken in the thirteenth century, from the Roussillon to Provence. Montady was the most emblematic, and one of the best documented. Nevertheless, things elsewhere were not always so simple: the draining of the five-thousand-acre Marseillette lake was a failure, while the archbishop of Narbonne preferred to keep his own lake at Capestang full of water because he deemed it more valuable as a source of salt. At Montady, the drainage gallery stands out because it created invisible connections with distant geographical and cultural expanses. Following the charter of 1247, bourgeois from Béziers who had acquired lands were expected to finance the tunneling works and their subsequent maintenance: "Across these plots of land, those who owned concessions could without let or hindrance build, or have others build, galleries, wells, canals, and ditches in whatever quantity they wished, wherever they chose, and do everything needful for draining and working the lake bed."

The vocabulary of the original Latin text deserves mention, being directly borrowed from the mining industry. Around the southern rim of the Massif Central, successful mine shafts had been opened within twelve to twenty miles of the lakes of the Languedoc. The terms of the Montady charter mentioned two main elements: the well shaft (*crosum*, a Latinization of the Occitan word *cros*) gave access to the gallery/tunnel (*balma*). Technically, how was this done? The horizontal gallery with its vertical shaft was not specific to mining; it was also used for building medieval underground aqueducts. With its sixteen vertical shafts (one every 275 feet on average), the Montady conduit is an impressive work of art, but it is not unique of its kind. Other lakes were drained by similar aqueducts, like Fleury-d'Aude or Saint-Gilles-du-Gard in the Languedoc, and also Canohès in the Roussillon. But one finds fewer such galleries away from the immediate vicinity of the Mediterranean.

In reality, these hydraulic works were inspired by an ancient and widespread practice, that of the *qanats* of the East. Necessary when the natural environment was particularly dry and arid, these underground canals were built to trap groundwater and then lead it to zones where people cultivated crops and needed irrigation. The canals could be deep and extend for long distances, sometimes thousands of miles. Their existence was already widespread during antiquity, in Mesopotamia on the Achaemenides plateau of Persia and in Egypt. In these regions, networks of irrigation proved indispensable for the development of agriculture. Archaeology and ancient texts have also revealed the same operations in reverse, draining water from areas where there was too much of it. This procedure — the same as for the *qanats* — was used in antiquity around the Mediterranean, wherever there were lakes and marshes. Fayum in Egypt and Lake Copais and

Lake Ptechai in Greece are examples. The Etruscans and the Romans followed the same procedure, most notably with the Italian lakes of Albano and Fucino (which had a gallery over three miles long). In southern France, the depression at Clausonne, near Nîmes, was drained in the same way in the first century CE, along the aqueduct that supplied the city with water and included the famous Pont du Gard.

As far as lakes and ponds are concerned, partial or total drying-out follows a protocol that unvaryingly repeats itself. Water is channeled by ditches that either surround the humid zone and/or cross it via the characteristic fan design; it is then evacuated through an outlet that can be in the open air if the surroundings of the depression are relatively low, but can be transformed into an underground aqueduct if a higher topographical relief requires it. At regular intervals, vertical shafts are drilled to facilitate the digging of the gallery, its maintenance, and its ventilation. The procedure was identical to that of the *qanats*, even though the objective was to drain and evacuate water rather than to transport it for irrigation purposes.

This basic technique for draining a closed-off depression (whether a lake, a pond, or a marsh) was copied in the Middle Ages, especially when it became necessary to reclaim land for cultivation. Accounts of it are manifold in Western Europe in the twelfth century. With exceptions such as the volcanic lake of Laach, in the Eifel mountain range in

Germany, most of the medieval underground aqueducts are, like Montady, close to the Mediterranean. Montady is thus the product of two thousand years of history, beginning in the Middle East and moving eastward into Afghanistan, and westward to the Maghreb in Northern Africa, where the channels were known as *foggaras*. The Islamization and Arabization of these regions extended this system of irrigation and drainage throughout the Iberian Peninsula and beyond to the Balearic Islands, as well as in medieval al-Andalus. Today, traditional *qanats* and *foggaras* are still used to capture and distribute groundwater in the southern Mediterranean and in the Middle East.

The ancient lake of Montady tells a story that is both local and global. Roman civilization and Arab hydraulic skills combined to spread the techniques of the *qanats* into southern France and beyond by the thirteenth century. Partly because of this technical mastery, southern France carved a distinctive path between, on the one hand, growing Capetian influence after Saint Louis's crusade against the Albigensians and, on the other, a Mediterranean world in which, as the example of hydraulics make clear, political and religious boundaries did not hinder cultural and technical exchanges.

Jean-Loup Abbé

1247

REFERENCES

Abbé, Jean-Loup. *À la conquête des étangs: L'aménagement de l'espace dans le Languedoc méditerranéen (XIIe–XVe siècle)*. Toulouse: Presses Universitaires du Mirail, 2006.

Briant, Pierre, ed. *Irrigation et drainage dans l'Antiquité. Qanats et canalisations souterraines en Iran, en Égypte et en Grèce*. Paris: Collège de France / Thotm, 2001.

Carrière, Pierre. "Le dessèchement et l'aménagement hydraulique de l'étang de Montady (Hérault)." *Bulletin de la Société languedocienne de géographie 14*, nos. 2–3 (April–September 1980): 199–229.

Goblot, Henri. *Les Qanats: Une technique d'acquisition de l'eau*. Paris / The Hague / New York / Paris: Éditions de l'École des Hautes Études en Sciences Sociales, 1979.

Grewe, Klaus. *Licht am Ende des Tunnels. Planung und Trassierung im antiken Tunnelbau*. Mayence: Philip von Zabern Verlag, 1998.

Squatriti, Paolo, ed. *Working with Water in Medieval Europe: Technology and Resource-Use*. Leiden: Brill, 2000.

RELATED ARTICLES

5800 BCE, 212, 719, 1287

1270

Saint Louis Is Born in Carthage

With the reign of Louis IX, France emerged from the
realm of myth and entered the realm of history as a
sovereign state — never fully inhabiting one or the
other. The king's death in Carthage in 1270 provided the
Capetian dynasty with a saint, and offered a name and a
protector to French settlements throughout the world.

The death of Louis IX, king of France — of a fever on the
side of a hill in Carthage on August 25, 1270 — marked the
birth of a new saint in the Catholic Church. Unlike the many
holy evangelizing and confessor kings of the High Middle
Ages, was Louis a sanctified layman, or the incarnation
of the Capetian plan to sacralize the monarchy? First and
foremost a dynastic saint who infused thaumaturgy with
royal blood, Louis became a "national" saint in large part
due to the new ideologies that inspired European states to
forge territorial identities in the early 1300s. Cancelling
out a Germanic *and* a Roman Saint Charlemagne, whose
canonization in 1165 would forever remain unofficial, "Saint

Louis" became more than an object of national memory. His death outside the French territory created a name that would proclaim France's presence throughout the world.

By the end of the sixteenth century, Europe was teeming with parishes called "Saint-Louis-des-Français." They were founded in Lisbon (1572), Istanbul (1581), Rome, by far the most famous (1589), and then Madrid (1613) and Seville (1730). One such parish was even built in Moscow in 1788. By the seventeenth century, "Saint-Louis" had become a worldwide toponym through colonial conquests and a French monarchy that embraced the "cult of Louis." The influence of the name "Louis" was so great that no other name was given to a French king between 1610 and 1824. In 1600, the Mexican town of Potosí added its patron saint's name to that of the town, now known as "San Luis Potosí." Before Champlain established a base in Quebec in 1646, Charles des Vaux founded São Luís in Maranhão in 1612, a French presence in the Brazilian antecedent of Guiana. French colonial expansion and missionary work attached the name "Saint-Louis" to towns, trading posts, simple churches, and fortresses from the shores of Senegal (1659) to the banks of the Missouri (1764), from Guadeloupe (1648) to the town of Saint-Louis-du-Sud in Haiti (1677), from Pondicherry (1704) to Mauritius (1735). The Jesuits, whose Paris headquarters were naturally dedicated to Saint Louis (in 1627), fulfilled a mission that was both universal and national, combining Catholic conversion with French commercial interests throughout the world. Finally, through the Church at Les Invalides (1670), patron of the "diocese of armies," Saint Louis became the protector of the French who ventured beyond national borders.

To what extent did the two crusades Louis IX undertook in 1248 and 1270 ("death-adventures," as chronicler Jean de Joinville called them) produce the mythical inspiration of this vast colonial patronage? This question is all the more important given that historians such as Paul Alphandéry and Alphonse Dupront hesitated to consider the Capetian's two overseas passages "crusades" at all.

By equating Louis's death with his lengthy captivity, Saint Louis's first hagiographer, Geoffrey of Beaulieu, promulgated a skewed conception of the Crusade. Following forays into Egypt and the crushing defeat at Al Mansurah in 1250, Tunisia became the next Muslim target. Defending the Holy Land was but a pretext, in fact abandoned (in part) in favor of a wide-ranging diplomatic strategy that extended as far as Mongolian central Asia. Intertwined within hagiographic narratives, Saint Louis's two "crusades" were experiments in which political and cultural confrontation melded through captivity and negotiation an irrepressible desire to convert with de facto exchanges with "infidels." As it happens, "Sanluwis ibn Luwis," as Saint Louis was called in Arabic, is also a figure in Middle Eastern historiographic narratives, both Christian and Muslim. Ibn Khaldun, like other Arab chroniclers before him, painted an ambiguous portrait of Saint Louis, at once ignorant crusader and treacherous conqueror.

Why did Louis IX pick up the Cross once again in 1267? And why did he target Carthage, a destination that remained secret up to the last minute? Though historians still debate the matter, they tend to agree that geopolitics proved less important than an ideological plan the Mendicant orders had been advocating for a half-century: to convert the Hafsid emir Al-Mustanṣir, who had just proclaimed himself caliph upon the fall of the Abbasids, defeated by the Mongols in Baghdad in 1258. French royalty embraced the missionary designs of Francis of Assisi toward Sultan Al-Kamil in 1219. At the very least, it was a way of supporting the local preaching of the Dominicans, whose Arabic study institute, the Studium Arabicum, founded in Tunis in 1250, had been violently shut down in 1267. The king knew he was ailing, moreover, and he felt compelled to redeem his failure in Egypt. To die in the land of the infidels would open the path to martyrdom.

The king's death was above all a new birth, all the more mystical in that it coincided with the day, twenty-two years earlier, when Louis IX had left Aigues-Mortes and France on the first "crusade," which was completed on April 24, 1254, the anniversary of the day of his birth. Transfigured into an eternal crusade, his death in a non-Christian land was scrupulously portrayed in ritual (he was said to have died on a bed of ashes, as a sign of humility) and words imitating those of Christ. Historian Jacques Le Goff has drawn attention to the way the king's last words (reported in 1272 by the confessor Geoffrey of Beaulieu) — "Father, I place my soul in Your hands" — identified the French ruler with the Messiah, completing a process that had begun in 1238 with the acquisition of Christ's crown of thorns and the construction of the Sainte-Chapelle. In 1239, the pope bestowed the name "*Dei filius*" upon Louis IX while calling for the deposition of Holy Roman Emperor Frederick II, whom he called the Antichrist. Beyond the Holy Roman Empire, the French monarchy outlined its own universalist mission. Within a dynastic and soon a national framework, the kingdom of Jerusalem could come into being here and now, on this expanse of the "Extreme West," open to the sea.

The passage of 1270 also entailed the maiden voyage of an autonomous fleet, with the commissioning of vessels and the creation of the rank of "admiral" of France, a word that shows the linguistic transfer of the Arabic "emir" into the French language. It was a foundational myth, of course, but one that would be resurrected with the advent of a true royal navy. Every French port would have its "Saint Louis" church, from Rochefort (1686) and Toulon (1707) to Brest (1702) and La Rochelle (1741) and the construction of a Port-Saint-Louis-du-Rhône (1737) and a Napoleonic church Saint-Louis in La Roche-sur-Yon (1808).

The singular Tunisian "crusade" forces us to ponder the political significance of Louis IX's long stay in the East, a six-year exile from royal government (1248 to 1254). Beyond the stated desire to colonize Egypt by providing farm equipment in Damietta, it provided a clear sign that a fledgling modern state could function autonomously, without its monarch. Despite the death of the regent Blanche of Castile in 1252, Louis IX managed — unlike his grandfather in 1190 — to complete negotiations with the sultans of Aleppo and Cairo. These negotiations revolved less on the possession of earthly Jerusalem than on the fortification of the Holy Land, now ranging from Gaza to Sidon. After buying back his freedom following his unfortunate capture at the Battle of Al Mansurah in 1250, Louis IX unintentionally got an education in the culture of the Middle East. As an eyewitness to the Mamluk coup d'état that took place at the time of his liberation, and then offered the sultanate of Cairo by an infidel, the king may have learned to view the world in a less binary way.

Louis saw how heterogeneous the "infidels" were and understood that the rumor of Mongolian terror was an unlikely divine sign of the coming of Gog and Magog. From Cyprus in 1248, Louis sent ambassadors bearing gifts to the Mongolian khan. Did he hope to convert the "son of Heaven" in order to outflank the Islamic powers? Perhaps — but this was also a desire to understand and explore Asia by bringing the Middle East closer. Until 1269, the king maintained a delegate, Geoffrey of Sergines, in the Holy Land. His embassies bore fruit. Until 1289, the King of France received letters from China. Though the encounter did not happen, contact had been established; the world was shrinking. It is not impossible that Louis IX also prolonged his stay to await the return of William of Rubruck, who had set out to meet the Mongolian khan in 1252.

On the whole, the king's travel represents a unique form of political communication, as seen in a letter he wrote to all his subjects in August 1250 to justify his decision to remain in the East. The possibility of maintaining a relationship with the Other was real. In 1272, Geoffrey of Beaulieu dared to assert that by founding a library in the sacristy of the Sainte-Chapelle upon his return, Louis IX was in fact following the lead of the sultan of Cairo and his court, with whom he had spent time while in captivity. This odd cultural transfer supports the notion of an "Enlightenment" Islam at the heart of a West that was hence recognizing its own ignorance.

In the 1280s, despite military and diplomatic failures, the king's two Eastern adventures earned him uncommon, if not global, renown. Singling him out from other "Frankish Bedouins," Ibn Wasil described him as the "ridafrans"

(Ibn Khaldun would follow suit). Here we see the name "France," not yet established in official titles, consecrated by the Arabic language. Despite the control exerted by later hagiographic sources, Louis IX's captivity and martyrdom left the missionary king's figure and legacy open to posthumous uses. With the exception of John II, a voluntary hostage in London in 1364, Louis IX was the only French monarch to die outside French territory, and the only one to die in a non-Christian land. That extra-territoriality required the dispersal of his body on either side of the Mediterranean. His remains became relics in Palermo as early as 1271; six hundred years later, Cardinal Charles Lavigerie obtained a fragment for the Chapelle Saint-Louis de Carthage, the Primatial Cathedral of Africa and home base for his missionary group, the White Fathers.

Like those exported remains, the legend of Saint Louis was subject to unexpected appropriations. In the early days of France's conquest of North Africa in the 1830s, it was said near Carthage that, rather than dying in 1270, Louis IX had converted to Islam and become the marabout known as Sidi Bou Saïd. This late canonization was astonishing, not least because this African Saint Louis could both serve and contest the French colonization of minds and even bodies.

Yann Potin

REFERENCES

Eddé, Anne-Marie. "Saint Louis et la septième croisade vus par les auteurs arabes." *Cahiers de recherches médiévales* 1 (1996): 65–92.

Hélary, Xavier. *La dernière croisade*. Paris: Perrin, 2016.

Le Goff, Jacques. *Saint Louis*. Translated by Gareth Evan Gollrad. Notre Dame, IN: University of Notre Dame Press, 2009.

McCannon, Afrodesia E. "The King's Two Lives: The Tunisian Legend of Saint Louis." *Journal of Folklore Research* 43, no. 1 (2006): 53–74.

Potin, Yann. "Saint-Louis l'Africain: Histoire d'une mémoire inversée." *Afrique et histoire* 1 (2003): 23–74.

RELATED ARTICLES
800, 1095, 1662, 1763, 1798, 1931, 2003

1282

"Death to the French!"

The rebellion of the Sicilian Vespers in 1282 marked the end of French rule over the Italian island, which had started some twenty years earlier when a Capetian prince, with the pope's intervention, won Sicily by force of arms. But the rebellion also disrupted the political equilibrium in the Mediterranean, turned Italy upside down, destabilized the papacy, and crystallized political passions and national identities up until the nineteenth century.

On Easter Monday, 1282, or possibly the next evening, during an annual spring festival that gathered the inhabitants of Palermo for a pilgrimage to the Church of the Holy Spirit, a quarrel broke out between French officers in the service of Charles of Anjou and some young men from the local nobility. The brawl degenerated into a massacre in which all the French and Provençal residents of Palermo were killed, to cries of "Death to the French!" Several hundred died. Neither women nor children were spared, and the bodies lay unburied, prey to dogs and vultures.

The uprising in Palermo spread to the hinterlands, reaching the town of Corleone first, and gradually engulfing other towns and communities around Sicily. Messina was the last to be overtaken, on April 28, and only a few French troops managed to withdraw to Calabria. On May 7, the pope issued a bull forbidding all aid to the rebels and ordering the insurgents to submit to their sovereign, Charles of Anjou, king of Sicily by papal investiture. The Sicilians refused to comply, turning for help to Peter III, king of Aragon and Count of Barcelona, who was widely considered the legitimate heir to the Sicilian throne because of his marriage to Constance of Hohenstaufen, daughter to the late King Manfred of Sicily. After a stop in Tunisia, Peter III landed in Trapani on August 30 and was proclaimed king in Palermo on September 4.

The rebellion of the Sicilian Vespers — the term was coined during the Renaissance — brought to a bloody end a remarkable adventure that had begun twenty years earlier when the youngest brother of King Louis IX of France tried to build a Mediterranean empire as outsized as it was ephemeral.

Back in 1265, the pope had chosen a prince from the Capetian dynasty, Charles, Count of Anjou and Maine, and by his wife Count of Provence and Forcalquier, to be his champion in the fight against the successors of Emperor Frederick II of Hohenstaufen, who inherited the Norman kingdom of Sicily from his mother. The Sicilian territory, under the pope's suzerainty, included the island itself and the southern portion of the Italian Peninsula. In the course of two military campaigns, which the pope elevated to the rank of crusades, Charles of Anjou successively eliminated Manfred, Frederick's son, who died on the battlefield at Benevento in 1266, and Conradin, Manfred's nephew, captured at the Battle of Tagliacozzo and executed in Naples in 1268. Charles thus stamped out the Hohenstaufen line, that "race of vipers," in the words of Innocent IV, which had been in conflict with the papacy since the twelfth century.

Once crowned, and with the support of the French royal house and the Roman Church behind him, Charles launched a hugely expansionist policy. He started by establishing hegemony over Italy, taking the Piedmont region, strengthening the ruling papal party in the northern and central Italian cities, and placing Sardinia under his indirect dominion. Then he subjugated the sultan of Tunis, acquired claims in the Holy Land, and obtained the title of King of Jerusalem. He also seized the Frankish principality of Achaea (the Peloponnese) and was proclaimed king of Albania. Two further developments — the accession to the papacy of a Frenchman friendly to his cause (Pope Martin IV, in 1281) and a naval and commercial alliance with Venice — led Charles to begin planning a final enterprise, again cast in the light of a crusade: the conquest of

Constantinople and the remaining vestiges of the Byzantine Empire. The Sicilian Vespers rebellion, which burned the French fleet in Messina and sowed chaos at the very heart of Charles's rule, stopped his progress cold.

Many factors led to the uprising. Papal support notwithstanding, Charles of Anjou's legitimacy was on shaky ground. The public execution of Conradin, which was out of step with the political norms of the time, had damaged his reputation as a knightly prince. But above all, the conquest of Sicily had been unusually brutal, and the rebellion of 1268 and 1269 by nobles in exile in Tunis led to harsh punitive measures against the island population. The rule of Charles's Anjou faction took on a frankly colonial aspect — the *mala signoria* or "misrule" denounced by chroniclers. It combined a purge of local aristocrats, often replaced by French or Provençal nobles, a rigorous central administration, increased taxation (all the more sharply felt because the collection of taxes was entrusted to Italians from the continent), and the transplant of the capital from Palermo to Naples.

Historians are still debating the part played by the court of Aragon's diplomacy. A chronicle of the rebellion written in Messina in the late 1280s, one of the oldest texts in the Sicilian language (and one later taken up by Petrarch and Voltaire), makes John of Procida the hero of the affair. Born to a noble family in Campania, he was exiled and became chancellor to the King of Aragon, from which post he purportedly directed an intricate political plot. In this scenario, the court of Aragon would have contracted an alliance with the new German emperor, Rudolf of Habsburg, as well as with the emperor of Byzantium, Michael Palaiologos. But while it is well known that letters passed between the Aragonese court and certain members of the Sicilian aristocracy, it seems impossible to make John of Procida the uprising's instigator. If there was a plot, it developed within Sicily. Besides, the insurgents initially chose a form of political organization that was current in north-central Italy: on the model of the Lombard League, each town, governed by its own body of magistrates, joined into a league with all of the other towns. Only when the pope threatened the insurgents did they decide to offer the crown to the King of Aragon.

The uprising had considerable effect. More final even than King Louis IX's defeat at Tunis in 1270, the Sicilian Vespers spelled the end of French ascendancy in the Mediterranean. The short-lived "Aragon Crusade," started by King Philip III of France in an attempt to help his uncle in 1284 and 1285, quickly fell flat. There followed a long struggle between the partisans of Charles of Anjou and the Aragonese, which turned into something like an alternative Hundred Years' War in the Mediterranean, briefly interrupted between 1302 and 1321, but ending only with the entry of Alfonso V of Aragon into Naples in 1442. In Italy at large, the Sicilian Vespers disturbed the political landscape. The former kingdom of Sicily was now divided in two, on either side of the Strait of Messina. In the cities of northern and central Italy, the Franco-papal faction was everywhere in retreat before Habsburg and Aragonese partisans. Factional strife within the papal state reached such proportions that the pope left Italy for France. Clement V eventually settled in Avignon in 1309, where he was soon joined by the papal curia.

The Sicilian Vespers attest to the rise of what we might call a "national sentiment" among Sicily's aristocracy and urban elites. All of our sources confirm the violently anti-French aspect of the uprising. The fact is somewhat surprising given that Sicily had been receiving successive waves of foreign immigration since the tenth century (Arabs, Greeks, Normans, Lombards, Germans); that a variety of religions and sects lived together there willy-nilly (Latin and Orthodox forms of Christianity, Islam, Judaism); and that the island was accustomed to being governed by foreign rulers (Arabs, Greeks, Normans, and Swabians). The Sicilian Vespers revolt therefore signals the end of one era and the beginning of a new awareness of "Sicilianism." The Count of Anjou's men were seen as unalterably foreign and French because of their political allegiance to the royal house of France, their imperfect command of the local language, and their brutal code of chivalry. It mattered little that Charles of Anjou's partisans were in fact of varied origins and included "Frenchmen" from Île-de-France, Champagne, and Picardy; Angevins and Manceaux (from the counties of Anjou and Maine); Provençaux (from Provence); and some Lombards and Amalfitanos.

The Sicilian Vespers have given rise to as many political mythologies as there were sides to the conflict. The Spanish and the French have, unsurprisingly, put the event to different uses. Charles of Anjou's claims were one of the reasons King Charles VIII of France embarked on the First Italian War in 1494, whereas the Spaniards who ruled southern Italy claimed a modicum of legitimacy because of the uprising, noting that it had been "popular" in origin. This rivalry lasted into the seventeenth century, as we can tell from the famous exchange reported by the Jesuit Baltasar Gracián in 1648. King Henry IV of France bragged that he could conquer Italy in a day: "I will attend Mass in Milan, have my midday meal in Rome, and dine in Naples." To this, the Spanish ambassador replied, "Sire, at that rate Your Majesty might end up the same day at Vespers in Sicily."

But it was especially in Italy that the Sicilian Vespers were appropriated for many ends. By the end of the thirteenth century, Dante was making the uprising an object lesson for what happens to a tyrannical power when it tramples on the common people. This line of thinking, often admixed with nationalism, was reprised and amplified in the nineteenth century and directed at the Spanish House of Bourbon-Anjou and the Austrian monarchy. While the liberal or radical ideas of the French Revolution spurred on the social and political changes of the Risorgimento in nineteenth-century Italy, the uprising received a scholarly treatment in Michele Amari's *La guerra del Vespro Siciliano* (1842), written while the historian was in exile in Paris during the 1830s and 1840s, and a more popular one in Giuseppe Verdi's *I Vespri siciliani*, performed for the first time in Turin on December 26, 1855. A final avatar of these successive reimaginings can be found in a fanciful etymology of the term "Mafia" that was advanced in the 1860s. Napoleon III's policies toward Italy had provoked considerable hostility, and in that context, "Mafia" was said to be composed from the first letters of the words chanted by the Palermo rebels, "*Morte alla Francia Italia anella*" ("Italy aspires to the death of France"). From one era to the next, the memory of the Sicilian Vespers continued to provide a mirror for national identities and to weave ambivalent bonds between France and Italy.

Florian Mazel

REFERENCES

Barbero, Alessandro. *Il mito angioino nella cultura italiana e provenzale fra Duecento e Trecento*. Turin: Deputazione Subalpina di Storia Patria, 1983.

Bresc, Henri. "La *mala signoria* ou l'hypothèque sicilienne." In *L'État angevin: Pouvoir, culture et société entre XIIIe et XIVe siècle*. Rome: École Française de Rome, 1998.

————, and Laura Sciascia. "Mort aux Angevins!" In *Palerme 1070–1492. Mosaïque de peuples, nation rebelle: la naissance violente de l'identité sicilienne*, edited by Henri Bresc and Geneviève Bresc-Bautier, 120–35. Paris: Autrement, 1993.

Dunbabin, Jean. *Charles I of Anjou: Power, Kingship and State-Making in the Thirteenth-Century Europe*. London/New York: Longman, 1998.

Runciman, Steven. *The Sicilian Vespers: A History of the Mediterranean World in the Later 13th Century*. Cambridge: Cambridge University Press, 1958.

RELATED ARTICLES

1287

In 1287 the French stonecutter Étienne de Bonneuil sailed
to Sweden to oversee construction of Uppsala Cathedral.
This voyage — and this invitation — bear witness to
the radiance of Parisian Gothic art and more generally to
the cultural influence of Paris and its beacon monument,
Notre-Dame Cathedral. That influence was rivaled only
by the technical excellence of its artisans.

Was Sweden an inaccessible if not hostile destination for a
subject of King Philip the Fair? Assuredly not. From the
vantage point of France, which had long sent out waves
of pilgrims and conquerors, Scandinavia seemed a safe
place, though not as beguiling as the Holy Land. While the
Hanseatic League's monopoly over commerce prohibited
merchants from becoming rich in Sweden, the clerics who
made the journey to spread Christianity beginning in 1100
and the artists and artisans who aided them in this task found
in this Nordic world a wonderful outlet. There, they could
put their skills to work in the service of a new church and

351

new places of worship that would endure throughout time.

Paris's great cathedral work sites were at a standstill at the end of the summer of 1287, with no new royal ventures on the horizon. Specialized laborers who had toiled on the prestigious architectural projects that had flourished thanks to Saint Louis's commission were finding it increasingly difficult to secure work. And so on August 30, the stonecutter Étienne de Bonneuil appeared before Guillaume Saint-Martin, one of the sixty clerics whom in 1270 Louis IX had appointed to draft acts under the legal authority of the provost. In a notarized document, written on parchment, Étienne acknowledged that he owed two students forty *livres parisis* (equivalent to a skilled worker's annual salary), a sum he had received as advance payment for an unusual mission: overseeing the construction of the Uppsala Cathedral. Étienne intended to reimburse his creditors upon his arrival, assuming of course that he and the workers he brought along to complete the task did not perish at sea.

Was Étienne's mission a success? The evidence points in that direction: an authentic copy of a construction document (bearing no official diplomatic seal) that was discovered in the Uppsala Cathedral archives; the mention of a "master Étienne" in a local deed; and most important, official plans for the Swedish cathedral, the largest Gothic edifice in the Scandinavian world.

It is worth noting just how much the twenty-two lines of

that little parchment of 1287 tell us about this undertaking's human dimension. The document strikes us as modern due to the language in which it was composed. Instead of the Latin we would expect, it is written in clear French, suggesting that its Swedish readers were familiar with the language of Parisian schools. Unsurprisingly, the parties involved covered considerable ground. The two men who had lent Étienne funds, "Sir Olivier" and "Sir Charles" (also known as Olaf and Carl), were both canons in Uppsala and students in Paris, where they hired an agent to recruit an entire team for a voyage across land and sea that would involve a stay in Bruges and last at least two months.

Convinced that a mission of this nature must have been approved by the King of France — something that may or may not have been true — historians have long refused to acknowledge that there was such freedom of circulation among artisans. This said, the scribe who penned the document above conformed to the statutes of the building trades that provost Étienne Boileau had established twenty years earlier, under the aegis of Saint Louis. This document thus clarifies the architect's uncertain status in Paris, where the Rayonnant Gothic style now prevailed. The word "architect" would not be commonly used in France for another two centuries, and yet Étienne deserves the title. This "stonecutter" joined the highest category of masonry workers and surrounded himself with experienced men who were either independent (*compagnons*) or else oversaw the work of others (*bacheliers*). Because he had been appointed "master in the building of the church [Uppsala Cathedral]," we may consider him an architect regardless of whether he conceived the work or simply carried it out.

How did these Normans become so familiar with Paris, its clerics, and its artisans? From its beginnings, the University of Paris was the principal purveyor of graduates for the Scandinavian clergy. As Étienne reached Uppsala, seat of the archdiocese of the peninsula since the twelfth century, the city was setting up a branch of its cathedral school in Paris. No other city in the region had done so. In 1286, Andreas And, provost of the Uppsala chapter who had obtained his master's degree in Paris, had bought a building on Rue Serpente to house and teach students from his diocese. Five years later, he gave this house to his church. The correlation between the foundation of that school, whose statutes were inspired by the Sorbonne's, and the involvement of Parisians in the construction of the Swedish cathedral is anything but a fluke. After all, the sponsors of Étienne's mission belonged to And's community. Parisian Gothic art would not have been transplanted so firmly in Sweden were it not for that country's thirst for scholarly culture and the lack of a local university center, which forced Swedish intellectuals to travel abroad.

But what was the exact nature of that transplant?

Generations of archaeologists have debated the respective roles of Étienne and other anonymous master artisans by imagining the layout of the Swedish cathedral, a task complicated by the fires of 1572 and 1702 and the extensive restoration of 1885. The 1287 document clearly states that Étienne was to oversee the work. The new cathedral had been under construction since 1271, and its chevet was partially functional by 1281 at the latest. Étienne's task, therefore, was to serve as project manager (as it were) for a venture that was faltering or had been delayed through various political and economic setbacks. He was expected to relaunch and coordinate an enterprise that had been undertaken by local brick workers. Commonly used in Sweden for large construction projects, brick proved technically challenging for this Parisian and his team of stonecutters. The latter in fact played a crucial role: they designed the entrances to the transept, adopting the iconic look of Paris-style portals with their lithic carvings and geometric lines. The original design of the chevet, conceived fifteen years earlier, is attributed to a predecessor who was already familiar with the great French cathedrals of the mid-thirteenth century, which combined Parisian know-how with French or even Germanic provincial accents.

From the many architectural influences that can be detected in its design, it is obvious that the Uppsala Cathedral ultimately freed itself from the French models from which it borrowed. It did so to a much greater extent than the great Gothic cathedrals in the kingdoms of Naples and Cyprus, for example. Still, Paris was the ultimate point of reference for the cathedral's patrons. A contemporary text states that "some lords, the elector of Cologne, and the abbot of Corvey were the guarantors that the forenamed French architect would build the church following the same form as Notre-Dame of Paris." This intention to imitate (whose motivations remain elusive) echoes the Wimpfen chronicle of circa 1300, which tells of the intervention, around 1269, of a "mason newly arrived from Paris in France to construct the church in the French style, out of cut stone." Art historian Marc Schurr has shown that the phrase "French style" (*opus francigenum*) written here was probably apocryphal, either imagined by the chronicler or wrongfully claimed by the architect, whose stylistic references owed more to the Lorraine or Alsace regions.

In truth, the dynamic world of architecture in the years 1270–1280 in Baden-Württemberg, Switzerland, and other peripheral areas of Europe and France revolved less around a precise geographical identity (French in this case) than technical excellence in stonecutting. The latter allied the technique of stereotomy with the refinement of architectural design that combined rigorous geometrical lines and ornamental delicacy. And ever since the construction of the Sainte-Chapelle and, above all, the metamorphosis of

Notre-Dame, such excellence was recognized everywhere as the mark of practitioners from the Île-de-France, the area surrounding Paris. In this regard, the 1287 document explains more clearly what constituted the renown of an architect in the second half of the thirteenth century than does the title *doctor lathomorum* pompously bestowed upon Pierre de Montreuil in his 1267 epitaph in the abbey of Saint-Germain-des-Prés. Archaeologists, who have not always paid strict attention to lexical matters, have turned Étienne de Bonneuil into a sculptor who was primarily responsible for the figures on the south portal of Uppsala. However, it is an architectural feature of Uppsala, the great rose window of the north façade, that most explicitly shows its connection to Notre-Dame, reproducing as it does (with some modifications) that cathedral's south rose window, designed around 1260 by Pierre de Montreuil.

De Bonneuil, about whom we know nothing except that he must have been a native of one of the Île-de-France parishes bearing his name, did not merely bring with him sketched models of monuments from his country: he also labored on the construction sites of Notre-Dame. When work started to wane there in 1270, he had no choice but to seek his fortune elsewhere. Motivated by multiple factors, his departure for Uppsala in the summer of 1287 should not be seen as the birthdate of an international Gothic for which France long remained a point of reference. As early as

357

1271, Uppsala had welcomed an architect carrying multiple references from the continent. A century earlier, while its first archbishop, Stephan, was being consecrated by the pope in Sens, Burgundy, and the Swedish abbey of Alvastra was being built in the severe style of the French abbey of Fontenay, French architect William of Sens was rebuilding the Canterbury cathedral and making sure the new Île-de-France architecture would enjoy irreversible dominance over European archiepiscopal construction. Builders of the Norwegian cathedral in Trondheim would find direct inspiration in that Gothic tradition.

The 1287 deed nonetheless reveals a key stage in France's role in the development of that new Gothic aesthetic, which, in the last quarter of the thirteenth century, saw Notre-Dame de Paris become synonymous with French-style architecture. (This would remain the case for more than fifty years.) This document deserves our attention, finally, as one of the oldest primary sources in the vulgate to reveal objectively — insofar as a notarized document can do so — the far-reaching borrowings within the network of Western cathedral construction, the importance of clerics in facilitating that kind of circulation across political borders, and the advent of a new type of individual in Western society: the sought-after architect, free and bold.

Étienne Hamon

REFERENCES

Aubert, Marcel. "Les cathédrales de Paris et d'Uppsala." *Konsthistoriska Sällskapets Publikation* (1923): 5–17.

Bony, Jean. *French Gothic Architecture of the 12th and 13th Centuries.* Berkeley/Los Angeles/London: University of California Press, 1983.

Frisch, Teresa G. *Gothic Art, 1140–c. 1450: Sources and Documents.* Engelwood Cliffs, NJ: Prentice Hall, 1971.

Lovén, Christian. "La neige, les briques et l'architecte français: La cathédrale d'Uppsala 1272–." In *Regards sur la France du Moyen Âge*, edited by Olle Ferm and Per Förnegård with Hugues Engel, 20–51. Stockholm: Runica et Mediaevalia, 2009.

Mortet, Victor, and Paul Deschamps, eds. *Recueil de textes relatifs à l'histoire de l'architecture et à la condition des architectes en France au Moyen Âge (XIe–XIIIe siècle).* 1929. Reprinted by Léon Pressouyre and Olivier Guyotjeannin. Paris: Comité des Travaux Historiques et Scientifiques, 1995.

Schurr, Marc. "L'*opus francigenum* de Wimpfen im Tal: transfert technologique ou artistique?" In *Les Transferts artistiques dans l'Europe gothique*, edited by Jacques Dubois, Jean-Marie Guillouët, and Benoît Van den Bossche, 45–56. Paris: Picard, 2014.

RELATED ARTICLES
1215, 1456, 1682, 1913

1336

The Avignon Pope Is Not in France

In 1336, the papacy's acknowledgment that its move to Avignon might last forever led some in Europe to believe that the church had become, as it were, French. Hence the paradox of the "Avignon Popes": While the French monarchy's grip on the Holy See was weaker than commonly believed, the papal presence in Avignon turned the city into a center of European culture and a testing ground for new forms of government.

In 1895, Jean Alboize, editor of the review *L'Artiste*, declared:

> At a time when archaeology and the historical interest of ancient monuments were low on the list of French administrative concerns, the Popes' Palace in Avignon, whose massive walls overlook the city and its surrounding countryside, was converted into an army barracks. The palace is still an army barracks today...but now the municipal council has unanimously approved M. Pourquery de Boisserin's project, namely, the restoration of the palace and the

conversion of a huge building that was once the seat
of the French Papacy into a museum of Christianity.

The conversion was duly undertaken ten years later, and
yet, did Avignon's Palais des Papes deserve, at the end of
the nineteenth century, the designation "seat of the French
Papacy"?

To understand, we need to go back to a date that is
rarely mentioned today: June 27, 1336. On that day, in the
city of Avignon, Pope Benedict XII presented the bishop
with a new palace on the site of today's Musée du Petit
Palais. By way of exchange, the bishop officially ceded to
the pope his own episcopal palace, in which the papal court
had been effectively residing for the last twenty years. The
legal act of transfer included a provision of vital importance,
that "this building, which in the past was commonly called
the 'Episcopal Palace,' shall henceforth be known as the
'Apostolic Palace.'" With this, the pope gave new meaning
to the papal presence on the banks of the Rhône.

He effectively acknowledged that this presence might
become permanent.

Until that time, the presence of the popes in Avignon
had seemed provisional — the result of a long and intricate
history. The papacy of the twelfth and thirteenth centuries
was often on the move. During these two hundred years, the
popes spent about half their time in Rome. Unable to control

this city that was prey to feuds between great aristocratic families, they shuttled between their palaces of the Papal States, in central Italy, frequently tarrying for long periods outside the Italian peninsula. Innocent IV and Gregory X did so in Lyon, holding two important papal councils there in 1245 and 1274. 1305 saw the coronation — in Lyon — of Clement V, commonly considered the first of the Avignon Popes.

Formerly archbishop of Bordeaux, Clement ascended the throne of Peter two years after the end of the confrontation between the French King Philip the Fair and Pope Boniface VIII. As long as Rome and part of northern Italy were hostile to the papacy, the new pope chose to stay in the immediate vicinity of the kingdom of France, without permanently living there. Thus it was that in 1309 Pope Clement V settled in the Dominican convent of Avignon. At that time, the town was not in France: it belonged to the counts of Provence, who were also the kings of Naples; but the region that surrounded it, the Comtat Venaissin, had been a pontifical possession since 1274. In sum, Clement V's presence in Avignon was part of a logic that was both feudal and apostolic.

After Clement's death and the election in 1316 of Pope John XXII (another "Frenchman," born in Cahors), another stage was completed when he moved into the bishop's palace. In 1336, Benedict XII thus began converting this building into an apostolic palace, both materially and legally, initiating the construction of the present north side of the Popes' Palace, known as the *Palais-Vieux*, the Old Palace. Although he had originally toyed with the idea of returning to Italy and setting up shop in Bologna, Benedict finally opted to settle permanently in Avignon. His successor Clement VI (1342–1352), who had been born in the diocese of Limoges, took the same line, completing the construction of the new palace with his *Palais-Neuf*, New Palace. He then went on to purchase the city of Avignon outright from Queen Joanna of Naples, in 1348. Thus, within a few decades, the Holy See contrived to secure an independent territorial principality of its own, on the left bank of the Rhône.

This initiative was roundly criticized by contemporaries. At the very moment when Clement VI was buying the city of Avignon, the poet Petrarch was writing letters castigating the papacy and holding up his sojourn in Avignon as a new "Babylonian exile," notorious for its extravagance and moral corruption. Major spiritual figures of the fourteenth century — among them St. Bridget of Sweden and St. Catherine of Siena — backed him up, denouncing the papal abandonment of Rome, which according to them was the only legitimate seat for the heirs of St. Peter. This polemic spawned the dark legend of an Avignon papacy that was "altogether too French," a legend that explains the paradox of the Avignon popes in collective memory. Historians of both Catholic Italy and Protestant Germany have persistently viewed the Avignon interlude as a time of crisis, while nineteenth-century French scholars determined that it had no place in the national narrative. Jules Michelet's 1855 *History of France* gives it short shrift: "Rome lent its pope to Avignon; wealth and scandal abounded. Religion had been decaying in these regions ever since the Albigensians; it was finally killed off by the presence of the popes." The picture remained gloomy in another *History of France*, this one edited by Ernest Lavisse at the beginning of the twentieth century: "The dignity of the papacy was much dented by its exile in Babylon. The French popes, surrounded by French cardinals and a French court, appeared even more shackled to France than they really were. They were openly accused of betraying the interests of the church."

In the eyes of posterity, only the artistic taste of the Avignon popes — as demonstrated by a palace converted into a barracks and then reconverted into a museum — would appear to redeem the heritage of the pontifical sojourn in Provence.

This "French papacy" was "French" in the minds of people observing Avignon from Christian territories more than in its connection to Capetian France. In the fourteenth century, the latter abruptly ended on the right bank of the Rhône. Like the Comtat Venaissin, Provence was part of the

Holy Roman Empire. Bertrand de Got (Pope Clement V) began life not only as a subject of the King of France, but also as a vassal of the Duke of Aquitaine, who also happened to be the King of England. Clement's immediate successors hailed from the Limousin and Quercy regions and their mother tongue, shared with their followers, was basically Occitan. "French" at that time encompassed a northern area of present-day France, between the Île-de-France and the Orléans regions, heartland of the Capet dynasty. To be sure, the administrative and ecclesiastical staff at the papal court of Avignon included a strong contingent of clerics from the kingdom of France, and it is probably through this prism that we should approach the "French" dimension of the papacy.

At the same time, papal politics sought to maintain the balance of power among the great princes of the West and, in this way, preserve the pontiff's theocratic predominance and his position as political arbiter. In 1344, Pope Clement VI, who in the past had served the French monarchy, tried — and failed — to broker an end to the conflict between the kings of France and England. In the same way, the Avignon popes fought to regain a footing in Italy while meddling in the successions to the thrones of Spain and the Holy Roman Empire.

When the papacy decided to designate its palace in Avignon as the Holy See, it was already intervening in all kinds of political matters. Locally, the goal was to fashion a territorial principality resembling the monarchical states taking form in France and England. Regionally, the papacy maintained close ties with southern France, especially its administrative and clerical personnel, and northern France, especially the world of the court and the university. It also looked to Italy, which remained its main political and cultural horizon. After all, writers such as Petrarch and artists such as Simone Martini and Matteo Giovannetti spent considerable time in Avignon. The Avignon papal court helped create a new culture that encompassed the international Gothic style and budding humanism and whose main characteristic was its European dimension. Ecclesiastic bureaucracy, both fiscal and spiritual, likewise took form across the Christian world. Broadly, the papacy's universal ambitions led it to embrace older notions of crusade, to establish new connections with the Byzantine, Greek, and Armenian worlds, to launch missions to Asia, and to pay close attention to Spanish and Portuguese voyages on the Atlantic.

The Avignon papacy of course had an impact on the kingdom of France, in the short-term (cultural exchanges, diplomatic proximity) and also in the long-term. After all, it coincided with the beginning of the Great Western Schism (1378), the emergence of the Gallican Church, and the creation of a pontifical enclave in Provence that was to last for more than five hundred years. But above all the experience of Avignon was pivotal to the future of the papacy itself from the fifteenth century onward. Avignon stabilized the institution, strengthened its administration and its fiscal policies, and generated new forms of government dependent on territorial domination.

The stamping of the Avignon papacy with the equivocal seal of "France" (strictly speaking, this meant the Latin *Gallia*) is nevertheless highly significant. The Avignon papacy was "French" without actually being French. It never claimed to be French; and its history attests to the sixteenth-century preeminence of cultural identity over identifications that were political and territorial (i.e., "national," in today's parlance). While the Hundred Years' War strengthened a collective awareness of the French kingdom, Avignon signaled in the eyes of English diplomats and Italian humanists the advent of a new collective imagination that melded cultures, a geographic perception of territory and eventually political subjection. The incorporation of Avignon and the Comtat to Revolutionary France — voted by the French population in 1791 — was in this sense the epilogue of a long history of confrontation between two models. With the Revolution, the ancien régime state that France embodied, with religious ambitions made manifest by Gallicanism, finally substituted itself territorially for a universal church placed under the authority of the pope, Vicar of Christ.

Étienne Anheim

367

REFERENCES

Aux origines de l'État moderne: Le fonctionnement administratif de la papauté d'Avignon. Rome: École Française de Rome, 1990.

Bueno, Irene, ed. *Pope Benedict XII (1334–1342): The Guardian of Orthodoxy.* Amsterdam: Amsterdam University Press, 2018.

Favier, Jean. *Les Papes d'Avignon.* Paris: Fayard, 2006.

Guillemain, Bernard. *La cour pontificale d'Avignon (1309–1376).* Paris: De Boccard, 1962.

Rollo-Koster, Joëlle. *Avignon and its Papacy, 1309–1417: Popes, Institutions, and Society.* Lanham, MD: Rowman & Littlefield, 2015.

Theis, Valérie. *Le gouvernement pontifical du Comtat Venaissin (v. 1270 – v. 1350).* Rome: École Française de Rome, 2012.

Vingtain, Dominique, ed. *Monument de l'histoire: Construire, reconstruire le palais des Papes (XIVe–XXe siècle).* Avignon: RMG, 2002.

Zutshi, Patrick. "The Avignon Papacy." In *The New Cambridge Medieval History.* Vol. 6, c. 1300 – c. 1415. Edited by Michael Jones, 653–673. Cambridge: Cambridge University Press, 2000.

RELATED ARTICLES

1282, 1494, 1572

THE GREAT
MONARCHY
OF THE WEST

There it is, recognizably, unmistakable in outline. France appears on the western edge of the world in the *Catalan Atlas* belonging to the library of King Charles V in 1380, the trace of its coastline interrupted by the names of its port towns. Its eastern boundary, formed by four rivers (the Scheldt, the Meuse, the Saône, and the Rhône), is less well defined. This boundary, which came into its own at the end of the fourteenth century, evokes the Treaty of Verdun (843), when the three sons of Emperor Louis the Pious divided up the empire of their grandfather Charlemagne. The *Catalan Atlas*, though, makes no mention of "France." The country did not yet exist as a territorial entity, closed in on itself, speaking one language, and welded by a common sense of nationality — as historians of a later date would imagine it. At the time, it still consisted of an amalgamation of principalities whose rulers, though contractually obligated to the king, sometimes followed an independent course. This was the case with the Duke of Brittany, until his duchy was reunited with the French crown in 1494; and it was particularly the case with the Duke of Burgundy, known as the "Grand Duke of the West," who embodied the contemporary revival of knighthood and the possibility for a principality to endure without being subsumed under a monarchy. This lasted until 1476, when the duke's death put an end to Burgundy's dream.

But let us reexamine the picture: over the still unnamed territory of fourteenth-century France we can already discern banners. The kingdom presents itself as a distinct territory where the limited power of a monarch applies, a monarch who, through his confrontations with the universalist claims of the papacy, has managed to impose himself as an emperor within his own kingdom. In the fifteenth century, the French clergy and the royal faction rallied around the notion of Gallicanism, which defended the independence of the Catholic Church in France against the pope, who was held to have spiritual authority only.

The consolidation of this monarchy in its administrative and sacred roles was without doubt the primary business of the period from the second half of the fourteenth century to the start of the seventeenth. The state took shape in the midst of crisis and in response to crisis: the cycle of calamities that began with the Black Death of 1347, at a time when the population was already in decline from a reversal of circumstances in the early 1300s and possibly from a systemic crisis to the feudal economy. Founded on the premise of continual expansion, this economy suffered when there were no further lands to be cleared in the latter part of the thirteenth century. The feudal system had reached its environmental limits, and its yields decreased, along with seigneurial levies on the labor of the peasantry.

How, then, were knights to continue living nobly? In short, through the profits that could be made from wars. Luckily for the warrior aristocracy, the latter became a constant. The conflict between the Capetian and Plantagenet dynasties had not yet become a war between the kings of France and England, as the Plantagenets, in their capacity as dukes of Aquitaine, were still vassals of the Capets. What began as a simple feudal quarrel lasted from 1328 to 1456, years that saw the state expand its military and fiscal authority. Subsequent historians called it the Hundred Years' War, but for the common people, it was but one more calamity. Before the saga of Joan of Arc, it was experienced primarily as a civil war, for there existed an "English France" that was favorable to the Plantagenets.

This specter of civil war still haunted Europe in the sixteenth century, as religious conflicts intensified after the twin shocks of the Protestant Reformation and the Roman Catholic Counter-Reformation. Culminating in 1572 with the Saint Bartholomew's Day massacre, which ended the great period of atrocities, the cycle came to a close with the assassination of King Henry IV in 1610 at a time when all of European Christendom was at loggerheads, divided between two antagonistic blocks defined by their religious beliefs. With Catholic Spain on one side and Protestant England on the other, France could no longer articulate its history on its own. Here again, our modern categories fail to convey the substance of history: religion no more encompasses all the events of the sixteenth century than nationhood encompasses all those of the fifteenth. In both cases, the need to avert a civil war obliged rulers to champion both war and justice for their people. Warfare was financed by constant taxation in this early modern age, and a sovereign could only justify taxing his subjects as long as he waged war. But he also had to deal with representative assemblies (in France, the Estates General) and therefore accept certain principles and practices regarding representation, negotiation, and contractual agreement. War, paradoxically enough, was the driving force behind the structure of the modern political state in Europe.

When Claude de Seyssel, archbishop of Turin, wrote *La Grant Monarchie de France* in 1519, he wanted to describe the great power that the kingdom of Louis XII and Francis I had become. He also wanted to argue for a political system: a hybrid monarchy moderated by a balance of power between provincial assemblies, central authorities, leading aristocrats, and the urban bourgeoisie. But the monarchy in France was driven by imperial ambitions, not to be constrained by this "kingdom of four rivers" that certain historians have long viewed as the endpoint of the country's historical destiny. The pull of the Mediterranean must account for one of the kingdom's early bids for empire, when the kings of France — from Charles VIII in 1494 (with the conquest of Naples) to Francis I leading the Battle of Marignano in 1515 — took part in the European conflict known as the Italian Wars. Italy was the threshold to the great world beyond, with Naples as the jumping-off point for Jerusalem, and the spirit of the Crusades was rekindled by the hope of new El Dorados — until other destinations, on the far side of the Atlantic, took their place.

1347

The Plague Strikes France

Did it come from Central Asia, Kurdistan, or the Volga region? Regardless, the plague spread through an Old World filled with populations that were increasingly connected to one another. As it made its way up the Rhône Valley, the pandemic made apparent the growing urbanization of the French territory and revealed this territory's integration within a broader community of dangers and fears.

Hong Kong, 1894: the Franco-Swiss doctor Alexandre Yersin, commissioned by the Institut Pasteur and the French government to study the plague epidemic that, after originating in Mongolia, was decimating southern China, identified the plague bacillus just ahead of his Japanese counterpart Kitasato Shibasaburō. First called *Pasteurella pestis* (by Shibasaburō, in homage to Louis Pasteur), the bacterium was renamed *Yersinia pestis*. Four years later, in Karachi, the French doctor Paul-Louis Simond pinpointed the role of the rat flea in the transmission of the disease.

Though scientists still debate the respective roles of human fleas and rat fleas in the transmission of the plague in the Middle Ages, progress in paleomicrobiology has eliminated all doubt regarding one thing: samples taken from mass graves in the cemeteries of Saints-Côme-et-Damien (Montpellier) and Saint-Laurent-de-la-Cabrerisse (a village in the Aude) have shown that *Yersinia pestis* was the infectious agent responsible for the great pandemic that struck France as well as a wide swath of the Old World in the middle of the fourteenth century. Between 1347 and 1352, the disease, which took two forms — bubonic, striking mainly in the spring and summer, and pulmonary (almost always lethal) in the winter — probably killed a third of the population of Europe and up to half the inhabitants of cities. It was that great *mortalitas*, to borrow a word from that time, or, as it has been called since the sixteenth century, the Black Death or Black Plague.

The Black Plague was neither the first nor the last appearance of *Yersinia pestis* on French territory. In the middle of the sixth century, a pandemic known as the "plague of Justinian" had decimated the Mediterranean Basin. Noted in Constantinople in 542, its appearance in Arles was mentioned by Gregory of Tours in year 549 of his *History of the Franks*. In 1720, it landed a final time in Marseille via bales of cotton carried by the *Grand Saint-Antoine*, a ship returning from the Levant, and then spread to surrounding Provençal cities: Arles again, and Avignon, where it died out in 1722.

But France and the world of 1348 no longer resembled the world of Justinian or the land of the Franks in the time of the bishop of Tours. Fourteenth-century France and the wider world looked much more like they did in the eighteenth century. The disease was only contained in Provence thanks to advances in prophylaxis that had resulted from the struggle against the Black Plague: for instance, a return of quarantine and the establishment of lazarets — hospitals for patients afflicted by infectious diseases (the first lazaret surfaced in Venice in 1423; there was also one in Marseille in 1526). To understand the pandemic's ravages in mid-fourteenth-century France, we must consider broader transformations. In the span of three years, the world had become a "carpet that should have been rolled up with everything on it," to quote Ibn Khaldun, a witness to the plague in Tunis in 1348. This world of the Black Plague — the Old World, the world without America, Oceania, or most of interior Africa south of the Sahel — took form in the wake of the Medieval Climate Optimum, a warm climate that lasted from roughly 950 to 1250, and a resulting demographic surge. The fourteenth century, however, witnessed a deterioration of weather conditions, food crises, and the return of wars. At the same time, this world was more interconnected than it had ever been before.

While China was once again playing a leading role, it is highly unlikely that it was the source of the pandemic, as the Andalusian doctor Ibn Khatima believed. Experts have identified three possible sources: Central Asia (where *Yersinia pestis* appeared twenty thousand years ago); the mountains of Kurdistan; and the lower Volga valley. But in 1331, China might have been the location of the first settled basin that was affected by the awakening of the bacillus, shaken from its ecological nest by the movement of Mongol armies. Sacked by Genghis Khan in 1215, Beijing became in 1271 the capital of the Mongolian Yuan dynasty, whose domination extended a few years later to southern China. The 1351 rebellion of the Red Turbans, whose uprising would prove fatal to the Yuan, was likely connected to the devastation of the plague.

The establishment of the Pax Mongolica from the Pacific Ocean to the Volga had encouraged the movement of people and goods over caravan routes that traveled through Eurasia. Persian, Arab, Jewish, Greek, and increasingly Venetian and Genoese merchants provided relay stops for this trade by virtue of contracts made with the Mongol khans of the Golden Horde, who controlled the steppe from western Siberia to its ports on the Caspian and Black Seas. Beyond, in the Mediterranean, trade was mostly monopolized by Italian city-dwellers, whose only competitors were Catalan and Languedoc merchants.

Yersinia pestis thus struck a world in which the Eurasian steppe provided an unprecedented continuum from China to Eastern Europe, a world in which Italian trade networks connected the ports of the Black Sea and those of the Levant to the entire western Mediterranean Basin. Circulating between these two spaces, the Mongol armies that crisscrossed Eurasia make for ideal culprits of transmission now that the bacillus was raging through Central Asia. This is supported by the high death rate at the end of the 1330s in the Nestorian community of the Issyk Kul oasis, south of Lake Balkhash. Still, the tale of the Golden Horde catapulting the bodies of dead infected soldiers over the ramparts and transmitting the plague to besieged Genoese in Kaffa, on the Crimean Peninsula, is no doubt a legend. No matter. The disease, which in 1345 had already ravaged the Horde cities of Saray and Astrakhan, struck Kaffa and the Genoese trading post of Pera, opposite Constantinople, the following year. In 1347, the scourge advanced up the entire Genoese network in the Mediterranean: Messina and Alexandria at the beginning of autumn, Marseille in November 1347, and then Provence, the Languedoc, and the Rhône Valley.

Between November 1347 and November 1348, the plague appeared over the entire territory of present-day France, sparing only a few isolated regions, such as the mountains of the Béarn. Its progression, which crested in the spring and summer, reveals the territorial, political, and social dynamics of fourteenth-century France. Arles and Avignon were struck right after Marseille. The attraction of Avignon, seat of the Holy See since 1309, must have accelerated contagion. With some one hundred dead, including six cardinals, the curia paid a heavy tribute to the disease. From Avignon, the plague traveled up the Rhône Valley. But it was on the roads and in the ports of the Languedoc that it progressed most rapidly, moving toward Barcelona and Valencia. From Bordeaux, stricken in June 1348, it reached England by sea routes then crossed the Channel again, landing in Calais. The English crown had expanded its possessions on the continent out of the Calais region two years earlier, following the defeat of Philip VI in Crécy. The conflict — later called the Hundred Years' War — began in 1337, but was interrupted in 1349 due to the effects of the plague. The pandemic had reached Rouen in June 1348, then Paris, the capital of the kingdom and the largest city in the land, in August.

More than two centuries of urban expansion had created exceptionally dense cities, which were the first to be struck and suffered a disastrous toll. Although estimates are imprecise, fiscal registers, wills, and accounts by clerics reveal the extent of the disaster. The convents of the Mendicant orders, established as close as possible to urban populations — the focus of their preaching — were very often emptied by the plague, as happened in Marseille and Montpellier. It is more difficult to know exactly what took place in the countryside. The parish register of the small town of Givry, in Burgundy, may offer the most precise information about the ravages of the plague. In ordinary times, Givry buried four or five residents per month. In 1348, however, the vicar identified 110 fatalities in August, 302 in September, and 168 in October, when the scourge began to dissipate. While there were no weddings in 1348, eighty-six took place in 1349, half of them in the first two months of the year, when unions contracted at the height of the pandemic were probably made official.

In Paris, whose population hovered between 80,000 and 210,000 before the plague, it is impossible to measure the extent of the disaster. The authorities did take measures, however. Fulfilling the orders of King Philip VI, the masters of the University of Paris published a report in October 1348, the *Compendium de epidemia*, on the illness's proximate and distant causes and also on possible remedies. Lacking an understanding of plague transmission, they conveyed the prevailing medical theories of the time and deemed the corruption of the air responsible for the "pestilence." Their identification three years earlier of the remote cause of the epidemic in the alignment of the planets Jupiter, Saturn, and Mars in the constellation of Aquarius likewise corresponded to current modes of explanation: hot planets — Jupiter and Mars — increased toxic vapors, provoked an unusually warm winter, and corrupted the air. The *Compendium* was read across the kingdom and in all the afflicted European countries, all the way to Poland.

Scholastic reasoning was unable to prove the role of planets as a cause of the plague. In France, as elsewhere in Europe, Jews were accused, along with beggars and lepers, of poisoning the wells. The burning at the stake of two thousand members of Strasbourg's Jewish community on February 14, 1349, is the most lethal illustration of this social response to the disease. Yet *Yersinia pestis* did not disappear. The plague became endemic and broke out at regular intervals — the 1360–62 outbreak proved especially devastating — before losing some of its force in the fifteenth century and gradually disappearing in the seventeenth. The plague of anti-Semitism endured, however. Though it had reached its peak in the kingdom of France before the pandemic, it would find expression through other fears and recriminations and culminate elsewhere in Western Europe at the very end of the Middle Ages.

Julien Loiseau

REFERENCES

Audoin-Rouzeau, Frédérique. *Les Chemins de la peste: Le rat, la puce et l'homme*. Rennes: Presses Universitaires de Rennes, 2003.

Biraben, Jean-Noël. *Les hommes et la peste en France et dans les pays européens et méditerranéens*, vol. 1, *La peste dans l'histoire*, and vol. 2, *Les Hommes face à la peste*. Paris/The Hague: Mouton, 1975.

Byrne, Joseph P. *Encyclopedia of the Black Death*. Santa Barbara: ABC-CLIO, 2012.

Favereau, Marie. *La Horde d'Or: Les héritiers de Gengis Khan*. Lascelles: Éditions de la Flandonnière, 2014.

Green, Monica H., ed. *Pandemic Disease in the Medieval World: Rethinking the Black Death*. The Medieval Globe Books. Leeds, UK: Arc Humanities Press, 2014.

Weill-Parot, Nicolas. "La rationalité médicale à l'épreuve de la peste: Médecine, astrologie et magie (1348–1500)." *Médiévales* 46 (Spring 2014): 73–88.

RELATED ARTICLES

1832, 1891, 1894

1357

Paris and Europe in Revolt

Would a new world order emerge after the Great Plague?
Rumblings of political conflict were heard throughout
Europe. After the revolt led by Étienne Marcel in Paris,
the Great Ordinance of 1357 raised the crucial question
of the role of the Estates General in the balance of power.
The state's willingness to reform became its main claim to
legitimacy.

In 1357, France was in crisis. Devastated by the twenty years
of war it had been waging against England, weakened by the
plague, the country was still suffering from the successional
crisis triggered by the death of all three of Philip IV's sons
without male heirs. The extinction of the Capetian line
and the accession of the Valois to the French throne had
lengthy aftershocks, as there was no shortage of pretenders,
including Charles of Navarre and the English Edward III.
Alongside this political crisis, there was a financial one.
French kings no longer had the means to finance wars
from the proceeds of their seigneurial revenues alone. A

new system of taxation was needed, one that levied both direct and indirect taxes — as the English had been doing for more than a half century. But this required negotiating with the Estates General, the assembly composed of the king's principal vassals from the secular and ecclesiastical realms and representatives of the fortified towns. The latter pushed back against the king's overtures. Leading the revolt were the burghers or wealthy bourgeois of Paris, headed by Étienne Marcel, provost of the city's merchants. They had no objection to contributing to the state's coffers, recognizing that the defense of the realm was a sacred obligation that justified a heavy tax. But the bourgeois of Paris asked for certain concessions in return, chief among them the reform of royal institutions in the Capetian tradition, along the lines of the Great Ordinance proclaimed by King Louis IX in 1254. Furthermore, Parisians had political aspirations tied to their city. As with towns in Flanders, Paris guarded its autonomy and sought to defend its privileges by tightening its hold over the small towns and rural districts in the surrounding area.

The Estates General convened at least once a year from 1355 to 1358, and at those sessions the opponents of the Valois dynasty made their opposition felt. France's kings — Philip VI (r. 1328–1350) and John II (r. 1350–1364) — had racked up a string of defeats to the English. The French lost naval control of the English Channel at the Battle of Sluys (1340) and were further humbled at the Battle of Crécy (1346).

The following year, the English captured Calais, securing a bridgehead on the continent that they would keep for two hundred years. Then in 1356, King John II was captured at the Battle of Poitiers.

Each of these setbacks weakened the French monarchy further, forcing it into concessions. In December 1355, the Estates General granted the king a new tax, but also obtained the right to collect it themselves. After John II's capture at Poitiers, his dauphin, Charles, acquiesced to the demands of the most virulent opponents of his father's authoritarian, disorganized, and unpopular monarchy. The ordinance of March 3, 1357, largely inspired by Étienne Marcel and his supporters, outlined an English-style government where sovereignty was shared between the monarch and the Estates General, who together composed the mystic body of the kingdom. The ordinance reconfirmed the assembly's monopoly over taxation. A commission was formed to purge royal institutions, and representatives from the Estates General were given a seat on the Royal Council.

When the reformers tried to put their political program into effect, however, they met insurmountable obstacles. The taxpayers were no more willing to pay tax collectors from the Estates General than they had been to pay the king's. Tax rebellions erupted on all sides, with the encouragement of John II, who was afraid that the measures taken in his absence would delay negotiations with the English and consequently his release. Étienne Marcel and his supporters grew more radical, entering into an alliance with the pretender Charles of Navarre. When peasants revolted in Champagne and Valois in June 1358, a season of violence known as the Jacquerie, Marcel wavered in his response to the disorderly mob, driven to insurrection by the harshness of the warrior class and, no doubt, by the ever-increasing demands of an impoverished nobility whose military defeats left it discredited. In the end, Marcel met the same fate as Jacob van Artevelde, the wealthy brewer from Ghent who made a bid for power in Flanders. On July 31, 1358, he was assassinated by Parisian burghers who supported Charles, the dauphin. The rebelling peasants, meanwhile, were brutally punished. Charles was able to return to Paris and parade in victory before the bodies of Marcel and his friends.

The richly fraught political era from 1355 to 1358, which has evaporated from popular awareness of France's national history, long fascinated nineteenth-century historians. Jules Michelet, for instance, saw the ordinance of March 3 as "France's first action." The French people had for the first time manifested their desire to throw off the yoke of monarchy. In the years since Michelet, historians have restored the events of the mid-fourteenth century to a truer perspective. The Estates General represented only France's political and economic elites. And we shouldn't ascribe class consciousness to the bourgeois of the fortified cities, who were affiliated for the most part with the aristocratic factions dominating the political landscape. Today historians no longer study the Estates General as an organic structure in its own right. Instead, they try to identify the different networks of power that fought to obtain seats in the Royal Council, increase their influence in the king's household, and gain supporters in the Estates General.

Historians have also analyzed the institutional dialogue between the ruler and his subjects from the perspective of historical anthropology. In this view, the dialogue proceeded according to subtle stages, but always against a background of unanimity. No differences of opinion were acknowledged, and conflict between the governing and the governed was literally unthinkable. The medieval representative assemblies, whether the English Parliament, the Spanish Cortes, the German Diets, or the French Estates General, were among the privileged places where the realm's communal unity was on view. Consultations between the king and these assemblies could have only one outcome: immediate concession on the part of the subjects to their king's requests, which were usually fiscal in nature, coupled in return with a liberal granting of privileges or political concessions on the part of the king. This was not about appearances alone. All the players in this political game were sincerely convinced that good government was impossible without consensus.

It would be highly reductive, however, to describe the events of 1355 to 1358 as either a simple conflict between aristocratic parties or a stereotyped political ritual in which everything had been worked out in advance. What is more, personal conflicts such as this one do not necessarily prevent a debate of ideas. The most brilliant intellectuals of the day deliberated on the role of the sovereign, the limits of his power, the nature of the public good, the rights of the community, and the legitimacy of taxes in ways that strike us today as surprisingly modern. Political science came into its own at that moment, drawing lessons from a crisis that engulfed the whole continent.

These events in France must be understood within the European context. A large sector of the Christian world was simultaneously experiencing social and political convulsions. In the early fourteenth century, a decline in the cloth industry led to a wave of uprisings against the governing merchant elites of the leading Flemish towns. Insurrectional governments were established, which the King of England turned to his advantage in his war against the Valois dynasty in France. The rebellion in coastal Flanders had barely been crushed in 1328 when Jacob van Artevelde seized power in Ghent in 1338 and formed an alliance with the English king. Although van Artevelde was assassinated in 1345, his son Philip took up the cause after him in 1382.

In the meantime, Europe went through an apocalyptic cataclysm. The Black Death killed between a quarter and a third of Europe's population and wreaked havoc on its economic order between 1347 and 1349. Land became widely available, while manpower was in short supply. Wages shot upward, reaching levels in the late fourteenth and early fifteenth centuries that would not be matched for another four or five hundred years. In every corner of Europe, governments issued regulations limiting prices and wages, but they were unsuccessful. Though circumstances seemed to favor the poor, rebellions continued to erupt across the continent. How could one enjoy higher wages when war raged and the old economy fell apart?

After the Black Death, it seemed that a new world might emerge. It was a time of abundant opportunities for those who knew how to make use of them. Chaucer's *Canterbury Tales* mourned the disappearance of an idealized world order, whose workingmen took hard toil in stride and whose stern knights lived up to their social and political obligations. Chaucer denounced the unscrupulous landowners who were now putting their property to commercial use and driving off their workers to raise flocks of sheep and sell wool for export. Sheep were devouring men, as people put it. "When Adam delved and Eve span, who was then the gentleman?" asked the Lollards, rebels in rural England led by itinerant preachers. They marched on London in 1381. King Richard

II brutally quelled their rebellion after temporarily coming to terms with them. At the same moment in Italy, textile workers known as the Ciompi were taking over Florence's government.

In the 1380s, popular unrest lessened, and the revolutionary wave seemed to have subsided. But was it accurate to even describe these events as a wave? When historical materialism was the dominant ideology in universities, these massive uprisings were viewed as interconnected rebellions rooted in economic depression and social inequality. Those conditions certainly existed; to deny the primordial importance of social and economic factors would hamstring history's ability to present an overall theory. Yet if the popular uprising in Paris was influenced by the urban rebellions in Flanders, it would be inaccurate to talk of a coherent political movement that, across Europe, followed a common ideology.

In the end, this all-encompassing crisis, which occurred simultaneously on the demographic, economic, social, political, and spiritual fronts, allowed new social groups to emerge, but without fashioning a new world. In Florence and in other republican city-states, a new Italian elite drove out the old. After a few decades of relative political openness, the doors of the councils of government closed again for another half millennium. The European monarchies all emerged from the troubles strengthened. The French king even managed to strip his subjects of the right of consent to taxation. The Estates General would serve only to echo royal propaganda and provide the sovereign with legitimacy during periods of crisis. France, which according to a well-worn pun was the land of men who were "frank," or free, had become a country of serfs, taxable at will by their monarch.

Amable Sablon du Corail

REFERENCES

Arnoux, Mathieu. *Le temps des laboureurs: Travail, ordre social et croissance en Europe (XIe–XIVe siècle)*. Paris: Albin Michel, 2012.

Autrand, Françoise. *Charles V le Sage*. Paris: Fayard, 2000.

Blockmans, Wim, André Holenstein, and Jon Mathieu. *Empowering Interactions: Political Cultures and the Emergence of the State in Europe, 1300–1900*. Farnham: Ashgate, 2009.

Cazelles, Raymond. *La société politique et la crise de la royauté sous Philippe de Valois*. Paris: Librairie d'Argences, 1958.

Hébert, Michel. *Parlementer: Assemblées représentatives et échange politique en Europe occidentale à la fin du Moyen Âge*. Paris: De Boccard, 2014.

Henneman, John Bell. *Royal Taxation in 14th-Century France: The Captivity and Ransom of John II, 1356–1370*. Princeton: Princeton

University Press, 1976.

Mollat, Michel, and Philippe Wolff. *The Popular Revolutions of the Late Middle Ages*. London: Allen & Unwin, 1973.

RELATED ARTICLES

1347, 1789, 1848, 1871, 1968

1380

An Image of the World in a Library

The year Charles V died, the *Catalan Atlas* was added to
the collections of the Louvre's library, sometimes seen
as a precursor to the universalist project of the French
national library, the Bibliothèque Nationale de France.
This nautical map presents a picture of France, not as
geographical entity, but as a realm of kings.

In the fourteenth century, how could a king of France
apprehend his kingdom? Extended to perceptions of the
universe, this question about the politics of space cannot
elude the belated emergence of cartography as an instrument
of government. Whereas by the thirteenth century, royal
power rested upon a continuous state that was gradually
establishing its territory and subsequently its borders, it
wasn't until the 1380s that a French king could avail himself
of an "atlas," or rather a "mappemonde" — an "image of
the world."

For a long time, images of the world reflected a desire
to connect religious notions of time to those of physical

space: this space was a theological cosmos, a text to decipher much more than a region to explore. As a field of positive knowledge, geography was used to wage war or exchange goods; it was also subjected to restraints imposed by people's imaginations. There were no maps to authoritatively and completely contain a confusing reality, to unite the world as a space and a temporality. In the fourteenth century, both time and space began to gradually take on independent identities. The time of states — characterized by clocks, the oldest of which, found in France, dates from the reign of Charles V (r. 1364–1380) — became distinct from the time of the world.

Perhaps paradoxically, those same states — i.e., territories with shifting borders — were entering a world space that was being actively enlarged by explorers, from Marco Polo (between 1271 and 1295) to John Mandeville (between 1322 and 1356). A century before Vasco da Gama circled the globe, the world was indisputably opening up. As maps unfolded, time seemed to shrink. The disconnect was unprecedented, and perhaps generative. Still, how do we make sense of the era's contemporaneous representations of "France" and the "world"?

An extraordinary document, the *Catalan Atlas* (1375) was preserved in the royal collections of the Louvre Palace between 1381 and 1411. The king, or at least his advisers, were thus able to consult it. To what purpose? The only uses that historians have documented for certain revolve around pleasure and contemplation; after all, this graphic object was the only one of its kind in the library. Carefully woven together, text and images unfold in a polyptych of twelve vellum sheets on seven wood panels: an illustrated screen as much as a nautical chart that could be "read" in two directions and hence depicts the rotundity of the earth while superimposing images of the origins and the end of the world — i.e., of time. Halfway between the mappemondes found in the encyclopedias of the Scholastics and the portolan nautical charts that had been used by sailors on the Mediterranean since the end of the thirteenth century, the *Atlas* invites readers on a journey around a world surrounded by seas. Created in the Majorcan workshop of the Jewish cosmographer Abraham Cresques, this "quarto of the sea" written in Catalan displays what was known about physical space at the time of its creation.

Additionally, this document presents the world order as decreed by God, from the Creation to the Apocalypse, including the coming of Gog and Magog, locked up by Alexander the Great, who appears in the atlas at the feet of Christ the Savior. The "Extreme West," seen beyond an ocean that is starkly empty but features one of the first rose compasses ever drawn, connects with Earthly Paradise, which appears on the opposite end of the polyptych. At that tip of the original world we see the promontory of the Canary Islands and the African Río de Oro, which had been explored by the Majorcan sailor Jaume Ferrer in 1346. Jerusalem is predictably located at the center of the *orbis terrarum*, but the world no longer appears as a Western construct, for, in the *Catalan Atlas*, the beating heart of peoples, kingdoms, and riches of the world is found in the space of the Islamic empires. If Western Europe occupies two sections, the "Middle East" in the broad sense — from the Aegean Sea to the Indian peninsula — unfolds over three panels, while the last two are reserved for East Asia. On the other side of the world, the end of time is continental, enclosed in mountains located to the northwest of "Cathay" (China). This distant memory of the Mongols from the preceding century substantiated the terror linked to the army of Timur, in power since 1369 in Samarkand.

The world of the *Catalan Atlas* is foremost one of sailors. Islands are especially well represented, and the edges of the Mediterranean, the Black Sea, the Caspian, and the North Sea are easily identified. While the Persian Gulf is drawn, the Indian Ocean remains an "oneiric horizon" (as Jacques Le Goff put it) that is absent and thus not connected to the Red Sea. This explains why Africa remains collapsed on itself, with Ethiopia in the east next to Mali in the west. The *Atlas* primarily represents geographical entities that are accompanied by real captions in red and blue capital letters. Europe includes England, Castile, Lombardy, Poland,

Sweden, Germany, Bavaria, Hungary, and more, but the word "France" does not appear. We can easily recognize that famous "kingdom of four rivers," bordered to the east by the Rhône, the Saône, the Meuse, and the Scheldt, all of which appear on the map, but this space remains frustratingly unnamed.

The *Catalan Atlas* thus suggests that, in the eyes of the world, France did not truly exist at the end of the fourteenth century as a geographical entity. It remained the realm of a prince whose claims of sovereignty ebbed and flowed depending on the balance of power he maintained with his immediate neighbors at any given time.

A graphic detail in fact reveals an underlying logic of distinction and even competition within the work. Whereas African kingdoms and Eastern sultanates are represented by more or less allegorical figures, the territories that include Western Europe remain abstract, identified by banners that fly over the budding capitals of state powers, which were just beginning to lead separate lives from their rulers. The heraldic symbols themselves seem fluid. Fleurs-de-lis are indeed placed over the depiction of Paris, but they also decorate the scepter of the ruler of Mali, Mansa Musa.

Much of the meaning conveyed by the *Atlas* remains a mystery to us. Was it equally opaque for its owner? This "quarto of the sea" was an encyclopedia of images more than an instrument of power, a political and eschatological agenda more than a radioscopy of the world.

The *Catalan Atlas* was also a valuable collectible gifted to a king by an ally, the wife of the King of Aragon, which was an early prototype of a maritime empire, before Portugal. This ally was also a relative of the king. Violant of Bar, cousin of the young King Charles VI and wife of the Infante John I, had this unique object sent on the occasion of the new king's accession. It is possible, however, that the commission was older — ordered by Charles V himself, who was planning to add to the "knowledge-based treasure" he had inherited and grown through a politics of translation and scholarly compilation that followed the model set by Alexander. According to its four surviving inventories, the Louvre library contained more than 900 manuscript volumes, the equivalent of more than 1,700 original texts or works. With more than two-thirds of its contents in French, this library reflects the universal rise of a vernacular language that, from a primarily literary idiom, had become one of government and practical knowledge. Like the pope, the King of France strove to dominate the universality of knowledge, if not that of power. Translations of the Bible and the political works of Aristotle (Alexander's tutor) made it possible for an entire abstract and theoretical vocabulary to find expression in French. This included *politique* and *gouvernement*, but also *spéculation* and *autonomie*.

Further, Aristotle's *On the Heavens*, translated into

French by Nicole Oresme, gave the language the means to rival Greek and Latin in describing the entire world as a reality and as a representation. Along with *infini* (infinite), there appeared *différence* and *sapience* (wisdom), qualities that were now ascribed to a state that was gradually fixing the borders of its territory at the very moment when the world seemed not to have any. Following its purchase in 1424 by John, Duke of Bedford, the regent of France and England, the Louvre's holdings would be irremediably scattered. Being the personal property of rulers, the library did not yet belong to a nation-state even if its holdings made it possible to imagine and conceive such a thing.

A mirror of the world rather than an instrument for its exploration, in a world in which "France" existed only by default, the *Catalan Atlas* took its place on the shelves of a library as an encyclopedic treasure through which the prince convinced himself he could conquer all the knowledge of the world. In the sixteenth century, humanism determined a new policy for the transmission and control of the language. Seven years after the creation of the Collège de France in 1530, and two years before the Ordinance of Villers-Cotterêts (which ordered the use of French in legal acts and official ordinances), the Ordinance of Montpellier of December 28, 1537, codified the administration of knowledge and the regulation of books by requiring that copies of all "printed matter," including maps, be deposited in the king's library. The royal reader Oronce Finé deposited the oldest preserved "map of France" in 1553. The memory of Charles V's library was now cherished: King Francis I affixed his ex libris onto the inventory recovered in 1380, just as the *Catalan Atlas* was resurfacing in the personal collections of Louis XII.

Since then, the *Atlas* has been preserved without interruption in what, under the name of Bibliothèque Nationale de France, has become since the French Revolution the setting for a certain French claim to universality. Expanded through the confiscation and nationalization of ecclesiastical property after 1790, the library forged its own founding myth as a direct descendant of the library of Alexandria by appropriating the earlier, fourteenth-century collection. In 1995, François Mitterrand inaugurated the ultimate architectural avatar of the universal library with a cornerstone from a tower of the Louvre, an odd conflation in which the cult of national memory claims to contain the knowledge of the world.

Yann Potin

REFERENCES

Balayé, Simone. *Histoire de la Bibliothèque nationale, des origines à 1800.* Geneva: Droz, 1988.

Bertrand, Olivier, ed. *Sciences et savoirs sous Charles V*. Paris: Honoré
Champion, 2014.

Dauphant, Léonard. *Le Royaume des quatre rivières: L'espace politique
français (1380–1515)*. Paris: Champ Vallon, 2012.

Gautier-Dalché, Patrick. "Un problème d'histoire culturelle:
Perception et représentation de l'espace au Moyen Âge."
Médiévales 9, no. 18 (1990): 5–15.

Potin, Yann. "Des inventaires pour catalogues? Les archives d'une
bibliothèque médiévale: la librairie royale du Louvre (1368–
1429)." In *Bibliothek als Archiv*, edited by Hans Erich Bödeker and
Anne Saada, 119–39. Göttingen: Vandenhoeck & Ruprecht, 2007.

RELATED ARTICLES
1270, 1357, 1539, 1769, 1875

1420

The Marriage of France and England

"The infamous Treaty of Troyes," which in 1420 sealed the French military defeat at Agincourt, has been a potent symbol of national humiliation ever since. The treaty is said to have gifted France to a foreign power — until Joan of Arc came riding to the rescue. Another, more plausible version approaches the treaty as a serious attempt to build perpetual peace between two kingdoms under a single sovereign.

France–England, March 19, 2016: once again, the French rugby team was beaten by its favorite adversary, England, in the annual Six Nations tournament. Of the participating nations (England, France, Wales, Ireland, Scotland, and Italy), five adjoin or are close to the English Channel. As a rule, the welter of symbolism on display during this intensely competitive tournament is rivaled only by the accompanying manipulation of national memory. With the threat of Brexit looming and a general feeling of decline in the air, an ordinary sporting setback assumed an extra layer of gloom that year. Stung by a growing British disenchantment they saw as "Francophobic," the French media promoted the idea that France and England were bound together by links that were historically "sacred."

Around the same time, the aristocratic de Villiers family and the National Front were claiming the honor of securing Joan of Arc's personal ring, bought at auction from an English collector with the (alleged) personal support of Queen Elizabeth II. On April 22, the weekly *L'Obs* warned darkly that "three times in history, there have been attempts to unite France and England as a single country": namely, September 1956, on the eve of the Suez Canal crisis; June 1940, at the suggestion of Jean Monnet, following France's military collapse; and above all in May 1420, when the Treaty of Troyes consecrated a perpetual union of France and England under a single sovereign. The project of Anglo-French unity submitted by General de Gaulle to the head of government Paul Reynaud on June 16, 1940, affirmed that "in an hour of peril that will decide the destiny of the modern world, the governments of the French Republic and the United Kingdom make this declaration of indissoluble union.... The two governments declare that France and Great Britain will henceforth be separate nations no longer, but a Franco–British union."

In 2016, it thus seemed as though the specter of a British divorce from France and Europe was calling into question the foundations of a certain national identity. Did this display the contradictions exaggerated by journalism, or a genuine paradox of history?

After Brexit was decided in Britain's June 2016 referendum, nobody dared mention the sixtieth anniversary of the failed union negotiated by Guy Mollet and Anthony Eden, which was intended to support the influence of the old colonial nations in the Middle East against the new American and Soviet superpowers. On the other hand, amid a frenzy of nationalism on both sides of the Channel, the traditional parade of the royalist Action Française party that May was dedicated to "Joan of Arc, symbol of France for the French." Supporters of Action Française — released for the first time since 1979 from political vampirization by the National Front — shouted other slogans, such as "We want Jeanne d'Arc, not Brussels." Their banners proclaimed that the "shameful treaty of Troyes" had prompted the national heroine to take up arms for France.

Joan of Arc's canonization by the pope had come very late — on May 16, 1920, a few days prior to the five hundredth anniversary of the dismal treaty. Alert to the danger of leaving the Catholic Church in sole possession of St. Joan, the French Parliament responded by proclaiming May 8 as France's patriotic feast day. As a secular *and* Catholic saint, the Virgin of Orléans now had two feast days: May 8, to commemorate her staving off of the Siege of Orléans in 1429, and May 30, when she was burned at the stake as a heretic in 1431 in Rouen.

Thus Joan's legend was consecrated rather late and by competing memorials in the aftermath of World War I. The month of May — traditionally associated with weddings and the Virgin Mary — was an odd choice; and indeed the confusion and manipulation of these commemorative events was later to reach a discreet apotheosis, when, as luck (or de Gaulle's diplomacy) would have it, May 8 coincided with the final capitulation of Nazi Germany to the Allies in 1945, bringing World War II to an end on a date that was eminently French. This was bound to help erase both the memory of the defeat of collaborationist Vichy France, and the long dependence and subordination of the Free French to the United Kingdom.

An archaeology of the constructions of national identity pieced together during the nineteenth century must consider the ambiguous, quasi-reversible roles of Joan of Arc and the Treaty of Troyes. At stake was a schizophrenic, mythographic, all-but-religious dependence on the idea that defeat was somehow necessary if French identity was to be fully asserted. Still, the cult of a fantasy union between France and England would seem indissociable from the cult of Joan of Arc.

And in order that peace, tranquility and concord shall in future times perpetually exist between the realms of France and England…by the advice and consent of the three estates of the said realms…it shall be commanded and decreed that in the time when our son or any of his heirs shall assume the throne of France, the two crowns of France and England shall perpetually and forever remain together and united, and shall be vested in the same person…who shall be the temporal king and sovereign lord of both realms, as it is said, whilst preserving in all other things, for each realm, its own rights, liberties, customs, usages, and laws.

The peaceful utopia evoked by article 24 of the Treaty of Troyes is a simple one: with a view to reestablishing universal peace, King Charles VI of France, demented for a full thirty years, gave his daughter Catherine in marriage to Henry V, king of England, who thereby became his adoptive son through the principle of carnal union. As king of France and England, Henry became the guarantor of the customs and usages of both realms, fraternally united as they were despite their differences. To achieve this, another trick of history had been played, which was pithily summed up by Jules Michelet: "It had taken the King of England three years to conquer Normandy; the death of John the Fearless appeared to have given him all France in a single day."

Ever since 1407, when the Duke of Orléans was assassinated by John the Fearless, Duke of Burgundy,

Valois France had been torn between the Armagnac and Burgundian factions. This led to a civil war that made it possible to revive England's ancient claim to the French throne. The shocking defeat at Agincourt on October 25, 1415, was seen as a fresh punishment sent by God for the illegitimacy of the last Valois dauphin, Charles (the future Charles VII), suspected of being a bastard son of Louis d'Orléans and a feeble prince from an exhausted line. After the successive deaths of three of his elder brothers — Charles in 1401, Louis in 1415, Jean in 1417 — the dauphin could not resist the desire for vengeance of his Orléans and Armagnac cousins. By murdering his other cousin, John the Fearless, on the bridge of Montereau in September 1419, Charles committed an act of high treason that, according to the Estates of the city of Paris, disqualified him from holding any crown.

"By the advice and consent of the three estates of the said realms": in the nineteenth century, as the memory of the three constituent estates of the Estates General (clergy, nobility, and Third Estate [which included the rest of the population]) tended to reconcile constitutional royalists with republicans in a shared cult of collective democratic sovereignty, politicians avoided any mention of their "consent" as a precondition that conferred legitimacy on the Treaty of Troyes. Instead, these politicians personalized the drama of the treaty and, giving free rein to every form of xenophobia, condemned this "shameful treaty" as an "infamous" betrayal concocted by a German queen, Isabel of Bavaria, and a Burgundian cousin obsessed with Lotharingian independence. After all, Germany became France's new hereditary enemy after 1870.

And yet the Treaty of Troyes was anything but a historic coup de théâtre: it represented a quasi-performative triumph of collective representations, with shared beliefs governing events that seemed anodyne.

Historians have long emphasized the structural dimension of the Joan of Arc interlude. To galvanize his troops in 1429, the dauphin's propaganda outfit seized on an ancient prophecy attributed to Merlin, which suggested that France would be saved by a virgin. In the absence of any other political certainty, Joan herself found in this a rationale for her short life. This political fable was part of a fierce propaganda war. In its attempt to establish a "final peace" through the adoption of France by England, the Treaty of Troyes also sought justification in a prophecy by St. Bridget of Sweden (1303–1373). The treaty was realistic when it came to law, however. Western diplomats were for the most part keen on royal unifications in the fourteenth and fifteenth centuries. Witness the unification of Poland and the Grand Duchy of Lithuania at Krewo in 1385; the unification of the Scandinavian kingdoms at Kalmar in 1397; the unification of Poland, Bohemia, and Hungary during the same century; the unification of Castile and Aragon beginning in 1479; not to mention the Holy Roman Empire itself and the union of the crowns of France and Navarre between 1284 and 1328.

According to article 26 of the Treaty of Troyes, the agreement was extensible within eight months of its signature to the alliances contracted by the twin crowns of France and England, and thence to the whole of Christendom, which had been racked by schism since 1378. In his analysis of the treaty, historian Jean-Marie Moeglin has proposed a rewriting of the Hundred Years' War: From the end of the thirteenth century to the incestuous wedding at Troyes, the obsession with marriage between the reigning families of France and England was as much the effect as the cause of their conflicts. In this sense, the Treaty of Troyes was a response to a fundamental medieval belief whereby unity and universality constituted one and the same thing — with no connection whatsoever to "national" ideals. This episode in medieval political history was so magnified in later expressions of the national narrative that Joan of Arc has become a providential figure for republicans, royalists, Catholics, and secularists alike. But Troyes was actually an event of global ambition, as utopian and prophetic as it was "family-based." In stark contrast, the republican cult of Joan of Arc was founded in 1839 by the concerted erudition and narration of historians Jules

Michelet and Jules Quicherat in response to an account of Joan's trial by the German Catholic historian Joseph Görres.

In short, this whole story is a sublime example of the engendering of the self by the other. Later, it would guide the first steps of Jean Monnet, one of the founders of modern Europe, who invoked the Treaty of Troyes as a supreme example when, in June 1940, he attempted to accomplish the impossible: a European Union.

Yann Potin

REFERENCES

Bonenfant, Paul. *Du meurtre de Montereau au traité de Troyes*. Bruxelles: Palais des Académies, 1958.

Bove, Boris. *La Guerre de Cent Ans*. Paris: Belin, 2015.

Guichard, Jean-Pierre. *Paul Reynaud, un homme d'État dans la tourmente (septembre 1939–juin 1940)*. Paris: L'Harmattan, 2008.

Moeglin, Jean-Marie. "Récrire l'histoire de la guerre de Cent Ans: Une relecture historique et historiographique du traité de Troyes (21 mai 1420)." *Revue historique* 664 (2012): 887–919.

Potin, Yann. "1420, traité de Troyes: Le rêve oublié d'une paix perpétuelle." In *Histoire du monde au XVe siècle*, edited by Patrick Boucheron, 320–324. Paris: Fayard, 2009.

RELATED ARTICLES
1051, 1137, 1662, 1790, 1858, 1913, 1940

1446

An Enslaved Black Man in Pamiers

Unlike serfs, whose harsh bondage entailed legal rights,
enslaved people in the Middle Ages were no more than
personal property. They were trafficked heavily from the
Black Sea to the Mediterranean. A trial in the town of
Pamiers gives us an insight into household slavery as it
existed in princely courts and the cities of southern France.

In Pamiers, in the county of Foix just north of the Spanish
border, a sensational trial was held in 1446 about the case of
an enslaved black man from Barcelona, Antoine Simon, who
had escaped and joined the household of Pierre Toc, a deputy
magistrate of the county. At the request of the slaveholder, a
Barcelona merchant named Pons Ferrer, the Count of Foix's
bailiff had arrested Antoine Simon and imprisoned him in
the castle. In his defense, Pierre Toc pointed to Pamiers's
customs, dating back to 1228, guaranteeing freedom to
all residents of the town. Otherwise, Toc said, he would
have let Simon continue on to Toulouse, a known haven.
The case was heatedly argued, and the hearing lasted three

days, with many citizens of Pamiers offering testimony. A merchant reported that during his father's consulship, a runaway Greek slave named George had been freed and welcomed as a resident of the town, as had another Greek named Nicholas, who belonged to the commander of the Tor hospital. The decretist in charge of the proceedings, Jean de Belaybre, confessed that he himself was the son of a once-enslaved woman, who had married and been freed after arriving in Pamiers. In his opinion, this freedom was a privilege, as it provided an exception to property rights. This responded to the Barcelona merchant's claims that he had paid a high price for Simon (100 Aragonese florins) and that Simon had thus committed robbery, the theft of his own person. As the head of a powerful family of merchants and shipowners, with operations extending down the African coast, Pons Ferrer had no intention of allowing a humble town council to deprive him of his property rights.

On October 31, 1446, after three days of hearings, Antoine Simon was formally freed and made a citizen of Pamiers in due and proper form.

Although we associate the Middle Ages with bondage of various kinds, slavery is not generally one of them. Slavery is more usually identified with the civilizations of ancient Greece and Rome or with the modern colonial powers and their slave trade. Yet throughout the early Middle Ages, the classical world's tradition of slavery persisted, particularly in the barbarian kingdoms. There is clear evidence on the European continent until the mid-eleventh century and in the British Isles until the early twelfth.

Where Latin was spoken, it is difficult to tell the slave from the serf, since both are referred to as *servus*. In Old English, though, it is easy enough to follow the use and eventual disappearance of the word *theow*, which meant slave. Evidence of a gradual and massive reduction in the ownership, sale, and trading of enslaved people continues into the Carolingian period, petering out toward the tenth century. The more characteristic form of subjection during medieval times, serfdom, differs from slavery in that the social inferiority of the serf exists within the context of seigneurial holdings. The ownership of serfs could be transferred with the land on which they lived, but there was neither a market nor traders, as had existed for slaves in Verdun in the ninth and tenth centuries. The serf was born on the land, a homegrown native, whereas slavery implies the removal of a person from his native soil and his introduction into an alien social and cultural context. A new word was coined in the late Middle Ages for this radical subjection, *esclave*, from which our word "slave" derives, gaining its modern meaning in parts of southern Italy that were under Norman domination and Byzantine cultural influence. The word was first accepted into spoken Romance languages, then in the twelfth century into literature, before replacing *servus* in charters and legal deeds.

After slavery disappeared on the continent, the abduction and sale of human beings continued around the Mediterranean Basin. A geographical division took shape: slavery was unknown throughout France and northern Europe, but it continued to exist and even abruptly increased in every region of the Mediterranean. In all the zones of contact between Christians and Muslims, men and women continued to be captured and taken into captivity as casualties of war, privateering, or piracy, in the context of the centuries-old conflict between Islam and the Christian world.

There are three major periods in the history of medieval slavery as it relates to the Christian lands of the western Mediterranean. Up to the mid-thirteenth century, captivity was restricted to "Moors" and "Saracens," that is, to Muslims from Spain, North Africa, and the Mediterranean islands. Slavery went hand in hand with the *Reconquista*, the retaking of the Iberian Peninsula from the Moors, and the Frankish conquests in Italy and Sicily. At the end of the thirteenth century, ports in the western Mediterranean saw a new influx of enslaved people from the East thanks to the commercial shipping routes that sprang up after the Genoese opened a trading mission on the Black Sea in 1261, in the Crimean port of Kaffa. The slave markets trafficked in Russians, Tatars, Turks, Bulgarians, as well as Greeks and Albanians, swelling the coffers of Italian and Catalan traders. The third period, starting in the fifteenth century, saw a massive shift to enslaving Africans, a consequence of Portuguese expeditions down the Atlantic coast of Africa, which supplanted the overland caravans crossing the Sahara to Libya. The trading post on the island of Arguin in Mauritania became a transit point for tens of thousands of souls, traded on a hitherto unknown scale.

France took no part in this traffic. Enslaved people escaping from Catalonia were constantly taking refuge in one of the towns that safeguarded their freedom, such as Pamiers and Toulouse, where the aldermen strictly enforced the custom that by setting foot within the town's precincts, a person was declared free. In the early years, a few towns on the Languedoc coast such as Montpellier and Narbonne allowed slaves to enter. In Narbonne, the tariff established in 1153 was five sous for the sale and three sous for the transit through town of a Saracen man or woman. There are later instances of Montpellier merchants and Narbonne shipowners taking part in the slave trade in Marseille or Barcelona, but slavery seems to disappear from those towns by the fourteenth century, or to continue only sporadically.

Still, slavery remained in existence in the county of Provence, which was part of the Holy Roman Empire, and in the Roussillon, a dependency of the kingdom of Aragon. Records of slave sales in Marseille are found among the earliest extant notarial deeds, dating from the mid-thirteenth century. There were many enslaved people in the major cities, Marseille and Perpignan; in the ports along the southern coast, Toulon, Fréjus, and Nice; and in the towns of the interior, including Avignon, Tarascon, Arles, and Aix. The geographic limits of slavery coincided with the boundaries of the counties of Provence and Roussillon. Slavery was nonexistent farther north in the Rhône Valley, in Valence and Lyon.

Where they were found, enslaved people lived mostly in cities or small towns, but a few lived in the countryside: in Roussillon, in 1271, a farmstead was sold "with garden, outbuildings, donkey, and Saracen." Most worked at household tasks, though it is often difficult to pinpoint their status because the source materials — basically deeds of sale — are far from prolix. A Tatar woman was sold as a slave in Marseille in 1367, allowing the buyer "to have her, keep her, give her away, sell her, exchange her, and do with her what he pleases." In the fourteenth and fifteenth centuries, eastern slaves, often from Russia or the Caucasus, could serve as wet nurses or be hired out by their owners according to need, while others were forced into prostitution. Some enslaved people became apprentices, particularly those belonging to artisans: in Perpignan they could work as skivers, dyers, tanners, and in naval yards. Where slavery was practiced, in Provence and Roussillon, it penetrated deep into the social fabric. Enslaved people were found not only in the households of the aristocracy and the high clergy, but also among millers, butchers, tailors, fishermen, and a great many merchants. In late medieval times, then, slavery was essentially an urban and domestic phenomenon, but it was also a feature of princely courts. Anticipating later developments, slaves were seen as luxury items and symbols of social status, a trend that extended well beyond the edges of the Mediterranean and was seen, for example, in the Burgundian court, the courts of the dukes of Berry and Orléans, and in the royal court of France itself.

Unlike serfs, who enjoyed legal rights, however limited, slaves were treated as items of personal property and subject to property law, as Pons Ferrer had claimed in Pamiers. Lawsuits about slaves were argued in commercial courts, such as the Maritime Consulate in Perpignan, or, if the owner was a cleric, before an ecclesiastical council. On the slaveholder's death, his slaves were bequeathed in his will, but some slaves might be freed as an act of piety, especially after a long period of cohabitation. In 1381, a man from Marseille freed an enslaved woman, Lucy, in his will; she had lived with him for thirteen years and borne him several children. The release from slavery might be immediate and unconditional, or it might occur after a variable length of time and require a series of payments. Christine, an enslaved Tatar woman who belonged to a wealthy merchant from

Marseille and had borne his son a child, was freed in 1376, in return for a sum of twenty-eight gold florins, payable at the rate of four florins a year over seven years, due on Michaelmas Day.

With their lives at the mercy of their owners, these men and women often faced cruel conditions. In 1377, a woman from Marseille sold an enslaved woman, Anthonia, who was white and baptized, to a grocer from Montpellier, but she kept Anthonia's one-year-old son, Antoine. In 1465, Pascal de Galdis, a noble and a Marseille shipowner, bought a pregnant black woman and her four-year-old son; three years later, he sold the little boy to a merchant from Aix. Catalonian slaves were forced to wear distinctive clothes and a prescribed haircut as well as chains.

Serfdom in the medieval period was largely a rural phenomenon, an aspect of seigneurial holdings, but slavery — which defined men as merchandise or cattle and as objects to be traded on the public square — coexisted with it. The extensive Mediterranean slave trade mixed populations together and generated a lucrative traffic. It can be considered a preliminary stage that made the condition of servility acceptable, a precursor to the black slave trade across the Atlantic.

Hélène Débax

REFERENCES

Guillén, Fabienne, and Salah Trabelsi. *Les esclavages en Méditerranée: Espaces et dynamiques économiques*. Madrid: Casa de Velázquez, 2012.

Hanss, Stefan, and Juliane Schiel, eds. *Mediterranean Slavery Revisited (500–1800), Neue Perspektiven auf mediterrane Sklaverei (500–1800)*. Zurich: Chronos, 2014.

Heers, Jacques. *Esclaves et domestiques au Moyen Âge dans le monde méditerranéen*. 2nd ed. Paris: Hachette, 1996.

Lahondès, Jules de. "Un procès d'esclave au quinzième siècle." In *Mémoires de la Société archéologique du Midi de la France XIII* (1883–1885): 334–42.

Rio, Alice. *Slavery after Rome*. Oxford: Oxford University Press, 2017.

Verlinden, Charles. *L'esclavage dans l'Europe médiévale*. Vol. 1, *Péninsule Ibérique, France*. Bruges: De Tempel, 1955.

———. *L'esclavage dans l'Europe médiévale*. Vol. 2, *Italie, colonies italiennes du Levant, Levant latin, Empire byzantin*. Gent: Rijksuniversiteit te Dent, 1977.

RELATED ARTICLES

600 BCE, 719, 1484, 1998

1456

Jacques Coeur Dies in Chios

After amassing vast wealth and serving as a councillor
to the King of France, Jacques Coeur was arrested on
false charges and died in exile. The criminal trial of this
powerful merchant illustrates a recurrent theme of French
history: state control interfering with "entrepreneurial
spirit." If the surviving memory of Jacques Coeur holds
that he mixed business and affairs of state, it forgets
his passionate support for the Crusades and his hope of
reconquering Constantinople.

In 1456, once more traveling to the Levant, where he had
adventured in his youth, Jacques Coeur joined an ultimately
fruitless campaign to reconquer Constantinople (as the
former capital of the Eastern Roman Empire was known).
Pope Nicholas V, with whom he had good relations, had
called for a crusade. When Nicholas died, his successor,
Calixtus III, renewed the call to the princes of Christendom
and took charge of operations, dispatching Coeur at the
head of a fleet of ships. But he never made it: along the way,

Jacques Coeur died on the island of Chios, which would stay in Genoese hands for another hundred years.

The controversies that developed a few years after his death and the questions about his true role in the administration of the crusade reflect both the rarefied place Jacques Coeur held as one of the best-known figures of his time and the ambivalence historians experience when confronting his life. Two quite different images emerge: on one side, the national hero with the incredible life story; on the other, the meticulous inventory of the many business deals in which Coeur engaged during his thirteen years as the king's *argentier*, or steward of the royal expenditure and court banker. The man's flamboyance leaps out from the historical saga that was his life, and also from a sculpted portrait of Coeur and his wife, Macée de Léodepart, that adorns the exterior of his palace in Bourges: the stone spouses lean out of adjacent stone windows, gazing lovingly at each other while resting on the balustrades. Ultimately, though, to understand his business dealings, historians are fortunate to have a contemporary source that is rich, detailed, and rigorous: the accounts drawn up by the solicitor general, Jean Dauvet, in prosecuting his lawsuit (1451 to 1453).

Legal troubles in France led Coeur to board the galleons built and outfitted by the pope and subsequently to meet his death in the Levant, far from his native city of Bourges and his homeland. Condemned to death in 1453 for crimes against the king, a sentence commuted to life in prison, Coeur managed to escape in 1454 to the Italian Peninsula and Rome, where, drawing on relationships established earlier, he was welcomed by the pope with open arms and shown every honor due to a powerful man. In his earlier life, he had conducted business with large Italian companies, particularly the big Florentine trading houses, and the papal court. He had even helped finance a silk-manufacturing workshop in the Tuscan capital. His partners on the far side of the Alps knew him as *Giacchetto Cuore*.

History has retained the story of how this son of a "humble" artisan rose unstoppably to wealth and power in a country that looked down on money and individual success — though his father was in fact a supplier of furs to the households of John, Duke of Berry and dauphin. The kingdom ruled by Charles VII was, it is said, a country with strong traditions, whipsawed by its complex relationship with money. From this comes the myth of Jacques Coeur as a lone man against the world, a man uniquely capable of understanding how wealth could be generated by large-scale trading, on the model of the great merchant families of the Italian city-states. Having apparently landed on French soil ahead of his time, he ran afoul of an aristocratic and administrative caste that was incapable of recognizing his genius. This idea — that France dislikes self-made men and is unable to recognize the value of its own people — was seized on and expressed by poets and other chroniclers as early as the fifteenth and sixteenth centuries.

The picaresque tale of Jacques Coeur marks an important inflection point for France, after the ravages of its conflicts with England and its civil wars. The fact that the French navy, acting with the ethics of corsairs, captured a great number of foreign galleons suggests that there was at least some understanding among French military, political, and financial leaders of the importance of long-distance international trade, and some knowledge of the routes it followed and the merchandise it carried. The French, too, could reap benefits from this trade. Jacques Coeur was one of the men who helped France put its roots down into the wider world of the fifteenth century, especially by developing connections with the Middle East and its markets, with the powerful figures of the day — kings, popes, wealthy merchants and nobles from the city-states of the Italian Peninsula — and by carrying this off with great energy and flair for success.

Jacques Coeur was also able to delegate capable intermediaries to see that his businesses ran smoothly and that his funds were circulating. Although his company could not rival in size the organizations of the great merchant bankers of Tuscany, he had many representatives working for him along the byways of France and Europe and many allies in positions of importance. His business presence extended along the Atlantic seaboard, from the North Sea to the Mediterranean, proof that the spirit of enterprise could exist in the kingdom of France, and that many people in that country were capable of supervising and conducting a variety of financial and commercial dealings. France had become a part of the world around it. Nothing proves this more directly than the fact that many of Coeur's fiercest accusers at his trial had originally come from the Italian Peninsula, and more particularly from Florence.

The construction of Jacques Coeur's grand house in the center of Bourges, near the government district, demonstrates that it was possible to accumulate great wealth fairly quickly in France, now that wars had become less frequent and the business climate more favorable. The structure of the house, built between 1443 and 1451, survives today as one of the greatest monuments to lay Gothic architecture. For those who had the "entrepreneurial spirit," as Coeur did, France offered innumerable opportunities. The king appointed him as his *argentier* in 1438, and Coeur continued to accumulate positions that gave him a strong hand in many markets, one of them being the salt market, for which he was both a merchant and the king's inspector general. Through his alliances and political postings, through his business dealings and partnerships, he provided an international environment in which his affairs might flourish.

And yet, his palace seemed the symbol — outrageous to some — of the economic and social success of an upstart. His success struck his competitors as altogether too rapid, and in the end it was risky. Lending money to powerful figures may be a way to advance one's career, but when the sums are too large the borrower may simply choose to wreck that career. Furthermore, major creditors had come to a bad pass in England as well: when the king declared bankruptcy in the fourteenth century, the Florentine banking houses that had backed him all failed spectacularly. The fact that Jacques Coeur held oversized loans may have been a reason for his many rivals and enviers to eliminate him. Had he lent too much money to the king? Had he made too much money too quickly, in a small society riven by internal conflicts?

At any rate, Jacques Coeur's career offers a perfect illustration of the intermingling of matters of state and private commerce, as was often the case in Europe at the time. He is credited with linking France to the south and the east of the Mediterranean Basin by sending his galleons to trade directly with the Levant — a Levant that he had long known and where he would eventually be buried. Though the French ships could not compete with the systems put in place by the Genoese, the Venetians, and the Florentines, they did make certain high-demand items more widely available, notably silks and spices. Other Frenchmen, southerners in particular, may have been trading with the

Levant already, but Coeur secured the monopoly because of his position in King Charles VII's court. He raised himself to the rank of the European merchant bankers with ties to the papacy and other centers of power, people who shared in the dynamic economic growth of the times.

Jacques Coeur's moment in the spotlight was an important juncture in the commercial history of France, and also one in which France asserted itself as one of the great powers.

Matthieu Scherman

REFERENCES

Farr, James R. *The Work of France: Labor and Culture in Early Modern Times, 1350–1800*. Lanham: Rowman & Littlefield, 2008.

Heers, Jacques. *Jacques Cœur (1400–1456)*. Paris: Perrin, 1997.

Mollat, Michel. *Jacques Cœur ou l'esprit d'entreprise au XVe siècle*. Paris: Aubier, 1985.

———, ed. *Les Affaires de Jacques Cœur: Journal du procureur Dauvet, procès-verbaux de séquestre et d'adjudication*. 2 vols. Paris: Armand Colin, 1952–1953.

Reyerson, Kathryn. *Jacques Cœur: Entrepreneur and King's Bursar*. New York: Pearson Longman, 2005.

RELATED ARTICLES

1202, 1270, 1720, 1860, 2011

1484

A Turkish Prince in Auvergne

His name was Cem, but in the little town of Bourganeuf
he was known as Zizim. The tower in which he was kept
prisoner, from 1484 on, took on the same name. The son
of Mehmed II, conqueror of Constantinople, Cem was a
pawn in a far-flung game of diplomacy whose purpose was
to rein in Ottoman power. The key players were the King
of Hungary, the Mamluk sultan, Pope Innocent VIII, the
French court, and the Knights Hospitaller.

Bourganeuf, the county seat of the Creuse district in central
France, was the headquarters of the "langue d'Auvergne,"
the Auvergne chapter of the Order of Knights of the
Hospital of Saint John of Jerusalem. A walled burg with
fortified gates, this commercial town hosted a commandery
of the Order of Saint John, which was itself protected by
ramparts and, on one side, a natural escarpment and a pond.
The compound was comparable to neighboring castles in its
design and its rugged beauty. But in 1484, plans were made
to supplement its main tower, known as the Lastic Tower,

429

with a second, the Great Tower or Tower of Zizim. "Zizim" was a debased version of the name of the Ottoman Sultan Cem, its first inhabitant and the man for whom it was built, at great expense. Cem's unlikely presence in this remote location was a consequence of chance and necessity.

At his death in 1481, Mehmed the Conqueror was survived by two sons, Cem and his half-brother, Bayezid II. The rules of succession gave them both an equal right to the throne, with the prize going to whoever acquired it first — in this case, Bayezid. Cem contested his brother's accession, but he lost the ensuing civil war. After a period of exile in Mamluk Egypt and a second, failed attempt to take the Ottoman throne, Cem fled to the nearest foreign land, Rhodes, with his brother's troops in pursuit. Rhodes received him with every honor, but his fate was henceforth in the hands of the Knights Hospitaller, who ruled the island.

Now under the control of the unbelievers, Cem posed a serious threat to his brother. The enemy could use him to destabilize Ottoman politics and prepare the ground for further crusades. Cem was eager to join forces with the King of Hungary to make another run at his brother's throne. Meanwhile, believing that an anti-Ottoman league would never coalesce, the Knights' Grand Master Pierre d'Aubusson and the council of the Order of Saint John decided to put their guest to advantage in a different way. Before concluding an agreement with Sultan Bayezid on his brother's fate, the knights insisted on a treaty that granted them important concessions. Negotiations over Cem then followed: the Order of Saint John would keep him under guard, in return for an annuity of forty thousand Venetian ducats. In addition to its financial benefits, this arrangement had the appearance of a tribute, which could give an otherwise squalid pact some luster of glory in Western eyes.

Pretenders to the Ottoman throne had previously found refuge within the Byzantine Empire, but this was the first time an Ottoman prince had put himself in the hands of a Western Roman power. While the Knights Hospitaller were sovereign in the eastern Mediterranean, they came under the pope's authority and had bases throughout Catholic Europe, where their commanderies provided them with revenue. It was quickly decided to send Cem westward, on the pretext of arranging his safe passage to Hungary, but in fact to improve the knights' bargaining position and keep Bayezid from making designs on his brother's life.

Joined by thirty companions and twenty enslaved Turks, Cem disembarked at the port of Villefranche in the Duchy of Savoy on October 16, 1482. Louis XI, who was then on his deathbed, refused him entry, not wanting a Muslim to sully his territory. Cem then went to Nice, and, when driven out by the plague, to Les Échelles, near Chambéry, the capital of Savoy, arriving in February 1483. Bayezid's spies were thick on the ground both in Savoy and in neighboring Italy. When the dukes of Savoy and Lorraine tried to help Cem escape, he was moved to Le Poët-Laval, near Montélimar, in June 1483. His guards responded to the escape attempt by increasing their surveillance, sending twenty-nine Turks in his entourage back to Rhodes and moving him from one Knights Hospitaller stronghold to another. In March 1484 — Louis XI had died on August 30 the previous year — Cem traveled with a reduced group of twenty Turks and a few knights of the Order of Saint John to Bourganeuf, where he stayed for three weeks in March and April. The town must not have seemed safe enough, because the decision was made to build the Great Tower.

During its construction, the little company spent two months in the nearby town of Le Monteil-au-Vicomte, two more months in the Morterolles commandery, and two years in Bois Lamy, before returning to live for two years in the Great Tower in Bourganeuf (from August 1486 to November 1488). All were isolated localities, meant to protect Cem from attempts at abduction or assassination. There was another factor as well: Pierre d'Aubusson had been born in Monteil; Bois Lamy belonged to Antoine, whose brother Guy de Blanchefort, the prior of Auvergne, was a future grand master of the Order of Saint John. Not only was the region safe, but the grand master and his circle had access to a local network of family and clients to whom they could entrust their precious hostage with complete confidence.

While Cem may have been sequestered from the world in tiny towns in central France, the world did not forget his existence. Some sovereigns — the King of Hungary and the Mamluk sultan of Cairo — wanted Cem for an offensive against the Ottomans. Pope Innocent VIII hoped to mount a crusade. The Venetians thought the hostage would be better used as a shield against Ottoman aggression, which coincided in the main with the opinion of the Knights Hospitaller. The Duke of Lorraine tried to abduct Cem a second time, and another escape was foiled. Meanwhile, there was considerable diplomatic maneuvering. Bayezid II, while overtly trying to arrange his brother's return to Rhodes, was secretly making tempting offers to the French king to keep him on French soil. A Hungarian embassy, on the other hand, was trying to negotiate Cem's delivery. But it was the papal nuncios who won out, with the Order of Saint John retaining the right of review over Cem's fate, responsibility for guarding him, and a quarter of the annuity. Cem left Bourganeuf on November 10, 1488, whisked out of France in haste — the Ottoman government was offering terms that were making the French court reconsider — and arrived in Rome on March 13, 1489. The papal plans for a crusade fizzled, but Cem was not done with either crusades or France. In January 1495, Charles VIII of France stopped in Rome in the course of his Italian campaign and took Cem with him on his progress south, claiming his intention of sailing for Ottoman lands. But Cem died in Naples on February 24, 1495.

Cem's Ottoman biographer painted a joyous picture of his early sojourn in Nice, and, according to Paolo da Colle, a Genoese informer of Sultan Bayezid, the knights were lavish in providing hunting parties, women, and a sumptuous table for Cem while in Savoy. He received many visitors there. As his guards grew more concerned about security, his freedom gradually decreased. The design of the Great Tower provides some insight. More spacious than other residential towers in the region, it offered some comfort: a wine cellar on the first floor, kitchens on the second, the quarters for Cem's retinue on the third. The captive lived on the fourth floor, with his guards on the sixth and the attic reserved for Christian artisans. But the entire tower was cut off from the world. Access was from the fortified town, past the walls of the commandery, up to the second floor of the Lastic Tower, and through a gallery raised thirty feet in the air that made a bridge to the Great Tower. One of Bayezid's secret emissaries did catch a glimpse of Cem on the town's main square; Cem maintained some contact with the outside world, if only through his companions. But an escape plan, hatched by one of them in collusion with the Duke of Bourbon, brought an increased level of surveillance that further isolated Cem.

Cem's interactions with local society were therefore

slight, probably limited to the Hospitallers who guarded him. It must have been in their company that he learned the "Frankish" language, as his Ottoman biographer tells us: French, or rather a form of Italian. One or two of his companions chose to remain in Bourganeuf, where, as converts to Christianity, they melted into the community without making a ripple.

Historians have always been aware of Cem, but he came into literature relatively late. Today, his memory is cherished in Bourganeuf, which has a Turkish community, but the only concrete trace of his stay there is the Tower of Zizim itself. For the Ottomans, he remained an important historical figure. His unusual adventure may have aroused their curiosity, but it was also morally suspect, as any long-term stay among unbelievers would have to be. This sentiment is probably responsible for our having the *Vā'iât-i Sulân Cem*, a biography of the sultan written by one of his companions (who himself had to justify belonging to Cem's retinue in a Christian country). It is full of vivid and well-informed accounts: of artificial prairies, fish farming in man-made lakes, and the Great Tower, but also of the Lyons commercial fairs and the election of popes. Although only two manuscript copies survive, the book is known to have been in wide circulation. Yet while some readers were likely drawn to its exoticism, Ottoman society generally gave it little importance. The accounts, although true enough, were meant to cast the adventures of a fiery but unfortunate prince in a wondrous light, relating the extraordinary adventures of an exceptional man.

The sojourn of this Turkish prince in Auvergne is more than an anecdotal episode: Cem's adventures were both the cause and the telltale sign of a new development. Henceforth, the Ottoman Empire would take part in the diplomatic dance. At the end of the fifteenth century, the quarreling states of Italy no longer hesitated to make the Sublime Porte (as the Ottoman government was known) a factor in their politics. That the sultan's brother was in the West accelerated this development and greatly increased the exchange of missions and envoys between Europe and the Ottomans. It also made the Porte realize that France had emerged as a major player: France held the fate of Cem in its hands, and to some extent therefore the fate of Bayezid as well, all because the grand master in Rhodes came from the French province of Auvergne. Bayezid made diplomatic overtures to the French king on matters that went well beyond his brother's release. Nothing came of these, but they laid the groundwork for a rapprochement during the reign of Francis I. Cem also provided the two countries with a shared memory: during a joint naval campaign in 1543–1544, the French king's representative reminded the Ottoman admiral that Cem had once lived in Nice.

Nicolas Vatin

REFERENCES

Delhoume, Didier. *Le Turc et le chevalier: Djem Sultan, un prince ottoman entre Rhodes et Bourganeuf au XVe siècle*. Limoges: Culture et patrimoine en Limousin, 2004.

Ménage, Victor L. "The Mission of an Ottoman Secret Agent in France in 1486." In *Journal of the Royal Asiatic Society* 97, no. 2 (1965): 112–32.

Thuasne, Louis. *Djem Sultan: Étude sur la question d'Orient à la fin du XVe siècle*. Paris: Ernest Leroux, 1892.

Vatin, Nicolas. *Encyclopaedia of Islam*. 3rd ed., s.v. Leiden: Brill, 2007.

———. *Les Ottomans et l'Occident (XVe–XVIe siècle)*. Istanbul: Isis, 2001.

———. *L'Ordre de Saint-Jean-de-Jérusalem, l'Empire ottoman et la Méditerranée orientale entre les deux sièges de Rhodes (1480–1522)*. Paris: Peeters, 1994.

———. *Sultan Djem, un prince ottoman dans l'Europe du XVe siècle d'après deux sources contemporaines: Vâı'ât-ı Sulân Cem, Œuvres de Guillaume Caoursin*. Ankara: Société Turque d'Histoire, 1997.

RELATED ARTICLES
1446, 1456, 1715, 1771, 1923

1494

Charles VIII Goes to Italy — and Loses the World

At the time when the sovereigns of Spain and Portugal were dividing the world between them at Tordesillas, the young king of France, Charles VIII, was dawdling in Naples, bewitched by the charm of Italy. Was this a setback in the building of the kingdom of France? Quite the contrary, claimed historian Jules Michelet: this "immense and decisive" event hastened the Renaissance.

The young King Charles VIII of France entered Italy by way of Mont Cenis, the route habitually taken by pilgrims to Rome. He "vaulted the wall of Italy," just like every other would-be Western conqueror, from Charlemagne to Napoleon. Two hundred years later, in 1692, the elderly military architect Sébastien de Vauban bumped and creaked along the same route in his mule carriage, when he was called upon to design a system of defensive Alpine fortifications around the French border town of Briançon. From Briançon, the frontier ran along a ridge beside the pass, beneath which Minister of War André Maginot buried the Mediterranean end of his famed "Maginot Line" of fortifications in 1932.

In 1494, Charles VIII was "young and willful," as Philippe De Commynes noted in his *Mémoires*. The king marched out of Grenoble on July 28, 1494, at the head of an army thirty thousand strong. On September 5, he was acclaimed in Turin; but as far as he was concerned Turin was only a way station, for his dreams were fixed on Naples and Jerusalem beyond. Charles was convinced it was his destiny to change the world and bring about Christ's return to earth. At the time he was only twenty-four; less than four years later, on April 7, 1498, he died suddenly on his way to the tennis court, after banging his head on a stone lintel in his castle of Amboise. This misfortune befell him even though he was "somewhat short in stature," according to the discreet Commynes. The waspish Italian humanist and diplomat Pietro Martyr d'Anghiera, more forthright, called the French king "a kind of pygmy" in a series of letters from the Spanish court that broke the story of Christopher Columbus's American discoveries to a fascinated Europe.

The coincidence between both events later proved acutely embarrassing to Charles's descendants, despite the fleeting triumphs of his army. 1494 was the year of the Treaty of Tordesillas (June 7), by which the kings of Spain and Portugal carved up the discovered (and undiscovered) world between them by means of a meridian passing 370 leagues to the west of the Cape Verde islands in the Atlantic Ocean. Tordesillas basically apportioned one hemisphere of the globe to the realm of Portugal, and the other to the crowns of Castile and Aragon. Through his own judgments, the pope himself had been sanctioning this universalist aspiration to *dominium mundi* since 1493. So we have to be quite clear: as Charles-André Julien, the great historian of North Africa, wrote in 1948, "France's share in the great overseas discoveries was to all intents and purposes nil."

It is true that the archives reveal few early French explorers. In his 1669 description of a voyage along the coast of Guinea, the explorer Villault de Bellefond suggested that in 1364 Norman merchants had maintained a colony known as le Petit-Dieppe in the south of Cape Verde, formerly Portuguese property. Later the Norman mariner Jean Cousin was said to have embarked from the port of Dieppe in 1488 with Martín Alonso Pinzòn (who captained the *Pinta* during Columbus's first voyage to the New World), thus discovering Brazil well ahead of the Portuguese fleet of Pedro Álvares Cabral in 1500. Vague claims like these have long encumbered French historians, to the point that the anthropologist Claude Lévi-Strauss seems still to have believed them when he wrote his *Tristes Tropiques* in 1955. They were born of an intense historic frustration, which was rendered all the more acute when, in the time of Villault de Bellefond and Vauban, the France of Louis XIV was dreaming seriously of Spanish-style world domination.

The fact is that ever since the reign of Louis XIV, French historians have blamed Charles VIII for missing the boat of history in 1494 — France's best chance to take the world. As they have repeated over and over again, when he reached Naples, Charles, like the dog in the Aesop fable, dropped his prey and grasped its shadow.

First of all, what exactly was the King of France doing in Naples?

After weathering a few crises, Charles had begun his reign quite well. When he came to the throne in 1483 on the death of his father Louis XI, he was only thirteen years old and under the strict guardianship of his sister Anne de Beaujeu. His brother-in-law Louis d'Orléans (who was later to succeed him under the name of Louis XII) led a rebellion of assorted other princes that became known as the *Guerre folle* (the Mad War). Once order had been reestablished, Charles made it his business to do what the history books of the Third Republic might have expected of a French monarch. He put an end to the war of the succession in Brittany and, by his marriage to Anne of Brittany, heiress of the duchy, at Langeais on December 6, 1491, he engineered its reattachment to the crown of France, thus completing the grand design of Louis XI. Nine months later, on October 11, 1492, Anne promptly produced a male heir. Everything was perfect, right up to the child's Christian name,

Charles-Orland; unless of course this Frenchification of the Italian "Orlando" (which itself was an Italian version of "Roland," the Carolingian French beau ideal) betrayed an ominously early fascination with romantic Italian chivalry.

Perhaps it was to clear the way to Italy that the young king went to unusual lengths to establish peace along his frontiers. On November 3, 1492, he signed the Treaty of Etaples with Henry VII of England. This was followed on January 19, 1493, by the Treaty of Barcelona with Ferdinand II of Aragon, and on May 23 by the Treaty of Senlis with Holy Roman Emperor Maximilian. In the process, Charles ceded Cerdagne and Roussillon to Ferdinand and presented Maximilian — who was doubtless mortified that his fiancée Anne of Brittany had slipped through his fingers — with the regions of Artois, Franche-Comté, and Charolais.

Perhaps he was overgenerous in giving away all this territory. It might have been better, in the light of the political and territorial promises of his predecessors, had he confined himself to the reforms demanded by the Estates General of Tours in 1484. Modern historians are routinely exasperated that Italy (the "peninsular outlet," to borrow a phrase from Emmanuel Le Roy Ladurie) seems to have distracted Charles from the traditional, patient Capetian policy of amassing territory for the French state. Certainly, many in his entourage, whether in his council of state or in city assemblies all over France, expressed their hostility to what they called *l'emprise* (from the Italian *impresa*): the king's Italian enterprise.

The latter has been branded by French history as the obstinate project of a fanciful, fragile personality. Charles's head was filled with prophecies and chivalric romances, and there you had it. Commynes describes the obsequious way the Milanese ambassadors truckled to the king, generally spreading the "smoke and glory" of Italy and presenting him with a copy of Honoré Bonet's *The Tree of Battles*, a fourteenth-century handbook of chivalric warfare that the Parisian bookseller Antoine Vérard published in 1493. The Duke of Milan, Ludovico Sforza, was singled out for blame, on account of his efforts to lure Charles into the Italian political game by convincing him to claim the ancient dynastic right of the house of Anjou — of which he was the heir — to rule the kingdom of Naples.

In reality, Italian diplomacy was not nearly so subtle. Italy itself had been a focus of the struggle for European hegemony since the 1470s; now this struggle had broken into the open and engulfed everyone. A whole political system was being swept away by the "Italian wars" and the forces they had unleashed. The Florentine diplomat and historian Francesco Guicciardini wrote that in 1494 "a flame and a plague entered Italy, which changed the Italian states, the systems by which they were governed, and their methods of waging war." Close to thirty thousand men formed the army that Charles VIII took to Italy, along with the first artillery train seen in Europe, and a permanent fleet such as no state besides the Ottoman Empire had ever mobilized before.

Indeed, there can be little doubt that the French king's true target was that same Ottoman Empire. On March 13, 1494, he proclaimed himself king of Naples and Jerusalem. The bloody Ottoman campaign in Otranto and Apulia in 1480–1481 had aroused a Europe-wide dread that the Turks would overwhelm all Italy. It was fully expected that another crusade against them would soon be raised. And had not Pope Pius II told Charles's father Louis XI that "only the King of France is capable of delivering the Holy Sepulcher"?

From Francis of Paola at Plessis-lèz-Tours to Girolamo Savonarola in Florence, all prophecies concurred that these were momentous times. Global in scope, this eschatological fever spread across Islam: 1494 marked the beginning of the tenth century of the Hijrah, precipitating the hope of a new *mujaddid* (messenger) in the Maghreb, Anatolia, Iran, and even India. Like the Prophet before him, this messenger would reorganize the known world. Historians today are well aware that the expeditions of Christopher Columbus, just like those of the Portuguese navigators under Manuel I, would be incomprehensible if not viewed against this messianic background.

Such was the world dimension of the "Italian enterprise" of Charles VIII in 1494. Its details matter little, although we should note, for the record, that the King of France was received in triumph in Lombardy, and then drove the Medici out of Florence, imposed an agreement on the pope in Rome, and entered Naples in February 1495 as a liberator, without shedding a drop of blood. This sovereign display left contemporaries stunned: "With a shake of his head he shook the world," the Florentine humanist Marsilio Ficino wrote, a bit grandiosely. But disillusion quickly followed, matching and then exceeding the hopes Charles had aroused. Derogatory pamphlets and satirical songs began to circulate among the Italians. As stories of "barbarian" licentiousness and cruelty spread, a new appreciation of "Italian-ness" (*italianità*) was born. Venice took the lead in founding a Holy League for the "consolation of Italy" by raising a military alliance strong enough to confront the French army as it retreated homeward. A battle at Fornovo proved bloody on July 6, 1495, but its outcome was indecisive. The French thought they had won because their retreat had not been cut off, while the Venetians celebrated victory because they had captured the French king's treasure, which was brought back to Saint Mark's Basilica as a trophy of war.

In any event, on his return to France, Charles VIII found himself helplessly looking on as his recently acquired southern realm fell apart. Before long, nothing remained of his Italian enterprise save the syphilis contracted by a few French soldiers. Known at first as the "Neapolitan disease," syphilis was destined to spread throughout Europe; having originated in America, it was doubtless the earliest bacteriological consequence of globalization.

In 1855, Jules Michelet uncovered another legacy in the expedition: nothing less than the Renaissance. Michelet began the eighth volume of his *History of France* with the descent of Charles VIII into Italy in 1494 (the seventh volume had ended with the convocation of the Estates General in 1484) and entitled it *The Renaissance*. Such was the significance he bestowed upon this episode in French history. Whether we like it or not, this invention has persisted to this day.

Michelet boldly stated that "the discovery of Italy had an infinitely greater effect on the sixteenth century than the discovery of America." Milan, Rome, Naples: Charles VIII had accomplished a "crescendo of marvels" that led him to imitate, in the Loire Valley, something of their accumulated beauty and, with that, the political models they had expressed. "This barbarity blithely collided one morning with high civilization: it was a collision of two worlds, but even more so, a collision of two ages that had seemed altogether distant from each other. The collision generated a spark; and from the spark, there arose the column of fire that was called the Renaissance." So it was that France's historic grandeur and its role in the history of the world were rescued by its very barbarity.

Patrick Boucheron

REFERENCES

Abulafia, David, ed. *The French Descent into Renaissance Italy (1494–1495): Antecedents and Effects*. Aldershot: Ashgate, 1995.

Boucheron, Patrick. "Les laboratoires politiques de l'Italie." In Boucheron, *Histoire du monde au XVe siècle*, 53–74.

Delaborde, Henri-François. *L'Expédition de Charles VIII en Italie: Histoire diplomatique et militaire*. Paris: Firmin-Didot, 1888.

Gilli, Patrick. "L'armée de Charles VIII franchit les Alpes." In Boucheron, *Histoire du monde au XVe siècle*, 417–420.

Julien, Charles-André. *Les Voyages de découverte et les premiers établissements (XVe–XVIe siècle)*. Paris: Presses Universitaires de France, 1948.

Schaub, Jean-Frédéric. "Le traité de Tordesillas." In Boucheron, *Histoire du monde au XVe siècle*, 421–423.

RELATED ARTICLES

1515

Whatever Led Him to Marignano?

A celebrated milestone in the drawn-out Italian Wars, the Battle of Marignano is nonetheless opaque. Historians have long tried to fathom the true intentions of King Francis I of France in bringing his armies to Italy. The ideals of knight-errantry and the dream of a universal monarchy may have played their part, but the battle mostly makes clear the financial power of the French state and the military power of the Swiss Confederacy.

The lure of Italy that enticed successive kings of France seems to play into a rejection of the modern. The crusader Charles VIII set off to conquer the distant kingdom of Naples in order to create a secure base for his campaign to free the Holy Land. The great feudal landowner Louis XII, wanting to reclaim the rights of his grandmother, Valentina Visconti, made it his lifelong obsession to conquer the Duchy of Milan. And Francis I, adopting his predecessors' claims as his own, aspired to nothing less than a universal monarchy, that old medieval ideal. Gaining control of

Naples and Milan would ensure his ascendancy over the Italian Peninsula, which at that time was the spiritual, cultural, and economic heart of Europe.

These three kings had moved a long way from the cynical realism of their immediate predecessors, Charles VII and Louis XI, who had patiently built France into a contiguous and homogenous realm. For both of them, respect for local particularities was a form of political prudence, paving the way for a thorough program of assimilation. Two generations later, the renaissance of classical literature and the revival of the chivalric ideal would go hand in hand. The works of Polybius, Caesar, and Frontinus, along with *Amadís de Gaula*, a romance of knight-errantry that omits none of the genre's tropes, were common touchstones for the aristocracy of Europe. The resurgent continent had a sharp desire for exploits and adventures. As much as the compass, the sternpost rudder, Toledo steel, and the crossbow, this hunger was responsible for bringing Christopher Columbus to Hispaniola and Hernán Cortés to Mexico. It would lead Francis I to camp at the gates of Milan and present himself at the imperial election of 1519.

Were the mad ambitions of the King of France within his reach? In 1515, they certainly were. At that time, his future archenemy, Charles, the Habsburg prince who would become Holy Roman Emperor, ruled only over the

Low Countries, which he had inherited from his great-grandfather, Charles the Bold. He had been promised Spain, but his grandfather Ferdinand II still ruled it with an iron fist. His other grandfather, Emperor Maximilian I, was absorbed with internal government reforms and had not yet moved to safeguard his succession by having Charles elected king of the Romans.

Chivalric notions and the new power of the modern state would soon shake up the world. The new power was for the moment confined to France, the most populous and most absolute monarchy, and the one leviathan on the European continent. "The peoples of France are humble and highly submissive; they hold their king in great veneration," wrote Machiavelli. A population of sheep, said Maximilian; a population of cowards, said John Fortescue, the eminent English lawyer. It is true that only the King of France could raise taxes at that time without prior authorization from a representative assembly such as the English Parliament, the Spanish Cortes, or the German Diets.

No power in Europe could match France's financial resources, which were five to ten times greater than those of its Spanish, English, Austrian, or Milanese rivals. In the summer of 1515, Francis I raised an army of 45,000 men to carry out his plan of conquest. Only one out of five of his soldiers spoke French. The entire infantry consisted of German mercenaries — the redoubtable landsknechts — and Gascons. France's aristocrats formed the heavy cavalry of the companies of men-at-arms and oversaw the artillery, the jewels of the French army.

A miscellaneous and divided coalition tried to keep these forces from crossing the passes through the Alps. Its backbone was an alliance between the Swiss Confederacy and the pope, who exercised a protective and self-serving tyranny over the young Duke of Milan, Maximilian Sforza. The alliance, a joint political project of Pope Julius II and Matthäus Schiner, the cardinal of Sion, had the grandiose ambition of restoring the temporal power of the church over the Christian world. The Swiss Confederacy would provide Julius the armed force he needed to rid Italy of French, German, and Spanish barbarians; afterward, it would bend the Italian states to his will.

Switzerland was at the height of its power, having brought down the "Grand Duke of the West," Charles the Bold, in 1477; defeated Maximilian in 1499; and humiliated Louis XII in 1513. Feared and actively hated by many, Switzerland was courted by all. After the confederacy drove the French out of Italy in 1512, it made the Duchy of Milan a protectorate whose tax revenues served to maintain Swiss garrisons in all its major towns. But confronted by the enormous army gathered by King Francis I, the opposing coalition split apart. The Milanese towns, staggering under their tax burden, teetered on the edge of rebellion, and neither the pope, Julius II's indecisive successor Leo X, nor the Spaniards wanted to assume the colossal bill that would be owed to the Swiss army.

The French expedition was meticulously planned. Driven by a strong chivalric impulse, Francis I directed his army not as a king and a knight but as a captain, a diplomat, and at times an accountant. He would not fall prey to the glorious uncertainties of war. Others might show a haughty disdain toward the prospect of victory, and the Chevalier de Bayard might say that "in time of war, one time you win, one time you lose," but Francis I made a point of putting every chance on his side.

After wrong-footing the Swiss and crossing the Alps at the Maddalena Pass, when they were expected to cross much farther north at Mont Cenis or Montgenèvre, a major strategic coup, the French forged ahead into the Piedmont. Their triumphal advance brought on the defection of their former enemies and the capitulation of Italian towns. First the city-state of Genoa sided with the French, then the Duchy of Savoy. Harassed by the French cavalry, abandoned by their allies, and starving, the Swiss began to waver. The Swiss Confederation, a league of thirteen cantons, each a sovereign mini-state with its own set of interests and political priorities, was riven by deep fractures. The patrician cities of the western plateau, Bern, Fribourg, and Solothurn, looked toward France and sought to expand toward Savoy, while the cantons of the interior, Uri and Schwyz in particular, thought only of consolidating their hold over the Ticino Valley and the Duchy of Milan.

French diplomats attempted to exacerbate these tensions in time-tested ways. Since the reign of Louis XI, French gold filled the cantons' public vaults, the private coffers of the merchants and nobles who controlled the government councils, and the purses of thousands of young men whose dream was to serve in the French royal army. But when the Swiss joined with France's enemies in 1510, the stream of French gold was deflected toward the landsknechts of Gelderland, Swabia, and Tyrol, the direct competitors of the Swiss on the mercenary market. The renewed flow of French money quickly eroded the opposition of a majority of the cantons, and the council of Swiss captains decided to engage in talks. On September 8, less than a month after Francis I crossed the Alps into Italy, the Treaty of Gallarate was signed. For the sum of one million gold écus, eleven of the thirteen cantons agreed to abandon their allies, recognize France's sovereignty over the Duchy of Milan, return the Alpine districts seized in 1512, and supply the king with as many mercenaries as he might require. Francis I's victory was complete.

Yet five days later, on the afternoon of September 13, the gates of Milan disgorged twenty-five thousand Swiss soldiers to attack the French, encamped a few miles away at Marignano. Reinforcements from Switzerland and the energetic intervention of Cardinal Schiner had managed to sway the soldiers. During a contentious council of war, with the captains on the verge of a fistfight, a supporter of Cardinal Schiner burst into the room to announce that skirmishes with the French had begun. The undecided now threw in their lot with the confederacy.

Faithful to their military culture, which looked contemptuously on danger and the adversary, the bare-headed and barefoot Swiss footsoldiers hurled themselves at the French lines, armed with pikes and halberds. Sixteen hours later, after the deaths of twelve thousand men, they admitted defeat. There had been a bloody hand-to-hand encounter, a deluge of fire from the French artillery, and several dozen cavalry charges in the heat and dust of the day, continuing into the cold and damp of the night, before the Swiss infantry retired to Milan at mid-morning on September 14. Already planning their next action, the French had pursued them half-heartedly. A few days later, Francis I made his entry into Milan. A year after that, on November 29, 1516, a treaty of peace and friendship known as "Perpetual Peace" was signed in Fribourg by the King of France and the Swiss Confederacy. This was followed five years later, in 1521, by a pact of alliance that made most of the Swiss cantons client states of the French monarchy.

Meanwhile, the wheel of fortune had turned. All of

France's gold failed to buy the German electors, and Francis I lost his bid to become emperor. Archduke Charles was chosen in his place, becoming Charles V, Holy Roman emperor, king of Aragon and Castile, ruler of the Low Countries and the Austrian states, lord of the first colonial empire on which the sun never set. In 1521, Milan rose up against the French. The following year, the French king's own Swiss mercenaries suffered a bloody defeat at the hands of the imperial forces. In 1524, a French army was routed without a fight, and the Chevalier de Bayard was killed while vainly trying to cover its retreat. On February 24, 1525, in the mud and mists of Pavia, Francis I's Italian dream would turn into a nightmare when his army was soundly defeated by an alliance of Habsburg forces. Captured and imprisoned, the king wrote to his mother, "All is lost to me save honor and life, which are safe," before signing the humiliating Treaty of Madrid. To save face, the erstwhile new Caesar, "subjugator of the Helvetians," assumed instead the inglorious but honorable role of doleful knight, ever true to his word. So it is when political messaging takes the place of true accounting.

Amable Sablon du Corail

REFERENCES

Deruelle, Benjamin. *De papier, de fer et de sang: Chevaliers et chevalerie à l'épreuve de la modernité (ca. 1460–ca. 1620)*. Paris: Presses de la Sorbonne, 2015.

Knecht, Robert J. *Renaissance Warrior and Patron: The Reign of Francis I*. Cambridge: Cambridge University Press, 1994.

Leduc, Antoine, Sylvie Leluc, and Olivier Renaudeau, eds. *D'Azincourt à Marignan: Chevaliers et bombardes (1415–1515)*. Paris: Gallimard / Musée de l'armée, 2015.

Le Fur, Didier. *Marignan: 13–14 septembre 1515*. Paris: Perrin, 2003.

Le Gall, Jean-Marie. *L'Honneur perdu de François Ier: Pavie, 1525*. Paris: Payot, 2015.

Mallett, Michael. *Mercenaries and Their Masters: Warfare in Renaissance Italy*. Barnsley: Pen and Sword Books, 2009 [1974].

Michon, Cédric. *François Ier: Les femmes, le pouvoir et la guerre*. Paris: Belin, 2015.

Potter, David. *Renaissance France at War: Armies, Culture and Society, c. 1480–1560*. Woodbridge: Boydell Press, 2008.

Sablon du Corail, Amable. *1515, Marignan*. Paris: Tallandier, 2015.

RELATED ARTICLES

1534

Jacques Cartier and the New Lands

He, too, ventured westward to find a trade route to the
riches and marvels of Asia. In 1534, the Saint-Malo
navigator Jacques Cartier gave Francis I an account of
his first voyage to the "new lands" of the North Atlantic,
reporting the information he had gathered among Iroquois
princes. The conquest rested on words as much as deeds.

At the foot of the fourteenth-century dungeon built by the
Duke of Brittany to control the mouth of the Rance River, a
wooden cross still reminds Saint-Malo residents of the one
erected in July 1534 by one of their distant ancestors, Jacques
Cartier. That cross was planted thousands of kilometers
from Saint-Malo, in Gaspé, part of eastern Quebec but
at that time neither New France or Canada. In the river's
estuary, the simplicity of the wooden beams contrasted with
the solemn grandiloquence of the inscription at its center:
"Long live the King of France." That declaration must have
resonated oddly for Bretons, who had been attached to the
kingdom of the French kings only since 1532, and also for

the two hundred fifty Native Americans before whom the cross had been planted and the proclamation made. The customary *vivat rex* of royal ceremonies had a strange ring indeed in the Americas, which was not yet wed to Europe. It brought together worlds that were not yet deemed inherently distinct and reduced to their respective ferocious capabilities.

For the French at the beginning of the 1530s, the world beyond France consisted first of the Duchy of Brittany, which was only connected to the King of France through family ties — and remained so until the estates of the province, assembled in Vannes, demanded its official unification with the crown. Beyond Brittany, there was Naples, Florence, Milan, and Rome, and also Egypt and Constantinople, the land of crusades and the horizon of an empire to which, since Charles VIII, the Valois rulers laid claim. It was there that messianic dreams combined with rabid worldly appetites, where hopes for salvation encountered the satisfaction of more profane desires. The French world also encompassed the lands of Marco Polo and Jean de Mandeville, the Eastern lands of gold and spices — and, finally, the islands that, far to the west off the coasts of Brittany and Labourd, attracted their sailors.

When Jacques Cartier's first voyage to the "new lands" of the North Atlantic was being planned, the Spanish had just conquered possessions of the great Incan Atahualpa

(1531–1533), and before that those of the Aztec Empire of Moctezuma (1519–1521). The explorations that the Portuguese Estêvão Gomes and the Spaniard Lucas Vázquez de Ayllón undertook off American coasts, from North Carolina to Newfoundland, in 1525–1526 also rendered obsolete the French cartography produced by Giovanni da Verrazzano. Vázquez de Ayllón had established a colony north of Florida in order to show that the Iberian powers would cede nothing of the papal arbitration of 1493 or the Treaty of Tordesillas of 1494, which guaranteed their monopoly over maritime routes and granted them the privilege of discovering the New World. The world Christopher Columbus encountered in 1492, full of indigenous Lucayan, Taíno, and Arawak people who were, he thought, subjects of the Great Khan, resembled the one discovered by Pedro Álvares Cabral in 1500: rich with that red wood — pau brasil — coveted by European dyers.

Jacques Cartier's voyage can be seen as a Breton reaction to the outfitting of Verrazzano's expedition by an association of Norman traders and Italian bankers in Lyon. The main objective was to identify a route to the "Indies of Cathay" and "Cipango" (China and Japan) and its riches (gold, gems, spices). Eastern access to Asia had been made more difficult since the fall of Constantinople in 1453. Indeed, it seemed more distant and dangerous than ever now that the size of Africa seemed to have doubled, with Bartolomeu

Dias rounding the Cape of Good Hope in 1488. The western maritime route, made possible by the roundness of the Earth, seemed the logical choice. Cartier's three voyages in 1534, 1535–36, and 1541–42 were ordered by Francis I: following his Italian setbacks, he had set his sights on new lands for his empire and for the riches that, in 1519 and 1525, had been refused him in Europe. Cartier explored the mouth of the Saint Lawrence River and then, going up the river to the Iroquois town of Hochelaga (the future Montreal) and to Stadacona (near present-day Quebec), obtained for the French ruler the lion's share of the American profits after which Francis I had been lusting. The king had forced open the door of the colonial powers club, and in 1533 convinced Pope Clement VII to interpret in his favor certain of the clauses of the 1493 Bulls of Donation by which his predecessor Alexander VI had granted the Portuguese and Spanish monarchs exclusive rights over future colonized lands.

Those three voyages cannot be reduced to a list of progressive discoveries or to the accumulation of ever more precise cartographic information. They were not mere links in a chain of colonial expansion or the growing exploration and delimitation of an American space in which French interests would prosper and initial discoveries feed a policy of long-term colonization. Examples of such colonization could be found in the "Charlesbourg-Royal" settlement Cartier founded near Stadocona, close to the Saint Charles River in August 1541, or in the "France-Roy" fort, established the following summer on the ruins of Charlesbourg-Royal by Jean-François de La Rocque, Sieur of Roberval.

By considering the underside of what some call the French colonial movement in the Age of Discovery, going beyond lists of heroic and inaugural events that may feed French pride, we will understand the French Atlantic adventure for what it truly was: a matter of words as much as deeds. Words were used to convince, persuade, engage in trade, seduce, dupe, and trick. Words were weak and insufficient and sometimes incomprehensible; they had to be interpreted, and sometimes they did not produce mutual understanding between these historical actors. In fact, the overseas adventure was an affair of words before it was even undertaken. The impotent eloquence of Bartholomew Columbus in 1490 did not convince the regent, Anne of France, to fund the expedition of his brother, Christopher, who could have crossed the Atlantic on behalf of the King of France. There was no need however for Anne, the daughter of Louis XI, to seek wealth — without guarantees — in the Indies when Brittany, conquered two years earlier by the strength of her armies, was a prosperous new world allied to the crown of her brother.

461

Today, Jacques Cartier is generally seen as a sort of Jules Verne figure belonging to the club of "great voyages and great voyagers," reflected in the series of *Extraordinary Voyages* Verne published in the 1870s. Indeed, posterity has depicted the Saint-Malo captain as an energetic navigator, as witnessed in the statues that, whether in Saint-Malo in 1905 or Quebec in 1926, depict him with his hand on the helm of his boat (or proudly standing, left hand on the knob of his sword and right raised in front of him as if to flag down the world to join him in this voyage of modernity, as in the 1893 statue in Montreal). Two little-known paintings, however, captured the essence of the French adventure of the years 1534–1543, which was above all a story, or rather an intertwining of tales and legends in which the main subject is less Cartier or Francis I than the Iroquois kings and princes.

Around 1910–1911, the painter Frank Craig depicted the French explorer upon his return from his first voyage of 1534. In the gardens of Fontainebleau, the sailor kneels to tell the story of his discoveries to the king who, on horseback, in the shade of a dais, listens to this marvelous tale about the exploration of new lands. Regardless of all that Cartier and his crews had failed to accomplish — finding the passage to China, uncovering riches beyond worthless animal pelts — this story provoked tremendous excitement. Dressed in black, Cartier contrasts with the courtiers surrounding the king and the audience of young men and women wearing leopard skins and luminous white dresses. To the glory of the nymphs and fauns of Greece, to the marvels of antiquity and the grandeurs of Rome that the humanists and artists brought to life in the king's palaces, Cartier added the tale of a world full of delights and promise. With its white men and their wool blankets, its gold and rubies, the kingdom of Saguenay — this northern transposition of the El Dorado of Iberian America — was within grasp. The moral seemed to be: French people, a bit more effort and the windfall will be yours!

The tale of the riches of Saguenay had been told to Cartier by the Iroquois chief Donnacona, who claimed to have visited it. The two Amerindian princes Domagaya and Taignoagny — his sons or nephews, whom Cartier brought back to France in 1534 — retold the story of those treasures. And when the explorer returned from his second voyage in 1536, it was the chief of Stadacona himself who told the tale once again, this time to Francis I, who fell under his charm. This most promising land, a marvel awaiting further exploration and carrying the promise of an enchanted world, floated against a horizon of desire. This beacon would guide the French trans-Atlantic adventure. Unsurprisingly, it also provided the title of Cartier's account of his second voyage, published in Paris in 1545. A second painting, by Lawrence Robb Batchelor around 1933, shows Jacques Cartier in the

Iroquois town of Hochelaga, seeking to convince its "lord" and inhabitants of the advantages that trade, an alliance, and good relations with the French would yield.

Words again — but doubly misleading this time. The kingdom of Saguenay would lose its illusory charms, as false as the rumored "diamonds of Canada," and this alliance between the French and the Native Americans, weakened by Cartier's abductions and bungling, would degenerate into an ephemeral colony that the French abandoned quickly in the summer of 1543. They left the shores of this New World and did not return for fifty years. Ultimately, these new lands were nothing but places of desire. Maybe that was not so bad for a territory that around 1511–1512 the Spanish navigator Juan de Agramonte had described to Queen Joan of Castile as plainly insignificant and empty: "*acá nada.*"

Yann Lignereux

REFERENCES

Cook, Ramsay. *The Voyages of Jacques Cartier*. Toronto: University of Toronto Press, 1993.

Havard, Gilles, and Cécile Vidal, *Histoire de l'Amérique française*. Paris: Flammarion, 2006.

La Charité, Claude. "Jacques Cartier élève d'Ouy-dire dans le *Quart Livre* de Rabelais." *Méthode! Revue de littératures* 20 (2012): 79–88.

Pioffet, Marie-Christine, ed. "Nouvelle-France: fictions et rêves compensateurs." *Tangence* 90 (2009): 37–55.

Taylor, Alan. *American Colonies*. New York: Penguin Books, 2001.

Trudel, Marcel. *Histoire de la Nouvelle-France*, t. 1: *Les vaines tentatives (1524–1603)*. Montréal: Fides, 1963.

RELATED ARTICLES
1494, 1763, 1769

1536

From Cauvin to Calvin

The ideas of the Reformed Church were propagated
across Europe through an underground network whose
members embraced a single book, the *Institutes of the
Christian Religion*, that was composed in Latin, published
in Frankfurt in 1536, and then translated into many
languages. Upon publication, its author, a French humanist
named Jean Cauvin who had left Paris for Switzerland two
years earlier, became Calvinus.

Winter 1534: Jean Cauvin is forced to flee Paris, to leave
Babylon behind, without ever turning back. In France,
after anti-Catholic posters had surfaced in various cities,
"votaries of Jesus Christ" — those hot-headed believers
whose souls were inflamed by ideas from Germany and
elsewhere abroad — were persecuted. They believed that
God alone could save; that the pope, the church, the holy
mass, the saints, the miracles, and even human works could
not contribute to salvation. These men and women would
soon be known as Protestants. Cauvin, or *Calvinus* in

Latin, was one of them. This humanist and lawyer who had studied, like so many others, at the University of Orléans was not yet well known. He was an autodidact when it came to theology, newly won over by the ideas of Martin Luther, the German monk who had started it all in 1517. Unless Luther had instead ended it all. For it came to seem like the end of a world, the end of Christianity. In 1534, Calvin was twenty-six, and he would seldom return to Paris. He would remain a refugee, looking at France from the outside, far from the center. A sentinel on the fringes of the kingdom, he would launch ideas to conquer Europe.

To be precise, it was a book that conquered the world. In January 1535, Calvin sought refuge in Basel, Switzerland, taking up residence with the printer Conrad Resch, among the first to distribute Lutheran books in France. Basel, the city to which Erasmus had retired, accepted the Reformation under the influence of the German humanist Johannes Oecolampadius. It was there that, in the spring of 1536, during the Frankfurt fair, Cauvin became John Calvin with the publication of the work that would make him famous and spread "Calvinism" far and wide. Composed in Latin, the language of international communication, the five-hundred-page *Institutes of the Christian Religion* came in a small size. Easy to carry, easy to hide, it was an apologia framed as catechism and also a cry of alarm that, by presenting a synthesis of new religious ideas, tried to convince King Francis I of France to extinguish the fires that were everywhere being lit to burn Reformers at the stake. Six chapters in all. The first four revolved around the law (an explanation of the Ten Commandments); faith (the Apostles' Creed); prayer (the Lord's Prayer); and the sacraments (baptism and communion). There followed two further chapters, one on the "false sacraments" (penance, confirmation, extreme unction, order, and matrimony) and the other on Christian freedom, the church, and the state.

The first printing sold out within a year. There would be more than twenty subsequent editions in the sixteenth century alone. Even the author was surprised at his book's success — particularly as it contained little that was really new. There were traces of Calvin's humanist readings — of Seneca, about whom he had published a commentary in 1532 — but it mainly rehearsed the bolder theses of "protesting" Europe, which Calvin had read with passion and now presented in a new configuration. He never hid his admiration for Luther. The organization of the *Institutes* and many of its ideas were borrowed from his *Catechism*, published in 1529, and from his great classics, *On the Babylonian Captivity of the Church and On the Freedom of a Christian* (1520). The success of the *Institutes* earned Calvin an invitation to Geneva from William Farel, who had just persuaded his city to adopt the Reformed religion. In Geneva, from 1536 to 1538, Calvin had his first experience of pastoral duties, which he broadened in Strasbourg after his expulsion from Geneva, working with the Alsatian theologian Martin Bucer. Basel, Geneva, Strasbourg: he was always near borders, near margins. Calvin would always be a pastor for the edges of the world.

In Strasbourg from 1538 to 1541, Calvin was a pastor to French Protestant refugees who had fled the persecution at home. He gave numerous sermons and extended his knowledge of the discipline and structure of the church. He also kept reworking his *Institutes*, whose final edition would come out in 1559. In 1539, he revamped the first edition, influenced by the *Loci communes* of Philip Melanchthon, Luther's closest disciple. Calvin also absorbed the work of the Swiss reformers Ulrich Zwingli and Heinrich Bullinger. Gradually, the concepts took on a more personal character. Calvin tried to reconcile Protestant theologians on the subject of the mass, which he called the Lord's Supper, rejecting the position that it was a sacrifice but also Zwingli's idea that it was no more than a "memory" of Jesus's Last Supper. Calvin believed that the Eucharist contained the "true presence" of Christ, but "in spirit"; the bread remained bread while hosting the body of Christ thanks to the intercession of the Holy Ghost.

Most importantly, in the 1536 edition of the *Institutes* Calvin developed the Calvinist concept par excellence, the doctrine of "double predestination": God has from eternity divided the elect from the fallen, with the former preordained for eternal life and the latter for eternal damnation. Some have found predestination terrifying, but it is also, as the historian Denis Crouzet has argued, a panacea against anxiety. Blind and sinful creatures since their exile from the Garden of Eden, human beings can do nothing by their own actions to ensure their salvation. It is enough for them to have faith and put themselves in the hands of a just and all-powerful God. By offering respite from actions, prayers, and traditional religious processions, predestination relieves the pressing anguish that so often cripples believers. Freed from impossible calculations about their fate on Judgment Day, men and women could peacefully go about their lives on earth, no longer tortured by the afterlife.

Calvin quickly realized that he would need to translate his *Institutions* out of Latin. In order for the merchant, the tanner, the mother to receive the Word, it had to be couched in their own language. How else could the divine message be conveyed without go-betweens? Calvin himself translated his book into his native French. This was the first time the language had ever been used so ambitiously in a defining theological treatise or entrusted with deploying abstract arguments. Calvin raised French to the ranks of a language of reasoning, suitable for philosophical exposition. *L'Institution de la religion chrétienne* was acclaimed as "the prime monument to French eloquence." Its linear sentences and sequences of arguments were Calvin's direct contributions to the invention of France's "classical language." This bears reiteration: the decisive impetus toward the creation of modern French came from a man under sentence of banishment, living beyond "national borders," from Strasbourg first and then from Geneva, where Calvin took up permanent residence in 1541 and published the first French edition. The work was immediately banned by the appellate court of Paris and listed by the Sorbonne on the Index of Prohibited Books. Nonetheless, it made its way into France, smuggled through back channels and finding its way into the hands of anxious, clandestine souls looking for certainty.

The ball was now rolling, and the text was translated into Spanish in 1540 by Francisco de Enzinas, a native of Burgos and a friend of Philip Melanchthon, also a protégé of the archbishop of Canterbury, Thomas Cranmer. Then came an Italian translation, in 1557, by Giulio Cesare Pascali, a young poet who had sought refuge in Geneva. Others followed: into Dutch in 1560 by Jan Dyrkinus, a lawyer and native of Ghent who emigrated to Emden; into English in 1561 by Thomas Norton; into Basque in 1571; into German in 1572; into Polish (in excerpts) in 1599. And then a Czech translation in 1617 by Jirik Strejc, a Hungarian translation in 1624 by Albert Molnár, and others yet. Having founded

471

an academy in Geneva in 1559 to educate pastors who would preach the reformed message across Europe, Calvin was equipping them with the *Institutes*, an indispensable manual of Christian life.

In a famous quip, historian Robert Kingdon coined the term "Calvintern," on the model of "Comintern," to suggest the Calvinist international, the underground of men and ideas that fanned out from a headquarters in Geneva to undermine the Catholic world. Their proselytism paid off. Numerous reformed churches were established, with confessions of faith derived from the *Institutes*: in Hungary in 1557, the Hungarian Confession; in France in 1559, the La Rochelle Confession of Faith. The Scottish theologian John Knox and the Walloon Guido de Bres, both of whom spent time in Geneva, imported the Scots Confession (1560) and the Belgic Confession (1561) to their countries. Calvinism also penetrated into Germany despite the strong presence of Lutheranism. In 1563, Frederick III, Elector Palatine, converted to the Reformed religion and oversaw the drafting of the Heidelberg Catechism, which enjoyed enormous success in Poland, Hungary, Bohemia, and the Netherlands. To adopt Calvinism was also to reject the Habsburgs.

In a strange twist, persecution played an important role in the spread of Calvinism across national borders. The repressive policies enacted in Spain, Italy, France, and

England not only created martyrs but launched thousands of Calvinist dissidents onto the roads of Europe. As early as the 1540s, evangelists were leaving northern Italy for Zurich and Geneva; Walloons were taking refuge in Wesel; and residents of Flanders, Brabant, and Holland were fleeing to London and Emden. Some five thousand English Protestants emigrated to Geneva during the reign of Queen Mary I (r. 1553–1558). In France, where the Huguenots (or Protestants) represented 10 percent of the population, the French Wars of Religion drove thousands of them to seek haven in England and Germany. In the early seventeenth century, the exile's path expanded globally. Calvin's *Institutes* boarded the *Mayflower* with the Pilgrims in 1620 and landed in North America, where the first book printed, in 1640, was the *Bay Psalm Book*, which was none other than a Calvinist psalter. After the revocation of the Edict of Nantes in 1685, 180,000 Calvinists fled France, scattering across Europe and to America, South Africa, and Russia.

We will stop the story of this diaspora there, at the dawn of globalization. Today, some 75 million faithful from South Korea to Nigeria, by way of Massachusetts, Indonesia, Uganda, and Brazil, embrace the tenets expounded in Calvin's *Institutes*. While innumerable factors have contributed to this worldwide success, John Calvin is in no small part responsible. Exile is integrally bound with Calvinism, this "Reformation for refugees"

(Heiko Oberman). In Geneva, Calvin considered himself a soldier posted to a military camp, the pastor for an army whose parish was the whole globe (to paraphrase historian Patrick Cabanel). Tirelessly, he called on the elect to leave their towns and countries in order to travel to congregations where they would lie in wait to take power or live clandestinely — sleeping cells for the Gospel. Predestination is also the refugee's comfort. It gives the believer the certainty of being saved "as long as he is assured of belonging to the aristocracy of salvation, comprising the small number of the elect" (Max Weber). Because it consists of the elect, the empire of Calvinism cannot form a uniform entity; it is made of archipelagos, ready for submersion or insurrection.

This rootless identity also explains the worldwide success of John Calvin's ideas. The man who was born in Noyon, in the province of Picardy, in 1509, declared in his *Institutes*, "If heaven is our country, what can the earth be but a place of exile?"

Jérémie Foa

REFERENCES

Cabanel, Patrick. *Histoire des protestants en France (XVIe–XXIe siècle)*. Paris: Fayard, 2012.

Calvin, John. *Calvin: Institutes of the Christian Religion*. Edited by John
    T. McNeill. Translated by Ford Lewis Battles. Louisville, KY:
    Westminster John Knox Press, 2001.

Cottret, Bernard. *Calvin: A Biography*. Edinburgh: T & T Clark, 2003.

Crouzet, Denis. *Jean Calvin: Vies parallèles*. Paris: Fayard, 2000.

Gordon, Bruce. *John Calvin's Institutes of the Christian Religion:
    A Biography*. Princeton: Princeton University Press, 2016.

Oberman, Heiko. *John Calvin and the Reformation of the Refugees*.
    Geneva: Droz, 2009.

RELATED ARTICLES
1572, 1685, 1751, 1840, 1920, 1949

1539

The Empire of the French Language

The Ordinance of Villers-Cotterêts is the most venerable
legislative disposition surviving in French law, and the first
measure to establish the King's French as the language of
jurisprudence. Did it respond to the confusing diversity
of France's regional tongues, or rather to the decline of
spoken Latin? Whatever the case, it implied an attitude to
linguistic expansion that was more imperial than national.

Villers-Cotterêts, the birthplace of Alexandre Dumas *père* in
the Aisne department of France, today has a population of
ten thousand, a Renaissance château, and an extreme-right
Rassemblement National–dominated municipality. When,
in March 2014, its newly elected mayor skittishly refused to
participate in ceremonies celebrating the abolition of slavery,
the town briefly found itself under the microscope of the
national press, and France was duly reminded that an important element of the national identity had been crafted there
nearly half a millennium earlier. By the grace of King Francis
I, who happened to be staying at his newly built château in

the game-filled woodlands of Retz between August 10 and 25, 1539, a decree was enacted that is still applied in French law. Indeed, the Ordinance of Villers-Cotterêts is conventionally described as the original royal directive establishing French as the national language of France.

Is this so certain? We owe the Ordinance of Villers-Cotterêts, also known as the *Loi Guillermine* — comprising the rules by which French courts hear and determine what happens in civil, criminal, or administrative proceedings — to a distinguished advocate of the French bar, Chancellor Guillaume Poyet, after whom it was named. The culmination of a period of intense legislative activity spurred by the 1498 Ordinance of Blois, whereby Henri III's minister Cardinal Georges d'Amboise had begun codifying French laws, the *Loi Guillermine* consolidated, in a single majestic list of 192 articles, all the rules of procedure affecting civil and criminal trials (no distinction between civil and criminal law was settled in France until 1670). The preamble of this document announced that its goal was to "provide, for the good of our system of justice, an abbreviated system for trials for the relief of our subjects." This goal was to be achieved by guaranteeing the accessibility, coherence, and perpetuation of a standard parlance for all French law.

Thus, in the field of notarial registration, article 51 of the ordinance ruled that registers of baptisms be kept and recorded (in French) at the offices of every bailiwick and seneschalship; while article 175 made it obligatory for notaries to keep registers and protocols (in French) of every will or contract they might draw up or receive from others.

The law had to be rendered visible, if the extent of what it could control was to be broadened. The need for absolute clarity was expressed by article 110: "And in order that there may be no occasion to doubt the intelligence of the said judgments we wish and command that they should be made and written so clearly that there may not and cannot be any ambiguity or uncertainty, nor grounds for any to request their further interpretation." Article 111 follows on directly, affirming that "these judgments must be expressed in the French mother tongue and not otherwise." Yet by a delicious paradox, this passage — which appears to command the administrative use of the French language to satisfy a need for clarity — is anything but clear in the original French.

It may even be that its survival in French law is due to this very ambiguity.

The ordinance specifically forbade the use of Latin in French law, but did it also exclude provincial languages and dialects? Not quite. The first jurist to comment on this was Pierre Rebuffe, who pointed out in 1580 that the King's French was not the mother tongue of every inhabitant of his realm, inasmuch as French people habitually spoke the dialects of the provinces in which they lived. Since those provinces were unquestionably French, Rebuffe reasoned that the dialect of each was no less a "French mother tongue" than the King's own. This, for him, was the only possible interpretation that could fit with the royal demand for clarity: "For were it to be otherwise, and should the judgments of the Occitanians have to be written in French, they would prove obscure to the point of unfathomable."

Rebuffe's interpretation prevailed, on the whole, until the jurisprudence of the nineteenth century. At that time, French judges began invoking the ordinance of 1539 not so much to link their decisions to a solemn and majestic principle handed down from the past, but as a nod to the attachment to their *"petites patries"* (home regions) of those subject to their jurisdiction.

This was very different to the repressive and outright Jacobin outlook of Ferdinand Brunot — a fervent republican known to the French as the "citizen-linguist." In the second volume of his staggeringly erudite *Histoire de la Langue française des origines à 1900*, Brunot advocated in 1906 a "linguistic monarchy [that] will dominate the vanquished and fallen dialects," as though the Third Republic could achieve some kind of synthesis between the enlightened ancien régime of Francis I and the revolutionary Abbé Grégoire's 1794 *Rapport sur la nécessité et les moyens d'anéantir le patois, et d'universaliser l'usage de la langue française* (Report on the Necessity and the Means of Annihilating the Patois and Universalizing the Use of the French Language). It took the energy of the *Annales* school historian Lucien Febvre to explode this compelling narrative in a 1924 article in *Revue de synthèse historique* entitled "Politique royale ou civilisation française?" Contending that the use of French had been slowly penetrating the south of France since the Middle Ages, Febvre wrote: "The southern regions did not abruptly obey the cry of a herald who, after three blasts of a trumpet, read the Ordinance of Villers-Cotterêts to an abject population."

And so it proved: if the *Loi Guillermine* had an immediate effect on the drafting of parliamentary legislation, this was because there was general approval of the vernacular as the language of administration, as historian Serge Lusignan has shown. In the northern towns of Arras, Saint-Omer, and Douai, acts drafted in French first appeared in 1230; within forty years they had spread across the southwest of France while skirting the heartlands between the Loire and the Seine. The fact was that the King's French was no provincial language, but an invention of the cities, which spread through France around the edges of the northern langue d'oïl regions. As for the penetration of French into the langue d'oc regions, this also began at a very early date: the scribes of the Dauphiné states forsook Latin for French and Franco-Provençal from the thirteenth century onward, well before the Dauphiné's attachment to the realm of France in 1343.

The Ordinance of Villers-Cotterêts was mainly aimed at legal Latin, a language known only to initiates. The latter fought, as jurists, to maintain their grip on the royal function through the obfuscating double language of medieval government. This linguistic transformation had been gradually advancing within the fourteenth-century royal chancellery, but the process was in no way linear. While 80 percent of royal charters were drafted in French by 1330, the process stalled with the accession of King John the Good in 1350, when Latin made a comeback that lasted until the reign of Charles V, who preferred French as the language of learning. This hot-and-cold process left its mark on the language itself. As they gradually abandoned Latin, notaries tended to Latinize their French spelling, as if they wished to bedeck the King's French with all the dignity of the Latin tongue of sacred majesty they had learned so well. This explains the proliferation in modern French of silent consonants and other orthographic oddities, of which the purists are so proud. Hence *le tens* (this was how the word was spelled in old French) became *le temps*, by slipping in a *p* from the Latin *tempus*.

In 1539, the challenge was not only to stamp out the lingering remnants of judicial Latin in order to clarify the king's justice and make it easier for his subjects to understand; it was also to gain traction for a new language of authority that would express the formal discourse of government. The same year of 1539 saw the publication of Robert Estienne's *Dictionnaire François-Latin*, the first dictionary of translation from French into Latin (rather than the opposite), thereby rounding off a decade that had been decisive for the grammatical solidification of the language. Poets then picked up the gauntlet. In 1549, Joachim du Bellay published *La Defence et Illustration de la Langue Française*, which passed for a manifesto of the *Pléiade*, a group of seven prominent writers whose ambition was to renew the French language and free it from the shackles of Latin. The idea of linguistic unity for the kingdom meant little to these humanists; they saw the linguistic expansion of the French language in imperial rather than national terms.

All of them had read Italian humanists like Lorenzo Valla, who posited a Latin-speaking empire extending far beyond the boundaries of the old Roman one. By the same token, Jean Bodin suggested in his *Six Books of the Commonwealth* (1583) that Arabic had become an imperial language. Thus by renouncing the ghost-tongue of a former power, Francis I created the linguistic framework for a French imperial project against a fiercely competitive European backdrop. To take a single example: on April 17, 1536, in Rome, Holy Roman Emperor Charles V challenged the French king — in Spanish — to either conclude a peace or fight a duel. When the two French ambassadors objected that they did not understand Spanish, the emperor resumed his speech — in Italian.

Francis I was the friend of many French poets, but he also did much to promote Latin, Greek, and Hebrew studies. His own library, wrote the diplomat and linguist Guillaume Postel, was remarkable for its variety of works "in Latin, Greek, Hebrew, French, and Italian." The teaching of Greek and Hebrew was the task of the "royal readers" of the Parisiis Trilingue Collegium, an extension founded in 1530 of the grand European humanist dream that had begun at Alcala, Leuven, Oxford, Rome, and Milan. To call this establishment the ancestor of the Collège de France — for so it is — is to admit that the French language carries within it the imperial ambition of universalism.

So is this "imperial ambition" the secret of what has been described ever since as the "genius of the French language" — namely, a clarity of expression that is all the more unique for being opaque to much of the rest of the world?

On June 6, 1782, the Berlin Academy held a competition in which the following questions were asked: What makes French the most universal language in Europe? How does it deserve this prerogative? Does it still? This must have seemed pertinent at a time when Casanova was crisscrossing Europe with French as his only means of expression, and when even the Ottoman chancellery was using French as its diplomatic language. A protégé of Voltaire, Antoine de Rivarol, won the Berlin competition with an essay that aroused more enthusiasm in Germany (notably from the Brothers Grimm) than in France. Rivarol had a way with words: "The books of France constitute the library of the human race," he wrote; and also "The time has come to speak of the *French world* as we used to speak of the *Roman world*." Twelve years later, in June 1794, a report submitted to the French revolutionary Convention by Abbé Grégoire noted (somewhat sourly) that this universal language was "very badly spoken by the French themselves."

When the ratification of the 1992 Treaty of Maastricht obliged the countries of the European Union to declare their official languages, French jurists were forced to admit that the Ordinance of Villers-Cotterêts was not quite as explicit as had been claimed for centuries. In consequence, the French Constitution of 1958 was modified on June 23, 1992, with an addition to article 2: "The language of the Republic is French." This in no way prevents the militant monolinguists of the French elite from invoking the intangible principle of 1539 as a reason not to ratify the European Charter of Regional and Minority Languages. This charter was adopted by the Council of Europe in 1992 and signed by France in 1999. It remains unratified.

Thus, in a curious reversal of history, France's collective consciousness has so upended the Ordinance of Villers-Cotterêts that it has become a memory more national than imperial, and an issue more defensive than expansive.

Patrick Boucheron

REFERENCES

Boulard, Gilles. "L'ordonnance de Villers-Cotterêts: Le temps de la clarté et la stratégie du temps (1539–1992)." *Revue historique 301*, no. 1 (January/March 1999): 45–100.

Fumaroli, Marc. "The Genius of the French Language." In *Realms of Memory: The Construction of the French Past*, edited by Pierre Nora and Lawrence D. Kritzman. New York: Columbia University Press, 1998.

Knecht, Robert J. *Renaissance Warrior and Patron: The Reign of Francis I*. Cambridge: Cambridge University Press, 1994.

Lusignan, Serge. *La langue des rois au Moyen Âge: Le français en France et en Angleterre*. Paris: Presses Universitaires de France, 2004.

Merlin-Kajman, Hélène. "L'étrange histoire de l'ordonnance de Villers-Cotterêts: Force du passé, force des signes." *Histoire Épistémologie Langage* 33, no. 2 (2011): 79–101.

RELATED ARTICLES
842–843, 1105, 1380, 1515, 1683, 1804, 1883, 1992

1550

The Normans Play Indians

On October 1, 1550, the joyous entry of King Henry
II into the good city of Rouen was celebrated with a
spectacular Brazilian festival. Tupinambá people played
their own roles: "good savages" and commercial partners.
The scene represented a dream of an alliance between
peoples — far from the racial categories and human zoos
that would come later.

It was a boisterous festival, with two hundred and fifty
participants, mainly men, most of them naked (though some
were chastely dressed), with belts of leaves covering their
genitals. They seemed ferocious with their large bows, oval
shields, and long wooden clubs. A few sported feathers on
their heads or perhaps tattoos on their skin, painted red.

These savages were Normans — sailors disguised as
Tupinambá Indians from the coast of Brazil — performing
in Rouen on October 1, 1550, before Henry II, the new king
of France who, after Paris and Lyon, had come with his
court to this city in Normandy.

Alongside fifty American Indians, who may have arrived from the lands located between Pernambuco and Salvador on the northeast coast of Brazil, these Normans walked among trees that had been painted red, climbed on palm trees, and pursued monkeys. They danced, carried tree trunks aloft, cooked, hunted birds, embraced, and rested in hammocks. As they engaged in mock battle with equally naked savages, huts and cabins caught fire in the heat of combat. This Brazilian festival was but one scene among many in a Royal Entry, a ceremony that, drawing from the Italian Renaissance, combined ancient carts, arches of triumph, mythological figures, and allegorical tableaux to instruct and delight the monarch. Still, it was exceptional, and made Rouen's celebration stand out from the festive and political competition that the French realm's good cities waged against one another. All were eager to show their respect and display their qualities to the new sovereign in order to secure his good graces and favors.

From the Chaussée des Emmurées, between the city and the Seine, the king, his courtiers, and ambassadors who had been dispatched to the realm could view replicas of Tupinambá, or Tupi, villages and observe the lives of the American Indians who inhabited them. A portion of the left bank of the river had been transformed into a Brazilian forest full of parrots, monkeys, and fruit trees. As they admired these marvels, Henry II and Catherine de' Medici were astonished at the extravagance of a foreign world with which, it must be said, Normans had been growing increasingly familiar since the beginning of the sixteenth century. Because the city's trade with this new world was prospering, a "trading post" was installed for the Royal Entry onto the shores of this Norman Brazil (a "French port" at the mouth of the São Francisco river is indeed indicated on a Portuguese map, even though since 1494 that part of the South American continent had been controlled by Portuguese interests).

The three accounts of the Entry that were written between the autumn of 1550 and 1557 enable us to reconstruct the sequence of reenactments. After "trading" animals and brazilwood to the French in exchange for axes and iron sickles, the Tupinambá defeated a marauding band of enemies and burned their village. This mock victory by France's allies was followed by another battle that proved equally flattering to the interests of the kingdom of Henry II: a naumachia, or mock naval battle, that portrayed a French ship's attack on a Portuguese caravel. These symmetrical battles involved the Tupinambá's enemies, the Tupiniquim, allies of the Portuguese in Brazil.

The festival of Rouen celebrated an alliance crowned by the success of weapons. It spoke of a relationship with the Indians unlike those of the Spanish, Portuguese, or English. The famous saying by Francis Parkman, the great nineteenth-century US historian — "Spanish civilization crushed the Indian; English civilization scorned and neglected him; French civilization embraced and cherished him" — is false and unfair, as demonstrated by France's pitiless war against the Natchez and Fox Indians. All the same, we must note that something unique was formed in that relationship between the French and the Tupinambá. The reenactment of Rouen does not suggest the infamous "human zoos" and indigenous reconstructions that proliferated in France at the end of the 1870s, first in Paris (notably at the Jardin d'Acclimatation) and then, as these human exhibitions became professionalized, in the provinces as well, within colonial and universal expositions that were staged during the following fifty years. Depicted among other exotic fauna and flora, traveling "black" or "Senegalese" villages and ethnological fairs portrayed a racialized human alterity, necessarily subaltern and subjugated.

The 1550 spectacle depicted neither vanquished American Indians nor the superior white man. It did not dramatize a so-called racial hierarchy or represent masters of the world on one side and the people who merely inhabited it on the other. It did not tap colonial images of indigenous people as children to be disciplined and educated or as animals to be broken and tamed. It did not turn the Indian into an abominable cannibal.

Instead, the spectacle introduced spectators to beardless savages who were indispensable commercial partners as well as valuable allies. And perhaps more. The ease with which, according to contemporary chroniclers, Norman sailors "naively" copied the gestures and speech of the Tupinambá, "as if they were natives of the same lands," suggests a common transatlantic identity, transcending religious and cultural boundaries, rather than irreducible differences. This sense of familiarity resulted from the conditions of commercial trade between the French and the Indians. The Normans who negotiated for wood had to spend long weeks with their hosts while awaiting the sought-after tree trunks. Even if European axes accelerated the work, delivering the trees would take time, and this time facilitated mutual understanding within Tupi villages. As Brazilian anthropologist Beatriz Perrone-Moisés suggests, these Norman sailors were reenacting their own experiences of the Brazilian land while impersonating American Indians. This extended comingling with the Tupinambá, whose language the Normans learned, contributed to the military alliance and commercial trade.

That mutually beneficial association began with an event that, while part of the symbolic narrative of the first encounters between the Europeans and the inhabitants of the new Atlantic lands, established the unique quality of a relationship founded less on a conquest — in the name of a sovereign or the Christian God — than on an alliance (in the word's etymological sense of "binding") of two peoples. During one of his voyages, a captain from Honfleur, Binot Paulmier de Gonneville, encountered headwinds that took his ship, headed for the Indies by way of the African Coast, to the Brazilian coast, where it shipwrecked in January 1504. It is said that on Easter Day, during his stay with the American Indians, with whom he traded, the Norman captain erected a large cross, a "marker" to prove that Christians had disembarked on that land. Raised with the help of natives, it reportedly contained several inscriptions: on one side, the names of the pope, the King of France, the admiral of the kingdom, Paulmier de Gonneville himself, and "bourgeois and companions of support, the greatest to the poorest"; on the other side: *Hic sacra paimarius posuit gonivilla binotus; grex socius pariter, neustraque progenies.* (Here Paulmier de Gonneville raised this sacred monument, thereby intimately associating the native people and the Norman lineage.) At the dawn of modernity, the alliance of the Normans and the American Indians established a relationship founded neither on the subjugation of a people by a state or the forced conversion to a church, but on the civil faith of a republic that knew its limitations yet meant to follow the logic of its expansion. The rights of the pope and king were certainly not forgotten, but their absolutist pretensions faded behind the intimacy of an alliance between peoples, of an association that mirrored what could be called the *"polity"* of the kingdom of France (before the state-driven turnaround of the following century). This was the empire of nations within a French republic envisioned in the 1539 Ordinance of Villers-Cotterêts, whose promulgation of French over Latin in the acts of the chancelleries of the kingdom reflected less the imperialism of the French language than an imperial use of the king's language.

Let us conclude by returning to the incomplete accuracy of the Norman reenactment. The spectacle of war and the victory of the French allies were in fact partial, for something was missing from this scene of military valor. The viewer's gaze turned abruptly from the edges of the Brazilian forest to the naumachia on the Seine. This diversion hid the ritual sacrifice and anthropophagic consumption of the defeated warriors. The Tupinambá were cannibals; this was a known fact that contemporary accounts did not hide. But the French did not portray these man-eaters cutting up their victims and roasting their flesh. Instead, they endowed the Tupinambá with a bucolic identity that was not rooted in a singular, immutable essence.

This freedom of being may still have resonated with Michel de Montaigne when he witnessed another Royal Entry — that of Charles IX into Bordeaux in 1565 — and another encounter with Brazilians. Montaigne dared to liken his contemporaries to barbarians worse than the savages of the West Indies, and their conquerors to men even more horrible than their cannibal victims.

Yann Lignereux

REFERENCES

Arnould, Jean-Claude, and Emmanuel Faye, eds. *Rouen 1562: Montaigne et les Cannibales*. Publications numériques du CÉRÉdI, Actes de colloque 8 (2013).

Bonnichon, Philippe. "Image et connaissance du Brésil: Diffusion en France, de Louis XII à Louis XIII." In *Naissance du Brésil moderne (1500–1808)*, edited by Kátia de Queirós Mattoso, et al., 9–31. Paris: Presses de l'université de Paris-Sorbonne, 1998.

Dickason, Olive P. *The Myth of the Savage and the Beginnings of French Colonialism in the Americas*. Edmonton: University of Alberta Press, 1997.

Perrone-Moisés, Beatriz. "L'alliance normando-tupi au XVIe siècle: La célébration de Rouen." *Journal de la Société des américanistes* 94, no. 1 (2008): 45–64.

Wintroub, Michael. "Civilizing the Savage and Making a King: The Royal Entry Festival of Henri II (Rouen, 1550)." *The Sixteenth Century Journal* 29, no. 2 (1998): 465–94.

RELATED ARTICLES
1494, 1840, 1889

1572

Saint Bartholomew's Season

First in Paris, then in dozens of cities across France, Protestants were massacred. The shock wave traveled across Europe. What was King Charles IX's role in the spread of violence? Would this civil war spread beyond France's borders? Unable to impose its narrative on the events, the French monarchy was buffeted by an intense political dispute.

Dawn on August 24, 1572. Paris was officially at peace, although tensions had recently been mounting. Then the church bells rang the alarm. For many Catholics, this signaled a Protestant attack. Their reaction was violent. Members of the citizens' militia joined by private individuals attacked Huguenots in the street, convinced that the king supported their action. After Admiral Gaspard II de Coligny, the foremost Calvinist leader, was assassinated, the Catholic Henry I, Duke of Guise, who led the dawn foray, cried out, "The king commands it!" Massacre was the order of the day.

Less than a week earlier, Paris had been celebrating the marriage of King Charles IX's sister, a Catholic, to Henry of Bourbon, king of Navarre and first among Protestant princes, on the square before Notre-Dame Cathedral. The alliance was meant to defuse religious tensions, a process that had begun with the Peace of Saint-Germain in August 1570, a treaty that ended the third War of Religion. The French king and his mother, Catherine de' Medici, were trying to reassure Catholics, many of whom resented the heretics' right to worship, and also Protestants, who formed too small a minority to feel secure. The peace presumed that all earlier conflicts would be forgotten. But Admiral Coligny sat on the king's privy council, and it was hard to forget that he had been burned in effigy on the streets of Paris only a few years earlier for offenses against the sovereign authority. Paris, the spear tip of Catholic reaction, was sweltering in the summer heat, the price of wheat was high, and tempers were anything but calm.

The other European powers questioned how France could survive after making the extraordinary decision to recognize two religions within the same political space. The Peace of Augsburg in 1555 allowed the ruler of a state in the Holy Roman Empire to choose his own faith as his subjects' official religion. Conflicts over religious faith were testing almost every country, from the Catholic rebellion in England in 1569 to the ongoing war between Philip II of

Spain and his Protestant subjects in the Netherlands. And though France, which was more than 90 percent Catholic, would never become a Protestant nation, the chance that it might support the rebellion in the Low Countries was very real. Coligny had urged the king to intervene. When the king's council refused to take official action, the admiral decided to rescue his co-religionists at the head of an army. His departure was set for August 25, after the wedding festivities.

But on August 22, an assassin tried to kill Coligny as he was leaving the Louvre Palace. There are indications that the Guise family were behind this, carrying out a family vendetta: they held Coligny responsible for the murder of François de Guise in 1563. Anger mounted among the great Protestant lords who had gathered at the French court for the royal wedding. The day of August 23 was decisive. Convinced that the Huguenots were planning to take revenge for the attempt on Coligny, the king and his council decided to act preemptively by executing the Protestant leaders. The operation was launched at dawn on August 24, the feast of Saint Bartholomew.

But as the first victims fell — Coligny among them, stabbed to death in his bed — soldiers and the Paris mob attacked every Huguenot they could find, including women and children. Several thousand would die that day. While many French Catholics saw the Huguenots as heretics, others were primarily concerned with the threat they posed to the safety of the city. Yet others took advantage of the volatile atmosphere to settle personal scores or kill Protestants and loot their possessions. This said, a majority of Catholics held back from the massacre, and many Huguenots owed their lives to Catholics, whether that assistance was disinterested or not (or quite simply a sign of indifference). Among the survivors were many who, like Henry of Navarre, would renounce their Protestant faith under duress. It was the one time during the Wars of Religion when the king instigated a mass killing.

Still, we must distinguish between two "massacres": the massacre of the "warrior Huguenots," which the king and his close advisers had called for, and the massacre carried out by the mob, which Charles IX never approved. The bloodbath lasted for a month in Paris; in a dozen other cities, it only ended the following October. "Saint Bartholomew's was not of a day, but of a season," historian Jules Michelet would say, and the fact pointed to the king's difficulty in imposing his authority. After linking the massacre to the Guises' private vendetta, Charles IX took responsibility for the decision to execute the Protestant leaders, saying it was necessary politically to forestall the resumption of civil unrest and a possible war with Spain. But the killing of ordinary Protestants was held to have been unwarranted, particularly as the king intended the provisions set by the

Peace of Saint-Germain to remain in effect.

The massacre sent a strong shock wave through Europe, carried by the accounts of ambassadors and witnesses, by the flood of refugees who left France, and by engravings that soon appeared and tended to linger on Coligny's death. Reactions were at logical extremes. In France itself, some interpreted the events as miraculous, others as punitive. In Rome, the pope held a Te Deum service of thanks and commissioned a commemorative medal. Philip II of Spain congratulated Charles IX, the "Most Christian King," on his action. Protestant countries, on the other hand, reacted with terror. French diplomats found themselves hard put to justify their country's politics — particularly those who, after explaining that it was a private vendetta, then had to backpedal, and those who were in Poland, a country that admitted multiple faiths, to support the candidacy of Charles IX's younger brother to the throne.

Debate broke out at once — and still rages among historians — about who was truly responsible for the various phases of the massacre. Conspiracy theories were rampant — in fact wasn't the king responding, as he would later explain, to the threat of a Protestant plot?

Many blamed the massacre on foreign governments — Spain in particular, eager to be rid of the heretical and warmongering Coligny. This scenario had Spain mounting its own conspiracy and using the Guises or the king's counselors to carry it out. It is difficult even today, after consulting the best books on the subject, to come up with sure conclusions. Many contemporary sources are available, advancing a host of hypotheses and giving voice even to the faintest rumors. In view of the complexity of events, the large number of decision-makers, and the fatal seriousness of the consequences, a bitter fight between competing versions broke out very early. Many were convinced that the massacres had been premeditated, the result of canny calculation or heinous villainy. Especially widespread was the belief that the royal wedding constituted a trap to draw Huguenot leaders to Paris. Many also believed that all of the massacres were carried out on the king's orders. But the most likely explanation is that commentators attributed after the fact reason and planning to events that snowballed unpredictably.

The variety of interpretations also attests to the crown's inability to impose its stamp on the affair. Not coincidentally, the massacres were a setback for the king, as they failed to save the peace and instead launched the country into another civil war. Yet the war remained within France's borders, and, at least on the international scale, the massacres' effect was limited.

The events surrounding Saint Bartholomew's Day also caused intense political reflection. The king claimed that he had been forced by extraordinary circumstances to take extraordinary judicial measures. Although the privy council's heated debates failed to prevent the mob's excesses or keep the country from civil war on August 23, they at least produced a notion of reason of state.

For Protestant thinkers, who would soon be branded as opponents to the monarchy, the massacre reflected the king's tyranny and not just the influence of a few bad counselors. This raised the question of whether resistance was called for. If there had been abuse of power, then the king's subjects needed better safeguards for their rights, possibly a contract. Yet the latter was no more than a last resort and hardly represented progress, being the result of a national trauma: a loss of confidence in the king, and an end to the people's love affair with the monarchy. A year later, in 1573, a publication called for an annual commemoration of this "day of treachery" and denounced as pure pretext the claim that Protestants had been plotting rebellion.

For Catholics in France, the trauma had a different aspect. Despite the decimation of the Huguenots, some killed and many more forced to renounce their faith, the heresy had not been eradicated. The Saint Bartholomew's Day massacre marked a turning point all the same, being the last massacre of Protestants in France. Catholics looked back uneasily on the events and were disposed afterward to blame the ineradicable stain of the heresy in France on their own sins. But on their side too, the massacres generated a desire for political reform.

Catherine de' Medici, believed by many to have inspired the grisly events, came to exemplify a negative model. Being foreign, female, and a disciple of Machiavelli, she was seen to wield a power antithetical to all things French. For an ultra-Catholic faction to take its inspiration from Machiavelli, whose writings were on the papal Index of Forbidden Books, may strike us as the height of paradox. At all events, the Florence-born queen further tarnished the image of Italians, who were accused of invading the king's privy council and ministry of finance.

The characterization of the events as a massacre quickly gained currency. In 1574, the Huguenot Henri de Montmorency would justify his armed rebellion by alluding to the "massacre carried out on Saint Bartholomew's Day." But what he mainly decried was the massacre of the nobility. In the popular imagination, the event came increasingly to center on religious fanaticism, whether a king driven by "mystical frenzy" (according to the French revolutionary Jean-Paul Marat) or "members of the Parisian bourgeoisie, rushing off to assassinate…their fellow citizens who failed to attend Mass" (Voltaire). This view became a staple of anticlerical polemics, reinforced by the durable alliance between the French throne and the clergy.

Philippe Hamon

REFERENCES

Bourgeon, Jean-Louis. *Charles IX devant la Saint-Barthélemy*. Geneva: Droz, 1995.

Crouzet, Denis. *La Nuit de la Saint-Barthélemy: Un rêve perdu de la Renaissance*. Paris: Fayard, 1994.

Diefendorf, Barbara B. *Beneath the Cross: Catholics and Huguenots in Sixteenth-Century Paris*. Oxford: Oxford University Press, 1991.

Jouanna, Arlette. *La Saint-Barthélemy: Les mystères d'un crime d'État (24 août 1572)*. Paris: Gallimard, 2007.

Joutard, Philippe, Janine Estèbe, Élisabeth Labrousse, and Jean Lecuir. *La Saint-Barthélemy ou les résonances d'un massacre*. Neuchâtel: Delachaux & Niestlé, 1976.

Sutherland, Nicola Mary. *The Massacre of St. Bartholomew and the European Conflict (1559–1572)*. London: Macmillan, 1973.

RELATED ARTICLES
177, 1095, 1683, 1794, 1942

1610

The Political Climate in Baroque France

The assassination of King Henry IV on May 14, 1610,
launched a race to control information. The news traveled
quickly across the globe, all the way to Mexico. But
although no one realized it at the time, this political event
coincided with a development of much longer duration, the
gradual warming of the earth's atmosphere.

The fact is widely accepted, though it came to light only
recently. An era of unprecedented climate change began
in 1610 because of the deforestation of a portion of the
Americas in the wake of the vast movements of people,
domestic animals, and diseases initiated by the European
discovery of the New World. We owe this conclusion to
two British researchers, Simon Lewis and Mark Maslin, who
have demonstrated a slight decrease in atmospheric carbon
dioxide in the period from 1570 to 1620. Many factors
contributed to this: the reduced use of fires to clear land in
North America, and the death of 90 percent of the native
population in South America from infectious diseases.

The demographic catastrophe allowed forest lands to regenerate and the attendant jump in biomass increased the sequestration of atmospheric carbon. For Lewis and Maslin, the year 1610 marks the beginning of the Anthropocene, the period when the earth's climate and ecosystems began to be fundamentally altered by human action. In the highlands of New Guinea, the memory of this ecological crisis and of the famines caused by the drop in temperature persist.

Across the Atlantic, a different event was roiling public life and drawing the attention of European chroniclers: King Henry IV of France had been murdered, stabbed by a Catholic from the town of Angoulême, François Ravaillac, on May 14, 1610. Historians have generally linked the episode to a rise in absolutism, or seen it as a symbol of religious zealotry. We will be less concerned here with the lead-up to the regicide than its aftereffects. Historian Michel Cassan has charted them by examining the way the event was recorded in the municipal archives of 240 French towns. The murder of the king takes its place in a long line of political assassinations in France that started in the Middle Ages, the most sensational being that of King Henry III on August 2, 1589. In examining how the information was passed on, there is clear evidence of political reframing of the event, as the Catholic League of France imprinted its interpretation on the news, even while transmitting it.

Because it offered a replay of the 1589 episode, the

assassination of Henry IV prompted the authorities to come up quickly with an official version of the event. Paul Phélypeaux de Pontchartrain, Nicolas Potier de Blancmesnil, and Antoine de Loménie, along with Marie de' Médici, applied themselves to the task of writing official dispatches. In that context it was not anecdotal to note that the attack took place at 4 p.m. on the Rue de la Ferronerie, that the Parlement of Paris was ordered to assemble by the chancellor at the Augustinian monastery, and that by 7 p.m. it had declared Marie de' Médici regent of the realm. With the Duke of Épernon urging the pace, an exceptional session of parliament was hastily convened the following day, May 15, to provide a solemn confirmation of royal justice. The young King Louis XIII, age eight, presided. It was not the custom, however, for a king of France to appear in public between the death of his predecessor and the funeral ceremony. This serious break with established ritual, writes the historian Sarah Hanley, "occasioned a reformulation of the constitutional ideology" and shocked contemporaries. Maximilien de Béthune, the Duke of Sully, complained in his *Memoirs* that to enthrone the king in this way was to rob the sacrament of its value as investiture.

Town hall deliberations, municipal correspondence, and ledgers tell us how a strategic sector of the French elite reacted at a time when, after the Wars of Religion (1562–1598) and the formation of the Catholic League, the crown had reassumed many city-related powers. One hundred fifty-three townships made special mention of the assassination, most of them in southern France. As the primary concern was to dispel any rumors that might set off a general panic or arouse popular sentiment, speed was of the essence. The postal network that the Duke of Sully, the superintendent of finances, had put in place allowed the information to travel widely, with towns situated along major roads receiving the news that day. By May 21, every town in France had been contacted. Supplementing this channel of communication were the letters sent out by local governors, which gave context and form to the news as it spread. A second concern was that the royal policy toward Protestants might change. When the towns published news of Henry's death, they used the occasion to reaffirm the guarantees the king had given Protestants in his 1598 Edict of Nantes, thereby forestalling any political violence.

The event was not purely an internal matter to France, and its interpretations reflected the diplomatic tensions with the Habsburgs. The French fear and mistrust of Spain was reawakened, resulting in acts of hostility toward Spanish representatives. Looking once more across the Atlantic, we find the news reached New Spain in September, after being relayed through Madrid and Seville.

On Wednesday, September 8, 1610, the news came to Mexico from Spain:

We learned that they had killed the king of France, don Henry IV, and that the man who killed him was a vassal, one of the king's servants and pages; he was not a knight, not a noble, but a man of the people. We learned that he cut the king's throat in the street as he was in his carriage with the bishop-nuncio. To cut his throat, [the servant] handed the king a letter in his carriage so the king would have to lean out to read it. He then cut his throat, though no one knows why. The king was making his rounds of the city, and he had ventured down a street to see that it was suitably decorated for the festivities about to be held for his wife, who was going to be crowned queen of France.

This passage, from the annals of Aztec chronicler Domingo Francisco de San Antón Muñón Chimalpahin Quauhtlehuanitzin (commonly known as Chimalpahin), has been masterfully glossed by historian Serge Gruzinski. The various details given by the Nahua annalist indicate to Gruzinski a decentered perspective on this French event: first, there is the portrait of Ravaillac as a man of the people; next, the reading of the letter before the king's murder; and finally the presence of the nuncio, which no doubt reflects a Spanish and Catholic interpretation of the event. As it happens, the church is very much in evidence in Chimalpahin's journal. Just before relating Henry IV's death, Chimalpahin described the beatification ceremony for the Jesuit Ignatius of Loyola. The episode also shows the doubts that the Hispanic world harbored about Henry IV's conversion from Protestantism to Catholicism, particularly as he was planning to resume hostilities with Spain and the Holy Roman Empire. That an event of this kind should figure in a Mexican chronicle indicates that it was a period of political uncertainty not only in Europe, but around the world. Discussed in Mexico, the event was also indirectly present in Japan, where painters represented the King of France next to other sovereigns from across the globe, including the Ottoman sultan and the King of Ethiopia. As Gruzinski writes, Chimalpahin's annals are "perhaps emblematic of another version of the modern, which is not to be confused with the irresistible march toward absolutism, and even less with a trend toward rationality in modern thought — Descartes by way of Montaigne. Rather, it suggests a state of mind, a sensibility, an understanding of the world that arises when a vision of world domination comes into contact with other societies, other civilizations."

Looking at the records of the king's assassination from the French provinces to Mexico City or Nagasaki shows we must venture beyond exclusively religious interpretations to understand the various reactions to the event. The circulation of information did not merely record (or confirm) a political news item, but instead created an information-sharing order that was becoming global in scope and whose every detail spoke to the power and uncertainty of local situations. This shift invites varied avenues of exploration. We could, for instance, delve further into the repercussions of this regicide within the French possessions and colonies taking shape in America under the Duke of Sully. From this, we could follow the general mobilization of French authorities outside Europe and the multiple conflicts that arose in the New World towns where French Protestants had settled.

Should we conclude that environmental crises and political assassinations are irremediably separate? Or should we locate their points of convergence? We might ask ourselves how, in the colonial context, the murder ushered in a new stage in the French administration of nature in the early seventeenth century. It is an odd coincidence, if we consider that the assassination of Henry IV has been interpreted as the founding act of what would become Cartesianism, which sees man as nature's owner and master. In the same way that English historians have tried to connect the history of the British Empire, the works of Sir Francis Bacon, and the environmental crisis, it might prove a fruitful exercise to join disparate entities by using analogy and collapsing chronologies.

For the moment, the effort to open up historical writing by crossing geographic and thematic boundaries is aimed less at demonstrating the global import of the French king or the universal power of the French state than at raising questions about a political regime in which dynastic stability and the monarchical principle guaranteed the safe continuation of a cosmos against wars and political violence. This regime also shaped a vision of the world and nature at the start of the seventeenth century.

Stéphane Van Damme

REFERENCES

Cassan, Michel. *La Grande Peur de 1610: Les Français et l'assassinat d'Henri IV*. Seyssel: Champ Vallon, 2010.

Gruzinski, Serge. *Les Quatre Parties du monde: Histoire d'une mondialisation*. Paris: Points Seuil, 2006.

Hanley, Sarah. *The "Lit de Justice" of the Kings of France: Constitutional Ideology in Legend, Ritual, and Discourse*. Princeton: Princeton University Press, 1983.

Lewis, Simon L., and Mark A. Maslin, "A Transparent Framework for Defining the Anthropocene Epoch." *The Anthropocene Review* 2, no. 2 (2015) 128–46.

RELATED ARTICLES

12,000 BCE, 1347, 1572, 1685, 1816

ABSOLUTE POWER

A King "sovereign in his own state, owing his crown to none but God": this is what the delegates representing the Third Estate (all French subjects except for the clergy and nobility) requested at the Estates General in 1614. Still traumatized by the assassination of Henry IV in 1610, they wanted the king to have absolute power, to be unshackled from the contractual arrangements that had characterized the modern state since the end of the thirteenth century. While this might seem a paradoxical position for representatives of the towns and the people, it reflects a deep distrust of the aristocracy and a corresponding confidence in the model of political theology. It also shows how few political alternatives were available.

From the appointment of Cardinal Richelieu to the Royal Council of ministers in 1624 up till the death of his successor, Cardinal Mazarin, in 1661 — both of them powerful figures in the Catholic Church and unswerving servants of royal power — France was traversing a pivotal period. Louis XIII's reign (1610–1643) is notable for the expansion of the central administration, with royal functionaries, the *intendants*, and a tighter system of fiscal and financial oversight. This system would be extended under Louis XIV by the mercantilist policies of his leading minister, Jean-Baptiste Colbert, who created inspectors to regulate the manufacturing industries.

Facing tax revolts, the political power of the Huguenots, and a rebellious aristocracy intent on defending its warrior-class privileges against the royal court, the Most Christian King of France became a king of war. The royal state hence dealt harshly with the Fronde (1648–1653), the rebellion by aristocratic magistrates and nobles of the sword (led by the princes of Condé and Conti) who took advantage of Louis XIV's minority to claim old privileges. The monarchy's severe response strengthened its power.

War justified this state of exception. It was accordingly the motif of the ceiling panels Charles le Brun painted in the Hall of Mirrors in the Palace of Versailles. The paintings "appalled the nations," according to the Duke of Saint-Simon, the great memoirist of court life. Indeed, they were the epitome of the royal propaganda churned out by artists, the great "artisans of glory" at the court of the Sun King. The central panel depicts Louis XIV's elevation to divine status. The king who extolled his accession to power in 1661 as a world revolution and made "the splendid embassies of neighboring powers" bow down to him did not even need to compare himself to Alexander the Great. Had not the Jesuit missionaries confirmed that the Huron chieftains of New France accepted "the Kynge of France as Lord of all the earth"? Following a century of religious violence, the Treaty of the Pyrenees (1659) allowed France to challenge Spain for hegemony over Europe. The treaty not only established a new border between the two countries, it set diplomatic boundaries to contain the influence of the Habsburgs and Spain, with its vast overseas empire.

But predominance was not the only goal: to shine like a beacon seems to have been the Sun King's great concern. He mobilized the artisans of glory to fashion his own image alongside those of France and the state, since, in the words of royal historiographer Nicolas Boileau, "the whole state is in him." Expressed in sumptuous court ceremonies where, increasingly, Louis XIV stood alone, this ritual narrowing of kingship to his person had the paradoxical effect of making the monarchy more fragile, confounding as it did the sovereign's two manifestations: the eternal body of kingship and the mortal body of the fallible man who incarnated it. Until that time, political doctrine had maintained the distinction.

Yet power has its charms, and French historians of the *Grand Siècle* (as the seventeenth century is known) can seldom resist it. Those were the days in which the idea of greatness was forged, and it plays an essential part in the exaltation of the literary *patrie*. How could historians resist that image, when the idea of France as a beacon of influence is so constant in the national debate, and when the stature of every Frenchman ambitious for power, from

515

Voltaire to Charles de Gaulle, has been measured against Louis XIV?

It is certainly the image of the classical state that prompts the identification of French genius with power, the "clear and distinct ideas" of Descartes with the sovereign symmetry of Versailles. The era that began to unfold in 1630 would see the scientific revolution and the growth of a community of scientists, the mathematical modeling of the world and of sovereignty itself, which, as the jurist Cardin Le Bret wrote in 1632, "is no more divisible than a point is divisible in geometry." It is well to remember that this "century of saints" also saw the philosopher Blaise Pascal write about the hidden God of the Jansenists, these intransigent Catholics who drew the Sun King's hostility. The dancing light in the mirrors at Versailles grew dimmer before the waning years of his reign, when France, surrounded by the "iron frontier" of Vauban, the military engineer who became marshal of France, found itself bled dry, taxed to excess to pay for wars whose brutality troubled Europe. Truth be told, this also happened in England, where the king taxed his people even more heavily, and with the full consent of Parliament. Absolutism, then, was not the last word in the history of France. It was at most a temptation, shared by many political forces, but always constrained by other and more powerful ones. This temptation is best apprehended on a broader scale, in the imperial designs suggested by the ships plying the seas on the globes of Vincenzo Coronelli.

1633

Descartes Is the World!

Galileo's June 1633 conviction for heresy stunned all of
learned Europe. Descartes reacted from Amsterdam, amid
a flurry of letter-writing with correspondents shaken
by the news of the world. A long tradition has turned
Cartesianism into a sort of specifically French genius.
And yet, René Descartes was above all a peripatetic
philosopher.

Descartes has for a long time been considered the
embodiment of French "genius," and the decade 1630–1640
the advent of a "philosophical revolution" symbolized by
his *Discourse on Method* (1637). In the nineteenth century,
political appropriation of Descartes revealed contradictions
and tensions surrounding the national question. Condemned
by the right-wing Action Française due to his rationalism,
Descartes was adopted by the Communist Party after World
War II as their philosopher of freedom. That designation
was by no means limited to the confines of France. The
globalization of the Cartesian reference is clearly found in

the wake of decolonization in the 1950s, as well as in North America and Asia, where Descartes was identified with French technocratic culture.

This representation of Descartes as philosopher of freedom, patiently constructed over several centuries, says little, however, about the Cartesian *eccentricity*, that is, his risky and de-centered position in the intellectual and scholarly world of the seventeenth century. The current association of Descartes with a French-style universalism thus conceals the highly problematic reality of his situation as a scholar exiled to the Netherlands. Without falling into excessive celebration of an intellectual nomadism that does not correspond to the reality of the philosophical world of the ancien régime, we can nonetheless explore the genealogy of a French passion in the way historian François Azouvi does, through an approach that takes seriously mobility, spaces, and the necessary diversity of perspectives. To approach philosophy from the perspective of movement enables us, first, to avoid the fetishism of the French national narrative and, second, to approach Descartes and Cartesianism on several levels. Would Descartes have been Descartes without such mobility? Without speaking of a Republic of Letters, it remains that, through his journeys and his residency in the United Provinces of the Netherlands, Descartes understood the great intellectual problems of his time through a lens that fashioned philosophical inquiry through a comparison with other spaces.

After joining forces with the Protestant Maurice de Nassau, stadtholder of the United Provinces, Descartes traveled extensively from 1619 to 1628, going from Denmark to Italy, passing through Germany and Paris. He lived in the French capital from 1625 to 1627, frequenting social and scholarly circles revolving around Jean-Louis Guez de Balzac and the priest Marin Mersenne. In 1628, he settled in the United Provinces and began to develop a complete philosophy that would encompass all realms of knowledge, from geometry to music, from treatises on physics to reflections on metaphysics and morality, as well as mechanics and subjects relating to medicine. Politics alone appeared to be missing. Facing ecclesiastical objections in the United Provinces and in France in the 1640s, he began corresponding with Princess Elisabeth of Bohemia in 1645. Later, at the invitation of Queen Christina, Descartes was welcomed at the Swedish court in 1649, where he died of pneumonia on February 11, 1650.

Through his travels, the itinerant scholar had developed another view of the social world, a competence rooted in mobility and the absence of fixed roots. By avoiding an exclusively French perspective, or an anachronistic celebration of French glory, we can see the strengths and the limitations resulting from the international circulation of ideas in the middle of the seventeenth century.

In the early modern era, the culture of mobility itself raised questions. According to historian Daniel Roche, it required "a departure from a fundamental stability that expected everyone to have a hearth and home and fit into the framework of a society classified according to accepted appearances and conditions." Breaking with the quotidian organization of time, mobility also appeared as a moral disruption, or the creation of a tension between travel and rootedness. Descartes was thus torn between his desire to communicate at a distance through letters and his thirst for social interactions, direct conversation, and the rituals of social calls, as he expressed in a letter to Hector Pierre Chanut dated March 6, 1646:

> I complain that the world is too large, due to the lack of honest people one finds in it. I wish all those men would come together in a town and then I would gladly leave my hermitage to live amongst them, if they would like to include me in their company. For though I flee the multitudes, on account of the many impertinent and objectionable people one encounters, I continue to think that the greatest thing in life is to enjoy the conversation of people one admires.

This Cartesian description of learned exchange matters because it modifies the usual notion of an intensification of international communication within the Republic of Letters.

Having arrived in the Netherlands, Descartes wrote: "Where else in the world can one find all the conveniences of life, and all the curiosities one might desire, all of which are so easily found here?" Seventeenth-century mobility was still difficult and dangerous in a European continent torn apart by the Thirty Years' War, whereas a specific place, in this case the Dutch city, remained conducive to the philosopher's freedom.

But the United Provinces were far from an ordinary place. Amsterdam has been described by Adam Boussingault as that "shop of the universe" where all books were published, and by historian Harold Cook as that "warehouse of the world" open to distant lands, from South America to Insulindian lands. The port was indeed the shop of the universe if one considers how prosperous the economy of the printed word was in the United Provinces at that time. Descartes worked continually with Dutch printers, engravers, and booksellers. Amsterdam was also the warehouse of the world because from New Amsterdam (founded in 1626) to Batavia, the Dutch East India Company strove to broaden Dutch horizons. Already at the University of Leiden in 1587, scholars delved into the riches brought back from Indonesia by the East India Company (Amsterdam and Utrecht would follow suit in 1610). Often undervalued, ignored, or reduced to a haven of controversy by historians of philosophy, the United Provinces were thus not simply an inert background against which the French philosopher developed his work. One found an earlier openness to the world in the Netherlands, a deeper taste for exoticism among the savants of the United Provinces than in France. The connection between the United Provinces and Spain can be found in the correspondence of the Dutch botanist Carolus Clusius. Historian Krzysztof Pomian notes that the United Provinces distinguished themselves from Italy in the attention they paid to the exotic *naturalia* of tropical zones. Whereas Italian *naturalists* sought above all to compare their observations with bookish knowledge derived from classical authorities, Dutch scholars were eager to confront a complete unknown. Descartes's stay in Amsterdam took place within the context of an expanding world, one that made the United Provinces an obligatory stopping point, challenging the certainties of what he had learned in the Jesuit school of La Flèche.

Another element that weighed on this intellectual adventure can be found in contemporary understandings of intellectual risk-taking, of control over intellectual mobility. The off-center French point of view was conveyed by a questioning of Catholic universality that had been given new life by the Counter-Reformation. Since the sixteenth century, Catholic universality was challenged by the norms of the Protestant world and the dynamism of the active Jewish diaspora in Amsterdam. In the face of increased royal and religious censorship, the Cartesian "revolution" was founded on prudence. Galileo's conviction in June 1633 for his *Dialogue Concerning the Two Chief World Systems*, an apologia for heliocentrism and a denunciation of Aristotelianism, had strong repercussions throughout learned Europe. The Galileo affair had a lasting effect on thinkers, and undoubtedly led Descartes to write and publish less. Here is Descartes on this matter, in a letter to his friend Mersenne:

> I considered sending you my *World* for the New Year, and just two weeks ago I was still quite resolved to send you at least part of it, if the whole couldn't be copied in time. But I will tell you, that these past few days in trying to find in Leiden and Amsterdam Galileo's *System of the World*, because I thought I had heard it had been published in Italy last year, I was told it had in fact been published, but that all copies had been burned in Rome immediately afterward, and that Galileo had been sentenced and fined. This shocked me so greatly that I almost decided to burn all my papers, or at least not to show them to anyone.... Because I couldn't imagine that Galileo, who is Italian, and even loved by the Pope, so I've heard, could be condemned for having simply attempted to establish the movement of the Earth. I knew well that it had once been censured by some cardinals, but I thought it was still being taught openly, even in Rome. And I confess that if

his theory is false, then all the foundations of my philosophy are as well, because it obviously comes out of them....But since I absolutely don't want to write anything in which the slightest word might be disapproved by the Church, I prefer to suppress it, rather than publish a censured version of it.

Following that episode, Descartes worried on many occasions about the reactions of Jesuits or Protestant theologians to his work. In 1642, he wrote to the philosopher Constantijn Huygens: "Perhaps these scholarly wars will result in my *World* soon being seen in the world." The pressure of censorship, which he expressed on several occasions, and an increase in controversies shaped the production and reception of a Cartesian philosophy that lacked the support of an institution. Like the mystics of his time, Descartes engaged with physical and social sites of knowledge production under political control. Concern with such control was omnipresent at the time; it also yielded a new economy of knowledge that was in every way contrary to the dogmatism of the Scholastics. Dissemination and inclusion are the twin features of a process that enabled Cartesian philosophy to obtain recognition while remaining fragile and uncertain. As the philosopher André Glucksmann put it in his 1987 essay *Descartes c'est la France*, the Cartesian "revolution" does not lend itself to a story of defense and worship of French philosophy. Descartes witnessed and contributed to the reshaping of a continent that was opening to the world. He was less a master of truth than a traveler with doubts.

Stéphane Van Damme

REFERENCES

Azouvi, François. *Descartes et la France: Histoire d'une passion nationale*. Paris: Hachette Littératures, 2006.

Cook, Harold. "Amsterdam: A Knowledge Warehouse in the 17th Century." *Revue d'histoire moderne et contemporaine* 55, no. 2 (2008): 19–42.

Fabiani, Jean-Louis. *Qu'est-ce qu'un philosophe français?* Paris: Éditions de l'École des hautes études en sciences sociales, 2010.

Kolesnik-Antoine, Delphine, ed. *Qu'est-ce qu'être cartésien?* Lyon: Éditions de l'École normale supérieure, 2013.

Van Damme, Stéphane. *Descartes: Essai d'histoire culturelle d'une grandeur philosophique (XVIIe–XXe siècle)*. Paris: Presses de Sciences Po, 2002.

RELATED ARTICLES
1215, 1751, 1875, 1903, 1961, 1965, 1984

1659

Spain Cedes Supremacy and Cocoa to France

With the Treaty of the Pyrenees, signed on November 7, 1659, France loosened the Spanish stranglehold on Europe by ratifying its conquests in the Netherlands. Peace was sealed by the marriage between Louis XIV and María Teresa of Austria, daughter of King Philip IV of Spain. Now that France had triumphed over its longtime rival, the time had come to advance its colonial designs.

The year 1659 marked the most important date for the history of chocolate in France. A certain David Chaillou, husband of Olympia Mancini, niece of the king's powerful minister, Cardinal Mazarin, had traveled through Spain despite the prevailing state of war between the two monarchies, and while there learned to prepare the precious beverage and confection. He became France's first *chocolatier*, having been granted a twenty-nine-year permit ("letters patent") in November 1659 specifying that he could "process & sell chocolate as a liquor, a confection, or any other form of his choosing." Chancellor Pierre Séguier's bureaucracy was slow to seal these letters patent, however, so slow that State Secretary Loémie de Brienne had to send an urgent missive on June 5, 1660, to the justice minister to get the business settled. The problem was that, by that time, the entire court had relocated to the Pyrenees, between the coastal town of Saint-Jean-de-Luz and nearby Ciboure, to attend the wedding of Louis XIV to María Teresa de Austria. But once the royal privilege in question was registered, Chaillou opened the country's first chocolate shop on the Rue de l'Arbre-Sec in Paris, halfway between the royal palace at the Louvre and Les Halles, between throne and marketplace.

It was whispered that chocolate was one of the new French queen's guilty pleasures. Daughter of Philip IV of Spain and Elisabeth of France, María Teresa de Austria was twice a cousin to Louis XIV. Raised at the Spanish court, she had acquired many of its manners and tastes, including a fondness for certain products brought from the Americas. The marriage of the two cousins at a town adjoining the border between the two monarchies brought the war to its official end. By 1659, the plenipotentiaries designated by Mazarin and Luis Méndez de Haro, the favorite of the Spanish king, had negotiated the articles of a much-anticipated peace. Talks had begun three years earlier. Satisfied with their conquest of several towns and strongholds in the regions of Hainaut, Flanders, Artois, and Luxembourg, the French were ready to consolidate their gains. Spain was resigned in 1648 to signing peace with the largely Protestant United Provinces in the Low Countries, and still hoped one day to reconquer Portugal, separated from the Spanish throne since 1640. The end of hostilities with France meant that it could now focus its political and military energy on the Iberian Peninsula and its Italian possessions while bolstering security in the Mediterranean and the Americas.

The Treaty of the Pyrenees in 1659 ratified the French conquests in the Southern Low Countries. The French committed to relinquishing their claim to the county of Barcelona, along with the lands of Burgundy and Franche-Comté. But in Catalonia, the territories located to the north and east of the crest of the Pyrenees, i.e., eastern Cerdagne and Roussillon, had now entered the French kingdom for good. In essence, the treaty stated that the Pyrenees, which had once split Gaul from Spain, would again be the point of partition for these same two kingdoms. Commissioners from both sides would come together in good faith to determine precisely which stretches of mountain would constitute the boundary. That system of expert bipartite commissions laid the groundwork for practices still in force to this day.

The marriage of the chocolate-loving Spanish princess to the young Bourbon king mirrored the double marriage in 1615 between Louis XIII and the Infanta Ana de Austria, on the one hand, and between future Spanish King Philip IV and the princess Elisabeth of France, on the other. In 1659 as in 1615, peace talks took place on Pheasant Island, as the Spanish called it, or Hospital Island, according to the French, located in the Bidasoa River. The matrimonial capitulations included a dowry payment of 500,000 ducats by Philip IV to his daughter. Financial shortfalls, however, prevented the Spanish monarchy from making good on this particular treaty article. In 1667, two years after the death of Philip IV, Louis XIV seized the occasion, and in defense of his wife's interests, demanded her due. The Sun King thereby triggered what came to be called the War of Devolution, at the close of which, in lieu of the unpaid dowry, he annexed a few towns and strongholds in the Southern Low Countries.

France was now triumphant over the rival that had dominated it since the captivity of Francis I in 1525, during the reign of Charles V. This revenge took a particular turn: not only had Louis XIV prevailed over Spain, but he now intended to unseat it. Louis, the *Rex Christianissimus* (Most Christian King), having gradually erased any trace of Protestantism at home, now aimed to add the title of *Rex Catholicus* at the expense of his cousin in Madrid. France was no longer wedged between Habsburg lands, and Spain was now subjected to French conquests. Loosening Spain's grip on Europe produced a parallel effect: it allowed France to enhance its colonial presence, particularly in its territories and channels across the Atlantic. Since the fifteenth century, Spain and

Portugal had always claimed monopoly status in the Americas and along the African coasts. Any initiative undertaken by a rival power, necessarily a latecomer to maritime expansion, would be considered an act of aggression. In reality, the two Iberian monarchies were incapable of controlling all the vast territories in which they claimed to enjoy exclusive rights.

Ever since Portugal reconquered the formerly Dutch-held territories of Pernambuco in 1654, the French islands, Martinique in particular, witnessed an influx of Jewish families fleeing the reinstatement of the Inquisition in Brazil. Among these exiles, the Portuguese trader Benjamin da Costa de Andrade played an important role in converting local crops to sugarcane. He is also believed to have established the first French cocoa plantation in Martinique, around 1660, right when David Chaillou was opening his shop on the Rue de l'Arbre-Sec. Development of the French Antilles relied on contractual agreements, a form of non-free labor whose duration was limited and negotiable, as well as on African slave labor.

The switch to a sugar economy took place between 1655 and 1660, when sugar replaced tobacco as the commodity in which levies were paid. This transformation brought with it a spectacular increase in the population of enslaved people, first in Guadeloupe, but also in Martinique and Saint-Christopher Island. When purchasing slaves, it was crucially important for the French to bypass the Iberian traders and middlemen. Thus, they had to begin operating the way the English and Dutch merchants had already done, by short-circuiting the Portuguese trading posts on the West African coast and the Gulf of Guinea. In this respect, 1659 is also an important date because that is the year that Finance Minister Jean-Baptiste Colbert revived his trading interests by creating a trading company, the Compagnie du Cap-Vert et du Sénégal. Soon thereafter, a fort was built that would constitute the core of the West African city of Saint-Louis, on Ndar Island at the mouth of the Sénégal River. This new creation resulted from negotiations with the *brak* of Waalo, sovereign of the Wolof realm in the marshy estuary.

A long process begun forty years earlier was now reaching tentative completion. As far back as 1612, contractors from Rouen had attempted unsuccessfully to settle in Gambia, where English and Dutch dealers were bypassing the former trade routes set by the Portuguese. A while later, in 1638, two gentlemen from Dieppe, Captain Thomas Lambert and Claude Jannequin de Rochefort, mandated by Émery de Caen's Compagnie Normande, constructed a building, a cross between a warehouse and a blockhouse, on Brieur Point at the mouth of the Sénégal River. Five years later, this first iteration of the Saint-Louis fortress was swept away by a tidal wave. Likewise, in 1658, Louis Caullier, sent out by the Compagnie du Cap-Vert et du Sénégal, witnessed the collapse of a building whose construction he had overseen on Bokos Island. With the establishment of the new Saint-Louis fortress on Ndar Island, the West Indies Company took over in 1664. The French took their cue from the Portuguese, who had always opted to settle on islands right off the African coast rather than venturing farther inland. Like them, they traded in Sudanese gold, ivory, gum arabic, and most especially, in enslaved Africans destined for plantations in the Antilles.

Like the Spanish and Portuguese before them, the French colonists in West Africa set up a triangular trade system to satisfy the demand for slave labor in the Caribbean plantation economy. As did their Iberian predecessors, they had to cope with environments for which they were culturally and physically unprepared. They were often obsessed by the fear of going native, of drifting away from standards of behavior deemed proper in France, even when accompanied by French men of the cloth. In a memoir about his first voyage to the African coast in 1685, Michel Jojolet de la Courbe notes that he witnessed French settlers playing a kind of handball wearing only undershorts and shirts, which he found utterly ridiculous. This breakdown of custom affected more than mere dress code. Other contemporary testimony expresses revulsion at the European settlers' sexual promiscuity with African women and at the unsavory emergence of "half-breeds." In their view, it was not their willingness to brutalize Africans and turn them into tradable merchandise that signaled the slide into barbarity, but rather their inclination to get too intimate. In the image of its long-time Spanish rival, France was proving itself a colonial power.

Jean-Frédéric Schaub

REFERENCES

Barry, Boubacar. *Senegambia and the Atlantic Slave Trade*. Cambridge: Cambridge University Press, 1997.

Hugon, Alain. *Philippe IV: Le siècle de Vélasquez*. Paris: Payot, 2014.

Nordman, Daniel. *Frontières de France: De l'espace au territoire (XVIe–XIXe siècle)*. Paris: Gallimard, 1998.

Rediker, Marcus. *The Slave Ship: A Human History*. New York: Penguin Books, 2014.

Schaub, Jean-Frédéric. *La France espagnole: Les racines hispaniques de l'absolutisme français*. Paris: Seuil, 2003.

RELATED ARTICLES

1572, 1808, 1919, 1920

1662

Dunkirk, Nest of Spies

Conventional wisdom has it that during the reign of Louis XIV, France settled into its so-called natural borders and fulfilled its destiny as a maritime power by taking control of its coastline. But when the king annexed Dunkirk, an infamous pirate lair that the Dutch nicknamed "the Algiers of the North," he acquired a most cosmopolitan port.

Starting with the annexation of Normandy in 1203, various wars of succession, marriages, and peace treaties enabled France to adjoin a coastal rim to what had until then been an exclusively land-bound state. Royal propaganda, echoed later by the French Republic, insisted that, through these territorial acquisitions, France was finally settling into its "natural" borders. What such a narrative conceals, however, is how fortuitous these maritime additions to the country's margins really were. Although some of these conquests were gained by fire and sword, many territories were secured through negotiation.

On October 27, 1662, Dunkirk was purchased from

England by Louis XIV for five million pounds. The whole city, with its citadel, fortresses and strongholds, cannons and munitions, fell once again — and for the last time — under the aegis of France. However French it may have become officially, though, it never ceased to be a world city. Over the long term, it kept its Flemish character with regard to language, religion, and trade, and cultivated close ties with Spain, the Netherlands, and England. Down through the centuries, the Flanders port town had shuttled among rival European powers. One event in particular symbolizes the singular fortune of the "church in the dunes" (*Duinkerk* in Flemish). After the Battle of the Dunes on June 14, 1658, the then-Spanish town surrendered to the Franco-English army led by the Vicomte de Turenne and Sir William Lockhart. Within a few hours, Cardinal Mazarin, the de facto ruler of France, had gifted it to the Commonwealth of England's lord protector, Oliver Cromwell — the fruit of an alliance negotiated with England against Spain. This was the "wild day," as Dunkirk's first historian Pierre Faulconnier described it, when the town was "Spanish in the morning, French at noon, and English by evening." Dunkirk represents an intersection of France's history in Europe.

Almost immediately, France regretted giving Dunkirk away to the English, but circumstances would soon conspire for its return to Louis XIV's portfolio. Back in power in the British Isles in 1660, King Charles II deemed the garrison and fortress too costly and decided to sell the city to the highest bidder. It was thus France, not Spain or the United Provinces of the Dutch Republic, that inherited the Flanders port town. This was a replay of a 1658 event, though the actors now switched roles. Whereas Louis XIV had turned the city over to England four years earlier, he now made a triumphant entrance on horseback through the Bergues gate. French royal propaganda celebrated the town's return to the Catholic fold after four oppressive years under heretical Anglican rule. Back in Britain, however, critics deplored the ignominious handover of the last British foothold in France. Some suspected that the Earl of Clarendon, who had negotiated the sale, may have taken a large slice of the proceeds for himself. His London mansion acquired the nickname of "Dunkirk House."

France's annexation of Dunkirk illustrates the heightened role of the sea in the country's strategy and economy. Located at the juncture of the English Channel and the North Sea, the port also marked one of the French kingdom's farthest flung boundaries; indeed Louis XIV was pushing the borders of his realm ever northward. Dunkirk helped protect France from invasion via the Flanders route; it became a vital link in the defensive chain designed to protect the country's perimeter by the military engineer and adviser to the king Sébastien Le Prestre de Vauban.

Surrounded on all sides by ramparts, easily isolated from its backcountry by floodplains, Dunkirk also helped spearhead Secretary of State for the Navy Jean-Baptiste Colbert's maritime policy. Major engineering work was undertaken to transform a silt-clogged harbor that could accommodate only shallow-draft boats into a top-tier naval base and commercial port. Between 1670 and 1680, thirty thousand soldiers dug canals, basins, and a special channel to curb the silting of the harbor. The engineers overcame huge technical difficulties, such as the construction of Fort Risban on a shifting sandbank. An impregnable citadel was erected based on a scheme that Vauban described as "the grandest and most beautiful fortifications design in the world." Demonstrating the importance he attached to this project, the Sun King made several inspection tours of the work in progress. In fact, throughout his long reign Louis XIV would pay more visits (six) to Dunkirk than to any other port in the realm. During one inspection tour, in 1680, he wrote to Colbert: "Dunkirk will be the most beautiful place in the world." It was a model port, a showcase proudly exhibited to ambassadors from Siam in 1685.

The issue of Dunkirk's fortifications would cause unending friction in France's relations with Great Britain. Irish philosopher and theologian John Toland expressed his alarm. If the British allowed the Dunkirk fortifications to stand, they might just as well let the French fortify Dover.

The 1713 Treaty of Utrecht eventually required that France tear down its battlements, raze forts and bastions, fill in the harbor, and destroy the city's jetties and sluices. Throughout successive wars, however, the fortifications and port would be reconstructed, only to be destroyed and rebuilt again.

A veritable pirate haven, Dunkirk had already been dubbed the "Algiers of the North" by the Dutch in the sixteenth century, a comparison to the lair of the Barbary pirates, because of the havoc the town's corsairs wreaked on the high seas in the service of the Spanish crown. Not only did the French monarchy not put a stop to these activities, it encouraged them, particularly in Saint-Malo and Bayonne. A large-scale privateering policy was undertaken, replacing naval squadron engagement by the end of the seventeenth century. This mixed economy mobilized the merchant marine in support of the royal war effort.

A commoner born in Dunkirk in 1650 to Dutch parents, Jean Bart was the most famous of this new generation of sailors. He quickly rose to prominence, gaining royal recognition. During the war against the United Provinces (1672–1678), his nimble ships easily navigated the shallow waters, and ended up capturing fourteen warships and eighty-one merchant vessels. Vauban became his protector and brought him into the Royal Navy, with the rank of lieutenant. Over the next two decades, from Bergen in Norway to Lagos and Portugal, Bart waged combat, attacking pirates from Salé, ransoming herring fishers and cargo vessels in Dutch waters, and sinking dozens of enemy ships. At the Battle of Texel in 1694, he recaptured from Rear Admiral de Frise, who was in command of a Dutch and English fleet, a convoy of one hundred twenty vessels loaded with wheat, which earned him a knighthood. After 1789, this same knighted pirate was remembered as a popular revolutionary French hero, son of a lowly merchant, who had served the despotic monarchy against his own will; he now provided an example for the common people, freed from the nobility. A statue glorifying the great man was erected in Dunkirk's town center in 1845, and his exploits were extolled in nineteenth-century history books. Still, Jean Baert (this was his birth name) spoke Flemish, the language still spoken in Dunkirk during the Revolution.

Words like "national" and "foreign" are not easily defined when applied to these maritime fringes. In order to secure the loyalty of the population, whose family allegiances were torn among several states, the monarchy granted them special economic, fiscal, and religious privileges. Sailors, whether French or foreign, could avoid having to serve in the Royal Navy. The city was exempt from paying tallage or salt taxes, while members of the clergy, "considered foreigners," were not allowed to collect tithes. Wines from Bordeaux, salt from La Rochelle, fabrics from the Levant, and canvas from Flanders came ashore to the warehouses of Dunkirk, whose population more than doubled between 1662 and 1685. Business boomed thanks to Louis XIV's tax exemption, which remained in force until the Revolution. Like Marseille and Lorient, Dunkirk was dubbed "an effectively foreign country." Its merchants could trade duty-free with foreigners, even while there was a customs border separating the city from the rest of France. This special status fueled sizable smuggling networks throughout the eighteenth century.

This widespread trafficking in Dunkirk came in many shapes, some very original. Locally referred to by the word "smogglage" (the French translation of the English "smuggling" and the Flemish "smokkelen"), contraband trading involved merchants of all origins as well as thousands of English and Irish *smogleurs*. Between 1765 and 1787, an average of nine hundred smuggling ships entered the port of Dunkirk, rising to 1,285 on the eve of the Revolution. By this means, tea from China or India, coffee from San Domingo, cognac, and brandy were purchased in France and fraudulently reexported across the Channel. According to the Colbertism that pervaded French economic thought at the time, trade constituted the lifeblood of war. England's gold guineas flowed freely in France while British customs were deprived of millions of pounds' worth of import duties.

Never rejected or feared as enemies, Dunkirk's foreign communities were, on the contrary, protected by the municipal government and the city's powerful mercantile interests, brought together into France's first chamber of commerce in 1700. The French navy defended them against local corsairs in the name of national interest. Briefly interrupted during the French Revolution, this activity came roaring back during the first French Empire. In 1810, Napoleon authorized smugglers to enter Dunkirk and Gravelines, thereby circumventing the continental embargo. Throughout the eighteenth century, European countries had competed to attract foreign traders, offering them subsidies, fiscal enticements, and access to the rights and privileges of the bourgeoisie. These situations of extraterritoriality complicated feelings of national belonging. Outwitting official state borders, merchant networks redeployed from port to port.

The finest hours of France's saga on the sea owe much to men born outside its borders. The nostalgic refrain of "France's maritime vocation" often overlooks the contribution that thousands of foreigners, whether fishermen, privateers, or smugglers, made to the prosperity of its coastal façade.

Renaud Morieux

REFERENCES

Cabantous, Alain. *Dix mille marins face à l'Océan*. Paris: Publisud, 1991.

Faulconnier, Pierre. *Description historique de Dunkerque, ville maritime & port de mer très-fameux dans la Flandre Occidentale*. Bruges: P. vande Cappelle, 1730.

Grose, Clyde L. "England and Dunkirk." *The American Historical Review* 39, no. 1 (1933): 1–27.

Morieux, Renaud. *The Channel: England, France and the Construction of a Maritime Border in the Eighteenth Century*. Cambridge: Cambridge University Press, 2016.

———. "Diplomacy from Below and Belonging: Fishermen and Cross-Channel Relations in the Eighteenth Century." *Past and Present* 202, no. 1 (February 2009): 83–125.

RELATED ARTICLES

1682

Versailles, Capital of French Europe

By May 1682 — well before the painter Charles Le Brun had finished decorating the Hall of Mirrors — the French court was fully installed at the Palace of Versailles. The ultimate fusion of civilization and French genius, the palace's interior, gardens, and new surrounding town became the admiration of Europe.

Today, the Palace of Versailles attracts millions of visitors from all around the world. It is viewed as the state palace *par excellence*, overshadowing the other residences of European royalty and the hunting lodges built by earlier hunting-mad French monarchs as they wandered through their realm in search of game. In 1682, Versailles became the official seat of the court and government of France, a move that reflected Louis XIV's desire to draw all eyes to himself as king and the embodiment of a nation whose destiny was to amaze all Europe with its feats of arms, its language, and its arts.

The mechanisms of modern tourism have amply endorsed the political discourse so dazzlingly represented by Versailles; the sun symbol appropriated by Louis XIV has even become the logo of the national museum. In his palace's Hall of Mirrors, the sovereign allowed himself to be portrayed by Le Brun as a mythic warrior commanding his troops in person and triumphing over European armies during the Franco-Dutch War (1672–1678). This iconographic language, devised as he consecrated Versailles as his kingdom's capital, would tell the world that a new European order had taken the place of the old, that the King of France had replaced the Habsburg emperor at the summit of the hierarchy of princes. His Hall of Mirrors would become the centerpiece of the French monarchy — for the reception of special visitors, ambassadors on special missions, and ordinary people from home and abroad. As the king reminded his son, "If there is a special characteristic to this monarchy [of France], it is the fact that our subjects have free and easy access to their prince." Henceforth foreigners too would be able to avail themselves of this access. Astonishingly, it remained possible until the end of the ancien régime to wander through the king's own apartments on Sundays in the company of more than a thousand other visitors.

Versailles was deemed an expression of French genius because it was the king's masterwork. This universal attraction would make it possible to wage war by other means: foreign tourists would bring with them some of the precious metals then circulating in Europe, from which France's mercantilist political economy was bound to benefit. In 1756, the officer of the King's *menus plaisirs* (in charge of court ceremonies and festivals) was still defending his outrageous expenses by arguing that "the court should stage events that might excite the curiosity of foreigners, occasioning thereby a circulation and consumption of goods that would be advantageous to the state." With its buildings and pleasures, the court became the backdrop for a spectacle whose political value rested on the participation of foreigners. Visitors were targeted by a raw propaganda that extended into official descriptions of the palace. Louis XIV himself drafted no fewer than six versions of his own *Manière de montrer les jardins de Versailles* (Exhibiting the Gardens of Versailles) between 1689 and 1705. In 1720, Jean-Baptiste de Monicart's *Versailles immortalisé* introduced itself as a

> volume [that] will be much sought-after by foreigners and French people alike, Versailles being the most magnificent and the most renowned of monuments and marvels that has ever appeared in the world. More than three hundred million livres were spent on it before the end of the reign of Louis XIV, and it continues to be faithfully maintained, at great cost, under the present king. Foreigners who may have already seen Versailles will believe themselves transported back there when they read

the diverting and easily understood pages of this book; and those who have not yet visited will learn in advance how its marvels will be impressed upon them.

In the eighteenth century, hope for a lasting peace in Europe as well as the development of exchanges and ideas for a new "European civilization" began to change the emphasis of the claims that guidebooks — which themselves represented a new and fast-developing genre — made about Versailles. Indeed, an alternative reading of the palace began to emerge, whereby its mythological frescoes and aesthetic qualities communicated a rather less warlike message than the images in the Hall of Mirrors — which began, ever more frequently, to be passed over in silence. While this cultural interpretation diverged from the objectives of Louis XIV, it remained inherently political. Though diplomats and philosophers like Voltaire bemoaned the monarchy's failure to promote the French language and French theater — a poor use of what we would now call soft power — Versailles was still deemed eminently *curious* by the learned academies patronized by the monarchy. In this fashion, the place remained the focus of an imaginary worldview wherein French genius and world civilization were one and the same thing.

The reaction of German visitor Sophie von La Roche emphasized the hybrid nature of this complex project, with its myriad facets imported from the rest of Europe. In 1785, after visiting the estate of Marly on the grounds of Versailles, she wrote that "the interiors date back to Louis XIV. They are magnificent, but their form differs greatly from today's taste. Indeed, I expect that a French visitor coming upon decors like these in a German palace, would exclaim: 'Here is proof that the Germans have no taste whatever!'"

Sophie von La Roche clearly thought that the passage of time had changed tastes and made national labels redundant. But from the outset — in 1682 — Versailles was far from an exclusively French novelty. Its likeness to Spain's Escorial Palace, an earlier example of the distancing of a royal residence from its capital city, has been much commented on. There were other plagiarisms. The façade overlooking the gardens is Italian (though fronted initially by a terrace that was later covered to accommodate the Hall of Mirrors). The avenues stretching away from its central rotunda are also Italian, in the style of the Roman *trivium*. As for the stratified progression of grander and grander halls leading through to the royal bedroom, this plan had been adopted much earlier by the Spanish and English monarchies. Versailles itself was later copied in all kinds of lesser ways, though its lightning-fast construction — to become out of nothing the suburban capital of a great kingdom — has yet to be emulated and probably never will be.

Moreover, having begun as part of a powerful system

for the glorification of the monarchy, before very long Louis XIV's palace had become a whipping boy whereby France's hegemonic ambitions could be denounced and laughed at. In 1679 already, Duchess Sophie of Hanover, while visiting her niece, Louis XIV's sister-in-law, fulsomely pretended in her letters (which she knew were being opened by the French intelligence service) to admire the " grandeur" of France's curial system of representation. Later, in memoirs written under the benign eye of her protégé, the philosopher and mathematician Gottfried Wilhelm Leibniz, she just as vigorously condemned it. The stories ambassadors and travelers told about the French court, and Versailles in particular, embellished by sundry engravings, gazettes, and pamphlets, fed a black legend about Louis XIV. This image his enemies in England, Prussia, and the Dutch United Provinces gleefully exploited.

The travelers sent by foreign potentates to investigate the aesthetic and political effectiveness of Versailles acknowledged, though less than systematically, the spell it cast. In 1686 Christoph Pitzler, an architect commissioned by the Duke of Saxe-Weissenfels to visit Versailles (among other European sites), left a highly personal description, blending his own notes and sketches with official accounts. His conclusions clearly showed that he was more interested in technical details and decorative features than in the allegorical significance of the Hall of Mirrors. Indeed, there was no serious imitation of Versailles, in its entirety, in Enlightenment Europe. The only comparison might be the New Palace of Herrenchiemsee, fifty miles from Munich, built by Ludwig II of Bavaria in the nineteenth century.

Like Pitzler, any sovereign who ventured to "imitate" Versailles could only do so by selectively mining the resources it had to offer. These were principally the gardens (witness the work of landscape architect André Le Nôtre's disciples at La Granja in Spain and Drottningholm Palace in Sweden), architectural elements such as the Ambassador's Staircase, which was reinterpreted at Het Loo Palace by William of Orange, and pictorial decoration (Frederick William I of Prussia had himself depicted, Louis XIV style, as a ruler and lawgiver at the Stadtschloss royal castle in Berlin). In addition to the construction of numerous suburban residences, it was Versailles's spatial arrangement, set off by a new town, which most clearly demonstrated the grand concept behind it. This concept was enthusiastically adopted in principalities of the Holy Roman Empire, where the most striking example is Karlsruhe; but also in St. Petersburg and in Washington, DC. Just as the plays in the repertoire of French theater were adapted for the benefit of the different royal courts of Europe, so Versailles was figuratively taken apart and put together again for other purposes.

Echoing these diverse appropriations, travelers of the

Enlightenment who experienced Versailles firsthand were split between fascination and disenchantment. Giacomo Casanova concluded in 1750 that "Fontainebleau...was much more brilliant than Versailles," whereas Sophie von La Roche claimed that she and her friends "laughed heartily, because they could not believe that this was indeed the Château de Versailles. Paintings and prints had led us to believe the place would be much more sumptuous." While Versailles was hardly obligatory in the Grand European Tours that aristocrats, writers, and other members of Europe's wealthy elite undertook to complete their cultural education, these travelers could always expect assistance and protection there. In 1763, the Scottish philosopher David Hume was enchanted by the compliments paid to him by the grandsons of Louis XV; he saw Versailles as the reception room of a philosopher king, stating without hesitation that "greater honor is paid to letters in France than in England." As for the economist Alessandro Verri, he was dazzled by the "sublime gardens" that were such a relief after the sour bickering of Paris. The ritual of court life may have repelled many, but these two eyewitness descriptions show just how useful Versailles could be in forging links between France's absolute monarchy and the European Enlightenment.

Pauline Lemaigre-Gaffier

REFERENCES

Auzépy, Marie-France, and Joël Cornette, eds. *Palais et pouvoir: De Constantinople à Versailles*. Saint-Denis: Presses universitaires de Vincennes, 2003.

Da Vinha, Mathieu. *Le Versailles de Louis XIV: Le fonctionnement d'une résidence royale au XVIIe siècle*. Paris: Perrin, 2009.

Duindam, Jeroen, Tülan Artan, and Metin Kunt, eds. *Royal Courts in Dynastic States and Empires: A Global Perspective*. Leiden: Brill, 2011.

Kolk, Caroline zum, Jean Boutier, Bernd Klesmann, and François Moureau, eds. *Voyageurs étrangers à la cour de France (1589–1789)*. Rennes/Versailles: Presses universitaires de Rennes/Centre de recherche du château de Versailles, 2014.

Markovits, Rahul. *Civiliser l'Europe: Politiques du théâtre français au XVIIIe siècle*. Paris: Fayard, 2014.

Papillon de La Ferté, Denis-Pierre-Jean. *Journal des Menus Plaisirs du Roi: 1756–1780*. Clermont-Ferrand: Paléo, 2002.

Sabatier, Gérard, and Margarita Torrione, eds. *Louis XIV espagnol?: Madrid et Versailles, images et modèles*. Paris/Versailles: Maison des sciences de l'homme/Centre de recherche du château de Versailles, 2009.

RELATED ARTICLES
800, 1336, 1380, 1686, 1715, 1871, 1921

1683

1492, French-Style?

What do the bombardment of Algiers (intended as
a crusade against Islam in the Mediterranean), the
publication of a royal edict on slavery and the slave trade
(the Code Noir), and the ideal of religious purification
have in common? They all reflect the French monarchy's
embrace of its imperial status.

On July 26, 1683, Mezzomorto Hüseyin Pasha, the dey of
Algiers, ordered that the Lazarist missionary Jean Le Vacher
be bound to the mouth of a cannon. The Ottoman governor
was defying the French fleet that had been battering the city
from the harbor. According to the apostolic vicar Poissant,
"As soon as the shot was fired, among Mr. Vacher's body
parts floating in the water a pillar of fire rose into the air.
This was a sign from God glorifying his servant." Divine
presence seemed ubiquitous during this battle. Not a single
Turkish soldier or local Jew had been willing to light the
cannon's fuse. In the end, they found a renegade to do the
irredeemable deed. Witnesses reported that he lost an arm

in the act, and that the cannon itself was damaged beyond repair. Louis XIV's navy was engaged in a holy war against the Turks in the western Mediterranean. The Sun King was taking over what had once been Spain's mission since the conflict between his forefather Charles V and Suleiman the Magnificent. The bombing of Algiers in 1683 needed to be all the more spectacular, since that same year, Louis XIV had failed to come to the rescue of his Habsburg rival Leopold I, who was fending off the Ottomans in Vienna.

In 1683 as in 1682, naval operations against Algiers were led by an admiral from Dieppe, Abraham Duquesne. In the twilight of his otherwise brilliant career, this grand septuagenarian seaman had always steadfastly refused to renounce his Protestant faith, despite mounting pressure by Louis XIV's regime. On October 18, 1685, the king signed the Edict of Fontainebleau, thereby revoking the provisions of the 1598 Edict of Nantes that had granted religious freedom to the Huguenots. The most radical measure was found in article 4, which mandated the expulsion of Protestant pastors, a move that would make regular worship practically impossible. "We enjoin all ministers of the said R.P.R. [the So-Called Reformed Religion], who do not choose to become converts and to embrace the Catholic, apostolic, and Roman religion, to leave our kingdom and the territories subject to us within a fortnight of the publication of our present edict, without leave to reside therein beyond that period, or, during the said fortnight, to engage in any preaching, exhortation, or any other function, on pain of being sent to the galleys." Duquesne chose not to emigrate, unlike the vast majority of Huguenots. The King himself authorized him to remain in France, provided he made no public display of his Protestant loyalties.

In step with the protocol followed by Spain in the fifteenth century to deal with its Jews, seventeenth-century France was the theater of a two-stage approach: a pressure campaign in favor of conversion, followed by an expulsion of officiants. In much the same way Portuguese King Manuel I had decided to get rid of his country's Jews in 1497 while allowing those who converted to stay, Louis XIV also wished to keep his Huguenots so long as they ceased to be Protestant. Since the early 1680s, the king's *dragonnades* were out in force, a coercive policy of intimidation consisting of unruly troops billeted in Protestant households. This policy led to tens of thousands of Huguenots converting to Roman Catholicism to escape the abuse and persecution mandated by Versailles.

The year 1685 was the pivotal moment that marked the passage from the first phase to the final tragedy. In a letter dated July 16 addressed from the Secretary of State for War, the Marquis de Louvois, to the *intendant* of Béarn, the political plan of action against the Protestants was clearly laid out: "You are under orders from His Majesty to oblige the gentlemen of Béarn to come forward with their titles, that you might conduct a verification, such that only those who are truly gentlemen will enjoy the privileges attributed to that nobility. And seeing as His Majesty's sole purpose is to obtain that these gentlemen convert, He deems it right that you conduct your search solely against those who remain obstinate in their refusal to comply." As this extract shows, an essential feature for understanding seventeenth-century France is the blurring of lines between politics and religion.

While the king and his ministers were cleansing France from within, they encouraged its outward expansion. The Compagnie de Guinée was created in January 1685, for a duration of twenty years. Its scope of action covered the coastal stretch from the Sierra Leone River all the way to the Cape of Good Hope. The king assigned it the task of running the slave trade, with the target of shipping every year one thousand enslaved Africans to the French Caribbean. In March of that year, a royal edict was issued whose first print edition in 1718 would bear the title of Code Noir. This set of sixty articles represented the result of compromise and converging interests between the king's magistrates in Martinique and the slaveholding plantation proprietors, who were growing mainly sugarcane and indigo. Based on a reference text drafted in 1685, the edict underwent significant changes depending on the territories that registered it into law, from Guadeloupe in 1685 all the way to Louisiana in 1724. The point was to set statutory rules for organizing social life within the various slaveholding communities. In other words, through this act of positive law, the French monarchy saw itself as a political entity whose basic character was defined by slave labor and human trafficking.

While this will come as no surprise to historians specializing in the seventeenth century, it bears repeating that the first eight articles of this edict deal with religious issues. Even more remarkable, the first article stipulates: "We enjoin all of our officers to expel from our islands all the Jews who have taken up residence there...We command them to be gone within three months of the day of issuance of the present [order], at the risk of confiscation of their persons and their goods." Who were these Caribbean Jews? Descendants of families originally from Spain and Portugal who had resided in the Dutch colony of Pernambuco in Brazil. They would scatter after Portugal retook the region in 1654, thereby escaping forced conversion and the rigors of the reinstated Inquisition. The edict of March 1685 was but the most recent chapter in the long history of persecution of Iberian Jews, and a preamble to the regulation of the lives of enslaved Africans in the French islands.

The articles that follow have to do with the status of slaves, considered as chattel; with their offspring, who were the property of their mother's owner; and with all manner of prohibitions, starting with that of assembly. Other articles concern criminal law, especially harsh where slaves were concerned. Others have to do with business law, since economic life had to be regulated. Article 57, for instance, establishes that a slave, once emancipated, was assumed to be a subject of the King of France like any other, without any process of naturalization, even when the subject was native of Africa. Taken together, these provisions assert that a society organized around a slave economy was neither outrageous in the eyes of the law nor aberrant in matters of religion.

French royalty readily performed its imperial and colonial roles, aspiring even further to a universal monarchy. It is perhaps symptomatic that this trend should coincide with a publication in the *Journal des sçavans* (April 24, 1684) by François Bernier, disciple of Pierre Gassendi and inveterate traveler, who was at one time family physician to the Grand Mughal of India: "A New Division of the Earth, According to the Different Species or Races of Men Who Inhabit It." This text breaks down humanity into four distinct races. The first encompasses all of Europe except the Tatars of Muscovy, but including what we now call the Arab World as well as Ottoman central Asia and the Mughal Empire of Delhi. Native Americans also belong to this first race. The second race is made up of black Africans in all their diversity; they are described in pejorative terms. The third combines a number of Asian cultures, from central Asia to China and Japan, including the Malay Archipelago. The fourth race consists of the Sami people, described as "nasty animals." Bernier broke with the tradition whereby climate explained variations in physiology and physiognomy, positing that hereditary characteristics alone determined visible differences. According to his "division," racial unity could exist even among peoples with distinct physical traits. Within the first race, for example, the skin colors of Scandinavians and Egyptians are quite different. But the variations were seen as relative. On the one hand, in places where the majority of people have deeply tanned skin, the elites might have lighter coloring. In another, the "swarthiness" of the Spanish indicated that one of France's neighbors could be as dark-skinned as the inhabitants of far-flung lands.

The first race is made up of all populations that, in Bernier's conception, have neither the black skin and textured hair of the Africans nor the epicanthic folds of the Asians. In the second part of his article, Bernier describes the physical beauty of women from the different regions. He claims to have seen women in Africa who "in my opinion, would obliterate the Venus displayed in Rome's Farnese Palace." His firsthand knowledge of central Asia and India allowed him to distinguish the female charms of these regions, with first prize in beauty going to the

Georgians and the Circassians he saw at slave markets. This text speaks to the geographic scope of one particular vision of the world. It challenges the prevailing explanations of human diversity, which were a mix of climatic, religious, cultural, and genealogical considerations. Bernier cannot be accused of wanting to rank the beauty of the races in favor of Europeans. But in his article, the transmission of natural traits through inheritance wins out over any other explanatory factor. By limiting the range of causality, he marks a turning point in the history of the racial definition of populations.

Crusades against Islam in the Mediterranean, religious purges, conversions and expulsions, colonial ambition, mass enslavement, supremacist ideology: such were the ingredients of this French-style 1492. And it was all remotely controlled from Versailles. At the midpoint of his personal reign, Louis XIV implemented a religious policy based on an increasingly intransigent Catholicism that was looking less and less Gallican. Defying prevailing understandings of the balance of power, the Sun King could conceive no limit to his pursuit of geopolitical dominance in Europe and overseas. He might well have made his own the watchword *Plus Ultra*, "further beyond" — the motto of Holy Roman Emperor and ruler of Spain Charles V, whose power knew no bounds.

Centuries later, historian Ernest Lavisse was well advised to deem Louis XIV very much a Spanish king.

Jean-Frédéric Schaub

REFERENCES

Boulle, Pierre-Henri. *Race et esclavage dans la France de l'Ancien Régime*. Paris: Perrin, 2007.

Labrousse, Élisabeth. *La Révocation de l'édit de Nantes: Une foi, une loi, un roi?* Paris: Payot, 1990.

Niort, Jean-François. *Le Code noir: Idées reçues sur un texte symbolique*. Paris: Le Cavalier bleu, 2015.

Peter, Jean. *Les Barbaresques sous Louis XIV: Le duel entre Alger et la Marine du roi (1681–1698)*. Paris: Economica, 1997.

Schaub, Jean-Frédéric. *La France espagnole: Les racines hispaniques de l'absolutisme français*. Paris: Seuil, 2003.

RELATED ARTICLES
1494, 1791, 1804, 1894, 1958

1685

France Revokes the Edict of Nantes, All of Europe
Reverberates

Protestants in France had enjoyed a measure of freedom
to pursue their religion since the reign of Henry IV, but
Louis XIV broke with his predecessor's spirit of tolerance
to reimpose a strict Catholicism. The persecution of the
Huguenots and their mass exodus from France caused
outrage throughout Europe and, in the balance, weakened
France.

No event stands more squarely at the intersection of
France's world history and its purely national history than
the Edict of Fontainebleau, dated October 17–18, 1685.
Its passage revoked the Edict of Nantes, which, in April–
May 1598, had brought an end to the Wars of Religion,
effecting a compromise that accurately reflected the forces
on the ground. Catholicism had been confirmed as the state
religion and the king's faith, and its sway was reestablished
across the kingdom. Protestantism was tolerated wherever
it existed, along with its pastors and churches, but was not

allowed to spread. Members of the Protestant faith had free access to every position in society. In addition, safe havens and a subsidy for troops offered them military protection, making the Protestant community as much a political party as a church.

This fragile equilibrium lasted for about sixty years. The military protections were withdrawn after a series of armed campaigns by Louis XIII and his minister, Cardinal Richelieu, effectively putting an end to the Protestant party — but not its churches. The Peace of Alais (1629), as the treaty was known, supported all the religious freedoms granted by the Edict of Nantes. Much as the Catholic faithful might have wished Richelieu to use his military victory to suppress Protestantism, the cardinal held firm. In fact, the Thirty Years' War (1618–1648) raging beyond France's borders was bringing the French monarchy into alignment with Protestant rulers against the (Catholic) Habsburgs. And during the Fronde, the French civil wars of the mid-seventeenth century, the Huguenots proved undeviatingly loyal to the young king Louis XIV, as fervent in their royal absolutism as the Catholic theorists. The decades from 1630 to 1650 could well be called a relative golden age for French Protestants.

Everything changed in 1661, when the now-adult Louis XIV, alone in the seat of power, started to interpret the edict more strictly and tighten the restrictions hemming in the

Protestant reformists, as though to gradually choke off the heresy altogether. Interestingly, the pressure lifted in 1669: for a while, Protestants were paid to convert to Catholicism. Louis XIV had just attacked the Dutch Republic, a Calvinist state, and wanted to avoid the appearance of an anti-Protestant crusade so as to maintain his alliance with the Protestant German rulers. The moment the war was over, the persecution resumed.

A symbolic measure passed in 1681 allowed Protestant children from the age of seven to convert. That same year, the king's agent in the province of Poitou, René de Marillac, correctly reading the king's intentions, began quartering troops, or dragoons, in Protestant homes as a means of "converting" their residents to the true religion. The practice, formerly applied to tax shirkers, was known as the dragonnade. The authorities would increase the number of dragoons billeted at a household until the occupants converted, with the soldiers having full license over their hosts, short of causing death. The method was remarkably successful, leading to numerous Protestant conversions. Far from being censured, the practice was widely imitated, spreading in 1685 to Béarn and the Languedoc in southwest France and then in the fall to the Huguenot bastions of the Bas-Languedoc and the Cévennes. The accounts that reached these districts from the neighboring provinces were so horrendous that the Protestant reformers rushed to register their conversion at the word that the troops were approaching. Reports of the Catholic victory poured in. The king, convinced that Calvinism was now a thing of the past in France, decided to revoke the Edict of Nantes without further ado. This was formally accomplished by the Royal Council, and the new Edict of Fontainebleau was signed and sealed on October 18.

The text is very short, just a preamble and twelve articles. The preamble justifies the royal decision. The king was simply respecting the wishes that his grandfather and father were unable to put into effect, the former because of his premature death, the latter because of war. The restoration of peace and the conversion of the "pretended reformers" allowed religion in France to be reunited under one roof. The Protestant faith was forbidden, and its churches were to be destroyed. Its pastors had a choice between conversion and immediate exile accompanied by their spouses and children below the age of seven. Ordinary congregants were not permitted to go into exile, contrary to the rules in force in other nations, where the chance to emigrate provided a counterbalance to the ruler's right to impose his religion. Having made emigration unavailable, the edict offered a last article contradicting the rest of the text: the remaining "religionists" were allowed to stay in France on the condition that they not practice their religion. But local authorities, acting with the consent of the monarchy, ignored this provision and sent dragoons into any households who had not shown up at church. Worse yet, the authorities in parts of the Languedoc forced residents to perform the Catholic sacraments of confession and communion during Easter 1686.

What brought about this momentous decision has long been debated. Although the king was primarily responsible, some historians have emphasized religious concerns and pointed to the pernicious influence of his father confessor, François de la Chaise, and his morganatic wife, Madame de Maintenon. But the evidence strongly suggests that the edict mirrored Louis XIV's political will and his view of extensive royal power, which gave him the authority to govern the conscience of his people.

The international context came into play as well — in two ways. Europe was at a culminating moment. Not only had Louis XIV just won a great victory against the Spanish Habsburgs in the War of the Reunions, but he had signed a twenty-year truce in Regensburg in 1684. Furthermore, a Catholic, James II, had ascended to the throne of England in February 1685, ensuring neutrality from that quarter. There was a second factor. Two years earlier, in 1683, the Ottomans had laid siege to Vienna. The Holy Roman emperor and the pope had called for help. Louis XIV studiously looked the other way, opening himself to the charge of breaking ranks with his co-religionists. What better way to display amity toward Catholicism than by eradicating the Protestant heresy from his territory, while sidestepping his differences with the papacy.

The international repercussions of the revocation were far reaching. Louis XIV's image was permanently tarnished, and his network of alliances with the Protestant German rulers was compromised. But the most serious consequences affected England. The existence of a Catholic sovereign was unpopular, but it was understood that he would be succeeded by his Protestant daughter Mary, married to William of Orange, stadtholder of the Dutch Republic. But in 1688, James II was presented with a Catholic son and heir, who replaced Mary in the line of succession. There is no question that the tales of persecution that circulated both before and after the revocation of the Edict of Nantes played a role in fanning popular alarm at the prospect of a Catholic dynasty, as did the testimony of Protestant refugees from France. British Protestants opened negotiations with Mary, and a few months later William of Orange arrived in England with an invading army captained by refugee Huguenot nobles. Its commander was the Duke of Schomberg, one of Louis XIV's most celebrated generals, who had chosen exile over conversion.

The tide of Huguenot emigration in fact began long before the reign of Louis XIV. The Saint Bartholomew's Day massacre of the previous century had opened the floodgates, and more emigrants fled after the Siege of La Rochelle by Richelieu's troops in 1627–1628. There were Huguenots in the Helvetian provinces, the Dutch Republic, and the British Isles. After the revocation, however, a much greater number of Protestants braved coercive measures and prohibitions and left France clandestinely, mostly from the northern and Atlantic provinces. The number of emigrants is estimated between 150,000 and 200,000.

More important than the number, however, was the kind of people who opted for emigration, and the places where they found welcome. Their outsized effect explains why their numbers and their impact on the French economy are often overestimated. The consequences were primarily felt outside of France. To illustrate the types of emigrants, let us cite two examples: the officers already mentioned who had assisted in the revolution in England, and the pamphleteers who lent unparalleled breadth and influence to the press in Holland. Paradoxically, these intellectuals imparted prestige to the French language as Enlightenment Europe was coming into being.

As to the places that received them, the most remarkable was Prussia. Acting rapidly and with great skill, Frederick William, elector of Brandenburg, encouraged Huguenots to emigrate to his country, offering them numerous benefits. His Edict of Potsdam, dated October 28, 1685, attracted at least fifteen thousand French Protestants, who would play a decisive role in the cultural and economic development of the Electorate of Brandenburg and comprise a key element of its army.

Whatever Louis XIV may have hoped, the revocation of the Edict of Nantes weakened French power in the world and strengthened the growing influence of Anglo-Saxons in Europe.

During much of the eighteenth century, the communities that welcomed the Protestant refugees maintained their identity. Some of their inhabitants gave support to the Protestants who, having remained in France, had rejected the revocation and now sought to preserve their religion despite the absence of pastors. Across Europe, exiled Protestants gave publicity to this resistance movement, particularly during the Camisard war (1702–1704), bringing fame to hitherto unknown locales, such as the Cévennes in south-central France.

The revocation was never annulled, not even after Louis XIV's death or during the Enlightenment. An entire population was thus deprived of civil status because its members refused to be baptized or married in Catholic churches. The persecution persisted, though on a more moderate scale, until the middle of the eighteenth century: the last Protestant to be executed was in 1762, and the last to be condemned to the galleys was in 1765.

This century of persecution and resistance forged a

strong memory among the Huguenots. They would be enthusiastic participants in the French Revolution and later strong supporters of the Third Republic and its secular schools. It was also the memory of past persecution that led some Huguenot strongholds — in the southwestern village of Le Chambon-sur-Lignon for instance — to rescue many Jews during World War II.

Philippe Joutard

REFERENCES

Benedict, Philip, Hugues Daussy, and Pierre-Olivier Léchot, eds. *L'Identité huguenote: Faire mémoire et écrire l'histoire (XVIe–XXIe siècle)*. Geneva: Droz, 2014.

Cabanel, Patrick. *Histoire des protestants en France (XVIe–XXIe siècle)*. Paris: Fayard, 2012.

Garrisson, Janine. *L'Édit de Nantes et sa révocation: Histoire d'une intolérance*. Paris: Seuil, 1985.

Labrousse, Élisabeth. *"Une foi, une loi, un roi?" Essai sur la révocation de l'édit de Nantes*. Geneva: Labor et Fides/Paris: Payot, 1985.

Magdelaine, Michelle, and Rudolf von Thadden, eds. *Le refuge huguenot*. Paris: Armand Colin, 1985.

RELATED ARTICLES
177, 1534, 1536, 1572, 1858, 1942

1686

Siam: A Missed Opportunity

If the ambassadors of the King of Siam were received with
extravagant honors at Versailles in 1686, it was because
the French were competing hard with the Dutch for their
Asian trade. But a palace revolution at Ayutthaya thwarted
them, leading to France's long-term withdrawal from the
Asian commercial scene.

On September 1, 1686, Louis XIV received a delegation
representing the King of Siam, Phra Narai (Ramathibodi
III). Although he was suffering from an agonizing fistula,
the French sovereign personally welcomed the three
emissaries from Ayutthaya, the capital of Siam, in his Hall
of Mirrors at Versailles. A First Ambassador (*ratchathut*),
the Ok-phra Wisut Sunthorn — known as Kosa Pan — led
the Siamese delegation. The delegation included, in order
of importance, a Second Ambassador (*uppathut*), the Ok-
luang Kanlaya Ratchamaitri; a Third Ambassador (*trithut*),
the Ok-khun Si Wisan Wacha; eight representatives of the
titled nobility (*khunnang*); a few lower-rank mandarins

(*khunmun*); a dozen young men who had come to learn about French arts and crafts; and a throng of servants.

The three ambassadors approached the throne with circumspection, before falling to their knees with their heads bowed and offering the Sun King a finely worked box containing a letter from their own monarch.

This ceremonial intrigued the poet and diplomat Simon de la Loubère, whom Louis XIV dispatched to Siam in 1687. De la Loubère noted in his classic travel book *The Kingdom of Siam*, published in 1691: "An ambassador in the Orient is no more than a messenger of his sovereign: his person is of little consequence by comparison with the respect given to the letter of credentials he carries with him." In southeast Asia, letters from monarchs, richly illuminated, were viewed at this time as authentic royal regalia imbued with the majesty of those who had sent them. They were entitled to the same ritual attentions as those surrounding the raja himself, should the latter be present in person. A chronicle of Malay royalty, the *Sejarah Melayu* (*Malay Annals*), composed in 1612 at Johor, devotes almost a full chapter to the subtle protocols that governed the writing, transport, and delivery of a letter addressed by the sultan of Malacca, Muzaffar Shah, to the King of Siam:

> The letter was read to the Sultan, who approved
> it from beginning to end. It was then carried on
> the back of an elephant to the state pavilion. A

knight riding the elephant held it, a herald led the elephant itself, and a minister walked beside as an escort. The procession was shaded from the sun by two ceremonial parasols white in color; it was accompanied by the music of trumpets, fifes, and drums.

Not surprisingly, Kosa Pan handled the missive of his sovereign with the utmost delicacy at Versailles.

For his own part, Louis XIV did not stint in the matter of pomp and grandeur. His silver furniture — throne, torchères, and girandoles — was set out on the royal platform. Fifteen hundred people attended the audience, which the gazette *Mercure galant* qualified as a huge success. Kosa Pan and his compatriots were subsequently invited to admire the marvels of Versailles, from the hydraulic machinery at Marly to the cages of the menagerie, by way of the *Cabinet des Estampes* with its vast print collection.

Behind all this, the diplomatic intentions of the French could not have been more evident. Even though peace had been signed with the United Provinces of Holland in 1678 after six years of brutal conflict, France intended by every means available to break into the Asiatic trade of the Dutch East India Company, which at the time covered a broad network of sources of merchandise from the Cape to Hirado, Japan. Although it had been led in the beginning by François Caron — a defector from the Dutch East India Company who had served in Ceylon (now Sri Lanka) and Japan — the French East India Company set up by Jean-Baptiste Colbert in August 1664 had so far failed to establish itself east of the Malacca Strait. The French believed, however, that there would be room for them in Siam, where the Dutch had only managed to keep a small trading outpost founded in 1608. A first envoy — André-François Boureau-Deslandes — traveled from Surat, India, to Ayutthaya in 1680. The following year, three Siamese ambassadors embarked at Banten, in northern Java, aboard the flagship of the French East India Company's fleet, the thousand-ton, sixty-gun, three-master *Soleil de l'Orient*, which sank with all hands off Madagascar on November 1, 1681. The shipwreck may have been caused by a pair of elephants chained up in the ship's hold; these were intended as modest gifts that Phra Narai thought might amuse Louis XIV's grandsons, the dukes of Burgundy and of Anjou. As it was, they inaugurated a strange animal-driven diplomacy between the two nations. After the governor of Pondicherry offered a Surat lion to Phra Narai in 1684, the King of Siam responded in 1686 by sending two baby elephants and a rhinoceros directly to Louis XIV.

In January 1684, Phra Narai dispatched two more emissaries to France on the advice of his new commercial superintendent of foreign trade, the Greek Constantine

Phaulkon. Born into a patrician Cypriot family who had settled in Cephalonia, and married to a Luso-Japanese woman who had converted to Catholicism, Phaulkon reached Siam in 1678 on a British ship. Within a few years he had imposed himself, thanks to his mastery of the Portuguese, Thai, and Malay languages, as an essential intermediary for serious commerce at Ayutthaya. Concerned as he was to counterbalance the growing influence of the Dutch, Phaulkon strongly advised Phra Narai to cultivate the French. To this purpose, in 1682 he appointed a French missionary, brother René Charbonneau, as governor of the port of Phuket, with the title and rank of Ok-phra. Three years later he supervised the 1685 signing of an agreement authorizing the French to station 650 soldiers in two fortified commercial outposts, Mergui and Bangkok. The French hence took the place of other foreigners — Bengalis, Persians, Turks, and Portuguese — who had served the dynasties of Ayutthaya in various civil and military capacities since the beginning of the seventeenth century.

But the close alliance between Phaulkon and the French was spectacularly exposed by the "Macassar Conspiracy" of 1686. In 1664, a prince of the kingdom of Macassar (Sunda Islands), Daéng Mangallé, established himself at Ayutthaya with 250 people in his train. Having opposed the policy of Sultan Hasanuddin, which he judged too favorable to the Dutch, Daéng Mangallé had no other choice but to flee the vengeance of his sovereign. Because they were Muslims, the exiles were lodged in the Malay *kampung* (quarter) at the gates of the royal city. But the disgrace of the Persian Minister Aqa Muhammad Astarabadi, in 1677, and the subsequent rise of Phaulkon led Muslim refugees in Siam — mostly Malays from the Peninsula and Sumatra, and Chams from Vietnam — to fear discriminatory measures. Daéng Mangallé unwisely associated himself with a conspiracy to sack the Royal Palace; the plotters were betrayed and the Macassar prince was summoned to the palace to beg for his life before Phra Narai. He refused to go, barricading himself instead in the Malay *kampung*. Phaulkon responded by ordering the Count de Forbin, who was in command of the Bangkok garrison, to cut off the fugitives' retreat along the river. Then, at the head of a small group of French and British troops, he himself mounted an assault on the *kampung*. Daéng Mangallé was killed in the fighting, but two of his sons were captured and handed over to the French for transportation overseas. The two boys arrived in Paris on September 1687. They were entrusted to Jesuits who baptized them with much fuss in 1688 before packing them off to the royal marine school at Brest. Throughout this affair, the French behaved as docile allies of Phaulkon, much to the annoyance of the Muslim merchants of Ayutthaya.

Thus the 1686 mission to France was a kind of

consecration of the pro-French diplomacy of Phaulkon. The Siamese emissaries were lavishly entertained by Louis XIV. We know, from a fragment of Kosa Pan's travel journal that has survived in the Foreign Missions Archive in Paris, that the port of Brest and the châteaux of the Loire Valley convinced him of France's power.

Alas, a palace revolution was to nip in the bud any chance of a lasting friendship between the two countries. In Ayutthaya, the growing influence of Phaulkon had alienated a section of the *khunnang* aristocracy, who saw his pro-European policies as mere adventurism. The Buddhist clergy of the *sangha* also feared the hold on the Royal Court acquired by the Jesuits, who displayed their knowledge of astronomy. In March 1688, Phra Narai fell gravely ill with dropsy and announced his intention to abdicate in favor of his daughter, Krom Luang Yothathep, on condition that she marry either his adoptive son Mom Pi, or the commander of the royal elephant guard, Phra Phetracha. The latter — whose mother had been the wet-nurse of Phra Narai, and who had as a consequence an almost brotherly relationship with the king — refused the subordinate role offered to him. He had Phra Narai arrested on May 17 and Phaulkon beheaded in mid-June, after which he proceeded to execute nearly every other member of the royal family. Phra Narai himself died in prison in mid-July. On August 1, the triumphant Phra Phetracha was crowned, choosing

577

as his minister for foreign affairs his devoted supporter...
Kosa Pan, the erstwhile leader of the 1686 Siamese mission
to France.

Kosa Pan immediately turned against the French in
spectacular fashion. Threatened with frontal assault and
certain annihilation, the Chevalier de Beauregard was
forced to evacuate the fortress of Mergui on June 24. The
other stronghold of Bangkok, held by General Desfarges,
was besieged for four months by an army of forty thousand
men, until the French agreed to sign an act of surrender that
enjoined them to leave the country at once. They returned
to Pondicherry aboard the warship *Oriflamme* in November
1688. After their expulsion, Siamese commerce reverted
to its former Malay and Chinese/Thai networks, an
arrangement that lasted for another two centuries without
interruption.

For the French, the failure of their Siam enterprise
resulted in a long-term withdrawal from the entire region.
Although they obtained, either by force or by concession,
a few supplementary outposts in India — Chandernagore
(today's Chandannagar, established in 1688), Mahe
(1721), Yanam (1731), and Karaikal (1739) — successive
French East India companies fell back on the Mascarene
Archipelago in the southern Indian Ocean (notably the
Bourbon Island, today's Réunion). Meanwhile, the Dutch
tightened their grip on Indonesia, and the British penetrated

the Malay peninsula and Burma (now Myanmar). The French did not reestablish a foothold in Southeast Asia until July 1885, when they overran the Vietnamese imperial city of Hue.

Romain Bertrand

REFERENCES

Diary of Kosa Pan: Thai Ambassador to France, June–July 1686, The. Edited by Dirk Van der Cruysse and Michael Smithies. Translated by Visudh Busayakul. Chiang Mai: Silkworm Books, 2002.

Jacq-Hergoualc'h, Michel. "La France et le Siam de 1680 à 1685: Histoire d'un échec." *Revue française d'histoire d'outre-mer 82,* no. 308 (1995): 257–75.

Kheng, Chea Boon. *Sejarah Melayu (MS Raffles no. 18).* Kuala Lumpur: Malaysian Branch of the Royal Asiatic Society, 1998.

Pelras, Christian. "La conspiration des Makassar à Ayuthia en 1686: ses dessous, son échec, son leader malchanceux. Témoignages européens et asiatiques." *Archipel 56,* no. 1 (1998): 163–98.

Smithies, Michael. "The Lion of Lopburi." In *Seventeenth Century Siamese Explorations: A Collection of Published Articles.* Bangkok: The Siam Society Under Royal Patronage, 2012.

———. "French Governors of Phuket, Bangkok and Mergui in the 17th Century." In *Seventeenth Century Siamese Explorations: A Collection of Published Articles.* Bangkok: The Siam Society Under

Royal Patronage, 2012.

Van der Cruysse, Dirk. *Louis XIV et le Siam*. Paris: Fayard, 1991.

RELATED ARTICLES

1534, 1550, 1715, 1863, 2003

1712

The Thousand and One Nights: Antoine Galland's Forgery

Overwhelmed by the success of his translations of
tales from the East — and in a tearing hurry to bring
out another volume — Antoine Galland added to his
Thousand and One Nights some stories supposedly told
to him by an Arab traveler from Aleppo. Is the story of
"Aladdin and His Wonderful Lamp" a French invention?
Whatever the case, there is no doubt that Galland, a
respected scholar from the Collège Royal, acted just as an
Arab compiler might have done.

No text in existence is more representative of Arab literature
in the eyes of the French public than *The Thousand and
One Nights*, a compilation of tales told by Scheherazade,
daughter of the sultan's vizier. The literary device therein
was that each story was interrupted at a particularly
thrilling juncture, every morning at dawn, so as to oblige
her listener — the Sultan Shahryar, a deceived husband
transformed into an exterminator of the female sex — to

suspend for yet another day his order for the narrator's execution, simply because he wanted to know what would happen next.

Nevertheless, the French text that introduced *The Thousand and One Nights* to Europe at the beginning of the eighteenth century and made them so popular, was in no way a faithful translation of an Arab original, but a bastardized work that owed its success to the initiative of Antoine Galland (1646–1715), one of the most eminent "scholars of oriental languages" of his time.

In 1704, Galland published the first volume of his *Thousand and One Nights*, which he followed with seven others at more or less regular intervals right up to 1709. A long hiatus followed, during which, we are told, people would assemble under his window at night to clamor for new stories. But it was not until 1712 that the next two volumes appeared, one of which contained the now famous story "Aladdin and His Wonderful Lamp" and "The Adventures of the Caliph Harun al-Rashid," an emblematic figure in the collection. Like the preceding volumes, these collections were put into the mouth of the beautiful storyteller Scheherazade. Nothing about these stories led anyone to suspect that they were not from exactly the same stable.

But this was not the case. At the end of the nineteenth century, the orientalist Hermann Zotenberg discovered, in Galland's journal, that the origins of all the tales in the four final volumes of the Arabian Nights — with the exception of "Story of the Sleeper and the Waker" — were different from those of the eight earlier volumes, which had been drawn directly from Arab manuscripts. In fact, the last batch contained tales the author had heard from Hanna Dyâb, a Maronite from Aleppo who visited Paris in 1709. Galland noted all the stories' essentials in his journal, without however qualifying them as authentic *Thousand and One Nights* productions. Of the story of Aladdin, he mentioned only the title, but did indicate that he had received a copy of it in Arabic from Dyâb. He also obtained from Dyâb a written version of the "Adventures of the Caliph Harun al-Rashid" and perhaps of the "Story of Ali Baba."

None of these copies have survived; the only clues still in existence are the summaries jotted down by Galland. While Arabic manuscripts relating the story of Aladdin and the story of Ali Baba were discovered at the end of the nineteenth century and the beginning of the twentieth in France and in England, in no way did they prove that these stories belonged to a written tradition prior to Galland. These manuscripts, in fact, were forgeries taken from Galland's own version. Ultimately, the first two-thirds of Galland's work were taken from tales belonging to the written tradition of *The Thousand and One Nights* while the remaining third were borrowed, as modern scholars have shown, from multiple oral traditions — Middle Eastern but perhaps also European — brought by a "man from Aleppo" at the beginning of the eighteenth century.

The initiative taken by Antoine Galland to introduce into his "translation" a series of tales from well outside the main bulk of the *Arabian Nights* was due to the fact that he very quickly found himself unable to obtain from the Levant any manuscripts more extensive than those he had already translated. Only the first of these, which contains 282 stories, and which he received from Aleppo in December 1701, remains in existence today (*BnF, ms. ar. 3609–3611*). Already in volume 8 of Galland's work, the Barbin publishing house had introduced (without his knowledge) two stories from a Turkish collection translated by François Pétis de la Croix, the secretary-interpreter of the king. After moving from Barbin to another publisher, Delaulne, Galland inserted a notice at the beginning of volume 9: "The two tales with which volume 8 ends are not taken from *The Thousand and One Nights*....Care will be taken, in the second edition, to omit these two stories as being foreign to the work." Justified though this declaration may have been, it could hardly fail to buttress the impression — later on — that the stories in the volumes that followed volume 8 really did belong to *The Thousand and One Nights*.

Why would the upright Galland carry out such a spectacular hoax?

When he published his "Arab tales," Galland was

already elderly. Despite his admission in 1701 to the Académie des Inscriptions et Belles-Lettres and his nomination to the Arabic chair at the Collège Royal (the future Collège de France) in 1709, his important work in the field of numismatics and his scholarly translations from Arabic, Persian, and Turkish were still languishing in the form of manuscripts. The only books he had published were works of popularization such as *De l'origine et du progrez du café* (Of the Origins and Progress of Coffee, 1699) or *Les Paroles remarquables, les bons mots et les maximes des Orientaux* (The Remarkable Utterances, Quips, and Maxims of the Orientals, 1694). With *The Thousand and One Nights*, he became famous overnight (so to speak). Overcoming the bitterness of a genuine scholar who might have hoped for a deeper sort of recognition, he decided in 1712 to publish a new volume of *The Thousand and One Nights*, at the price perhaps of truth. He had begun piecing it all together in November 1710, spurred possibly by the appearance of imitators like Pétis de la Croix, whose *Thousand and One Days* was selling like hotcakes in Paris. Did Galland have second thoughts? Maybe. Volumes 9 and 10 appeared in 1712, but it was not until 1717, two years after he died, that the two final volumes were published, ending with a denouement whereby, after a thousand and one nights, the sultan finally pardons Scheherazade.

Another question entirely is how, a full eighteen months

after hearing them told by Hanna Dyâb and working from basic summaries and some copies, Galland was able to write tales that the reader can in no way distinguish from the earlier ones drawn from manuscripts of the *Arabian Nights*. At this point his work ceased to be that of a translator; he was now a creative writer, able to use narrative structures whose vagaries he respected as frameworks for stories of far higher quality. Thus a summary of "The Story of Prince Ahmed and the Fairy Pari-Banou," which occupies seven pages in his journal dated May 22, 1709, blossoms into a story nearly two hundred pages long in volume 12 of *The Thousand and One Nights* (published in 1717). Galland composed his texts by tapping knowledge drawn from his life's work in orientalism; thus the evocation of a Hindu temple in "The Story of Prince Ahmed" is based on one by Abd al-Razzāq al-Samarqandī (1413–1482) in his account of the Timurids (*Matla-us-Sadain wa Majma-ul-Bahrain*) translated from the Persian by Galland himself a few years earlier. The description of the Valley of the Sogde in the same tale comes from the *Bibliothèque orientale* (1697), a summary of oriental knowledge by Barthelémy d'Herbelot (1625–1695), again completed and introduced by Galland.

Original writer that he had now become, Galland the orientalist began to draw on his personal experience of the Levant, where he had spent nearly fifteen years between 1670 and 1688. We find in his *Arabian Nights* a number of notations that already figure in the journal he kept of Constantinople in 1672 and 1673. The magnificent processions in his story of Aladdin echo the pomp of the "great lord" leading his army out on a campaign — a scene he had himself observed at Adrianople. Some details are reiterated exactly as in their first formulation, like the orchestra with its "concert of trumpets, kettledrums, tambours, fifes, and oboes" that accompanied the sultan's army into battle, but which, in the later tales, is transposed into much more festive circumstances.

In addition to enriching the material furnished by Hanna Dyâb, Galland also had to preserve the general unity of his series. He succeeded in this largely by observing, in the second part of his collection, the same literary conventions as in the first, where he had adapted the tales from his Arab manuscripts. In an era when translators were all too liable to embroider far too richly on their originals, translation, just as much as creative writing, demanded that its authors obey certain rules of propriety, which scarcely admitted realistic descriptions of the material world. Thus, Galland turned palaces and detailed portraits of young princesses into abstract evocations or else made them stylized: "women of matchless beauty" inhabit rooms with "domed ceilings painted in the Arab manner," furnished with "sofas." No doubt a faithful translation of the Arab sources would have been judged unreadable, and if Galland profoundly modified the presentation of his tales, he also refrained from outrageously over-Frenching them, as certain other translators of his time did by, say, portraying Aeneas in the trappings of a French knight. Galland set out to please, but he also sought to be instructive. Since the classic aesthetic was not against the evocation of morals, customs, and religious practices, he went ahead and evoked them, and even explained them if he felt it to be necessary.

Galland's writing in the last volumes of his *Arabian Nights* is based on his earlier ones, whereby a form of expression devised for oral delivery by a storyteller was transformed into elegant French classical prose. At the same time, he has a distinctive way of developing his source material, giving psychological ballast to his characters, skillfully amplifying their dialogue. He also cultivates the art of transition with great skill to make acceptable a mixture of genres that was considered unrefined by his contemporaries. With this we can begin to understand how Galland, grappling with Arabian tales of extraordinary richness, contrived to pass them on to us in such a personal form.

Galland's is obviously but one version among many of *The Thousand and One Nights*. Some of the other translators and tellers even ventured to take the title literally, as with a monumental Egyptian effort in the late eighteenth century that was translated into European languages by translators as celebrated as Richard Burton. Yet none went so far as Antoine Galland, who in a way followed the example set by the original Arab compilers when he filled out the collection, to contribute to the worldwide spread of the tales of Scheherazade. Above all, Galland imposed real uniformity, stamping these tales forever with the seal of the written word.

Sylvette Larzul

REFERENCES

Abdel-Halim, Mohamed. *Antoine Galland: Sa vie et son œuvre*. Paris: A.G. Nizet, 1964.

Bauden, Frédéric, and Richard Waller, eds. *Le Journal d'Antoine Galland (1646–1715: la période parisienne)*, vol. 1. Leuven: Peeters, 2011.

Irwin, Robert. *The Arabian Nights: A Companion*. London: The Penguin Press, 1994.

Larzul, Sylvette. "Further Considerations on Galland's *Mille et une Nuits*: A Study of the Tales told by Hannâ." In *The Arabian Nights in Transnational Perspective*, edited by Ulrich Marzolph, 17–31. Detroit: Wayne State University Press, 2007.

———. *Les traductions françaises des "Mille et Une Nuits": Étude des versions Galland, Trébutien et Mardrus*. Paris: L'Harmattan, 1996.

May, Georges. *Les Mille et Une Nuits d'Antoine Galland ou le Chef-d'Œuvre invisible*. Paris: Presses Universitaires de France, 1986.

Schefer, Charles, ed. *Journal d'Antoine Galland pendant son séjour à Constantinople (1672–1673)*. Paris: Leroux, 1881. Reprint Maisonneuve & Larose, 2002.

Sermain, Jean-Paul. "Galland traducteur et créateur." In *Les Mille et Une Nuits*, 80–86. Published in conjunction with an exhibition at the Institut du Monde Arabe, November 27, 2012–April 28, 2013. Paris: Hazan, 2012.

RELATED ARTICLES

1143, 1539, 1751, 1771, 1842

1715

Persians at the Court of Louis XIV

Looking for an alliance against the Ottoman Empire and
other hostile Sunni powers, Safavid princes of Persia
arrived in Versailles to witness the decline of the Sun King.
The memoirist Saint-Simon would turn the encounter into
a narrative while Montesquieu made it a political fable.

It is one of the great scenes from the last stages of Louis
XIV's reign. The French court is assembled at the far end
of the Hall of Mirrors in the Palace of Versailles, and the
Persian ambassadors bow low before the dais bearing the
throne. The aged king, gaunt, his features pinched, adrift
in his diamond-embroidered robes, sits before the Persians
in his chair of gilded wood. Etiquette called for a prince on
either side of the throne: on the right was the dauphin, Louis,
five years old, as handsome a child as he was inexpressive;
on the left was the Duke of Orléans, the king's nephew and
the future regent. The Duke of Saint-Simon, who attended
this audience on February 26, 1715, reported that Claude
Gros de Boze, a recent member of the Académie Française,

and Antoine Coypel, a history painter, were at the foot of the throne, the first to write a description and the second to memorialize the ceremony on canvas.

The French court had deployed all of its splendors in welcoming the ambassador, Mohammad Reza Beg, and his entourage. After landing in Marseille on October 23, 1714, the ambassador had made a ceremonial entry into the city, hosted banquets and been hosted in return, and attended two operas by Jean-Baptiste Lully: *Amadis* and *Bellérophon*. His slow progress from Marseille to Paris was marked by receptions in every city, speeches by dignitaries, and gifts — nougats in Montélimar, fruit jams in Valence, candles and exotic fruits at Nevers. In Paris, where the delegation arrived with great pomp on February 7, 1715, the Persians were ensconced on the Rue de Tournon at the townhouse for ambassadors extraordinary.

The royal audience on February 19 was a repeat of the ceremony used in welcoming the doge of Genoa in 1685 and the embassy from Siam in 1686. Mohammad Reza and his train of attendants were met in the forecourt of the Palace of Versailles, where two thousand soldiers of the French and Swiss Guards were drawn up, their hats decorated with plumes and cockades, their drums beating in the ambassador's honor. Proceeding to the royal courtyard, the Persian found the guards of the gate and the house guards waiting at attention. Mohammad Reza mounted the Ambassadors'

Staircase, crossed the State Apartment and Hall of Mirrors, made his way through a throng of courtiers, and finally reached Louis XIV, to whom he presented a letter from Sultan Husayn, shah of Persia. But the ambassador embarrassed the king by engaging in conversation with him rather than offering the customary speech. During the whole audience, the French royals remained bareheaded, though Mohammad Reza Beg, in true Muslim style, never removed his turban. The leave-taking audience, a simpler ritual, took place on August 13, three weeks before Louis XIV's death. It was his last public act.

Thanks to Saint-Simon, the Persian embassy remains linked to the king's death. Viewed as insignificant in itself, the visit is seen as a prelude of sorts to his demise, the "beginning of the end," as the memoirist would characterize it. Saint-Simon was not the only one to cast the episode in an unflattering light. The rumor in 1715 was that Mohammad Reza Beg was an impostor, that the gifts he brought Louis XIV were of no value, and that the whole embassy had been staged by the king's entourage to distract him. The king, in this version, was the victim of a deception somewhat like the Turkish ceremony at the close of Molière's *Bourgeois Gentleman*. The ambassador's stay in Paris, which gave rise to many humorous incidents, also raised doubts about the seriousness of his mission. Parisian idlers collected to watch him drink his coffee or tea, savor his sorbets, smoke his pipe, take his bath, and practice throwing the javelin on the city ramparts. Mohammad Reza had a host of women admirers and managed to seduce a young lady of good family. From this perspective, the Persian mission of 1715 was a nonevent that heralded another nonevent: the death of a royal who had long ago stopped being the Sun King.

Yet the dark picture painted by Saint-Simon and a few of his contemporaries deserves some retouching. It may be true that the king who died on September 1, 1715, had dimmed in glory since the triumphant decades of the 1670s and 1680s. In 1697, with the Treaty of Ryswick, Louis XIV was forced to give back some of the conquests made during his heyday. Still, France remained undefeated on land. In 1713 and 1714, with the Treaties of Utrecht and Rastatt, drawn up after unprecedented military defeats, he again gave up territory but managed to keep the Spanish crown for his grandson Philip V. The France of 1715 may no longer have been predominant, but it remained the most populated and powerful country in Europe. Though Louis was worn out — he sometimes fell asleep during sessions of his council — he was not senile; in fact, he was working at preserving through diplomacy what had been won through wars. By recreating Versailles's resplendence one last time for the Persian emissaries, and especially with his display of military might, the king meant to show the public in France and abroad that his country had not lost its greatness.

Prudence and negotiation rather than adventure and the politics of power: this became the watchword of his ill-loved nephew, Philippe, Duke of Orléans, when he became regent after his uncle's death.

Despite recent setbacks, France's royal administration and its business sector had many plans in the works for commercial and colonial expansion. The country's navy had emerged greatly diminished from the War of Spanish Succession, but the navy and the Bureau of Foreign Affairs were casting a covetous eye on the Indian Ocean and Spain's holdings in America. The ruling group in France was trying to draw what lessons it could from the recent war, whose outcome owed much to the financial might of the English and the Dutch. The rise of John Law, the brilliant economist whose speculations brought such chaos to the French economy, was not far off.

The embassy, however, was initiated by the Persians. Its official intent was to conclude a treaty of friendship and trade that had been under discussion for fifteen years. In fact, however, the mission's purpose seems to have been primarily political and military. Shiism was the official religion of Persia under the Safavids, and the surrounding countries were hostile Sunni states: the Ottoman Empire, the Mughal Empire, the Khanate of Bukhara, and the Imamate of Oman. Persia maintained a tenuous peace with all of them. Omani pirates were raiding its shipping in the

Persian Gulf and terrifying its coastal towns. Persia thus sought an alliance with the French against the Omanis. In return for favorable trade concessions, the French navy would secure the port of Muscat, which had been disputed since the early sixteenth century by the Portuguese, the Ottomans, the Persians, and the imams of Oman. Once established in Muscat, the French fleet could police the flow of trade in the Persian Gulf.

The Persian embassy of 1715 was one of a series of diplomatic missions that Muslim rulers sent to Europe around the turn of the eighteenth century: the Ottoman embassy of 1669, the Moroccan embassy of 1699, and the Ottoman embassy of 1721. These belonged within the traditional diplomatic strategy of forming alliances with partners to the rear of one's enemy, a practice known in France as an *alliance de revers*. They also corresponded to a growing awareness within the Muslim world of the technological advances the West was making, particularly in the arts of war. Eager to learn about European innovations, Eastern potentates invited Christian experts to work in their countries. The voyages of Peter the Great to Europe from 1697 to 1698 and from 1716 to 1718 arose from similar motives.

But Persia's outreach to France came too late. Given the slow pace of communications and the turnover of political actors in both countries, negotiations dragged on until

1722. In that year, the Afghans, who had rebelled against the Safavid state, launched an attack on Isfahan, the capital of the Persian Empire. They destroyed the imperial army despite its numerical superiority and its artillery division under the deputy command of a Frenchman. After a lengthy siege, the Afghans entered the capital. Persia then sank into chaos and disappeared from the European diplomatic agenda for almost a century.

On the French side, the Persian embassy of 1715 was void of diplomatic and military consequences, but rich in philosophical and literary ones. Though the Persian travels of Jean-Baptiste Tavernier and Jean Chardin were already available to French readers, direct observation of the customs of the Persian embassy gave Louis XIV's subjects a firsthand lesson in cultural relativism. After Baron de Breteuil, the French chief of protocol, was greeted by Mohammad Reza Beg sitting cross-legged by the fireplace, the Baron retained the distinct first impression of the ambassador as "a large monkey crouched by the fire." "I have no doubt," the courtier continued, "that the first time the Persians saw a European seated on a chair, they thought his posture as ridiculous as the ambassador's seemed to me at first sight." The visit to Paris of the shah's emissary aroused much curiosity and speculation, which soon resulted in one of the early monuments of the Age of Reason: Montesquieu's *Persian Letters*, published in 1721. If the shock of an alien culture let the French see through new eyes, they trained their gaze not on the East, but on the West itself.

Thierry Sarmant

REFERENCES

Herbette, Maurice. *Une ambassade persane sous Louis XIV, d'après des documents inédits*. Paris: Perrin, 1907.

Matthee, Rudi. *Persia in Crisis: Safavid Decline and the Fall of Isfahan*. London/New York: Tauris, 2012.

Sarmant, Thierry. *1715: La France et le monde*. Paris: Perrin, 2014.

Touzard, Anne-Marie. *Le Drogman Padery: Émissaire de France en Perse (1719–1725)*. Paris: Geuthner, 2005.

RELATED ARTICLES
1550, 1682, 1685, 1771

1720

Law and Disorder

How to pay off the debt left by Louis XIV? Philippe II,
Duke of Orléans, was won over by the bold ideas of
Scotsman John Law: create a general bank that issues
stock. This early experiment in financial markets ended in
bankruptcy, resulting in mutual suspicion between the state
and the creditors.

John Law's System was a radical finance experiment carried
out in Regency France. A quick overview of the man behind
it: John Law (1671–1729), son of an Edinburgh goldsmith,
spent a dissipated youth in London, where he fought in a
duel that landed him a death sentence, which he evaded with
outside help. Law then spent twenty years crisscrossing
Europe, getting acquainted with financial markets and
proposing bank projects to various royal courts. At that
time, any business larger than a partnership required a royal
privilege (or authorization), and Law did not want to become
a mere investment banker, working on his own. He aspired
to replicate the success of the Bank of England (founded in

1694) by adapting the model to local circumstances. Though hardly the first or the only contemporary to mastermind such a venture, he went about it in a distinctive way. He presented his bank not as a fiscal expedient, but as a tool of economic policy, based on highly advanced theoretical reasoning half a century before the writings of his fellow Scotsman Adam Smith. For Law, a currency based on well-regulated credit rather than precious metals would prove more reliable, and would stimulate economic activity by supplying liquid assets and lowering interest rates.

When he arrived in France in late 1713, the realm had just emerged from the War of Spanish Succession, a conflict that affected the whole of Europe. Although France was able to limit its losses, the war years had depleted its coffers, leading to partial bankruptcy and heavy tax increases. What Law submitted to Louis XIV, and later to the regent, the Duke of Orléans, after the king's death in 1715, had definite appeal. However, it could not spare the regent recourse from adopting harsh measures between 1715 and 1718: lowering of interest on national debt, consolidation of floating debt into state notes of dubious value, monetary tampering, and tax increases. Nevertheless, the regent was enticed by Law's intelligence and vision, and managed to convince his government to give the Scotsman a chance.

Law's System unfolded in three stages. First, a bank was established in 1716 by offering bearers of state notes the option to exchange them for bank shares, which amounted to trading sovereign debt for shares in a potentially lucrative venture. The bank would issue bearer notes, convertible on demand into coins of fixed weight, and would purchase commercial bills. Though the notes were not legal tender as such, they were soon accepted for payment of taxes and made convertible among tax collectors. This well-managed bank proved profitable, and the protection granted to notes against the monetary reform of May 1718 further enhanced their popularity.

Meanwhile Law launched the second stage in 1717 by creating a trading company, here again through the exchange of state notes for shares. The Company of the West, as it was then called, was created to develop the colony of Louisiana, which at the time comprised the entire Mississippi Basin, a vast territory acquired thirty years earlier but that remained unexploited. Business was slow at first, but the company soon acquired a series of other commercial and fiscal ventures. Share prices rose, and the company was able to finance its acquisitions by issuing new shares. In 1719, it absorbed the Indies Company and took on its name, thereby dominating most overseas trade.

The third stage took place in the summer of 1719, when the company carried out two simultaneous operations. First, it won the leases to collect indirect taxes, thanks to which it now owed the crown a fixed amount for the value of taxes levied, keeping for itself whatever losses or gains accrued. Furthermore, it offered to lend the king sufficient funds to reimburse the entire national debt at an advantageous rate. It financed this loan through a massive share issue, for which it accepted existing debt obligations. The operation essentially amounted to converting fixed interest national debt into shares of a company that collected, in addition to profits from its monopolies on foreign trade, the surplus of (variable) state revenues on its fixed expenditures. The state funded itself not by fixed-rate borrowing (that resulted in bankruptcy in the worst cases), but through variable dividend stocks that shared risks. Law was providing France with a boldly modern finance system, and with it, the prospect of raising necessary funds in the event of a future armed conflict. The brief war with Spain in 1718, for instance, was won without even a ripple in financial markets.

Law's increasing influence over the regent was such that he eventually became the general comptroller of finances in January 1720. His triumph was so complete that Great Britain saw fit to imitate France. In that same year of 1720, England's South Sea Company persuaded Parliament to convert the entire national debt into stock, and London was soon engulfed in feverish speculation. A similar financial bubble would emerge the same year in Amsterdam.

But Law's project failed. The price at which the older loans were converted into shares was fixed, but Law felt it necessary to raise share prices to encourage lenders to convert. Though the income he foresaw for his company was reasonable, he justified the high target by the drop in interest rates that monetary abundance should have brought about, or so he predicted. To support stock prices, he used banknotes, at first behind the scenes, then more overtly. To support the value of banknotes, he made them legal tender, while varying and finally demonetizing gold and silver currencies. The now uncontrolled monetary creation caused exchange rates to weaken and gave rise to inflation. In order to backtrack, Law reduced stock prices and the face value of banknotes on May 21, 1720. This dealt a fatal blow to general confidence. Emotion was running so high that Law was temporarily removed from office and his measure rescinded — though Law was reinstated at the Company in an attempt to save the venture. The price of shares and of banknotes in gold were both in freefall. Law attempted to reabsorb the mass of paper money in several ways, reestablishing the national debt, issuing new bonds, and creating bank accounts on the Bank of Amsterdam model. Nothing seemed to work. Banknotes were gradually demonetized. Meanwhile state revenues were collapsing and the Company was unable to meet its payments. Law was dismissed and secretly escorted to the border that December.

Public finance was not the only thing in disarray. The wild speculation on stocks and other instruments, the incomplete reimbursement of the national debt, and especially the forced valuation of paper money, a windfall for debtors, had disrupted many a fortune. The job of cleaning up the mess fell to the Pâris brothers, experienced financiers who designed the "Visa," a plan to save the Indies Company, liquidate the Bank, and settle the Law System's debts while limiting, to the extent possible, injustices and undue profits. Over a half million submissions were processed and liquidated, which is to say, reduced according to the origin of the asset and converted into new public debt instruments.

What survived this experiment? First of all, the Indies Company. After retroceding its tobacco monopoly and the Louisiana Territory in 1731, it focused on trading with the East and supplying France with luxury products from India and China, and competed with its Dutch and British counterparts. Although it was a private company, it was closely monitored by the government, which had an interest in its success, but lacked the necessary resources to support it in the event of military conflict. After the defeat following the Seven Years' War, the Company was liquidated and its trade reopened to competition.

Law's experiment also yielded an organized financial market. The quaint stock-jobbing on Rue Quincampoix, sometimes encouraged and at other times suppressed, was given a location and a regulatory framework in 1724.

Government bearer bonds were traded, but the leading security was stock in the Indies Company, whose quotation, advertised in all European newspapers, represented the financial barometer of France. A capital market was thus in the making, though the state was unable to leverage it. Interrupted by the Revolution, the Bourse (or stock market) made its comeback at the end of the eighteenth century, under the Directory, and expanded throughout the following decades.

Still, the experiment left scars. First, the state's borrowing power, especially during wartime when public spending was so massive, remained limited by the memory of ill-treatment of the creditors. One might assume that the Visa softened the blow somewhat. But breaches of faith persisted for quite some time, with suspensions of payment in 1759 and 1788, and forced reduction of the debt in 1771 and 1797. The collapse of the Royal Bank deprived France of a resource that its Dutch and British rivals enjoyed; it would take another half century before the Caisse d'Escompte, ancestor of the Bank of France (1800), was established in 1776.

The Law experiment was also a missed opportunity. The French ancien régime, briefly open to new ideas and possibilities for far-reaching reform, retreated instead into inertia and fear of innovation, which the 1720 disaster seemed to justify. One can only imagine what royal absolutism would have become if faced with a state (of shareholders) within the State.

François Velde

REFERENCES

Faure, Edgar. *La Banqueroute de Law*. Paris: Gallimard, 1977.

Lévy, Claude-Frédéric. *Capitalistes et pouvoir au siècle des Lumières*. 3 vols. Paris: Mouton, 1980.

Murphy, Antoin E. *John Law: Economic Theorist and Policy-Maker*. Oxford: Clarendon Press, 1997.

Neal, Larry. *The Rise of Financial Capitalism: International Capital Markets in the Age of Reason*. Cambridge: Cambridge University Press, 1990.

Velde, François R. "Was John Law's System a Bubble? The Mississippi Bubble Revisited." In *The Origins and Development of Financial Markets and Institutions*, edited by Jeremy Atack and Larry Neal, 99–120. Cambridge: Cambridge University Press, 2008.

RELATED ARTICLES
1357, 1456, 1860, 1973, 2011

ENLIGHTENMENT NATION

From the philosopher Denis Diderot to the revolutionary Maximilien Robespierre, from the first publication of the multivolume *Encyclopédie* in 1751 to the provisional survival in 1794 of the young French Republic, bloodied from the Reign of Terror, history seems to have accelerated during these pivotal years. The French Revolution, which had long been brewing, was only cut short by its own progress. The astronomer's image of the earth's revolution is worth considering here. Literally and figuratively, the French Revolution sought to restore harmony to the cosmos by regenerating mankind. After all, the monarchy had identified itself with the sun, suggesting that the world was a system of stars and planets. Once the sun had disappeared behind a veil, the Revolution seemed more like a foundational act, sacralizing politics and desacralizing religion.

The movement that caused the centers of power to undergo a revolution did not drop from the sky. It was the outcome of an extraordinary collective aspiration, multifaceted and often contradictory, inspired by an optical and geometric vision. The "Enlightenment," which reexamined social reality under the glare of reason, was an indispensable precursor to the revolutionary moment. The desire for social change was "global" in the sense of wanting to be in step with the movement of mankind or even the universe. In an act that had powerful symbolic import, the newly formed National Assembly chose the astronomer Jean-Sylvain Bailly as its first president, in June 1789. Now that the sun of the absolutist state had declined, the source of light (in this *siècle des Lumières*) would henceforth be the collective sovereignty of the French people, emanating from the earth's surface.

Though it has a long history, this French claim to embody universality through the particulars of its own people came to a head in the second half of the seventeenth century. The circulation of books, newspapers, and knowledge created a new order that leapt across social and cultural boundaries. Information and the shaping of public opinion made society into a will and a representation, destabilizing the traditional means by which states ruled. Yet as society became a public space, there was a corresponding rise in Freemasonry and secret societies, the very obverse of the Enlightenment's political equation between knowledge, freedom, and transparency. But if the guiding light now emanated from a new source, it was also that a new effort was underway to bring man's rational faculties into harmony with his emotional being. This ideal ran through the writings of contemporary thinkers, from Jean-Jacques Rousseau to the Marquis de Sade, to the point where it started to dictate behavior. The profusion of representational styles in theater and the dramatic arts and the conflicts among these styles reflected a society intent on finding salvation.

This was the substrate from which, by bringing human passions and hopes onto the stage, a new mystical-political alliance sought to turn citizens into integral moral beings. This new idea of humanity, emphasizing freedom and natural rights, found justification in the discovery of populations scattered across a globe that one could now circumnavigate. Here again, the earth's revolution provides an apt and resonant image. Humankind, because of its identification with the terrestrial globe, could come into its own as a political principle *and* a demographic entity.

As dominion over the seas extended, the world stopped being an object for mystical speculation. Instead, it was the subject of rational inquiry and exploration. By the end of the eighteenth century, a fifth "oceanic" continent had been added to those already known, after the voyages of James Cook, Louis-Antoine de Bougainville, and Nicolas Baudin. Having explored the world from end to end, European rulers now began to believe it was their destiny to rule over it. The Seven Years' War, however, saw France losing its commanding position in the race toward empire, and for the next century and a half, the foremost world power would be the British Empire. French nostalgia for global domination soon focused on an intensive and speculative economic colonialism. Slave ownership, which the Revolution came to deem intolerable in mainland France, was practiced intensively in the French Caribbean, making a mockery of the equal rights of man.

The regeneration of the minds required the physical emancipation of bodies. Inspired by the American Constitution, the sudden, near-religious surge of the French Revolution sought to accomplish its vision through the blessing of law, the virtue of education, and the exercise of fraternity. Revolutionary Paris was the long-awaited stage for the reconciliation of the political and the natural orders, gathered in a terrestrial Eden that the new National Museum of Natural History foreshadowed.

But was it possible to bring perpetual peace to the world without resorting to force and, before long, waging war? Clear-eyed about the political designs coming out of France, the kingdoms of Europe rebuffed the new French Republic, seeing in its claims to political and moral universality a pretext to rule over them. The heirs to the Enlightenment made, unmade, and then remade their revolutions, whose deviations from their true course did not happen without a reason.

1751

All the World's Knowledge

Denis Diderot and Jean le Rond d'Alembert's *Encyclopedia*,
whose publication began in 1751, reflected the universal
vocation of French learned culture. Grounded in
the country's still indisputable economic powers and
strengthened by an increasingly urban society, the
dominance of French Enlightenment thinkers mirrored and
nourished a radiance that was political, and then symbolic.

On May 4, 1751, the Faculty of Theology at the University
of Paris retroactively authorized the publication of
the first volumes of Georges-Louis Leclerc, Comte de
Buffon's 1749 *Natural History, General and Particular* —
a wide-ranging enterprise to catalog human diversity that
would continue throughout the century. For Buffon, human
variety stemmed from the natural differences making up the
habitats of the Earth's populations. Voicing a Eurocentric
point of view that echoed the prejudices of his time, he
argued that Europe's natural conditions made it the most
conducive environment for perfecting individuals and

societies. As an extension of that idea, he placed Europeans at the top of a hierarchy of civilizations. Many of Buffon's contemporaries believed that within Europe, France — or rather, Paris — was the seat of universal civilization and the capital of reason and civility. No self-respecting traveler could bypass the French capital.

Another work published in 1751 captures the French pretension to enlighten the universe. That year, a Parisian bookseller named André-François Le Breton and two members of a transnational community of scholars known as the Republic of Letters, Denis Diderot and Jean le Rond d'Alembert, began the publication of their intellectually and commercially ambitious *Encyclopedia*. The project sought to offer a select European readership the sum of all knowledge. By exporting its scientific institutions and substituting its language (to the detriment of Latin) as the lingua franca of elites, Paris seemed to dominate the world and embody the ideal of progress at the heart of the European Enlightenment.

The French kingdom pulsed with new energy after the misfortunes of the final years of Louis XIV's reign. Between 1700 and 1750, the urban population grew from 2.7 million to 3.1 million residents (out of a total of nearly 24 million in 1725), reflecting true demographic, economic, cultural, and military vibrancy. In 1737, Louis XV was quick to send his troops to restore order in Geneva, thereby reaffirming

France's role as Europe's police. Paris was the capital city of a vast, ever-expanding empire that extended into Africa, Asia, and North America. Thanks to sustained immigration, the metropolis grew from 400,000 to 450,000 residents between 1700 and 1750. Francophone and Francophile European elites flocked in search of the curiosities and pleasures provided by spaces of discussion and sociability, now divided between the city itself and the royal court in Versailles. Embodied by Voltaire, Buffon, and other figures whose reputations and epistolary networks far exceeded France's borders, thinkers of the French Enlightenment (a term that was coined later) established a space for discussion that reflected the vitality of the Republic of Letters and the emergence of public opinion at the European scale.

The universalist aims of French culture were grounded in solid economic and material bases, symbolized by the commercial growth of its Atlantic port cities. Bordeaux, Nantes, and La Rochelle embraced the triangular slave trade with the Caribbean islands (especially Saint-Domingue). This trade in turn generated significant revenue for a thriving middle class eager to conform to social codes established by the nobles. They invested in land (which led to the development of Bordeaux wines marked for export) and, with the help of prominent officials, undertook large-scale urban projects to make French cities more functional. Conflicts with old urban or clerical elites were rife as maritime commerce became an engine for more general development, encouraging the circulation and flow of people, goods, and ideas. The authorities now invested in roads (thanks to *la corvée royale*, an in-kind tax established in 1738 that provided the state with free labor) and canals, which were devised by a reorganized Corps of Bridges and Roads (the Royal School of Bridges and Roads was founded in 1747 to train its engineers). Together with the general vitality of urban centers, this growth led to deep transformations in eating practices and clothing fashion, which, in this appearance-based culture, became important cues for determining social hierarchy. Calico, a painted or printed cotton first imported from India before being manufactured in Europe, became synonymous with French fashion.

To be sure, such changes did not apply to all the king's subjects, and the benefits of this general vitality were only felt by a small segment of society. The vast majority of the French population was made up of peasants, who, aside from the essential labor they provided, remained unaffected by these transformations. Although major scourges such as war, famine, and plague were kept at bay (the last outbreak of plague occurred in Marseille in 1720), rural and urban residents continued to live in difficult conditions, under the social and cultural domination of a minority group of aristocrats and bourgeois. It is nonetheless thanks to this mostly urban-dwelling, highly selective elite that the cultural activities and intellectual practices that became hallmarks of French civilization took off.

The court of Versailles remained the seat of artistic and intellectual life. Madame de Pompadour, Louis XV's official mistress, was a social magnet who encouraged royal patronage and played a vital role in the development of the arts. Meanwhile, the royal academies continued to act not only as cultural arbiters but also as places for artistic and intellectual experimentation. Starting in the 1730s, members of the Royal Academy of Sciences, under the direction of Pierre Louis Maupertuis, used their clout to introduce Newtonian ideas, which had previously faced hostility from French thinkers. Academy members (especially the mathematician Alexis Clairaut, whose work confirmed Sir Isaac Newton's ideas and Edmond Halley's calculations) contributed to the radiance of French science by, for instance, initiating maritime expeditions (to Peru in 1735 and Lapland in 1736). Though they sought to confirm theories about the shape of the globe, these expeditions owed as much to science as to economics, diplomacy, and a colonial machine that served royal interests and those of scholarly institutions (e.g., the Royal Garden, today's Jardin de Plantes, which Buffon began overseeing in 1739). In terms of the arts, the Royal Academy of Painting played a major role in establishing a new space for publicizing and critiquing artistic creations when it began organizing exhibitions in 1737. These four- to five-week-long free biannual events were an immediate success, with almost 15,000 people gathering at the Louvre for an exhibition in 1750.

A variety of lively social locales developed alongside royal and scholarly institutions, making their mark on the changing urban culture and encouraging the emergence of a true public sphere. Under the regency of the Duke of Orléans (1715–1723), places of Parisian sociability reserved for members of the nobility and the elite bourgeoisie were restored. This fostered a type of worldly civility that would undergird the new notion of "civilization," a term used in 1756 by Victor de Riqueti, the Marquis de Mirabeau. At the beginning of the eighteenth century, the Marquise de Lambert's salon at the Hôtel de Nevers rivaled Louise Bénédicte de Bourbon's "Court" of Sceaux, a social group steeped in old aristocratic norms. After 1764, the salon of Mademoiselle Lespinasse on Rue Saint-Dominique vied against that of Madame du Deffand, her aunt and former guardian, for the most famous men of letters and artists.

Although women played an important role in salon life, some men, mostly rich collectors or amateurs, held their own. The Paris salons promoted conversation, etiquette, and good manners, values which over time were upheld as models throughout Europe. At the same time, the salons fashioned a complex set of codes as a value system for high society (literary, scientific, and artistic reputations were forged in such salons) and a means of excluding those deemed unworthy of their ranks. Other, less restrictive spaces for social life also contributed to cultural and intellectual change: cafés, where reading rooms provided the humbler middle and lower-middle classes with access to periodicals and books; Masonic lodges (established in France in 1715–1720 and proliferating after 1730), where these same readers could seek spiritual answers, new cultural practices, and entertainment. By providing access to a wide array of cultural resources, such spaces helped change modes of behavior and habits. The impact was mostly urban at first, but over time, priests and salespeople and other cultural mediators brought cultural and intellectual change to rural areas as well.

All of this was cause for concern and even opposition. From the 1730s on, members of the clergy waged war against new cultural practices that seemed to call into question the church's moral authority. The offensive gained momentum with the expansion of the book market and the emergence of supposedly perverse reading practices, which were believed to harm first and foremost women and servants. Enlightenment thinkers and philosophers were accused of destroying the political and social order. Diderot's and d'Alembert's *Encyclopedia* became the target of the offensive: the work was condemned in 1759 by the King's Council, the Parlement of Paris, and the pope, but its circulation continued in secret thanks to the help of Malesherbes, the official who oversaw the press and censorship. Still, the one hundred and fifty contributors were for the most part members of the administration and thus in favor of the monarchy. Most *Encyclopédistes* and philosophers fought against "excesses" and "abuses" (in religious, tax, and legal matters) that weakened the prince's power and prevented general well-being.

These conflicts, which extended far beyond France's borders, helped solidify France's influence as a civilizing power throughout Europe. But were the 1750s the peak of that movement? Over the course of the decade, the kingdom experienced a series of crises: attacks on royal authority by noble elites who made use of judicial courts, the *parlements*, to prevent tax and legal reforms; agitation within the urban populace, inflamed by the brutal execution of Robert-François Damiens, the servant who sought to assassinate Louis XV in 1757; a sharp cleavage within the Catholic Church around the issue of Jansenism. All of this weakened the foundations of a French civilization that now faced ascendant English and Prussian competitors. The military defeats and diplomatic failures that accompanied the end of the Seven Years' War in 1763 revealed the limits of France's universalist aspirations.

Jean-Luc Chappey

REFERENCES

Caradonna, Jeremy L. "Prendre part au siècle des Lumières: Le concours académique et la culture intellectuelle au XVIIIe siècle." *Annales. Histoire, sciences sociales* 63, no. 3 (2009): 633–62.

Chappey, Jean-Luc. *Ordres et désordres biographiques: Dictionnaires, listes de noms et réputation, des Lumières à Wikipédia.* Seyssel: Champ Vallon, 2013.

Charle, Christophe, ed. *Le temps des capitales culturelles (XVIIIe–XXe siècle).* Seyssel: Champ Vallon, 2009.

Darnton, Robert. *The Business of Enlightenment: A Publishing History of the Encyclopédie 1775–1800.* Cambridge, MA: Belknap Press, 2012.

Lilti, Antoine. *The World of the Salons: Sociability and Worldliness in Eighteenth-Century Paris.* Translated by Lydia G. Cochrane. Oxford: Oxford University Press, 2015.

Regourd, François, and James McClellan III. *The Colonial Machine: French Science and Overseas Expansion in the Old Regime.* Turnhout: Brepols, 2011.

RELATED ARTICLES

1380, 1536, 1633, 1712, 1795, 1875, 1900

1763

A Kingdom for an Empire

The Treaty of Paris of 1763 enshrined the emergence of
the British Empire and put an end to France's claim to
universal imperial domination. The expulsion of the Jesuits
from France and its colonies the following year completed
a "national" shift, a scaling back of France's world power
to a more manageable economic colonization.

Voltaire was back home at his Ferney château in October
1760. Banished from Paris by Louis XV, and denied right of
abode in Geneva, here he was on the Swiss border, near his
estate at Tournay, welcoming throngs of enthusiasts who,
from all corners of Europe, flocked to this tiny, cosmopolitan
outpost in the Gex region that was fast becoming the
news hub of the world. This same world happened to be
undergoing what might be called a first world war, touched
off by an assassination in 1754, the very year of Voltaire's
ostracism. That year, one of the king's officers sustained a
fatal tomahawk blow to the head while on mission in the
Ohio territory. The European rivals, France and England,

were exporting their clashing armies and their vying claims to world hegemony to America, Africa, and Asia. Voltaire had invited friends to his château to celebrate, not so much the recent British victory in Montreal, which followed their triumph in the Battle of the Plains of Abraham (Quebec) a year earlier, as the French defeat itself. The king's troops were incapable of holding on to "a few acres of snow" in a war where both countries spent "much more than all of Canada was worth," as the peace-loving Voltaire had written two years earlier in the satirical novel *Candide*.

Though Voltaire probably had yet to realize it, this celebration was contemporaneous with the plight of a certain Jesuit, the superior of his order's mission in the West Indies, who had purchased a sugar plantation/trading company in Martinique in the hope of boosting his underfunded apostolic activity. But with England's maritime supremacy confirmed by a decisive victory over France in the Seven Years' War (or French and Indian War, as it is known in the Americas) and sealed at the 1763 Treaty of Paris, Father Antoine de La Valette's plantation was put out of business by the British sea blockade and its occupation of part of the French Caribbean, which impeded France's highly profitable transatlantic traffic. To the contingencies of war was added an epidemic that ravaged his plantation's workforce, precipitating the final collapse of his commercial venture. Two associates of this business-minded cleric, Provençal traders named Gouffre and

Lionci, took their case to court in Marseille, suing the Society of Jesus to recover what was rightfully owed them.

The Jesuit order, figuring it could not be held responsible for the debts of a bankrupted enterprise it hadn't approved in the first place, had the lawsuit moved to a higher court in Aix-en-Provence, which ended up ruling against the Jesuits, forcing them to appeal to the *parlement*, or appellate court, of Paris. The conclusion of the Paris trial was the prelude to the catastrophic "wrecking" of the Society of Jesus, in the words of one of its fathers, the preacher Charles Frey de Neuville. Having been expelled from Portugal in 1759, the Society was in effect convicted by Parisian judges in 1762 of being "inadmissible by its very nature in any civilized State." It was abolished by royal edict in November 1764 and banished from the realm in 1767.

Voltaire and his guests might well have toasted a double victory at that fete in Ferney. The first toast would have marked the demise of France's colonial illusions in Canada and the folly of its blind warmongering. The second would have celebrated the failure of a clerical order that, to Voltaire's mind, was too closely linked to the despotism of Louis XV, having spearheaded an offensive against the Enlightenment and ensuring a year earlier that two landmark works, Denis Diderot and Jean le Rond d'Alembert's *Encyclopedia* and Claude-Adrien Helvétius's *De l'esprit*, be placed on the Index of Forbidden Books. The struggle against "the loathsome" (*l'infâme*), the all-powerful church and its religious orders, was now underway. Earlier in 1760, Voltaire had in fact locked horns with the Jesuits in neighboring Ornex over an issue involving six orphans and their rightful inheritance. Despite the respect he felt for the Jesuit teachers of his youth, he went after the Society fathers with vengeance, calling them "foxes" and "stinking animals" while denouncing their greed and harmful influence.

All of these disparate locations — Ohio, Quebec, Martinique, Paris, Marseille, Gex — have something noteworthy to say about the history of the French kingdom. The provocative toast by the Anglophile Voltaire, coming as it did precisely as the Jesuits were embroiled in their own political-juridical battles, calls attention to the unraveling of certain political configurations in the mid-eighteenth century, whether it be France's relations with the rest of the world or the prevailing metaphor of the body as sole political framework of the realm.

The 1763 Treaty of Paris settled a war that had proven disastrous for France, forcing it to relinquish all its continental American possessions to Britain, maintaining only a few fishing rights and harbor privileges for its ships. France was also made to surrender everything it had been working toward in Africa and India, retaining only what Napoleon would much later call "the confetti of empire," its scattered island possessions. The key word here is "empire." For what was at stake in this negotiation, if not the colonial conversion of France's former world politics? In the geography of overseas France, the choice was clear: Canada was turned over to the English on the condition that France could retain its Caribbean islands. In other words, what might have become an empire was traded for what was already a functioning colonial system. There was more at stake here than a diplomatic arbitration over a land dispute settled at the final whistle of international negotiations. France was choosing a way of being in the world; it was opting for sugar plantations and slave labor in the Caribbean, a "plantocracy" run by large plantation owners over a form of imperial governance that might have accommodated — dare I write this? — encounters with the Other that would not rest on antagonism, contempt, indifference, or misunderstanding.

To be sure, we must not romanticize. One cannot deny the racialized character of political, social, and cultural relations by the turn of the eighteenth century. This profoundly altered the terms of the initial alliance between the French and the Native Americans of the vast territories of New France. Nor is it a secret that there were slaves in Canada and that the Code Noir, adopted in Louisiana in 1724 by the Superior Council of New Orleans, was far harsher with regard to the treatment of slaves than its initial version, promulgated by Louis XIV in his Caribbean possessions. Nevertheless, the years 1759 to 1767, from the fall of Quebec to the expulsion of the Jesuits, with the Paris Treaty at the epicenter, bear witness to a reconfiguration of France and its relationship with its overseas holdings.

Historian Pierre-Yves Beaurepaire has highlighted the fact that the Duc de Choiseul, Louis XV's foreign minister, sought the favor of the various *parlements* to register the fiscal edicts required to reestablish the Royal Treasury after the Seven Years' War. By *ceding* the Jesuits to the Gallican magistrates who had been waging battle with them for two centuries, the minister hoped to weaken the pious party that was standing in the way of his political designs.

This maneuvering accomplished far more, however. It is worth revisiting the text of the Parlement of Paris's decree of August 6, 1762, that formally dissolved the Society of Jesus in France. The Society was condemned as an "institute inadmissible by its very nature in any civilized State... tending to introduce into the Church and the States...a political body whose essence consists of a sustained activity with the purpose of achieving, by means both direct and indirect, covert or public, an absolute independence, and eventually of usurping all authority." Was it not incumbent upon the *parlement* to defend the monarchy when it was so blatantly under attack? "Monarchy" here meant the body of the man himself, the king, the father of the nation, whom the servant Robert-François Damiens's infamous penknife had wounded in an assassination attempt in January 1757, reviving a latent association in people's minds, dating back to 1610, between Jesuits and regicides. The assassination attempt, two years later, against the King of Portugal, did nothing to dispel this imaginary linkage.

Defending the monarchy also entailed pushing back against the prerogative, held by those Paris magistrates, to speak to the king on behalf of the nation. These *parlement* judges had been waging a real battle, the stakes of which were brought into perspective by Louis XV himself in March 1766 in the scathing response by which he sought to quash their challenge to his authority. The king could not abide "that there should arise in his realm an association that would cause the natural tie of shared duties and obligations to degenerate into a confederation of resistance. Nor that an imaginary body should find its way into the monarchy and disturb its harmony." In what has been called his Flagellation speech, he reminded his audience that "the rights and interests of the nation, of which some would dare to form a body apart from that of the monarchy, are necessarily at one with the King's own."

By expelling the Jesuits, deemed a foreign body subservient to Rome and universal Catholicism; by reining in the judiciary, returning the sovereign courts to their position of subordination and political relativity, turning them away from the notion that they could represent the nation by freeing themselves from the single body of the king; and by abandoning the imperial ideal and choosing to preserve a colonial system of slave-owning plantations, Louis XV's France was succumbing to an obsession in the 1760s. *Obsession* should be understood in its older, more military meaning: *besieged*. This was an obsession with a regime of political and cultural identities that was coming undone. Like a wounded body that turns inward to protect its own vulnerability and deaden the pain, the country had to be called to order — to a national order, brought back to impassable borders and the simple body of the sovereign. As the political philosopher Elsa Dorlin has recently demonstrated, this order rested on a powerful colonial and sexual matrix, governed by fathers and white masters whom the unruly sons and brothers of the 1789 Revolution and the rebellious slaves of Saint-Domingue in 1791 would soon bring down.

Dreaming of a better tomorrow, these revolutionaries and slaves would sing a popular 1785 tune that mocked the clergy's crackdown on Enlightenment ideals: *C'est la faute à Voltaire, c'est la faute à Rousseau*. This tune would later be sung by another young rebel at yet another tipping point of the nation and the people, the final barricade, Rue de la Chanvrerie, of the Paris insurrection of June 1832. Victor Hugo would immortalize this refrain as a rallying cry, even if a bullet silenced Gavroche's song.

Yann Lignereux

REFERENCES

Beaurepaire, Pierre-Yves. *La France des Lumières (1715–1789)*. Paris: Belin, 2011.

Belmessous, Saliha. "Assimilation and Racialism in Seventeenth and Eighteenth-Century French Colonial Policy." *The American Historical Review* 110, no. 2 (2005): 322–49.

Dorlin, Elsa. *La matrice de la race: Généalogie sexuelle et coloniale de la nation française*. Paris: La Découverte, 2009.

Havard, Gilles. *"Les forcer à devenir Citoyens*: État, sauvages et citoyenneté en Nouvelle-France (XVIIe–XVIIIe siècle)." *Annales. Histoire, sciences sociales* 64, no. 5 (2009): 985–1018.

Vidal, Cécile, ed. *Français? La nation en débat entre colonies et métropole (XVIe–XIXe siècle)*. Paris: Édition de l'École des hautes études en sciences sociales, 2014.

RELATED ARTICLES

1270, 1494, 1534, 1804, 1913, 1931, 1960

1769

The World's a Conversation

Bougainville's return home after his voyage around the world disappointed the scholars of Europe as much as it thrilled the worldly and literary elite of French society. The reality was that French naval power was a shadow of its former self, and Bougainville comes across as a holdover whose Tahitian adventure achieved little more than the idealization of a lost paradise.

On March 16, 1769, the frigate *La Boudeuse*, commanded by Louis-Antoine de Bougainville, docked in the port of Saint-Malo. In her wake was *L'Étoile*, a converted warship that had served as the naval explorer's supply vessel. This tiny flotilla had completed a two-year voyage to Rio de Janeiro, Tahiti, the Moluccas, and Île-de-France (now Mauritius), among many other exotic places. Aboard the *Boudeuse* were roughly a dozen naval officers, two hundred sailors, and a young Tahitian named Ahutoru, whom Bougainville had consented to bring to France.

The safe return of the *Boudeuse* caused an immediate

sensation. It was the first time a ship of the French Royal Navy had circumnavigated the globe. Bougainville himself was received at Versailles by Louis XV and feted in the salons of Paris, where he was able to relate his adventures at leisure and in detail. Encouraged by the fervor surrounding him, he wrote a detailed account of his expedition, which was published two years later, in 1771. The book was an immediate best seller.

Conventional history would have it that Bougainville was a pioneer who opened a new era of spectacular maritime exploration. In the early centuries of the modern age, merchants, conquerors, and missionaries had sailed the oceans, gradually broadening Europe's horizons to include the rest of the globe; but now the time had come for the kind of scholarly explorers and philosophical observers suggested by Jean-Jacques Rousseau years earlier. As a man of the Enlightenment, a competent mathematician, and the younger brother of Jean-Pierre de Bougainville, an eminent member of the Académie Française, Louis-Antoine de Bougainville fit the bill perfectly. He announced in advance that his goal was to discover and understand the world, not enslave it; moreover he would be accompanied on his voyage by a respected naturalist, Philibert Commerson. A few years later, another explorer, the Comte de La Pérouse, attempted to follow where Bougainville had led, only to come to grief on the rocks of Vanikoro. After him came the great explorers of the early nineteenth century, but their travels are open to a much more sinister interpretation. Were they not eager to advance colonial expansion?

This is the conventional story — legend is perhaps a better word — surrounding Bougainville. In reality, although his *Voyage autour du monde* was a spectacular literary and publishing triumph, he aroused little interest among genuine scholars, who were more enthralled by the discoveries of Captain James Cook. While Cook had explored Australia, New Zealand, Hawaii, and the American shores of the Pacific, sending back priceless specimens and exact maps of what he found, Bougainville seems to have crossed the Pacific in a furious hurry, writing only notes and descriptions that were picturesque but vague and colored by utopian fantasy. Cook and Bougainville could scarcely have been more different, even in death. Bougainville expired in his bed at the age of eighty-one, a senator and a count of the French Empire rather than a hero of science. Cook's violent death on a Hawaiian beach in 1779 remains one of the most famous and debated stories of the initial contact between Europeans and the native inhabitants of the Pacific.

It may be that this contrast was created by contemporary notions of national psychology and geography of temperament. In the eyes of the philosopher Denis Diderot, Bougainville was a "true Frenchman," by which he meant a witty, good-tempered man of the world "who loved women, the theater and fine food," but who was also a philosopher, given to subtle comment and acute generalization. This blend of dilettantism and intellectual ambition constituted both his charm and his weakness. Bougainville was a quintessential man of his time and social background. He belonged to an elite that divided its time between literary squabbles and military campaigns while lacking the self-sacrifice and seriousness needed to bring great enterprises to fruition over years of hard work. Moreover, his popular *Voyage autour du monde* disappointed the scholars of Europe for exactly the same reason that it delighted writers and ordinary readers: despite Bougainville's qualities of observation and empathy, in him the picturesque and exotic always came before precision and rigor. His relationship to the world was limited to what might generate agreeable conversation.

To judge Bougainville solely in the light of the scientific accomplishments of his voyage is to fly wide of the mark. By the same token, to see him as a precursor of scientific exploration would be not only idealistic but also an anachronism, given the specific military and diplomatic context of his expedition. In 1763, the Treaty of Paris brought an end to the Seven Years' War, which has sometimes been described as the first authentic world conflict and which ended in defeat for France, its imperial ambitions wrecked. In general, the war led to a terminal decline of the French presence in North America and India, all to the advantage of England. Bougainville himself had known the bitterness of his country's defeat, having served from 1756 to 1760 as the Marquis de Montcalm's aide-de-camp in Canada, where he was an impotent witness to the fall of Quebec.

Bougainville's voyage around the world can only be understood within the context of the commercial and colonial rivalry between France and England. As soon as the peace was signed, he began pestering the Duc de Choiseul, Louis XV's minister for foreign affairs and Bougainville's own protector, to authorize a settlement on the Falkland Islands in the South Atlantic (known to the French as the Malouines Islands, a name given to them by Bougainville in 1764). His objective was to preempt the British by obtaining for France a strategic outpost on the western route from Europe to India. Despite the vigorous objections of Spain, Bougainville did claim possession of the Falkland archipelago for the French crown in April 1764, and his later expedition around the world was in part an attempt to further pursue this endeavor. Bougainville would first surrender the Falklands to the Spanish monarch, in the hope of obtaining in exchange a commercial foothold in the Spanish-controlled Philippines.

Second, Bougainville would reconnoiter the unexplored territories of the South Pacific on the route to China, and take possession, on behalf of France, of any he judged "useful to French trade and shipping," according to the instructions that had been given to him by the French monarchy. These instructions were nothing if not explicit: "His Majesty commands the Seigneur de Bougainville to find, if he can, an island within range of the coast of China which may serve as a base for the Compagnie des Indes (the French East India Company) for future trade with China." The fact is that behind the benevolent, cosmopolitan science of the Enlightenment lurked the commercial and strategic ambitions of France. Its rivalry with Great Britain had shifted geographically. Having lost Canada and India, it was to the Pacific, with the lucrative Chinese trade on its horizon, that France now turned.

Here again Bougainville's voyage was a disappointment. He seized a few islands in the immensity of the Pacific, but failed to discover any southern continent and never reached China or the Philippines. Worse, he was largely preceded by the English naval explorer Captain Samuel Wallis (in Tahiti, for instance) and was himself closely followed by Captain Cook. In the short term, his discoveries were of no real commercial or political consequence.

So ultimately the importance of Bougainville's circumnavigation of the world was concentrated in a single port of call, the island of Tahiti, on which he spent exactly ten out of the eight hundred days his expedition lasted. Tahiti mattered not because its so-called discovery had immediate consequences, as Bougainville might have hoped, but rather because the enthusiastic echoes he brought back to Paris fixed a new ideal — the paradise island — into the mental maps of many Europeans. Thanks to him, Sir Thomas More's island of Utopia, imagined two centuries earlier, was supplanted by an all-too-real island, endowed with rich natural beauty and hospitable inhabitants.

Bougainville's naturalist, Philibert Commerson, was the first to construct the myth of Tahiti. He did it with a spellbinding description of "New Cythera" — Cythera in Greek mythology being the birthplace of Aphrodite — that he published in the *Mercure de France* in November 1769. "These people" he wrote, "are anything but a horde of brutal or bestial savages; everything about them shines with the most perfect intelligence....Born under the loveliest skies, nourished by a land that needs no cultivation, ruled by family patriarchs and not by kings, they have no other god but love." These islanders on the far side of the world were not savages but harbingers of wisdom, living in complete harmony with nature. There was no question of converting them or making them "civilized," only of admiring their innocence and envying their happiness.

Bougainville added some comments of his own to this description, notably after his discussions with the young Tahitian Ahutoru, who gave him a glimpse of the violence that simmered beneath the surface of the island's hierarchical society, including the local practice of human sacrifice. No matter — for the French philosophers who had been bickering for half a century over the benefits of progress and civilization and the historic specificity of Europe, the Tahitian myth seemed to give new momentum to the ideals of Rousseau. It compelled them to confront head-on the ambivalence of civilization and the dangers of colonialism. During this veritable crisis of the European conscience, Diderot grappled with the questions of the age in a work nowadays revered as a classic. With his *Supplément au voyage de Bougainville*, his ironic play of smoke and mirrors — typical of philosophical dialogue — baffled readers, who are left to wonder whether his idealization of Tahiti was a sincere critique of the excesses of civilization, or a literary palliative to contemporary anxieties.

In fact, Diderot and his fellow philosophers gave scant credit to the Tahitian myth. Their suspicion of travelers' tales and their passionate faith in the material and cultural progress of Europe made them doubt that there was any such thing as the noble savage. All the same, Tahiti forced on the French a measure of self-awareness and self-criticism. There were precedents. In the sixteenth century, Montaigne had exercised his wit on the subject of the supposed barbarity of cannibals in his writings about the Tupi Indians. But now the situation was different. At the very moment when philosophers were becoming aware that European expansion had engendered "a revolution in trade, in the powers of nations, in the habits, industry and government of all peoples," as the Abbé Raynal, author of *A History of the Two Indies*, had written, Tahiti invited introspection from deep within the conscience of modernity.

This new voice — call it the voice of a bad conscience — was a European creation. The anticolonialist stance of the old Tahitian, a character in the *Supplément au voyage de Bougainville*, resonated because people recognized in it, as Diderot noted, "European ideas and European turns of phrase." Diderot had actually met an honest-to-goodness Tahitian in Paris. But that Tahitian, who never learned French, had been infinitely less interesting to Diderot than the fictions he drew from Bougainville's account. The time of ethnography had not yet come.

Antoine Lilti

REFERENCES

Bougainville, Louis-Antoine de. *Voyage autour du monde (1771)*. Edited by Michel Bideaux and Sonia Faessel. Paris: Presses de l'université Paris-Sorbonne, 2001.

Cheney, Paul. *Revolutionary Commerce: Globalization and the French Monarchy*. Cambridge, MA: Harvard University Press, 2010.

Diderot, Denis. "Supplement to Bougainville's Voyage." In *Diderot's*

Selected Writings, edited by Lester G. Crocker. New York: Macmillan, 1966.

Gascoigne, John. *Encountering the Pacific in the Age of the Enlightenment*. Cambridge: Cambridge University Press, 2014.

Liebersohn, Harry. *The Traveler's World: Europe to the Pacific*. Cambridge, MA: Harvard University Press, 2008.

Taillemite, Étienne. *Bougainville et ses compagnons autour du monde (1766–1769)*. Paris: Imprimerie nationale, 1977.

RELATED ARTICLES

1380, 1550, 1793, 1869, 1907, 1931

1771

Beauty and the Beast: An Opéra Comique at the Court of France

On the occasion of the betrothal of the heir to the crown in 1771, a performance of *Zémire et Azor* celebrated sentiments cherished by the Enlightenment. This representation, which sealed the advent of opéra comique, gave worldwide fame to a story first published in 1740 by Gabrielle-Suzanne Barbot de Villeneuve.

Scene: Persia. A merchant from the Strait of Hormuz rashly picks a rose in the garden of Azor, a terrifying monster. To expiate his crime, he must sacrifice Zémire, one of his three daughters, to Azor. The trembling Beauty comes to the palace of the growling Beast. So familiar today, the plot did not faze the courtiers of Louis XV who, on November 9, 1771, gathered to witness a performance of *Zémire et Azor* brought to the stage by librettist Jean-François Marmontel and composer André Grétry. Their opéra comique, celebrating certain sentiments dear to the Enlightenment, signaled the advent of this genre not only in France but also in the rest of Europe. Its subsequent history contributed to the spread of an archetypal narrative across the world.

The story, which originated as a tale in the Roman writer Apuleius's *Metamorphoses* (called *The Golden Ass* by Saint Augustine), appeared in two best-selling books in the mid-eighteenth century. In 1740, Gabrielle-Suzanne Barbot de Villeneuve published a fairy tale entitled "Beauty and the Beast" in her collection *La jeune Américaine et les contes marins* (The Young American Girl and Sea Stories). In this version, a Creole girl, educated in metropolitan France, returns to the home of her wealthy planter parents in Saint-Domingue. Her long transatlantic voyage is enlivened by the "sea stories" told by her fellow passengers and the ship captain to amuse her. The first tale, told by the young heroine's maid, is "Beauty and the Beast." Soon after, writer Pierre-Claude Nivelle de la Chaussée adapted this story in his play *Amour pour amour*, which was performed in 1742 at the Comédie-Française. Next, Jeanne-Marie Leprince de Beaumont offered an abridged version — popular but moralistic and toned down — in a pedagogical work entitled *Le Magasin des enfants* (The Children's Store), published in London in 1757. Marmontel and Grétry based their libretto and score on this last version.

There was nothing unusual in the early 1770s in the choice of such a libretto for a musical spectacle. The wondrous had often been used in French lyrical tragedies performed by the exclusive Royal Academy of Music, as well as by fairground theaters that found in it an inexhaustible source of allegory and drama. The oriental echoes of the *Zémire et Azor* version of the Beauty and the Beast story were bound to delight a literate public that had already been won over by the mirages of *The Thousand and One Nights,* translated into French by Antoine Galland earlier in the century.

On the other hand, it really *was* audacious in November 1771 to offer the French court a musical genre so closely linked to fairgrounds — a light opera characterized by alternating scenes of dancing and singing — and to have it acted by the company of the Comédie-Italienne. What is more, the piece was performed at the château of Fontainebleau, on the occasion of royal ceremonies celebrating the betrothal of the dauphin, the future Louis XVI, and Marie Antoinette, born an archduchess of Austria. Certainly the ambitious choreography, the richness of its original costumes and sets masked its humble origins. Indeed, the libretto's first printed edition soberly referred to a *comédie-ballet*, thus laying a claim to the traditions of French ballet and Molière's theater. But the fact was that on November 9, 1771, Marmontel and Grétry's *Zémire et Azor* brought opéra comique into the most prestigious cultural space imaginable: the court of the King of France. In doing so, they gave notice that the norms regulating French musical life in and around Paris were ripe for a change. The old hierarchy of the theatrical and musical genres, which the royal system of privilege had kept in place since the reign of Louis XIV, was under attack.

French theater, dominated by the Comédie-Française, and French lyrical tragedy as devised by the Florentine Jean-Baptiste Lully as the head of the Royal Academy of Music — of which the operas of Jean-Philippe Rameau had become emblematic — no longer won unanimous approval. Lighter forms of theater, often inspired by Italian comedy and opera buffa, were becoming much more popular. This was not just a matter of taste; it had also to do with an eminently political question that involved the building of a certain French identity. Reviving the quarrel between the Ancients and the Moderns, the *Querelle des Bouffons* was a war of words that broke out after the 1752 performance of Giovanni Pergolesi's *La serva padrona* by an Italian troupe at the prestigious Royal Academy of Music, pitting partisans of French music and those of Italian opera against one another. Enchanted by Pergolesi's delightful score, Jean-Jacques Rousseau claimed in his *Confessions* that the confrontation between opera buffa and French lyrical tragedy "unblocked the ears of the French." The controversy went way beyond disagreements about the symbolic and hierarchical divisions among Paris-dominated theater genres. By calling into question the cultural superiority of French music and prosody, it threatened the very identity of France and its "national genius." Was it really necessary for that identity to be so firmly on the side of reason and virile nobility, and for its dramatic art to be bound so firmly to words? Why should it reject the exuberant, chaotic character attributed to the "Italian nation," as expressed through Italian language and music?

Since the first performance at the Saint-Germain fair on February 3, 1715, of Lesage and Fuselier's *Télémaque*, a parody of the lyrical tragedy of the same name then being performed at the Royal Academy, opéra comique had been outmaneuvering these national affiliations just as it derailed traditional dramatic conventions by including sung pieces as spoken ones, and vice versa. The productions of Charles-Simon Favart, which parodied French operas of the 1730s and 1740s, and then those of Antoine Dauvergne, notably his *Troqueurs* performed on July 30, 1753, at the Foire Saint-Laurent with a libretto by Jean-Joseph Vadé, were huge popular successes.

André Grétry, who had started at a parish choir school in Liège before spending several years in Rome perfecting his talents, slipped easily into this line of musicians who mixed musical influences and generally exploited the opportunities offered by the French capital. In the musical geography of Europe, distinguished by the clear supremacy of Italian opera houses, Paris was unquestionably a secondary musical destination, but it was an attractive one, as Mozart's two prolonged stays in the city attest (1763–1764 as a child, and 1778 at the beginning of his adult career). The city was notable for the dynamism of its musical publishing, the proliferation of musical venues, and the vigorous intellectual debate around the subject.

Grétry arrived in the French capital in 1767, following the advice Voltaire had dispensed at Ferney: "It is from there that one flies to immortality." After 1768, Grétry went into partnership with Marmontel, an established literary figure and contributor to the *Encyclopedia*, the recognized author of *Contes moraux* (*Moral Tales*), and a member of the Académie Française. The first opéra comique born of their collaboration, *Le Huron*, was put on by the Comédie-Italienne in 1768 to considerable public acclaim. The young composer's first spectacle was praised as "a masterpiece that raises its author without any possible doubt to the highest rank," in the words of the *Correspondance littéraire*, which also emphasized its "purely Italian" style. Other triumphs quickly followed for Grétry, with Marmontel and then Michel-Jean Sedaine, to whom he owed the libretto of a "historic" opéra comique, *Richard Coeur de Lion* (1784). Through his productions, his writings on his career and on music in general, and his frequent exchanges with his friend Denis Diderot and other enlightened thinkers who viewed music as a philosophical and political matter, Grétry made a huge contribution to the legitimation of opéra comique.

This cultural promotion was consolidated by a progressive institutionalization of the genre. In 1715, the traveling theater group of Catherine Baron and Gauthier de Saint Edme had been the first to receive the authorization to present an opéra comique and take the name of an eponymous company; in 1762, the Comédie-Italienne merged with the company of the Opéra-Comique, moved to the Hôtel de Bourgogne theater, and obtained the status of "royal theater," thereby accelerating the process of cultural accreditation. It was in fact on the stage of the Hôtel de Bourgogne that the second performance of *Zémire et Azor* occurred on November 16, 1771, a week after its inaugural production before the royal court at Fontainebleau.

In the wake of this success in Paris, the opéra comique spread rapidly across Europe, accompanied by hasty translations of Marmontel's libretto. Charles Burney, crisscrossing the continent to compile an inventory of musical practices, attended a performance in French in Brussels on July 15, 1772. On August 6, he saw it again at Mannheim, but this time in German. In 1774, *Zémire et Azor* reached the court of Saint Petersburg, and on July 22, 1778, it was presented for the first time in Swedish, at the palace of Drottningholm in the presence of Sweden's royal family. The following year, it arrived at the King's Theatre in London.

Marmontel and Grétry's work was regularly reprised on the French stage until the 1860s; after then, productions were few and far between. In the twentieth century, the cinema placed its technical magic and visual power at the service of the fantastic — and of the tale imagined by Madame de Villeneuve. In 1899, the Pathé brothers presented a short film inspired by this wonderful narrative. In 1946, with a potentially much larger international audience, Jean Cocteau produced his *La Belle et la Bête*, starring Josette Day and Jean Marais in the title roles. The film — which received the prestigious Louis-Delluc Prize — made the monstrous Azor's leonine mane and general hairiness iconic in the public imagination.

Indeed, Cocteau's model has inspired all subsequent adaptations of the story, whether aimed at younger Disney audiences (1991) or older spectators seeking a blend of fantasy and eroticism. More recently, the plot's erotic aspect has been well served by the film directors Christophe Gans (2014) and Bill Condon (2017). The modern opera created in 1994 by Philip Glass — with a score directly inspired by the images of the film — probably remains the most faithful to Cocteau's vision. Having traveled from the court of France to the studios of Hollywood, the romance of Zémire and Azor continues to honor the sincere sentiments so cherished by the encyclopedists of the eighteenth century.

Mélanie Traversier

REFERENCES

Charlton, David. *Grétry and the Growth of Opéra-Comique*. Cambridge: Cambridge University Press, 1986.

De Beaumont, Jeanne-Marie Leprince, Nivelle de La Chaussée, Caroline-Stéphanie-Félicité Du Crest Genlis, and Jean-François Marmontel. *La Belle et la Bête: Quatre métamorphoses (1742–1779)*. Texts prepared and annotated by Sophie Allera and Denis Reynaud. Saint-Étienne: Publications de l'Université de Saint-Étienne, 2004.

Demoulin, Bruno, and Françoise Tilkin, eds. "Grétry, un musicien international dans l'Europe des Lumières." *Art & Facts* 32 (2013).

Traversier, Mélanie. "Musique virile et airs futiles: Génie national et genre musical au miroir de la rivalité entre deux capitales lyriques, Paris et Naples (vers 1750 – vers 1815)." In *Anticléricalisme, minorités religieuses et échanges culturels entre la France et l'Italie: De l'Antiquité au XXe siècle*, edited by Olivier Forlin, 219–49. Paris: L'Harmattan, 2006.

Vendrix, Philippe, ed. *Grétry et l'Europe de l'opéra-comique*. Liège: Mardaga, 1992.

RELATED ARTICLES
1712, 1715, 1946

1784

Sade: Imprisoned and Universal

On an order from the king, who followed a request from the Comte de Sade's mother-in-law, the infamous writer was imprisoned at Vincennes in 1777, and remained under lock and key, including five years at the Bastille prison, until 1789. Prison gave him the freedom to write his first book, *Justine, or the Misfortunes of Virtue*, which, along with the publication of many subsequent books after his death, led to the spread of "sadism" from England to the Romantics.

On an Easter Sunday in 1768, in what became known as the Arcueil affair, the twenty-seven-year-old Comte de Sade (who had inherited his title after the death of his father a year earlier) made headlines with his blasphemous behavior and mistreatment of a young working girl and occasional prostitute, Rose Keller, who was able to secure a dowry out of the event. But it wasn't until 1772, with the Marseille affair, that Sade gained an international reputation as an outrageous libertine. In 1790, Jean-Paul Marat complained that his "ears rang" in 1773 and 1774 with talk of "M. de Sade, his involvement in all manner of licentious affairs, and his supposed imprisonment at the Châtelet."

On July 25, 1772, a letter was brought to the attention of the editors of a popular chronicle in which Monsieur de Montyon, intendant of Provence, described a scandal involving prostitutes in Marseille. The women complained of complications related to some experimental aphrodisiac pills forced upon them by Sade and his valet, Latour. The pills were made from dried beetles. Coming three days after the event itself, the written account depicted a sordid moral affair as a frightening orgy: "Everyone who took [the pills] was overcome with burning and shameless desire, giving into all manner of lustful excesses. The night degenerated into a lascivious gathering worthy of the Romans." The chronicle did not hesitate to spread this inflammatory account from London, where it was supposedly published.

As early as 1768, Madame du Deffand, a well-known *salonnière* and epistolarian, had alerted Horace Walpole, a pillar of London's political and literary scene, to Sade's despicable actions. "This nation's taste for our deeds, and especially for the scornful mistreatment of some toward others" would not be denied. The curse of the libertine Sade was to have drawn and aroused the attention not only of the Parisian police but also of London's literary society.

In 1778, the court of Marseille cleared Sade, for the

most part. But thanks to his mother-in-law, Madame Marie-Madeleine de Montreuil, the king kept him under arrest in Vincennes before transferring him to the Bastille in 1784. I write "thanks" to her because without Sade's time in the Bastille he may never have become an author, the *Marquis de Sade*.

Two days after a court divested him of the management of his estate, Sade began writing *The Misfortunes of Virtue*—the first version of *Justine, or the Misfortunes of Virtue*. This debut novel, published in 1791 after he was freed by the Revolution, is a testament to the kind of freedom of expression — unbound by ideas of moral decency — promoted by Robespierre in the same year. The book's six or seven editions circulated underground across Europe. After Sade's death, they could be found in library collections. Its success was phenomenal, leading to what is commonly deemed the complete edition, published "in the Netherlands in 1797" (the date and place are both fictional). Jean-Jacques Pauvert, the twentieth-century French publisher, deemed *The New Justine*, which included four volumes and "a title page and forty carefully drawn engravings," followed by the six-volume *Juliette* about Justine's sister, illustrated with sixty engravings, the most ambitious underground pornographic publication ever conceived.

With *Justine*, Sade was baptized as an author. *Philosophy in the Bedroom*, for example, was first published in 1795 in Paris (not London) with a note advertising that this was a "posthumous book by the author of *Justine*."

Yet Sade, who actually died in 1814, vehemently denied being the author of *Justine*. Still, *this* book allowed him to enter the nineteenth century's pantheon of forbidden books. On November 30, 1818, Thomas Moore remarked in his diary, "A debauched society exists in Paris based on the ideas presented in *Justine*...which is called Sadism." In 1834, the *Revue de Paris* published a sensationalist article titled "The Marquis de Sade," in which the journalist Jules Janin describes how a poor young man who had dared to borrow the book — a wax-sealed "confessional repository" — from his clerical uncle's library turned into an epileptic moron after reading it. The word "sadism" does not appear in Janin's article.

For the eighth edition of Pierre-Claude-Victor Boiste's *Dictionnaire universel de la langue française*, published in 1836, the writer and librarian Charles Nodier added a considerable number of words, including "sadism," which he defined as: "An appalling aberration and debauchery; a monstrous, anti-social system that goes against nature." The etymology of "sadism" is: "From Sade, a proper noun."

For Nodier, "neology" was the "art" of creating new words that capture "the attention of readers and provide them with new ideas, expressed in a new way, with a word that makes those ideas more striking and *memorable*." With his corpus difficult to find (Sade's work was banned in France upon his death in 1814 until 1957) and lacking images of the man's face and body, posterity has remembered Sade through the word "sadism." But as literary critic Jean Paulhan suggested, sadism (or perversion) may have been quite alien to Sade: "I don't know if Sade was sadistic. His trials do not shed much light on the subject. In what is today his best-known affair, the Marseille trial, Sade shows himself to be more of a masochist, which is the complete opposite of sadism."

The first appearance of the word in French, in 1836, was followed by the qualifier "seldom used." And indeed, it often went missing. Although a biography of Sade was included in Pierre Larousse's *Grand dictionnaire universel du XIXe siècle* (1864–1876), there is no entry for sadism, which tended to be seen as an exclusively French affliction. The word was similarly left out of *Néologie; or the French of Our Times: Being a Collection of More than Eleven Hundred Words, Either Entirely New or Remodernized* (1854).

"Sadism" did not come into the common vernacular until it became an adjective, that is, when it could be used to describe ways of being separate from the Marquis de Sade. In other words, "sadism" owes commonplace usage to "sadistic." As early as 1862, before becoming a diagnosis — Krafft-Ebing's *Psychopathia Sexualis* was published in 1886 —

and a half century before psychoanalysis adopted it as a perversion — Sigmund Freud completed *Three Essays on the Theory of Sexuality* in 1905 — literature began promoting and legitimizing the transformation of Sade's greatest legacy, his name, into an adjective. A play on words that was derived from layers of legends shackled Sade to an infamous reputation. Has he ever been freed from that prison?

The word "sadistic," which emerged in a reactionary period, is perhaps less a contribution to science than it is a literary strategy — a critique of modernity. "I would posit, without fear of contradiction, that Byron and Sade...were perhaps the two main inspirations for our modern thinkers: one flaunted and visible; the other hidden, though not too much. As you read some of our fashionable novelists... never forget this insight," wrote the celebrated critic Charles Sainte-Beuve in 1843.

Twenty years later, Sainte-Beuve discovered a "bit of sadistic imagination" in Flaubert's *Salammbô*. But rather than read Flaubert in Sade's terms, he referenced Chateaubriand's *The Martyrs* — a more staid and safer literary choice. Sadistic? After his acquittal in the obscenity trial over *Madame Bovary*, Flaubert would no doubt have rejected the compliment. Was *Salammbô* sadistic? Whatever the case, the novel would never overcome this excoriation.

In 1882, one of Edmond de Goncourt's characters, George Selwyn (*La Faustin*), is explicitly described as "sadistic." De Goncourt did not make a secret of the fact that George Selwyn was modeled after an English collector of erotic books, Frederick Hankey, and an English poet, Algernon Charles Swinburne (as well as an eighteenth-century English politician and sexual eccentric, George Selwyn). Edmond de Goncourt and his brother Jules were initially interested in Swinburne because they detected his influence on Flaubert's prose: "We admire the poetry of the Englishman Swinburne in Flaubert," they wrote in their journal on February 28, 1875.

Although the French public was unfamiliar with Swinburne's work (which had not yet been translated), his reputation was well known in Parisian salons thanks to the novelist Guy de Maupassant, who from 1875 to 1892 published several different accounts of his bizarre chance meeting with the poet, much to the delight of literary society. Sexual relations with monkeys, taking in pornographic photographs while sucking a finger on a stuffed hand, intercourse with young servants sent from England: Algernon Charles Swinburne was a rich source of inspiration not only for Maupassant but also for the writer Auguste Villiers de L'Isle-Adam in his 1888 literary portrayal of "English sadism," *Histoires insolites*. But it was not until 1897, through the field of legal medicine, that the English became infected with the French disease of sadism, which encouraged them to commit hitherto unthinkable crimes.

Anne Simonin

REFERENCES

Barnes, Julian. "An Unlikely Lunch: When Maupassant Met Swinburne." *The Public Domain Review*, 2012. https://publicdomainreview.org/2012/01/24/an-unlikely-lunch-when-maupassant-met-swinburne

Goncourt, Edmond de, and Jules de Goncourt. *Pages from the Goncourt Journals*. Edited and translated by Robert Baldick. New York: New York Review of Books, 2006.

Pauvert, Jean-Jacques. *Nouveaux (et moins nouveaux) visages de la censure*, suivi de *L'Affaire Sade*. Paris: Les Belles Lettres, 1994.

———. *Sade vivant*. Paris: Le Tripode, 2013.

Sade, Marquis de. *Justine, or the Misfortunes of Virtue*. Translated by John Phillips. Oxford: Oxford University Press, 2012.

RELATED ARTICLES
1633, 1842, 1852, 2011

1789

The Global Revolution

The storming of the Bastille on July 14, 1789, changed the course of French history, but its effects rippled throughout Europe and the world. An exemplar for some Europeans, anathema to others, the French Revolution inspired patriots in their quest for freedom and equality.

"For the first time, a great people freed itself from its shackles and peacefully secured the constitution and laws it believed suited to public happiness." Jean-Antoine Nicolas Caritat de Condorcet, the Enlightenment philosopher, was not referring here to 1789, but rather to the events of 1776–1783, when the thirteen colonies of North America threw off the British yoke. The impact of this event on European struggles for freedom was more widespread than is commonly thought today, as witnessed in a letter in which the French champion of the American cause, General Lafayette, expressed pleasure that the "ideas of liberty have spread rapidly since the American Revolution." Not only did this revolution convince ordinary people that they could challenge the crowned heads of Europe, but it also seemed to win over the French monarchy, which provided support to the rebels. Indeed, in 1785, it sided with the Dutch patriots who were revolting against their ruler, and gave them refuge two years later, when the Prussians invaded the United Provinces and restored William of Orange to power. During this same period, King Louis XVI initiated reforms to refill France's coffers, depleted by its support for the American war of independence. These efforts would exacerbate factional conflicts within French society.

Before examining the global repercussions of 1789, we should acknowledge that the French Revolution's origins were transnational, not least because the French noblemen who fought alongside George Washington returned home with potent political ideals: a written constitution, natural rights, and of course "no taxation without representation." In early 1788, this is what Lafayette had in mind. If the 1776 mystique gradually faded on the European continent, it is because the revolution that followed in France took place on an entirely different scale: 26 million inhabitants and a capital city of some 600,000 residents as compared to a young country of just 2.5 million inhabitants, which experienced slavery and indentured servitude but not feudalism, hereditary succession, or religious intolerance in the French mold. Condorcet made the comparison in 1794, concluding that the French Revolution had been "a more total revolution than the one in America, and as a result, less peaceful within its borders." The same held true outside the country, for many years to come.

The French revolutionaries fought for the same ideals as oppressed peoples across Europe. The Republic of Geneva had already undergone several failed revolutions, including one in 1782 that sought to broaden the electoral franchise and forced many revolutionaries into exile. The Austrian Netherlands — today's Belgium — rose up in autumn 1789 and strove to form the "United Belgian States." And then there were the Dutch patriots, who conspired to channel their expertise into the French revolutionary firebrand Honoré Mirabeau's political circle, which produced many pamphlets and papers on the status of insurgent movements to the north. For these foreign revolutionaries, the French example nurtured hope that they might one day return home in triumph. They adopted the French rebels' cause for their own, and schemed incessantly to push France to declare war on their oppressors. Resisting this warmongering, France's Constituent Assembly declared peace to the world on May 22, 1790. However, it could not resist annexing foreign enclaves in Alsace and the Comtat Venaissin (formerly part of the Papal States) to the French territory.

There was nothing revolutionary about such land-grabbing. After all, Prussia and Austria had just carved up Poland yet again. But the French Revolution had seemed — for a short while — to herald respect for popular sovereignty. Successive annexations between 1790 and 1793 rounded out the country's borders under the pretense that local peoples on the periphery wished to become French and hence accede to freedom. The first Belgian campaign in the winter of 1792–1793 was waged along these lines, leading to the "liberation" of the Dutch province of Brabant, complete with trees of liberty and tricolor flags. Liberation proved ephemeral, as did the reunification of Belgium with France. Following the defeat of French general Charles François Dumouriez at Neerwinden in March 1793, Belgian and Dutch patriots returned to the fold of their masters, the prince of Orange and the Habsburg monarchy.

Phase one of the emancipation of European subjects ended in failure. But this setback did not prevent revolutionary ideas from spreading across the continent, much to the displeasure of neighboring rulers and political thinkers, including Edmund Burke and William Pitt, who responded by discrediting a bloodthirsty French Revolution that filled them with terror. This myth would prove enduring.

France's defeat in 1793 arguably explains why French revolutionaries curtailed their annexation and "liberation" policy. Following the lead of Georges Danton, the National Convention (the representative assembly elected in 1792) vowed in March 1793 to cease meddling in the affairs of foreign governments. So much for the emancipation of oppressed peoples; so much for the decree of November 19, 1792, which had proclaimed fraternity and succor to all people yearning for freedom. This decree had sparked fury among many European governments, which deemed it contrary to international law. Ordinary people, however, welcomed the promise made by French representatives a month later to eliminate the tithe, feudalism, and the nobility and its privileges, all in the name of "liberty, equality, and fraternity."

This string of decrees and promises demonstrates the French Revolution's internal conflict, torn as it was between the resolve to emancipate people across Europe and the temptation to turn inward. As Danton put it in the spring of 1793: "Consider first and foremost the preservation of our political body, and establish French greatness... France, through her enlightened ideas and her energy, will draw in all peoples." This retreat was but temporary; the emancipation policy reclaimed the upper hand the following year when French legislators framed it once again as support for oppressed peoples everywhere rather than a raw desire for conquest.

Still, France was not always the initiator of such liberation schemes. Foreign revolutionaries or "patriots" who had taken refuge in Paris exerted enormous influence on foreign policy. When France went to war in April

1792, it was partly at their incitement and partly because revolutionary messianism mingled with political strategy in the domestic diplomatic committees.

In 1794 and 1795, a series of French military victories reunited Belgium and "liberated" the Netherlands, bringing friendly republics into being near the country's borders. The Batavian Republic of January 1795, which superseded the Dutch Republic that had ruled in the Netherlands since 1581, was first among them. Soon to follow were Italy and Switzerland, where dissenters and exiles attempted to persuade France to help them win their independence from local rulers by dangling the advantages of an honest alliance. It was therefore not the French authorities alone who steered foreign policy, but countless individuals at the fringe — mostly foreign patriots, and local generals and diplomats — who expressed the will of countless others. Italy is the most flagrant example. By sending troops there in 1796, under the command of Napoleon Bonaparte, French leaders had no intention of "revolutionizing" the Italian states; they were focused on keeping the Austrians at bay and securing financial resources. Caring little for what Paris might think, however, Bonaparte began creating republics in the peninsula. He opened the way to a policy of expansion that no one had initially envisioned.

Won over by the principles of the French Republic, foreign patriots were nonetheless determined to "nationalize" their revolution, to make it their own and avoid France's mistakes. The French Directory (the regime that followed the radical Convention and lasted from 1795 to 1799) had learned its lesson and promulgated a middle-of-the-road course in the countries it governed. Thus, Dutch radicals had trouble prevailing, whereas in Italy, governments came and went to the rhythm of Paris's shifting agenda. Conversely, Holland and Switzerland succeeded in implementing constitutions and declarations of rights that were not pale imitations of the French example. France was as much a counterexample as an example to emulate. Foreign patriots hence sought to perfect this French model rather than simply copy it. Indeed, a genuine dialogue took place among the revolutions of the European continent, whence the notion that France had created a constellation of "sister republics."

The sisters in question saw themselves as rivals, however, and so they did not adopt the "sisterly" designation. The first occurrence of the term dates to 1794, when, upon arriving in Paris, American diplomat James Monroe invoked the special relationship between the United States and France. The title of *Grande Nation*, mother to these newly created republics, was a different matter altogether. The latter's very existence depended upon the success of the French armies. Holland, Italy, and Switzerland felt close to one another only when threatened by the perils of 1799, when France was compelled to abandon them after the French army suffered major defeats, notably against Austrian and Russian forces. From that point forward, a certain solidarity arose among the "sister" republics. This lasted only a short while, however, since Napoleon would soon refashion European geopolitics and turn the young republics into kingdoms that he oversaw. While the drive to "republicanize" the continent had from the start struggled with the resistance of the great European powers, Napoleonic policy dealt the death blow by "monarchizing" the revolutionary legacy and betraying its ideals.

For a short while, then, principles of liberty and equality had carried the day in Europe. Under Napoleon they remained an unfulfilled promise and were achieved only in the Americas before rebounding to the Old World in the 1820s. This movement resumed when the anti-Napoleon Constitution of Cádiz (1812) inspired the revolutionary governments of Sicily, Spain, and Portugal as well as the South American states. Thereafter, these ideals have enkindled the hopes of peoples struggling for freedom worldwide. 1789 was not for naught!

Annie Jourdan

REFERENCES

Condorcet, Jean-Antoine-Nicolas C. *Sketch for a Historical Picture of the Progress of the Human Mind*. Translated by June Barraclough. London: Weidenfeld and Nicolson, 1955.

Jourdan, Annie. *La Révolution batave entre la France et l'Amérique (1795–1806)*. Rennes: Presses universitaires de Rennes, 2008.

————. "Tumultuous Contexts and Radical Ideas (1783–1789): The 'Pre-Revolution' in a Transnational Perspective." In *The Oxford Handbook of the French Revolution*, edited by David Andress, 92–108. Oxford: Oxford University Press, 2015.

Lafayette, Marquis de. *Memoirs, Correspondence and Manuscripts of General Lafayette*. New York: Saunders and Otley, 1837.

RELATED ARTICLES

1357, 1808, 1848, 1871, 1948, 1968, 1989

1790

Declaring Peace on Earth

The declaration of peace that France made to the world in 1790 came with a declaration of unconditional hospitality, founded on the brotherhood of the human race. But in 1793, the advent of total war in Europe made every citizen of a foreign country a counterrevolutionary suspect. From that point on, "hospitality" could only be the expression of friendly, reciprocal links between allied peoples or citizens.

With its declaration of peace to the world on May 22, 1790, the French Constituent Assembly affirmed that the only legitimate war between human beings was a defensive one. Thereafter, the French people claimed to reject any relationship of domination or conquest of any other people. Reciprocal liberty among individuals belonging to sovereign nations, and their mutual recognition of one another, were expected to generate a new form of fraternity through what the philosopher Immanuel Kant, in his *Perpetual Peace: A Philosophical Essay* (1795), called a "cosmopolitical" act. Thereby all free citizens became responsible for their own government — and every free nation became directly responsible for world peace.

On July 14, 1790, thirty-six foreigners in Paris made a formal request — in the name of the human race — to participate in the first Festival of the Federation and honor the Revolution. They belonged to a "committee of men of all nations" who claimed to be citizens of countries that were still ruled by tyrants. "The Phrygian cap of liberty raised by these men will guarantee the deliverance of their unfortunate fellow citizens," declared their representative, "orator of mankind," the Prussian baron Anacharsis Cloots, who had rushed to Paris in 1789 to partake in the revolutionary events. The Americans among the thirty-six — free since winning their war against their British oppressors — petitioned to swear an oath of friendship to the people of France, as fellow citizens and brothers who likewise cherished the marriage of liberty and peace. As for the British, they considered themselves free but were somewhat loath to renounce the idea of domination. The idea of fraternity — by which was understood the alliance of free peoples — was supposed to ensure "order in the world." Everyone in Paris, free or otherwise, whether or not they supported total equality or a form of domination that fell short of community, was given hospitality at the Festival of the Federation.

Thus the 1790 Festival proclaimed a new era for the

human race and a virtually unconditional welcome on the part of the French to all foreigners. "A free people has no enemy but the enemies of the rights of man," declared a revolutionary decree. Jules Michelet, writing in 1847, described the event as a "prophetic symbol" and "a general union of the world."

The union was short-lived. By August 3, 1793, Garnier de Saintes, elected to the National Convention, was submitting a proposal for a law to regulate the presence of foreigners in France. Article 7 of this law was presented to the recently elected republican assembly as follows: "Foreigners who obtain a certificate of hospitality will be obliged to carry on their left arm a tricolored ribbon on which will be marked the word *hospitalité*, followed by the name of the country wherein they were born."

The demand to identify at a glance all guests admitted to France has echoed down the ages. The status of the foreigner has changed little since that time. Foreigners remain a perpetual source of suspicion, sometimes mild, sometimes severe. Already the tricolor ribbon proposed by Garnier de Saintes was far from a badge of honor, and Article 8 of his projected law clearly confirms this: "Foreigners may not discard this ribbon at any time or walk abroad without their certificate of hospitality; and in the event that they disobey one or other of these regulations, they shall be deported as suspects." The final version of the decree rejected the proposition of the tricolor ribbon, but maintained the certificates of hospitality. Thus the stranger remained ipso facto an object of suspicion.

The tricolor had been bestowed to strangers before. "Foreign deserters will be welcomed with friendship and fraternity and will immediately receive the tricolor cockade as a sign of their adoption," stated the decree of April 29, 1792. This honor was extended to such deserters less than ten days after the French declaration of war on the Emperor of Austria. The cockade was offered to all those who sought asylum and the protection of the law in France, and to all those who might already be considered refugees from conflicts between revolutionaries and counterrevolutionaries. On May 1, 1792, the revolutionary Charles Duval had declared that it was precisely at the moment when "peoples were most crushed by monarchs who were themselves in revolt against liberty" that it was necessary "to prove to them that we are their friends and brothers and that everywhere — in their own homes or in ours — they will always have our help and comfort." Duval saw the national law as a "guarantee of the fraternal affection that should bind all people together." If French justice had in view a humanization of social and political relationships by the recognition of a universal legal norm, which would — or at least should — be valid everywhere and at all times, the law of the nation was also universal.

Never mind if deserters from foreign armies had no knowledge of this law, they would soon learn to love it. For how could anyone not know and love the Declaration of the Rights of Man and of the Citizen, when every French child practically learned to read by deciphering it?

The tricolor was indeed a symbol of universal fraternity, under the auspices of the Declaration; and hospitality was a key feature of this new fraternity. Yet Garnier de Saintes's law of August/September 1793 seemed to put an end to all this. A project that had been emblematic of the revolutionary system ever since the declaration of peace to the world and the inaugural Festival of the Federation might come to an end.

Six months earlier, when the declaration of war on Great Britain broadened the war already being waged on the Emperor of Austria, the firebrand revolutionary Bertrand Barère and some others had declared that the French had to "preserve our hospitality and the protection of our laws not only toward those English and Batavians who are currently on the soil of the Republic, but also toward those who might wish to come here and benefit from the blessings of free government. Citizens, may you differ in this from your enemies! How keenly it will be felt, this difference in the conduct of a free people from that of a despotic government, when you are seen to be generous and hospitable at the very moment when your enemies show tyranny and barbarism toward your fellows."

The question of fraternal hospitality was also at the heart of certain propositions made by another radical, Louis Antoine de Saint-Just, during the constitutional debate of April 1793. "The French nation declares itself to be the friend of all other peoples; it will respect religiously all treaties and all flags; it will offer the safety of its ports to the world's ships; it will give succor to the great and virtuous of all nations; its vessels shall protect foreign ships from storm and tempest. Foreigners and their customs shall be respected within France. The Frenchman living in a foreign country, like the foreigner living in France, shall be able to inherit and buy, but shall never be able to alienate." Obviously the foreigner should not behave as a conqueror, nor should he manipulate his host country through commerce. But beyond the constraints placed on conquest and colonization, foreigners had a right to scrupulous consideration. Hospitality was deemed virtually unconditional, indeed an absolute duty, for the human race constituted a political and social entity in which every human being could claim the same rights as his neighbor.

In the same constitutional debate, Robespierre proposed to regulate all relationships between nations and also between citizens in the coming declaration of human rights. Robespierre set forth the following four articles: "*Article I*: Men of all countries are brothers, and different peoples should help one another as it may be in their power to do so, as if they were citizens of the same state. *II*: Any man who oppresses one nation declares himself the enemy of all. *III*: Those who make war on the people to halt the progress of liberty and abolish the rights of man should be pursued by all, not as ordinary enemies, but as rebellious murderers and brigands. *IV*: Kings, aristocrats, and tyrants, whoever they are, are slaves who have risen up against the sovereign lord of the earth, which is the human race, and against the lawgiver of the universe, which is nature."

But by September 1793, the foreigner was no longer an allegory for the universality of revolution. Likewise, the risk of resembling despotic regimes in other parts of the world had ceased to be a consideration. What could have brought so abrupt an end to France's fraternal hospitality, whose only limits had been the rejection of conquest, colonialism, and domination?

First, obviously, there was the hostility of the counterrevolutionary coalition of European powers marching against France. Next, the generous hospitality and friendship offered in the past seemed to have been betrayed, and it was now considered important to place limits on the practice. However, this had to be done without entirely giving up the idea of a community of nations capable of acting according to the same principles. Unconditional hospitality had to be suspended — but in the name of a cosmopolitan project founded on reciprocal values. Thus, those who did not belong to a free and allied people could no longer be trusted, unless they were vouched for by several "good citizens."

The risk of confusing different types of foreigners was clear. From that time on, it became imperative to distinguish between good foreigners and spies in the pay of foreign monarchies. Garnier de Saintes himself, commenting on the law of August/September, declared: "The French people, generous in their politics and rigorously just, will not confuse the returning prodigal with the masked conspirator, nor the peaceful foreigner who loves our laws with the hypocritical intriguer who speaks of them with respect, only to betray them." But in practice the condition imposed on foreigners if they were to be admitted to French hospitality — guarantees from two patriotic citizens — simply replaced an unconditional public hospitality supported by legal protections with a conditional civic hospitality supported by the virtue of patriots. In each case, the hospitable character of patriotic citizens was reaffirmed. They alone would know how to play their role as members of a free people and they alone would know how to guarantee the rights of man. In their own limited spheres, they would be tasked with ensuring that the idea of peace declared to the world would survive, along with the rejection of all wars of conquest.

Heavy responsibilities indeed.

As Saint-Just wrote in his *Fragments on the Republican Institutions* (1794): "There have been freer peoples who have fallen from greater heights." Alas, nobody can say when — or where — this particular fall will end.

Sophie Wahnich

REFERENCES

Belissa, Marc. *Fraternité universelle et intérêt national (1713–1795): Les cosmopolitiques du droit des gens*. Paris: Kimé, 1998.

Bell, David A. *The First Total War: Napoleon's Europe and the Birth of Warfare as We Know It*. Boston: Houghton Mifflin Harcourt, 2014.

De Francesco, Antonino, Judith Miller, and Pierre Serna, eds. *Republics at War (1776–1840): Revolutions, Conflicts, and Geopolitics in Europe and the Atlantic World*. London: Palgrave Macmillan, 2013.

Mathiez, Albert. *La Révolution et les étrangers: Cosmopolitisme et défense nationale*. Paris: La Renaissance du livre, 1918.

Wahnich, Sophie. *L'Impossible citoyen: L'étranger dans le discours de la Révolution française*. Paris: Albin Michel, 1997.

RELATED ARTICLES
1420, 1920, 1927, 1948, 1974, 2003

1791

Plantations in Revolution

On the night of August 22, 1791, an unprecedented slave revolt flared up in the French colony of Saint-Domingue. Human and political rights had to exceed the bounds of white colonial privilege. This uprising led to Haiti's independence and the abolition of slavery, the first time in modern history that the practice was outlawed.

On August 14, 1791, dozens of slaves gathered at Bois Caïman, a clearing in the woods of northern Saint-Domingue (Haiti today), to perform a voodoo ceremony they sealed with a blood pact. The sacrifice of a pig, likely inspired by a Dahomean ritual, marked the slaves' solemn entry into revolution. At the gathering, the black leaders of the Northern Plain (a vast sugar-producing region) committed to carrying out a plan hatched a week earlier, on a plantation. The conspirators' aims were modest in scope: to obtain a third day of rest per week and to end punishments by whipping. The means of achieving these goals — destroying plantations, massacring their owners, occupying the island's main port, Cap-Français — were more radical. Astonishingly, the uprising also aimed to bolster Louis XVI — who faced threats from radical revolutionaries in France after his failed attempt to flee the country — and was carried out under the colors of the French monarchy, whose political model more closely resembled African kingdoms. The French National Assembly, under pressure from plantation owners, had done nothing to improve conditions for "the blacks of Saint-Domingue." Still, many slaves demanded to be afforded the rights outlined by the Declaration of the Rights of Man and of the Citizen. The uprising of August 22 was multifaceted in symbolic scope: a turning point in the French Revolution, a major event in the history of Africa and its diaspora, a rupture in the world history of colonization, and a foundational moment for the nation of Haiti.

The revolt was particularly significant due to the considerable economic weight of the French colony of Saint-Domingue in the late eighteenth century. This small territory on the western side of Hispaniola island was the leading producer of sugar and coffee in the world, representing most of France's colonial commerce. The prosperity of Nantes, Bordeaux, Le Havre, and even Marseille owed much to the massive expansion of the slave trade, which peaked in 1789–1791. To ensure France's commercial power, more than 500,000 slaves, two-thirds of whom were born in Africa, worked in Saint-Domingue in horrendous conditions, with dismally low life expectancies. Nevertheless, this enviable economic powerhouse ran the risk of arousing the attention of France's imperial rivals, Spain and Great Britain.

This economic context nourished an explosive social and political climate. Long before the slave revolt, white plantation owners, emboldened by their financial success, had demanded political authority and the creation of colonial assemblies in line with the British model. Raising the specter of American independence, and demanding the right to trade with foreign nations, the colonists expelled the king's representative as soon as they got wind of the storming of the Bastille. Violently patriotic, the insubordinate plantation owners were by no means abolitionists — quite the contrary. Their preferred targets were none other than the mainland's "philanthropists," who made up the Société des Amis des Noirs (Society of the Friends of the Blacks) — Jacques Pierre Brissot, Abbé Grégoire, and others who fought for the gradual abolition of slavery and an international ban on the slave trade.

But these "patriotic" colonials were primarily in conflict with other slave owners and free people of color — freed slaves or descendants of freed slaves who sought political equality with whites. Although they fulfilled the criteria required to obtain full citizenship, they were denied access to revolutionary assemblies on the basis of what contemporaries called "epidermis." In October 1790, confronted with unwavering opposition by white elites, Vincent Ogé, a mixed-race merchant, formed a small army to claim the rights of free people of color. Poorly organized, the attempt was quickly stamped out. Ogé and his men were eventually forced to retreat, taking temporary refuge in the Spanish part of the island. Saint-Domingue's authorities ceded control over the rebels' fates to the white plantation owners, who captured them and subjected them to a torture device known as the breaking wheel. This begat a civil war, with free people of color and colonials mobilizing their own armies of slaves.

Yet, the rebels radically changed the stakes in August 1791. They demanded recognition of their human rights, and refused to be exploited by colonial elites. Although members of different social and racial groups might occasionally combine forces, the slaves would in no way be pawns of colonial manipulators. In fact, the borders between these different groups were far more porous than the era's political discourse suggests. While the Catholic Church justified the colonial enterprise, for instance, some priests fought side by side with the slaves. Toussaint Louverture, who would play a key role in the Revolution several years later, was both a freed man and a slave owner. Likewise, the insurgents of 1791, men as well as women, represented a diverse range of profiles and backgrounds. Under the label of "Congos," most of the rebels had African ancestry, and they mixed with island-born Creoles, who shared their language. Some, like the leader Jean-François Papillon, were former slaves and runaways; others had just arrived from Africa. Moreover, these classifications do not account for the diversity of histories, dialects, and occupations. As the revolts spread throughout the colony, alliances between social and racial groups were forged within provinces or even parishes, taking many forms. All of this speaks to the complexity of the strategies and stakes.

Seen from mainland France, the uprising was understood in much simpler terms — as a brutal and savage mob. News of the revolt did not reach Paris until late October 1791, when rumors of the events spread throughout the mainland, where they were interpreted in the light of mainland political events. The deep divide within the Jacobin club, provoked by the king's escape attempt and the Champ-de-Mars Massacre on July 17, 1791, had colonial ramifications. It was not a coincidence when the Feuillants, who sought to "stop the Revolution," named a major plantation owner in Saint-Domingue (Viénot de Vaublanc) to represent them at the Assembly. These "moderates," many of whom had been thrown out of the Jacobin club for opposing any concessions to the nonwhite free population, made a habit of recycling appalling reports promoted by colonials. One image came to occupy the public imagination: that of a white child cruelly impaled by rebel slaves. While the brutal repression of the uprising was concealed, the heads of the rebels, including that of their leader, the Voodoo priest Dutty Boukman, were placed on prominent display throughout the city of Cap-Français. The link between Africanness and savagery was uniquely explicit in media coverage of the revolt.

The Society of the Friends of the Blacks, far from cheering on the insurrection, attributed the troubles to royalist counterrevolutionary tactics. Professions of support for Louis XVI lent credibility to their argument about rebel slaves. Jacques Pierre Brissot, a leading Jacobin voice at the Assembly, alleged that the slaves had been duped by the "aristocrats." He suggested that the violence of August 1791 was simply an imitation of the plantation owners' earlier rebellious actions. However, Brissot made sure to add that he would consider himself a "monster if he'd been so cruel as to inspire the rebellion of a single black person." Taking their cues from the Marquis de Condorcet and United States abolitionists, the Society of the Friends of the Blacks remained committed to gradual emancipation, spread out over several decades as a means of "preparing" Africans for freedom. The process was meant to manage colonial interests by giving them time to progressively adjust to wage labor. To that end, abolitionists were determined to subdue the uprising. They backed the white plantation owners and people of color who would "reestablish order" in Saint-Domingue.

The meaning and implications of the insurrection varied according to one's location. While people had trouble grasping what was happening more than four thousand miles away, the revolts in Paris and Dunkirk against rising sugar prices in January–February 1792 show how much the French urban population had grown accustomed to these semi-luxury products. On a global scale, the troubles in the "pearl of the Caribbean" threatened the fragile, already fraught equilibrium of nearby slave societies — Jamaica, Cuba, Venezuela, and the United States. Plantation owners, slaves, free people of color, and merchants fashioned their own readings of the uprising depending on their respective fears, hopes, emotions, and interests.

At the end of 1791, the outcome remained uncertain. Although slaves occupied the Northern Plain, they had not managed to seize Cap-Français. Insurrection leaders Jean-François Papillon and Georges Biassou attempted to negotiate amnesty, but failed in the face of uncompromising colonials and tougher demands from their own troops, who now wanted general freedom. Two years elapsed before the revolutionaries extended their supposed universal citizenship to former slaves. The decree of 16 Pluviôse Year II (February 4, 1794) cannot, therefore, be seen as a logical extension of July 14, 1789. It took sustained pressure from slaves, the advent of the Republic, heightened conflicts between parties, and the needs of a world war against Great Britain, which justified a massive enlistment of citizen-soldiers from Africa, for the "new people of Saint-Domingue" to obtain political rights.

On 17 Pluviôse, the Convention invented the notion of a crime against humanity for slave owners and solemnly recognized human dignity for all. The abolition of slavery, though short-lived within the French Empire (1794–1802), would serve as an essential stepping stone for the nation of Haiti, which became the second independent state in the Americas in 1804. The 1791 revolt would long remain a taboo subject in France, since it laid bare some of the period's contradictions and ambiguities. It would also constitute a source of anxiety for slave societies and a major point of reference for the black Atlantic world.

Manuel Covo

REFERENCES

Dorigny, Marcel, and Bernard Gainot. *La Société des amis des Noirs (1788–1799): Contribution à l'histoire de l'abolition de l'esclavage.* Paris: UNESCO, 1998.

Dubois, Laurent. *Avengers of the New World: The Story of the Haitian*

Revolution. Cambridge, MA: Harvard University Press, 2009.

Fick, Carolyn E. *The Making of Haiti: The Saint Domingue Revolution from Below*. Knoxville: University of Tennessee Press, 2004.

Geggus, David. *Haitian Revolutionary Studies*. Bloomington: Indiana University Press, 2002.

Serna, Pierre. "Que s'est-il dit à la Convention les 15, 16 et 17 pluviôse an II? Ou lorsque la naissance de la citoyenneté universelle provoque l'invention du 'crime de lèse-humanité." *La Révolution française: Cahiers de l'Institut d'histoire de la Révolution française* 7 (2014).

RELATED ARTICLES
1446, 1683, 1848, 1919, 2008

1793

Paris, Capital of the Natural World

The founding in 1793 of the National Museum of Natural
History contributed to the French Revolution's project
of moral and political education. Heir to the Jardin du
Roi (the Royal Botanical Garden), the Parisian museum
confirmed France's preeminence in the field of natural
science for several decades to come.

How was Paris made into the universal capital of the natural
sciences? The revolutionary-era creation of the National
Museum of Natural History, on June 10, 1793, fits into the
overall project of rethinking the sciences while carrying
forward the cosmopolitan message of the Enlightenment.
The natural sciences, brought together and exhibited in the
museum and its garden, were meant to display to the world
the importance of a rejuvenated France, and to consolidate
its influence.

This founding belongs to a whole lineage, that of
the Royal Botanical Garden, or Jardin du Roi, which had
ascended to international prominence during the eighteenth

century, giving rise to numerous replicas throughout Europe. A center for the collection of artifacts and natural specimens, the garden was a symbol of Enlightenment universalism. Travelers brought back specimens from all over the world. Georges-Louis Leclerc, Comte de Buffon, intendant from 1739 to 1788, had set up a vast network of European correspondents. As it was customary to attach sachets of seeds to letters, the exchange of plants multiplied. Furthermore, acclimatization projects for rare or "exotic" plants spoke to the determination to make the garden a microcosm that would compile all the living species of the globe, classifying, labeling and ranking them. According to the same rationale, the Royal Garden was also designed as a tool of domination, manifesting the sovereign's power over far-flung lands and their wealth.

The Revolution challenged none of this. Quite the reverse: the creation of the Museum of Natural History pushed the endeavor forward by making the institution available to the public (access to the garden had previously been reserved for a privileged few). For the Jacobins, the purpose was to turn the contemplation of nature into a project of moral and political education. This ambitious venture, which went hand in hand with the new central art museum at the Louvre (founded a few weeks later), would impart patriotic knowledge to the people and regenerate France.

Granted relatively free rein, a new administrative structure, and more extensive prerogatives than the old Royal Garden, the museum became a national institution, with public classes open to all. The chair-holders, whose number jumped from three to twelve, received equal salaries and lived together on the garden grounds. Combining the resources of botanical gardens with those of old naturalist cabinets of curiosities, the institution's scientists devoted themselves to the three kingdoms of nature (animal, vegetable, and mineral). The Revolution's confiscations enlarged the collections and made manifest the museum's central position in the world of naturalists. These confiscations also had heuristic effects. Scientist Georges Cuvier, for instance, found in the collection that had belonged to the Dutch stadtholder some elephant skulls from Ceylon and Cape Town that allowed him to confirm the existence of two distinct living species of elephants. By observing specimens coming from the other side of the world, and matching his observations to drawings exchanged with foreign naturalists, he published a series of works that proved decisive for fossil anatomy.

More broadly, the museum model extended beyond national borders: the Zoological Museum of Naples — created by the French government in 1813 and opened in 1845 thanks to Giosuè Sangiovanni, a student of Cuvier and the naturalist Jean-Baptiste Lamarck — included two galleries designed from the same floor plan as the avian gallery of the Paris Museum. Indeed, many of the students attending classes in Paris were foreigners, at least until the 1830s and 1840s. For a long time, English and Italian students were among the most numerous. The museum's international reach took yet another form: the spread of theories, such as Lamarckian inheritance, throughout Europe.

This pedagogical venture, whose range thus extended beyond national boundaries, had political overtones. As the man of letters Jacques-Henri Bernardin de Saint-Pierre pointed out in 1792, "our political relations require that we set up a menagerie." In May 1794, the creation of such a menagerie in the garden met the need for a place to accommodate gifts from royalty the world over. This is where, in 1827, a giraffe given to Charles X by the pasha of Egypt, the first specimen of the species to enter France, found refuge. It lived there for eighteen years, inspiring fashion, design, and even political pamphlets, before being stuffed and mounted in the museum.

Natural history was also intended as a useful science, allowing for the development of agronomy and the progress of agriculture. André Thouin, appointed "professor of crop science" in 1793, endeavored especially to introduce exotic plants into the garden and provincial botanical gardens, with an eye toward the rural economy. The museum became a repository for far-flung species that it then redistributed to colonial botanical gardens. In 1798, the director of the botanical garden of Cayenne, French Guiana, who was a former student of the Royal Garden, brought back to the museum breadfruit trees that had originated in Tahiti, and which he had succeeded in acclimating to the Caribbean. The most useful breadfruit tree, tasked with ensuring food security in the colonies, made its way from one botanical garden to another around the world before finally earning a place at the museum. Through collection and attempts at naturalizing and acclimating exotic species, the museum contributed to a vast endeavor to control the world. As France's first colonial empire in the Caribbean began to unravel in the wake of slave revolts and emancipation, it became urgent to acclimate a number of exotic plants in order to lessen the country's dependence on colonial ties.

The enthusiasm of the revolutionary period, the initiatives of Thouin and Cuvier, and the significant enrichment of its collections allowed the museum to remain at the forefront of natural science for a few more decades. The institution's central position, however, lasted only a generation. Foreign institutions did not confine themselves to merely sending samples or receiving research from Parisian naturalists: they also emulated this research and innovated. London's Grant Museum of Zoology and Comparative Anatomy thus owes a great deal to Cuvier and the Parisian gallery of comparative anatomy. But when the American naturalist and Harvard professor Jeffries Wyman visited Paris in 1841, he found Cuvier's collections in a state of neglect, and concluded that the London museum had become the most important in Europe. By the 1830s, in numerous areas of natural history, English and German institutions had outpaced Paris.

Moreover, in the age of empire, it appeared that the museum, devoted as it was to pure science at the expense of commercial interests, was falling behind. On an individual basis, museum professors got involved in colonial trade, via the Geographical Society or the Acclimatization Society. With professors taking part in scientific missions and museum representatives now sitting on the French Ministry of Public Education's new Travel Commission, this patronage system endured for decades, guaranteeing the enhancement of collections through distant expeditions. In 1889, the Paris Exposition Universelle, or Universal Exhibition, included an enormous greenhouse that, on museum grounds, both displayed and tamed exotic nature. In 1895, the museum's Exposition Zoologique, Botanique et Géologique de Madagascar expressed support for France's recent colonial conquest of that island. France, like other imperial powers, increased the number of trial gardens in the colonies: Algiers as early as 1832, Saigon in 1863, Libreville in 1887, Tunis in 1891, and Madagascar in 1897, to cite only a few examples.

Some had close ties with the museum while others maintained a looser connection.

While the National Museum of Natural History thus kept step with imperial expansion in the nineteenth century, it did so with some diffidence. The magnificent Buitenzorg Garden in the Dutch colony of Java welcomed scientists in residence from all over the world, featured laboratories and its own journal (in French, as it happened), and became a reference in the field. Great Britain, with its unmatched network of botanical gardens at Kew, and by virtue of the sheer size of its empire, enjoyed an overwhelming advantage. Thanks to the richest herbarium in the world, a museum of applied botany, and an unequaled network, the British imposed their own taxonomic standards.

The National Museum of Natural History seems to have missed the imperial turn. Though it came to include a department of colonial crop science in the latter part of the century, this impetus remained modest. The Kew model, which centralized and directed all colonial gardens and appointed directors trained at the home office, was not replicable in the French setting. The museum's scientists were unwilling to follow utilitarian orders issued by colonial pressure groups. Furthermore, the juncture between Public Education — the museum's home Ministry — and the Ministry of the Colonies was far from easy. In 1899, the creation of a new colonial garden in Nogent-sur-Marne, close to Paris, on grounds belonging to the museum but financed by the colonies, provides a pertinent illustration. The mere existence of this new site demonstrates the disconnect between the museum and the colonial sphere. It is in Nogent that future directors of colonial trial gardens would be trained, and that plants would be reproduced in special greenhouses and then shipped off to the tropics.

Between 1793 and the end of the Bourbon Restoration (1830), the National Museum of Natural History believed, and convinced others to believe, in France's role as leader in the natural sciences. Its influence was indeed broad. But as the world changed, the roles were redistributed. Over the course of the nineteenth century, natural history lost its prestige. New disciplines such as biology reconfigured the natural sciences and thereby marginalized the museum's model. Other European institutions asserted their prominence, notably in the area of botany and acclimation. The leadership of Kew Gardens in the second half of the century points to the new directions taken by the natural sciences, in particular the economic value placed upon plants in imperial contexts. It also shows that in a changing world, the centrality of scientific institutions was bound to remain transient.

Hélène Blais

REFERENCES

Blanckaert, Claude, Claudine Cohen, Pietro Corsi, and Jean-Louis Fischer, eds. *Le Muséum au premier siècle de son histoire*. Paris: Éditions du Muséum national d'histoire naturelle, 1997.

Bourguet, Marie-Noëlle, and Christophe Bonneuil, eds. "De l'inventaire du monde à la mise en valeur du globe: Botanique et colonisation (fin XVIIe siècle – début XXe siècle." *Revue française d'histoire d'outre-mer* 86, no. 322–323 (1999): 7–38.

Bourguet, Marie-Noëlle, and Pierre-Yves Lacour. "Les mondes naturalistes: Europe (1530–1802)." In *Histoire des sciences et des savoirs, de la Renaissance à nos jours, t. 1: De la Renaissance aux Lumières*, edited by Stéphane Van Damme. Paris: Seuil, 2015.

Lacour, Pierre-Yves. *La République naturaliste: Collections d'histoire naturelle et Révolution française (1789–1804)*. Paris: Éditions du Muséum national d'histoire naturelle, 2014.

Spary, Emma C. *Utopia's Garden: French Natural History from Old Regime to Revolution*. Chicago: University of Chicago Press, 2010.

RELATED ARTICLES

1794

The Terror in Europe

The coup d'état that destroyed Maximilien Robespierre's
government on July 27, 1794, utterly transformed Europe's
attitude to what was happening in France. The story
about the "Reign of Terror" that took hold afterward
made it possible for the European monarchies fighting the
French to condemn their revolution as a vehicle of brutal
repression. In reality, the methods of the Terror had been
regularly used by other European states since at least the
1780s.

Few periods of French history have raised higher passions
than the months between the spring of 1793 and the summer
of 1794. The name given to this period — *"La Terreur"* or
"the Reign of Terror" — portrays a sequence of events
that have been seen as both obscure and frightening.
Four years after the ecstatic storming of the Bastille, the
Revolution had, according to popular lore, succumbed to
a dictatorship of a kind that had never been seen before,
buoyed by radical Jacobin ideology and personified by the

famed revolutionary Maximilien Robespierre. The country at large was plunged into a state of generalized violence, which some believe foreshadowed the age of totalitarianism and the gulags of the Soviet Union.

But was the Terror a purely French phenomenon? Certainly not.

The myth of the Terror was hatched in the summer of 1794, or more precisely in the days following July 27, 1794 (9 Thermidor Year II, in the revolutionary calendar), when the conspirators who had just seen Robespierre and his allies beheaded spoke, one after the other, at the bars of France's various elected assemblies. In justifying the political masterstroke they had just accomplished, they contrived to invent one of the most tenacious fictions in the history of France and Western Europe.

Their narrative was very simple. On July 29, the day after Robespierre was executed at the Place de la Révolution (now the Place de la Concorde), his nemesis Bertrand Barère excoriated the dead man's government as one of "total centralization." A month later, on August 28, Jean-Lambert Tallien — Barère's co-conspirator and a former leader of the "Terrorists" in the French provinces — coined the expression "system of terror." The following day, Laurent Lecointre, also a powerful early supporter of Robespierre, condemned his "system of oppression and terror." Prepared for several months in advance by numerous personal attacks and campaigns of destabilization, and fueled by rumors that Robespierre was preparing to reestablish the ancien régime by having himself crowned king, the story, fabricated by those who in spite of their diversity were somehow united as "Thermidorians," was in fact a total fabrication.

Robespierre, who like Georges Danton and Jean-Paul Marat before him was a favorite of the people, had no special political powers and absolutely no ambition to exercise personal dictatorship or occupy any sort of throne. All the same, in the summer of 1794 the myth put about by his enemies took a firm hold in France and abroad, purely because it sorted out a complicated situation.

For many European states, the Reign of Terror narrative came as an unexpected blessing: an admission from the French themselves that the Terror had truly taken place, that proved beyond a doubt the existence of the monster the French Revolution had become, and that justified the war the other European empires had been waging against it ever since 1792. In France, the fiction whereby Robespierre had to die if the principles of 1789 were to be preserved made it possible to institute a critical change. The excesses of the Terror could now be blamed on a single man and his supporters, however much of an invention that might be; at the same time the Republican regime, which henceforward would turn away from the idea of radical revolution, could remain in place. This story — or rather this interpretation of events — gave birth to a completely new regime in France: the five-member Directoire, or Directory, which effectively replaced the revolutionary Committee of Public Safety.

And yet the crucial date, which is still commonly known in France as the "9 Thermidor," was anything but the clean break with the past that it has so often been called. The framework of the regime that ruled France in 1793 and 1794, for which the Thermidorians blamed Robespierre, had been hastily cobbled together to deal with the desperate conflicts then engulfing France. And yet, many months after the coup, that framework was still in place. Another savage political repression was now unleashed against those who publicly opposed the Directory. The *grande police* law presented in the spring of 1795 by Emmanuel Joseph Sieyès, the famed author of "What Is the Third Estate?", was just as repressive as similar laws that had been voted on during the Terror. In fact, political tension and violence in France were continuing unabated and it was only the *appearance* of a return to order that enabled the Convention to effect another political metamorphosis. Though true peace and national reconciliation had been rendered theoretically possible by the liquidation of Robespierre's party and a repudiation of the immediate past, these ideals were actually out of the question, so firmly did the Directory's regime commit itself to crushing radicals and excluding the ordinary working people who formed the real backbone of the nation.

Many people deemed this imperfect regime a great deal better than the Terror, whose echoes continued to generate morbid nightmares within Gothic and Romantic novels and, more broadly, the European imagination. The real reason that the Franco-European political fiction of the Terror had taken hold so easily was that it conformed to an imaginative universe that had taken shape much earlier.

Well before the 1790s, "terror" was a familiar word throughout the continent. Having designated for many centuries the fear of God's punishment, the term also evoked the kind of paralyzing dread, far worse than fear, that was used by despotic governments to dominate their peoples and prevent them from rebelling. After the 1750s, the word was increasingly used in politics, literature, science, and aesthetics, adding to the options available for exploring human emotions. This possibility fascinated not only scholars, but also theorists of government looking for ways to control people, physically and psychologically.

All over eighteenth-century Europe, jurists and philosophers agreed that civilized government consisted of preemptively terrorizing anyone who threatened public order. The idea was to reduce them to frightened impotence rather than to crush them afterward. In England, the United Provinces, Naples, Geneva, and the Habsburg-dominated Netherlands — all hotbeds of the Enlightenment — the policy of terrifying people with daily spectacles of punishment meted out in public had deterred crime while minimizing the public use of force. In Geneva, various penal reforms were aimed at "striking terror into crime." Thus it was that, well before 1793, terror had become an instrument of government. Widespread though by no means uncontroversial, it was now stigmatized as a barbarian holdover, now practiced as a technique for domination and the maintenance of order while economizing on the actual use of violence.

This ambiguity explains why, after the French Revolution began in 1789, the word "terror" was used by supporters of the ancien régime to denounce revolutionary violence or call for the reestablishment of a strong authority that could restore order. In the opposing camp, terror was sometimes embraced: good "patriots" needed to know how to inflict terror on the enemies of the nation and thereby protect public safety. When civil war broke out between French revolutionaries and counterrevolutionaries in 1793, it became a matter of urgency to turn the weapon of terror against so-called "terrorists." The Committee of Public Safety's dictatorial rule and the state of exception that they gradually put in place were intended to both terrorize and eliminate counterrevolutionaries. Danton expressed this succinctly in his famous pronouncement of March 10, 1793: "Let us be terrible, and spare the people the need to be so"; Jacques Nicolas Billaud-Varenne, one of the key architects of the Terror, gave the idea further coherence with his theory of the "Terror-response." In the royal courts of Europe, it seemed clear that the French were playing with fire in seeking to transform the most powerful human emotions into a veritable system of government. Nevertheless, "exceptional measures" and "provisional suspensions of ordinary political activities" were all too familiar to foreign critics of the French Terror, who had seen them applied in their own countries in other times of crisis.

The French Revolution quickly led to an international crisis that threatened to destabilize every state in Europe. The consequence was a general wave of repression, violently targeting anybody suspected of partiality to radical ideas. In this climate of generalized suspicion, it is a fact that terror was an instrument routinely used by states that were at war with France.

Though Great Britain was viewed by European patriots as the home of constitutional liberties, even the British did not escape a surge of authoritarianism coinciding with the French Terror. As early as 1792, a repressive policy was introduced to counter the spread of the "Jacobin conspiracy." A "state of exception" was declared and in June 1792 the Middlesex Justices Act centralized the police force and placed it under the government's overall authority. This was vigorously opposed by some members of Parliament, who saw it as a betrayal of fundamental liberties. For example,

"Clause D" of the act authorized magistrates to carry out preemptive arrests of individuals merely "suspected of ill-intent." In May 1794, the 1679 Habeas Corpus Act was suspended, making "treason" an exceptional crime and enabling the police to detain individuals for a greater length of time before bringing them to trial. Tens of thousands of "suspects" were now placed under surveillance.

Responding to a similar situation of war and international crisis, British and French legislation more or less simultaneously commenced the repression of foreigners, who were identified as possible enemies. In the colonies of both nations, the practice of terror was routine. Rebel populations in the French Caribbean were subjected to extreme violence, while almost the whole of colonial Ireland was ruled by emergency laws between 1796 and 1798, at which time a British military repression took the lives of tens of thousands of people in the space of a few months.

At roughly the same time, in 1798, the American federal government — which was not at war with anyone — passed a series of extraordinary laws suspending the rights affirmed in its Constitution with a view to protecting itself from revolutionaries coming from Europe. The Alien and Sedition Acts repressed both inflammatory publications and inflammatory foreigners; even certain members of Congress were placed under surveillance. At the same time, in the Netherlands, radicals and moderates fought each other tooth and nail over a series of emergency laws that each camp denounced as terror measures. Meanwhile, the Austrian government called a halt to the liberal experiments it had been gingerly testing in Belgium since the 1780s. In one country after another, revolutionary wars led to authoritarian clampdowns.

In this context, the dictatorship of the French Committee of Public Safety was only partly exceptional. The revolution in France was the most recent of a series of movements that had shaken Europe in the 1780s, but as it was more radical and more destabilizing than the others, it sparked conflicts of far greater importance. Because the French emergency measures were introduced against a backdrop of European war as well as civil war in France itself, they were particularly extreme; in the eighteen months of the Terror, a staggering 35,000–45,000 people were executed for political crimes. All the same this savage repression did not make the French "state of exception" any different from the others, except insofar as its brutality obliged ordinary working people to become the driving force of events. After 1792, they called for legal and social compensations in exchange for their support — without which the revolutionary regime could not survive. As a result, the political regime that prevailed between 1793 and 1794 took unprecedented steps toward economic redistribution and social cohesion. Thus, behind the cliché of France's Terror lurks a history that is European in scope and infinitely more complex than we have been led to believe; a history of transitions and changes in the habitual functioning of the political status quo, at a time when that status quo was threatened by vast crises of war and revolution.

Guillaume Mazeau

REFERENCES

Baczko, Bronisław. *Ending the Terror: The French Revolution After Robespierre*. Translated by Michel Petheram. Cambridge: Cambridge University Press, 2007.

Brunel, Françoise. *Thermidor: La chute de Robespierre (1794)*. Bruxelles: Complexe, 1989.

Jourdan, Annie. "Les discours de la terreur à l'époque révolutionnaire (1776–1798): Étude comparative sur une notion ambiguë." *French Historical Studies* 36, no. 1 (2013): 51–82.

Martin, Jean-Clément. *La Terreur, part maudite de la Révolution*. Paris: Découvertes Gallimard, 2010.

Mazeau, Guillaume. "La 'Terreur,' laboratoire de la modernité." In *Pour quoi faire la Révolution*, edited by Jean-Luc Chappey, Bernard Gainot, Guillaume Mazeau, Frédéric Régent, and Pierre Serna. Marseille: Agone, 2012.

RELATED ARTICLES
1610, 1789, 1871, 1958, 1989

A HOMELAND FOR
A UNIVERSAL
REVOLUTION

France does not monopolize the idea of revolution, but the country was most certainly one of its most emblematic wellsprings until the mid-nineteenth century. In the painting Frédéric Sorrieu painted to commemorate the "Spring of Nations" in 1848, France leads other nations toward emancipation under the benevolent gaze of Marianne (the allegory of the French Republic) and a hovering Christ looking down from the heavens. Paradoxical though it might seem, this same France which, only fifty years before, had subdued the entire continent of Europe under the rule of Napoleon continued to embody the ideals of freedom and brotherhood from the First Republic, declared in September 1792, until the proclamation of the Second, in February 1848.

The execution of Maximilien Robespierre brought the Terror to an end in the month of Thermidor (July) 1794. The revolutionaries who had survived the violence unleashed during the preceding years attempted a return to institutional stability under the Directory (1795–1799). This much disparaged regime, known for its infighting and a bourgeois rather than radical interpretation of Revolution, was overthrown by one of its most brilliant generals. Basking in the glory of his victorious campaigns in Italy (1796–1797) and Egypt (1798–1799), Napoleon Bonaparte, "son of the Revolution," claimed to safeguard the gains of 1789 by staging a coup on 18 Brumaire Year VIII (November 9, 1799). The road to a true "republican monarchy" was now wide open, but the fiction of power-sharing under the Consulate (1799–1804) gave way to full-blown autocracy when Napoleon proclaimed the Empire in 1804. The supreme ruler revived the system of royal symbols and social distinctions that the revolutionaries had sought to eradicate in 1789.

Yet even this collapse of republican institutions could not tarnish the aura of those universal principles trumpeted throughout the 1790s. Indeed, they were taken up by peoples who, across the world, sought either to imitate France's revolutionary spirit or to contest its imperial vision. The enslaved laborers of Saint-Domingue, France's most prosperous colony, were the first to demand that the 1789 Declaration of the Rights of Man and of the Citizen be applied to them. Although Napoleon had reestablished slavery in 1802 and sent an expeditionary force to the island to quell a rebellion, the insurgent slaves won their independence and founded the new republic of Haiti on January 1, 1804. In Europe, meanwhile, many peoples embraced France's newly exported ideals, whether its famous Napoleonic Code, adopted in 1804, or its vision of a universal French culture, whose diffusion was intended to improve the fate of mankind while serving French interests, and then turned them against the occupying

Napoleonic forces. In Italy, Spain, and the Germanic territories, the advance of Napoleon's armies stimulated feelings of national entitlement, which combined with powerful desires for reform and modernization.

Another general, Simón Bolívar, took advantage of Napoleon's occupation of Spain to undermine the foundations of the Iberian empire in the Americas. The notions of constitution, republic, and nationhood were crisscrossing the Atlantic just as Napoleon's European domination bogged down in the frozen slog of the Russian campaign (1812). The disintegration of the "Grand Empire," which by then included some twenty-eight million Frenchmen and fourteen million foreign-born individuals, left in its wake millions dead, a much diminished and occupied French territory (Louisiana was sold to the United States in 1803), and peoples now subject to the will of the victorious Holy Alliance, a coalition of Russia, Austria, and Prussia intent on restoring order and monarchical rule. British hegemony now rose triumphant.

The fall of Napoleon brought the Bourbon dynasty back to the throne some twenty years after the beheading of its last king, Louis XVI. At the Congress of Vienna (1814–1815), Austrian Chancellor Klemens von Metternich and Russian Czar Alexander I set the scene for France to restore the political, religious, and social values of the ancien régime. Still, the short-lived Bourbon reign (1814–1830) could not erase the indelible imprint of liberalism left behind by the revolutionary period. A great sense of uncertainty prevailed during these transition years, politically but also climatically (as illustrated by the scientific debate over the infamous "Year Without a Summer" in 1816 and its catastrophic impact on crop yields and food distribution, all caused by a volcanic eruption thousands of miles away in the Dutch East Indies).

And yet, the guiding light of revolution never dimmed, despite deep political divisions between left and right that further fractured a still very rural and motley country. The peoples of Europe did not resign themselves to the silence imposed by the police, armies, and censors of the restored monarchies. Two visions of Europe and the world were now at loggerheads: one embraced principles of dynasty, religion, and natural rule by traditional social elites; the other sought broader freedoms, equality, and national independence. In the early 1820s, hopes for national emancipation gravitated toward the Mediterranean, where Italian, Spanish, and Portuguese radicals sought in vain to disrupt the political order established in Vienna. The Greek struggle against the Ottomans triggered an unprecedented outpouring of solidarity and humanitarian zeal, backed by Europe-wide philhellenic networks, with Paris as one of their most active hubs.

By 1830, France was once again at the epicenter of

a sweeping revolutionary movement. Over just three days in July, the Parisian people revolted and forced the Bourbon King Charles X, symbol of authoritarian, reactionary values, to abdicate. Louis-Philippe, heir to the Orléans dynasty, acceded to the throne. Drawing inspiration from this episode, the Belgians had within a few weeks secured their own independence and adopted a liberal constitution. The Russia-dominated Poles, on the other hand, would not be so lucky: their appeals to France and other European countries went unanswered. Louis-Philippe and his coalition of liberals and conservatives sought to avoid the possible return of either republic or empire; they had no desire to see revolutionary fervor spread. Subversive activities nonetheless slipped over the borders, in much the same way as a new disease from Asia, cholera. The epidemic, which set off a panic in 1832, led bourgeois European elites to pay closer attention to the lower classes, if only to ensure their own survival.

Refugees from all over Europe flocked to Paris throughout the 1830s, among them Adam Mickiewicz, Heinrich Heine, and Karl Marx. Poets, painters, and writers contributed to the Romantic revolution, an early form of cultural globalization that brought French novelists, the likes of Victor Hugo, Stendhal, Honoré de Balzac, and George Sand, to a readership beyond national borders. Bankers, industrialists, and merchants — the leading protagonists of Louis-Philippe's July Monarchy — were laying the groundwork for a new capitalism based on railroads, textile, and manufactured semi-luxury goods. The glorification of hard work and savings, cardinal virtues of this middle-class era, did not eradicate subsistence crises and epidemics, however. Despite the regime's repressive turn in the mid-1830s, social and political protest grew steadily more vociferous. It was during this time that France became the cradle of countless utopian projects that sought, with characteristic ambition, to revamp the human race. The disciples of the utopian socialist Henri de Saint-Simon (1760–1825) imagined a reconciliation of East with West while the Icarians, driven by the ideas of Étienne Cabet, set sail for the United States to create what proved to be short-lived experimental communities.

Others saw in Algeria — under French control since the expedition launched by Charles X in 1830, weeks before his downfall — a new El Dorado provided the atrocities committed by the French army were brought to a halt. General Thomas-Robert Bugeaud's enfumades suffocated Algerian civilians who had sought refuge in caves that became death traps when the soldiers lit great bonfires at the entrance. There was outrage in France, to be sure, but also support for such tactics in the name of a new liberal imperialism and French greatness.

Faced with a devastating social crisis and a grassroots

campaign in favor of universal suffrage, the French authorities refused any broadening of the voter base. This obstinacy led to yet another revolutionary episode, in February 1848. This would be the final death knell for monarchy in France. The ousted king withdrew in favor of a new Republic, the second one in recent French history. Unlike 1830, the protest movement now spanned all of Europe. Within a matter of weeks, Berlin, Vienna, Prague, Milan, and Budapest witnessed uprisings that forced absolute monarchs to concede constitutions and a variety of liberal measures. This "Spring of Nations" espoused as its symbol the street barricade. A protest tool once belonging exclusively to the people of Paris, the barricade, entered the European revolutionary mainstream.

The ideal of emancipation borne by revolution once again crossed the Atlantic. Even before the proclamation of the abolition of slavery by the French government on April 27, 1848, those enslaved on Guadeloupe and Martinique were rising up against their masters. Along with the adoption of universal male suffrage in Paris in 1848, this reconfigured the outlines of French citizenship.

Just as in 1830, however, France did not live up to its own revolutionary aspirations. The bloody repression of French workers in June 1848, the refusal by the new Republic to aid Italian patriots struggling against the Papacy and Austria, the election to the presidency of

Louis-Napoleon Bonaparte, nephew of the emperor — all
of this shook the confidence of republican true believers
at a time when the forces of conservatism were regaining
control. On December 2, 1851, a new coup d'état put
an end to the ephemeral Second Republic, which had
provided so much hope a mere three years earlier. In
the name of universal suffrage and pan-European peace,
the new Bonaparte reestablished an empire (the Second
Empire) and took on the title of Napoleon III. Ironically,
a country that symbolized liberty renounced dreams of
political emancipation that other peoples continued to
deem inherently French.

1795

"The Republic of Letters Shall Give Birth to Republics"

October 25, 1795, saw the creation in Paris of the National
Institute, a learned society that would gather together
all the scientists, men of letters, and artists of the world.
Would the propagation of moral and political sciences
herald universal peace or imperial domination?

"Just as the vegetation of various parts of the globe acclimatizes
to each land despite the resistance of ground temperature,
so the institutions most useful to improving political bodies
also adapt there." On 7 Germinal Year IV (March 27, 1796),
presenting his thoughts on how best to perfect the political
sciences, on the occasion of a public lecture at the Institute, the
Abbé Grégoire, bishop of Blois, pledged that the principles
of the French Revolution would soon acclimate to the entire
planet. Grégoire, a former deputy who had fought to abolish
slavery and universalize the French language, refrained
from downplaying the sheer magnitude of the work to be
undertaken: "The two great principles of separation of powers
and of representation," he went on, "have thus far emerged in

but a few corners of the globe; elsewhere, they have made
fleeting inroads, and always as unwelcome intruders." Yet
by cultivating the science of governments, that science which
despots had willfully neglected and dissimulated in favor of
the agreeable and frivolous arts, morality would finally catch
up to enlightenment.

Grégoire made these remarks at a public lecture given
before the National Institute, which had been created
a few months earlier, in 1795. On 3 Brumaire Year IV
(October 25, 1795), a decree inspired by the philosopher
Nicolas de Condorcet had parted ways with the ancien
régime's academism by integrating the Institute into a
radically new project of public education. Elementary
schools as well as Écoles Centrales and Écoles Spéciales
would be linked together and crowned by the Institute.
At the heart of this framework was the Class of Moral and
Political Sciences (to which Grégoire belonged), situated
between the Class of Mathematics and Physics and the
Class of Literature and Arts. The Institute was to become
the beating heart of a planetary scientific body, bringing
together a "family" of scientists, men of letters, and artists
"scattered across the globe" through a "combined system
of vast correspondence." All of this would "accelerate the
circulation of thought and discovery," making way for a
fusion of languages. In this manner, promised Grégoire,
"the republic of letters [would] give birth to republics."

In order to become truly universal and serve others besides the powerful, this new science of man had to change in both form and content. History would no longer limit itself to accounts of conquest and princely marriages; rather, it would speak of the people and be written collectively, thanks to the contributions of local correspondents who would confer with village elders. Metaphysics would be replaced by a study of sensations and ideas grounded in physiology and analytic methods. Law would become social science and legislation. Morality would be freed from theology, and political economy would, in its republican incarnation, become "public economy." Even geography, traditionally in the service of conquerors, would shift its way of looking at the world. The description of a new island, asserted the geographer Philippe Buache on 22 Floréal Year IV (May 11, 1796), would no longer be "a title deed for the powers whose flag is on display." As "a Confederation unprecedented in history," the Institute would reorganize the world Republic of Letters with Paris as its center. Grégoire made clear, however, that those undertaking this endeavor were in no way aspiring to supremacy of any kind, since literary and scientific sovereignty was, like its political equivalent, by nature shared.

Reality proved somewhat trickier in a context where France had also resolved to defend the republic by force of arms. It was through war that the moral and political

717

sciences first spread. Louis-Marie-Joseph Maximilian Caffarelli du Falga, general in the republican army and nonresident member of the Analysis of Sensations and Ideas section, joined Napoleon's Egyptian expedition and died, sword in hand, in the Holy Land at the Siege of Acre in 1799. With other members of the Institute's second class (distributed among its six sections), he had contributed to founding the Institut d'Egypte, in which he held the first chair in political economy. Within the European sister republics of Italy, Switzerland, and the Netherlands, which republican troops had conquered, the introduction of moral and political sciences required that France find willing collaborators on the ground. Such was the case, in the Cisalpine Republic, of Francesco Soave, translator of Locke and member of the Classe di Scienze Morali e Politiche of the Istituto Nazionale Italiano, which was founded in Bologna in 1802.

Such intermediaries were not devoid of all critical thinking. Imposing moral and political sciences at gunpoint blatantly contradicted Grégoire's project, which held that everything should stem from scientific communication. Could knowledge alone, then, convert people? Analyzing the failure of the Neapolitan revolution in 1799, the Italian historian Vincenzo Cuoco contrasted France's all too universalizing and rationalist school to what he called the *scuola delle scienze morali e politiche italiana* of Machiavelli,

Gravina, and Vico — a school he considered more attentive to circumstances and popular emotions. In 1808, the Royal Society of Naples, founded for the new kingdom of Naples by Napoleon's brother Joseph and headed by the same Cuoco, included a third class of Scienze Morali, Politiche, ed Economiche, even though its French counterpart had been dissolved in 1803.

As instruments of imperial domination, the moral and political sciences could acclimate to other areas only by becoming more provincial. The Faculty of Moral and Political Sciences that was created in 1803 within the new Imperial University of Vilnius was a legacy of a former Polish university, now under Russian domination and reengineered by Alexander I. In choosing this title, in publicizing its public essay contests in French periodicals, and in inviting the Genevan Jean Charles Léonard de Sismondi to teach political economy, the Imperial University asserted its commitment to openness to the West. But it remained quite distinct from the Parisian second class in including theology in its version of moral and political science.

Paradoxically, it was in Great Britain, where Thomas Robert Malthus wrote his famous *Essay on the Principle of Population* (1798) against the "French" notion of infinite perfectibility, that moral science alternatives to the Paris model were elaborated and disseminated. In reaction to the Revolution's education agenda, the elite universities of Oxford and Cambridge were quick to reinstate the study of classical humanities in the late 1790s, or rather to reinvent them in favor of a natural theology that went on to function as Anglican moral science. Elsewhere, however, radical philosophers such as William Godwin and Jeremy Bentham echoed this French project of a science of human perfectibility. In Scotland, the common-sense philosophy of Thomas Reid and Dugald Stewart posited, for its part, a moral science that, while similar to the ideals of the French Revolution, also served the interests of the Whig party and the proponents of commercial expansion. In 1848 at Cambridge, a moral science tripos was founded that operated within an Anglican framework that gradually opened up to different traditions after 1860.

This institutional model of moral sciences, which was embedded in higher education rather than in the academies that now structured the Republic of Letters, had been tested in the Americas before taking root in England. In the late eighteenth century, the colleges that trained the new republican elites on the other side of the Atlantic borrowed from various European traditions while crafting their curricula. When Bernardino Rivadavia, then a government minister for the United Provinces of the Río de La Plata, recast the Colegio Unión del Sud (Buenos Aires) into the Colegio de Ciencias Morales, the College of Moral Sciences, in 1823, he drew on the ideas of two of his friends: Bentham and French philosopher Antoine Destutt de Tracy. This college was to become the seedbed to the future "generation of 1837" that struggled to free itself from Spanish cultural heritage as the provinces and surrounding territories came together as Argentina. In the United States, the prospects for brotherly commercial and philosophical ties with France were dashed with the 1797 presidential election of John Adams, hardly a Francophile. Thus, in East Coast colleges, the moral science course taught in the final year of study, most often by the president of the college himself, drew, depending on his religious orientation, from English and Scottish sources.

The opposition between these two institutional frameworks, one centered on academies and the other on universities, extended into the nineteenth century. In 1832, French Minister of Education François Guizot espoused a return to the spirit of the decree of 3 Brumaire Year IV, by founding the Academy of Moral and Political Sciences and, shortly thereafter, passing a major law on primary education and establishing a Committee on Historical and Scientific Works whose major task was to collect documentary traces of the national past. This time, moral and political sciences were less about conquering Europe than civilizing France. They would henceforward give priority to a national objective, shedding a part of their cosmopolitan ambitions. Still, the French academy model, founded on the establishment of a hierarchical caste of members, some full and others "correspondent," was often replicated. Entire academies, or academic sections devoted to the moral and political sciences, were established in Brussels (1843), Geneva (1853), Madrid (1857), Naples (1864), and Rome (1874).

Meanwhile, the university version of those sciences was disseminated overseas via Great Britain, where political economy, logic, moral philosophy, and law colleges held pride of place for the training of civil and colonial administrators. "Moral science" thus became, in the latter half of the nineteenth century, an important issue for institutions of higher education that were designed to train Indian elites. From the 1830s on, Scottish missionaries like Alexander Duff had marshaled this science into an instrument of regeneration for India — against Hindu "superstitions." In 1860, the manual of physician-philosopher John Abercrombie was introduced into the curriculum of the University of Calcutta. The notions it outlined on the intellectual powers of the Western subject were already familiar to India's educated classes in the country's large port cities. Having long kept up with trends in European thought, they knew how to put such notions at the service of their own struggle for rights and freedoms. In 1898, Kishori Lal Sarkar, judge at the High Court of

Calcutta, wrote *The Hindu System of Moral Science*, in which he proclaimed the existence within Hinduism of not only a metaphysics but also an independent moral philosophy.

Admittedly, everything did not unfold as a consequence of the institutional dynamics initiated in 1795. The writings of authors such as John Stuart Mill and Auguste Comte, who played a major role in developing this scholarly arena, circulated outside institutions explicitly devoted to moral science. In Germany, Mill's *System of Logic, Ratiocinative and Inductive* (1843) paved the way for the grand debate on the *Geisteswissenschaften* (sciences of spirit) at the turn of the century. In China, which Voltaire and Quesnay saw as the mythical land that originated moral science, translations of Mill and Comte coincided in the early twentieth century with attempts to assimilate Chinese intellectual heritage into an institutional framework for higher education that was imported from the West.

Despite its heterogeneous nature, the institutional web of moral science represented an important space of circulation for the human sciences until the late nineteenth century, when it was marginalized by the surge of "disciplines" fashioned within German and American research universities. If the world republic of moral science acquired such a wide purview, it is because it managed to transcend its Parisian origins.

Julien Vincent

REFERENCES

Bayly, Christopher A. *Recovering Liberties: Indian Thought in the Age of Liberalism and Empire*. Cambridge: Cambridge University Press, 2011.

Leterrier, Sophie-Anne. *L'Institution des sciences morales: L'Académie des sciences morales et politiques (1795–1850)*. Paris: L'Harmattan, 1995.

Mémoires de l'Institut national des sciences et arts, pour l'an IV de la République: Sciences morales et politiques. Paris: Baudouin imprimeur de l'Institut national, 1798.

Sartori, Andrew, and Samuel Moyn, eds. *Global Intellectual History*. New York: Columbia University Press, 2013.

Staum, Martin S. *Minerva's Message: Stabilizing the French Revolution*. Montreal: McGill-Queen's University Press, 1996.

RELATED ARTICLES
1380, 1751, 1793, 1815, 1891, 1903

1798

Conquest(s) of Egypt

Napoleon Bonaparte set out on May 19, 1798, from the port of Toulon at the helm of a three-hundred-and-fifty-ship expedition sailing for Egypt. However short-lived France's military conquest turned out, Egypt proved a tremendous testing ground for political and scientific "modernity."

The Institut d'Égypte in Cairo had an important announcement to make at its thirty-first session on 1 Thermidor Year VII, or July 29, 1799: a certain French engineer had made a chance discovery of a trilingual stela, or carved stone slab, during some work on fortifications in the foundations of a Mamluk-era fortress near the town of Rosetta (Rashid, in Arabic), east of the Bay of Abukir. Four days earlier, the French Army of the Orient had won the Battle of Abukir against Ottoman troops brought ashore by the British navy, at the very spot where this same English fleet had wiped out the flotilla that had dispatched Bonaparte and his army to Egypt a year earlier. The stela was transferred to

725

Cairo. In 1800, a preliminary study appeared in *La Décade égyptienne*, the Institute's periodical, produced on the first printing presses set up in Egypt by the French. And then, in the summer of 1801, right when it was about to be shipped off to France from Alexandria, accompanied by the members of the Arts and Sciences Commission that had sailed to Egypt with Bonaparte, the stela was confiscated, along with other treasures, by the English following French General Jacques-François de Menou's surrender. Ever since, it has been famously housed at the British Museum. The Rosetta Stone, with its triple transcription in hieroglyphics, demotic (the cursive script of ancient Egypt) and Greek, would allow Jean-François Champollion (or, as he fancied himself in Arabic, al-Saghir) to identify phonetic characters in certain hieroglyphs in 1822, paving the way for future decipherers of ancient Egyptian inscriptions.

In their own way, the Rosetta Stone's tribulations tell the story of how, in the late eighteenth century, a military, technical, and scientific venture gave birth, first, to the brief French occupation of Egypt (1798–1801), then to the protracted publication of a multivolume *Description de l'Égypte* (1809–1818), and finally to a special relationship between France and Egypt. This bond, rooted in a shared passion for Pharaonic civilization and yet much more complicated, has endured to the present.

The three-year Egyptian campaign was piloted by

Bonaparte from May 1798 until his return to France in October 1799, commanded by General Jean-Baptiste Kléber until his assassination in Cairo in May 1800, and then ended by General Jacques-François de Menou, a nobleman and Muslim convert also known as Abdallah de Menou, who was forced to surrender in Alexandria on August 30, 1801. But this was hardly just another episode among others in the serial warfare that pitted English against French on the world's seas since the mid-eighteenth century. When an invasion of England was judged too hazardous, the expedition that left the port of Toulon on May 19, 1798, seemed the next best thing, with its nearly three hundred vessels escorted by some fifty warships. The idea was to attack English interests by gaining control of a crucial leg on the passage to India. Pursued by Admiral Horatio Nelson's armada from Toulon to Malta to Alexandria, the French fleet was destroyed in the Bay of Abukir. It was aboard British vessels that Mamluk troops were transported from Istanbul, in a bid to bring Egypt back into the Ottoman fold; it was again aboard British ships that the vanquished French Army of the Orient sailed back home to Toulon. Egypt was forever the high-stakes prize of the Franco-English rivalry, whether it involved Thomas Young and Champollion vying for preeminence in deciphering hieroglyphics, or a few decades later, the bid for control of the Suez Canal.

But the Egyptian campaign also launched the wars that

France would be waging in the Middle East for the next century and a half, right up to the bombing of Damascus in May 1945 in the waning hours of the French mandate in Syria. The epic version of Napoleon's drive into Egypt unsurprisingly highlights his victory over the Mamluks at the Battle of the Pyramids on July 21, 1789. Egypt had been experiencing political disruption since 1775 due to clashes among rival Mamluk factions, those warriors that the Sublime Porte imported into Egypt from Georgia and Armenia in the venerable tradition of military slavery. Having freed themselves from Ottoman oversight, the Mamluks reigned over the local Egyptian population, who detested them and yearned for deliverance. The conditions were set for Bonaparte to step in as their liberator. Let us not forget, however, how prosperous the Mamluk government had become in the mid-eighteenth century, a prosperity that ushered Egypt into the era of modern capitalism.

The defeated Mamluks then entered into Bonaparte's service and were mobilized against their former paymasters, the Ottomans, who had sent troops to regain control of Egypt. Of the 1799 French expedition into Palestine, from Gaza to Acre, the imperial epic once again selectively remembers only the taking of Jaffa and Bonaparte's compassion for his plague-stricken soldiers. The massacre at the Jaffa garrison, the French defeat in Acre at the hands of Ahmad Pasha al-Jazzār ("The Butcher"), Bonaparte's desertion of wounded and plague victims, the scorched-earth return to Egypt, sparing only Gaza, which alone remained faithful to the French: all these episodes belong to the future emperor's dark legend.

But the campaign's harshest treatment was meted out in an altogether different theater, and its victims, neither Mamluk nor Ottoman, were noncombatants. On two separate occasions in October 1798, and again from March 20 to April 22, 1800, the population of Cairo rose up against the French, who brutally repressed the revolt, sparing no one, not even the *ulema* who had sought shelter in the Great Mosque of Al-Azhar University, which was then bombed by the occupying force. The *ulema*, learned clerics who had traditionally acted as go-betweens for their fellow Egyptians and the foreign rulers to whom they were beholden, had been co-opted into the Egyptian government by the French, who set up a *Divan*, or Council, where the grand *ulema* of Cairo would assemble. The first of these gatherings took place on July 25, 1798. This kind of assembly was in fact consistent with the Ottoman Empire's consultative tradition, but the context of the French occupation turned the Cairo *Divan* into an unprecedented political experiment, casting the *ulema* as representatives of the Egyptian nation. To be sure, the political modernity foisted upon Egypt by the French was neither consensual nor mutual. But on a practical level, from census-taking to traffic policing and law enforcement, from locally printed Arabic-language circulars and public notices to the protocols for celebrating the anniversary of the founding of the French Republic, the political culture that the French imported into Egypt was unquestionably modern.

Egypt proved particularly conducive to yet another modernity, technical this time. The one hundred and fifty members of the Sciences and Arts Commission who had sailed with Bonaparte in 1798 — engineers and graduates of the newly founded École Polytechnique school as well as printers, scientists, and artists — were expected to bolster the military expedition by devising means of exploiting the country's resources. This mission rested upon the conviction that modern technology would revive, within this ancient cradle of civilization, millennia-old scientific, industrial, and artistic knowledge that had been forgotten or corrupted over time. The *ulema* understood what was afoot. How could they not, given their interest in engineering projects, technical innovation (whether that meant wheelbarrows or windmills), and the scientific instruments, astronomical ones in particular, introduced by the French.

That said, the Institut d'Égypte was hardly a place in which knowledge was shared, even if the scholar Abd al-Rahman al-Jabarti, one of the most important chroniclers of his era, made use of its library. Rather, it was a place where knowledge could be co-produced. The engineers, artists, and scientists who made up its four sections (mathematics, physics and natural history, political economics, and finally literature and the arts, divisions modeled after France's National Institute) were to leverage the knowledge and skills of learned locals and artisans in the service of an extraordinary undertaking: an exhaustive description of the country, its topography and natural resources, and its inhabitants, with their customs and promising technologies such as mortar mills and proto-incubators for hens. Last but not least, the project inventoried the country's past and monumental remains, granting Islamic architecture the same pride of place as Pharaonic-era antiquities. In November 1799, the Institut d'Égypte decided to compile all of this information into a collective work, the *Description de l'Égypte*, which conferred equal dignity to all the bodies of knowledge about the country that the French had systematically gathered.

The *Description*'s timeline both precedes and exceeds that of the Egyptian campaign itself. The commission charged with its publication met for the first time in 1802, though the "imperial edition," the first volume of which appeared in 1809, was not completed until ten years later, under King Louis XVIII. The *Description* was grounded in a well-established scientific esprit dating back to its grand Enlightenment forerunner, the *Encyclopedia* (1751–1772). Divided into three parts — Natural History, Antiquities, and Modern State — its inventory had been prefigured in travel narratives such as Comte de Volney's *Voyage en Égypte et en Syrie*, published in 1787. But the *Description*, produced as it was in the wake of a French military campaign, was the first to marry scientific ambition, knowledge of the arts, and imperial conquest. In this regard, it laid the groundwork for later editorial projects, such as the *Exploration scientifique de l'Algérie*, published in 1844.

The outgrowth of scientific conquest proved immeasurably more beneficial than the bitter fruits of a fleeting military victory. But the real legacy of 1798 reads more like a love story. Beguiled by their ephemeral conquest, the French have ever since flocked to Egypt in search of a dream, an ideal, a new homeland. Throughout the nineteenth century, engineers, doctors, and architects would devote the best years of their lives to the push for modernization initiated by Muhammad Ali Pasha and carried forward by his descendants. French orientalists made a major contribution to the science of Egyptology, understood as the study of the civilizations that had followed one another along the banks of the Nile. The Museum of Egyptian Antiquities, the Middle East's first archaeological museum, was founded in 1858 by Auguste Mariette, a Frenchman who spent a quarter century in the service of the khedive of Egypt as director of antiquities. He would end his days in his country of adoption, where his remains rest in a modern sarcophagus in the Cairo museum garden.

Julien Loiseau

REFERENCES

Bourguet, Marie-Noëlle, Daniel Nordman, Vassilis Panayotopoulos, and Maroula Sinarellis, eds. *Enquêtes en Méditerranée: Les expéditions françaises d'Égypte, de Morée et d'Algérie*. Athens: Institut de recherches néohelléniques de la Fondation nationale de la recherche scientifique, 1999.

Laurens, Henry. *L'Expédition d'Égypte (1798–1801)*. Paris: Le Seuil, 1997.

Parkinson, Richard, et al. *Cracking Codes: The Rosetta Stone and Decipherment*. London: British Museum Press, 1999.

Pouillon, François, ed. *Dictionnaire des orientalistes de langue française*. Paris: IISMM-Karthala, 2008.

Raymond, André. *Égyptiens et Français au Caire (1798–1801)*. Le Caire: Institut français d'archéologie orientale, 1998.

Solé, Robert, and Dominique Valbelle. *La Pierre de Rosette*. Paris: Le Seuil, 1999.

RELATED ARTICLES

1804

Many Nations under One Code of Law

On March 21, 1804, two months before France emerged
as an empire, Napoleon issued a law rounding up separate
"civil laws into a single body." This demiurgical decision
was a tactic. Using the law as a tool, Napoleon sought to
conquer a form of universal sovereignty. Future iterations
of what became known as the Napoleonic Code would
ensure its global reputation into the twentieth century.

March 21, 1804: a new law merged thirty-six civil legislative
texts adopted under the French Consulate into what the
legislators called "a single body of laws, under the title
Civil Code of the French People." Much is said in the
wide-ranging Code, which comprised 2,281 sequentially
numbered articles and, though technical in form, reached
beyond strictly civil matters while repealing Roman laws
and rolling back royal ordinances and customs. Although all
of the Code's thirty-six laws had been enacted on separate
dates, the history of their application as a unified body began
on that 21 of March — eight days after Napoleon adopted a

measure to reinstate the study of law and two months before the Napoleonic Empire was established. On that day, the Civil Code was implemented throughout the departments then making up France (eighty-three created in 1790, nine in present-day Belgium and Luxembourg, the department of Léman and Geneva, four in the Rhine, and six in Piedmont). Across the land, it cleared the legal slate. From then on, a single civil law applied to the French people.

That did not mean, however, that this new legislation was democratic. Indeed, Bonaparte had forced otherwise recalcitrant lawmakers into adopting the Code, personally attending half the assembly meetings where the matter was to be discussed. The emperor's commitment to this process was rewarded when the law became known as the "Napoleonic Code" in 1807. From then on, his name would be associated and dissociated with the Code in step with his reputation's rise and fall. In 1814, once the Bourbons had regained power, the Code was "rid of the usurper's name" only to be reinstated in 1854 under Napoleon III, before falling out of usage again in 1870, when France became a Republic again. Private publishers, who had made a fortune off the text, eventually settled on a name adopted by all legal scholars: the Civil Code.

It is important to emphasize that this was indeed a "Civil Code for the French People," applying to all of France. To be sure, it was not the first French legal code, a title which

735

goes to the Penal Code of 1791. But it was the first code in the world to be established on the basis of nationality (the "French quality," as expressed at the time), and not on that of residence. Unsurprisingly, given that France was again at war with England in 1804, the new law was rather restrictive when it came to the civil rights of foreigners. In civil matters, the Code unified "French law," an expression dating back to the sixteenth century to speak of all Roman rules, customs, and canonical doctrine that, together with royal legislation, formed the legal apparatus used under the French monarchy. Until March 21, 1804, French law could be described as a mosaic of documents and internal jurisdictions. With the Code, that piecemeal legal system was absorbed into a single civil document.

The Civil Code is inconceivable as a French document without the French Revolution. The prerevolutionary monarchy never would have dared meddle with a long-standing distinction between customary and written law. Nor would it have undermined the privileges enjoyed by members of the clergy or aristocracy. Even legal experts did not begin to speak of codifying civil law before 1789: Jean Domat, Robert Joseph Pothier, and other jurists never so much as dreamed of a civil code. Only utopians familiar with the work of Frederick II of Prussia (like revolutionist Honoré Gabriel Riqueti de Mirabeau) would have entertained such a thought. The French Constituent Assembly made the development of a civil code into a constitutional objective when it stated in the Declaration of the Rights of Man and of the Citizen that law was "the expression of general will," and "the same for all, in protection and punishment." Indeed, the French Constitution of 1791 proclaims, "A Code of civil laws common to all the Kingdom shall be made."

The performative power of law did not mean, however, that this desire to establish a cohesive legal code yielded substantive law at once. Revolutionary lawmakers proved incapable of adopting any of the three code proposals put forward by statesman Jean Jacques Régis de Cambacérès. Nevertheless, the French Revolution paved the way for a consolidated Civil Code that abolished the feudal system (more radically than elsewhere in Europe), secularized marriage, instituted divorce, emancipated Jews, acknowledged the rights of children born out of wedlock, established free trade, authorized loan interests, and organized a judicial system under the aegis of the Court of Cassation (a high-instance court). Generations of French nationals have embraced this legacy each time they have cast their ballots.

The Napoleonic Code did roll back some of the reforms gained by the French Revolution. It leaned on old aristocratic institutions and borrowed from both longstanding customary law and written laws. But it did so as a means of bridging divides between traditionalists and modernists and marrying the customary laws of Northern France with the written laws of Southern France. Article 8 — "All French people shall enjoy civil rights" — is a clear reference to article 6 of the Declaration of the Rights of Man of 1789. Both texts were molded out of the French language and both show a semantic and symbolic wealth that does not cease to amaze.

Looking beyond France, legal historians situate the French Civil Code between the Prussian Civil Code of 1794 and the Austrian Civil Code of 1811. Although it is considered to be part of this "first wave of codifications," the French Civil Code features unique, almost incomparable characteristics. Later, Max Weber would see it as an archetype of codification and even, at least for the nineteenth century, as an outer limit of possibility.

In 1804, the French Civil Code began to spread outside of France's traditional borders. Its jurisdiction covered all the departments of the French empire from Hamburg to Rome, with one odd exception: the small Swiss town of Simplon. Napoleon put pressure on his vassal states to adopt it as well. While he succeeded in Italy and Poland (excluding civil marriage), his influence was more limited in Germany. Napoleon never attempted to introduce it in Spain. An 1814 cartoon shows Napoleon and his "brethren" headed for Elba Island, a Civil Code tucked under his arm. By 1814, the Code's influence was waning, but it was still in force in the

Netherlands (until 1838, when a Dutch Code was written). And despite that new code, independent Belgium (1830) and Luxembourg embraced the French Code. Residents of Prussian Rhineland and Bernese Jura fought for nearly a century for the Civil Code to be applied there.

Naples, Parma, Piedmont, many Swiss cantons, and other Restoration regimes copied parts of the Civil Code, but left out its most revolutionary measures, including civil marriage and equal inheritance rights. As early as 1808, the Napoleonic Code inspired the state of Louisiana's civil code. In 1816, it was introduced in Haiti, even though the nation had risen up against France in 1804, becoming the first republic established by former slaves. In 1828, a small group of anonymous legal experts in the state of Oaxaca translated a slightly modified version of the Civil Code into Spanish. It was subsequently adopted there, paving the way for the further influence of the French Code throughout Latin America. The Code also inspired Quebec's Civil Code in 1866. And in 1859, on the Italian Peninsula, when a war against the Austrian Empire proved instrumental in the country's unification, the French Code was adopted to jubilant fanfare: "Long live the kingdom of Italy, long live Victor Emmanuel, king of Italy, long live the Napoleonic Code!" Italian lawmakers would rely on this document as they drafted their own Italian Civil Code of 1865.

At the same time, the Napoleonic Code received

sharp criticism from the German Historical School of Jurisprudence and legal scholars such as Friedrich Carl von Savigny. Burned at nationalist gatherings, the document was the subject of heated debate in early-to-mid-nineteenth-century Germany. Hegel cited it as an example; Marx, who lived under its jurisdiction in Rhineland, saw it as a case of legislation co-opted by the bourgeoisie. By the time the German and Swiss Civil Codes were written, the influence of the French Code was on the decline. In other cases, such as Japan in 1896 and Turkey in 1926, it was combined with new models.

Although France refused to apply the Civil Code to "natives" and "subjects" of its colonies, the influence of the Code spread with French imperial conquests in Africa and Asia. The French mandate in Lebanon (1920–1946) gave birth to a Code of Obligations and Contracts in 1932. And although the British may have taken Saint Lucia from France in 1804, its Civil Code of 1879 was based on Quebec's. Meanwhile, Pondicherry's residents, having renounced Hindu law during the colonial period, are still ruled by the French Civil Code.

To speak of the present day: since 2012, several dozen Lebanese couples desiring a civil marriage and finding obstacles in religious law have asked notaries to apply the Civil Code, which has not been repealed since the French mandate. A story of globalization could be pieced together from the places touched by the Civil Code. Which is not to say, of course, that the Code has not come under attack, for instance during the recent controversies on gay marriage in France. Ultimately, the Code's afterlives tell a double story of social change and enduring symbolic resonance within and beyond French borders. After all, the Code was the first document to establish our right to marry the person of our choosing.

Jean-Louis Halpérin

REFERENCES

Audren, Frédéric, and Jean-Louis Halpérin. *La culture juridique française: Entre mythes et réalités (XIXe–XXe siècle)*. Paris: CNRS Éditions, 2013.

Caroni, Pio. *Saggi sulla storia della codificazione*. Milan: Giuffrè Editore, 1998.

Halpérin, Jean-Louis. "Deux cents ans de rayonnement du *Code civil des Français?*" *Les Cahiers de droit* 46, nos. 1–2 (2005): 229–51.

———. *L'Impossible Code civil*. Paris: Presses Universitaires de France, 1992.

Martin, Xavier. *Mythologie du Code Napoléon: Aux soubassements de la France moderne*. Bouère: Editions Dominique Martin Morin, 2003.

1804

The Coronation of Napoleon Bonaparte

As an iconic moment in the history of France, the coronation of Napoleon stands alone. The events that took place at Notre-Dame Cathedral married historical memories of Charlemagne's own coronation with nascent modern political strategies. Still, by consigning the imperial title to a dynasty — his own — Napoleon Bonaparte nevertheless made his own contribution to the dismantling of the notion of universal empire.

On Sunday, December 2, 1804, 11 Frimaire Year XIII of the French Republic, shortly after the stroke of noon, Emperor Napoleon and Empress Joséphine, followed by a grandiose train of people, proceeded up the nave of Notre-Dame in Paris to the strains of Jean-François Le Sueur's "Marche du sacre" (Coronation March). Twelve thousand guests, for the most part government officials, crowded the cathedral's galleries. When the imperial couple arrived at the chancel, they settled in their chairs whilst Pope Pius VII descended

742

from the throne on which he had been waiting patiently to sing the hymn "Veni Creator Spiritus." This done, Napoleon and his wife divested themselves of their imperial trappings, which were laid on the altar. After an interval of prayer, they knelt before the pope, who anointed them three times with holy unction before performing high mass. Napoleon then seized one imperial insignia after another: the ring, the sword, the coronation robe, the baton topped by the Hand of Justice, and finally the scepter. He passed the Hand of Justice to his archchancellor and the scepter to his archtreasurer, then went to the altar, took the circlet of golden laurels in his hands, turned to the congregation, and placed it on his own head.

Then came the moment immortalized by Jacques-Louis David in his famous painting: Napoleon grasped in his hands the laurel coronet of the kneeling Joséphine, stood before her, and crowned her in turn.

Descending now from the altar, Napoleon took back his scepter and Hand of Justice and recrossed the nave to a tall throne close to the cathedral entrance, while the choir sang *Vivat imperator in aeternum*. After repeating the same invocation to the Almighty, Pope Pius sang a Te Deum for good measure and continued with his mass, which came to an end at 3 p.m.

When Pius VII had at last withdrawn to the sacristy, the emperor laid his hand on the Bible and pronounced the constitutional oath: "I swear to preserve the integrity of the Republic, to respect the rules of the Concordat [France's 1801 treaty signed with the Holy See] and of freedom of worship and ensure they are obeyed; to respect and ensure respect for equality under the law, political and civil liberty, and the irrevocability of all sales of nationalized property [during the French Revolution]; neither to raise existing taxes nor to levy new ones other than according to the law; to maintain the institution of the Legion of Honor; to govern with no concern other than the best interest, happiness, and glory of the French people."

Whereupon the principal herald solemnly proclaimed: "The most glorious and august Emperor of the French is hereby crowned and enthroned. *Vive l'Empereur!*"

"*Vive l'Empereur!*" dutifully responded twelve thousand voices.

There have been many descriptions, both official and independent, of this extravagant ceremony. All are slightly at variance as to the detail of what took place, which was anything but spontaneous, and the attitude of the people who were present. Some depicted Napoleon as pale, somber, and deeply moved; others described him as a fastidious despot fearful that the holy unguents would stain his clothes, struggling to stop himself yawning during the interminable mass. The official reports related the enthusiasm of the crowd, the glittering sunshine that miraculously flooded through the cathedral windows when the emperor crossed the nave. Less friendly witnesses focused on the blunders that occurred, real or otherwise, many of which have survived to amuse posterity. While carrying Joséphine's train, one of Napoleon's sisters sulked, another buried her nose in smelling salts, and the third tugged the material so hard that her sister-in-law nearly fell over backwards. Napoleon fumbled badly when adjusting his wife's diadem, while the public appeared more gleefully agog than awestruck by the proceedings.

Worst of all, the ceremony went on so long that many of the guests were seen to pull food from their pockets and snack as they watched. Even Pope Pius was not spared by the onlookers: Jean Jacques Régis de Cambacérès, who had been second consul under Napoleon, chided: "One could have wished that the pope's expression had been a trifle more dignified. It displayed nothing but resignation and impatience." Napoleon himself had told his council of state shortly before the ceremony: "From the sublime to the ridiculous is only a step." Before being celebrated by David's sumptuously sycophantic painting, the imperial coronation was brutally satirized by the English caricaturist James Gillray, who depicted it as a gigantic farce.

Of course it was easy to jeer at the outlandishness of this ceremony. With the age-old coronations of French monarchs at Rheims and the solemn rituals of enthronement

745

made familiar by the Capets as a backdrop, the upstart emperor claimed an imaginary Carolingian heritage, with Pope Pius VII expected to consecrate him in 1804 in the same manner that Leo III had crowned the Holy Roman Emperor Charlemagne, formerly King of the Franks, in 800. The resultant ceremonial was a hodgepodge of French and Roman ritual, the result of long negotiations between the Holy See and Napoleon's government. The décor of Notre-Dame on the day was partly neo-antique (eagles, trophies, and triumphal arches), partly neo-Gothic (the porch set up by the architects Percier and Fontaine before the façade of Notre-Dame was one of the earliest examples of the style). The goal of all this was to exalt the Catholic Church and the new monarchy while embracing the conquests of the French Revolution: nationalized property, freedom of worship, a pledge to put all taxation to the vote. "I reflected much on this crass alliance of charlatans, on religion crowning tyranny in the name of human happiness," wrote Stendhal in disgust.

Yet the coronation of Napoleon in December 1804, like the Concordat between the Vatican and France and like the empire itself, did not emerge from some kind of nostalgia for the ancien régime. The venture was both realistic and rational. Like most of the political theorists of the preceding century, Napoleon considered that republican rule was only suitable for smaller states. Great nations needed something altogether grander. Monarchy, for the emperor, was the best guarantee of unity of action, continuity of power, and institutional solidity. The rest was no more than ideological hot air, as he was wont to say of philosophical and liberal ideas. He was convinced that the empire would ensure a living legacy for the Revolution's achievements much better than a republic ever would. This was the essence of a speech Napoleon delivered as first consul to a group of deputies and senators who had been given the task of ensuring "the heredity of the supreme magistrate." Much the same thing was proposed to him by Second Consul Cambacérès when he reported the *senatus consultum* (senate decree) of May 18, 1804, to First Consul Bonaparte and proclaimed him Emperor of the French even before the text had been approved by popular vote. When a plebiscite was eventually held, its result — made public on August 2 — was 3,521,625 in favor and 2,579 against.

Napoleon's legitimacy as emperor of the Republic proceeded from a senate decree and a plebiscite, in the same way that the legitimacy of the former kings of France proceeded from their royal birthright. An imperial coronation added luster in the eyes of the nation. The emperor agreed with Voltaire that the people needed religion to hold them together. He took the title of emperor because it was "more grand" than the title of king, because it eluded rational explanation and provided "something that awes the imagination." A coronation on this scale would hence endow his power with an aura of mystery. As a ruler, Napoleon's rationale was that his subjects seldom obeyed reason.

But historians make a big mistake if they think this explanation covers everything. Obviously, the evolution of France's first consul into an emperor satisfied Napoleon's own insatiable lust for the material advantages and symbolic satisfactions that power procured. The senate decree of May 18, 1804, installed not only a supreme hereditary lawgiver, but also a dynasty and an imperial court, with their distinctive pomp and circumstance. Imperial rank was declared hereditary in the male line of Napoleon himself, and in the event he had no issue, in that of his brothers Louis and Joseph. The sum appropriated annually to pay the expenses of the emperor and his household was fixed at the same level as that of Louis XVI — 25 million francs a year. The members of the imperial family took the title of "princes of the French." The senate decree instituted grand dignitaries and officers of the empire, both civil and military, who were the embryos of a new nobility. The seven most powerful officials of the empire all belonged to Napoleon's immediate family and entourage: Joseph Bonaparte, grand elector; Louis Bonaparte, constable; Cambacérès, archchancellor of the empire; Cardinal Joseph Fesch, high almoner of the empire and Napolean's uncle;

Charles-François Lebrun, archtreasurer; Joachim Murat (the emperor's brother-in-law), high admiral; Eugène de Beauharnais (the emperor's adopted son), archchancellor of state. The Bonaparte family, enriched as it was by various skullduggeries during the mid-1790s, continued its steady ascent, not so much on account of the supposed talents of its members as because it was the only group on whose loyalty Napoleon felt he could depend. Thereafter the family became inseparable from its head, who abandoned the name Bonaparte for that of Napoleon and obtained from the same senate decree absolute authority over his relatives. Finally, there would be "an organization of the Imperial Palace in accordance with the dignity of the throne and the greatness of the nation." The way was open for a brand new court to thrive.

Napoleon's preference for the title of emperor over that of king, the allusion to Charlemagne, and the splendor of the coronation foreshadowed, beyond the French Empire, the Grand Empire of 1806 onward. Imperial France's first task was to replace the crumbling Holy Roman Empire as the principal power in the hierarchy of European states. Accordingly, under pressure from the French, the Holy Roman Empire disappeared completely in 1806, and the former Holy Roman emperor's title was limited to the hereditary emperorship of Austria. There were no limits to Napoleon's ambition: he saw himself as master of Europe and the world, as well as sovereign of France. "I am Charlemagne," he wrote grandly to his uncle, Cardinal Fesch, on January 7, 1806. In his federative system, the Grand Empire embraced France itself along with a cluster of client states, at the heads of which were placed the princes of his family or those allied to it. Napoleon made himself King of Italy, "Protector" of the Confederation of the Rhine and "Mediator" of the Swiss Confederation; Joseph was King of Naples and then Spain; Louis, King of Holland; Jerome, King of Westphalia; Eliza, Princess of Lucca and Piombino, and then Grand Duchess of Tuscany; Pauline, Princess of Guastalla; Murat and his wife Caroline, Grand Duke and Grand Duchess of Berg and then King and Queen of Naples. It never entered Napoleon's mind that any of these puppet sovereigns might have wills of their own or take any action independent of him.

With time, Napoleon began to believe in his quasi-legitimacy as a divine right, viewing the Bonaparte dynasty as a fourth royal line after those of the Merovingians, Carolingians, and Capetians. As the years went by, reminders of the dark, revolutionary origins of his power became less and less agreeable to him. On November 11, 1812, during the retreat from Moscow, he wrote to Cambacérès from Smolensk, outlining a project for a "solemn and religious" ceremony in the church of Les Invalides, during which a pronouncement would be made

750

with a view to reestablishing in all its purity the fundamental maxim of monarchy: "In France the King never dies."

The magician had finally been taken in by his own magic.

Thierry Sarmant

REFERENCES

Cabanis, José. *Le Sacre de Napoléon (2 décembre 1804)*. Paris: Gallimard, 2007.

Cambacérès, Jean-Jacques Régis de. *Mémoires inédits.* Présentation et notes de Laurence Chatel de Brancion. Paris: Perrin, 1999.

Lentz, Thierry, ed. *Le Sacre de Napoléon (2 décembre 1804)*. Paris: Nouveau Monde, 2003.

Sarmant, Thierry, Florian Meunier, Charlotte Duvette, and Philippe de Carbonnières, eds. *Napoléon et Paris: Rêves d'une capitale*. Paris: Paris Musées, 2015.

RELATED ARTICLES
800, 1763, 1921

1808

Napoleon and Spain: An Atlantic Affair

In January 1808, Napoleon's armies swarmed southward
across the Pyrenees. It was the beginning of an occupation
that lasted until 1814 and devastated the Spanish monarchy.
In the longer term, the Napoleonic invasion of Spain
changed the face of Spanish America, prompting a liberal
backlash and creating new republics.

In San Sebastián, in the Spanish Basque country, every 20th
of January there is a great festival during which townspeople
wearing the uniforms of early nineteenth-century soldiers
thump on empty barrels and sing the "Marcha de San
Sebastián." The *tamborrada* parade, as it is called, dates
back to the Napoleonic invasion; it commemorates the
"War of the French" of 1808–1814. On the other side of the
Pyrenees, this war has been more or less forgotten — largely
because the French lost — but in Spain its lasting upheavals
remain very much alive in popular memory. In the wake
of the invasion, the Spanish monarchy became the theater
of a liberal revolution that led, in unexpected ways, to the

independence of every region of the Spanish Empire of America, with the exception of Cuba.

When Napoleon's legions tramped across his border, Carlos IV had been on the throne of Spain for two decades. Though indecisive and pusillanimous, the king was fixated on the idea of preventing the spread of French revolutionary ideas in his realm. His prime minister and favorite, Manuel Godoy, had nonetheless negotiated a diplomatic rapprochement with France after the War of the Pyrenees of 1793–1795. The Franco-Spanish Treaty of San Ildefonso, signed on August 17, 1796, established a military alliance against Great Britain, a common enemy of Spain and France. Carlos IV's goal with this treaty was to protect his American possessions, whereas the French needed a counterbalance to the strong alliance between Britain and Portugal. After a first conflict with Britain that lasted from 1796 to 1802, the European war resumed in 1805 and almost immediately brought about a shocking disaster for Spain. The greater part of the royal fleet was utterly destroyed at Trafalgar on October 21, cutting off all communications with Spain's empire — or rather, its colonial possessions.

In November 1806, Napoleon, now Emperor of the French, set up his Continental System, a blockade whereby neutrals and allies of France were forbidden to trade with Great Britain thus (hopefully) bringing the "nation of shopkeepers" to its knees. Two years later, the need to extend his blockade to the whole of Europe convinced him to invade Portugal. This required the cooperation of Spain. Applying the secret terms of the 1807 Treaty of Fontainebleau with King Carlos, French troops entered Spanish territory in January 1808. But instead of marching across the country to invade Portugal as promised, the French army turned aside to secure the strategic strongholds of Pamplona and Barcelona. At the beginning of March, Marshal Joachim Murat's army marched on Madrid: by then it had become crystal clear that Carlos IV's unreliable ally had betrayed him.

Weakened and discredited by this setback, the Spanish monarchy began to totter. On March 18, the enemies of Godoy — led by Prince Ferdinand, the heir to the throne — launched a palace revolution. Godoy fled, and Carlos was forced to abdicate in favor of his son. On March 23, Ferdinand entered Madrid to a triumphal welcome.

Napoleon's lightning response to this dynastic crisis was to make Spain another client state of his empire. At the beginning of May, he summoned the members of the Spanish royal family to Bayonne, where both Ferdinand and his father were compelled to abdicate in favor of Joseph Bonaparte, the emperor's brother.

For the people of Spain, this double abdication was a cruel humiliation. Overnight, their country had become, in their own words, an orphan or even a monster, with a foreign head grafted to its body, infested by deeply unpopular and feared French soldiery. The figure of Napoleon himself now fitted all the wicked stereotypes of the French revolutionaries, especially in their attitude to religion. The Revolution, it must be remembered, had turned Catholic priests into civil servants, whereas Napoleon was excommunicated by the pope in June 1808. Out of loyalty to the old system of monarchy but also out of necessity, the Spanish authorities rallied reluctantly to the new King "José I," earning themselves the contemptuous title of *afrancesados*, the Spanish equivalent of collaborators. Initially, Joseph set out to change the nature of Spanish government root and branch. To do this he appointed a constituent assembly, the Cortes of Bayonne, which gave Spain its first written constitution. But this constitution was never enforced: hamstrung by his dictatorial brother who did not hesitate to intervene forcefully in Spanish affairs whenever he chose, and by the presence of a bevy of powerful French generals who refused to obey his orders without consulting Napoleon himself, Joseph signally failed to become king of all the Spaniards.

His difficulties came to a head when the people of Madrid rose against the French.

The savage repression that ensued would be famously immortalized by the painter Francisco Goya in his depiction of a firing squad, *The Third of May 1808*. Thereafter the principal cities of the country joined the capital in intermittent rebellion. Prominent citizens across Spain formed government assemblies, or juntas, which claimed the right to govern in the place of the absent king. This ambition was based on an ancient but still relevant rule that if the legitimate monarch was prevented from governing, his sovereignty reverted to the communities or *pueblos* that formed the body of his realm. A provisional government, the Supreme Central Junta, was formed on this basis on September 25, 1808.

On the pretext of protecting the rights of the king, a liberal revolution was soon under way. A constituent assembly, the Cortes, met in Cádiz at the end of September 1810, in a context that was rendered precarious — to say the least — by the presence nearby of French troops ravaging Andalusia. Among the hundred or so Cortes deputies elected by the free cities, the representatives of the occupied regions of Spain, and the Spanish American colonies, only a handful of radicals gathered around the poet Manuel Quintana were directly inspired by the French Revolution. Nevertheless, the turmoil in Cádiz made it possible for them to impose their ideas: the Cortes would welcome individual representatives (rather than social orders such as the clergy or nobility); the assembly was constituent by nature; and its first act was a declaration of national sovereignty. After this, the Cortes adopted several important measures (freedom of the press, abolition of feudal rights, sale of the property and effects of religious and military orders) and endowed the monarchy, in March 1812, with the Constitution of Cádiz (otherwise known as "La Pepa"), which became a model for liberal Europe. Until the end of the war, in December 1813, the Cortes set about reforming the monarchy in a way that was partly inspired by the ideals of the French Revolution — that is to say, the relatively moderate ideals of 1789 rather than the more radical ones of 1792, which led to the decapitation of the French king and queen.

Meanwhile, Spanish America felt the repercussions of the crisis of the Spanish monarchy. The news of the French invasion in 1808 caused deep anxiety and contradictory reactions in the colonies. Nevertheless the dominant sentiment was redoubled loyalty to the crown, along with a determination to protect the Catholic religion and the possessions and the rights of the king. In every province of the empire, Ferdinand VII was acclaimed and the Central Junta was recognized as a substitute for his authority. The proclamation of equality between these two elements of monarchy worked in favor of such a solution, which was considered most legitimate.

But all this fell apart in 1810 with the invasion of Andalusia by the French, the dissolving of the Central Junta, and the general conclusion that the Spanish peninsula was now lost. The idea that the monarchy itself could break with Europe, escape Napoleon's clutches, and survive in South America began to gain traction. Between April and September 1810, the capitals of the overseas regions (Caracas, Buenos Aires, Santiago, Bogotá) formed juntas of their own that rejected the authority of the Regency Council and the Cortes. Other cities, notably the imperial bastions of Lima and Mexico, persisted in their loyalty to the authorities of the peninsula. Thus the former Spanish Empire became a patchwork in which autonomous and loyalist cities and regions fought one another. From this standpoint, the wars of colonial independence were above all civil wars between American former subjects of the Spanish king, divided between supporters of absolutism and the status quo, and partisans of change and self-government.

Just as it had in peninsular Spain, the devolving of sovereignty onto the *pueblos* offered basic legitimacy to the new regimes and brought about the rise of liberal principles in the Americas. This happened along lines peculiar to the Hispanic world. Far from being inspired by the French Revolution, *libertadores* like Simón Bolívar and José de San Martín were firm Spanish liberals. Witness in Paris to the rise of Bonaparte between 1802 and 1806, Bolívar was appalled by his coronation as emperor. San Martín fought Napoleon's armies as an officer of the Spanish army; the self-proclaimed emperor, and San Martín's own experience of Jacobin excesses, inspired in San Martín nothing but contempt.

With the exception of a few isolated cases, it was not from revolutionary France but from liberal Great Britain and liberal Spain that the patriotic elites drew their references, which were colored by traditional attitudes and a fierce attachment to the Catholic faith. The ideals of liberty and equality, dramatized worldwide by the events in Haiti, were much cherished by both the enslaved and free blacks of the Caribbean coastal countries of Venezuela and Colombia, so much so that white slaveholders and landlords began to fear a possible race war. The sovereignty of the people was on the march; revolutionary governments were consolidating power by broadening political representation and organizing elections. Assemblies were formed and constitutions adopted; patriotic regions followed the lead of Venezuela in 1811, declaring independence one after another. Even in the loyalist camp, the application of the Constitution of Cádiz after 1812 made possible the further spread of liberal principles.

In a distant but thunderous echo of the War of the French, by 1814 all Spanish America was convulsed by revolution. By contrast, the end of the European conflict and the return of the Spanish monarchy disappointed many. When the longed-for King Ferdinand VII returned to claim his throne in Spain, instead of endorsing the reforms that had been made in his name, he swept them away with a stroke of his pen and let it be known that he thought the American patriots no better than rebels. Counterrevolutionaries saw this as a sign of a return to order, especially when Ferdinand contemplated sending military expeditions of reinforcement and reconquest to the other side of the Atlantic.

It was too late, however. Although much weakened, the armies of San Martín in the South and Bolívar in the North held the initiative. Within a few years all the Spanish regions of South America had been liberated. Finally, in 1820, a liberal revolution broke out among the soldiers of an expeditionary force that was about to embark for South America, forcing the king to reestablish the constitution and the Cortes. The following year, Mexico declared its independence and its support for the anticlerical politics of the Cortes while Peru, the last redoubt of royalist Spain, was "liberated" and constrained to independence by San Martín's army in the 1820s.

But even as these new South American republics were rising from the ruins of the Spanish empire, a French expedition into Spain — the "Hundred Thousand Sons of Saint Louis," sent by King Louis XVIII to support his royal cousin Ferdinand VII in April 1823 — brought an end to this liberal interval and made possible the reestablishment of absolutism in the mother country.

Events had come full circle. The occupation of Spain by Napoleon's troops in 1808 had had the direct, paradoxical consequence of bringing about the sovereignty of the people, new liberal regimes, and the birth of independent nations in South America — all from the womb of a Spanish monarchy that since 1789 had remained steadfastly aloof from the "excesses" of the French Revolution.

Geneviève Verdo

REFERENCES

Busaall, Jean-Baptiste. *Le spectre du jacobinisme: L'expérience constitutionnelle de la Révolution française et le premier libéralisme espagnol (1808–1814)*. Madrid: Casa de Velázquez, 2012.

Demélas, Marie-Danielle, and François-Xavier Guerra. "The Hispanic Revolutions: The Adoption of Modern Forms of Representation in Spain and America (1808–1810)." In *Elections Before Democracy: The History of Elections in Europe and Latin America*, edited by Eduardo Posada-Carbó, 33–60. London: Palgrave Macmillan, 1996.

Gomez, Alejandro E. *Le spectre de la Révolution noire: L'impact de la Révolution haïtienne dans le monde atlantique, 1990–1886*. Rennes: Presses Universitaires de Rennes, 2013.

Guerra, François-Xavier. "Révolution française et révolutions hispaniques, filiations et parcours." *Problèmes d'Amérique latine* 94 (1989): 3–26.

Hamnett, Brian. *The End of Iberian Rule on the American Continent, 1770–1830*. Cambridge: Cambridge University Press, 2017.

Hocquellet, Richard. *Résistance et révolution durant l'occupation napoléonienne en Espagne, 1808–1812.* Paris: La Boutique de l'Histoire, 2001.

Rodriguez, Jaime E. *The Independence of Spanish America.* New York: Cambridge University Press, 1998.

RELATED ARTICLES

1889, 1973

1815

Museums of Europe, Year Zero

After the fall of the Napoleonic Empire in 1815, France
returned much of the artistic heritage it had seized
across Europe after the revolutionary victories. Still, this
restructuring of the "universal museum" allowed the
Louvre to convince the rest of the world that it was the first
public museum in the West and also the template for its
newly national counterparts.

> The same feelings which induce the people of
> France to wish to retain the pictures and statues of
> other nations would naturally induce other nations,
> now that success is on their side, to seek the return of
> artistic objects to their rightful owners....Besides, it
> is desirable for France's happiness and the world's
> that the country understand that, regardless of the
> partial and momentary domination it wielded over
> other European powers, the day of restitution must
> come.
>
> — The Duke of Wellington, 1815

The summer of 1815 was filled with dread and uncertainty — with the Congress of Vienna concluding on June 9, ultimate defeat for Napoleon at Waterloo on June 18, lingering doubts about the emperor's surrender until mid-July, and allied armies occupying Paris and the galleries of the Louvre, which had been renamed the Napoleon Museum in 1803. Through November, thousands of works of art were making their way along the roads of continental Europe. In a letter dated September 23, 1815, while the tyrant was sailing down the Atlantic on the *Northumberland* (he wouldn't arrive at Saint Helena until October 15), the Duke of Wellington sanctioned the ransom of victory. In the absence of formal diplomatic negotiation on the subject, the words he addressed to Lord Castlereagh, secretary of state for foreign affairs to the British crown, constituted the sole justification for taking back, with no prior warning, the "artistic conquests" of the Revolution and First Empire.

By transforming the restitution of war trophies into a military (if not a divine) trial by ordeal, Wellington's letter was meant as an act of political communication on a European scale, expressing British domination over Europe when it came to moral arbitration. Translated into several languages, this open letter was published on October 18, 1815, in the *Journal des débats*. Thirteen years after ambassador Lord Elgin had gained permission from the Ottoman sultan to transfer the Parthenon frieze to London,

Wellington was adopting the manners of his former rival, exiled at last to the ends of the earth, by dismissing prior treaties as mere legalistic quibbling. Power alone mattered. The victor's arguments made the rare voices who had been critical of Napoleon's project — an incessant expansion of the Louvre's collections in order to transform it into an ideal "universal museum" through imperial conquests — sound prophetic. Petitioning against the transfer of the first waves of Bonaparte's artistic plunder to Paris, Antoine-Chrysostome Quatremère de Quincy, archaeologist and diehard royalist, had anticipated the irredeemable danger of "tying the future of timeless monuments of art to the chariot of victory."

It must be acknowledged, however, that the fall of Napoleon fostered a restitution that was no more legal than the confiscations that had ensued over the previous two decades. This same October 18 was the two-year anniversary of the victory of the army opposing Napoleon (a coalition of Russian, Prussian, Austrian and Swedish troops) over the Grande Armée at the Battle of Leipzig. The redistribution of looted art works therefore seemed a fitting compensation for this victory, also known as the "Battle of Nations." On this same October 18, a few months before its cathedral was to become the symbol foreshadowing future German unity, the population of Cologne fervently processed through the town to celebrate the return of Rubens's *Crucifixion of Saint Peter*, a work long considered the city's palladium, the artist having spent many years in that Rhineland city. Its return had been awaited since 1800.

Still, can we conclude that the dismantling of the Napoleon Museum was the prelude to the nationalization of artistic heritage?

The Treaty of Paris of May 30, 1814, was deliberately silent on artistic restitution, for its signatories knew that the French Bourbons, in power for the first time since 1792, were also among the victors. By its backward-looking counterrevolutionary designs, the treaty aimed to reestablish the sovereign's private patrimony, believing it could bring this unfortunate revolutionary interval to a close with the stroke of a pen. Two issues were at play. For one, when King Louis XVIII declared to the Chamber on June 4 that "the glory of the French armies is in no way breached; the monuments to their merit subsist, and the artistic masterpieces now belong to us by rights more stable and sacred than those of victory," the Louvre and its collections became "royal" once more. Allied sovereigns, for their part, felt they were supporting the French king's popularity, all the while earmarking for the future and for the sake of diplomatic appearances a complimentary restitution of certain masterworks. The latter would remain "in reserve," agonistic and dynastic entitlements that would not be exhibited in the galleries of "the most beautiful museum in the world."

The final race for the "public display" of these works was on. Dominique Vivant, Baron Denon, director general of the Louvre since 1803, rushed to line the public galleries with the masterworks France fully intended to keep for its ideal museum. In the spring of 1815, to the delight of the city's occupiers, he organized an exhibit of German and Italian "primitives," sprinkled with a few Spanish works it likewise had no intention of restituting. By refusing to give up on the idea of a universal museum, patiently built up in the wake of Napoleon's victorious armies, Denon sought to maintain an illusion that was not quite lost, all the while laying the aesthetic groundwork for national arts.

The situation was quite the reverse when it came to the public domain of states. Article 31 of the treaty required that "all archives, maps, plans, and documents belonging to the ceded countries, or anything concerning their administration, be faithfully restored to those countries upon their ceding." According to traditional reasoning, archives alone were deemed intrinsic to state (if not quite national) sovereignty. Successive territorial annexations of Belgium, the Rhineland, and also of the Papal States and part of northern Italy had — since 1794 and even more so after 1809 — called for a monumental "palace of the archives of Europe." Nearly all the pontifical archives, parts of the archives of the Castilian crown, and a few coffers-full from the emperor in Vienna were scheduled to be deposited into what Pierre Daunou, head archivist of the empire, called an immense "treasure of charters." Starting in August 1812, architect Jacques Cellerier erected a massive quadrangular depository in iron and stone at the foot of the Palace of the King of Rome — a complex intended to be a residence for Napoleon's infant son. By the time the empire fell, Paris was still awaiting the *archivio* of the Grand Duke of Tuscany and the papers of the King of Holland.

The historian Jules Michelet evoked best the deeper meaning of this material translocation of universal power through archives: "At that time, the archives of France were becoming those of the world." To wit: the end of the *imperium* gave way to a massive and legitimate backflow of papers, barely interrupted by the One Hundred Days debacle, during which Napoleon returned from exile to seize power again. One grand theft justified another, precipitating a dramatic legal and symbolic turn of events. In the eyes of the allies, the guilty party was no longer the emperor, but rather a national army in revolt against one of their own. Military defeat prevented Louis XVIII from giving Denon any instructions. Denon could thus not stop the occupants from seizing artworks as both payback and symbols of national sovereignty: art as heritage. Already, the Prussian representative reclaimed the works belonging to the regional princes under his authority. Antonio Canova, commissioner to the pope, likewise recovered a large share of the pieces from northern Italy. This headlong rush to restitution redrew the potential new map of Europe in the time it took to pack the crates.

Before submitting his resignation to Louis XVIII on October 3, Denon, known as "Napoleon's eye," mounted one last stand by refusing to surrender to Austria what remains to this day the largest painting in the Louvre, Paolo Veronese's *The Wedding at Cana*, which had been seized from the Palladian refectory of the monastery on the island of San Giorgio Maggiore in Venice in 1797. In order to hold onto the image of Christ's first miracle, Denon convinced his former rival Antonio Canova to take in exchange a painting by Charles Le Brun, an item from Louis XIV's royal collection representing Christ in the House of Simon a few days before his Passion. Skilled at the staging of symbolic value, Denon was able to accomplish, in a testamentary gesture, a kind of appeasement: he relinquished the sign of the Passion so that the vanquished could better conserve the memory of the miracle. The Veronese painting, perfectly adapted to its original monastic setting, has been considered ever since its theft and installation in the Louvre as the vestige of a stubborn misunderstanding: the painting is hung in the worst possible place, two feet from the floor, and directly opposite the *Mona Lisa*, which visitors flock to see, turning their back on the Veronese and all it represents.

This same misunderstanding presided over a paradoxical

origin myth: that the sacrifice of the Central Arts Museum, created in 1793 and then transformed into the Napoleon Museum, brought about the invention of the *public* museum. The Louvre's claim was double. First, it was universal because it was public; second, it was public in order to be universal. This cast a shadow on preexisting museum styles. From Florence to Dresden by way of Dusseldorf, there were already countless galleries, princely ones to be sure but open to the public at large. In reality, the Louvre, a belated experience compared to the rest of Europe, merely endorsed an earlier movement. It most certainly did not mark the *birth* of public museums, but rather the adoption of an international movement toward the opening of museum collections to the public.

After all, the universal museum was not as "open" to the public as it was said to be. The galleries were in fact closed in 1806 and 1808 and through most of the following two years. Increasingly subsumed to the needs of an intrusive imperial court, Denon's galleries were by the end of the First Empire exhibiting "only" twelve hundred paintings. This included some of the finest artworks, but paled in comparison with the public gallery of the Elector of Saxony in Dresden, which had been displaying some three thousand works a half-century earlier.

Far from constituting a legal precedent for international law on cultural property, which would not emerge until

World War I, France's massive restitution within a few epic weeks — twenty-one hundred paintings, six hundred statues and busts, two thousand vases, cameos and enamels — undoubtedly spawned the myth of a continental European patrimony. This locked the Western artistic tradition into the less-than-universal celebration of a seemingly rearguard gathering in a single place of *all* the treasures of the various regions: Italian (over half the items), German and Flemish (nearly 40 percent), French, and Spanish (less than 10 percent). This was the archaic territory of the Holy Roman Empire and the papacy, the beating heart of cultural patronage that, as it happens, would come to an abrupt end in the nineteenth century. As art historian Édouard Pommier has suggested, the "compulsory redistribution" of France's plunder constituted the catafalque of an imperial monopoly on universal art. The new nation-states now sought to inscribe the universal within the narrower confines of national patrimonies.

This "dissemination of the universal museum into national museums" was thus a major moment in European history, opening the floodgates of the collective imagination. The double translocation of artworks within two decades anticipated a massive legal counter-transfer. The new continental powers in Berlin, Vienna, and Rome were also centralizing the art that had once adorned churches and monasteries. The dynamic of restitution, triggered by a

French political conflagration, gave rise to a secularized art in which public authority merged with collective property. Accessibility (or at least its appearance) now became a matter of public good. All told, this multilayered story of restitution conserves for France the ownership of an idea: the universal museum. Despite its struggles to put this idea into practice, France has maintained a worldwide reputation for a universal and accessible artistic heritage that it continues to export, all the way to the Louvre Abu Dhabi and the globalized shores of the Persian Gulf.

Bénédicte Savoy

REFERENCES

Bordes, Philippe. "Le Musée Napoléon." In *L'Empire des muses: Napoléon, les arts et les lettres*, edited by Jean-Claude Bonnet, 79–89. Paris: Belin, 2004.

Perrot, Xavier. "De la restitution internationale des biens culturels aux XIXe et XXe siècles: Vers une autonomie juridique." PhD diss., University of Limoges, 2005.

Pommier, Édouard. "Réflexions sur le problème des restitutions d'œuvres d'art en 1814–1815." In *Dominique-Vivant Denon: L'œil de Napoléon*, edited by Marie-Anne Dupuy, 254–257. Paris: Éditions de la Réunion des musées nationaux, Musée du Louvre, 1999.

Poulot, Dominique. *Musée, nation, patrimoine (1789–1815)*. Paris: Gallimard, 1997.

Savoy, Bénédicte. *Patrimoine annexé: Les biens culturels saisis par la France en Allemagne autour de 1800*. 2 vols. Paris: Éditions de la Maison des sciences de l'homme, 2003.

RELATED ARTICLES

34,000 BCE, 1287, 1380, 1793, 1798, 1907, 1914, 1940

1816

The Year without a Summer

With Europe only just recovering from the Napoleonic Wars, a bleak harvest stoked general unrest in the summer of 1816. What contemporaries called "the disturbance of seasons" also kicked off massive debates both inside and outside of France on the root causes of climate change.

For many countries, 1816 became known as the "Year without a Summer." Today, that phrase could readily describe a year with an unusually rainy August. But, in the aftermath of Mount Tambora's 1815 eruption, it indicated a much more dire scenario, with cascading calamities and disasters in the form of food shortages and political strife.

The eruption occurred in April of 1815 on Sumbawa Island in Indonesia. The initial impact on local surroundings was devastating. The disaster obliterated three local kingdoms and forced the area's few survivors to choose between famine and slavery. From a climate standpoint, the debris and ash spewed into the atmosphere settled back down to earth in the days following the event, resulting in minimal impact. What wreaked widespread havoc were the sulfate aerosol particles, which lingered in the atmosphere and spread across the globe. Traces could even be found in ice cores of the polar regions. When combined with water molecules, sulfur creates a veil that reflects solar energy toward space and interacts with weather patterns. That climatic phenomenon had historic, global consequences.

In China's prosperous Yunnan province, low rice yields led to widespread famine. Historians now believe that, well before the arrival of European gunboats, this demographic devastation caused an economic crisis that would plague China throughout the nineteenth century. Tambora can therefore be seen as a contributing factor to what historians call the "great economic divergence" between China and Western Europe.

In India, the 1816 monsoon was weak, but the summer of 1817 experienced heavy flooding of the Ganges Delta. Meanwhile, this period also marked the country's first cholera epidemic. Until then, the disease had been contained to the Bay of Bengal. For European doctors trained in Hippocratic medicine, the confluence of events was far from random. Indeed, most documentation from the time links the outbreak of this global pandemic to the weather troubles.

In Europe, the years 1816 and 1817 represent the continent's last great subsistence crisis. The economic downturn can be seen in a decline in marriage and birth rates; people made strategic decisions. The cost of grain shot up, sharpening inequalities. Large-scale farmers took advantage of the price hike, while urban laborers and workers experienced a collapse in purchasing power. Across Europe until the fall of 1817, marketplaces became the stage for bread riots. Desperate populations threatened to seize stocks if grain sellers did not lower their prices. Looters spoke of a "moral economy" based on "fair prices" to justify their actions, insisting on a right to subsistence and community access to grains. For the most part, the purpose of these riots was to prevent grains from being carried off to capital cities, where residents benefited from state-subsidized food purchases.

In France, the government made the political decision to defend market prices and free trade. This was a risky move for Louis XVIII, who could appear to neglect his duties as father of his people. To make matters worse, the populace still remembered the measures taken by Napoleon's government to limit the price hike during the previous food shortage of 1811–1812.

The food shortages of 1816–1817 forged a direct link between the weather and politics. Fearful of further social agitation, political stakeholders leaned on climate experts to further their own agendas, downplaying the importance of the weather event with respect to food shortages.

These learned elites pointed to the climate's immutability and then cast around for factors that might explain these social disturbances. England's Tories, like laissez-faire policymakers in France, either minimized the high price of grains by claiming that the said shortage would prove temporary, or else shifted blame to the behavior of the crowds at the marketplaces. Nature did not cause social unrest, they claimed; on the contrary, riots had upset the market and hence created the illusion of a cataclysmic climatic event.

Thus, as two cold, wet years nourished a prerevolutionary climate, London intellectuals scrambled to publicize signs of global *warming*. Their findings were based on what they believed was a discovery of melting glaciers in the North Pole. In the late summer of 1817, teams of whalers reported a sensational piece of news: an ice barrier in northern Spitsbergen had vanished. The news was reassuring given the spread of bread riots during this cold spell: nature seemed to be making up for recent excesses. The issue was especially important for scholars such as Joseph Banks, president of the Royal Society and representative of landowner interests, who defended the Corn Laws, a set of tariffs and trade restrictions on grain, and promoted the idea of a self-sufficient England through crop production, soil management, and acclimation. A cooling of England's climate would have stymied his plans.

In Switzerland, famine ravaged mountain communities, riots broke out in Geneva, poverty became rampant, and more and more residents migrated to the United States and Russia. However, this general misery and violence gave rise to one of the most important scientific advances in climatology: the Ice Age Theory. In October 1817, the Swiss Academy of Natural Sciences organized a public essay contest on the cooling of the Alps. Ignaz Venetz, a Swiss engineer, paid attention. In his daily work on behalf of regional authorities, Venetz encountered the effects of both the Year without a Summer and the Little Ice Age (a period of cooling that occurred from the sixteenth to nineteenth centuries). Indeed, he had to manage dangerous situations in which glaciers blocked rivers and created reservoirs of water. For his essay, Venetz devised an innovative study on ice accumulations and argued that glaciers had taken up much more space in the past. His conclusions flew in the face of a prevailing notion of global cooling put forward by French naturalist Georges-Louis Leclerc, Comte de Buffon. For Venetz, the Swiss climate was not at present subject to an inexorable drop in temperature. In fact, it had been exposed to much colder conditions in the past — during what would soon be known as the Ice Age.

France also became preoccupied with the weather in the summer of 1816. It was then that the idea of a "disturbance of seasons" gained lasting traction with the public. Meanwhile, respected scholars like François Arago began to study historical weather patterns as a means of calming fears. One of the most renowned explorers and scholars of the time, the Comte de Volney, argued that the strange weather was purely accidental and did not suggest global cooling. His hypothesis linking the eruption of Mount Tambora with the recent weather phenomena became a plausible explanation for the Year without a Summer.

Yet, in contrast with the rest of Europe, the summer of 1816 launched in France a debate on the impact of deforestation on the climate. Discussions on logging practices in national forests emerged in the context of low crop yields in 1816 and 1817. The issue was primarily political: national forests had been established in 1789 through government expropriation of land once belonging to the clergy and emigrated nobles, and since the Restoration, their fate was at the heart of conflicts pitting ultra-royalists, who rejected the French Revolution and its legacy, and liberals, who sought to reconcile a constitutional monarchy with the values of 1789. Government after government argued that the privatization of national forests played a crucial role in convincing creditors to invest in public bonds, with one official even coining the term "forest security." The implication for the state was clear: national forests were a means of quickly paying war reparations, which in turn would lead to a withdrawal of Prussian,

Austrian, and Russian forces from occupied territories; they served to reassure investors who had purchased aristocratic or clerical property during the Revolution and now feared it might be taken away; and they mollified foreign powers, who could be called upon in the event of future uprisings.

The sale of public forests would mean that the state's credit now rested on natural holdings that belonged to the nation. This proved unpalatable to ultra-royalists, who pushed back against this dangerous scheme. They insisted that, by connecting credit to forests, the state would alter France's climate. A prominent counterrevolutionary, Louis de Bonald, claimed that, "An enemy seeking to destroy France…could not make our seas run dry, our soil barren, or our air unclean, but he could sell our forests." The ultra-royalist general and statesman Marquis de Castelbajac drew on an example from the nation's southern departments, which were "devastated every year [by storms] since the plundered peaks of our mountains saw the passage of revolution." In March 1817, when food shortages reached their peak, the writer and royalist politician François-René de Chateaubriand addressed the upper house of parliament: "Everywhere that trees have been cut down, man has been punished for his improvidence. I am better equipped to speak on these matters, dear sirs, and on the consequences of the presence or absence of forests, since I have seen the pristine lands of the New World, where nature is newborn, and I have seen the deserts of old Arabia, where creation has all but died."

If the issue of climate change became a government affair in France during the Restoration (1815–1830), it was because Mount Tambora's explosion and Napoleon's 1815 defeat at Waterloo happened to coincide. In 1821, the ultra-royalist Bourbon government launched a national inquiry into climate change, capping a period marked by meteorological upheaval across Europe, the financial fallout of defeat in France, the end of the Little Ice Age, and the aftershocks of revolution.

Jean-Baptiste Fressoz and Fabien Locher

REFERENCES

Fressoz, Jean-Baptiste, and Fabien Locher. *Le climat fragile de la modernité*. Paris: Le Seuil, 2019.

Jong, Berenice. "Mount Tambora in 1815: A Volcanic Eruption in Indonesia and Its Aftermath." *Indonesia* 60 (1995): 37–59.

Post, John D. *The Last Great Subsistence Crisis in the Western World*. Baltimore: Johns Hopkins University Press, 1977.

Wood, Gillen D'Arcy. *Tambora: The Eruption That Changed the World*. Princeton: Princeton University Press, 2015.

RELATED ARTICLES
12,000 BCE, 1247, 1610, 1793, 1973

1825

Rescuing Greece

Between 1821 and 1832, Greek revolutionaries were locked in a bitter war of independence with the Ottoman Empire. Their struggle aroused a wave of sympathy in the rest of Europe, but especially in France. On February 28, 1825, a philhellenic committee was created in Paris. Its members included liberals, conservatives, and high society ladies, all of them fervent admirers of the Greeks and "the glory that was Greece." This transnational mobilization launched a completely new form of humanitarian interventionism.

There are moments in human history when nationalistic, ideological, and social emotions cross frontiers with unprecedented ease. It is not so much that they swirl and eddy wherever they please, only that for a while there is no urge to prevent them spreading.

The Romantic, post-Napoleonic age is a supreme example.

In 1770, Voltaire tried to awaken French public opinion to the fate of Greeks rebelling against Turkish oppression.

His efforts were in vain: he neither won the backing of Catherine II of Russia nor galvanized anything like a rebirth of Christian solidarity. By contrast, the romantic awakening of the Hellenes in the 1820s gave a powerful jolt to the European conscience and generated a wave of emotion that thrilled not only France but much of the West. This time the shock was deeply felt; indifference was impossible. The Greek cause resonated in people's hearts more powerfully than in their heads.

From Lisbon to London and from New York to St. Petersburg, the Greek–Turkish conflict was seen — against all odds — as a major event of world history, to such a degree that, despite the oblivion that surrounds this war today, it still intrigues historians. Everything began in Morea in the spring of 1821, with the revolt of the *klepht* mountain people against the Turkish occupation. While the uprising secured the support of an ardent Greek diaspora across the world, the Greeks who did the fighting and those who had chosen exile soon espoused different political views. The former sought to recover the long-lost radiance of Byzantine orthodoxy; the latter hung on the words of Adamantios Korais, a leading figure of the intellectual Greek diaspora in Paris, who dreamed of building a modern nation-state. But after France, Great Britain, and Russia had annihilated the Turkish–Egyptian navy in the Bay of Navarino on October 20, 1827, and after full Greek independence had been achieved in 1830, the face of the new Greek state satisfied nobody. Their heroic struggle notwithstanding, the Greeks found themselves saddled with a Bavarian monarch, following a succession of suspicious transactions between the great powers. They were certainly not granted autonomy. They were not even given the frontiers they wanted.

All this was to come later. In 1825, about one thousand volunteers from all nations rushed to help the Greeks. Though they quickly acquired mythic status, these fighters were in reality a mixture of soldiers from the Napoleonic Wars and wild young romantics stirred to action by the cause and the charismatic presence of Lord Byron. Far more significantly, large numbers of men and women mobilized at a distance, founding hundreds of committees of support for the Greeks around the world. In getting clothing, food, and money to the insurgents, they deployed forms of philanthropic savoir faire that have since become standard practice: subscriptions, door-to-door requests for contributions, exhibitions on behalf of the Greeks, charity balls and concerts, education of orphans, and the manufacture of philhellenic objects and clothes. In March 1826, women of Parisian high society raised a considerable sum in this way, finding donors from all social backgrounds. Using similar methods, other ladies' committees sprang up in French provincial towns as well as in foreign countries, using the French blueprint as a model.

For philhellenic France, 1825 marked a turning point. At that time Paris became the undisputed center of worldwide mobilization on behalf of the Greeks. By then the French had progressed beyond their first flush of enthusiasm. In 1821, early tremors were felt when the first volunteers set out for the East from Marseille. They increased the following year with the news of the Turkish massacre at Chios, amid scenes soon to be immortalized by the painter Eugène Delacroix. They grew even stronger with the first embryonic committees, such as the Parisian Société de la Morale Chrétienne. But in those years, the main impulse was coming from Switzerland and the German states. This remained the case until disillusioned reports began to filter back from the first German military volunteers and Klemens von Metternich's growing pressure began to shift the movement's center of gravity. A second phase then began, this time directed from London, where the creation of a committee in February 1823 injected new energy into the movement of international solidarity with the Greeks. Philhellenic rhetoric tilted in the direction of Benthamite utilitarianism. This did not last long. The death of Byron at Missolonghi in April 1824, followed by a succession of financial scandals in the City of London linked to Greek loans, handed the leadership back to Paris.

So on February 28, 1825, a new Parisian philhellenic committee broke on the scene. It was broad-based, vigorous, and inventive. For two continuous years thereafter, the Greek movement steadily widened in scope. New committees formed — or reformed — throughout the continent: in about thirty French cities, in Piedmont, in Tuscany, in Switzerland, in the Low Countries, in Bavaria, and even in Prussia and Scandinavia. The overriding goal of their vaguely pacifist, moralizing, evangelical pitch was one of philanthropy; but seven committees, led by Paris, refused to hide their military and political intentions.

With each new generation, the movement's center and periphery shifted a bit, fastening new networks of interdependence. Still, the gravitation back to Paris made it possible to revive impulses that had earlier waned and, above all, to build stronger systems of coordination. There were tensions, obviously, but in the end the collective logic of international cooperation won the day against narrow national considerations. This was especially so in 1826, at the time of the Siege of Missolonghi, when the funds collected in Europe were centralized in Paris. The incessant comings and goings of men, funds, and skills generated a transnational philhellenic network, at once active and powerful. Never before Greece had the international community ventured quite so far in sponsoring a single national culture. Ever on the watch for potential conspiracies, the defenders of the Holy Alliance (the coalition created by the great monarchist powers of Russia, Austria, and Prussia), suspected that all this activity heralded the emergence of an alternative "greater European state," whose objective was the annihilation of the political system established by the Congress of Vienna.

Greece was not a country like any other: as the common matrix of Western civilization, it held a deep pull on European minds. Half a century of neoclassicism had brought the great authors and artists of Greek antiquity back into fashion, relegating the Romans to the level of pale imitators. Greek sculpture was a thing of fascination, to the point that French, British, and German antiquaries — they were not yet known as archaeologists — all wanted a piece of the crumbling remains of a heroic Greek era. The Venus de Milo found its way to the Louvre in 1821. Two decades later, the French School of Athens was inaugurated. It was a genuine sentiment, widely felt, that modern civilization owed an incalculable debt to the Ancients. How could Europeans fail to repay the (presumed) descendants of the Hellenes by restoring the civilization that their fathers had so generously bestowed on Europe? Gratitude, the necessary gift given in return, was the true raison d'être of philhellenism.

A few doubting "Mishellenes" questioned any direct descendance between ancient and modern Greeks, but they remained too much of a minority to have any effect. As for the local Greeks — the ones who dealt on the spot with the European volunteers and then with the regular French soldiers of the Morea Expedition of 1828 and the Bavarians after 1833 — they remained baffled by all the philhellenic fuss, which kept referring them back to a very distant and, to them, nebulous past.

If the war between the Greeks and the Turks touched so raw a nerve in France, Europe, and America, it was also because it raised the possibility of a number of other readings and interpretations. Some saw their hatred of Islam revived and justified — a new crusade taking shape on the horizon. Here this conflict offered nothing less than the reconquest of the cradle of the West, which had remained for so many centuries beneath the boot of the infidel. There was also the charm of exoticism, which gave life to reflexes of attraction and repulsion for what was seen as the cruel, sensual, and mysterious Orient, personified by the vast Ottoman world.

Moreover, the conflict was shot through with political resonance. In post-Napoleonic Europe, the partisans of liberty — and especially the exiles and rebels who formed the liberal International — saw in the struggle of the Greeks the last hope of a cause that had been defeated everywhere else. As for the conservatives, they were eaten up with ambivalence and guilt. To intervene against the sultan was to attack a sovereign — the sultan — who was considered to be legitimate and hence risk destabilizing the European framework established by the Congress of Vienna in 1815. To *refuse* to intervene, however, would be to abandon other Christians, even though they might be schismatics, to the bloodthirsty cultists of the Crescent. After twenty years of ceaseless warfare on the continent, and shortly before its final fragmentation into national units, these philhellenic years appeared to Europe as a time of manifest unity. The reanimated Turkish enemy reminded Europeans of their shared origins.

The debate proved most acute in France. Very early on, Classicists and Romantics took possession of Greece's profuse source material   Jacques-Louis David and Eugène Delacroix on their canvasses, Casimir Delavigne and Victor Hugo in their verse — to the point that French philhellenism was turned into a kind of hybrid, unexpected cultural distillation. In the political field, Greece came to transcend partisan differences. The Greeks were seen as martyrs of the Cross as well as of liberty. The reactionary Louis de Bonald and the liberal Marquis de Lafayette were both ardent philhellenes, defying traditional political cleavages. The Paris committee, the largest in Europe, covered a surprisingly wide spectrum of opinion. The reason, as everyone quickly understood, was that a cause such as this made it shameful to pursue any kind of short-term calculation. Nobody could remain passive before such exactions. Whether real or fictitious, the atrocities attributed to the Ottomans — of which the Greeks themselves, being Christians, were deemed incapable — fostered indignation and a political connection thousands of miles away.

But the truth remains that with this distant suffering a tipping point had been reached in terms of a collective sensibility. Europe had remained indifferent to Greek hardship in the 1770s largely because the thresholds of tolerance for the pain of distant peoples were much higher at that time. In the interval, against a backdrop of affirmation of humanitarian ideals, a progressive redefinition of the frontiers of acceptable morality had taken place, including what was tolerable and intolerable in terms of foreign policy.

So in this sense the great transnational philhellene mobilization was a key, inaugural moment in the broader history of humanitarian intervention. It also launched a debate on another sensitive topic: the right to intervene in the affairs of other countries.

Hervé Mazurel

REFERENCES

Barau, Denys. *La cause des Grecs: Une histoire du mouvement philhellène (1821–1829)*. Paris: Honoré Champion, 2009.

Espagne, Michel, and Gilles Pécout, eds. "Philhellénismes et transferts culturels dans l'Europe du XIXe siècle." Special issue of *Revue germanique internationale* 1–2 (2005).

Klein, Natalie. *"L'humanité, le christianisme et la liberté": Die internationale philhellenische Vereinsbewegung der 1820er Jahre.*

Mainz: Philipp Von Zabern, 2000.

Mazurel, Hervé. *Vertiges de la guerre: Byron, les philhellènes et le mirage grec*. Paris: Les Belles Lettres, 2013.

Roessel, David. *In Byron's Shadow: Modern Greece in the English and American Imagination*. New York: Oxford University Press, 2002.

Saint Clair, William. *That Greece Might Still Be Free: The Philhellenes in the War of Independence*. London: Oxford University Press, 1972.

RELATED ARTICLES

600 BCE, 1095, 1143, 1202, 1936, 1954

1832

France in the Time of Cholera

Do rich and poor have the same basic rights? In France, this became a burning question when the regime that emerged from the revolution of July 1830 delivered political inequality and unbridled liberalism in equal measure. Then, in the spring of 1832, a mysterious, seemingly incurable Asian epidemic spread across Europe, shaking France's confident bourgeois elite to its very core.

On May 16, 1832, in the early morning, the death was announced of Casimir Perier, president of the French Council of ministers. This industrialist and former member of Parliament had been asked to form a government by the new King Louis-Philippe in March 1831. The nascent July Monarchy, a regime born of the 1830 revolution in Paris, had come under pressure from many sides: radicals frustrated by the survival of the monarchy (even if there had been a change of dynasty from the Bourbon to the Orléans line); royalists who remained faithful to the Bourbons (they were called legitimists); and hordes of silk workers who, in

Lyon, campaigned for higher salaries. Having dashed the hopes raised during the summer of 1830, the unpopular government was caught in the middle. Casimir Perier was the leadership choice of the more conservative liberals around Louis-Philippe, a strong figure who was expected to restore order and embody the elite nature of the new regime.

No one was prepared for the arrival of a different and terrifying threat, against which even wealthy politicians were defenseless. In March 1832, a deadly disease that had originated in Asia suddenly broke out on French home territory. *Cholera morbus*, arriving by way of the North Sea coastal ports and the Rhine valley, reached Paris on March 26. Within weeks, more than one hundred thousand people had perished in France, twenty thousand of them in the capital. Many died within hours of showing the first symptoms, after intense diarrhea and vomiting. France's ruling classes were convinced that only the illiterate, unwashed poor were seriously at risk.

On April 6, in an attempt to show his sympathy with those afflicted, the king sent his son the Duke of Orléans and his chief minister, Casimir Perier, to visit the cholera victims crowding the Hôtel-Dieu hospital in Paris. This philanthropic act of heroism, fully in line with the middle-class morality of the time, proved fatal to poor Perier, who fell ill within twenty-four hours and died weeks later, despite being treated by the best physicians in the country. Among these physicians was Dr. François Broussais, who had done his utmost to convince contemporaries that cholera was not contagious. Following the death of the minister, the leading lights of France could no longer defend the idea that only people living in poverty, hunger, and dirt were at risk.

The advent of the epidemic, the worst of its kind in France since the plague of Marseille in 1720, was hardly a surprise. In 1831, Casimir Perier himself had ordered a stiffening of health controls. The irresistible nature of cholera was already well-known to the medical profession; it had appeared for the first time in Bengal in 1817 and by 1824 it had reached the fringes of Europe. The worldwide movement of British troops and British trade were laying the groundwork for a future pandemic, one that would eventually explode across the Indian subcontinent to the Urals and the shores of the Caspian Sea. Already in Java, close to one hundred thousand people had died. In 1826, a second wave struck in the heart of Europe before crossing the Atlantic with Irish immigrants traveling from their native country to Quebec. From India to the United States, no nation was spared. The disease continued to baffle the medical profession. Though it clearly skipped from person to person, nothing was understood about the vectors of its contagion, for *cordons sanitaires* and other traditional quarantine measures appeared to have no inhibiting effect whatsoever.

Above all, cholera exacerbated social and political tensions. The revolutions of 1830 in France and Belgium, the independence of Greece, and the uprisings in Italy had borne witness to the increasingly transnational character of political opposition since the early 1820s. In its own way, the disease exposed the interdependence, both political and biological, of the European countries of the Holy Alliance. For example, it was the Russian soldiers sent to put down the Polish uprising of 1831 who carried the plague from the eastern regions of Eurasia to its western borders. Cholera and revolutionary passion leapfrogged over frontiers in tandem, to the deep distress of conservative powers. For liberal elites, the epidemic bore witness to a broader scourge, that of the "social question" raised by exposing the peril inherent to the noxious conditions — the stagnant, putrid miasmas — in which the common people languished. Further connecting class and vulnerability, the celebrated physician Louis-René Villermé led an inquiry that brought home the inequality of social conditions surrounding the disease. The fate of Casimir Perier and other prominent figures also made it clear that those in power could not simply ignore the dying urban masses. A concern for public health, spurred on by a desire not only to help the poor but also to protect the rich, came to the forefront in the 1830s and 1840s.

Meanwhile, for the people of Paris and more generally for the opponents of the July Monarchy, the cholera epidemic was part of a vast conspiracy. In the French capital, but also in other parts of Europe, there were strong suspicions that the disease was really a mass poisoning, as if political leaders had been unable to find any other solution to resolve the question of proletarianization other than to eradicate the men and women who suffered the most in the new industrial economy.

The second cholera pandemic, which occurred between 1826 and 1827, was followed by five more as the misery persisted right through to the dawn of the twentieth century. Badly affected in 1832, France was struck even more gravely in 1853–1854, after a third pandemic spread from China to South America. This time, French soldiers involved in the Crimean War were at once the main vectors of the disease — they carried it from the Mediterranean coast to the Black Sea — and its principal victims. More than 140,000 French citizens were cut down by this new outbreak. At the same time, on the other side of the Channel, the British researcher John Snow at last identified water as the most frequent source of contamination, concluding that the fouled wells from which city dwellers drew their drinking water were mostly to blame. This discovery strengthened the conviction of the British that before they even knew the exact pathology of cholera they should make serious improvements in conditions of hygiene and cleanliness, notably by modernizing water conveyance and drainage systems. London invested heavily in this, and after 1866 there were no more cholera outbreaks in Great Britain.

In Paris, however, the epidemic continued to smolder right up to the early 1890s. In 1883 at last, during the fifth pandemic, the German researcher Robert Koch managed to isolate the cholera bacillus, a full thirty years after early experiments by the Italian Filippo Pacini had revealed its existence. The subsequent discovery of germs by Louis Pasteur and his colleagues finally settled the medical and scientific debate which had raged since 1832: it was now clear that cholera was caused not by foul air or miasmas, but by a pathogen spreading via contaminated water, dirty clothing, and human sweat.

Prolonged scientific uncertainty regarding the nature of cholera explains the profound disagreement on the best ways of countering it. Government actions were only logical if they were carried out transnationally. It was obvious that troop movements, migrations, and trade all followed the routes by which the disease was spreading — ever more rapidly, as new means of communication like railways and steamships were introduced. But to win the battle against epidemics like cholera, was it necessary to sacrifice free commercial exchanges, which according to the British held out such bright promise of peace and prosperity? Those who doubted the contagionist hypothesis joined forces with commercial interests in their rejection of quarantine measures, which were anyway proven to be as expensive as they were ineffectual. Generally, the farther a country was from the sources of the epidemic, the more it responded with improvements in hygiene and disinfection and the less it restricted movement. France dithered about this for much of the century, but when in 1851 the first international health conference was held in Paris, with a dozen countries in attendance, the main item on its agenda was a loosening of the quarantine rules. In effect, France had adopted the British position.

However, the cholera epidemic that struck Mecca in 1865 totally discredited the free exchange credo that had been favored by the government of French Emperor Napoleon III since 1860. Indeed, after 1865, the holy places of Islam were viewed throughout Europe as major breeding grounds for epidemics (including the plague) that might later spread from East to West. The attention of the European powers shifted to the Ottoman Empire and Egypt, which they saw as forward positions in the battle against cholera. As long as they imposed strict surveillance of ships, migrants, and merchandise at the entrance of the Suez Canal — the new choke point between the Persian Gulf and Mediterranean Europe — they could relax controls within their frontiers. French physicians, who had been present for a very long time in the Middle East, took a leading part in building a network of health controls in the region, establishing hospitals and quarantine areas all around the Red Sea. By the end of the century, the combined policy of the colonialist European powers was to take all necessary measures to prevent Eastern epidemics from entering Europe. By 1907, the efforts of French researchers and diplomats to establish an efficient system of international health surveillance had led to the creation of the International Public Health Bureau. Its headquarters were in Paris, and it is in the French capital, likewise, that four of the eleven international conferences organized between 1851 and 1903 took place.

In sum, the struggle against cholera lay at the core of France's social tensions, political confrontations, scientific debates, and international strategies for seven decades — from the death of the hapless Casimir Perier in 1832 to the dawn of the twentieth century.

Nicolas Delalande

REFERENCES

Baldwin, Peter. *Contagion and the State in Europe (1830–1930)*. Cambridge: Cambridge University Press, 1999.

Bourdelais, Patrice, and Jean-Yves Raulot. *Une peur bleue: Histoire du choléra en France (1832–1854)*. Paris: Payot, 1987.

Bourset, Madeleine. *Casimir Perier, un prince financier au temps du romantisme*. Paris: Publications de la Sorbonne, 1994.

Chiffoleau, Sylvia. *Genèse de la santé publique internationale: De la peste d'Orient à l'OMS*. Rennes: Presses Universitaires de Rennes, 2012.

Evans, Richard J. "Epidemics and Revolutions: Cholera in Nineteenth-Century Europe." *Past & Present* 120–1 (August 1988): 123–46.

Hamlin, Christopher. *Cholera, a Biography*. Oxford: Oxford University Press, 2009.

Jorland, Gérard. *Une société à soigner: Hygiène et salubrité publiques en France au XIXe siècle*. Paris: Gallimard, 2010.

RELATED ARTICLES

1347, 1816, 1891

1840

Utopian Year

In 1840, Paris was the world's breeding ground of social
utopias, buzzing with political exiles and intellectual
ferment. Dreams of a different world were emerging, and
French utopians were exporting their projects to Algeria,
Brazil, and even the United States.

Belleville, July 1, 1840: the "first communist banquet"
brought together more than one thousand people, including
artisans and tradesmen, all gathered into a spacious hall
decked in tricolor flags. This event signaled the emergence
of communism as an idea and an incipient organization.
Thanks to foreign press reports, news of the Parisian
event immediately spread throughout the world. Polish
exiles were present, as was Wilhelm Weitling, member
of the League of the Banished, created in Paris in 1836 by
persecuted artisans compelled to flee the German States.
The communist idea was steadily gaining momentum. The
success of Étienne Cabet's landmark communitarian novel,
Travels in Icaria, and the publication of brochures such

as *Comment je suis communiste* (How I Am a Communist) brought the term itself into circulation. By 1840, radical reformers, communists, and socialists — though the term "socialism" was rarely heard at the time — were speaking out through their brochures, books, newspapers, almanacs, and songs. While the grand theoretical treatises of Henri de Saint-Simon and Joseph Fourier had been published earlier, it was around 1840 that their disciples began to organize, to strategize, to sow the first seeds of a radical transformation of the world. Political reform was falling short: it had to be matched by a grassroots reorganization of labor and more equitable and harmonious social relations. Economist Louis Reybaud was right in step with the times when he published that same year a study of Saint-Simon, Fourier, and their Welsh counterpart Robert Owen that claimed for these new theories the status of "universal science."

Some of the most important works in the French and international radical and socialist traditions came out in 1840: Louis Blanc's *The Organization of Labor*, Cabet's *Travels in Icaria*, Pierre-Joseph Proudhon's *What Is Property?*, and Pierre Leroux's *De l'humanité* (On Humanity). Fourier's followers banded together behind Victor Considerant, whose publications spread the master's message. His book on France's role in Europe appeared that year, with works on the utopian phalanstery system and the foundations of positivist politics following soon after. The list also includes the *Code de la communauté* by Théodore Dézamy, one of the organizers of Belleville's communist banquet. France unquestionably occupied a central position in framing the intellectual and political issues that mattered at that time. Apart from the more economically liberal United Kingdom, embroiled in its own Chartist wrangling, the rest of Europe was dominated by conservative, authoritarian governments. In this setting, London and Paris became laboratories for social utopia, forging the fresh worlds of tomorrow.

Despite governmental deadlock and rampant economic woes, hope remained alive on the French left in 1840. Even while legislation was outlawing strikes and associations and seizing newspapers, secret societies and attempted regicide were on the rise. Backers of the Republic launched petitions and organized banquets calling for institutional reform. One of the hottest issues had to do with Prime Minister Adolphe Thiers's decision early that year to build a new reinforced wall around Paris to prevent the city from falling into foreign hands, as it had in 1814. This "imprisonment of Paris" quickly became the very symbol of the regime's repressive policies. By summer of the same year, tens of thousands of Parisian workers went on strike to demand better conditions and true social justice.

Defying harsh reprisals, the underrepresented masses spoke out in both the streets and the press. The first workers' newspapers, with titles such as *La Ruche populaire* and *L'Atelier*, flourished during this period, their chief concern being to defend and represent the "working class," a notion that was starting to make sense despite the variety of working conditions in mid-nineteenth-century France. The squalid side of Paris, as visible as in other major cities, was becoming increasingly intolerable. Not surprising, then, that this period witnessed some of the first large-scale social investigations into the everyday lives of workers, prostitutes, and others. They were conducted by journalists and economists such as Eugène Buret, doctors such as Louis-René Villermé, and Flora Tristan, the famed writer and activist who, in her *Promenades dans Londres*, described the glaring social wreckage left in the wake of British industrialization. By 1840, social issues were front and center in the political and intellectual arenas, thoroughly redefining key issues and points of friction.

But the social utopias forged in 1840 sought not only to improve the conditions of French laborers. They aspired to nothing short of the wholesale regeneration of humankind. What the so-called utopians were writing around 1840 varied tremendously in tone and form, but all point to the same universal project. They would found a social science, taking on the herculean task of intellectual reconstruction, reinventing social bonds, countering the prevailing every-man-for-himself mentality, and hence forging universal, everlasting peace. Naturally, there were disagreements over which path to take, particularly when it came to the use of violence and revolution, or matters of equality. Where the communists espoused absolute parity and community-held assets, the followers of Fourier and Saint-Simon defended private property and sought not to eliminate, but rather to smooth out income disparities. Such discrepancies notwithstanding, these utopians converged in significant ways: they condemned pervasive competition, believed to be the root of poverty; they harshly denounced bourgeois self-centeredness; and they expressed serious concern about industrialization and new, unbridled technologies such as the railroad and steam engines.

All this utopian agitation testifies to France's complex presence on the world scene. On the one hand, the world found its way to France thanks to the exile population, the widely circulated printed materials, and the various revolutionary experiments that, especially in Paris, fed intellectual and ideological radicalism. On the other hand, homegrown ideas rapidly spilled over national and notional borders, imagining life beyond capitalism through a heady mix of science, messianic religiousness, and community-building. In other words, a feedback loop of writings and circulation paved the way for a utopia that drew on foreign experiments and broadcasted its results back out into the world. To cite one important instance, the so-called utopian French socialists were influenced by Robert Owen, father of the cooperative movement and British socialism. Étienne Cabet met him while in exile in England in the late 1830s and carried on his legacy.

Many adherents were equally concerned by colonial issues during this period of imperialist expansion. They expressed horror at the massacres perpetrated by the French military in Algeria, and they denounced slavery, still persistent in the Caribbean and America, linking it to the proletarian condition back home in Europe. Barthélemy-Prosper Enfantin, former leader of the Saint-Simonians, traveled to Egypt after his indictment for endangering public morality in 1832, and even worked as an ethnographer on the official Commission in Charge of Research and Exploration in Algeria. He sharply disapproved of colonization and denounced the deeds of the French military in a work entitled *Colonisation de l'Algérie*, published upon his return in 1843.

French publications were soon circulating on the continent, kindling underground unrest and dreams of social renewal. As the capital of European intellectuals, Paris acted as a laboratory: exiles flocked from all corners of Europe, rubbing shoulders with fellow radicals and socialists, soaking up their ideas and joining in their feuds. Many of Fourier's disciples were in fact foreigners, such as the Belgian Zoé de Gamond or the Pole Jan Czyński. Some came from further afield, like Albert Brisbane, Fourier's main American follower, who'd met the master in the 1830s. A keen stateside propagandist of Fourier's ideas, he laid out the latter's doctrine in his *Social Destiny of Man*, published in 1840. In England, though the movement never quite gained the same momentum, a core of phalansterians did emerge, also around 1840, spurred by the Irishman Hugh Doherty. In fact, a weekly review, *The London Phalanx*, was published in London from 1841 to 1843, with the purpose of spreading Fourier's ideas. In Germany, meanwhile, Marx avidly consumed works by French socialists — works he would soon claim to supersede with his "scientific socialism."

The socialist reformers of 1840 were quick to spread their networks, influence, and experiments across the world. Faced with an unyielding political situation at home, Fourier's believers pulled up stakes and moved to ostensibly virgin territories in which their communitarian ideas might take hold. In 1841, hundreds of Fourierist artisans and laborers settled in the Santa Catarina region of southern Brazil to test their alternative lifestyle. In the capital Rio de Janeiro, they presented their projects to the young Emperor Pedro II. In 1846, a pro-Fourier officer in the French colonial troops obtained a land grant in Algeria in order to contribute to social progress through a marriage of capital and labor. Cabet's communist followers, for their part, created an "Office of Icarian Immigration," a first step toward the foundation of a utopian community in the United

States. Thus, in February 1848, shortly before Revolution broke out anew in Paris, some sixty colonists boarded a ship in Le Havre for a long crossing that would propel them toward their New World venture.

François Jarrige

REFERENCES

Beecher, Jonathan. *Victor Considerant and the Rise and Fall of French Romantic Socialism.* Berkeley: University of California Press, 2001.

Bouchet, Thomas, Vincent Bourdeau, Edward Castleton, Ludovic Frobert, and François Jarrige, eds. *Quand les socialistes inventaient l'avenir (1825–1860).* Paris: La Découverte, 2015.

Cordillot, Michel. *Utopistes et exilés du Nouveau Monde: Des Français aux États-Unis de 1848 à la Commune.* Paris: Vendémiaire, 2013.

Fourn, François. *Étienne Cabet ou le temps de l'utopie.* Paris: Vendémiaire, 2014.

Johnson, Christopher H. *Utopian Communism in France: Cabet and the Icarians, 1839–1851.* Ithaca, NY: Cornell University Press, 1974.

Maillard, Alain. *La communauté des égaux: Le communisme néo-babouviste dans la France des années 1840.* Paris: Kimé, 1999.

Riot-Sarcey, Michèle. *Le réel de l'utopie: Essai sur le politique au XIXe siècle.* Paris: Albin Michel, 1998.

———, Thomas Bouchet, and Antoine Picon, eds. *Dictionnaire des utopies.* Paris: Larousse, 2002.

Vidal, Laurent. *Ils ont rêvé d'un autre monde*. Paris: Flammarion, 2014.

RELATED ARTICLES
1789, 1848, 1858, 1871, 1968

1842

Literature for the Planet

When Honoré de Balzac sketched the outline of his *Human Comedy* in 1842, he struck a rich vein that would make the French novel both a worldwide genre and a shining symbol of his country's culture. Ever since that time, French literature has had an unrivaled array of descriptive tools with which to define nations and scrutinize the societies these nations represent.

In the 1820s, when Honoré de Balzac decided to become a writer, the novel was a minor literary genre in France. Like Voltaire, educated French people preferred poetry and grand tragedy, wherein virtue, truth, enthusiasm, and hope marched solemnly across the page. As a result, contemporary French novelists were almost ashamed of their prose. Many published under pseudonyms — the men because their tone tended to be light, schoolboyish, and edgily anticlerical; the women because they knew to expect prim, frowning disapproval if they openly wrote for publication.

Then the sentimental novel began to win popularity. Writers such as Adelaïde de Souza, Sophie Cottin, Germaine de Staël, Madame de Genlis, and Madame von Krüdener gravitated toward Jean-Jacques Rousseau's 1761 *Julie, or the New Heloise*, enriching its approach to prose with fresh narrative procedures that realist novelists would later adopt. With remarkable precision, these authors analyzed contemporary dilemmas regarding, for instance, the post-revolutionary longing for individual freedom and the enduring weight of social conformity. In foreign countries, they came to represent a sparkling inventiveness that was entirely French; the English, in particular, appreciated this inventiveness, comparing it to their own Samuel Richardson and Ann Radcliffe. Meanwhile, the Germans applied it in their attempts to explain the dichotomy between *Moralität* and *Sittlichkeit* (individual morality and the collective ethic).

The contemporary French sentimental novel exported well to the rest of Europe, though most modern literary histories would have us forget it ever existed. The fact was that between Paris, London, and Weimar a Romantic genre was circulating; the French variant, largely produced by women, offered non-French people a keener understanding of the literary specificity of France than the idiosyncratic prose of the Romantic François-René de Chateaubriand or Benjamin Constant. Indeed, these sentimental novels alerted sensitive observers all over Europe to the painful destinies of fictional characters who lived as outcasts from their own existences, and also to the French approach to a human predicament that was as noble as it was vulnerable. Literature, in the first three decades of the nineteenth century, was much concerned with human passions at odds with social norms, and it tailored itself directly to readers — especially women — who now sought to define themselves through their characters rather than their conditions. Natural sensibility became the equivalent of a literary passport.

Then came Sir Walter Scott. The Edinburgh-based poet of *The Lady of the Lake* and author of *The Bride of Lammermoor* swiftly became world famous as the author of the Waverley novels. In 1814, when he began his mighty series, Scott was already noted for his poems and stories. Waverley inaugurated a sensational new writing manner and method, which was translated and reprised by others throughout the nineteenth century, from Sweden to Portugal and from Brazil to Japan. The global Waverley mania is hard to imagine today; but Harry Potter and Stieg Larsson's Millennium trilogy might be reasonable comparisons.

There was a threefold novelty about Scott's fresh brand of historical fiction. To start with, the fabric of his stories was resolutely national. Scott's theme was the people of Scotland; his literary mission was to convey, through fiction, the cultural and social autonomy of a country which could aspire to political independence. In place of the abstract humanity of the sentimental novel, Scott described the community of a nation in the making.

Scott's Waverley novels, whose titles placed end to end — *Ivanhoe*, *The Fair Maid of Perth*, *Quentin Durward*, *Guy Mannering*, *Waverley*, etc. — followed the chronological history of the Scottish nation from the eleventh to the nineteenth century, crystallized a broader national turn within European literature. This exploration of the national past injected the energy of a real future into a community that was groping for its identity. To succeed, the novel would have to appear believable, credible. Scott thus weaved his plots into the customs and legal frameworks of ancient periods. Documentary evidence, discreet though it was, gave his fiction a truthfulness and authenticity that had never been seen before. Scott expressed historical truths, drawn from existing archives, through the prism of art.

This daring new approach to literature proved fascinating to French historians and novelists. Augustin Thierry, Prosper de Barante, Jules Michelet, Alfred de Vigny, Prosper Mérimée, and Victor Hugo were galvanized by Scott's "patriotic erudition." So, too, was Balzac, beginning with *The Chouans*, his 1829 novel on the French Revolution. In the end, he proved more faithful to Scott's model — a series of linked novels — than any of his contemporaries. Like the great Jules Michelet, author of a nineteen-volume history of France, Balzac believed that historians should concentrate "on the people, not only on its leaders or institutions." Unlike Michelet, he deemed it imperative to describe and understand the manners and customs *of his own time.* Half a century after the dramatist Louis-Sébastien Mercier first attempted to classify social types in his *Tableau de Paris*, the French nation was still in search of itself following the maelstrom of the Revolution and the Napoleonic Empire. Balzac believed it was his duty as a French writer to revisit Paris and the provinces and show what his country had become. Literature had an important role to play as a symbolic space in which his compatriots could come together, identify and repair the injustices caused by the market and social mobility, and restore a semblance of community to France.

Thus the world of his *Human Comedy* is emphatically not that of the sentimental novel. Balzac's stories are not set in Russia, the East, or America, but in Paris and the French provincial towns of Tours, Angoulême, and Douai. Here, exoticism begins at home and cultures collide when French people encounter their neighbors. When a French soldier gets lost in Upper Egypt ("A Passion in the Desert"), he falls in love with a leopard; perhaps, being French, he finds it easier to cross the animal frontier between species than the cultural frontier separating nations. Every social bond in Balzac's literary universe is formed between groups whose members know themselves to be compatriots. His networks of bankers, shopkeepers, judges, doctors, soldiers, elected officials, artists, and intellectuals overlap within a dense social and urban space, a common territory laden with history and rich with a shared future. Balzac's novels create their own community within the strict confines of an imagined country, inviting readers to recognize one another in the social types that thronged post-revolutionary France: the upstart, the parvenu, the bankrupt, the shell-shocked soldier, the genius, the woman obsessed with a fickle lover, the domestic housewife, the unscrupulous seductress, the subservient daughter, the betrayed cousin, and so on ad infinitum.

Balzac's characters, when they are not French, are most often German, English, Italian, Spanish, or Brazilian. Their nationality is expressed in their manners or their accents. By having the Baron de Nucingen speak with a recognizable German accent, for instance, Balzac exaggerated a difference for which the defining criteria were national. The humor rested on the distance now separating the French spirit from a common history, culture, and wit. Readers were expected to laugh at this German because he was not French — even though he may have had other sterling qualities.

Scott's worldwide success released a flood of nation-centric novels elsewhere. Balzac's novels embraced this assignment for literature: assembling — or reassembling — a nation. In their wake, writers across the world declared themselves "realists" — by which we should understand that they tapped Balzac's realism to write histories of the current era (rather than Scott's distant eras) and explore contemporary tensions within newfangled national communities. The worldwide transformation that French literature made its own and announced in 1842, when the first volume of the *Human Comedy* came out, was dual: the separation of cultures into nations and the globalization of literary universes, now confined to nation-states.

And yet…another form of literary cosmopolitanism was reinventing itself within the walls of the French university. In 1830, Claude Fauriel was appointed inaugural professor of "foreign literature" at the Sorbonne. A polyglot translator who had come late to higher education, Fauriel built upon the comparative grammar of the Enlightenment while turning his attention to pre-Romantic German philology. He felt that if certain peoples create literature, then it is up to anthropology to find the reasons why; not so much through philosophical speculation about the origins of languages and poetry as through the application of rigorous historical research to literary exchanges. The notion of "world literature" (*Weltliteratur*) suggested by Goethe between 1827 and 1832 rested on a similar conviction: the idea of literary nationality, which is but an exception in the history of mankind, should never obscure the fact that cultural exchanges have always predated political borders.

Fauriel devoted a chapter of his *History of Provençal Poetry* to the influence of the Arabs on French literature. It is rare that this idea is given much thought anymore. Nevertheless, one might be forgiven for wishing that it could be more widely discussed in our own time.

Jérôme David

REFERENCES

Cohen, Margaret. *The Sentimental Education of the Novel*. Princeton: Princeton University Press, 1999.

David, Jérôme. *Balzac: Une éthique de la description*. Paris: Honoré Champion, 2010.

Espagne, Geneviève, and Udo Schöning, eds. *Claude Fauriel et l'Allemagne: Idées pour une philologie des cultures*. Paris: Honoré Champion, 2014.

Moretti, Franco. *Atlas of the European Novel, 1800–1900*. New York: Verso, 2015.

Thérenty, Marie-Ève, ed. "Les mystères urbains au prisme de l'identité nationale," *Médias*, no. 19 (2013). www.medias19.org

RELATED ARTICLES

1066, 1712, 1771, 1784, 1984, 2008

1848

Paris, Revolution Ground Zero

The February 1848 Revolution toppled the July Monarchy. In a matter of weeks, barricades went up across Europe, slavery was abolished in the colonies, and cries for democracy and freedom erupted in Asia and South America.

French premier François Guizot stepped down on February 22, 1848, following protests against his decision to outlaw a political assembly by activists seeking to expand voting rights. News of his departure sent jubilant crowds into the street in front of his former office to celebrate what was seen as a people's victory, the Campaign of Banquets. Suddenly, a shot was fired, followed by a loud boom coming from the guardroom. Bodies fell onto the cobblestones and were quickly picked up by the crowd, some thrown into a nearby wagon. The scene turned riotous, soon growing into a full-scale revolution. The next day, barricades were erected throughout the city. Bloody skirmishes erupted, with insurgents often winning out. As the established regime of King Louis-Philippe, the July Monarchy, exited power after eighteen years of rule, a new republic emerged. This regime held out the promise of a new beginning for all social strata: for the bourgeois class, it would be moderate and enlightened; for laborers, it would be democratic and socially minded; and for peasants, it would ensure the rule of law and freedom. But at the time, nobody could have anticipated the impact of the February shooting on French and even world history.

In truth, this was not an isolated event. Europe was seized by a severe economic crisis, and the Campaign of Banquets emerged out of larger forces: growing liberalism and nationalism among educated urban dwellers, as well as maturing socialist ideas. Switzerland was still reeling after the Sonderbund civil war in 1847. In Palermo, liberal movements clashed with King Ferdinand in 1848. But the February Revolution in Paris stood out in the landscape of European turbulence: it unleashed a wave of political upheaval known as the Spring of Nations across the European continent. Soon thereafter, the kingdoms and principalities of Italy rose up against Austrian rule. Austria itself was not spared: the vast, multinational empire was shaken by a revolution that seized the capital city of Vienna on March 13. After Paris, Vienna emerged as the second beacon for revolution. In Berlin, King Frederick William IV attempted to quell the violence of March 16–18 by promising to adopt liberal measures, including a constitution. Calls for German unification grew more strident in German-speaking lands. Starting on March 31, liberal and democratic officials organized a "pre-Parliament" in Frankfort, in preparation for a national parliament that would be elected through universal suffrage. The movement spread to Greater Poland, sending tremors throughout all of Europe.

Although the forms, motivations, and outcomes of these uprisings varied greatly, the influence of the Paris revolution could be felt throughout the continent. Barricades erected in the center of France radiated out into the streets of Milan and Berlin. In Vienna, insurgents forced the government to create a National Guard on the French model; in Württemberg, revolutionaries planted liberty trees, symbols they associated with France. Yet France was not so much a model of revolution (many were wary of the French Republic) as it was an apt reference for insurgents with diverse motivations and situations.

The spirit of Europe's Spring of Nations reverberated in France as well. It nourished a sense that the world was being reborn in the image of ideals of Liberty, Equality, and Justice. Some even believed they were creating a "universal republic" of countries freed from the yoke of monarchy. The poet Alphonse de Lamartine lyrically placed France at the head of this movement: "We shall not impose premature or incompatible structures that would go against a people's nature; but if the lights of freedom rising up in Europe glow alongside ours…then France is there! The French Republic is more than our homeland, it is also a soldier for future democracy!" But the poet, who also happened to be the minister of foreign affairs, was diplomatic when asked to provide foreign insurgents with military or political support.

Across Europe, the violence of February 1848 had long-lasting consequences. In France, the French Republic became less and less republican with each new election. And it did not support more radical movements that would next emerge in Baden, Germany, and Rome. As the year wore on, a drastic shift began to take place across Europe as authorities struck back. In April, Prussia broke its promise to acknowledge Polish sovereignty, while its army slaughtered Poles in Austrian Galicia. That provoked a massive wave of support in France. On May 15, crowds in Paris marched to the Palais Bourbon and stormed the Assembly in an attempt to seize power. The effort failed, but May 15 still came to represent a decisive turning point in the increasingly tense relationship between the street and the new government. The French Republic was torn between ideologies: on the one hand, monarchists who imagined a representative republic that respected social order and, on the other, republicans who envisioned a democratic and social republic that would support the working class. Tensions between these two groups reached their peak in

June. The elimination of a government work program providing unemployed Parisians with jobs (the National Workshops) led to violent clashes and massacres that shocked all of France and Europe.

The action did not remain confined to Western Europe. Revolution spread to the colonies. Following February 1848's events, the provisional government abolished slavery on April 27 and sent representatives to the colonies to enforce their decree. But English ships brought news of abolition to the slaves before official word arrived. Their revolts created so much pressure that slaves in Martinique and Guadeloupe were freed on May 23 and 27. Guiana and Réunion followed suit on August 10 and December 20. Eventually, the abolition of slavery would free 250,000 people, if we include the Four Communes of Senegal and the French possessions in India. All of them could now elect representatives to the French National Assembly.

Driven by the memory of 1789 and the Haitian Republic of 1804, the newly freed residents of Martinique and Guadeloupe formed political clubs and newspapers that reported on the elections, which had universal male suffrage. But with mounting pressure from plantation owners and worry on the mainland, the situation would here again be subject to rapid change. The question of socio-economic conditions was not considered, and the clubs and political papers were closed by September. Later that fall, on November 4, the new French Constitution declared that although the colonies and Algeria were part of the French territory, they were subject to special laws. The law of March 15, 1849, reduced the number of colony representatives, and many of its measures excluded Senegalese Muslims, who did not enjoy civil rights, and deprived the French possessions in India of parliamentary representation. Here as on the mainland, reactionary measures quelled the tide of freedom born out of the spring of 1848.

Still, things did not return to the way they were before. The major powers in Europe could no longer deny nationalism's aspirations, which forced authoritarian regimes to incorporate aspects of liberalism into their governing process. And while living conditions remained abject for most colonial subjects, slavery was abolished, giving rise to an immense, lasting swell of hope. That hope would eventually become a driving force for future independence battles.

The Spring of Nations sent a shock wave across the globe. And although opposition and conflict movements may have arisen in very different contexts, their sheer number suggests a worldwide trend. Some were able to turn events in Europe — especially in France — to their advantage as they made demands for change. If, as is often claimed, the United Kingdom escaped revolutionary contagion, its colonies did not. In Ceylon (present-day

Sri Lanka), colonial surgeon and conservative Baptist Christopher Elliott saw the fall of King Louis Philippe as a model for locals in his fight against new tax measures. In Australia, Wellington radicals took a cue from French activists and planned banquets in February 1849 as a means of supporting reform movements. To be sure, these practices were not exactly revolutionary, but they do show the political and cultural power of the 1848 events. Other places, such as Latin America, felt a more direct impact from the European revolutions. In Colombia, after radical liberals arrived to power in 1849, work programs modeled after the National Workshops in France were created. Later, during the 1854 military insurrections, some groups inspired by French democratic and social ideas as well as the memory of Simón Bolívar sought to form a republic of artisans. In Chili, the Santiago Society for Equality was established in 1850 on these same ideals. It was one of the first democratic organizations in the country.

Generally speaking, the events of 1848 influenced the spread of radical and social ideas through multiple pathways. But to be clear: the transmission occurred through distinctive processes in which local actors borrowed ideas and refashioned them to fit their own needs. Nevertheless, France left a palpable mark on the revolutionary trend.

And so the events of 1848–1850 reached a global scale. Although it cannot exactly be argued that France was the single cause of this tendency, the strife that erupted on February 22, 1848, had a significant impact on worldwide ways of living and thinking. France was but one point in a complex network of relationships and struggles. But its capital was indeed ground zero for revolution.

Quentin Deluermoz

REFERENCES

Aprile, Sylvie, Raymond Huard, Pierre Lévêque, and Jean-Yves Mollier. *La Révolution de 1848 en France et en Europe*. Paris: Éditions sociales, 1998.

Gazmuri, Cristián. *El "48" chileno: Igualitarios, reformistas radicales, masones y bomberos*. 2nd ed. Santiago: Editorial Universitaria, 1999.

Gribaudi, Maurizio, and Michèle Riot-Sarcey. *1848: La révolution oubliée*. Paris: La Découverte, 2008.

Sperber, Jonathan. *The European Revolutions (1848–1851)*. Cambridge: Cambridge University Press, 1994.

Taylor, Miles. "The 1848 Revolutions and the British Empire." *Past and Present* 166, no. 1 (2000): 146–80.

RELATED ARTICLES
1357, 1789, 1871, 1968

1852

Penal Colonization

At a time when its prisons were causing moral outrage
at home, France sought to move its incarceration system
offshore, following Britain's Australia model. In 1852, the
South American territory of French Guiana was turned
into a prison colony whose profit-making designs took
the guise of a rehabilitation effort, but was anything but
civilized.

On May 10, 1852, the *Allier* made landfall in the Salvation
Islands, just off the coast of French Guiana, and offloaded
three hundred and one convicts who had sailed from the
port prison of Brest. This convoy marked the beginning
of France's century-long experiment in penal colonization
in the remote corners of its empire. Over one hundred
thousand prisoners, tried and convicted in mainland France
or its home colonies, would end up serving sentences in penal
colonies located in French Guiana and New Caledonia.
Following the lead of the British, who had pioneered this
sort of settlement in Australia, lawmakers gambled on

what they assumed would be a win–win strategy; namely, enabling petty criminals and paupers to found a new society while enhancing the wealth of the fatherland. The goals were many: to rid the port prisons of Brest, Toulon, and Rochefort of their unsavory inmates, to remove them from mainland France, to provide the colony with a steady supply of cheap labor (thus boosting local development), and to allow the most worthy and hardworking of the convicts to become full-fledged colonists once their sentences were served.

Ten years after Britain began abolishing the transportation of convicts (completed in 1868), France decided to launch its own venture. For close to a century, its exceedingly arbitrary policies would shift according to the political and social winds shaking the country.

A decree issued on March 27, 1852, designated French Guiana as the site that would accommodate the convicts. The few previous attempts at free migration to this territory had all ended in failure, and the abolition of slavery in 1848 had led to a massive labor shortage. But what made Guiana so ideal as a land of exile was its geographic location, far enough from Europe to preclude any likelihood of return should a convict attempt an escape. During the French Revolution, three hundred priests who had resisted the new laws subordinating clergy to the secular government were shipped out, followed shortly thereafter by seventeen revolutionaries who had lost out during internecine struggles. Later, the uprisings of 1848 and 1851 led to a decree that, in late 1851, ordered the deportation of 3,146 convicts. They were eventually granted amnesty in 1859, but politically motivated deportation went forward with a new law in 1895 that designated the walled compound of the Salvation Islands penitentiary, Devil's Island, as its destination. The first and most famous Guianese deportee was Captain Alfred Dreyfus, incarcerated on Devil's Island from March 1895 to June 1899. Thirty-seven others were to follow, mostly for incidents of treason committed during World War I, though, unlike the convicts transferred there from prisons, political detainees were not subjected to hard labor.

The fact is that France's penal colonization and settlement in French Guiana and New Caledonia effectively relied on prison labor. An 1854 law on hard labor, the so-called transportation law, required that these prisoners be "assigned to colonization's hardest work" and stipulated a "doubling," which is to say that those who were sentenced to fewer than eight years had to remain in the colony after their release for a period equivalent to their sentence. Those with longer sentences had to stay for life, a measure clearly intended to prevent them from returning to France or their colony of origin, and to induce them to settle in situ. Those with the best performance records could be assigned to work for private individuals, for the colony's public service sector, or for a company; they might even obtain a land grant or get married. By 1936, 52,905 convicts had been transported to Guiana. Settlements had started in the east of the country, chiefly in Cayenne, Montagne d'Argent, and Kourou, before moving west around 1857 with the creation of the town of Saint-Laurent-du-Maroni.

Still, the appalling death rate on the ground forced the authorities to backtrack. New Caledonia's milder climate, not unlike that of neighboring Australia, supported the idea of sending convicts from the French mainland to develop colonies there, and so, starting in 1867, this is where all Europe-based convicts ended up. From then on, Guiana received only the "colonial" prisoners, who were assumed to be more resistant to the horrendous equatorial climate. The numbers tell the story: from 1864 to 1931, over 30,000 convicts were shipped to New Caledonia: 22,057 convicts from mainland France, another 3,960 political deportees following the Paris Commune and the 1871 insurrections in Kabylia (part of France's Algerian holdings), and 3,772 repeat offenders, or relegated convicts. But, facing protests by the New Caledonian population, the convoys were by 1896 redirected to Guiana, which once again became the sole destination for convicts.

By then, France had invented a new category of convict: the *relegated*. In 1885, a law targeted delinquents with multiple convictions, sentenced mainly for theft and vagrancy, and 17,375 were sent to Guiana. Considered irredeemable, these petty thieves and drifters were deemed exceptionally dangerous according to the evidence provided by judicial statistics. The sentence for such relegated offenders was life internment in the penal colony. Those with enough financial wherewithal lived relatively unconstrained lives, though they were still not allowed to leave the colony. The indigent convicts, the vast majority, were not so fortunate. Classified under collective relegation, they were, like the other transported convicts, held in a penitentiary, monitored by wardens, and subjected to hard labour.

This shift in emphasis was matched by an attitudinal change toward penal colonization. The utopian ideal of the early days gave way to a hardening of prisoner treatment. The colony's mission no longer consisted of reforming the convicts in its charge; rather, the colony came to serve as a dumping ground for continental France and some of its colonies (mainly Algeria). To encourage the advent of settler colonization, women were shipped off to Guiana (394 regular convicts and 519 repeat offenders). Housed in a "penal convent" in Saint-Laurent, they were to enter into contractual marriages with male convicts. But their death rate was such that the program was abandoned in 1907.

Apart from the inmates of the Salvation Islands, Kourou, and Cayenne, most convicts were concentrated in the penal territory of Maroni, created by an 1860 decree. Saint-Laurent-du-Maroni became a penal collective in 1880, managed entirely by the prison administration. Two penitentiaries were located in this territory, Saint-Laurent for the regular convicts and Saint-Jean for the repeat offenders, as well as two outlying camps. The director of penitentiary administration ran the whole territory, overseeing what came to resemble a vast penal archipelago in which appropriate sentences were meted out to regular and repeat offenders.

There was a final set of convicts in the Guiana penal colony: "colonial lifers" or "category two transports." One thousand came out of French possessions in Martinique, Guadeloupe, and Guiana. And starting in 1931, there were also 535 Asian convicts, sent over from the prison camp of Poulo Condor, in Indochina. They were settled into camps located in the Inini territory, overseen by the local governor.

The move to abolish Guiana's penal colony started around 1923 when an investigation by news reporter Albert Londres alerted readers of the newspaper *Le Petit Parisien* to the inner workings of this ruthless, outmoded institution. In 1933, the Salvation Army settled in the colony to help release convicts and relieve their hardship. Concurrently, a politician named Gaston Monnerville, grandson of a slave and deputy representing Guiana in the French Parliament, pushed his fellow legislators to pass a law abolishing the penal colony. This finally happened in 1936 with the arrival of the Popular Front government. But the legislative decree signed on June 17, 1938, resulted only in halting fresh prisoner transfers to Guiana. It was only in the aftermath of World War II, when it was revealed that large numbers of relegated convicts had died of starvation and exhaustion (nearly 48 percent of the total population in 1942), that the decision was made to shut down the penal colony and gradually clear out its occupants. This move was completed in 1953.

The remnants of Guiana's penitentiaries have since undergone major recovery work. The Salvation Islands site, managed by France's space agency (which has operations in Guiana), now includes a museum devoted to the penal colony. The municipality of Saint-Laurent, awarded the rank of "City of Art and History" in 2007, has restored its prison camp and, since 2014, features a visitors' center for architecture and heritage. New Caledonia is currently in the process of promoting the same kind of heritage tourism, allowing visitors a glimpse into this harrowing chapter of France's correctional history.

Jean-Lucien Sanchez

REFERENCES

Anderson, Clare, ed. *A Global History of Convicts and Penal Colonies*. London: Bloomsbury, 2018.

Barbançon, Louis-José. *L'Archipel des forçats: Histoire du bagne de Nouvelle-Calédonie (1863–1931)*. Villeneuve-d'Ascq: Presses universitaires du Septentrion, 2003.

Criminocorpus: Museum of the History of Justice, Crime, and Punishment. www.criminocorpus.org

Donet-Vincent, Danielle. *De soleil et de silences: Histoire des bagnes de Guyane*. Paris: La Boutique de l'Histoire, 2003.

Lichtenstein, Alex, and Christian G. de Vito, eds. *Global Convict Labour*. Leiden: Brill, 2015.

Sanchez, Jean-Lucien. *À perpétuité: Relégués au bagne de Guyane*. Paris: Vendémiaire, 2013.

RELATED ARTICLES

1066, 1784, 1871, 1931, 1961, 1984

GLOBALIZATION IN THE FRENCH STYLE

A large number of Parisian articles (feathers, artificial flowers, umbrellas, combs, parasols, inlaid boxes, fans, buttons, toiletries), along with hectoliters of wine, hundredweights of books, and tons of bibelots were exported in the 1860s to the four corners of the world, mainly to members of the upper class in Europe, America, and the colonies. Engineers from the town of Lille built locomotives for Brazil and China, and public works projects (roads, bridges, viaducts, and canals) in Egypt and Russia. The meter, a French unit of measure, became a universal standard. French nuns and schoolteachers fanned out into the world bringing "French-style" education, with its emphasis on good manners and social graces, so that young women in Europe and America would learn piano and the art of conversation. Toward the end of the century, Sarah Bernhardt, the "empress of the theater," toured European and American stages with resounding success, at a time when the dramatic arts were becoming more broadly popular. Auguste Escoffier served up haute cuisine in Monte Carlo, Lucerne, London, and New York. French chambers of commerce and the Alliance Française promoted the French language and French manufactured articles abroad.

The global spread of France's influence accompanied the extension of its empire, as France gained territory in the Pacific (Tahiti, New Caledonia), Africa (Senegal,

Congo, Côte d'Ivoire, Benin, Niger, Mauritania, etc.), and Asia (Vietnam, Cambodia, Laos). This constituted France's second colonial empire, and republican ideologues pondered how best to civilize the "natives." The idea of France's "civilizing mission," popularized by the propagandists of colonial expansion, was inherited from the French Revolution, which invented the myth of the universal nation charged with educating other peoples. Colonizing on behalf of the universal values of the French Republic and the rights of man gave legitimacy to overseas expansion while consolidating the republican government at home. Backers of "assimilation" insisted that French colonies should be integrated into the juridical and administrative framework that prevailed in the metropole. In practice, however, from the 1880s on, all the territories of the French empire moved toward indirect rule. Protectorates were established in Tunisia (1881), Annam and Tonkin (1883), Madagascar (1885), and Morocco (1912). These Asian and African dependencies were considered ill-adapted to direct colonization and incapable of representative democracy.

Colonial France broke with republican law by drawing a distinction between subjects and citizens and abandoned the fundamental principles of civil law and secularization. Under the Third Republic, French colonizers excluded the indigenous populations from citizenship, while restricting their legal status and subjecting them to extraordinary judicial regulation, along the lines of the Code de l'indigénat, a specific legal code enacted in Algeria in 1881 and subsequently extended to other portions of the colonial empire. Assigning a separate legal status to the native population created both new offenses that did not apply in metropolitan France and collective penalties. It contravened the principle of the separation of the judiciary and executive powers.

Other forms of colonial violence (brutal repression of riots and demonstrations, as in Greater Kabylia in 1871, massacres of whole villages and summary executions, the burning of lands, expropriation, political repression, forced labour) broke with the Republic's standards of law and morality. The education of the native populations, presented by republican ideologues as the main prong of France's "civilizing mission," was in fact very limited. More than anything, the French feared the development of a French-speaking elite of natives, "evolved" but potentially déclassé, who could imperil the colonial order. If this "civilizing mission" made little headway, it was also because of the inadequate manpower and financial resources the French devoted to the colonies. Its colonial empire was chronically under-administered, with few French soldiers and settlers, because France itself was shorthanded.

France thus became a magnet nation for immigrants. The first population count occurred in 1851, which was also the first year that birth on French soil conferred citizenship. British mechanics settled in France, followed by Belgian day labourers, Jews fleeing the Russian empire, and workers from Italy, Germany, Poland, Switzerland, and Spain. This cosmopolitan France was further augmented during the universal expositions (1855, 1867, 1889, and 1900) that transformed Paris into the capital of modern life. French cultural practices were enriched by a new taste for the foreign, witnessed by the Anglophilia and keen admiration of all things British of the late nineteenth century. Dandies wore frock coats in the 1860s while French workers took up soccer in the 1890s. In the eyes of the rest of the world, people who traced their origin to other countries came to represent the genius of the French. The Countess of Ségur, author of the children's book Sophie's Misfortunes (1858), was Russian-born; the politician Léon Gambetta and the novelist Émile Zola were both of Italian origin; Baron Haussmann, the prefect turned urban planner who transformed Paris under the Second Empire, was of German origin, as was the composer Jacques Offenbach. The pioneering physicist Marie Curie, born Maria Skłodowska in Warsaw, and the poet Guillaume Apollinaire, born Wilhelm Kostrowicki, were both of Polish origin.

At the same time, foreign workers faced successive waves of xenophobic violence in the 1880s and 1890s, protectionist decades during which immigration became the subject of contentious political debate. The question of immigrant labour, bandied about in the popular press, was weaponized by politicians who claimed to be protecting the national workforce. Hatred for foreigners melded into a hatred for the French Republic itself.

The Third Republic arose after the defeat of Napoleon III at the hands of the Prussian Army at Sedan on September 2, 1870. But the new conservative government of Adolphe Thiers had to contend with the Paris Commune, a revolutionary experiment whose two-month radical rule, which lasted between March and May 1871, brought with it such innovations as the ten-hour workday, the separation of church and state, direct democracy and the election of delegates, the emancipation of women, and freedom of the press. After the bloody suppression of this insurrection, the transformation of France into a republic proceeded slowly and gradually. The "Marseillaise" became the national anthem in 1879, while July 14 was chosen as the French Republic's day of national celebration a year later. To shape France — a country divided along social, political, and religious lines — into a united nation, the leading figures of republicanism forged a new national narrative. Building on Second Empire precedents, they fashioned the concept of "our ancestors the Gauls," which supplanted the aristocratic thesis of the Frankish origins of France. Republicans also declared French the national language, often at the expense of the many regional languages, and made military service mandatory and primary school free, secular, and universal.

Paradoxically, this "Frenchification" and the crystallization of France's national identity came about precisely at a time when the country was reinventing its regional cultures and for the first time strongly experiencing globalization. The Félibrige association, inspired by the Provençal poet Frédéric Mistral, began promoting the Provençal language, or langue d'oc. Meanwhile, in 1904, the founder of the modern Olympics, Pierre de Coubertin, was using the word "globalization" to promote the Olympics as a philosophy and a movement that would use athletics for the betterment of mankind and the establishment of international peace.

1858

A Land of Visions

Four years after its proclamation as Catholic dogma, on
March 25, 1858, the "Immaculate Conception" appeared
at Lourdes, a small town in the foothills of the Pyrenees.
The vision of fourteen-year-old Bernadette Soubirous,
occurring beside a picturesque cave spring where
firmament and underworld met, was perfectly attuned to
the new phenomenon of mass coverage by photography
and the press.

Responding to new modernist currents, the French
theologian Alfred Loisy was wont to say in the early
twentieth century that "God is not a historical figure." By
this he implied that, for methodological reasons, God did
not belong to history as historians understood it, though his
traditionalist adversaries were quick to suspect him — not
without reason — of quietly deducing that the absence of
God from history suggested he did not exist at all.

But was the Virgin Mary any more a feature of the
history of France than God himself? This was a burning

question, because, unlike God, the Virgin seems to have appeared to French mortals on so many occasions in the nineteenth century that the experience has been given a technical term — *mariophanie* — in French religious anthropology. At the time France was the world's leading Catholic country (it has long since been supplanted by Brazil, among others), and in the last census to include a religious rubric, in 1872, more than 98 percent of French people considered themselves to be Roman Catholics.

Most of the nineteenth-century apparitions are forgotten today. Yet three of them have, with the blessing of the church, remained vividly present in the public consciousness. These are the apparitions of La Salette in the Alps on September 19, 1846; of Lourdes in the Pyrenees in 1858; and of Pontmain in the Mayenne (Loire region) on January 17, 1871, during the Franco-Prussian war. Of the three sites, Lourdes — a small town in the foothills of the Hautes-Pyrenees between Pau and Tarbes — is by far the most famous. Today's pilgrimage to Lourdes is the most important in the Catholic world. Every year, it attracts close to five million people, more than the Hadj pilgrimage to Mecca.

It all began with a series of eighteen visions, between February 11 and July 16, 1858, seen by Bernadette Soubirous, a fourteen-year-old girl from a poor family living in Lourdes. Bernadette had come with two friends to the banks of the Gave de Pau river to gather firewood in the vicinity of Massabielle grotto when she saw a woman who became known as the "white lady." Her most famous vision took place on March 25, when the figure, silent until that moment, suddenly began to speak French in the local dialect and presented herself as the "Immaculate Conception."

"*Qué soï l'immaculé counceptioú*," she said.

As time went by, believers and onlookers began to accompany Bernadette every day to the place where her visions had taken place, to the considerable irritation of the civil authorities. The latter were led by the notorious police commissioner Dominique Jacomet, who tried without success to stop the stampede. On July 20, 1858, Monseigneur Laurence, bishop of Tarbes, announced the creation of a special church commission whose task was to determine the authenticity of what was happening. This was just like the 1851 commission that had previously assembled at La Salette under similar circumstances and had returned a verdict acknowledging the vision of a weeping Virgin seen there by two children in 1848. The Lourdes commission went to work immediately and completed its own inquest in April 1860. Its conclusions were not made public until January 1872, giving the anxious bishop time to make material preparations for the building of the future sanctuary.

At the outset, Monseigneur Laurence was suspicious — particularly when at least thirty similar

845

manifestations cropped up all over his diocese in the wake of Bernadette's vision. But in the end the inquiry convinced him that the girl was telling the truth. In his authorization of January 18, 1862, he put forward three arguments to that effect.

Number one was the luminous personality of Bernadette Soubirous herself. Her sincerity, poise, and obedience inclined the bishop to reject any suggestion that she was either lying, hallucinating, or self-promoting. The nineteenth-century church, which tended to give greater importance than it had in the past to the personal experiences of clairvoyants, had interrogated more obdurate witnesses than Bernadette: the children Mélanie Calvat and Maximin Giraud at La Salette, for example. In 1866, Bernadette left Lourdes forever to take the veil (under the name of Sister Marie-Bernard) with the Soeurs de la Charité et de l'Instruction Chrétienne at Nevers, where she died in 1879. She was finally made a saint on December 8, 1933. To this day her embalmed body remains on view at Nevers, laid in a glass reliquary.

The bishop of Tarbes's second argument covered the positive effects of pilgrimage, with its beneficial effects on the human soul and body. These effects he prudently qualified as "extraordinary cures" (not miracles), though in no way did he exclude the possibility that a miracle or two might lurk among the various sensational cures suddenly being recorded at Lourdes. In 1883, an office of medical certification was set up to sort out which was which in a scientific manner. Of course the pilgrimages themselves had emerged spontaneously from the presumed virtues of the spring at Massabielle, but they did not take off until the 1870s, when the Pères de l'Assomption congregation and the Notre Dame de Salut association began using France's burgeoning railway network to organize national pilgrimages for the faithful, many of them ailing.

Monseigneur Laurence's final argument in favor of the reality of the Lourdes *mariophanies* concerned the "divine economy of Providence" on the site. The Virgin had introduced herself to Bernadette as the "Immaculate Conception," and this phrase offered a crucial — even God-sent — breakthrough for the Vatican. The fact was that "*Qué soï l'immaculé counceptioû*" conveniently proved the vital dogma proclaimed by Pope Pius IX four years earlier, with his *Ineffabilis Deus* decree of December 8, 1854, which stated that "from the first instance of her conception" and "by a singular privilege and graced granted by God," the Virgin Mary had been "preserved immaculate from all stain of original sin." At the time, influential voices within the church had objected that the scriptural bases of Pius's dogma were slender at best, and that the procedure used to force it through — a written consultation with the bishops followed by a definition promulgated by the pope

847

alone — were eminently arguable. But now that the Virgin Mary had arrived in person to confirm the validity of her Immaculate Conception, all debate about it abruptly ceased.

The fact that she had introduced herself as the "Immaculate Conception" and not, as one might have expected, as "Mary" or the "Immaculate Virgin," seemed a trifle strange, but the expression was not unknown to the literature of the time, and nobody lingered over it unduly. It would seem improbable, on the other hand, that Bernadette herself was unaware of the dogma prior to her vision, especially given that immediately after its proclamation spectacular celebratory feasts took place in every diocese in France, and these events made a lasting impression on every man, woman, and child who witnessed them.

One of the figures who contributed most to spreading the word about the visions of Lourdes, both nationally and internationally, was the famous Catholic journalist Louis Veuillot, editor of *L'Univers*, a newspaper that was much pored over in French rectories. Veuillot visited the site of Bernadette's visions, and after a thorough inquest published a detailed article on the subject at the end of August 1858.

"It would seem to us that what has happened at Lourdes throws an interesting light on the general origins of pilgrimages," Veuillot wrote:

> At the beginning there is an event like the one that has taken place here. An apparition, a revelation,

an image discovered, an unexpected state of grace fervently corroborated by ordinary believers and then denied by experts and intellectuals — or by people who consider themselves such. The popular belief persists and grows in spite of them.

"The church intervenes," Veuillot added, and decides either against, as in the case of the Tamisier affair in the diocese of Avignon in 1850–1851, or in favor, as in La Salette. Thereafter, "the pilgrimage gathers way; a torrent of prayer is drawn to these chosen places, flowing with a vigor that only strengthens with the passing centuries. Occasionally the flow may be staunched, but it always returns — and we see this in our own time — as full and irresistible as before."

A striking aspect of the events at Lourdes was their mix of ancient and modern characteristics. In a sense they reflect, as Veuillot states, the "Long Middle Ages" to which the medieval historian Jacques Le Goff refers. The "Long Middle Ages" were extended in some places well into the nineteenth and twentieth centuries, particularly in regions like that of Lourdes, where the Catholic faith had long been strong. The vision of Bernadette was rooted in a thoroughly local context, both as folklore and as a religious event. This context was afterward obscured by the symbolism and rituals of an international Catholicism that was more contemporary and dogmatic, but at the time it was especially influenced by the proximity of the sanctuary of Notre Dame de Garaison, which commemorated an appearance of the Virgin to a young girl of twelve, Angèle de Sagazan, at the beginning of the sixteenth century. When, in March 1864, Bernadette was shown the official statue of the Virgin of Lourdes executed according to her description by the Lyonnais sculptor Joseph-Hugues Fabisch, she refused to recognize in it the image she had seen; it seemed too big and too old, she said.

Yet alongside these elements of continuity linked to popular religion over the ages, the *mariophanie* of Bernadette relates to a more modern state of affairs. Lourdes can be seen as the earliest religious apparition of the media age. *Notre Dame de Lourdes*, the history of the visions that Henri Lasserre published in 1869, was one of the best sellers of the century, with one million copies sold by 1900. Bernadette herself was copiously photographed in front of pasteboard décors, sometimes in the dress of a Pyrenean country girl, on behalf of charitable causes. Her 1858 vision was likewise firmly at the forefront of the wave of devotion for the Virgin that was such a strong feature of the nineteenth century. In the 1850s, for instance, one in three little girls born in France was christened Marie. Likewise, the number of congregations, sanctuaries, statues, and brotherhoods that were placed under her patronage proved limitless.

All told, then, the 1850s were the most fruitful years of the century for French Catholics. A climate of optimism had unexpectedly returned; for a while the church even allowed itself to believe that the hideous revolutionary period that had befallen France at the end of the eighteenth century was finally drawing to a close.

It was not to be.

Guillaume Cuchet

REFERENCES

Bouflet, Joachim, and Philippe Boutry. *Un signe dans le ciel: Les apparitions de la Vierge*. Paris: Grasset, 1997.

Harris, Ruth. *Lourdes: Body and Spirit in the Secular Age*. London: Penguin, 2008.

Laurentin, René, Bernard Billet, and Paul Galland. *Lourdes: Documents authentiques*. 7 vols. Paris: Lethielleux, 1957–1965.

RELATED ARTICLES

23,000 BCE, 177, 511, 910, 1105, 1143, 1336, 1685, 1940, 1954

1860

The Other Free Trade Country

Heir to the liberal Saint-Simonian tradition, the "free trade" treaty of January 1860 drawn up between France and the United Kingdom was hardly a one-off event: it nudged French commerce toward increased exports and opened the way to what could be seen as a forerunner to the European common market.

For a long time, the trade agreement reached with the United Kingdom on January 23, 1860, was considered something of an aberration in France's record of deeply protectionist policies. Deemed a "customs coup d'état" by its opponents, it brought about free trade, "the root of all evil," as Gustave Flaubert sarcastically quipped in his *Dictionary of Accepted Ideas*. The notion lives on, even today, when Napoleon's Continental System and the Third Republic's entrenched protectionism still color the way we perceive nineteenth-century French economics.

And yet, this treaty was the high point of a French participation — more intense than is usually remembered — in what historians call "nineteenth-century globalization." By lifting the last import bans inherited from the Napoleonic era and replacing them with more moderate tariffs, the 1860 agreement harkens back to earlier attempts at liberalizing Franco-British trade: first, the Eden Treaty of 1786 (rescinded by the Revolution) and then a gradual reduction of customs barriers begun in the 1830s. Soon after the treaty went into effect, the sliding scale of duties on grain and the constraints placed on colonial trade dating back to the ancien régime (the infamous "Exclusif" system) were also abolished. The effect was dramatic: between 1850 and 1870, France's foreign trade experienced record-breaking growth, unequaled to this day, with export values quadrupling and imports quintupling. This surge fits the pattern of a new international division of labour rather than an attempt to catch up with the United Kingdom. France's cotton and steel industries could not compete with the British, but Lyonnais silks, wine production, and high-end *articles de Paris*, i.e., fancy goods such as gloves, furniture, and bibelots, experienced such a boom that they comprised 50 percent of French exports.

Despite the claims of disgruntled opponents, the treaty did not seek to indulge the dominant United Kingdom. Instead, it stemmed from an inherently French concept of free trade. Its initiator was Michel Chevalier, a brilliant professor of political economy at the Collège de France whose Saint-Simonian-based economics came across as unorthodox even if, by today's standards, their emphasis on financial markets, transport and communications networks, and educational policies that prioritized economically useful skills sound oddly familiar. Chevalier's reflections on global trade and production circuits, precipitated by the famed Crystal Palace Exhibition in 1851, would not seem out of place in the business pages of today's daily papers:

> The same product is or can be processed in one country, then further processed in a second or third country, and so on; it will thus cross five or six borders, being worked on five or six times before landing in the hands of the merchant who will sell it, at home or abroad, in his own town or in another hemisphere. Here's some muslin cloth woven in Saxony, perhaps, with Manchester-spun thread obtained through a blend of cottons harvested in Surat, India, Mobile, Alabama, and Egypt. It will then be embroidered in Nancy, to be sold in Philadelphia or Canton or Batavia [Java], after being warehoused in New York, Hong Kong, or Singapore.

Although the 1860 agreement is more often than not referred to, especially in English-speaking circles, by the name of its British signatory, Richard Cobden, Britain's "apostle of free trade" played a relatively minor role during the negotiations. The United Kingdom had unilaterally reduced most of its customs duties, and had little more to offer in 1860, apart from a readjustment of tariffs and excise taxes that lessened the unfavorable burden placed on French wine as compared to Portuguese wine and local beer.

It was also France, and not the United Kingdom, that broadened this treaty to the rest of Europe by signing similar agreements with the continent's major powers between 1861 and 1866. While the UK's unilateral adoption of free trade in the 1840s had had a limited impact on the customs policies of other countries, the full-scale bilateralism of France's trade-related diplomacy — amounting essentially to multilateralism thanks to the systematic inclusion of the favored nation clause in the agreements — introduced the building blocks of Europe's first common market. Beyond Europe, Napoleon III's navy provided significant support to the gunboat diplomacy deployed by the United Kingdom and the United States to open Asian and African markets to international trade. The unequal trade agreements between France and, among others, Siam (1856), Japan (1858), China (1860), and Madagascar (1868) look like the distorted reflection of the treaties drawn up in Europe.

In addition to this diplomacy of free trade imperialism, the Second Empire encouraged the export of French capital. The latter surpassed British foreign investment in the 1860s, particularly in Europe and the Middle East. During an international conference held in Paris in 1867, Napoleon III's regime even attempted to turn the Latin Monetary Union, established in 1865 with Italy, Switzerland, and Belgium, into a monetary unification of the entire continent. British hostility and Prussian reluctance alone scuttled the imitative. The Paris Universal Exposition of 1867 and the impressive opening ceremony of the Suez Canal in 1869 thus celebrated a specifically French brand of economic universalism.

As one would expect, this French drive to unify European and world markets also responded to self-serving geopolitical agendas. Michel Chevalier had long been concerned about raising French power to the level of Britain's and endowing the "Latin race" with as much prestige as the "Anglo-Saxon." At the same time, the 1860 treaty demonstrated that France's bid for dominance had become a matter of collaboration rather than confrontation with the British superpower. It was the logical follow-up to the rapprochement inaugurated in the 1830s and to France's military backing of the United Kingdom in the Levant and Far East, be it during the Crimean War against Russia (1853–1856) or the Second Opium War against China (1856–1860).

The British side sought first and foremost to boost political collaboration between the two countries. Thus, in 1859, Cobden, then a trade representative, wrote to Chevalier that the commercial solidarity model was "the method chosen by God to create an *entente cordiale*." That being said, the French and British presses still spent the century exchanging xenophobic broadsides. But the rhetoric framing England as a materialist, self-important "anti-France" should not overshadow the pragmatism of the policymakers. Likewise, the thunderous outcry provoked by the 1898 Fashoda Incident, an imperial territorial dispute in East Africa, soon gave way to a restored *entente cordiale* through an agreement in 1904 on respective spheres of colonial influence.

So why did this French-style economic globalization run out of steam? For one, the Second Empire's prosperity rested on shaky foundations. Population rates were starting to plateau around 1850, and specialized French industries were reluctant to embrace technological advances. Political factors and unforeseen events also hastened its demise. There was the failed French expedition to Mexico (1862–1867), motivated largely by commercial concerns and financial interests: on the one hand, the building of a second grand canal through the isthmus; on the other, securing a steady supply of silver ore to ensure the sustainability of the bimetallist standard for the French franc. Most crucially, there was the disastrous war with Prussia in 1870–1871. After that blistering defeat, the Third Republic increased French customs duties, failed to renew the 1860 treaty when it expired in the early 1880s, and opted for an outright protectionist policy: the 1892 Méline tariff, named after Prime Minister Jules Méline, one of the staunchest opponents to free trade. Along with Great Britain, France might thus have dominated the world economy for another decade, but not much longer.

In the end, why did this burst of French globalizing activism leave such a light footprint in collective memory? One might hypothesize that, like the entente policy with the United Kingdom, free trade was never really that popular at the time. On the evening the 1860 treaty was signed, British economist Nassau William Senior attended the gathering organized to celebrate the event. Apart from the co-signers themselves, Chevalier and Cobden, he reported a meager attendance, "some fifty free-traders, all that Paris could scrape together." Furthermore, this activism, even when it scored some successes, failed to win over leading republicans and large swathes of public opinion. Émile Zola's scathing critique of Second Empire profiteering in his Rougon-Macquart cycle of novels, notably in *Money*, captured and exacerbated deep-seated suspicion. One final factor: recent memory has clearly struggled to come to terms with a vision of France as champion of triumphant globalization.

Still, it is important to recall that the French have been more than just victims of the world economy's integration process. We might just as easily perceive in the Second

Empire's economic diplomacy initiatives the harbinger of a tradition that would go on to thrive in the twentieth century. History explains why French technocrats have taken a leading role in European economic integration, and the world economy's governing organizations, such as the IMF and the WTO.

David Todd

REFERENCES

Bairoch, Paul. *Commerce extérieur et développement économique de l'Europe au XIXe siècle*. Paris: Mouton, 1976.

Marsch, Peter T. *Bargaining on Europe: Britain and the First Common Market (1860–1892)*. New Haven: Yale University Press, 1999.

Nye, John V. C. *War, Wine, and Taxes: The Political Economy of Anglo-French Trade (1689–1900)*. Princeton: Princeton University Press, 2007.

Todd, David. *L'Identité économique de la France: Libre-échange et protectionnisme (1814–1851)*. Paris: Grasset, 2008.

Verley, Patrick. *L'Échelle du monde: Essai sur l'industrialisation de l'Occident*. 2nd ed. Paris: Gallimard, 2013.

RELATED ARTICLES

600 BCE, 1202, 1456, 1962, 1983, 1992, 2011

1863

"Algeria Shall Be an Arab Kingdom"

Turning recently conquered Algeria into an "Arab kingdom" and client-state of France was a doubly imperial project. Though supported personally by Emperor Napoleon III, who believed that an empire by its very nature should dominate vassal kingdoms, it nevertheless had many bitter opponents, not least the French settlers on the spot.

"Algeria is not a colony in the strict sense of the word, but an Arab kingdom. The natives there, like the settlers, have an equal right to my protection, for I am just as much the emperor of the Arabs as I am of the French." The letter containing this passage, written by Napoleon III to Marshal Aimable Pélissier, governor general of Algeria, on February 6, 1863, was followed in June 1865 by another that attempted to define a policy for Algeria, which the emperor now presented as an "Arab kingdom, a European colony, and a French military base." Widely disseminated around the country, the contents of this letter was perceived as a slap in the face by a majority of the French settlers, who — until Napoleon's fall in 1870 — furiously opposed a regime that they accused of imposing on them "an Arab kingdom," contrary to the best interests of the Europeans who had made Algeria their home.

Was Napoleon's plan a pipe dream or a real program for the future? What exactly was the project behind a statement that exposed, first, the emperor's uncertainty regarding the best mode of government for colonial Algeria, and, second, his hesitations over the place of the colony in the broader geopolitical arena of the Mediterranean?

In October 1852, Napoleon had reminded the dignitaries of Bordeaux that "We have, right opposite Marseille, an enormous kingdom that we must absorb into France." The term "kingdom" was used at the time to qualify the territory of the former Bey of Algiers, notably in the debates concerning the colonization of the regency and the forms that it might take. Auguste Cerfberr (author of *Du gouvernement d'Alger*, published in 1834) suggested that the best solution for organizing a territory that had been in the process of conquest and subjugation since 1830 was to set up a "kingdom of Algiers" independent of France "but linked to her by indissoluble treaties." This was necessary for domestic political reasons — but also to shore up a French colonial system that was still reeling from the ignominious loss of Saint-Domingue.

Who would rule Algeria? Some recommended indirect government for a few years by local chieftains. Henri d'Orléans, the Duke of Aumale (King Louis Philippe's soldier son and governor general of Algeria between 1847 and 1848), recollected, in 1865, that France "began by attempting to govern the populations of the interior using Turkish beys as intermediaries, then tried to group them under the authority of an Arab viceroy, or rather a sovereign allied to us." This "sovereign," who ruled after the signing of the Treaty of Tafna in 1837, was expected to be the emir Abd el-Kader, the charismatic leader of the Algerian resistance who had surrendered after a long struggle.

There was also a suggestion of a viceroyalty (subordinate to Paris) for the Duke of Aumale, who in 1847 had briefly taken the place of the ruthless military commander Thomas-Robert Bugeaud as governor general. Other propositions were made, but Napoleon III seemed above all determined to create a "separate kingdom of Algeria," though, when it came to its institutional organization, he hesitated between lieutenancy, vice royalty, and special ministry.

The "Arab kingdom" idea, all the same, marked a turning point in the Algerian policy of France. It is to be understood in the context of a wider Mediterranean policy, the Mediterranean being seen as a future French lake thanks to France's possession of Algeria and its determination to maintain a strong presence in the Middle East.

In effect, France had been politically engaged in the eastern Mediterranean ever since the expedition of Bonaparte to Egypt (1798–1801). At that time the establishment of a modern Egyptian state, a vassal of the Ottoman Empire, was mooted, hence Napoleon I's dispatch of battalions of experts in support of Muhammad Ali's attempt to reform the country. In the 1850s, French policy sought to balance France's alliances with Constantinople and London while at the same time affirming the country's presence in the Arab Mashriq countries (today's Lebanon, Palestine, Jordan, Syria, and Iraq). These moves, which lay at the heart of the great Franco-British game, became all the greater when work began on the construction of the Suez Canal in 1859.

The massacre of Christians in Syria during the summer of 1860 provoked the landing in Beirut of a French expeditionary force. Napoleon III thus reassumed Francis I's mantle of protector of the Christians of the Orient. In the space of a few dramatic weeks, the intervention of Abd el-Kader, then in exile in Damascus, allowed several thousand Christians to escape death. The French press, and especially the Catholic press, paid fulsome tribute to his actions. Had the emperor intended to harness the emir to French policy when he took the decision to send an expedition to Syria? It is hard to say; yet the historian Charles-Robert Ageron has shown how frequently the name of the emir was mentioned in contemporary French newspapers. Some editors even proclaimed that "a strong, civilizing government should be created" for Abd el-Kader to run as an "Arab state," and even "an Arab empire." The French authorities did indeed consider setting up an "Arab emirate of the Levant," recruiting Abd el-Kader in 1865 as head of state of "an Arab empire," or at least as governor of Syria. The emir duly declined the offer, but the project remained on the French agenda in the years that followed.

France's Syrian expedition itself was a success for the "active Arab and Oriental" policy in the Mediterranean — and in the Maghreb. More interested in the region during his first visit to Algeria in September 1860, Napoleon III himself opined that France should appear as the "savior of the Arab nation in Algeria." In 1865, the emperor went on to declare that "France, which everywhere embraces notions of nationality," could not justify its domination over the Arab people "without offering them a better existence." Algeria had to become "for the fifteen million other Arabs in the other parts of Africa and Asia, an enviable country." When that day came, "the glory of France would be acknowledged from Tunis to the Euphrates, securing for our country a fame that could make no man jealous, being founded not upon conquest but upon a respect for humanity and progress." According to the historian Henry Laurens, the idea was to render "the influence of France desirable by making Algeria a model of civilization for all other Arab-speaking nations within the Ottoman Empire."

Napoleon's letter of February 6, 1863, whose tenor rapidly became common knowledge throughout Algeria, was by no means the first text in which the emperor mentioned an "Arab kingdom." As early as November 1861, he was writing to Marshal Pélissier: "Our African possession is no ordinary colony, but an Arab kingdom." This echoed a speech made on September 19, 1860, in Algiers, during which he proclaimed: "Our first duty is to work for the happiness of the three million Arabs" who had recently come under French domination, and to raise them "to the dignity of free men." Both in its inspiration and its phrasing, the text of 1863 cleaves to the ideas of Ismael Urbain as expressed in his 1862 *L'Algérie française: Indigènes et immigrants* (French Algeria: Natives and Immigrants). Urbain, a brilliant journalist and former Arabic interpreter, was a close friend and confidant of Abd el-Kader. He was also a convinced Saint-Simonian, member of a group of young engineers and doctors who had proposed original solutions to the social and banking crises of the early nineteenth century. Urbain had real influence at that time in Algeria, and so did his colleagues: the geographer, historian, and former Prefect of Algeria Frédéric Lacroix in Paris, and Baron David, a former officer of the Arab bureau. All three called for an administration of the tribes by the intermediary of native leaders or *caïds* named by the Arab bureau. This would lead to a "veritable Franco-Arab association, preparatory to genuine fusion."

In the meantime, Frédéric Lacroix wrote in 1863 that "Algeria will be an Arab kingdom" on the model of India, an "Indian kingdom exploited by England." Decreed on April 22, 1863, this policy was presented as a guarantee of Algerian land ownership. When, after a five-week visit to Algeria in 1865, Napoleon III described the colony as "an Arab kingdom, a European colony, and a French military base," he also compared the French role to that of "the Spaniards of Mexico, who have brought together all the native inhabitants." His strategy was therefore to accustom the Arabs "to our laws, to make them used to our dominance, and to convince them of our military and institutional superiority." The emperor's other proposals concerning the natives were numerous enough, but their only legislative result was the Senate's decree on nationality (July 14, 1865), which allowed Algerian natives to become French citizens provided they abandoned the previous legal status they held as Muslims.

The imperial project was badly received in Algeria in 1865 if then governor general Patrice de MacMahon is to be believed. In his view, the expression "Arab kingdom" would worry the French public as well as settlers, who would "persuade themselves that what we want is to recreate an arbitrary Arab nationality as a solid entity that Europeans may no longer penetrate." According to the Duke of Aumale, the policy of autonomy underpinned by the "chimera of an Arab kingdom" would only serve to strengthen the "indigenous feudal system." It was even rumored that Abd el-Kader himself would be appointed viceroy — a solution favored by the French press baron Émile de Girardin, who campaigned vigorously on behalf of an autonomous Algeria under French suzerainty.

In fact, if Napoleon III ever meant to give a political role to the emir, it was one that he would be expected to fulfill not in Algeria, but in the Middle East. In August 1865, the emperor directed General Émile Félix Fleury, a diplomat specializing in Middle Eastern matters, to "assess the feelings of Abd el-Kader as to the creation in Syria of an independent Arab state of which he could be the sovereign." The emir's firm refusal to contemplate this notion put an end to this possible facet of France's Arab policy.

Several factors combined to kill the "Arab kingdom" idea: the ill will of the governors general, the hostility of the settlers, and the social effects of a series of natural disasters between 1867 and 1868 that were seen as the consequences of the emperor's pro-Arab policies. In addition, international developments distracted the sovereign's attention from the Algerian question. On March 9, 1870, the legislative body voted unanimously in favor of "a civilian regime, to reconcile the interests of Europeans and the native population." That April, the editors of the newspaper *L'Écho d'Oran* exulted in what they called the "Waterloo of the Arab kingdom," definitively buried as it was by the policies of assimilation of the first years of the Third Republic. Directed from Paris the new Algerian administration would override the particularities of a territory wherein native populations coexisted with Europeans whose socioeconomic and cultural backgrounds differed from their own. Only in 1899 did France confer upon its Algerian colony a relative autonomy and a budget of its own.

Claire Fredj

REFERENCES

Ageron, Charles-Robert. "Abd el-Kader souverain d'un royaume arabe d'Orient." *Revue de l'Occident musulman et de la Méditerranée* 8, no. 1 (1970): 15–30.

Laurens, Henry. *Le Royaume impossible: La France et la genèse du monde arabe.* Paris: Armand Colin, 1990.

Levallois, Michel. *Ismaÿl Urbain: Royaume arabe ou Algérie franco-musulmane? (1848–1870)*. Paris: Riveneuve, 2012.

Rey-Goldzeiguer, Annie. *Le Royaume arabe: La politique algérienne de Napoléon III (1861–1870)*. Algiers: SNED, 1977.

"ALGERIA SHALL BE AN ARAB KINGDOM"

RELATED ARTICLES
1270, 1712, 1798, 1869, 1958, 2003

1869

The Inauguration of the Suez Canal

The Suez Canal was inaugurated in November 1869
in the presence of French Empress Eugénie and the
Emperor of Austria. Made possible by the efforts of
Ferdinand de Lesseps and the investments of the Egyptian
Khedive Ismāʿīl Pasha, this massive brainchild of French
engineering became the vital artery of the British Empire.

On November 17, 1869, a long column of ships left Port
Said to make its way through the stretch of sand dividing
the Mediterranean and the Red Sea, now newly connected
by a thin thread of water. They were marking the occasion
of the inauguration of the Suez Canal, which would reduce
the distance between Europe and its Asian colonies by
about 40 percent. Empress Eugénie of France was the
first to pass the new canal on her yacht *L'Aigle*, leading an
armada of fifty-five ships that carried princes, ambassadors,
and other European and Middle Eastern notables. The trip
was not without trepidation for the captains navigating
the canal; Eugénie herself was in near hysteria given the

canal's narrowness and the excitement of the long-expected occasion. While staging the event, organizers made sure to follow French etiquette and welcome the empress with as much polite attention as possible. Stretching his tight finances to the limit, the Egyptian khedive Ismāʿīl even had the European-style Gezirah Palace built for Eugénie's reception in Cairo.

Do the opening of the Suez Canal and the role of Empress Eugénie make this event a component of French history? Or was Ismāʿīl's attempt to "make his country part of Europe" deeply anchored in Egyptian history? Should we, finally, situate it within British imperial history; after all, the canal soon came to be known as the highway of the British Empire? If we follow architectural critic Sigfried Giedion's notion that the sun is mirrored even in a coffee spoon, then despite its narrowness the Suez Canal was certainly large enough to encompass all kinds of global and local histories, including the global history of France. Yet global histories always carry specific perspectives. The question of where to situate the opening of the Suez Canal within global history thus leads to broader questions about the "ownership" of historical events, or whether the latter should have any owner at all. The answer will depend of course on one's viewpoint, but also on how we define chronology. When did the opening of the Suez Canal begin and when did it end?

The dream of connecting the Mediterranean and the Red

Sea to avoid a detour around an entire continent was born before construction began in 1859. Prior to the canal opening, the short stretch of land dividing the Mediterranean and the Red Sea at the Isthmus of Suez had become symbolically charged. At the crossroads of political rivalries, this desert took on multiple meanings. It was at once a strip of barren desert that had to be mapped and calculated and a mystical project that drew on cutting-edge technology while drawing from the legends of ancient Egypt and biblical lands.

The construction of the Suez Canal captures late-nineteenth-century attitudes toward "progress" and "modernity." And it is in this long nineteenth-century story that France took on a specific role. As in other European countries, Egypt loomed large in the imagination of French travelers and, later, scientists, engineers, and military leaders. Published in 1803, just after the Napoleonic expedition, Jacques-Marie Le Père's *Mémoire sur la communication de la mer des Indes à la Méditerranée par la mer Rouge et l'isthme de Soueys* deemed the canal impossible due to a ten-meter difference in height between the two seas. Several decades later, followers of Henri de Saint-Simon took up the project again, convinced that the Suez Canal would resolve the opposition between East and West. Saint-Simonian Barthélemy-Prosper Enfantin traveled to Egypt to lobby for his scheme.

Eccentric as Enfantin may have been, engineers were

becoming leading global actors now that large-scale infrastructural projects were the order of the day. In this context, the École Polytechnique, alma mater of both Le Père and Enfantin, developed into an international model for training engineers. Of course, French engineers also built bridges, towers, and railways — all of them symbols of modernity as well as technical feats. The Suez Canal was no exception.

Given the prestige of French engineering, it might not astonish that a Frenchman, Ferdinand de Lesseps, won the bid to construct the canal in the 1850s. His success rested largely on his connections, however. As the son of a diplomat, de Lesseps had not only befriended Eugénie, but also spent considerable time in the Ottoman Empire, and more particularly in Egypt. This enabled him to establish close ties with ruling elites. The canal's construction did not rest on French actors alone. During the preparatory planning, French engineers tapped the likes of Alois Negrelli, an Austrian oft-forgotten by historians who had been involved in Enfantin's Society for the Study of the Suez Canal. Once the actual building began, de Lesseps necessarily relied on all kinds of associates to raise capital and secure a local workforce. There were of course competitors and critics as well, above all Britons and Americans who, given the era's abolitionist climate, protested the use of forced labour. In order to finance the undertaking, de Lesseps could not simply rely on French stakeholders. He offered shares in numerous exchanges and pressured Ismāʿīl Pasha to buy up the ones he could not sell.

The same multilayered global structure surrounds the inauguration. Following the Saint-Simonian line, the Suez Canal Company presented the canal as a tool of global unification. This could mean at least two things: either Europeanization of non-European lands or else the fusion of "East" and "West" at this particular place. The Company avoided depicting the canal as exclusively French or European, emphasizing instead its "Oriental" and global dimensions. During the inauguration festivities, desert tents complete with Bedouins and snake charmers entertained the illustrious guests while showing how the canal would marry European technological modernization with Orientalist fantasies that fulfilled the expectations of European visitors. Other aspects of the opening ceremony advanced the idea of unification. The religious service and the benediction of the canal, for example, included Catholic, Greek Orthodox, and Muslim clergy. The building site manager, François Philippe Voisin, made this thinking explicit when he declared that "all languages, all races, all colors, all dresses [were] gathered in the wide streets of the nascent city." This idea of the world in one location was taken up by the Suez Canal Company and others, placing the role of France in this global story in proper perspective.

After its inauguration, the canal joined not just French and Egyptian histories, but — perhaps most importantly — British global history. Its opening, which coincided with the expansion of steamship navigation, increased passenger traffic and facilitated travel by migrants, tourists, and colonial officials. The canal found itself surrounded by metaphors in travel accounts and elsewhere: it was an artery, a jugular vein, the highway of empire, the wasp's waist connecting the British head to its Indian body. At the inauguration, British travel agent Thomas Cook had already called the canal the "greatest engineering feat of the present century." Authors such as Rudyard Kipling anchored it in the public imagination as the exact halfway point between Britain and India. Britain also contributed to this process in more tangible ways. When the khedive of Egypt was forced to sell his shares in 1875, Prime Minister Benjamin Disraeli seized the opportunity to become majority shareholder. The Rothschild bank contributed to this renowned financial coup.

In its daily operations, the canal became a place of competition between empires. The British and the French observed their rivals' troop transports to imperial possessions. Likewise, all kinds of global mobility were channeled, tabulated, and sorted out in the canal. Consider the pilgrims who journeyed from French North Africa to Mecca via this passageway and were accused of transporting epidemic diseases as well as dangerous and contagious political ideas into the Mediterranean. As illustrated by the scene Jules Verne set in this region in *Around the World in Eighty Days*, the canal became a checkpoint for the control of criminals, smugglers, alleged traffickers of women, and other forms of illicit mobility.

The Suez Canal thus requires many historical perspectives. French and British expansionism both provide legitimate angles, but so do Egyptian, Indian, and North African approaches. This history provides at once a history of global hierarchies connecting empires and nations and a history of the subversion of these very hierarchies. In this sense, the image of the sun mirrored in a single coffee spoon does not do full justice to the global history of a place like the Suez Canal. Instead, we need an entire cutlery set, with its innumerable reflections of light.

Valeska Huber

REFERENCES

Giedion, Sigfried. *Mechanization Takes Command: A Contribution to Anonymous History*. New York: Norton, 1969 [1948].

Huber, Valeska. *Channelling Mobilities: Migration and Globalisation in the Suez Canal Region and Beyond, 1869–1914*. Cambridge: Cambridge University Press, 2013.

Piquet, Caroline. *Histoire du canal de Suez*. Paris: Perrin, 2009.

Schweitzer, Sylvie. "Der Ingenieur." In *Der Mensch des 19. Jahrhunderts*, edited by Ute Frevert and Heinz-Gerhard Haupt. Essen: Magnus, 2004 [1999].

RELATED ARTICLES

719, 1095, 1247, 1484, 1769, 1900, 1962, 2003

1871

Local Revolution, Global Myth

The Paris Commune began on March 18, 1871, as an
experiment to counter Prussian defeat, defend city
freedoms, and emancipate workers. This local movement
was met with a bloody crackdown and expulsions from
France. For twentieth-century revolutionaries, it would
become a landmark event.

The Paris Commune holds a unique place in French and
international memories. For a long time, it was viewed as
an inspiration for future revolutions in Russia (1917) and
China (1949). Marxist readings of this revolution appeared
to cement its place in world history. But over time, its impact
seemed to recede and become more localized to Paris, its
status in history uncertain. Divided between conflicted
memories, it is poorly understood today.

The Commune takes its place within a longer sequence
of political and military events, beginning with the Franco-
Prussian War of 1870. The conflict between two of Europe's
major powers was one of the largest on the continent,

878

following the Crimean War (1853–1856), the Italian Wars in the 1850s and 1860s, and the Austro-Prussian War of 1866. The proximity with the American Civil War (1861–1865) did not go unnoticed on either side of the Atlantic. Contemporary interest in the conflict should not come as a surprise, therefore, especially when the French armies collapsed, when Napoleon III's Second Empire came to an end, and when a new Republic surfaced in France. At that point, the French cause became a republican cause. Thousands of international volunteers — Italians, Poles, Belgians, Greeks, Americans, Argentines — rushed to the aid of the "universal republic." The military feats of Italian General Giuseppe Garibaldi, the "hero of both worlds" who was placed at the head of the volunteer Army of the Vosges, embodied this widespread sentiment.

The breadth of this international radical movement should not be overstated, however. It was matched by a parallel phase of intense national mobilization, in France as well as in Germanic countries, which some historians have viewed as a forerunner to the "total" wars of the following century. Diplomacy also played a strong role. The newly established Third Republic sought official recognition from foreign nations. In the name of shared republican ideologies, the United States were the first to do so. This symbolic gesture elicited jubilant displays, with French and American flags waved in Paris and Marseille. Italy, Greece, Spain,

Portugal, Sweden, and Colombia followed suit and quickly recognized the French Republic. The United Kingdom and Austria were more reluctant.

Still, these displays of foreign support did not change the outcome of a war won with unrivaled firepower. The London Conference (January–March 1871) did little to change the plans of Prussian Chancellor Otto von Bismarck, who annexed part of France's territory (Alsace and Moselle) and levied heavy war reparations (five billion gold francs).

The evolution of French politics was strongly influenced by this international context and by preexisting dynamics, both national and regional. Bismarck, for instance, pushed French authorities into establishing legislative elections as a means of negotiation with a nationally representative assembly. And the war encouraged people to vote for peace. But the elections of February 1871 also revived earlier conflicts between radical republicans, liberals, and monarchists, while exacerbating latent tensions between cities and rural areas. In the end, with divisions as sharp as ever within each group, conservatives and especially monarchists (though they had been losing steam for years) won out against republicans. March 18, 1871 — the start of the Paris Commune — can be seen as an extension of these tendencies. If the head of the executive branch, Adolphe Thiers, sent the army to collect cannons from the National Guard in Montmartre, it was with the dual aim of ensuring the conditions for peace with Prussia and controlling an increasingly rebellious city. His efforts failed. The movement to reconquer the city from within grew first into a riot and then into revolution.

The Paris Commune was a high-visibility project to free the city and workers. It occurred in the capital city of the era's second largest economic and imperial power, after London. It stimulated similar tendencies in other French cities: Lyon, Marseille, Narbonne, Le Creusot, and even, although this is less known, Algiers. In short, the events of the Paris Commune drew the world's attention to France.

In addition, the Paris experiment was supported by Karl Marx's recently formed International Workingmen's Association. Established in London in 1864, the organization had undergone considerable growth in the late 1860s. Reticent advocates at the outset, members at the head office and local branches quickly became ardent supporters of the Commune. Rallies for the cause were held in London and Geneva in April. On May 25, German socialist August Bebel defended the Communards at the Reichstag. These groups brought increased visibility to the event. Nevertheless, their impact was overwhelmed by a wave of criticism in the official French and foreign press. "The gentlemen of Belleville [a working-class neighborhood] and French prisons are not wasting their time," wrote *The Times* in an ironic tone on March 25. "They know they can't hold onto power for long,

881

and above all their desire is to exact vengeance — as some would say, to give free rein to their madness."

In Paris, the local stakes of the event remained strong. Anti-Commune propaganda painted the movement as a cosmopolitan plot, pointing to the involvement of many members of the International Workingmen's Association. Even pro-Commune propaganda sought to link the Commune to a greater cause and depicted it as a beacon for future revolutionary movements. But, in truth, the leaders were the Parisian masses, who embraced politics as workers, Parisians, and socialists. Let us note also that most Communards espoused a universal republic, the emancipation of all workers, regardless of nationality, and the defense of the Commune itself, now at war with the official government in Versailles. Patriotism was part of the question. For Parisians, universal and nationalistic aims were not necessarily contradictory, even if the latter appalled Marx. The Commune's aim was not to collectivize property, but to establish a democratic and socialist republic anchored in previous revolutionary experiments, especially the early years of the Second French Republic (1848–1850). Its members voted for the separation of church and state and encouraged the development of unions and production cooperatives, such as a mechanics' union. They envisioned a federation of associations that would establish a bottom-up, concrete republic and equal exchanges between producers and consumers. For some, a scheme of federated free cities would constitute a "true" and fair republic.

The violent offensive by the regular French Army squelched such attempts. Their massacre of insurgents during what was dubbed the "Bloody Week" and the burning of several buildings by Communards (the Parisian City Hall, the Tuileries Palace, and many others) shocked France and the world. Between five and six thousand Communards went into exile in England, Switzerland, and the United States, as well as Argentina and Chile. Meanwhile, the International Workingmen's Association was banned or placed under scrutiny in many countries.

The Commune's multiple dimensions, too rich to lend themselves to simple classification, have been overwhelmed by such images of bloodshed and mayhem. That explains why the event has so often been appropriated by later political forces: French republicans after 1880, Bolsheviks in 1917, French patriotic groups in the 1920s, the French Communist Party after World War II, Maoists in the 1960s, and protesters in May 1968. The Paris Commune may be old history, but it is easy to understand why it remains relevant today, as occupations of public spaces grow ever more numerous.

Quentin Deluermoz

REFERENCES

Deluermoz, Quentin. *Le crépuscule des révolutions, 1848–1871*. Paris: Le Seuil, 2012.

Fournier, Eric. *La Commune n'est pas morte*. Paris: Libertalia, 2013.

Godineau, Laure. *Retour d'exil: Les anciens communards au début de la Troisième République*. PhD diss., Paris I, 2000.

Katz, Philip M. *From Appomattox to Montmartre: Americans and the Paris Commune*. Cambridge, MA: Harvard University Press, 1998.

Merriman, John. *Massacre: The Life and Death of the Paris Commune of 1871*. New Haven: Yale University Press, 2014.

Rougerie, Jacques, Tristan Haan, Georges Haupt, and Miklos Molnar, eds. "Jalons pour une histoire de la Commune de Paris." Special issue of *International Review of Social History* XVII, (1972).

Tombs, Robert. *The Paris Commune 1871*. London: Longman, 1999.

RELATED ARTICLES

1357, 1789, 1840, 1848, 1852, 1892, 1968

1875

Measuring the World

In the spring of 1875, seventeen nations came together
to sign the Metric Convention. Against a backdrop of
globalized exchange, the international agreement elevated
the French unit of measure, which had been invented under
the Revolution, to a universal scale. Still, muted national
rivalries and the United Kingdom's refusal to adopt the
system limited its reach.

From March to May 1875, Paris hosted an unusual summit.
The twenty attending nations were not there to manage
border disputes, avoid war, or divvy up the world. Rather,
the diplomats and scientists convened in France only had
eyes for the meter — the unlikely hero of this international
gathering.

After several weeks of discussion, seventeen nations
reached an agreement and signed the "Metric Convention,"
which created a new institute, the International Bureau
of Weights and Measures, soon thereafter established in
Sèvres, where it remains today. The bureau was tasked with

developing and preserving international prototypes of the meter and the kilogram in a neutral space. There, nations could compare their own standard weights and measures with indisputable references. The ultimate aim was nothing short of contributing to unifying humankind through the spread of the metric system across the globe. Falling short of creating a universal language, the meter could at least give humanity a universal system to compare weights and measures. It would not end armed conflict, but science, trade, and transportation infrastructure would certainly benefit.

In reality, this summit was the second of its kind. France had convened an international commission to discuss the meter once before, in 1799. The context then was quite different: the revolutionary nation was consumed with its universal mission and hoped to convince foreign scientists to lend authority to the work that two French astronomers, Jean-Baptiste Joseph Delambre and Pierre Méchain, had been labouring over since 1792. The two men had been tasked with supplying an accurate measurement of the revolutionary meter, defined as one ten-millionth of the arc separating the North Pole from the equator. With the Paris meridian as their point of reference, Delambre and Méchain used a triangulation method to calculate the distance between the northern French town of Dunkirk and Barcelona. They then offered a value estimate of a meter that would stand up to scrutiny. The globe itself would become the measure of all things, thereby preventing any single nation or people from imposing its own arbitrary system.

Although French scientists and politicians spearheaded this research, the enterprise was undertaken in the name of nature and science. The French revolutionaries imagined themselves as agents of a universal scheme that transcended personal or national interests. The list of countries represented at the 1799 conference showed the limits of this rhetoric, however. While French allies and territories were represented in the discussion, England and its associated powers found themselves excluded. Politics came into play: the merit of the meter — its precision and universalism — were vaunted precisely at the time France began exhibiting newfangled imperial ambitions. In matters of measurement diplomacy, science and power were inextricably linked.

A member of the French Academy of Sciences, General Napoleon Bonaparte showed a keen interest in metrological debates. Yet, shortly after the coup through which he seized power on 18 Brumaire Year VIII (November 9, 1799), he suspended widespread use of the metric system in France. The French revolutionaries had sought to impose the metric and decimal systems at the expense of a patchwork of measurement units inherited from the ancien régime. By implementing a universal system, they hoped to encourage the exchange of goods and ideas. The metric system, like the administrative division of the territory into departments and the new calendar with ten-day weeks, would imbue the French nation with a scientific spirit of reason and homogeneity. This was part of what the revolutionaries called "regeneration."

But however sincere such idealism may have been, it clashed with a lingering conservatism at play in French society. Loath to abandon their customs, many French men and women continued to count in aunes and bushels for day-to-day transactions. Eventually, Napoleon decided that overhauling and standardizing weights and measures was not worth the trouble. The venture was postponed. And so it was that while France promoted universalism, the country failed to overcome its incredible local variation. The metric system would not enter the day-to-day lives of French people until the late 1830s.

In the meantime, the system spread through a large swath of Europe and the world. New nation-states, including Belgium in 1830, South American countries in the 1850s, and Italy and Germany in the 1860s, were eager to adopt it as part of national unification projects. Scientific and industrial progress called for uniform, or at least easily convertible, weights and measurements. World's Fairs (starting with the Crystal Palace Exhibition in 1851), the first international statistics congresses, and the International Association of Geodesy (founded in 1862) bolstered advocates of an internationalized metric system. Meanwhile, growing rail, postal, and telecommunication connectivity required further coordination among nations. Established in 1865, the International Telegraph Union was one of the first organizations devoted to international technical cooperation and increased circulation. Even England, which had long been wary of the French metric system, was on the verge of giving in when, in 1863, the House of Commons approved a proposal making the meter mandatory. Alas, the bill was not confirmed by the House of Lords.

Growing Prussian interest in internationalizing the metric system caught the attention of Napoleon III. To make sure France did not lose its wonderful invention, he convened an international commission in Paris in July 1870. The Franco-Prussian War, which broke out that same month, disturbed these plans. And although the Second Empire fell that year, the meter survived. Discussions to develop an international system for improving and harmonizing weights and measures began again in 1872. A defeated and humiliated France, occupied by a lenient Germany, would soothe its wounded pride thanks to the meter, whose scientific prestige won international recognition. That was the context for the 1875 summit, devoted to the status and role of the future International Bureau. The defeated revolutionary nation could thus remain a model in technical and scientific matters, even if by 1889 the old, imprecise meter housed in the National Archives would be replaced by new international prototypes.

The diplomatic victory of 1875 was of course incomplete. The United Kingdom was the world's leading economic, commercial, and imperial power, and it did not authorize its representative at the summit, London's commissioner for weights and measures and monetary standards, to negotiate in its name. Despite progress made by local proponents of the metric system, the British remained unfailingly attached to their inches, feet, and yards. The international metric system was not adopted across the Channel (and in the Commonwealth) until the 1960s and 1970s, when the nation considered joining the European Economic Community. Meanwhile, the United States participated in the summit from the beginning, but, as we know, has never made the metric system mandatory. Much as contemporaries spoke of scientific neutrality, a civilized world, and international standardization, national rivalries persisted in the 1870s and 1880s. The meter may have won out in 1875, but parallel discussions about adopting a universal timekeeping system ended in stunning failure for French scientific diplomacy just nine years later.

In 1884, a Washington, DC, summit established the Greenwich meridian line as the international reference point for ship navigation and time telling, relegating Paris's meridian to a mere relic, pointing to a bygone time during which French scientists believed they could dominate the world. In an equally devastating blow, the British gold standard began to prevail on an international scale from the 1870s on, overshadowing France's initiative to establish an international monetary system based on the franc and its bimetallic anchor currency, the Latin Monetary Union.

The history of the metric system and France's stake in its invention and subsequent general use shows how absurd it is to contrast globalization with the construction of nation-states, as if one could undermine the other. In reality, France sought to standardize its domestic measurement system throughout the nineteenth century at the same time as it fought to make its system an international reference. France was an advocate for globalization, so long as it reflected French ideals.

Nicolas Delalande

REFERENCES

Alder, Ken. *The Measure of All Things: The Seven-Year Odyssey and Hidden Error That Transformed the World*. New York: Simon & Schuster, 2003.

French Ministry of Foreign Affairs. *Conférence diplomatique du mètre*. Paris: Imprimerie nationale, 1875.

Geyer, Martin H., and Johannes Paulmann, eds. *The Mechanics of Internationalism: Culture, Society, and Politics from the 1840s to the First World War*. Oxford: Oxford University Press, 2001.

Rosenberg, Emily S., ed. *A World Connecting: 1870–1945*. Cambridge, MA: Harvard University Press, 2012.

RELATED ARTICLES

1539, 1795, 1804, 1860, 1903, 1973

1883

From the Zambezi to the Corrèze, a Single World
Language?

July 21, 1883, marks the founding of the Alliance
Française, whose purpose was to spread French throughout
the globe, even as the language's status as lingua franca
of world elites and for that matter of French regions was
uncertain. We tend to forget the colonial roots of this
association, which has grown into the largest cultural
NGO on the planet.

"So, where did you pick up such good French?"

"At the Alliance Française [in Rosario, Argentina],
where else?" was the reply Ernesto Guevara is said to have
given in January 1959 to the French ambassador, who was
duly impressed by Che's fluency. This is the same Che
Guevera who, upon learning that his guerrilla fighters,
under orders from Fidel Castro himself, had shut down the
large Alliance Française in Havana, commanded that it be
reopened the next morning. After all, even the Bolsheviks
had spared Moscow's Alliance offices back in 1921. As the

quintessential language of enlightenment and emancipation, French made sense to revolutionaries like Rafael Guillén, the future Zapatista Subcomandante Marcos, who'd come to Paris in 1977 to take French classes at the Alliance, before sampling the more serious offerings of Louis Althusser and Michel Foucault. They would have been baffled upon discovering the imperialist origins of this venerable institution, founded in Paris in 1883 under the less than revolutionary name of French Alliance for the Propagation of the French Language in the Colonies and Abroad.

On July 21, 1883, a learned assembly met at 215 Boulevard Saint-Germain to "spread France's influence through the propagation of its language." The august gathering was convened by two fervent believers in the Republic: geographer Pierre Foncin and diplomat Paul Cambon, then serving as resident general in Tunis. They brought together a senior government official, an Arabic-speaking scientist, a former education minister, a member of the Protestant community, a Catholic missionary, and a representative of the Jewish community, all committed to promoting French interests in, of all places, Tunisia, which had become a French protectorate two years earlier. Their stated intention was to assert France's colonial power before Tunisia's massive Italian community by devising a new tool of influence. Inspired by Ernest Renan's *La reforme intellectuale et morale* (1871), this pedagogical, patriotic, and colonial project evolved in symbiosis with the geographical societies that were flourishing at the time.

Modeled after the Alliance Israélite Universelle, which had been active in Tunisia since 1878, the Alliance Française was partially financed by the state and comprised local volunteer committees that, in order to "alert people to the virtues of the French language," created and funded libraries and schools, organized meetings and lectures, and thus increased the number of "friends of France." The Alliance's mission soon expanded into a broader effort to supplement the inadequate educational infrastructure in the French overseas empire, to reassert the country's "civilizing mission" among colonized subjects, and to accrue cultural prestige following France's humiliating 1870 defeat by the Prussians. In 1884, an undistinguished professor at the University of Toulouse recalled the association's raison d'être: "The Alliance is absolutely right to be concerned first and foremost with spreading our language: our colonies will not be French in their hearts and minds until they understand some French....For France in particular, language is the crucial instrument of colonization. Emigration from France is not as strong as it is from England or Germany; and even if we encouraged it more, it would never amount to enough to provide the vast territories of Algeria, Tunisia, and Tonkin with French nationals who, by their mere presence, spread our ideas and influence."

This obsession with population decline, expressed here by the young Jean Jaurès, was shared by geographer Onésime Reclus, who coined the term "francophonie" in his 1886 book *France, Algérie et les colonies* to designate this new linguistic empire whose expansion he was advocating. He believed that language, more so than trade or race, was the glue that held the empire together, connecting Paris to the provinces and the colonies: "We accept as 'Francophones' all those who speak our language or appear destined to do so: Bretons and Basques of France, Arabs and Berbers of the Tell, whom we already administer." Although parts of Belgium, Switzerland, and Canada were included under this Francophone banner, Reclus was convinced that the colonial empire alone could make French a universal language. This imperial ambition appealed to Pierre Foncin, who directed the Alliance for more than three decades and urged a "moral conquest" of the colonized populations through rudimentary command of spoken French — enough to meet the needs and capacities of the "natives." This soft-power imperialism would prove far less expensive than coercive military measures: "It costs less to maintain a schoolteacher than a company of legionnaires."

Republican elites and Alliance board members such as Ferdinand de Lesseps, Ernest Renan, Louis Pasteur, and Jules Verne shared the same belief in the virtues of French as a "perfect language" that combined precision, clarity, and elegance. "French leaves no room for irrationality or equivocation," politician Jules Simon exclaimed without batting an eye in 1888, addressing an assembly of notables he'd won over to the cause. Philologists were reinventing the national language by emphasizing its indigenous roots, or more precisely its origins in Paris, the nexus of the Francien dialect that underpinned what evolved into modern French. The superiority of French, a turn-of-the-century truism, had been exalted twenty years earlier by Victor Hugo in his essay "William Shakespeare": "How does one recognize intelligence among peoples the world over? There is one sure sign: whether or not they can speak French." It was an undisputable fact that, since the eighteenth century, French had boasted both a body of classical literature and a status as idiom of choice for the worldly life of intellectual Paris. By way of aristocrats, journalists, writers, soldiers of fortune, and French-speaking schoolteachers, French had become the lingua franca of a large portion of the European, Russian, and American aristocracies — the language of diplomacy since the 1713 Treaty of Utrecht. French was also the language of literature, science, love, and all conversations worth having in lecture halls or salons.

The language's preponderance started to wane in the 1880s, when France found itself waging a "language war" against European rivals and suffered its first setback with the decline of French book exports. "When nations are not shooting it out on the battlefield, language is their most powerful weapon of war....Anglo-American missionaries first spread their Bibles throughout Africa, Asia, and the Pacific Islands, and the use of English followed soon after.... Our cross-channel neighbors are practical people who know that wherever English can be heard, British products will be purchased," wrote Alliance founder Foncin in 1888. German was rivaling French in the field of science, while Italian was rapidly gaining ground after the creation of the Dante Alighieri Society in 1889. Idealists hoping to reunite a humanity riven by these various linguistic imperialisms were minting brand new languages that, from Volapük (1879) to Esperanto (1887), now earned international recognition.

French may well have been the prerogative of a portion of the world's elites, but how much French was actually in use in France itself? Less than one might believe. In a lecture delivered in Bordeaux in 1884, the Alliance secretary general reminded his listeners that the battle had to be won at home first: "Without even leaving France, I see some dark areas: in the north, Flemish is spoken; in Bretagne, low Breton; on the Spanish border, Basque and Catalan; and in the south, various vernaculars derived from the old Occitan....As progress is made in elementary school education, these dark zones will gradually fade away, and we can envision a time when the French language will be understood and spoken by all the people of France." French did indeed make headway, and regional languages receded due to laws put forward by Education Ministers François Guizot (1833), Alfred de Falloux (1850), and especially Jules Ferry (1881–1882), who made primary education free, compulsory, and secular (*laïque*).

Laws notwithstanding, school inspectors uncovered evidence of patois resistance in a large portion of the country. In the southwestern town of Moissac, "a man from the north has a hard time making himself understood"; near the Pyrenees, "for most children, especially in rural areas, French is a foreign language, about as understandable to them as the Latin in their prayer books"; in a nearby department, "French might as well be Chinese" for the schoolchildren. Even taking into account the difficulty involved in conducting an accurate survey of non-French-speaking patois users, an 1864 study ordered by the Ministry of Education concluded that French was a minority language in large parts of Alsace-Lorraine, Bretagne, Ariège, Corrèze, Haute-Vienne, Hérault, and Alpes-Maritimes, including the cities of Montpellier and Nice, where the Montpellier and Nissart dialects reigned supreme. Practically no one spoke French in the regions of Aveyron, Gers, Var, and Corsica. Many historians argue that only at the turn of the century, thanks to compulsory, cost-free education, mandatory military service, and a surge in the market economy, did French make significant inroads in such regions.

Meanwhile, as ethno-essentialist ideas replaced ineffectual policies of "native" assimilation in the French empire, the Alliance Française began neglecting its original educational mission among colonial subjects. Like the French colonial state more generally, its influence was slight in the end. On the eve of decolonization, fewer than 10 percent of "native" children were enrolled in elementary school. Instead, the Alliance focused on adult courses and cultural activities in Europe, America, and France. As early as 1890, there were active committees in a range of locations: Barcelona, Mauritius, Mexico City, Rio de Janeiro, Havana, Melbourne, and Nîmes and other French towns. Language became the symbol and matrix of national unity and a main feature of French cultural diplomacy, as highlighted in a speech by Charles de Gaulle on October 30, 1943, in Algiers, marking the association's sixtieth anniversary even as the Nazis were shuttering the Paris Alliance offices and shipping its archives to Berlin: "It is through unimpeded relations of friendship, the mingling of our hearts and minds, among ourselves and with others," de Gaulle declared, "that our cultural influence can spread for the betterment of all, enhancing our own worthiness in the process. Organizing these relations, this is why the Alliance Française came into being, why it has lived on, and why it will pursue its mission into the future."

Across the world, foreigners have backed this

Francophone movement through committees that were revitalized in the 1960s by Cambodian leader Norodom Sihanouk, Tunisia's Habib Bourguiba, Niger's Hamani Diori, and Senegalese writer Léopold Sédar Senghor. Algerian novelist and poet Kateb Yacine wrote that the French language was among the former colonies' "spoils of war," a legacy that has made French one of the African continent's most important vehicles of communication and literary production.

Pierre Singaravélou

REFERENCES

Barko, Ivan. "L'Alliance française: les années Foncin (1883–1914). Contexte, naissance, mutations." *Documents pour l'histoire du français langue étrangère ou seconde* 25 (2000).

Casanova, Pascale. *La langue mondiale: Traduction et domination*. Paris: Le Seuil, 2015.

Cerquiglini, Bernard. *Une langue orpheline*. Paris: Minuit, 2007.

Chaubet, François. *La politique culturelle française et la diplomatie de la langue: L'Alliance française (1883–1940)*. Paris: L'Harmattan, 2006.

Vigier, Philippe. "Diffusion d'une langue nationale et résistance des patois en France au XIXe siècle." *Romantisme* 9, nos. 25–26 (1979): 191–208.

1883

RELATED ARTICLES

842–843, 1215, 1539, 1771, 1842, 1931

Pierre Singaravélou

1889

Order and Progress in the Tropics

1889, the hundredth anniversary of the French
Revolution, saw a successful military coup d'état in
Brazil — immediately after the Universal Exhibition
in Paris closed its doors. The new Brazilian Republic's
flag featured a blue disc, a starry sky, and a curved band
inscribed with the national motto "Ordem e Progresso."
The words were drawn directly from the work of the
French positivist philosopher Auguste Comte; their
adoption signaled a period of intense intellectual exchange
between France and Brazil, where positivist thought had
become a veritable religion of humanity.

Between May and October 1889, the tenth Universal
Exhibition — the biggest ever — was held in Paris.
Gigantic structures were erected over nearly 250 acres of
land to celebrate human environments, ways of life, and arts
from all over the world, all regions newly energized by the
spread of Western civilization and the march of science. A
triumph of modern technical prowess, the exhibition was

also intended to highlight the hundredth anniversary of the French Revolution and the permanence of the French Republic. *Le Petit Journal* printed the following report on May 8, 1889: "President Sadi-Carnot, speaking at the foot of the colossal metal tower erected by Gustave Eiffel, proclaimed yesterday that all France was celebrating the dawn of a great century which had opened a fresh era in the history of humanity. When given its freedom, the human spirit gathers energy and science takes flight; today, steam and electricity are transforming the world."

The underlying message of the exhibition was that there could be no progress without a republic and no republic without progress. Not surprisingly, it didn't please the monarchs of Europe one bit. Most were distinctly lukewarm about funding the installation of their national pavilions, which was left to rich donors or industrialists.

The exception was Brazil. The construction of a small palace, surrounded by greenhouses, tropical gardens, and a great pool filled with giant water lilies from the Amazon River, was fervently supported by Emperor Pedro II, who turned up in person. "He was the only sovereign who actually did this," noted the *Guide bleu du Figaro* of 1889. An elderly bourgeois king, enlightened, and Francophile to his fingertips, Pedro took the risk of exhibiting his agrarian nation, the last monarchy in America and (until May 1888) the last slaveholding society in the Western world, at the high mass of liberal and industrial modernity. He took this risk to conquer new markets, attract labour, and involve Brazil in the great movement forward of civilization.

Pedro II was in touch with the spirit of the times. The image he left behind was that of a sovereign convinced of the inevitability of his own downfall — which in fact took place on November 15, 1889. Barely a fortnight after the closure of the Universal Exhibition, a republic was proclaimed in Brazil. Announcing this event, the *Journal de Paris* amused its readers with an imaginary letter that the fallen emperor might have sent to Louis Pasteur from the ship carrying him into exile in Paris: "While I was occupied with astronomical observations of the highest interest, certain individuals of a less philosophical nature took over my government and kicked over the chair they called my throne....I hope they don't pretend they founded the new republic in Brazil. I am the one who founded it, who accustomed the Brazilians to the idea of liberty, who imported the great principles of France" (November 20, 1889).

This ponderous jest was way out of line. Brazil's Second Empire was actually a ruthlessly authoritarian regime that protected a racist, class-ridden society. Nevertheless, the shadow of France loomed large over the early years of the young tropical republic. The "revolution in Brazil" acclaimed in the French press had very little to do with the popular uprisings that France itself witnessed throughout the nineteenth century. Instead it was a coup d'état led by young republican military officers and condoned by an elite of slaveholding land barons who had lost faith in the empire. The ordinary people of Brazil had nothing to do with it.

Nevertheless, the country's radical republicans, who called themselves Jacobins, dreamed of reliving the French Revolution in the year of its centenary. Imagining their people taking to the streets, they founded political associations, decorated pamphlets with Marianne images and Phrygian bonnets, and pompously addressed one another as "citizen." "We spoke of our beloved France and of the influence of French culture; France was our reference in the smallest details of our political struggle. The 'Marseillaise' was our battle hymn, and we knew by heart every episode of the great revolution. Whenever we shouted 'Long live the Republic!' we were careful to add the words 'and long live France!'" remembered a Brazilian naval officer years later (*O Paiz*, November 20, 1912).

While the Jacobins were but a minority of Brazilian republicans, their fascination for the France of enlightenment and liberty was broadly shared among their compatriots. According to Brazil's progressive elites, ever since the 1860s France had represented the heart of civilization and the "brain of the world," as an editorial in the *Courrier du Brésil* stated on December 1, 1889. For educated Brazilians, France was a model of urbanity and good manners, the nursery of the world's greatest literary figures, philosophers, and scientific personalities — some of whom, like the botanist Augustin de Saint-Hilaire, had made Brazil their special area of research. Brazilian intellectuals and artists looked to France for a sense of history and inspiration for their own nation in its quest for progress, social justice, and liberty. Victor Hugo, for example, was immensely influential in Brazil, where he was seen as a prophet of revolution and the initiator of a new surge of romantic energy.

Steadily built up throughout the century, this ideal of France was fertile ground in the 1870s for the positivism of Auguste Comte, which was embraced by a new elite of Brazilian engineers, soldiers, medical doctors, and professors. Working from the heart of the Brazilian republican movement, which revolved around the country's military school, these men imposed Comte's stamp on the new regime. His precept "Order and Progress" has been emblazoned ever since on the starry blue disc in the middle of Brazil's national flag.

In the first phase of his career, Auguste Comte was the inventor of a philosophy of history that transcended religion and metaphysical introspection, suggesting instead that human populations developed unavoidably in the direction of a scientific and experimental relationship with the world. He claimed that this "positive" thought, applied to politics, would ensure the gradual reform of societies along with their secularization, their republicanization, their integration, and their technical and economic development. After 1845, Comte's thought took an abruptly religious turn: following a mad love affair with a young Catholic woman, Clotilde de Vaux, he founded what he called a "religion of humanity," an astonishing cult of the dead — and of his own thought — that was supposed to generate "affection" between human beings and establish the "positive state."

Comte's scientific positivism had a deep impact on Western thought in the second half of the century for the good reason that it turned the era's scientific optimism and confidence into a law of science. But it was only in Latin America — and Brazil in particular — that positivism's secular religious offshoot developed to such a degree. This is largely thanks to the strong support of the medical profession and the relentless proselytizing of Pierre Laffitte, Comte's successor and a doggedly literal interpreter of his final texts. Tightly controlled by Miguel Lemos and Raimundo Teixeira Mendes, leaders and "apostles" of Comte's religion of humanity, the Brazilian positivist movement broadened, became organized, created its own hierarchy, and played a central role in political debates during the second half of the century. At the same time, the Positivist Church of Brazil saved Comte's cult from oblivion in France. Known as the "Chapel of Humanity" to this day, its Parisian headquarters on Rue Payenne (the former home of Comte's muse, Clotilde) was bought in 1903 by a group of Brazilian positivists.

Comtism was so successful in Brazil because it offered the then-peripheral country a place in universal history and assigned to brand-new elites the mission and the tools for the struggle against the "absurd particularisms" — slavery, Catholic monarchy, and aristocracy — that might stand in the way. The positivist movement of the late nineteenth century was a progressive force, radically abolitionist and republican, favorable to popular education and the separation of church and state. This struggle, led by an enlightened avant-garde, was closely associated with an idealized image of the Third French Republic, in which liberty and progress seemed to have arrived side by side with order, the cardinal virtue of Comtist thought. Convinced of their intellectual and moral superiority, the frock-coated technicians of positivism could easily visualize themselves as such political trailblazers.

1889 was not a year in which new French transplants suddenly rooted themselves in Brazil: no republican models, universal historical thought-mechanisms, or positivist theories crossed the Atlantic. Brazilian politicians preferred to delve into the modern political repertoire that France made available. Looking for concrete tools rather than systems of thought, they read and adapted the works of lexicographer Émile Littré and pioneer investment banker

Jacques Laffitte in preference to Comte; they gravitated toward economist Pierre Paul Leroy-Beaulieu rather than Karl Marx. Their priority was to negotiate a path between national tradition and the theories running counter to it. Eventually, the political and constitutional battle in Brazil was won by the old elites, who by the end of the century had imposed a federal and oligarchical republic, neither socially nor politically inclusive.

Yet the founding influence of France on Brazil had powerful effects in the long term. First of all, it fostered a special relationship between scientists on both sides of the Atlantic. French intellectuals were not only seen as the Enlightenment personified: by the end of the century they were fulfilling Comte's promise — meaning science in its age of full maturity and the new discipline of sociology. Brazilian social sciences were birthed under a powerful French influence, as witnessed by the roles historian Fernand Braudel and anthropologist Claude Lévi-Strauss played in the creation of the University of São Paulo in the 1930s. Both men were overwhelmed by their firsthand experiences of Brazil, where they encountered indigenous populations and the legacy of the country's slaveholding past. "I became intelligent in Brazil," wrote Braudel. "What I saw was such a spectacle of history, such a model of social kindness that I began to understand life in a completely different way."

France was the preferred country of exile and training

for Brazilian intellectuals between the establishment of the authoritarian, corporatist Estado Novo (1937–1945) and the period of military dictatorship (1964–1985). Sociologist Fernando Henrique Cardoso, geographer Milton Santos, and economist Celso Furtado all studied at the Sorbonne. To this day, the authors of reference in Brazil's schools and universities — in the humanities — are mostly French.

Ultimately, the French positivist reading of history seems to have established an inner conviction in Brazil that the nation — perpetually dominated as it was by conservative oligarchies — had only half entered the history of an ordered, "civilized," industrialized First World in the twentieth century. With this conviction came another: that only a strong, enlightened central government could guide Brazil to the grandeur that was its natural destiny. This statist, modernizing ideal has been shared by a broad array of Brazilian political movements, from the populist left of Getúlio Vargas to the putschist military officers of the 1960s and 1970s.

Maud Chirio

REFERENCES

Alonso, Angela. "De positivismo e de positivistas: Interpretações do positivismo brasileiro." *Revista Brasileira de Informação Bibliográfica em Ciências Sociais (BIB)*, no. 42 (1996): 109–34.

Carelli, Mario. *Cultures croisées: Histoire des échanges culturels entre la France et le Brésil, de la découverte aux temps modernes.* Paris: Nathan, 1993.

Carvalho, José Murilo de. *A formação das almas: O imaginário da República no Brasil.* São Paulo: Companhia das Letras, 1990.

Castro Gomes, Angela de, Dulce Chaves Pandolfi, Verena Alberti, and Américo Freire, eds. *A República no Brasil.* Rio de Janeiro: Nova Fronteira, 2002.

Palti, Elias José. "Positivism, Revolution, and History in Brazil." In *The Worlds of Positivism: A Global Intellectual History, 1770–1930,* edited by Johannes Feichtinger, Franz L. Fillafer, and Jan Surman. New York: Palgrave Macmillan, 2018.

Queirós Mattoso, Kátia de, Idelette Muzart-Fonseca dos Santos, and Denis Rolland, eds. *Modèles politiques et culturels au Brésil: Emprunts, adaptations, rejets.* Paris: Presses de l'université Paris-Sorbonne, 2003.

RELATED ARTICLES

1550, 1808, 1840, 1973

1891

Pasteurizing the French Empire

In January 1891, Albert Calmette founded the first overseas Pasteur Institute in Saigon. At a time when the discoveries of Louis Pasteur were having next to no effect on public health in metropolitan France, the *pastoriens* were transforming colonial societies into laboratories for a global medical revolution.

The Pasteur revolution never took place — in France, that is. The discoveries of Louis Pasteur culminated with the holy grail of a rabies vaccine in 1885 and then three years later with the creation of the Pasteur Institute in Paris, but otherwise they brought about no change in the public health policies of France. By identifying microbes as the key to victory in the battle against infectious diseases, Pasteur's approach to medical science had captured the public imagination; nevertheless, spurned by a suspicious medical profession and obstructed by the maneuvers of politicians in parliament, it failed to fulfill contemporary dreams of social reform. The *pastoriens*, as the pupils of Pasteur were known

913

in his lifetime, like the researchers trained at his Institute after his death, did not modify sanitary conditions in France.

This fact takes on a different complexion if one thinks of France — like many of the *pastoriens* of the Third Republic — as merely another province of a wider overseas empire. In the colonies, a powerful alliance between the administration and those in the medical profession who favored Pasteur began to take shape at the close of the nineteenth century. As laboratories were set up, the dream of a society transformed by medical science took shape within the French Empire.

The story began in December 1890. Louis Pasteur, newly installed in his Institute, was eager to place it at the service of his country. He summoned Albert Calmette, a brilliant naval doctor and self-taught microbiologist with an excellent knowledge of the tropics, who had stopped for a few months in Paris to study Pasteur's techniques following a posting on the islands of Saint-Pierre and Miquelon. Having consulted the assistant secretary of state for the colonies, Pasteur suggested that Calmette create a laboratory in Indochina to produce vaccines and study local pathology.

The offer was accepted on the spot.

Calmette belonged to the first generation of *pastorien* true believers. The work of Pasteur was likewise fascinating to the doctors of the colonial health corps, created in

1890. Their enthusiasm fitted the purposes of the Institute inasmuch as they formed a legion of convinced and zealous disciples. Graduates of the naval medical school in Bordeaux were sent to study exotic pathologies at the École du Pharo in Marseille; they brought with them a new form of laboratory training whose practical applications were already numerous, from individual diagnoses to the general health of industrial workers. Thus the colonial health service and the Pasteur Institute, both of them relative newcomers to the French medical world, found themselves functioning in tandem as the "race for microbes" between the *pastoriens* and their German and British rivals shifted to Africa and Asia. Already in 1883, Pasteur's mission to identify the principal agent of cholera had returned defeated from Alexandria, overtaken in its quest by the German Robert Koch.

On his arrival in Saigon, Calmette set up his laboratory beside the military hospital. Most of the space was taken up by a stable, in which cattle and buffaloes were used to produce an anti-cholera vaccine. Just like Pasteur in Paris, Calmette played the "exhibitor of microbes," carrying out laboratory studies of the pathologies of patients from the area and showing a close interest in local "biological" products like opium and rice alcohol. He went on to rationalize their production by identifying the microorganisms involved, and thus dangled before settlers the promise of future industries, patents, and monopolies. Gradually, he turned his laboratory into a miniature Pasteur Institute. Queues formed around it for vaccinations against cholera, which was still rampant at the time; people bitten by dogs traveled great distances across Indochina to be delivered from the horror of rabies. Money poured in; the governor was satisfied.

Calmette returned to France in 1893, bringing with him copious notes and materials to continue his research, notably on the effects of snake venom. Back in Saigon, his laboratory continued to make steady progress, serving as a base for research missions that fanned out across the entire region. In 1894, for example, Alexandre Yersin isolated the plague bacillus in Hong Kong. In 1904, Calmette's original foundation became the official Pasteur Institute of Saigon — whereby its status as an offshoot of Paris was confirmed along with its autonomy vis-à-vis the local government.

The same scenario then repeated itself in many other French colonies. The central Pasteur Institute in France would send out a representative to set up a laboratory and produce vaccines; after a few years of trial and error, of networking and research conducted under the distant oversight of Parisian mandarins, the laboratory — which by then had made itself indispensable to the local administration — became an official Pasteur Institute.

By the end of the 1930s, Pasteur's disciples had installed themselves in Antananarivo, Brazzaville, Dakar, Algiers, Tunis, Tangier, Casablanca, Hanoi, Nha Trang, and Nouméa; they were even present in sovereign nations like Iran and Greece. The sun never set on the Pasteur Institutes.

Nor did *pastoriens* conceal their pride in the part they were playing in the colonial master plan. Vaccines, culture broths, serums, and mosquito nets were tools of empire. As strategic instruments for protecting the health of soldiers and colonists, they also served in the "conquest of hearts and souls." They made the work of colonization "eminently humanitarian and civilizing," wrote Calmette in 1905.

From the posts they occupied within the health service, the *pastoriens* helped the French Empire respond to a shortage of trained workers that hampered colonial development, especially in Africa. Doctor Eugène Jamot, deputy head of the Pasteur Institute in Brazzaville, perfected a treatment for sleeping sickness, a disease caused by parasites: mobile teams went from village to village with microscopes and syringes to screen and treat every single case. This collective and sometimes coercive approach to medicine made the health of the population ("the natives") paramount. For the first time, large numbers of African nurses were given a thorough training in modern medical procedures. Thus the *pastoriens* were at the forefront of an ambitious form of militarized social medicine. The goal was quite simply to eradicate endemic tropical diseases, sanitize Africa, and convert these natives to respect modern hygiene. This would be done by persuasion or by force. In 1939, when the fiftieth anniversary of the Pasteur Institute in Paris was celebrated with much fanfare, Louis Pasteur Valléry-Radot, Pasteur's grandson, promised the president of the Republic that "the Pasteur Institutes of our one and indivisible empire will remain vigilant as long as they are inhabited by the spirit of Pasteur and the soul of France."

Although they liked to borrow the vocabulary of propaganda, the "Pastorian missionnaries" (as Calmette called them in 1912) did not confine themselves to a utilitarian role. Their research was freed from the economic imperatives and demands of the mother establishment in Paris. Between the wars, Charles Nicolle turned the Pasteur Institute in Tunis into a thoroughgoing medical center whose dynamism rivaled that of the metropolis; Nicolle himself received the Nobel Prize in 1928 and was buried on the premises of his institute. Figures like Nicolle ("Le Tunisien") and Yersin, named director of the Saigon Institute in 1901, became emblems of the *pastoriens'* attachment to local cultures. With time, the brotherhood became cosmopolitan. The Saigon Institute began training Indochinese doctors from the 1920s onward, whereas the Pasteur course in Paris accredited colonial subjects (though the latter, when they went home, all too often faced a glass ceiling of racial hierarchy).

Pasteur's disciples were not content merely to spread a theory that, in Pasteur's own words, was "carried by a breath of truth toward the rich fields of the future" and, obviously, of the empire. Theirs was a two-way movement: their wanderings usually ended with a return to base. All the same, French medicine was indelibly marked by their achievements. Calmette, for example, created a Pasteur Institute in Lille shortly after his return, and from there he orchestrated a battle against the spread of tuberculosis among working people. Its sheer scale has never been equaled since. It was as if Calmette had brought home a way of thinking about medicine as a social endeavor, along with fine political skills that enabled him to finance his program, without waiting for public money, by relying on elites and philanthropists in northern France. For Calmette and many others, the colonies provided a valuable education. In the empire as in the French metropole, medicine constituted an investment in "human social capital."

Most astonishing of all was the revitalization of these Institutes after the wave of independences around 1960; in fact, new establishments were created in Africa. After embracing the Gaullist project of "cooperation" with France's former colonies, *pastoriens* would lead the fight against the epidemics of AIDS, Ebola, and avian flu. The international network of Pasteur Institutes subsequently reinvented itself at the close of the 1990s as a precious instrument of surveillance for world health. The colonial history of the Pasteur Institute thus became something of an awkward memory. Commemorated with unabashed fervor until the 1960s, nowadays it tends to be passed over in polite silence or — at best — romantically evoked by the adventures of Yersin in Indochina. Few in France point out that Calmette, who after his death in 1933 earned national honors on account of his BCG (*vaccin bilié de Calmette et Guérin*), had been a "great colonialist."

Guillaume Lachenal

REFERENCES

Dozon, Jean-Pierre. "Pasteurisme, médecine militaire et colonisation." In *L'Institut Pasteur. Contributions à son histoire*, edited by Michel Morange, 269–78. Paris: La Découverte, 1991.

Guénel, Annick. "The Creation of the First Overseas Pasteur Institute, or the Beginning of Albert Calmette's Pastorian Career." *Medical History* 43, no. 1 (1999): 1–25.

Monnais-Rousselot, Laurence. *Médecine et colonisation: L'aventure indochinoise (1860–1939)*. Paris: CNRS Éditions, 1999.

Moulin, Anne-Marie. "Patriarchal Science: The Network of the Overseas Pasteur Institutes." In *Science and Empires*, edited by Patrick Petitjean, Catherine Jami, and Anne-Marie Moulin, 307–22. Dordrecht: Kluwer Academic Publishers, 1992.

Pelis, Kim. *Charles Nicolle, Pasteur's Imperial Missionary: Typhus and Tunisia*. Rochester: University of Rochester Press, 2006.

RELATED ARTICLES
1347, 1832, 1931

1892

"Nobody Is Innocent!"

A series of anarchist attacks rocked Europe in the early
1890s. Paris was one of the most combustible spots
in a chain reaction that sparked fears across the continent
and generated international responses to terrorism.

The wave of anarchist terrorism that struck France in the
early 1890s represented a convergence between different
types of national and global events.

The industrial revolution had changed the social order,
giving way to a new "working class" whose demands seemed
to transcend borders. This new identity was accompanied
by the emergence of different currents of thought, including
socialism and anarchism. The latter was fueled by the
teachings of libertarian socialist Pierre-Joseph Proudhon,
Mikhail Bakunin (a Russian revolutionary anarchist),
and Peter Kropotkin (a Russian activist, scientist, and
philosopher). Exiled by the authorities but in contact with
one another, these men spread their ideas at an international
level.

Everywhere, Europe seemed to be at a crossroads: France, Great Britain, and Switzerland were safe havens for anarchists fleeing authoritarian regimes. At the same time, countries marked by the industrial revolution were fertile ground for these types of ideologies. And France stood out, perhaps because of its history. After all, Kropotkin viewed French revolutionaries as his "ancestors from 1793–1794," part of his movement's heritage.

Anarchist attacks in the 1880s and 1890s were nourished by the industrial revolution, with technological advances facilitating the circulation of people, ideas, and strategies for action. Dynamite, the anarchist weapon of choice, provides a salient example of this confluence of technology and communication. Nitroglycerine was discovered in 1846 and became commercially viable by 1864, thanks to experiments led by Alfred Nobel. The first plastic explosive was invented in 1875. Meanwhile, as literacy rates rose, media advances and a proliferation of publications gave an ever-growing readership easy access to information. One such publication, a user manual entitled *L'Indicateur anarchiste* (1887), a slim, forty-page pamphlet translated into French, Italian, English, German, and Spanish, had a wide readership among activist circles. Among other things, it explained how to make a bomb out of nitroglycerine.

France's national history and politics made it especially vulnerable to attacks. As the industrial revolution took hold, power dynamics between the French Republic and working-class activists hardened. Tensions began mounting as early as June 1848 and came to a head with the bloody repression of the Paris Commune in 1871 and the Fourmies shooting in 1891 (in which troops fired at peaceful protesters on France's first International Labor Day). The republican government attempted to stigmatize the working classes as dangerous social elements. In turn, many working people saw the governing class as an enemy.

This latent hostility between the working classes and the Republic was itself the expression of a larger anti-parliamentary movement nourished by the Paris stock exchange crash of 1882, revelations of a pay-for-honors scheme in 1887 (*l'Affaire des décorations*), and the Panama Scandals of 1892–1893. Such scandals discredited the regime's already tenuous authority and helped legitimize violence against the state. The Socialist leader Jean Jaurès voiced the growing sense of disgust toward the nation's leaders when, on July 26, 1894, he sought to amend an anti-anarchist law proposal (*les lois scélérates* or "villainous laws") with the following provision: "All public servants — ministers, senators, deputies — will be deemed to have provoked acts of anarchist propaganda if they profited from their office, received bribes, or participated in corrupt financial dealings, either by sitting on the board of a guilty company, or by advocating for such businesses, in the press or by their own word, before one or multiple persons."

Following the failures of First International (a labor federation formerly known as the International Workingmen's Association), those who supported "propaganda by the deed" grew increasingly numerous within anarchist movements. Their actions exposed the continent — and France in particular — to its first wave of terrorism.

However, to be clear: "propaganda by the deed" did not necessarily imply terrorism. The first proponent of violent actions was the Russian Peter Kropotkin, who founded the newspaper *Le Révolté* with French geographer Élisée Reclus. He would later repudiate that idea in 1891, condemning the violence he himself had set into motion. His hesitations capture a deeper ambivalence on the question of revolutionary violence within anarchist groups. Individual actions and violent attacks were divisive issues, adopted by a small but visible and highly publicized minority.

French and European society in the 1890s were deeply troubled by these attacks, the descriptions of victims and executioners, and the rumors of future violence. The press echoed and amplified what had become a public obsession. Collective paranoia and general suspicion set in. And whenever fears began to subside, terrorism struck again. For instance, after a peaceful strike at the Carmaux Mining Company in August 1892, anarchist Émile Henry placed a bomb at company headquarters to energize the workers' movement. Before going off, the bomb was discovered and transported to the police station on Rue des Bons-Enfants, where it exploded and killed five officers.

One of the paradoxes of anarchist terrorism was its dual aim to hold society hostage to fear and at the same time to create almost legendary figures in the media. Some of the infamous figures coming out of this period (1892–1894) have gone down in history. François Claudius Koenigstein, known as Ravachol, gained fame from his attacks and subsequent trial. Seeking revenge for three other anarchist activists — Henri Louis Decamps, Charles Auguste Dardare, and Louis Léveillé — who had been arrested after a shootout with the police (two were sent to prison, the third was acquitted), he placed bombs in the buildings of the examining magistrates and judges on the case. Sentenced to death, Ravachol went on to inspire Auguste Vaillant, Théodule Meunier, and even Émile Henry. Meunier set off a bomb in the café where Ravachol had been arrested. Vaillant committed an eminently symbolic attack, throwing a bomb at the Palais Bourbon while the Assembly was in session.

Émile Henry's background and calm demeanor made him a source of fascination and fear for newspapers and their readers. He came from a bourgeois family, dropped out of the prestigious École Polytechnique, and chose to bomb the Carmaux Mining Company, followed by Le

Terminus, a café in the Saint-Lazare train station. Clear-eyed as to the consequences of his actions, he turned his trial into a political spectacle, giving a detailed account of his "conversion" to anarchist terrorism and accusing the public in a single phrase, "Nobody is innocent!" For him, the enemy consisted of society in its entirety, including bystanders drinking coffee on a café patio. A month after his execution on June 24, 1894, another anarchist, the Italian Sante Geronimo Caserio (demonstrating the transnational character of the movement), avenged him by assassinating the president of the French Republic, Marie François Sadi Carnot, in Lyon. Anarchist attacks became a game of call-and-response, at times motivated more by revenge than by ideology. This vicious cycle (attack–crackdown–attack–reaction) forced European society to consider the role played by the media in the fight against anarchist terrorism.

Vaillant and Henry committed their crimes fully aware of the fate that awaited them. At his trial, Vaillant even admitted having contemplated suicide, but in the end, he opted for a death that would "serve the cause": "Weary of this miserable and cowardly life, I brought this bomb to the people responsible for social suffering." His trial was a political spectacle amplified by the media and broadcast beyond France's borders. Across the world, newspapers reported on each new attack, giving the impression that a massive conspiracy had the whole world in its grip.

Indeed, the wave of attacks of the 1890s spread across a large swath of the globe. By definition, anarchist terrorism was transnational in its ideology and its very procedures. Supporters traveled widely and carried out attacks wherever they were, without distinguishing between nationalities or borders. That is how an Italian came to assassinate the French president, and again how another Italian made headlines in French media when he assassinated Empress Elisabeth of Austria in Switzerland in 1898.

The response to anarchism was likewise international. More and more, police forces communicated at the European level, thanks in particular to modern methods developed by French biometrics researcher Alphonse Bertillon, the inventor of the mug shot. In 1898, an international summit against anarchist terrorism took place. While its impact was limited due to conflicts between authoritarian regimes and democracies, its existence shows that law enforcement agencies were beginning to view anarchist terrorism as a transnational problem.

In France, the government's severe response to terrorism matched the level of fear anarchy was engendering. The Republic began by making it clear it would never yield. Auguste Vaillant's attack at the Palais Bourbon served as a convenient symbol for government officials. Charles Dupuy, the lightly wounded president of the Assembly, insisted, "Sirs, the session shall go on! It is a question of dignity for the Assembly and the Republic. These attacks, whose source and motivation we do not know, must not disrupt our lawmakers."

Nevertheless, a few days later those same lawmakers adopted the first of what became known as *les lois scélérates*. On December 11, 1893, just two days after the attack, Jean Casimir-Perier proposed a law condemning those who advocated anarchist deeds and authorizing preventive arrests. On December 18, a second law authorized the arrest of members or sympathizers of anarchist organizations. On July 28, 1894 (one month after the assassination of Sadi Carnot), a third law prohibited all anarchist propaganda, though it did not specify a definition of anarchism, which made the law easier and more flexible to enforce. The *lois scélérates* represent the Third Republic's first legal attempt to establish exceptional methods of control. Though it was not labeled antiterrorist, this approach draws our attention toward the exceptional regimes of law — antiterrorist and otherwise — that continue to surface across France today.

Jenny Raflik

REFERENCES

Bantman, Constance. *The French Anarchists in London, 1880–1914: Exile and Transnationalism in the First Globalisation*. Liverpool: Liverpool University Press, 2013.

Bouhey, Vivien. *Les anarchistes contre la République: Contribution à l'histoire des réseaux sous la Troisième République (1880–1914)*. Rennes: Presses universitaires de Rennes, 2009.

Jensen, Richard Bach. *The Battle against Anarchist Terrorism: An International History, 1878–1934*. Cambridge: Cambridge University Press, 2013.

Maitron, Jean. *Le mouvement anarchiste en France*. 2 vols. Paris: Maspero, 1975.

Merriman, John M. *The Dynamite Club: How a Bombing in Fin-de-Siècle Paris Ignited the Age of Modern Terror*. New Haven: Yale University Press, 2016.

RELATED ARTICLES

1794, 1871, 1968, 2015

1894

Dreyfus, a European Affair

Charges filed against Alfred Dreyfus divided more
than just French society. The ensuing affair resonated
throughout a European continent in the grip of widespread
anti-Semitism. This moment marked the dawning of the
Zionist movement, while the name Dreyfus came to stand
for the struggle against all forms of injustice.

On a September Sunday in 1899, some fifty thousand
demonstrators gathered at Speakers' Corner in Hyde
Park, London. It was an unthreatening "petit bourgeois"
assembly, according to *The Times*, but the *Daily Telegraph*
reported Londoners protesting "despicable judges" who
were trampling "the fundamental principles of humankind"
in France. As soon as word of Captain Alfred Dreyfus's
second conviction hit the newsstands, a wave of outrage had
surged out of France into Europe and beyond, to the point
where there was talk of boycotting the Universal Exhibition
to be held in Paris in 1900.

Unjustly accused of spying for Germany, Captain

Dreyfus was first sentenced to deportation for life on December 22, 1894. Deprived of his rank, imprisoned, vilified, he was granted a retrial in 1899 thanks to his defenders' tireless efforts. Found guilty a second time, though with extenuating circumstances that clearly pointed to the judges' mounting unease, he was eventually pardoned and released from confinement, before full rehabilitation in 1906. More than a mere court drama, this case mirrors the history of France's tug-of-war between democratic principles and nationalist leanings, this time playing out in an atmosphere of political uncertainty within the faltering Third Republic.

But the shock waves were felt throughout Europe and the world, where the Dreyfus Affair, as it came to be called, recast the whole issue of anti-Semitism and forged a template for civic activism.

The affair opens like a time-worn spy novel: in September 1894, the cleaning lady at the German Embassy, also in the employ of the French secret services (the "Statistics Section"), happened upon an odd-looking document in a wastepaper basket, the infamous *bordereau*, as it would come to be known. It contained what was thought to be secret information, but which later proved to be the trivial concoction of a heavily indebted fellow officer, Ferdinand Esterhazy, the real culprit. Pressured to wrap things up fast, and swayed by their personal biases, the investigators steered their suspicions toward an Alsatian captain, Alfred Dreyfus. Wealthy, happily married, earning high marks from his superiors, the young officer aroused jealousy; the fact that he was Jewish, in an army still steeped in anti-Semitic prejudices, only made matters worse. Dreyfus was the convenient scapegoat, but he resisted pressure and protested his innocence. Realizing how flimsy their case was, the investigators leaked rumors to the press and fabricated enough false evidence for a court martial to convict him on December 22, 1894.

The Parisian correspondent for the Austrian *Neue Freie Presse*, Theodor Herzl, was troubled by what he observed in court. He had been in attendance at Dreyfus's official public degrading, on January 5, 1895, where he realized he'd witnessed the raw expression of a prevailing anti-Semitic mood that dashed what little remained of his hopes for the future. For eastern European Jews, targeted by pogroms that only intensified with the assassination of Czar Alexander II in 1881, the French Republic had emerged as a safe haven. The Yiddish expression "happy as God in France" speaks to that reality: Where else would Jews have been able to launch so promising a career as had Alfred Dreyfus? And yet, the four years Herzl had spent in France by that point allowed him to gauge the local population's mixed feelings over Jewish integration. Beginning in the 1870s, age-old Christian anti-Judaism was complicated by the perception of Jews as shrewdly powerful financiers and by biological theories that anchored anti-Semitism in pseudo-scientific racial prejudice. This exclusionary language was hardening and escalating, as demonstrated by the success of Édouard Drumont's racist pamphlet, *La France juive* (1886), whose rabid theses were echoed and amplified in his newspaper *La Libre Parole*, the first to denounce "Dreyfus the traitor."

In other words, the Dreyfus Affair came not as a decisive break, but rather as the latest stage in the intellectual journey that led Herzl to envision a "modern solution to the Jewish question." Assimilation had proven illusory, and "liberals had been deluded into believing that men could be made equal by some decree recorded in the official record." Henceforward, he would advocate for Zionism and a *Jewish State*, the title of the book he published in 1896. At the first Zionist Congress, held in Basel in 1897, loud applause welcomed the mention of the name Bernard Lazare, who in 1895 had led the movement to demand a retrial for Dreyfus.

The Dreyfus Affair became an enduringly powerful mobilizer for Jewish communities, who were deeply shaken by this individual human tragedy and by the winds of anti-Semitism gusting through French society, and Europe. In the far-off Russian shtetls, explained the lawyer Léon Baratz, "everyone felt co-indicted alongside Captain Dreyfus, and knew that world Judaism was on trial" in Paris. Reports of new pogroms in eastern Europe in 1900 proved his point. Even in the United States, where the press reported passionately on the case, worried immigrants were plunged back into memories of persecution, while well-to-do Jews started wondering: Isn't this Dreyfus as assimilated as we are and yet ruthlessly shunned? The affair thus revealed the second wave of a widespread anti-Semitism that flourished in Vienna, whose new mayor Karl Lueger professed hatred for Jews, and found sustenance in the widely circulated *Protocols of the Elders of Zion*, a fabricated screed contrived by the Russian secret police in 1901.

Beyond the issue of anti-Semitism, the name Dreyfus elicited heartfelt compassion as it appeared in headlines throughout the world. When the second conviction was handed down in 1899, Queen Victoria herself could not contain her outrage: "No words could convey my repulsion. If only all Europe would cry out in indignation!"

Still, had this international outpouring also reached remote locales? In the tiny Breton village of La Rablais, the gatekeeper was said to have asked the question, soon to be reprinted in columns all across the country, "Who is this Dreyfus? Never heard of him." Interviewed by the press, this "care-free fellow" who preferred to "tend to his chickens and vegetable garden rather than read newspapers" embodied what the city-dwelling elites wrongly considered the cultural isolationism of France's country-folk, whom they assumed indifferent to trends of opinion. But countless examples show that ordinary people rallied just as vigorously for or against the captain, whose travails they followed in their local gazettes. "Such a poignant plight, such splendid characters!" wrote Émile Zola, whose "novelist heart leapt with passionate admiration." The affair was turning into a serialized drama, with its long-suffering victims (the wretched exile on Devil's Island, but also his steadfast wife, Lucie, so brave and dignified), its heroes (Lieutenant Colonel Picquart, who uncovered the truth and dared to confront his superiors), and its countless plot twists.

The late nineteenth century was witnessing the birth of a genuine newspaper civilization borne along by rising literacy rates, technical advances, and growing freedom of expression. From the outset of the affair, the press played a major role as a vector of anti-Semitism, but it was also harnessed by advocates of a retrial, intellectuals and politicians who often had an inside track in the world of journalism. The pro-Dreyfus camp, the so-called Dreyfusards, endeavored to raise public awareness through whatever means available: press articles, brochures, and lectures, of course, but also rumormongering, barbs, and scandals. When all this advocacy was starting to flag around 1896, Dreyfus's brother Mathieu revived the affair with a whisper campaign, picked up by the London *Daily Chronicle*, that announced the captain's alleged escape. Two years later, on January 13, 1898, just when political authorities were on the verge of closing the case for good, Émile Zola challenged his opponents and sparked its reopening with his resounding article "*J'accuse*," published on the front page of the daily *L'Aurore*. Leveraging his fame to denounce those responsible for the miscarriage of justice, he ran the risk of prosecution. His indictment, when it came, aroused further cries of indignation. Zola sought refuge in Brussels, and in doing so, rekindled memories of the political liberals exiled under Napoleon III, in the 1850s and 1860s.

Outside France, however, people found it difficult to assess exactly what was at stake in this case, except perhaps in Belgium, where the clash of church and state proved as virulent as in France. The full scope of the Dreyfus Affair can be appreciated only within the larger framework of the Third Republic's brewing identity crisis. Should the regime veer to the right to better safeguard the nation (*la patrie*) and its institutions, or should it move forward with its project of emancipation, risking confrontation with the army and the church? The central questions looming over the political landscape in the 1890s came into sharper focus through this political affair. In this atmosphere of tension and political awakening, the liberal-leaning statesman Pierre Waldeck-Rousseau was asked by the president in June 1899 to form a "government of republican defense" that would galvanize the forces on the left against their twin enemies: despotic rule and, especially, clericalism.

After this political reshuffle, for which he unwittingly served as both pretense and enabler, Alfred Dreyfus quit center stage. Sentenced but then released in 1899, he was rehabilitated in 1906, and two years later, he attended the ceremony to transfer Émile Zola's remains to the Panthéon. On that day, tensions ran so high that gunshots were fired in his direction, a sign that nationalist hatred remained embedded in French society. The ceremony honoring Zola was the Republic's way of acknowledging the courage of the Dreyfusards, who had dared to shake up the regime's institutions in order to bring it back to first principles.

There were republican stalwarts whose quest for truth and cult of reason powered their commitment to just causes — from Lucien Herr, a strategist for the Dreyfus case, to Georges Clemenceau and the Socialist Jean Jaurès. These staunch Dreyfusards had already embraced the cause of the Armenians, massacred in the Ottoman Empire. When this high-minded "mystical" fervor (as writer Charles Péguy called it) turned into mere instrumental "politics," with its inevitable compromises, seekers of absolutes who had come of age in the heat of these struggles couldn't help being disappointed.

But neither the French Republic nor any other world democracy has given up on the universalist values that coalesced around the affair. Whenever a miscarriage of justice comes to light, the same values resurface. From

Jules Durand, the trade unionist falsely accused of killing a non-union worker in 1910, to financial trader Jérôme Kerviel, the "new Dreyfus" who in 2010 took the fall for widespread banking practices, any summoning of the original often devolves into a hackneyed argument for some legal maneuver, spinning out like a Godwin's law for Dreyfus analogies. But when cited and mobilized in other circumstances, such as the civil rights movement, the name Dreyfus now denotes a democratic critique of the distortions and disillusions of democracy itself.

Arnaud-Dominique Houte

REFERENCES

Aynié, Marie. *Les Amis inconnus: Se mobiliser pour Dreyfus (1897–1899)*. Toulouse: Privat, 2011.

Drouin, Michel, ed. *L'Affaire Dreyfus: Dictionnaire*. 2nd ed. Paris: Flammarion, 2006.

Duclert, Vincent. *Alfred Dreyfus: L'honneur d'un patriote*. Paris: Fayard, 2006.

Harris, Ruth. *Dreyfus: Politics, Emotion, and the Scandal of the Century*. New York: Metropolitan Books, 2010.

Joly, Bertrand. *Histoire politique de l'affaire Dreyfus*. Paris: Fayard, 2014.

RELATED ARTICLES
1105, 1347, 1683, 1942, 1962

1900

France Hosts the World

Over fifty million visitors flocked to Paris for the Universal
Exhibition of 1900. But what was the real purpose behind
this jamboree? Like its predecessors, yet more ambitiously,
the 1900 world's fair was meant to paper over the nation's
recent setbacks with a powerful display of French
enlightenment and progress.

France often comes across as a country that wants to pass
off its failures and defeats as symbolic victories, concealing
its points of weakness by displaying unrivaled strength in
such areas as fashion, letters, luxury, and the arts. In the
second half of the nineteenth century, this was demonstrated
by the Universal Exhibitions of 1855, 1867, 1878, 1889, and
1900. Having somehow found itself at the center of every
crisis, revolution, and disaster endured by the Western
world since the end of the eighteenth century, Paris was
ideally positioned for enterprises of this kind. In 1878, the
newly established Third French Republic was looking to
orchestrate a national resurrection following the calamitous

defeat against the Prussians in 1870 and the ensuing civil war between the new Republic and the Commune. In 1889 — despite a recent political crisis involving the populist general Georges Boulanger and the refusal of certain monarchies, among them Germany, to take part in the festivities — France celebrated the hundredth anniversary of the Revolution. By 1900, after temporarily (and less than gloriously) settling the Dreyfus Affair, the government was seeking to highlight the nation's unity and confidence at the dawn of a new century.

These ever more grandiose exhibitions could not conceal the fact that France was steadily losing ground to other world powers. If Paris had managed to be present at every rendezvous of recent history, it was thanks to the incomparable image of this capital in the eyes of the rest of the world, and also because regime after regime had vied with its predecessors to embody the inexorable march of progress. Each one had accordingly invested ever more money in Universal Exhibitions. But the exhibition of 1900, this encyclopedia of the world, was far more than a storefront displaying the planet's riches or an arena of peaceful competition between nations. Instead it represented a kind of French overview of the planet, designed to extend and magnify the spirit of the Enlightenment and the *Encyclopedia* of d'Alembert and Diderot. Its deeper purpose was to frame the future squarely within a French version of history to which precious few other nations were willing to subscribe at the time.

The statistics of Paris 1900 offer objective data that set this exhibition apart in the global history of France. In 211 days, no fewer than 50,860,801 people visited it, of whom 41,027,177 paid an entrance fee. The average number of daily entries was 241,046, peaking one Sunday at 409,376. In addition to local Parisians of every class, the traffic passing through French railway stations and seaports showed that the occasion was also massively attractive to provincials and foreigners. An unheard-of total of 102 million passengers surged through the Paris railway stations — 25 million more than in 1878 and 56 million more than in 1889, the other exhibition years. The *Album de statistique graphique* of 1900 went even further in its analysis of visitors' geographic provenance: 439,976 travelers came by rail from abroad and 150,763 by ship. Not surprisingly, the countries that sent the most visitors were the closest ones to France, and the visitors themselves belonged to the upper reaches of society. The countries of provenance were, in decreasing order, Great Britain, Belgium, Holland, Switzerland, Germany, Austria, and Italy. It was difficult to determine how many came from the US because so many Americans traveled on transatlantic liners and only crossed the Channel after disembarking in London or Liverpool. Visitors from distant regions showed the global reach of the exhibition:

more than 10,000 came from South America, 3,600 from China and Japan, and 8,000 from India and Australia. Over 14,000 Russians traveled by ship — with others taking the Moscow–Berlin–Paris train, mixing with the German contingent along the way. Over 28,000 visitors came from the eastern end of the Mediterranean, 59,753 from Algeria, 14,556 from Tunisia, and 2,974 from South Vietnam. In 1900, Paris matched London as a center of what was then called the "first globalization."

The area set aside for the exhibition was double that of 1889, with 540 acres divided into two sites (the Champ de Mars, the Esplanade des Invalides, and the hill of Chaillot being one, and the Bois de Vincennes the other). In aerial photographs, the clustered pavilions give the impression of a saturated space in which an attempt had been made not only to display all the corners of the world, but also to highlight the avalanche of new inventions that were already beginning to define the twentieth century: automobiles, cinema, aviation, radio, and ubiquitous electric lighting to roll back the night. The exhibition contained every conceivable architectural, artistic, and musical style. Curiously, the 1900 exhibition left fewer permanent monuments than its predecessors. In 1878, the first Palais du Trocadéro had been built on the hill of Chaillot; in 1889, this achievement had been capped by the controversial Eiffel Tower, 1,063 feet tall. In spite of the furor that surrounded its construction, this great lattice steel construction had by the turn of the century come to symbolize the French capital. Yet in 1900, the only major permanent buildings were the florid rococo Alexandre III Bridge, symbol of the Franco-Russian alliance that linked the right and left banks of the Seine, and the Grand Palais and Petit Palais, with iron and glass domes and naves, solemn classical façades, extravagant sculptures, and fantastical art nouveau vegetable motifs inside and out.

The world rendezvous of 1900 offered Paris an opportunity to catch up with London and Berlin in the matter of urban transport. Delayed for years, the construction of an electric metro system was finally initiated in 1898, and the metro line between the Porte Maillot and the Porte de Vincennes (a little more than ten kilometers) duly inaugurated on July 19, 1900. Over a period of five months, this pioneering rapid transport project, in a capital ever more crowded by velocipedes, automobiles, and horse-drawn vehicles struggling for space, immediately attracted more than ten million travelers — almost five times the population of Paris at that time.

The exhibition's city-within-a-city contained hundreds of construction styles from every epoch and every part of the world, as well as tens of thousands of artworks, machines, and objects, all competing to attract prizes and crowd attention. The general public, like the teams responsible for putting the exhibition together, was prey to nostalgia. Buildings positing the future had huge success, but so did those that reflected past traditions; for instance, the reconstitutions of a Swiss village and an old Parisian neighborhood. Italy offered a pastiche of Saint Mark's Basilica and the Doges' Palace, the Ottoman Empire a copy of a *yalı* waterfront house on the Bosphorus (designed by a French architect), and Spain a replica of the Giralda bell tower in Seville.

The colonial pavilions were assembled on the hill of Chaillot. Their straightforward purpose was to demonstrate the prowess of French, British, Dutch, Portuguese, and German colonialism overseas. People flocked to see a world in which the traditional past and European domination apparently lived in perfect harmony. There were Moorish cafés with throbbing music, languorous Javanese dancing girls, and traditional potters laboring with their wheels only yards from the gleaming, lethal machinery of heavy industry. In a fantastical pavilion called Around the World, monuments from sites thousands of miles apart lay within touching distance of each other. In a trice, observers could thus travel from India to Portugal, from Egypt to Japan, from Angkor to Beijing. In sum, 1900 saw the invention of the virtual, of the waking dream, of a world dominated by humankind, of time erased.

France itself had to triumph in the sphere of art, where it crushed its competitors in the Grand Palais with an exhibition celebrating the art of the nineteenth century. All told, 3,073 works were shown, from Jacques-Louis David to paintings by the youthful Picasso, who had recently arrived from Barcelona. The Petit Palais opposite displayed a retrospective of French decorative art with 4,774 works from its origins to 1800. This exhibition also included a number of profitable spectacles that generated more than twelve million francs: the most popular, held in the Palais de l'Optique, enabled visitors to learn about recent discoveries in the spheres of astronomy, biology, x-ray technology, and geology.

A form of popular amusement linked to the traditional image of Paris as a city of culture and entertainment, the 1900 exhibition also emphasized the French capital's centrality by hosting a large number of military, professional, and scientific congresses. For years, these congresses had been structuring the field of international knowledge. In 1855, three were held; in 1867, there were 14; in 1878, there were 48, and, by 1889, the total reached 101. In 1900, this doubled again to 203, with a total of 68,000 participants. Historians rubbed shoulders with firemen, economists with electricians, traveling salesmen with inventors, feminists with Sabbatarians. By bringing together professionals, experts, militants, and intellectuals from every walk of life, Paris showed itself as the true intellectual and political capital of the world. Participants in these congresses filled libraries with capacious volumes that contained proceedings of their deliberations and agendas for future discussion on subjects as diverse as labor law, international peace, and international regulations.

Today it is fashionable to doubt, with a mocking tone, the usefulness of early universal exhibitions, whose formula imprints our modern business conventions and theme parks. Obviously, the Internet has generated a world encyclopedia infinitely more complete than the Paris 1900 maze of pavilions, where countless visitors became hopelessly lost within minutes of their arrival. Yet Paris 1900 was probably the last occasion at which one could witness the encyclopedic project, the optimism of the Enlightenment, belief in the possible convergence between the world's nations, and the ambition to speak to intelligence as well as emotion, to human ideals as well as human interests, to crowds looking for diversion as well as knowledge and edification.

Yet, the ideal world of the 1900 Universal Exhibition, just like the ideal Paris of the affluent neighborhoods (divorced from the abject slums to the east of the capital), belied the actual position of France. It is only too clear that everything was beginning to change in 1900, not only for France but also for the rest of the world. European imperialism was still in high gear, but the new overseas empires of the United States and Japan now stood in its way. Rebellions against colonialism were under way, notably in China with the Boxer Rebellion. Industrial technology was challenging the fine arts, and avant-gardes of all kinds were rejecting outdated conventions. Above all, scientific discoveries were opening up vast new worlds that surpassed the clear reasoning of Descartes — for instance, the radioactivity discovered by Marie and Pierre Curie in 1898, or Sigmund Freud's exploration of the human unconscious in his *Interpretation of Dreams*. That earth-shattering work, too, was published in 1900.

Christophe Charle

REFERENCES

Birnbaum, Pierre, ed. *La France de l'affaire Dreyfus*, Paris: Gallimard, 1994.

Chalet-Bailhache, Isabelle, ed. *Paris et ses expositions universelles (1855–1937)*. Paris: Éditions du Patrimoine, 2008.

Higonnet, Patrice. *Paris: Capital of the World*. Cambridge, MA: Harvard University Press, 2002.

Kaiser, Wolfram. "Vive la France! Vive la République! The Cultural Construction of French Identity at the World Exhibitions in Paris 1855–1900." *National Identities* I, no. 3 (1999): 227–44.

Mandell, Richard D. *Paris 1900: The Great World's Fair*. Toronto: University of Toronto Press, 1967.

Rearick, Charles. *Pleasures of the Belle Epoque: Entertainment and Festivity in Turn of the Century France*. New Haven: Yale University Press, 1985.

Schroeder-Gudehus, Brigitte, and Anne Rasmussen. *Les fastes du progrès: Le guide des expositions universelles (1851–1992)*. Paris: Flammarion, 1992.

Schwartz, Vanessa R. *Spectacular Realities: Early Mass Culture in Fin-de-Siècle Paris*. Berkeley: University of California Press, 1998.

RELATED ARTICLES

1550, 1751, 1793, 1889, 1931, 1998

1903

With the coming of the new century, the third Nobel Prize
for Physics, funded by the will of the inventor of dynamite,
was given to Marie Curie — a Polish woman married to
a Frenchman — for her discovery of radioactivity. Thus
the birth of the nuclear world almost exactly coincided with
the establishment of international science's most coveted
award.

On the tenth of December 1903, in Stockholm, Henri
Becquerel stood alone to receive his half of the Nobel Prize
for Physics, awarded by the Swedish Royal Academy of
Science and presented by the King of Sweden "in recognition
of the extraordinary service rendered to humanity by his
discovery of spontaneous radioactivity." The other half
of the prize was awarded to Pierre and Marie Curie, "in
recognition of their extraordinary research into the ray
phenomena discovered by Professor Henri Becquerel."
The Curies were not present to receive their diplomas and
medals. Marie Curie was ill, and after her recovery she got

pregnant with their daughter Eve, which meant that the couple did not reach Stockholm until two years later, in June 1905.

What was the discovery that their prize rewarded? Between March and May 1896, Henri Becquerel had carried out experiments at the Natural History Museum in Paris to determine if the exposure to light of certain salts might produce an emission of the x-rays recently discovered by Wilhelm Röntgen. His first results were promising enough, but one overcast day he noticed a ray spontaneously emitted by his uranium salts, with no input of energy from any other source. He named this new phenomenon the "uranic ray."

Marie Skłodowska, a Polish woman born in Warsaw in 1867, had studied physical science and mathematics and moved to Paris in 1891, where she married the French physicist Pierre Curie in 1895. After the birth of their daughter Irène in September 1897, Marie wrote a doctoral thesis on the uranic rays discovered by Becquerel. Pierre then contrived a system to measure the electrical charges produced in the air by rays emitted from uranium. By measuring and systematically comparing the rays generated by uranium and its various components, Marie established beyond doubt that these "spontaneous" rays were properties of the atom. She then defined the property of spontaneous emission of rays as "radioactivity." The sheer intensity of these rays led her to conclude that another element — much more active than uranium — had to exist within the mineral. With Pierre, now her close collaborator, she went on to announce the discovery of polonium on July 18, 1898, and followed this on December 26 with the discovery of radium (in collaboration with the brilliant chemist Gustave Bémont). The rays emitted by the new elements were millions of times stronger than those from uranium. Almost immediately, the phenomenon of radioactivity became a subject of passionate interest to physicists and chemists the world over.

The Curies' research took place just after the death in December 1896 of Alfred Nobel, a Swedish chemist and industrialist who had discovered dynamite. Nobel bequeathed a vast sum to reward each year the most important research in five vital branches of human knowledge. The national and foreign members of the Royal Swedish Academy of Sciences were asked to propose nominees for these Nobel Prizes. Among the five allotted disciplines, the Nobel Prize had to be awarded "to the most important discovery or progress in chemistry" and "the most important discovery or invention in the field of physics." The initial prizes were given in 1901; the foundation was still in its infancy in 1903.

While chemistry and physics had built up identities of their own during the nineteenth century, recent work on atoms and molecules had shown that the frontiers of these disciplines were far from fixed. The first Nobel physics and chemistry prizes rewarded work on the understanding of the atom, which necessarily required an association of physical and chemical theory; the second chemistry prize was given to a line of research that combined chemistry and biology. Clearly, what is known today as interdisciplinary research was already underway in 1903.

As soon as it was discovered, debate broke out regarding radioactivity. Did these new elements belong to the sphere of chemistry or physics? There followed a series of discussions involving Sweden's most eminent scientists, including precursors of the discipline of physical chemistry. The Nobel Committee for Chemistry would have loved to bring radioactivity and chemistry together, but the award simply could not be shared with the committee's favorite candidate, Svante Arrhenius, a Swedish academic who was among the founders of physical chemistry. Therefore the chemistry committee surrendered Henri Becquerel and the Curies to the physics committee, on condition that their new radioactive elements, polonium and radium, be given no mention in the attribution of the prize. At the same time, it reserved the possibility of rewarding the discoverers of these elements with a Nobel Prize for chemistry some time in the future. In this way, future radioactivity research would be harnessed to the discipline of chemistry.

In 1902, Emil Warburg, a German, and Jean-Gaston

Darboux, a Frenchman, proposed Henri Becquerel, Marie Curie, and Pierre Curie for the Nobel Physics Prize, but all lost to Hendrik Antoon Lorentz and Pieter Zeeman. In 1903, Charles Bouchard, a French medical doctor, proposed Marie Curie (in second position after Becquerel, with Pierre Curie third). A single committee member, the chemist and politician Marcellin Berthelot, recommended Henri Becquerel alone. The four other French academics invited by the Nobel Committee to give their views proposed Henri Becquerel and Pierre Curie. When he got wind of this, Pierre wrote Henri Poincaré, who had great influence over other French scientists, to ask that the name of his wife be added to the list of nominees:

> I have learned that there is a suggestion that M. Becquerel and myself should be proposed for the Nobel Prize for the sum of our researches on radioactivity.... This would be a great honor for me, but all the same I wish to share it with Madame Curie and I beg that she and I be considered as a team in this, just as we have always been in our work. Madame Curie has studied the radioactive properties of uranium salts, thorium, and radioactive minerals.... It appears to me that if we are not considered a team in the present case it will be tantamount to declaring that her role has been merely preparatory, which would be inexact. Please forgive me if you think this letter is inappropriate,

for of course I have no right to air any views on the matter and by all rights I should not even be aware of what is in question.

Pierre Curie's request was duly forwarded, without his knowledge. He renewed it to Gösta Mittag-Leffler, a Swedish mathematician, in August 1903. It would seem that his views met no objection, because Pierre and Marie are both mentioned in the committee's correspondence. We have no way of knowing whether Marie was aware of the possible nomination of her husband or of his efforts to include her. In all likelihood, she knew nothing about either.

On November 14, 1903, the secretary of the Swedish Academy wrote the Curies to confirm its decision to grant the two of them one half of the Nobel Prize for Physics. He told them of the coming official ceremony and reminded them that according to the statutes of the Nobel Foundation, they were "bound to hold a public conference about the work for which they had been given the prize within six months of being presented with the award." Pierre duly held his conference, announcing his conclusions on the possible dangers and benefits of radioactivity. Like the energy of Nobel's own dynamite, the massive energy emitted by rays might serve just as much to build as to destroy, to cure as to kill. All the same, Pierre affirmed his deep faith in humanity: "I am among those who believe — like Nobel himself — that mankind will derive more good than harm from these new discoveries."

The attribution of the 1903 Nobel Prize for Physics was a crucial event in the history of science, in the history of women's rights, and in the history of the Nobel prizes. The first awards of 1901 had caused a sensation in the French press because the literature prize and half of the peace prize were won by French citizens. In that year, Frédéric Passy, the founder and first president of the French Association for Arbitration Between Nations, shared the peace prize with Henri Dunant, founder of the Red Cross. The literature prize was given to Sully Prudhomme for his "poetic perfection and qualities of heart and intelligence." The science prizes, won in 1901 and 1902 by German and Dutch scientists, were almost entirely ignored by French newspapers and received little attention from the public. But when the Nobel Prize for Physics was attributed to Becquerel and the Curies in 1903, the press seized on a subject that was previously thought too complicated for ordinary folk. Before long, the medical and social consequences of the discovery of radioactivity were known to all. Science, which had promised for decades to grapple with world problems like cancer, appeared to be finally keeping its word.

The Nobel Prize — itself a novelty — did not have behind it the long tradition of excluding women that was common to many older institutions. Marie Curie's prize did not go unnoticed; yet she continued for years to be presented as her husband's worthy assistant. Sometimes, too, she was portrayed as the exception that proved the rule, as if her success was accessible only to a minority of unusual women. Equality of ability between men and women was not openly claimed by French women until Irène Joliot-Curie took a public stand on the question in the 1930s.

Marie Curie, who was by then referred to as Marie Skłodowska-Curie, received a second Nobel Prize in 1911, this time for chemistry. It rewarded her discovery of polonium and radium, her isolation of pure, metallic radium (a feat accomplished with André-Louis Debierne), and her study of this remarkable new element. To this day, she remains the only woman ever to win two Nobel Prizes. After her death, she was admitted to the Panthéon, where her remains rest, alongside her husband's.

Natalie Pigeard-Micault

REFERENCES

Blanc, Karine. *Pierre Curie: Correspondances.* Saint-Rémy-en-l'Eau: Éditions Monelle Hayot, 2009.

Crawford, Elisabeth. *The Beginnings of the Nobel Institution: The Science Prizes, 1901–1915.* New York: Cambridge University Press, 1984.

Curie, Pierre and Marie. Papers. National Library of France, Paris.

Musée Curie, Paris. Archives of the Institut du radium.

Nobel Prize Nomination Archive Database. https://www.nobelprize.org/nomination/archive/list.php

Quinn, Susan. *Marie Curie: A Life*. Rev. ed. Boston: Da Capo Press, 1996.

Radvanyi, Pierre. *Les Curie: Pionniers de l'atome*. Paris: Belin, 2005.

RELATED ARTICLES
1215, 1247, 1380, 1751, 1793, 1875, 1891, 1960

MODERNIZING IN
TROUBLED TIMES

From the halcyon years of the belle epoque (spanning the late nineteenth century to World War I) to the postwar decades of economic growth (1945 to 1973), France modernized at a breakneck pace, despite faltering over the catastrophic events of the two world wars. The start of the twentieth century appears golden in retrospect. A booming economy, international peace, and a rising standard of living cheered the working classes, who sought their entertainment in music halls and their news in *Le Petit Parisien*, a daily newspaper that, in 1918, had one of the highest circulations in the world. France became the center of a powerful entertainment industry (first serialized literature and boulevard theater, then the cinema, invented by Auguste and Louis Lumière, who made their first moving pictures in 1895) that influenced fashions in other countries. "Paris was the twentieth century," said Gertrude Stein. "It was the place to be." The French capital was the cradle of the avant-garde and the birthplace of modern art. It was in his Bateau-Lavoir studio in the Montmartre district, in 1906 and 1907, that Picasso painted his groundbreaking *Demoiselles d'Avignon*.

In the summer of 1914, France was drawn into World War I by the web of alliances among European nations. The French Army managed to halt the German offensive, and a line of trenches more than 450 miles long hardened into a front, from the mud of the Vosges Mountains to the North Sea. New weapons were put to experimental use (airplanes, machine guns, tanks, mustard gas), and the great battles of Verdun and the Somme in 1916 each claimed hundreds of thousands of lives with no definitive result. In late 1917, French soldiers rebelled against the absurdity of the war, while the French population behind the front lines carried on as if nothing was happening. The United States' entry into the war on the side of the Allies on April 6, 1917, was to prove decisive in the following year's victory over Germany and its allies. Close to one and a half million soldiers died "for the glory of France," another four million were wounded, and one million children were orphaned.

With its strong pacifist movement — led by the politician Léon Bourgeois, winner of the 1920 Nobel Peace Prize, and Albert Thomas, first director general of the International Labor Office in Geneva — France was poised to play a leading role in regulating international relations and founding the League of Nations. Meanwhile, Paris was not only the center of an empire, where thousands of people from the French colonies subsisted in the shadows, but also the capital of anti-imperialism. Among those whose paths crossed there were Nguyen Ai Quoc (later to become Ho Chi Minh); Messali Hadj, proponent of Algerian independence;

Lamine Senghor, former Senegalese skirmisher; and Zhou Enlai, then a young Chinese militant. Several of these figures belonged to the French Communist Party and the General Confederation of Labour, the CGTU, an anarcho-syndicalist trade union, and wrote for the famous anticolonialist newspaper *Le Paria*, founded in Paris in 1921 by militants from Indochina, Madagascar, the French Antilles, and North Africa. They exchanged ideological doctrines and revolutionary know-how at a time when police repression in the French colonies was on the rise.

The world of culture in France was flourishing. Artistic movements such as surrealism, cofounded by André Breton, and art deco, under the lead of André Mare, were nourished by the many exchanges across national borders that characterized the Roaring Twenties. France, still considered the birthplace of the rights of man, attracted growing numbers of foreigners, refugees, and exiles. They numbered 2.7 million in 1931, among them Jolán Földes, a young student and worker, who would become the most famous Hungarian writer of the time with her novel *The Street of the Fishing Cat*, which tells the story of an immigrant family in Paris. By the early 1930s, somewhat later than its neighbors, France felt the effects of the Great Depression, which spread across the globe from the Wall Street crash of October 1929 and plunged the European continent into a series of dark years. France experienced a degree of economic hardship: the standard of living of the peasants and workers rose only very slowly, and the middle classes lost ground. This crisis abruptly curtailed immigration. In a few months, close to half a million foreigners returned to their countries of origin.

In the 1930s, the rise of communism and the lure of fascism, provoked by worldwide geopolitical tensions, agitated the political sphere, where rising unemployment and poverty were creating a deep social crisis. This was the context for the experiment of the French Popular Front from 1936 to 1938. This first Socialist government of the Third Republic initiated important social and political reforms that are mainstays of the French left even today: collective bargaining, a reduction of the work week to forty hours, paid vacations that make tourism accessible to everyone, and youth hostels. Democratization occurred, however, without the participation of women (who acquired the right to vote in continental France only in 1944) or colonized "natives" (who were first granted some electoral rights by the Deferre Law in 1956). Opposition movements gathered strength in the French colonies of Indochina, Morocco, Syria, and Tunisia.

In September 1939, the French declared war on Germany, hoping that a military confrontation would never occur. The "Phony War," as it is known, ended with the German offensive in the Ardennes in May 1940, which caught the French Army command off guard. The rout was total, and Marshal Philippe Pétain, who had assumed the leadership of the French government, now headquartered in Bordeaux, asked the Germans for an armistice. The document, signed on June 22, called for France to be divided into two main zones (with a few smaller ones along borderlands and coasts): the German Occupation Zone and the "Free" Zone to the south, under Pétain's government in the spa town of Vichy. Given full powers by the National Assembly on July 10, Pétain established an authoritarian regime that openly embraced collaboration with Hitler. The Vichy government persecuted Jews, Freemasons, Roma, and foreigners. Meanwhile, many of the French rallied behind the Free France government-in-exile and the Resistance and, to fight the Nazi occupation, scraped together resources from certain French colonies (the trading outposts of Chandernagore and Pondicherry in India, the New Hebrides, Tahiti, New Caledonia, Chad, Congo, etc.) as well as Britain and the United States. Thanks to the interventions of the United States and the USSR, which entered the war on the Allied side in 1941, the Axis powers were defeated in 1945.

Because a significant portion of France's infrastructure was destroyed during the war, a difficult period of reconstruction began during the immediate postwar era. The great reforms that followed the liberation of

France (nationalization of Renault and other concerns, economic planning, social security), together with financial help from the United States' Marshall Plan, allowed the economy to reboot. France again imported foreign labor even as it benefited from a spectacular rise in the postwar birth rate — the baby boom. By the mid-1950s, these changes, coupled with a mass exodus from rural to urban areas, paved the way for a new industrial consumer society, marked by the construction of urban housing developments that continued into the mid-1970s. Simultaneously, the contradictions of the colonial system proved intractable, and, between 1945 and 1962, the French colonies gradually gained their freedom through armed resistance. The empire had collapsed, and France turned toward Europe.

1907

A Modern Art Manifesto

Pablo Picasso's *Les Demoiselles d'Avignon* is a riotous
collection of references to ancient and modern times,
working-class life, Paris, the Iberian Peninsula, and
Africa. A new turn in art, this major painting completely
eluded Picasso's contemporaries.

Pablo Picasso painted *Les Demoiselles d'Avignon* at his studio
in the Bateau-Lavoir, an artists' residence in Montmartre,
Paris, in 1907. The large painting was unlike anything
anyone had ever seen before. While the work is considered
a groundbreaking experiment in modern art, at the time,
nobody knew what to make of it.

The large-format oil brothel scene (8 × 7.5 ft.)
originally bore a much racier title. Writer André Salmon is
rumored to have called it a "Philosophical Brothel" in 1912,
before suggesting the work's current name and replacing the
painter's chosen title, "Avignon Brothel." *Les Demoiselles
d'Avignon* — or Young Ladies of Avignon — was an apt
choice because Picasso lived in Barcelona, just paces from

Carrer Avinyo (Avignon), where he would buy his paper and paints. Also, his friend Max Jacob had a grandmother from Avignon and had initially been a figure in the painting, beside Picasso's then girlfriend (their relationship later soured) and Marie Laurencin, a young artist whom a lovestruck Guillaume Apollinaire had recently introduced to the Spaniard. And if the painter had depicted these three women at a brothel, well, it was all a "joke."

Picasso's initial intention was to paint a sailor sitting in a brothel full of naked women. Meanwhile, a medical student was to enter from the left holding a skull and a book. But the seven figures portrayed in the artist's preparatory sketch (now at the Kunstmuseum in Basel) were pared down. The male figures (self-portraits) disappeared, leaving five disjointed, mask-faced women against a blue and white background. A table stands in the foreground, with a small still life acting as a palpable acknowledgment of the patently erotic scene. Haunting statues emerge out of the artist's use of geometry and his proliferation of diagonal lines and twisted, sharp angles. On the left, the statue that came to replace the sailor draws back the curtain, forcing us to look at a dark and brutally lifelike spectacle.

This painting consumed Picasso throughout 1907. His subject evaded him, as can be seen in his repeated studies, across any and all media — from proper drawing paper to printed materials. That year, women's bodies and heads littered his work. One even finds them on a bank's marketing mailer and an erotic piece from a contemporary magazine, *Le vieux marcheur*. Picasso appears to have borrowed from all manner of sources: *The Turkish Bath* by Jean-Auguste-Dominique Ingres (discovered at the 1905 Salon d'Automne's Ingres retrospective), Eugène Delacroix's *The Massacre at Chios* and *Women of Algiers*, and Manet's *Déjeuner sur l'herbe*.

But in addition to finding inspiration in modern (and partly Orientalist) art, Picasso also looked to literature. He had recently discovered Arthur Rimbaud and the Marquis de Sade. And in 1907, Apollinaire dedicated his erotic novel *The Eleven Thousand Rods* to Picasso. Of course, other decisive influences were the pre-Roman Iberian pieces uncovered in Cerro de los Santos and Osuna in Andalusia, which debuted in Paris at the Louvre in early 1906. Picasso even unwittingly bought two stolen relics taken from the exhibit by the adventurer Honoré Joseph Géry Pieret. The Paul Gauguin retrospective at the Salon d'Automne of 1906 can also be credited with inspiring the *Demoiselles d'Avignon* adventure. That was where Picasso first laid eyes on Gauguin's strong Tahitian women. But his primitivism can also be traced to his trip to Gósol, Catalonia, and his encounter with a large-eyed twelfth-century Virgin.

Picasso shared his taste for saints, prostitutes, and primitivism with a handful of artists and writers seeking to create a counterculture against bourgeois norms and Western orthodoxy. From that point of view, Picasso liked the expressive deformation of form and color in André Derain's *Bathers* and Henri Matisse's *Blue Nude*, both of which he saw in 1907 at the Salon des Indépendants. That same year, he witnessed Paul Cézanne break down classical painting at the Salon d'Automne's retrospective of the artist. For him, these examples became creative rivals.

Picasso had also recently discovered what was then called "Negro art," thanks to a small wooden statue purchased by Matisse. Max Jacob recounts seeing his friend after this first encounter with the statue: Picasso drawing a large-format, one-eyed woman with an oversize nose where her mouth should have been and a lock of hair over her shoulder. The poet was mystified by the painter's dark mood and strange drawing. André Malraux's report in *La Tête d'obsidienne* of Picasso's reaction to a visit to the Trocadero Ethnography Museum sheds some light:

> I was looking at the figures, when it occurred to me: I too am against everything. I too think everything is unknown. Everything is the enemy. Everything! Not the details! The women, the children, the animals, tobacco, playing...Everything! I realized what the Negro sculptures were for. Why make sculptures like that? Why not do it differently? They weren't Cubists, after all! Since Cubism didn't exist! Surely, people made models and then other people

imitated those models. That's tradition, right? But all these idols served the same purpose. They were weapons. To help people free themselves. They were tools. If we give form to the spirits, we become free. The spirits, the unconscious (people weren't talking about that yet), emotions, it's all the same. I realized why I was a painter. Alone, in that dreadful museum…with masks, red-skin dolls, dusty dummies. *Les Demoiselles d'Avignon* must have come to life on that day, but it wasn't a question of form. Rather, this was my first exorcism painting!

The artist's catharsis was not appreciated by all. Indeed, critical response to the painting was catastrophic. Not even his friends spared him. The painting was beyond Guillaume Apollinaire and Félix Fénéon, who chalked it up as an exercise in caricature. The German writer Wilhelm Uhde saw something Assyrian about it, while the dealer Daniel-Henry Kahnweiler, on his first visit to the Bateau-Lavoir, expressed bewilderment. A stunned Derain speculated that Picasso would one day hang himself behind his giant painting. Matisse, who was already Picasso's rival and mimetic double, rightly judged it to be a critique of his own *Bonheur de Vivre* (1906). American collector Leo Stein was horrified, but his sister, Gertrude, embraced the artist's game-changing work. In 1910, despite the uproar, an American critic published a reproduction of *Les Demoiselles d'Avignon* in *Architectural Record* under the title *Study by Picasso*.

Contrary to what is often said, the painter did not immediately relegate the work to a dusty corner of his studio. In fact, it was again photographed in his Montmartre studio in 1913–1914. Only after its first, very short-lived public exhibition at the 1916 Salon d'Antin was it rolled up and stored. Picasso may have ceded to criticism, but some part of him still stood by his work, as when he told art collector Christian Zervos that each painting came to him from a far-off place, the product of his dreams, instincts, desires, and thoughts. The artist went on to say that the ideas behind his works incubated for a long time and emerged at times against his will. For him, the unconscious was just as important as the conscious in the creative process. Hence the impression given by *Les Demoiselles d'Avignon* that we are looking at a battlefield.

Ten years after the painting's completion, a hint of recognition emerged, not from the French state, which would not appreciate the value of Picasso's work for some time, but from French collector and art patron Jacques Doucet. He bought *Les Demoiselles* in 1923 on the recommendation of André Breton, who went on to publish a print of it in the fourth issue of *La Révolution surréaliste* in 1925. After Doucet's death, the painting was sold by the collector's widow in September 1937 to American antiques dealer Jacques Seligmann. The Museum of Modern Art acquired it at the end of the year for 28,000 dollars, thanks to a donation by Lillie P. Bliss. Its public existence would finally begin.

In the meantime, interpretations of the painting as a modern art manifesto began to emerge. In 1920, Daniel-Henry Kahnweiler and André Salmon depicted it as a starting point for Cubism. That same claim would be picked up by MoMA's director, Alfred Barr. Others felt that a comprehensive understanding of the piece's multiple perspectives required deeper critical work. To grasp its revolutionary scope, one had to place it within its individual, medical, social, and political contexts. For instance: the contemporary fears of venereal disease and the contrast between white and black prostitutes, a theme that had inspired François-Edmond Fortier's colonial photographs, some of which could be found in Picasso's personal collection. From a political perspective, this tension can also be found in the 1905–1906 debates in the Chamber of Deputies on colonial abuses against indigenous populations in the French and Belgian Congos.

The year 1907 also saw a bloody government crackdown on a "peasant revolt" led by Languedoc and Catalan winemakers. To understand the impact of the era on Picasso, it is important to remember the suicide of his dear friend Carlos Casagemas, a Spanish art student and poet. In his name, Picasso embraced a lifelong, nonmilitant form of anarchism (contrary to the claims made in a 1940 police report that denied him French citizenship) and resolved to fight the bourgeoisie. At Casagemas's request, Picasso signed the "Manifesto of the Spanish Colony Resident in Paris," published in 1900 by *La Publicidad* in Barcelona. Even as a card-carrying member of the French Communist Party, which he joined in 1944, he defended anarchists, continuing to blend elements from private and social life in his art. He never ceased representing his major preoccupations: war, love, and death.

As for *les demoiselles*, after years in the shadows, they did eventually have a lasting impact on art and beyond. Senegal, for instance, put them on a stamp in 1967. From the 1960s on, artists across the globe appropriated, recycled, and reimagined these ladies: Alain Jacquet, Richard Prince, Richard Pettibone, Mike Bidlo, Robert Colescott, Kathleen Gilje, Sophie Matisse, Gerri Davis, Julien Friedler, Faith Ringgold, Eileen M. Foti, Patrick Caulfield, Leonce Raphael Agbodjelou, Wangechi Mutu, and Jeff Koons, whose personal collection includes Picasso's 1925 painting *The Kiss*. Picasso was clear-eyed: a painter is a collector who builds his collection by painting the works he loves in the oeuvre of other artists.

Laurence Bertrand Dorléac

REFERENCES

Rubin, William, ed. *Picasso and Braque: A Symposium*. New York: The Museum of Modern Art, 1992.

Rubin, William, Judith Cousins, and Pierre Daix. *Picasso and Braque: Pioneering Cubism*. New York: The Museum of Modern Art, 1993.

Rubin, William, Hélène Seckel-Klein, and Judith Cousins. *Les Demoiselles d'Avignon: A Special Issue*. New York: The Museum of Modern Art, 1994.

Seckel, Hélène. *Les Demoiselles d'Avignon*. Paris: Éditions de la Réunion des musées nationaux, 1964.

RELATED ARTICLES

34,000 BCE, 1682, 1771, 1798, 1940, 1946

1913

A Promenade for the English

The grand opening of the Negresco "Palace" Hotel in Nice in 1913 marked the pinnacle of modern convenience and international tourism, a precedent set by a century of British travelers. On the verge of going mainstream, leisure society was still the preserve of a worldly industrial elite living in a universe of its own making.

On January 4, 1913, a 450-room beachfront hotel opened for business in Nice. With its stained-glass canopy and massive rotunda, its bronze statuary, crystal chandeliers, and marble floors, its frescoes, vast carpets, and American-style cocktail lounge, it was the undisputed talk of the town. The cost of room furnishings alone was astronomical. Guests enjoyed private telephones, a personal mail delivery service via pneumatic tubes, and electric lamps lit at the mere touch of a button. Heating was provided by five furnaces installed below sea level. A vacuum cleaning system linked all parts of the hotel to a turbine-driven centrifuge that could suction one thousand cubic meters of air per hour. Journalists covering this inaugural event were amazed. The only term to adequately describe such a building, its staff, and its standards, was one recently imported from English: *palace*.

The opening was quite the international affair, with seven crowned heads in attendance, according to the papers. The Dutch architect Édouard-Jean Niermans had already built hotels of this caliber in Paris, Biarritz, and Madrid. The director, Henri Negresco, was a Bucharest native — son of an innkeeper named Jean Negrescu — who had worked for all of Europe's grandest hotels. He lent his name, albeit slightly Gallicized, to this newest establishment. The Hotel Negresco quickly became a magnet for wealthy cosmopolitans who could otherwise be found in the first-class cabins of cruise ships and luxury trains.

The high society embarking on these five-star excursions around the planet may have been worldly but they were also relics of another, quasi-aristocratic age. Anecdotes from the period make them sound like something out of ancien régime Versailles. Rumor had it that the hotel's emblematic pink dome was modeled after the breast of Negresco's mistress, a story reminiscent of France's legendary royal concubines. These inveterate palace-hoppers soon came to be known by yet another English term: "globe-trotters." A few months after the Negresco opening, the wealthy and whimsical heir to the Vichy Saint-Yorre mineral water fortune, Valery Larbaud, himself a denizen of lavish international pleasure spots, published a novel that portrayed this new elite via an American protagonist: *A.O. Barnabooth*.

In hindsight, it would have made more sense for Larbaud's character to be British. It was in England and Scotland that, by the second half of the seventeenth century, certain habits of leisure travel first entered the upper-class agenda, grouped under the general heading of "the Grand Tour." Typically, once young male British aristocrats had completed their courses of study, they would leave for a long trip on the continent, often lasting two years. Italy was their favored destination, until the second half of the eighteenth century, when tastes shifted toward natural settings and mountain landscapes, making Switzerland the latest de rigueur venue.

Young noblemen from all over Europe were soon imitating the British model, while in France's heartland, British *tourists* — the word now a fixture of French vocabulary — had become the butt of mockery, and understandably so, as the local's curious eye returned the visitor's scrutinizing gaze. In the satirical magazines of the nineteenth century, the traveling Englishman was a standard comic figure, endlessly caricatured. Any Frenchman who ventured to imitate him paid the price: the author Stendhal was derided for titling his 1838 travel account *Mémoires d'un touriste*. The word sounded like an impossibly silly Anglicism.

Still, people were aware of the progress this new trend was enabling, in terms of comfort and convenience. As early as 1811, the writer François-René de Chateaubriand could state that travelers of all countries owed a huge debt to the English: "They are the ones who established fine accommodations all over Europe." Thanks to them, one could dine on roast beef and sip sherry all the way to the gates of Sparta. Likewise, it took the British traveling in the Alps to compel the Swiss to improve their hotel standards of comfort and sanitation (notably those English-style commodes that were now replacing chamber pots). Writer Gustave Flaubert lampooned the notion in his satirical *Dictionary of Accepted Ideas*: "Hotels — good only in Switzerland." It was generally assumed that the English were the most widely traveled people in the world, unlike the more sedentary French. The most famous travel agency in France in the late nineteenth century was founded by Thomas Cook. It is no coincidence that Jules Verne's protagonists are mostly Englishmen.

Throughout the nineteenth century, the French town of Vichy was the undisputed mecca for taking the waters, but the upscaling of spa tourism had been undertaken a century earlier across the Channel, at Bath, whose innovations spread later to spas on the continent. The same went for sea-bathing, whose therapeutic benefits had been demonstrated at Brighton in the latter half of the eighteenth century, giving rise to countless establishments in France, starting with Dieppe in 1825. The same was true of wintering resorts. Legend had it that the first one came into being after the Scotsman Tobias Smollett spent a season in Nice in 1763.

The custom of wintering in southern France gained popularity at the turn of the eighteenth and nineteenth centuries, with the British turning certain resorts into fashionable destinations. Scottish physician Alexander Taylor's 1842 study on the health effects of the climate of Pau, in the Pyrenees, helped launch that resort, just as Dr. James Henry Bennett's 1860 study put the coastal town of Menton on the map. The development of Cannes into a tourist town owes much to British statesman Lord Brougham, who took up residence there in the 1830s. As for Nice, British influence was written into the urban landscape in the mid-nineteenth century with the naming of a beachfront promenade right outside the Negresco: La Promenade des Anglais.

Tourists flocking to southern France for the winter months joined what was called the "British colony" or "wintering colony." Cultural habits changed. People took to playing billiards and whist and attended the racetracks built to satisfy the peculiar English taste for horse racing. Golf courses followed, the first of which opened in 1856 in Pau, whose mayor was Dr. Taylor's Irish-born translator.

This trend was accelerated by improved means of

transportation, starting with rail transport. Nice's train station was built in 1864, only three years after the region became part of France, enabling further growth of the wintering colony. Spas, beach resorts, and wintering havens all expanded, with alpine resorts soon to follow. All kinds of amenities sprang up around the cure facilities, along the wide avenues designed to foster healthy air circulation: hotels, theaters, concert and dance halls, reading rooms and museums. Having already adapted from Italian the term *villégiature* to dub such vacation spots, the French now borrowed another one: *casino*, which at the time designated not just a gambling hall but a concert and performance venue. The cosmopolitan society that thronged to the gaming tables came in for harsh criticism, as if this mix of nationalities was necessarily coupled with rapacity. The swindlers and card sharks who would come to conduct their shady business were called "Greeks."

Trends began to shift around 1913. Resorts were no longer reserved exclusively for the upper crust. For several decades, people had been calling for more equal access to holiday tourism. "Pleasure trains" now enabled factory workers to take weekend excursions. New vacation spots were developed for the middle class. One of the larger daily papers even published a guide to affordable holiday locales, *"petits trous pas chers,"* or cheap getaways. The French state's new National Tourism Bureau undertook a massive advertising campaign to promote the country's scenic beauty spots, complete with attractive new labels. The coastal region between Cassis and Menton was named Côte d'Azur in 1887, the shores around Saint-Malo and Dinard became known as the Côte d'Émeraude in 1894, the Atlantic coast of southwest France was called Côte d'Argent in 1905, and the area around Boulogne-sur-Mer on the English Channel was dubbed Côte d'Opale in 1911. With the invention of the postcard as a cheap marketing tool, the map of France was starting to look like an amalgam of regional advertisements.

A wave of democratization was sweeping across a large part of Europe, robbing the former elites of their political clout, which only made the high society that would occupy the 450 rooms of the Negresco more eager for luxury. In Great Britain, the Parliament Act of 1911 shifted power from the House of Lords to the House of Commons. Almost everywhere, the old aristocracy could only express its power through outward signs of its affluence, what American economist Thorstein Veblen called "conspicuous consumption" in his classic 1899 work, *The Theory of the Leisure Class*. The Negresco performed this new social function of showy display. But the crowned heads in attendance at the hotel's inauguration had become irrelevant to the course of world affairs.

The final curtain was falling on an era. Leisure would take a new turn, with a vacation revolution centered around summer beach holidays. On the Côte d'Azur, Juan-les-Pins and Saint-Tropez supplanted the older resort towns. But Henri Negresco, who died bankrupt in Paris in 1920, would not live to see this cultural transformation.

Sylvain Venayre

REFERENCES

Boyer, Marc. *L'Invention de la Côte d'Azur: L'hiver dans le Midi*. La Tour d'Aigues: Éditions de l'Aube, 2001.

Buzard, James. *The Beaten Track: European Tourism, Literature, and the Ways to "Culture," 1800–1918*. Oxford: Clarendon Press, 1993.

Schor, Ralph, Stéphane Mourlane, and Yvan Gastaut. *Nice cosmopolite (1860–2010)*. Paris: Autrement, 2010.

Venayre, Sylvain. *Panorama du voyage (1780–1920)*. Paris: Les Belles Lettres, 2012.

RELATED ARTICLES

1682, 1946, 1974, 1998

1914

From the Great War to the First World War

The conflict that broke out in the summer of 1914 was
not just another clash between European nations. It
was a global confrontation, something contemporaries
understood immediately. Within six months of the
mobilization of August 1, the French were already talking
about *La Grande Guerre* — the Great War.

One way of taking the true measure of World War I is to drive
along the D929 road between Amiens and Bapaume, across
the chalky Somme plateau. No other sector of the former
western front has such a varied concentration of military
cemeteries, each carefully maintained by a different country.
A few kilometers from the town of Albert, the imposing
Thiepval Memorial to the Missing of the Somme, dedicated
to the 72,000 fallen of the British Empire, dominates the
landscape. Farther on, a bronze statue representing a
caribou — the symbol of Newfoundland — recalls the
sacrifice of soldiers of the Newfoundland Regiment on the
battlefield of Beaumont-Hamel. The dead of South Africa

and New Zealand are buried at Longueval; those of China and India at Ayette. To the south, at Villers-Bretonneux, the Australian National Memorial designed by Sir Edwin Lutyens surrounds a cross of sacrifice and a tower memorial, on which are engraved the names of some 10,000 soldiers whose bodies lie buried in unmarked graves. Even though more than 65,000 French soldiers lost their lives in the slaughter of the Somme, everything here suggests that this is not so much a site of national memory as the location of worldwide tragedy — the last great battle in the history of the British Empire.

What is true of the Battle of the Somme (summer and autumn 1916) is also true of this war in general. A century later, it seems to us to have been a planetary event, immediately surpassing the borders of the European continent where it began. Nobody today would dream of writing a history of World War I solely from a national standpoint, in the way academics used to study the fluctuations of French demographics caused by the bloodletting of 1914–1918. The Great War cannot be crammed, either, into the framework of some kind of European civil war, even though most of the ten million who died fighting were killed in Europe. In its European theater it might have resembled a civil war in some aspects; but the fighting immediately drew in Australia, Canada, and Europe's African and Asian colonies, sucking men and raw materials from all quarters of the world into the European vortex. Three years later the United States and Latin America also entered the fray, ending a state of neutrality that was theoretical given that, from the end of 1914, the Americas had been providing the Allies financial support.

Even the regions farthest from Europe found themselves affected by the conflict, whether directly or through its indirect consequences, which included deadly epidemics and millions of refugees. Thus the grim paradox: a war breaking out as a petty regional conflict (and thus similar to so many others since the close of the nineteenth century), a war that should never have taken place grew so unimaginably colossal that it changed the global geopolitical map, annihilating four great empires and forging new relationships between the nations of the world.

For the French, this war was immediately recognizable as a break from previous conflicts; hence its name, the *Grande Guerre*. Their adversaries, the Germans, used the term *Weltkrieg*, meaning world war. In 1914 the fighting instantly spread beyond the European theater of operations. In the first days of August, the French and British took advantage of the opening of hostilities with Germany to attack its poorly defended African colonies Togoland and Cameroon. The ensuing war of skirmishes was waged over vast stretches of land by small, highly mobile units with no artillery — too cumbersome for the purposes of rapid movement. The soldiers carried machine guns on their backs instead.

All too often World War I has been summed up as trench warfare in the north and northeast of France, as if there had been nothing but the all-devouring mud Henri Barbusse described in his fictional memoir (*Le Feu*), Maurice Genevoix's description of Verdun (*Les Éparges*), the Somme where Ernst Jünger fought. The war actually extended its field of action to other environments, from the arid deserts of the Middle East to the savannas of Africa, and also the Alps, where soldiers were as terrified of avalanches and extreme cold as they were of the enemy, and the Balkans, where fever epidemics caused more deaths than the fighting itself. In all these theaters, Frenchmen were called upon to fight.

As the conflict spread across Europe and beyond, France turned to its colonies and began to train the "black forces" envisioned by General Charles Mangin in 1910. Unlike the British, who refused to deploy black African troops to Europe, the French were convinced of the need to bring colonial manpower home to fill the void threatened by their low birth rate. Harassed by compulsory recruitment, tens of thousands of potential African conscripts fled French colonies for British possessions, knowing that Great Britain would not send them to the trenches. But other colonial subjects saw the war as an opportunity for social advancement or a means of escaping patriarchal authority. Between 1914 and 1918, 270,000 soldiers were drafted in North Africa, 189,000 in French West Africa and French Equatorial Africa, 49,000 in Indochina, and 41,000 in Madagascar. Their losses were proportional to those of France's home army.

There was also a need to sustain the war industries, manufacture armaments, and feed the gigantic national armies. The colonies provided war-torn Europe with cereals, wood, and meat. After the appalling losses sustained by the French cavalry during the borderland battles of August 1914, hundreds of thousands of horses were imported from Argentina and the Great Plains of America. France's government also brought in colonial laborers to work in its factories and agriculture — 78,000 Algerians, 49,000 Indochinese, 35,000 Moroccans, Tunisians, and Madagascans. In addition, 140,000 Chinese — mostly from the province of Shandong — were sent to France after agreements signed with the Republic of China in 1916. The graves of some of these Chinese workers may be seen at Noyelles-sur-Mer, in the Somme; most died in the epidemic of Spanish flu at the end of hostilities.

With the advent of total war, France became the focal point of a vast movement of men, animals, and raw materials from all over the world. At the same time, the cultural issues at stake in the conflict became internationalized. To begin with, defensive patriotism was at the core of the French war effort: their country had been invaded, and the invader had to be expelled. France's priority was the protection of the motherland, its regions, and its people. In the summer of 1914, the French population embraced the war coalition government of L'Union Sacrée. Before long, however, both sides began to believe they were fighting for a certain idea of civilization, and not only for the defense of their respective nations. The "German atrocities" of the summer of 1914 were seized upon by French and British propaganda to create a toxic mix of fantasy, fear, and pity for civilian victims of the war. This also contributed to the globalization of the conflict.

In Great Britain, whose army was essentially composed of volunteers until 1916, stories of civilians massacred by the Germans in Belgium and the north of France were highly effective tools of recruitment. This was also true in Ireland. Reims Cathedral, bombed and burned by German troops on September 19, 1914, appeared on numerous British and — later — American propaganda posters. The war of images obviously went a lot further than the strict national framework. The ruins of Reims Cathedral were a perfect symbol of France broken but unbowed: one famous postcard even featured a confrontation between Joan of Arc and Kaiser Wilhelm II with the monument burning in the background. But Reims was not only a French symbol.

The place where the kings of France had been crowned for centuries became an illustration par excellence of a "cultural atrocity" — the term used at the time — committed by the enemy. "The barbarians, who take such vicious pleasure in destruction, set out willfully and intentionally to raze this temple and the glorious traditions it embodied," explained a contemporary. "All they achieved was to cover themselves with shame in the eyes of the civilized world."

The outcry against crimes against civilians, their property, and their heritage — in the name of the principles laid out by the Hague Conventions of 1899 and 1907 — led to aid programs for refugees and occupied populations, and then to the rebuilding of destroyed towns and villages. Naturally this meant generous assistance to the victims of war — especially the French and Belgians. But when it came to the humanitarian program led by Herbert Hoover from 1914 onward, or the aid organized by the American philanthropists J. P. Morgan and Edith Carow Roosevelt (wife of Theodore), the purpose went far beyond France. This was about the universal. Common humanity and basic human rights had to be preserved in the midst of a conflict that afflicted civilians and soldiers with the same unspeakable savagery. World War I marked the beginning of an era of global conflict. In the summer of 1914, war itself was changed forever — not only in its scale but also in its very nature.

Bruno Cabanes

REFERENCES

Audoin-Rouzeau, Stéphane, Annette Becker, and Leonard V. Smith. *France and the Great War*. Cambridge: Cambridge University Press, 2003.

Cabanes, Bruno. *The Great War and the Origins of Humanitarianism, 1918–1924*. Cambridge: Cambridge University Press, 2014.

Gerwarth, Robert, and Erez Manela, eds. *Empires at War, 1911–1923*. Oxford: Oxford University Press, 2015.

Horne, John, and Alan Kramer. *German Atrocities, 1914: A History of Denial*. New Haven: Yale University Press, 2001.

Winter, Jay, ed. *The Cambridge History of the First World War*. 3 vols. Cambridge: Cambridge University Press, 2014.

RELATED ARTICLES

52 BCE, 1137, 1420, 1763, 1794, 1940

1917

The View from New Caledonia

In April 1917, while Kanak soldiers from New Caledonia were fighting for France in Europe, their kinsmen at home found themselves waging a bitter guerrilla war against French colonists. The colonial system had made the Kanaks just French enough to die for France — but no more.

France originally took possession of New Caledonia on September 24, 1853, but it took the Great War in Europe, six decades later, to expose the divided political subjectivity that was forced upon the Kanaks by a colonial system that made them French (against their own will) and never fully accepted them.

In April of 1917, the people of New Caledonia in the Pacific balked at the idea of a second mobilization by the French Army to fight in Europe. Kanak soldiers who had previously enlisted had written home about the awful food, the cold, the isolation, and the extreme violence of the western front, warning of the all-too-likely death awaiting anyone rash enough to join the French forces. A flood of letters and postcards from the front, all saying the same thing, were read by brothers, fathers, and sons who, by that time, were actively challenging forced land seizures that had herded them into closed reservations, like the Native Americans. They rebelled against the conditions of work inflicted upon them and against the authority of the loyalist leadership installed over their heads by the colonial administration to keep its exploitation machine running. Why go out to die for France when France in return maintained a system that held their homeland in continuing bondage? In an attempt to throw off their oppressors, the Kanaks of the northern central region of New Caledonia (on Grande Terre, the main island) began attacking isolated colonists, mine guards, French soldiers, and any of their fellow Kanaks who backed the French counterinsurgency. The fighting on Grande Terre lasted for several months; afterward, French troops swept viciously through the pacified rebel zones until the end of 1918.

The Kanak people have never forgotten this miserable episode. The uprising of 1917 prompted a profound change in the way they viewed all local and global events, whether or not provoked by themselves, whether they took place before or after the conflict.

In their oral or written story-poems known as *ténô*, those Kanaks who could write in their own languages (Paicî and Cèmuhî) turned these facts into events. To do so they devised narrations in verse that condensed their history, thoughts, and emotions within exclusively Kanak criteria of truth. Their words cast a strong light on the original ways in which the colonized Kanaks perceived France, its policies, its enemies, and its allies at the turning point of World War I.

We need to go back to the Kanak mode of expression itself if we are to understand the impact of unprecedented historic experience upon the first residents of the New Caledonian archipelago. In works of strange and powerful beauty, formulated in a completely new way though based on narrative traditions that were much more ancient, these story-poems described technical, political, and warlike affairs among the Kanaks at the beginning of the twentieth century. They broadened the power of the vernacular to deal with the present, using specific formulas that went well beyond the age-old resources of their language. By enriching reality in this way, the Kanaks mapped out their local and international political world and the place they wished to occupy within it, whether for or against the cause of France. Above all, these texts show the extent to which the Kanaks' perspective on the world encompassed the behavior and attitudes of their colonizers.

Local Kanak leaders fought in the Great War in Europe and also fought at home against their compatriots, the 1917 insurgents who were determined to win a bare minimum of rights for the Kanak people. The Great War further complicated matters by involving Kanaks in a conflict pitting Christian nations against one another in an incomprehensibly murderous bloodbath. At the beginning of a long oral work relating the war of 1917 in the Paicî language, a rebel poet exclaimed:

> *Why are we in this state?*
> *What are they up to over there?*
> *Where are they turning like that*
> *and what are they preparing for Tiaoué*
> *when they act with France*
> *whirl for Wilhelm*
> *spin for Poincaré*
> *in a carousel of bullets*
> *stabbing with bayonets*
> *hauling cannons to the heights*
> *offering only likely death [pi-töpwö]*
> *gauging the path to war*

The Kanak poem-narrative captures the abrupt, historical break of this world event. Far from a repetition of the "authentic traditions" of the "savage," these verses express, first, surprise before the unprecedented situation facing the Kanaks and, second, a budding grasp of the multiple futures now made possible. It was so difficult to understand what was happening. The local leadership of Tiaoué was collaborating with the French authorities. Kanak soldiers were giving their lives (*pi-töpwö*) in Europe, but for whom, and why? *Pi-töpwö* (*pi*, meaning reciprocal, and *töpwö*, meaning to swap gifts) referred to the exchanges between people and groups that had always been a vital feature of Kanak social life. These exchanges brought people together by setting up a circulation of property beyond strict necessity. In this case, the poet wonders what will be the quid pro quo for the gift of Kanak lives to France. The asymmetry of the colonial relationship is noted with great bitterness.

The same is true of the following song in the Cèmuhî language, written by Kanak veterans of the Great War:

> *You were aware*
> *of our goodwill.*
> *You forced us,*
> *you pushed us to leave.*
> *Tossed on the sea*
> *we drifted blindly,*
> *choked by the night*
> *surrounded in darkness.*
>
> *Alas! What confusion,*
> *what evils*
> *we endured!*
> *We lay on the ground*
> *as Wilhelm's machine guns*

rained death upon us
but then we cried: "Aïpa!"
and faced them.

Today I am ashamed
I feel like a coward,
because I abandoned
my fathers and my grandfathers.
Their ashes enrich the soil, rotting far away,
We left them to their fate
for that was our wish.

The experience of simultaneous wars, in France and in New Caledonia, each contaminating the other, was inseparable from the colossal power of European weaponry, so much more destructive than the Kanak's own cudgels, slings, and spears. Horrified and yet amazed by this technical savagery, Kanaks dwelt on the new death-sounds of what Apollinaire had called the "simple, brutal symphony of war":

Bursting shells
dynamite splitting and blasting,
pistols and revolvers crack
shrieks from plumes of dust
clinging tongues of flame:
the knots of war drawn tight.

This text compares the efficiency of the new killing

machines with Kanak war rituals, notably those signaling a pact to give battle by the knotting of votive herbs around wooden stakes. These stakes are still known as "war taboos."

But while the technical advances brought by the whites altered the way people could die, they also contributed greatly to the comfort of living. The New Caledonia uprising of 1917 was unleashed in the hope of obtaining from the colonists at least a share of the new commodities and techniques. In vain.

We sleep, we dream,
we dream of happiness
Bring us the sugar
and the candles
fetch us the rubber
give us electricity…

The motion of the vessels taking them across the sea to Nouméa relaxed the captured Kanak warriors and lulled them to sleep. As they slept, they dreamed of the imported goods they associated with a better life. To understand the Kanak uprising, we must also understand their openness to the material advantages of modernity. Their chief motive truly was a quixotic hope for a better world, in which whites would admit Kanaks to the new forms of wealth they had discovered. There was nothing messianic, no cargo cult at work in their struggle: only a thirst for justice.

In 1917, the countries of Europe and the rest of the world were in some difficulty before Germany, whose offensive in Europe had met unexpected success. Australia joined the allies fighting against the expansion of the Austro-Hungarian Empire. France called for assistance from New Caledonia, and some Kanaks joined up at a time when their brothers were openly defying the imperial power. This political geography was defined by a long poem, originating with loyalist auxiliaries, which mentions several different continents and countries:

> *The English soldiers stand in ranks*
> *Paris carries a bayonet*
> *The German guns stand line abreast*
> *There are echoes in Italy*
> *Sydney joins in*
> *There is spitting in Germany*
> *Panic in Batavia*
> *Murmuring among the Allied countries*
> *They call for everyone's help*
> *And the Grande Terre answers.*
> *Caledonia can provide.*
> *They seek in their doubt*
> *They jump up and ask me*
> *They beg for a wall,*
> *A wall that protects and provides hope*
> *Stone to establish trust.*

1001

In Kanak tradition, the stone in question favored the growth of yams, but its powers encompassed support for other countries in wartime. Thus a propitiatory arrangement of a kind normally used in agriculture was here dedicated to the success of the Allied armies; such was the special ritual assistance that the Kanaks, in good faith, offered to France to help it prevail. At Houaïlou, in the north, the ethnologist and pastor Maurice Leenhardt and the young British zoologist and ethnographer Paul Montague joined a ceremony in which "a spell was cast over the Kaiser using a rare magic stone." Later, Leenhardt wrote that he had "not so much converted the Kanaks, as he has been converted by them."

Dui Denis Péaru, born in 1891, was recruited as a "volunteer" in June 1916 then arrested as a deserter in March 1917 before being sent to France in November of the same year. He was killed in action on August 28, 1918, at Le Bois-Roger in the Aisne. There is a cross to his memory at the Cemetery of Douaumont.

By contrast, his brother took the side of the two men who began the guerrilla war of 1917 on the west coast of New Caledonia; one of them was assassinated in 1918. The Péaru family was hit twice by the conflict: it lost a direct relative, who gave his life *to* France on the western front, and an indirect one, killed *by* France in the New Caledonia uprising (this was Noël Pwatiba, who belonged to a neighboring clan).

Pwënyî Ignace Péaru — Denis's great-nephew — keeps two photographs in a drawing box at his home in Atéu. One is of the cross at Douaumont commemorating the brother of his grandfather, Dui Denis, and the other is of the severed head of Noël Pwatiba, the hero of 1917. The two wars, the great one of 1914–1918 and the small one of 1917, yielded many such bitterly ambivalent memories, which remain lodged in the lore and identity of the Kanaks.

From wartime destruction to poetic resistance against oblivion and despair, the Kanaks found ways of overcoming and writing history, whether for France or against the colonial power. In concert with the Western literary outpouring that followed the Great War, the Kanaks used their ambiguous relationship to colonial domination to both borrow tools from the West — literature, guns, the ideal of liberty — and at the same time contest its dominance and assert their own narrative, ritual, and political power.

Alban Bensa

REFERENCES

Bensa, Alban, Kacué Yvon Goromoedo, and Adrian Muckle. *Les Sanglots de l'aigle pêcheur: Nouvelle-Calédonie, la guerre kanak de 1917*. Toulouse: Anacharsis, 2015.

Boubin-Boyer, Sylvette, ed. *Révoltes, conflits et guerres mondiales en*

Nouvelle-Calédonie et dans sa région. Paris: L'Harmattan, 2008.

Leenhardt, Maurice. *Gens de la Grande Terre*. Paris: Gallimard, 1953.

Naepels, Michel. *War and Other Means: Power and Violence in Houaïlou (New Caledonia)*. State, Society and Governance in Melanesia. Canberra: ANU Press, 2017.

Rivierre, Jean-Claude. *Dictionnaire paicî-français (Nouvelle-Calédonie)*. Paris: SELAF-Peeters, 1983.

RELATED ARTICLES

1852, 1931, 1940, 1961, 2008

1919

Two World-Changing Conferences

Two utterly different high-level gatherings were held
in Paris in 1919, each with the purpose of rethinking
international relations. The Versailles Peace Conference
and the second Pan-African Congress raised hopes
momentarily, only to disappoint in the longer term.

From February 19 to 20, 1919, a Parisian hotel hosted fifty-
seven delegates from fifteen different nations for the second
Pan-African Congress. The gathering was organized by
W.E.B. Du Bois, financed by the NAACP, and chaired by
the Senegalese deputy to the French National Assembly,
Blaise Diagne. Their collaboration mirrored what was
taking place at the Versailles Peace Conference that followed
World War I. There, for the first time on a world scale, great
expectations were on the horizon, particularly the hope of
mitigating the "color line" that, speaking at the first Pan-
African Congress held in London in 1900, Du Bois had
defined as the paramount problem of the twentieth century.

From January to June 1919, twenty-seven delegations

from every continent met to thrash out the conditions of a still fragile post–World War I peace. Fifty-two commissions were at work to redraw the map of Europe, determine the fate of Germany's colonies and certain provinces of the Ottoman Empire, and put forward a new set of international operating principles. For a period of six months, Paris was the furnace where the world's future was being forged. Meanwhile, France had only just begun demobilizing and tabulating its massive casualties — 1,300,000 killed in combat and many more disabled, widowed, and orphaned — and extensive material destruction. Persistent food shortages led to price hikes, requiring the government to supply the population with subsidized staples, which were sold from makeshift sheds set up in the streets of Paris, the *baraques Vilgrain* named after their creator, Ernest Vilgrain. The labor strikes that broke out that spring were particularly intense, and while Prime Minister Georges Clemenceau accepted demands for an eight-hour workday, he was unable to defuse hopes of sparking radical change, akin to the triumphant 1917 Russian Revolution.

Against this tense background, Du Bois and Diagne made the bullish gamble that France was the hub "where all races have gathered in mutual acknowledgement, and where, perhaps for the first time, a common danger will have truly kept alive the idea of universal brotherhood." Du Bois sought to research the military feats of African-American soldiers in order to demonstrate their bravery, even as black veterans were met with lynch mobs back in the US. As France's commissioner in charge of colonial military enrollments, Diagne managed to recruit 63,000 reserve troops in West Africa, including territories where the draft had triggered a full-blown insurrection. Building on the positive image of this army, he vowed to make good on an earlier promise to provide full citizenship for the colonized population.

The issue of equality among peoples and races, officially brought forward by the Japanese delegation at Versailles, was quickly removed from the peace conference list of objectives, even though it was such a topical discussion point. In the spring of 1919, Koreans were rising up in great numbers to reject the protectorate of their Japanese "big brothers"; in Egypt, Britain's refusal to authorize a nationalist delegation to attend the Paris meeting led to demonstrations and the creation of a new political party, Wafd ("delegation" in Arabic); in India, Gandhi was launching his first civil disobedience campaign against laws that upheld censorship and the state of emergency, a movement cut short when imperial troops opened fire on an unauthorized public gathering in Amritsar, killing some four hundred people. Not a single voice of contestation was raised in Paris to denounce these acts of imperial repression, which denied people their right to self-determination.

A staunch defender of this right, which he laid out as the basis of future peace in his famous Fourteen Points speech in January 1918, American President Woodrow Wilson met with a number of delegations in France, Great Britain, and Italy during brief visits. He held talks with Léon Jouhaux, secretary of the General Confederation of Labor (CGT), France's general labor union, but did not grant similar access to representatives of the colonized peoples. Among those to experience this bitter rejection were: Emir Khaled, grandson of Emir Abd el-Kader, leader of the first generation of Algerian freedom fighters against the French, who had seen eighteen months of combat for France, and wrote to Wilson on behalf of a group called the Young Algerians; Tunisian political activist Abdelaziz Thâalbi, who worked with a similarly oriented group, the Young Tunisians, turned their petition into a public manifesto, *La Tunisie martyre*, and created a new party, the Destour, calling for a constitution; and the future Ho Chi Minh, who had taken the alias Nguyen Ai Quoc, "Nguyen the Patriot."

The same kind of discrimination tainted the conference's geopolitical shuffling. One provision turned over Germany's Chinese territories to Japan, demonstrating that non-Western peoples in sovereign countries could be dispatched with the same heavy hand as colonized populations. Such flagrantly unequal treatment immediately cast doubt upon the fulsome rhetoric of the new treaties, especially regarding the "sacred civilizing mission" yet again attributed to Westerners by article 22 of the Covenant of the League of Nations.

The second Pan-African Congress took place at a moment when the peace conference had recessed for a month, allowing Wilson to return to the US. This satisfied Diagne without worrying the American and British officials, who had limited the number of participants by refusing to issue them proper authorizations. Although Clemenceau supported the Congress, colonial matters were low on his political agenda, and served essentially as bargaining chips during adjustment and compensation talks. His top priority consisted of hammering out an international arrangement whereby peace and collective security could be guaranteed, and Germany would be held to pay reparations commensurate with the casualties and material losses suffered by France.

A blueprint for the League of Nations, hashed out in February 1919, precluded any armed forces and required that all decisions be unanimous. The original French draft had been brushed aside by the American and British version, and by concerns about a hawkish hatred of the enemy, deep-seated among veterans and the French population at large. If this peace conference could hardly have been held anywhere but Paris, the choice of venue did not always serve French interests.

The Pan-African delegates were pinning their hopes on the League of Nations. They argued for the drafting of an international code of protection for indigenous peoples, to be enforced by a specially designed permanent secretariat within the league. They were concerned about the fate of "civilized blacks" who were not living in the colonies. Finally, they needed to make certain that the league would appeal to a hypothetical world opinion whenever the rights of people of black African descent were infringed upon, or whenever a state "deliberately excluded its civilized citizens of African origin from its political and intellectual circles." Like so many of their contemporaries, these delegates hoped that the League of Nations would resolve reemerging tensions between an internationalist worldview and a more nationalist, imperialist perspective. Diagne was undoubtedly torn between, on the one hand, Du Bois's worldwide antiracism struggle and, on the other, the possibility of becoming the new champion of assimilation within the French colonial empire.

And yet, dreams of universal brotherhood were rapidly dispelled by the texts outlining an exit strategy from the war. Peoples who were not yet considered "capable of governing themselves" became a category under international law in the Covenant of the League of Nations, encoding into law once again the time-worn distinction between so-called civilized peoples and "uncivilized," dominated peoples. The access to citizenship that France had promised to its colonial conscripts was drastically curtailed by the 1919 Jonnart law, which granted only local citizenship to Algerian veterans. In the other colonies, this denial of rights to war veterans justified a drastically Malthusian citizenship policy that coincided with economic objectives. The scope of physical reparations in mainland France forestalled any policy of investment in the colonies, where forced labor had become widespread. Indigenous populations were locked into an untenable status.

French officials rejected even the more prudent reforms linked to their territorial mandate, which they hoped to circumvent. In mainland France, some two hundred thousand colonial workers, forced into labor during the war, were sent home and replaced by European migrants. Even though black American writers, artists, and performers were given a warm welcome, the official segregation of colonial workers during the war left its legacy in ensuing decades, forcing colonial workers who chose to remain in France or who had come in search of freedom to hide from the authorities. Colonial soldiers also bore the humiliating burden of this double-speak. Those who took part in the occupation of the Rhineland were vilified by a racist international campaign that deemed the very presence of dark-skinned people an affront to Germans. There was an infamous term for this: *schwarze Schande*, the black shame.

Signed on June 28, 1919, the Treaty of Versailles hardly pleased anyone. Although the United States refused to ratify it, the compromises upon which it rested kept the peace until 1931. The Bastille Day victory parade of July 14, 1919, was the last outward sign of this concerted international effort. Like France, now retreating into a defensive position, this event mourned the Allied dead while celebrating victory. France was still negotiating its final exit from the war, but the trauma caused by the four-year conflict was already weighing on both its international status and its imperial policies.

Emmanuelle Sibeud

REFERENCES

Becker, Jean-Jacques. *Le Traité de Versailles*. Paris: Presses Universitaires de France, 2002.

Cabanes, Bruno. *La Victoire endeuillée: La sortie de guerre des soldats français (1918–1920)*. Paris: Le Seuil, 2014.

Manela, Erez. *The Wilsonian Moment: Self-Determination and the International Origins of Anticolonial Nationalism*. Oxford: Oxford University Press, 2007.

Stovall, Tyler. *Paris and the Spirit of 1919: Consumer Struggles, Transnationalism, and Revolution*. Cambridge: Cambridge University Press, 2012.

Winter, Jay, ed. *The Cambridge History of the First World War*. 3 vols.
Cambridge: Cambridge University Press, 2014.

RELATED ARTICLES

1920

"If You Would Have Peace, Cultivate Justice"

In January 1920, the socialist reformer Albert Thomas
was appointed director general of the International Labor
Office. Founded just after the end of World War I, the ILO
fostered dialogue among the former antagonist nations and
initiated a transnational legal system to protect the rights of
working people everywhere. Its first goal was to enshrine
the eight-hour working day in international law.

Millions of dead on the European fields of battle, hundreds
of thousands displaced or in exile, unprecedented
environmental destruction, and everywhere the legacy of
chaos, violence, and instability. The survivors of 1914–
1918 had to grapple with all of this, remedy the disasters
engendered by the conflict, reestablish relations between
the former belligerents, and above all rebuild and reinvent
the world on a completely new footing. Different visions
of the future squared off: on the one side, the communist
internationalism of the October Revolution, on the other,
veterans in their respective liberal democracies. "Do we

want Wilson or Lenin? We can follow the way of democracy born of the French Revolution, tried and tested by a century of struggle — or we can opt for the primitive, incoherent, brutal fanaticism of Russia. The choice is ours," was the blunt conclusion of socialist reformer Albert Thomas, in an article published by the French communist newspaper *L'Humanité* on November 19, 1918.

Albert Thomas had been the architect of industrial policy in France's wartime administration. In January 1920, he took control of the postwar International Labor Office, which soon became one of the most successful organizations of the era, a unique source of expertise for social and economic questions and one of the few forums where erstwhile enemies could discuss topics of mutual concern. Created by the Treaty of Versailles and based in Geneva, the ILO was expected to play a civilizing, regulatory role with the power to intervene across a wide spectrum of issues related to labor. For example, the agenda of its first conference, in Washington, DC, in October 1919, included discussions of the eight-hour day, the battle against unemployment, the protection of the labor rights of women before and after childbirth, the regulation of night work, and the minimum age for industrial workers. No fewer than forty countries sent delegates to this first major international meeting; before long they were joined by spokesmen for Germany and Austria, at a time when the former Central powers had yet to be admitted to the League of Nations.

The beginnings of a plan for an international organization of labor emerged from the wreckage of the war. *Si vis pacem, cole justiciam* was its motto. "If you would have peace, cultivate justice." In many ways, the ILO derived from the "sacred unions" forged during the conflict. "It was the war that gave labor legislation such urgency," explained Thomas. "The war forced governments to tackle the poverty and injustice afflicting workers. And it was the war that made organized labor understand that it needed strong legal protections, deployed across national borders, to obtain what it wanted."

As a student at the École Normale Supérieure, Thomas had been an influential figure in a reformist group. Among his friends were Mario Roques, a specialist in medieval literature who would become his chief of staff during the war before heading the Paris branch of the ILO; the great economist François Simiand, who ran the wartime Armaments Ministry; the sociologist Maurice Halbwachs; and the economist Edgard Milhaud, who oversaw the international inquiry into industrial production, labor, and consumption in 1925. The interlocking careers of these men illustrate the strong continuity between France's elite school network at the turn of the century, government circles during the war, and the leadership of the ILO in the 1920s.

It was Lucien Herr, legendary librarian of the École

Normale Supérieure since 1888, who charted the course. "We are all agreed about the things we must jettison: namely, world systems and value theories that have no interest whatever, philosophical waffle and childish polemic. I think the important elements now are socialist data, historical and critical study, factual enquiry and practical action." The social reformism championed by Albert Thomas and his friends turned its back on the romantic ideal of socialism that had marked the previous generation. From now on the emphasis was on scientific socialism, founded on fieldwork and intellectual proximity to German socialists. It was the era of great international congresses such as the Berlin conference of 1890, which advocated labor laws on a universal scale and set up an "epistemic community" of experts on social issues. This network spawned three major associations: an international association to combat unemployment, an international congress on workplace accidents, and an international association for the legal protection of workers. Cofounded by Arthur Fontaine, the latter laid the foundations for the first international labor legislation — bans on women's nighttime industrial work and on the use of white phosphorus in the match industry.

When World War I broke out, Albert Thomas abandoned pacifism and became a fervent patriot. In the spring of 1915, he entered the French government, first as undersecretary of state with responsibility for artillery and military equipment, and then for nine months from 1916 to 1917 as minister of armaments and war production. He was convinced from that time on that the social concerns he championed when he was reorganizing French war production (limitation of women's work hours, introduction of breastfeeding rooms) would remain relevant after the cessation of hostilities. The other continuity between his policies at the Ministry of Armaments and the line he adopted in Geneva at the beginning of the 1920s was bringing together governments, employers' organizations, and workers' unions, all of which were associated closely with the writing of industrial policy. What would later be known as "tripartism" had already been present (in embryo) within the ILO with the practice of arbitration and conciliation during the war. The impulses driving these ideas were not the same, however. During the war, Thomas could exploit the patriotism of both employers and workers, taking advantage of the fact that class loyalties were temporarily suspended during a time of national mobilization. With the postwar ILO, his concern shifted toward a transnational project involving various social partners in order to secure general recognition of universal social rights.

During the first years of his mandate as director of the ILO, Thomas saw through no fewer than sixteen conventions and eighteen recommendations on labor policy. The promotion of international norms was undertaken in tandem with an ambitious program of inquiries and publications. As time went by, however, the ILO had to grapple with a shortage of funding and the reluctance of national parliaments to vote into law a set of rules decided by experts sitting in distant Geneva. Little by little, the war receded into the past, as what historians now call the process of cultural demobilization gathered way. Pacifism was one of the leitmotifs in the rhetoric of war veterans, especially in France. It offered a form of renewed patriotism that linked love of France with love of humanity, loathing of the militarism that had precipitated the crisis of the summer of 1914, and hope that the Great War would never be repeated. This political and moral posture had its heroes (such as French Minister of Foreign Affairs Aristide Briand), its rituals (the solemn liturgy of November 11), and its solid achievements (the League of Nations, championed by the elder statesman Léon Bourgeois). To mount a common defense of their rights and promote better care for the war wounded, veterans from all over the world met at Geneva for an international conference of associations of the war-disabled and other military veterans. Adrien Tixier, himself war-disabled and an ILO official, and the eminent jurist and politician René Cassin organized these meetings.

The 1920s enthusiasm for transnational ideals — which resulted in the landmark Locarno agreements — could not obscure the facts that cultural demobilization took place at a snail's pace and that hatred for former enemies failed to disappear. In every country, but especially in France, the collective memory of the Great War was first and foremost a national affair, indissociable from the memory of those compatriots who had perished. The need to retain memories of the dead generated two contradictory imperatives. On the one hand, we find the pacifist message of *plus jamais ça* (never again), conveyed by veterans' associations. On the other hand, there was a moral taboo against reconciling too quickly with a recent enemy. Moving past the war was a betrayal of the fallen. Thus the great mathematician Émile Picard, who lost three sons in the conflict, continued in 1925 to request Germany's exclusion from all international congresses of European academics. Only six years had passed since the end of hostilities: "Too short a time for us to be drawing a veil over so many odious criminal acts," Picard declared, "especially when no regret has ever been expressed."

Bruno Cabanes

REFERENCES

Cabanes, Bruno. *The Great War and the Origins of Humanitarianism, 1918–1924*. Cambridge: Cambridge University Press, 2014.

Horne, John, ed. "Démobilisations culturelles après la Grande Guerre."

14–18 Aujourd'hui, Today, Heute, no. 5. Paris: Noésis, 2002.

Lespinet-Moret, Isabelle, and Vincent Viet, eds. *L'Organisation internationale du travail*. Rennes: Presses universitaires de Rennes, 2011.

Topalov, Christian, ed. *Laboratoires du nouveau siècle: La nébuleuse réformatrice et ses réseaux en France (1880–1914)*. Paris: Éditions de l'École des hautes études en sciences sociales, 1999.

RELATED ARTICLES
1420, 1659, 1914, 1948, 2003

1921

Chanel — A Woman's Scent for the World

In 1921, Gabrielle "Coco" Chanel, already a leading figure
in Parisian high society, expanded her millinery business
to include perfumes. Chanel No. 5, the signature scent she
launched with the help of Russian émigré Ernest Beaux,
met with phenomenal success. Celebrated by such figures
as Marilyn Monroe and Andy Warhol, the stylish little
Chanel flacon remains an iconic object and an enduring
symbol of French luxury.

Had the *Pioneer* and *Voyager* space probes of the 1970s
shipped a scent representing mankind to impress
extraterrestrial civilizations, there is no doubt that it would
have been Chanel No. 5. Until recently this was the world's
best-selling perfume, a mythical product that carried far
and wide the banner of France as a manufacturer of luxury
products. Still wildly popular, it has now been in production
for nearly a century.

In 1921, Gabrielle Chanel was thirty-eight, and her
hat-making business, which had quickly expanded to

include couture, proved increasingly successful in postwar France. Orphaned at twelve years old, left by her father to be educated by the sisters of the Cistercian nunnery of Aubazine in the rural Corrèze, Chanel had prospered in Paris, where she opened her headquarters at 31 Rue Cambon, just behind the Ritz Hotel. Several years earlier, she had finished repaying her dashing English protector Arthur Edward "Boy" Capel (killed in an automobile accident in 1919) the sums he had invested in her business. By now, she employed more than three hundred female workers. Chanel was also the mistress of Grand Duke Dimitri Pavlovich, grandson of Czar Alexander II, among whose close friends were the couple Josep Maria and Misia Sert. The latter belonged to a circle that included Pablo Picasso and Sergei Diaghilev (with whom Chanel worked on the ballet production *Parade*) as well as Igor Stravinsky and his family, exiled from Russia. The Stravinskys quickly became permanent guests at Bel Respiro, Chanel's villa in Garches, just outside Paris.

Most importantly, of course, Chanel championed — like Jean Patou and other contemporary Paris couturiers — a style freeing women to wear trousers, cardigans, jerseys, and suits that loosened, lengthened, and streamlined the look of their bodies. At the time she began diversifying her business to include perfumes, this market was particularly dynamic. Poiret had ventured into this market with great success ten years earlier. The principal manufacturers of the time were

Guerlain, Roger & Gallet, Piver, and — for the preceding fifteen years — Coty, whose Chypre, launched in 1917, had been hugely successful. Guerlain's L'Heure Bleue (1912) and Mitsouko (1919) were also highly prized. French perfume dominated the world.

Gabrielle Chanel met the perfumer Ernest Beaux in 1920, probably through the good offices of Grand Duke Dimitri. Having been technical director for Rallet, the leading Muscovite perfumery, Beaux had been forced into exile by the 1917 Russian Revolution. He recovered his own French business, which had been sold in 1896 to the Grasse-based company Chiris, and brought it home to La Bocca, a neighborhood in Cannes. In 1946, writing in the magazine *Industrie de la parfumerie,* he described how Chanel No. 5 had come into being:

> I composed No. 5 when I got back from the war. I'd campaigned with the military in northern Europe, inside the Arctic Circle, at a time when the sun was still shining at midnight and the lakes and rivers breathed a scent of an extraordinary freshness. That fragrance was fixed in my memory and I managed to reproduce it; not without difficulty, because the first aldehydes I was able to find were unstable and irregular in the way they were made.

Of course Chanel No. 5 was not, by a long shot, the first perfume to be composed using synthetic raw materials. By

1920, artificial molecules had been used in scent manufacture for about forty years. The originality of No. 5 is mainly due to the high proportion of aldehydes in its formula of some eighty components. Aldehydes, synthetic scent bodies whose individual odor is not especially pleasant, have the special property of sharpening the scents of the raw materials with which they are combined. Gabrielle Chanel was looking for "a women's scent with the scent of a woman." Beaux's aldehydes made it possible for him to transform the complex floral bouquet he was composing into a form of abstraction in which the natural raw materials — *rose de mai*, jasmine, and ylang-ylang — could be more closely blended and were less directly identifiable. Indeed, as Edmonde Charles-Roux observed, "No. 5 has the surprising character of an abstract creation." The major role the synthetic notes played in the scent was a notable innovation — and did not hinder its popularity. "This fragrance had — and still has — immense success. Few perfumes have been imitated and counterfeited as much as Chanel No. 5," Beaux wrote in 1946.

The choice of the name "No. 5," after a number which is a symbol of perfection in many cultures, also constituted a break with usual practice. For writer Paul Morand, it evoked "a future in which perfumes would no longer be called Trèfle Incarnat or Rêve d'automne, but would have numbers on them, like convicts." But Beaux himself revealed the real origin:

Why the name? Mademoiselle Chanel, who was running an extremely fashionable couture house in Paris, asked me to come up with a few fragrances that might suit her style. I offered two series, numbered 1 to 5 and 20 to 24. She selected some of them, including the one labeled 5, and when I asked her to suggest a name, she said: "I present my next collection on the fifth of May, which is the fifth month of the year. So let's name this scent after the number it already has — number five. That should bring it luck." She couldn't have been more right.

And yet, in 1921, the ingredients of success were not quite all there for Chanel No. 5. Fashion houses were now diversifying into the increasingly competitive field of perfumery. In 1923, the Jeanne Lanvin house moved into the market with a perfume called Irisé, composed by Madame Zed. In 1924, Jean Patou brought out Amour Amour, Que sais-je? and Adieu sagesse, all three created by the master perfumer Henri Alméras. And even though No. 5 was already on the market, Gabrielle Chanel did not have the means necessary to produce and distribute it on a large scale. Her meeting in 1923 with the Wertheimer brothers proved decisive in that regard.

Ernest Wertheimer had been the owner of the perfume maker Bourjois and Co. since 1898. Founded by Joseph-Albert Ponsin and bought in 1868 by his employee

Alexandre-Napoléon Bourjois, this company was famous for its Java rice powder, of which 2.5 million boxes had been sold yearly in the world since 1912. Bourjois and Co. had also owned a factory and building plots at Pantin, conveniently sited on the outskirts of Paris, since 1891. In 1923, Paul and Pierre Wertheimer, Ernest's sons, met Gabrielle Chanel through Théophile Bader, the cofounder, with Alphonse Kahn, of the Galeries Lafayette department store. With the possibility of major production at the Bourjois plant at Pantin, backed by a structure of distribution capable of serving a broad sales network, the conditions for success were now in place. The following year, the Parfums Chanel company was founded, with Ernest Beaux as its technical director. The initial contract agreement between the parties assigned 70 percent of the capital to the Wertheimer brothers, 20 percent to Adolphe Dreyfus and Max Grumbach, representing Bader, and 10 percent to Chanel. This collaboration, which grossly disadvantaged her, was later the cause of much bickering. In 1947, after the war, Chanel renegotiated the contract to bring her share to 2 percent of the annual turnover. In 1954, Pierre Wertheimer bought the 20 percent of the company still held by the Galeries Lafayette, and, when Chanel herself returned to couture, Parfums Chanel went on to buy the couture house. This left Pierre Wertheimer as owner of the entire Chanel group, at a time when the brand was once again immensely successful.

The 1950s saw a huge boost to Chanel No. 5 when a journalist happened to ask Marilyn Monroe what she wore in bed, and the actress famously replied: "Nothing but a few drops of No. 5." Although there is no trace of the original interview, in the years that followed Monroe was photographed several times with the perfume, notably during a shoot in which she posed naked under a blanket, and in an iconic portrait that pictures her with lowered eyelids clasping a huge flacon of No. 5. In a recording dating from 1960, which was unearthed by the Chanel company in 2013, she mentions the original interview and repeats the famous words. This recurrent association of the great actress with the perfume contributed significantly to its international fame and mythical status. The image of Marilyn — American, blonde, shapely, fizzing with energy — was the perfect complement to the image of Chanel herself — dark, cool, cerebral, and European. No. 5 became a perfume for all women — the very essence of femininity.

The inspired choice of a name that was easy to translate and imaginatively transparent made possible any number of readings and projections in cultures all over the world. Its unassuming packaging, too, allowed the perfume to stay abreast of the changing times and preserve its universal appeal. Spurning the bitter rivalries of contemporary flacon design, Chanel No. 5 appeared in a simple little bottle inspired by the vodka flasks of the old Russian imperial guard. "The sharp-edged, rectangular flacon Chanel epitomized an approach that was modern, logical, and crystal clear," declared the writer Edmonde Charles-Roux, author of *Chanel and Her World*. "Women were expected to want not so much the container as its contents; not so much the object as the soul within it. Their olfactory sense was aroused by the promise of this golden liquid, imprisoned in a cube of pure crystal, made elegantly manifest as a pure object of desire." In 1959, No. 5 and its simple bottle entered the permanent collection of the Museum of Modern Art. In 1985, Andy Warhol made it the subject of one of his series, consecrating it as an iconic object of the twentieth century.

The sobriety of the bottle, along with the abstraction of its name, made No. 5 a virgin canvas upon which the very essence of the Chanel brand could be expressed. By making her scent minimalist and elitist — the twin characteristics of her own style — but without locking it into a specific narrative, as was the case with Shalimar, Arpège, L'Air du temps, Opium, Poison, and so many other major twentieth-century perfumes, Chanel proved that the value of perfume resides in the image it projects. To lodge this image in a narrative is to make the product vulnerable to the passing of time. Conversely, to place the product above any conceivable narrative is to give it a chance to partake in all narratives, and even to make these narratives evolve, as time goes by, the better to seduce women of every era and every corner of the world.

No. 5's publicity campaigns have continued to reflect this position. While the women who have personified the perfume since the 1970s have usually been French (Catherine Deneuve, Carole Bouquet, Audrey Tautou), there have been others, such as the Australian Nicole Kidman and the Brazilian Gisele Bündchen, and even men, such as Brad Pitt in 2012. The image that is projected upon the perfume is not of a French ideal but rather of the markets it perpetually targets. We thus find 1980s American skyscrapers and Shanghai buildings. All told, Chanel No. 5's subtle balance projects to the rest of the world an ideal of luxury à la française whereas to France itself, it offers something even more exquisite: a French woman with the world at her feet.

Eugénie Briot

REFERENCES

Beaux, Ernest. "Souvenirs d'un parfumeur." *Industrie de la parfumerie* 1, no. 7 (October 1946): 228–31.

Charles-Roux, Edmonde. *L'Irrégulière: L'itinéraire de Coco Chanel*. Paris: Grasset, 2016 [1974].

Morand, Paul. *The Allure of Chanel*. Translated by Euan Cameron. London: Pushkin Press, 2017.

RELATED ARTICLES
1202, 1682, 1712, 1913

1923

Crossroads of Exile

In 1923, an Armenian couple named Aznavourian landed at the port of Marseille, among hundreds of other refugees from the East. The wanderings of Knar, Misha, and their daughter Aïda, who had fled the ruined Russian and Ottoman Empires, ended in Paris. In 1924, the Aznavourians had a second child. They named him Charles.

Just after World War I, the pontoon of a ship docked at the port of Marseille was probably as good a place as any from which to observe the human cost of political upheaval in the East. The refugees' papers, with their multiple nationalities, offered a last glimpse of the "Russian," "Armenian," and "Ottoman" microcosms to which their owners still belonged, even as they prepared to part company with their native lands. For some of those who arrived aboard the *Sphinx*, the *Lamartine*, or the *Madonna*, Marseille was just a stage on a much longer journey of migration. Some had chosen to head for Paris or try their luck in America; others encountered unexpected circumstances that redirected their journeys. All were connected by history to a patchwork of eastern territories, whether Ottoman or Imperial Russian, from which they had been expelled after the advent of Lenin's USSR and the authoritarian rule of Mustafa Kemal Atatürk in Turkey. Neither regime offered the least hope of return to people who — for a mix of political, ethnic, and religious reasons — had been stripped of the simplest rights conferred by nationality.

The Aznavourians, who arrived in Marseille in October 1923, had been rejected by both regimes.

Knar had grown up beside the Sea of Marmara, in the Ottoman city of İzmit, facing Istanbul on its western side and the high Anatolian plateau on its east. Her husband Mamigon — nicknamed Misha, in the Russian style — came from a small town in today's Georgia, formerly located on the Caucasian edge of the czarist empire. The couple first met during the war, when a lull in hostilities allowed Misha, a young singer in a light opera troupe, to leave the Russian Caucasus to perform in Istanbul. At the time, Knar was completing her studies in the same city. Misha himself had no idea that the Bolshevik revolution would turn his musical tour abroad into a lifelong exile, any more than Knar had the slightest suspicion that her entire family back in İzmit had perished following the deportations that marked the onset of the Armenian genocide in 1915.

At the end of the war, the Ottoman capital seethed with

hundreds of thousands of refugees. Placed under interallied control, the Bosporus was a strategic haven for those fleeing the violent, lawless militias that had filled the vacuum left by the old Russian and Ottoman orders. Among the desperate civilians seeking sanctuary were many thousands of Armenians from the eastern provinces of Turkey, who had managed to escape the genocide and survive the further deportations that followed it, only to meet with renewed harassment from Atatürk's nationalist forces after 1919. At the same time, between the spring of 1919 and the winter of 1920–1921, up to 230,000 Russian subjects poured across the Bosporus following the defeat of the czarist White Army. French and British naval vessels joined a gigantic rescue operation hastily mounted by the Imperial Russian fleet.

The refugees found themselves in limbo, forced to wait and contend with the collapse of legal norms. At the same time, they had high hopes for the ongoing peace negotiations. "The Bolsheviks will end up leaving at some point." The Russian émigrés consoled one another with this formula, convinced that the defeat of Lenin was a certainty. As for the Armenians, they contrived to make their voices heard at the Versailles Peace Conference that gave shape to the postwar European order. The Treaty of Sèvres (signed by the Central powers on August 10, 1920) included an assurance that the Turkish nationalist leaders responsible for the Armenian genocide would be judged by an international penal court, in place of the Ottoman military tribunals whose procedures had become toothless with the accelerated withdrawal of the occupying British Army in 1919. The Sèvres treaty also promised that an independent Armenian state would be established on the eastern side of Asia Minor, separated from Turkey and united with Caucasian Armenia.

So the refugees of the Bosporus spent the immediate postwar years vainly awaiting some political resolution. But the comings and goings of Knar and Misha around the western edge of the Ottoman Empire show that waiting did not necessarily mean idleness. Still, their movements were circumscribed, for it was essential to the Aznavourians — who were now part of the larger circle of an opera company — to remain in contact with local Armenian networks. Such networks existed in Constantinople and Smyrna; they were also solidly established in the Balkans, where the opera company regularly toured. In January 1923, the company was performing in Salonika when the couple's first child, Aïda, was born. By then the tide had turned. Atatürk's forces had made decisive advances during the preceding autumn, driving the Greek Army out of Smyrna in September and triumphing in Istanbul in October. The 35,000 Russians still present in the capital were given until January 1923 to find a country that would take them in; this was the decision of Mustafa Kemal himself, who basically wished to see all Christian minorities deported from Turkey.

From Salonika, Misha made his way back to Istanbul to fetch Knar's grandmother. This journey began a geographical turning point for the family. Like 65,000 other Armenians, and as many Russians, the Aznavourians now prepared to travel to France, whose consulates were impartially stamping entry visas on international passports, travel papers, laissez-passers, safe conducts, and other identity papers. In their diversity, these documents demonstrate the local arrangements that officials cobbled together to cope with the dislocations of two collapsed empires and their administrations. In the territories ruled by mandate — where the number of Armenian refugees now exceeded 100,000 — the agents of the French high commissioner of the Levant took it upon themselves to issue the necessary legal documents to emigrants who wanted to leave. At a time when the United States was beginning to close its frontiers to immigration, France linked the opening of its own to its national interests. The Great War had annihilated 10 percent of the active male population. It was hoped that a huge injection of foreign labor would make up for this loss of manpower, especially in heavy industry, a sector that French nationals were forsaking in favor of more qualified jobs.

Smelling a windfall, French industrialists began to scour for workers in regions with large reserves of manual labor, principally in Eastern Europe and the Middle

East. Beginning in 1924, the French state entrusted the employment of foreigners to an employers' organization that quickly became the sole interlocutor as regarded immigrants and labor. This was the Société Générale d'Immigration, assisted in its task by the Bureau International du Travail (International Employment Office). Their partnership brought hundreds of thousands of workers to France in the 1920s. Russians and Armenians, whose exile was often structured as work migration, took part in this process.

The *Sphinx*, the *Lamartine*, and the *Madonna* — but also the *Euphrates*, the *Maréchal Bugeaud*, the *Bulgaria*, the *Tourville*, the *Albano*, and the *Catharina*....The agents of the Marseille special police services noted the names of the ships that arrived one after another in the fall of 1923. Among them: the *Andros*, which had sailed from Piraeus and carried, among other passengers, three Aznavourians and Knar's grandmother. The women had followed Misha, the head of the family — a former subject of the czar — into the category of "Russian refugees" on the ship's manifest of passengers. That list is kept today in the departmental archives of the Bouches-du-Rhône, in southern France. Mamigon is registered with a forename — Mamimokou — as randomly spelled as his surname ("Arnavourian" here, it was altered to "Aznavourian" later, before Mamigon's son Charles finally settled on "Aznavour" when he made his stage debut).

At the time when the "Arnavourians" were authorized to enter France, international law had not yet defined the legal status of "stateless refugees." Several intergovernmental agreements had to be signed before the completion, in October 1933, of the first Geneva Convention. For the time being, in 1923, French legislators dealt with the situation as best they could. The designation "Russian refugee" entitled its bearers to a specific travel document, known as a Nansen passport. Mamigon got his from the Greek interior ministry, which guaranteed his identity and made it possible for him to embark for France.

The Nansen passport is still remembered today because it made its holders intimately aware of their banishment. This certificate, a piece of administrative tinkering hammered out by the League of Nations, also helped stabilize the postwar world by attributing the legal "Nansen" status to those who had been collectively victimized and deprived of their nationality by concerted state policies. Over a million Russian subjects were directly affected at the start, followed by hundreds of thousands of (formerly Ottoman) Armenians.

On the quays of Marseille, the French health authorities and the railway and port police were concerned by these waves of refugees. The officials who kept track of the disembarking nationalities — Russian, Armenian, and Ottoman — wrote alarmist reports that made their way up the bureaucratic chain. Brandishing the figures of the day, the week, or the month, the local prefect wrote his minister about the insufferable "congestion" of the port of Marseille.

In their concern to control the immigrants ever more tightly, the authorities began to ask each one to state a final destination. Their answers revealed lines of travel across the French territory — up the Rhône Valley to the major industrial cities of the north and then sometimes fanning out across the world. The Aznavourians opted for Paris, the preferred destination of many new arrivals. They hoped to join Misha's father in the Latin Quarter, where he had started a small business on the Rue Champollion. His restaurant, Le Caucase, attracted a clientele of Russians, Georgians, Armenians, and penniless students.

In 1924, the birth of a second child — a boy christened Charles, *à la française* — scotched the family's nascent plan to head for the United States. With that, Knar and Misha found an establishment on the Rue de la Huchette and opened a Caucase of their own. Dividing their time between kitchen work and theater, the young Aznavourians grew up in Paris. They entered talent shows and began to win cash prizes — a hundred-franc note here, fifty francs there. This helped to settle the family debts, relieve their parents, and launch their careers.

Anouche Kunth

1923

REFERENCES

Aznavour-Garaventz, Aïda. *Petit frère*. Paris: Robert Laffont, 1986.

Gatrell, Peter. *The Making of the Modern Refugee*. Oxford: Oxford University Press, 2013.

Gerwarth, Robert. *The Vanquished: Why the First World War Failed to End, 1917–1923*. London: Allen Lane, 2016.

Gousseff, Catherine. *L'exil russe: La fabrique du réfugié apatride (1920–1939)*. Paris: CNRS éditions, 2008.

King, Charles. *Midnight at the Pera Palace: The Birth of Modern Istanbul*. New York: Norton, 2015.

Kunth, Anouche. *Exils arméniens: Du Caucase à Paris (1920–1945)*. Paris: Belin, 2016.

RELATED ARTICLES

12,000 BCE, 1927, 1931, 1953, 1974, 1998

1927

Naturalizing

When a law was passed on August 10, 1927, to facilitate
access to French nationality, the effect was immediate: the
number of naturalized citizens doubled the following year.
The law, which both announced pro-immigration policies
and helped usher them in, was expected to fuel postwar
reconstruction, compensate for labor shortages, and allay
fears of population decline.

Born in Kalusz, then part of Poland, in 1893, David
Bienenfeld arrived in France in August 1922. Four and a half
years later, in December 1927, he tried his luck and applied
for naturalization at the police commissioner's office nearest
his Parisian residence. "Settled permanently in France,
which is much to his liking and where he sees a future
for himself and his family, he wishes to become French,
as did his two uncles before him, and hopes to obtain the
same status for his wife and children," he explained in this
application. Bienenfeld was granted French nationality by
decree in February 1928, according to the provisions of the

newly adopted August 1927 law pertaining to nationality.

At that time, immigration was not only encouraged, but considered in various circles useful and necessary. An outlier on the European continent, France had emerged as one of the world's magnets for immigrants. The geopolitical upheaval resulting from World War I accelerated the rate of population transfers and refugee movement, involving Armenians, Assyrian-Chaldeans, Russians, Bulgarians, Greeks, and Turks, among others. After the US drastically reduced its influx of immigrants through quotas in 1921 and 1924, France became their prime destination. For the first time since 1891, the 1926 census included an entire volume devoted to foreigners. The nonnative population increased by nearly one million in only five years: between 1921 and 1926, it surged from 1,532,000 to 2,409,000. In total, foreigners accounted for 6 percent of the French population, a proportion that would not be equaled again until 1975.

These population shifts were not entirely random: the French state provided the impetus during World War I, with its massive call for foreign labor, particularly from the colonies, to fill the factory jobs left vacant following the mobilization of workers. In the 1920s, management and public officials made common cause to set up a policy of large-scale recruitment of foreign workers who would make up for labor shortfalls. Workers recruited by the Société Générale d'Immigration, which since 1924 comprised all the main employer organizations, were channeled toward jobs in heavy industry, such as mining, metalworking, and steel. It was undoubtedly during this period that "foreigner" came to be equated with "immigrant worker."

Still, the hiring of cheap, acquiescent labor was not the only issue. In the 1920s, priority was also placed on repopulating the country through active immigration, the solution advocated by a flourishing movement supporting population growth in the battle against demographic decline. Since the end of the nineteenth century, powerful natalist organizations, such as the National Alliance for the Growth of the French Population, embraced an issue they presented as inherently patriotic. France's military readiness was at stake: military service, reserved for French nationals since 1872, became compulsory in 1905. That foreign residents should be exempted from this duty was deemed unacceptable at a time when diplomatic tensions were on the rise throughout Europe. France's million and a half dead from the Great War heightened demographic fears. There was a "distressing crisis of the French birth rate," explained the Radical deputy André Mallarmé, rapporteur of the 1927 law on nationality, to the Chamber of Deputies. Couldn't naturalization provide the answer? Couldn't an immigration flux produce new French citizens?

This is how the August 10, 1927, law was presented and defended before parliament by the pro-population lobby: it was their "lifeline," a "truly effective remedy to the illness afflicting the country, this disease that, like a cancer, is consuming it, but which we too often choose to ignore: I am talking about depopulation." The law was designed to make it easier for immigrant workers to gain French nationality, so that this "reservoir of men" might serve to "bolster our failing national resources." The law showed an unprecedented degree of leniency that has not been matched since. In order to apply for naturalization, migrants had to have lived in the country for a mere three years instead of the standard ten years required by an 1889 law. The paperwork was streamlined, and children born in France were automatically made citizens upon reaching the age of consent, provided they had not renounced French nationality in the interim.

French women who married foreigners would keep their nationality, breaking with the standing rule that required French women to relinquish their nationality and adopt their spouse's. The law also allowed women who married foreigners prior to its enactment to recover their original nationality upon simple written request. Though some accused the law of being feminist, let there be no mistake: women remained confined to their reproductive role, or more precisely, to their role as producers of young French nationals. Radical deputy Charles Lambert went so far as to argue that the law was a sign of "progress for feminism, not in the way the most ardent feminists understand that term, for although French women have not been given the vote, we are securing them the means to exercise their social influence for the good of the country and the future of the race. We ensure that their children remain French, that France can claim them as her own."

The 1927 law broke new ground. Until then, naturalization was assumed to be the final step toward assimilation, the watchword where interwar immigration issues were concerned. In practice, French officials had endeavored to check each applicant's preexisting degree of assimilation, using variable criteria, sometimes socioeconomic and sometimes ethnic, leaning toward racial categories. The reduction of the residency requirement to a mere three years modified all of this: naturalization was no longer the end point of assimilation, but rather its trigger. Individuals born in France to a foreign parent could automatically acquire French nationality provided they made the request before the age of twenty-one. Such citizens would be "French by declaration." Charles Lambert justified the measure: "Twenty-five thousand children are attending elementary schools in Paris. Their teachers will tell you that they have assimilated remarkably well, and that many are at the head of their class." In the future, "they will make excellent Frenchmen."

The 1927 law thus moved out of the era of diagnostics

and into that of prognostics, as explained by the Justice Ministry board responsible for its implementation. With France's economic and demographic future at stake, it was a wager worth making.

This wager was offset by a provision allowing for the possibility of stripping new citizens of their nationality. It targeted those who committed "acts jeopardizing the internal or external security of the French State," engaged in actions deemed "incompatible with French citizenship or contrary to French interests," or evaded military service. All of this was applicable for a ten-year period, and it included wives and children as well. This principle of forfeiture was hotly debated. For Justice Minister Louis Barthou, naturalization was "a favor that the government could grant or withhold." Some members of the left spoke out against the idea of "taking away with one hand what you so generously granted with the other." In the end, the amendment advocating the suppression of forfeiture was voted down overwhelmingly, and the law was enacted.

The effects were felt overnight. The annual number of naturalizations doubled the following year, and some six hundred and fifty thousand people were made French by decree between 1927 and 1940, in addition to the two hundred and fifty thousand children who became French by declaration and the nearly one hundred thousand who recovered their status as French nationals. In all, the 1927 law is credited with creating nearly one million new French citizens.

French, yes, though not entirely. Certain provisions of the text curtailed the rights of naturalized citizens, making them ineligible for a ten-year period. This was the flipside of the "prognostics" era, where naturalized citizens were placed in a sort of limbo between French and foreign, a temporary stage of Frenchness. In the xenophobic climate of the 1930s, virulent press campaigns targeted scapegoats for the ongoing economic crisis. A string of measures was gradually adopted to prevent anyone whose naturalization was less than ten years old from working in the civil service, the judiciary, or the medical professions. Naturalized Frenchmen were becoming second-class citizens. In 1938, the government of Édouard Daladier made new citizens ineligible to vote for the first five years after naturalization. The scope of forfeiture was broadened: any naturalized citizen sentenced to a year or more in prison might lose his or her French nationality.

Then came Vichy, which challenged the law head-on. On July 22, 1940, a few days after coming to power, Marshal Pétain began reviewing all the naturalizations that had been enacted since August 10, 1927. It was, in other words, a retroactive disavowal of twelve years' worth of citizenship acquisition. The Vichy state was settling its scores with the Republic by dismembering the 1927 law. In practice, this amounted to ejecting those it deemed "unworthy" of being French from the national community. A special Commission for the Revision of Naturalizations was set up for this purpose, with the Herculean task of reopening hundreds of thousands of files in order to rule on the merits of each.

Thus it was that in the spring of 1941, "Mr. David Bienenfeld and his family were taken aback by the awful news [that] their French nationality...had been revoked, by virtue of the July 22, 1940, law, leaving them greatly distressed." The cover page of Bienenfeld's file bore this handwritten note in the margin: "Jewish, no national interest." The Bienenfelds recovered their French nationality at the war's end, as did most of the fifteen thousand other individuals denaturalized by the Vichy regime, with the exception of those who died or disappeared. In 1945, the Nationality Code replaced the 1927 law: five years were now required before one could apply for French citizenship. To rebuild the country after the war, France was once again in need of labor, of children and nationals. It was the newly minted Ministry of Population that was henceforward responsible for matters of naturalization.

Claire Zalc

REFERENCES

Depoid, Pierre. "Les naturalisations en France (1870–1940)." *Études démographiques* 3. Paris: Imprimerie nationale, 1942.

Journal officiel de la République française. Débats parlementaires, Chambre des députés. (March 31 and April 7, 1927): 1100–10 and 1212–21.

Paxton, Robert. *Vichy France: Old Guard and New Order, 1940–1944.* New York: Columbia University Press, 2001 [1972].

Sayad, Abdelmalek. "Naturalization." In *The Suffering of the Immigrant*, edited by Abdelmalek Sayad. Translated by David Macey. Cambridge, UK: Polity, 2004.

Weil, Patrick. *How to Be French: Nationality in the Making since 1789.* Translated by Catherine Porter. Durham, NC: Duke University Press, 2008.

Zalc, Claire. *Dénaturalisés. Les retraits de nationalité sous Vichy.* Paris: Le Seuil, 2016.

RELATED ARTICLES

212, 1942, 1974, 1998

1931

Empire at the Gates of Paris

From May 6 to November 15, 1931, a miniature version of
the colonial world was on display at the Bois de Vincennes.
A propaganda stunt for some, the Paris Colonial
Exposition was also a world's fair, a celebration, and a
scientific event. But was it indicative of a French "imperial
state of mind"?

"Paris, a window on the world," boasted one of the many
posters for the Colonial Exposition organized at the Bois
de Vincennes in 1931. But to which world exactly did it
refer? The scale-model colonial world constructed on some
270 acres around Lake Daumesnil may have revealed more
about mainland France than it did about its empire. France
was having its moment, according to some, on the strength
of its many overseas possessions and its recent celebration,
in 1930, of the centenary of the Algerian conquest. Others,
however, saw a country in crisis, its tenuous identity
bolstered by exhibiting the colonial Other.

Repeatedly postponed and redesigned, the event was a

long while in process. It belongs to the protracted history of representations of colonial places and peoples, who occupied an ever-increasing share of universal and international expositions since 1855. The creation in 1906 of a National Committee on Colonial Expositions demonstrated how political these perennial events had become. But it was the "colonial party," a group of French politicians who embraced the country's imperial presence, who in 1910 came up with a dual idea: an exhibit-as-inventory coupled with the foundation of a permanent Museum of the Colonies.

In the wake of World War I, the Marseille Chamber of Commerce and the Municipal Council of Paris both vied for this project. A national colonial exposition was slated for Marseille in 1922, while a larger-scale international show featuring France and its allies was set to take place in Paris in 1925. The Marseille exhibit was approved, and the Paris one enacted by law on March 7, 1920. The interallied dimension would be scaled back once Britain declined to participate (although this did not prevent Palestine, the South African Union, and Canada from taking part). The 1924 British Empire Exhibition held at Wembley seemed sufficient to celebrate its imperial grandeur. In the end, only Belgium, Denmark, Italy, Holland, and Portugal were in attendance, along with the United States and Brazil.

Longtime colonial administrator Gabriel Angoulvant was put in charge of the 1931 Exposition, but Marshal Hubert

Lyautey, the empire-builder, took over in 1927 and raised the stakes by an order of magnitude. A massive urban planning scheme was launched in Vincennes, the working-class suburb of Paris chosen for this staging of "Greater France." Work began on November 5, 1928, with the extension of a Metro line to improve accessibility. Lyautey also wanted to make his political mark, and so the long history of France's colonial past would be given pride of place, with a tribute to missionary work and close attention to the economic aspects of the colonial enterprise. Lyautey devoted a set of pavilions to facts and figures about the French empire — useful information for financiers, manufacturers, and merchants. He also turned the Exposition into a teaching instrument. By displaying the empire's scope, diversity, and wealth, it would become "a justification and a response," so that "at last, the French people will feel the stirrings of a legitimate sense of pride and faith." Paul Reynaud, the Minister of the Colonies, made it clear in his inaugural speech that the whole point was to make the French people "aware of their empire," to win over hearts and minds, to persuade and educate: "Each and every one must feel that they are citizens of the Greater France, in the four corners of the globe."

To instill an imperial consciousness in French minds, and in doing so accentuate the radiance of France, the Exposition was broken into four sections: Metropolitan France, overseas France, international pavilions, and the Museum of the Colonies. It hosted twelve thousand exhibitors, and a whole array of buildings was constructed to provide "a trip around the world in a single day." Visitors could marvel at a reproduction of the Angkor Wat temple, discover a "French West African palace" modeled on the Great Mosque of Djenné, and peer into so-called "native" villages. But there were also novelties, such as a replica of George Washington's house in Mount Vernon, patriotic monuments like the one devoted to the overseas armed forces, and pavilions set aside for Catholic and Protestant missions. "Natives" were mobilized in great numbers to act out a fictitious daily life by pretending to busy themselves in the streets and alleyways of an ersatz Tunisian souk, crafting artisanal objects, marching in processions and parades, or performing dance numbers and musical or theatrical shows.

Vincennes also became a gigantic amusement park. Nighttime spectacles called "colonial nights" and light shows making use of water features added to the enchantment. Visitors could ride a camel or row a native canoe out on the lake or board the Scenic Railway roller coaster. The zoo alone received over two million visitors. But Vincennes was more than a massive fairground. Serious scientific gatherings also took place. An exhibit on prehistory and colonial ethnography opened at the Museum of the Colonies, while Alfred Martineau, professor at the Collège de France and founder of the *Revue de l'histoire des colonies françaises*, chaired the first Congress of Colonial History. The Institute of Phonetics and the Museum of the Spoken Word of the University of Paris produced, with the backing of the Pathé filmmaking company, 368 sound recordings of "music and speech from the colonies." Vincennes was a place where ideological, aesthetic, pedagogical, and scientific ambitions could freely mix. It was a crossroads where different readings of the world and history conveyed the complexity of what it meant to be on one or the other side of the colonial equation.

The Exposition enabled France to celebrate the progress that its "civilizing mission" rendered possible beyond its borders. The speeches made at the Exposition highlighted this steadfast colonial effort, emphasizing its energy and action, associating colonialism with virility and national grandeur. Organized at the same time, the General Feminism Conference offered a platform to women colonizers, but was a mere sideshow that drew little attention. At the behest of Lyautey and the exhibition's Deputy Commissioner Marcel Olivier, the staging of colonized societies made room for racial and civilizational diversity and showcased the distinctive "personalities" of each culture. The Exposition was thus not merely a "human zoo," but also an "encyclopedia of the colonial world," a world fair (an "imperialist" fair, according to the communist daily *L'Humanité*, on June 7, 1931), a celebration, a teaching opportunity, a work of propaganda, and a tourist hub. At the same time, by reasserting the foundational distinction between "Us" and "Them," by establishing and then staging a natural hierarchy among civilizations, the Exposition also fueled racism and nationalism, both of which found a breeding ground in a country in deep crisis in the early 1930s.

France still suffered the devastating demographic consequences of World War I and the economic ones of the Great Depression. It also faced resistance in the very colonies displayed in the Exposition. A few years earlier, the army had clashed with the rebellious Druzes in Syria, waged battle in the Rif region of Morocco, and put down an uprising of the Kongo-Wara populations in French Equatorial Africa. In Indochina, a mutiny among Vietnamese soldiers in February 1930 was followed by violently repressed demonstrations on May 1, 1931, just days before the Exposition's inauguration.

In the rest of Europe as in France, opposition voices were merging into a multipronged anticolonial campaign. On May 24, 1930, a plot to destroy the Angkor temple was reported to French government authorities. On January 23, 1931, the Anti-Imperialist League launched a "universal appeal" from Berlin, calling for mobilization against the Exposition. Pamphlets proclaimed "Do Not Visit the Colonial Exposition." International Red Aid printed and distributed one hundred thousand copies of *Véritable guide de l'Exposition coloniale* (The Real Guide to the Colonial Exposition) in late June. A counter-exposition, "The Truth about the Colonies," was organized by the Anti-Imperialist League, the French Communist Party, and the CGTU, the major trade union confederation. It opened on September 20 and would total around four thousand visitors. This was clearly a poor showing, but the action committees against the Exposition that originated in Marseille, Bordeaux, and Toulouse brought together several dozen militant Vietnamese and French communists. While the French Section of Workers' International and the Human Rights League never took a stand on the Exposition itself, they did denounce colonial abuses and violence.

Though they remained isolated, these radical and reformist expressions of opposition put a kink in the notion of a French republican consensus. As for the general public, it is difficult to get an overall sense of its reaction. Did the fact that over thirty-three million tickets were sold, that around eight million visitors — half of them Parisian, with three million from the provinces and another million from other countries — attended this event justify the claim that the Exposition gave rise to an "imperial state of mind"? Did the twenty thousand schoolchildren who saw the world in a day in the summer of 1931 become fervent partisans of colonization?

The director of the École Nationale de la France d'Outre-Mer, or École Coloniale, a training ground for future colonial administrators, was not so sure: "Have we got into the habit of thinking imperially? Most assuredly not." The rare opinion polls taken at the time suggest that the Exposition had limited success persuading people to embrace the imperial idea. This may help explain why the great Vincennes extravaganza spawned few follow-up events. Some material vestiges alone remain: the National Center for the History of Immigration located within the walls of the former Museum of the Colonies, the newly renovated zoo, the former Togo and Cameroon pavilions repurposed as the International Buddhist Institute — as well as the long-term impact on the way the French might imagine themselves and others.

Pascale Barthélémy

REFERENCES

Ageron, Charles Robert. "L'Exposition coloniale de 1931: Mythe républicain ou mythe impérial?" In *Les Lieux de mémoire*, t. 1: *La République*, edited by Pierre Nora, 561–91. Paris: Gallimard, 1984.

Blanckaert, Claude. "Spectacles ethniques et culture de masse au temps des colonies." *Revue d'histoire des sciences humaines* 2, no. 7 (September 2002): 223–32.

Hodeir, Catherine, and Michel Pierre. *L'Exposition coloniale: 1931.* Brussels: Complexe, 1991.

L'Estoile, Benoît de. *Le Goût des autres: De l'Exposition coloniale aux arts premiers.* Paris: Flammarion, 2007.

Zalc, Claire, et al. *1931. Les Étrangers au temps de l'Exposition coloniale.* Paris: Gallimard, 2008.

RELATED ARTICLES

1763, 1769, 1863, 1883, 1900, 1960

1936

A French New Deal

On May 3, 1936, against a backdrop of mounting fascism
and xenophobia across Europe, a far-left coalition party —
the Popular Front — won France's legislative elections.
The newly elected leader, Léon Blum, unveiled an
ambitious program of reforms. Not unique to France, this
historical moment reveals the difficulty of reconciling
patriotism with internationalism.

"I am French," insisted a defensive Léon Blum on the front
page of *Le Populaire* on November 19, 1938. "For as far back
as you can trace a family as humble as my own, you will see
that my heritage is purely French." This was not the first
time the politician was called upon to clarify his heritage in
the face of rumors and libel. For many of Blum's critics, the
Popular Front's politics were anything but French. As they
saw it, this coalition was headed by a Jew, followed orders
out of Moscow, and promoted foreign economic policies.
Detractors saw a foreign plot even if the Popular Front
had won the 1936 elections by historic margins that spring.

Postelection enthusiasm extended into the summer, reaching as far as Algeria, where left-wing activists and members of the Algerian Muslim Congress drafted plans for colonial reform. The social movement animating that spring and summer was unprecedented.

In France, these elections and the subsequent government have gone down in history as a symbol of the nation's internal strife leading up to the disastrous events of 1940. However, the Popular Front was not limited to France. Other countries had their own *Frente Popular*: Republican Spain with the successful election of a coalition led by Manuel Azaña in February 1936, Chile with the election of Pedro Aguirre Cerda in 1938. Everywhere in Europe and the Americas, people and parties had to position themselves politically, geopolitically, and economically vis-à-vis the crisis of liberal capitalism and the rise of fascism. The Popular Front was not really, as some narratives still describe it, an "improvement" or "escape" — a halcyon moment suspended in time — that later clashed with the realities of the world. From its beginnings in 1934–1935, the coalition was an assembly of socialists, communists, and radicals, as well as union groups and clubs, whose internationally minded aim was to improve the lives of the working classes and protect liberties. 1936 was therefore a test of the left's ability to reconcile patriotism with internationalism, internal purchasing power with openness to the world economy, and social reforms with military redress. It was up to Léon Blum, thirty years after Jean Jaurès laid the groundwork for this movement, to orchestrate this fragile balance.

It is impossible to grasp the rise of the French Popular Front outside the global struggle between fascism, communism, and democracy that began to emerge in 1933. Hitler's arrival to power quickly led to the arrest of communists and the exile of major figures of German socialism. In early February 1934, a workers' revolt erupted as a last effort by the Austrian left to counter Chancellor Engelbert Dollfuss's authoritarian rise to power. In Paris, the anti-parliamentarian riots of February 6, 1934, foretold the Third Republic's possibly fatal weakness. Warning signs abounded: fascist and authoritarian regimes from Europe to Japan rose to power at a dizzying pace, while democracy seemed to hang only by a thread.

In France, political and financial scandals played out against a backdrop of economic stagnation. But even so, the country became the epicenter of potential resistance. In a show of force, the left organized a general strike on February 12, 1934, proving that not all hope was lost. Activist groups attempted to unify the left and move beyond the gaping rift opened up in 1920, when some left-wing factions broke away to create what would become the French Communist Party. Within civil society, groups like the World Committee Against War and Fascism (1932–1933), the Watchfulness

Committee of Antifascist Intellectuals (1934), the Human Rights League, and the International League Against Racism and Anti-Semitism (LICRA) worked to raise awareness and organize.

A political trigger was pulled in Moscow. Concerned over the USSR's growing isolation from Europe, Stalin and Georgi Dimitrov, the new leader of the Communist International, reversed their strategy in 1934. Instead of opposing "socialist traitors," the communists would henceforth forge alliances in a common struggle against fascism. Formalized at the Communist International's seventh congress in the summer of 1935, this new policy would be enacted by emissaries (in France, that person was Eugen Fried, better known as "Comrade Clément"). Slightly disoriented, French Communist leader Maurice Thorez took it upon himself to spread this message of a united front. Together with Blum and centrist Édouard Daladier, he sealed an alliance of left-wing movements known as the Rassemblement Populaire. This harmonization of former enemy groups stood out in Europe. In Belgium, socialists Henri de Man and Paul-Henri Spaak participated in the 1935 government coalition headed by Catholic statesman Paul van Zeeland, but without communist support. In many countries, the sharp divide between social democrats and communists proved unsurmountable.

Paris therefore acted as a capital for political exiles and

Jewish refugees fleeing authoritarian regimes and the first waves of persecution. In a national context of growing insularism and an intransigent backlash to the newcomers from the legal and medical professions, the French right unflinchingly characterized migration as an "invasion." But although the Popular Front's policies toward immigration were conservative (a provisional arrangement was signed in July 1936 for a temporary improvement to protections for refugees from Germany), the party's vast network of activists, volunteer organizations, and unions ensured that migrants received aid. The outbreak of the Spanish Civil War, in July 1936, created a flood of thousands more refugees. The General Confederation of Labor (CGT) and other organizations formed aid groups to take in the fifteen thousand children of Spanish republicans evacuated into France. That was several years before the 1939 "Retirada" unleashed an international crisis, as hundreds of thousands of refugees poured out of Spain, many into camps in the south of France. Unfortunately, French soil was not a safe haven for everyone. Fascist hate hounded refugees in exile. In June 1936, brothers Carlo and Nello Rosselli, activists in the Italian Giustizia e Libertà movement and proponents of liberal socialism, were assassinated in Bagnoles-de-l'Orne by a commando force made up of members of a fascist-leaning organization, probably under orders from Fascist Italy. Borders vanished in what was now a European civil war.

These international tensions did not prevent Léon
Blum's government from establishing an ambitious program
of economic and social reform in the spring and summer
of 1936. Blum's detractors would later suggest that such
policies weakened the nation's economy and power, as if
France's defeat in 1940 stemmed directly from forty-hour
work weeks, paid vacations, and union agreements. This
short-term view, which historian Marc Bloch discredited
in his classic account of France's military debacle, *Strange
Defeat* (1940), missed the essential point: the Popular Front
was one attempt among many to respond to the global crisis
created in 1929 by liberal capitalism. By the mid-1930s, few
people were prepared to defend liberal orthodoxy (forced
deflation, budget cuts, free circulation of capital). Between
the failure of free-market exchange (historians speak of
a period of "deglobalization" to describe the 1930s) and
the expanding appeal of authoritarian approaches to the
economy (Soviet engineering, Nazi interventionism, and
Italian totalitarianism), a narrow middle-ground reconciling
capitalism and democracy was badly needed.

This "great transformation" (as Karl Polanyi called it),
which would give birth to mixed economies after the war,
was in a phase of experimentation at the time. Blum and his
close advisers had closely followed Franklin D. Roosevelt's
arrival to power in the United States in 1933. American
Democrats, who were neither dangerous communists

nor shy socialists, supported federal intervention in bank regulations and Social Security (1935). In Sweden, the social democracy compromise that would become a model for the world was making great strides. And in France and Belgium, a massive general strike ended in June 1936 with the adoption of the forty-hour work week and wage increases.

Were these the first steps of a "Keynesian revolution"? It was too early to tell. The great Cambridge-trained economist published his *General Theory of Employment, Interest, and Money* in early 1936, and few world leaders (with the exception, in France, of Georges Boris, who helped chart Blum's economic program in March–April 1938) understood the book's full significance. After the currency devaluation of September 1936, Blum and Finance Minister Vincent Auriol were again accused of selling out national sovereignty. In reality, after the pound and dollar abandoned the gold standard in 1931 and 1933, nobody believed in the intrinsic stability of currency. The Popular Front was at the forefront of policymaking as it experimented with what Anglo-Saxon historians view as a veritable French New Deal. The experiment led to radical transformations in the relationships between government, markets, and civil society. These policies would be furthered during the war by the National Council of the French Resistance, and through measures adopted after liberation.

Despite these developments, never had government

officials been the subject of such scorn and slander. Tragically, the Popular Front's minister of the interior, Roger Salengro, committed suicide after being falsely accused of deserting during World War I. Anti-patriotism was not located where one expected, however. In February 1937, Blum suspended reform projects, largely because he refused to sacrifice rearmament spending and implement unilateral capital controls. Meanwhile, French capital was flowing across the Swiss border. Jean Jaurès's famous phrase ("Some internationalism casts us away from the nation; much internationalism brings us back into the fold") never rang so true as during these years of great uncertainty.

Nicolas Delalande

REFERENCES

Horn, Gerd-Rainer. *European Socialists Respond to Fascism: Ideology, Activism, and Contingency in the 1930s*. Oxford: Oxford University Press, 1996.

Jackson, Julian. *The Popular Front in France: Defending Democracy, 1934–38*. Cambridge: Cambridge University Press, 1988.

Keren, Célia. *L'Évacuation et l'accueil des enfants espagnols en France: Cartographie d'une mobilisation transnationale (1936–1940)*. PhD diss., École des hautes études en sciences sociales, 2014.

Marynower, Claire. "Le moment Front populaire en Oranie:

Mobilisations et reconfigurations du milieu militant de gauche."
Le Mouvement social 236 (2011): 9–22.

Monier, Frédéric. "Léon Blum: les socialistes français et les réfugiés dans les années 1930." July 2016. Fondation Jean Jaurès.

Nord, Philip. *France's New Deal: From the Thirties to the Postwar Era*. Princeton: Princeton University Press, 2011.

Patel, Klaus Kiran. *The New Deal: A Global History*. Princeton: Princeton University Press, 2016.

RELATED ARTICLES

1789, 1848, 1894, 1953, 1989

1940

Free France Emerges in Equatorial Africa

On August 28, 1940, Brazzaville became the capital of
Free France. French Equatorial Africa lent territorial
reality to a nascent state with no political legitimacy or
international recognition. Still, Free France in Africa was
not tantamount to independence for the Africans.

In the wake of the military debacle of May–June 1940, the
incipient Free France amounted to an expatriate movement
of dubious legitimacy, led by a still relatively obscure
general, Charles de Gaulle. Some contemporaries harked
back to the perils and pitfalls of emigration, referring to the
waves of victims and opponents who had over the centuries
fled France for Great Britain, from the Huguenots to the
counterrevolutionaries and the critics of Napoleon III. By
the summer of 1940, Free France was deficient in several
areas besides its questionable international status. It could
muster few fighters, and even fewer bids of confidence from
the outside, apart from the personal support of Winston
Churchill. Most importantly, it had no territorial base, which

only worsened its persistent shortfalls in manpower and supplies. De Gaulle's radio appeals for support in June 1940 sought to address this. Few officials answered his heartfelt calls, however, and even fewer territories came forward. Off the record, the maverick general opened up to the scholar Denis Saurat in an almost Shakespearian monologue: "Give me some land...some land that is France. Anywhere. A French base, somewhere to start from."

It was overseas that the general rustled up such places. The Franco-British New Hebrides rallied to his movement on July 20. Other specks on the map, such as France's trading posts in India, soon joined the cause. But the most significant territories to rally around General de Gaulle throughout 1940 were indisputably French Equatorial Africa (FEA) and Cameroon.

Contrary to common belief, Free France was not primarily based in London, at least not in constitutional, military, or territorial terms. Rather, from late August 1940 to May 30, 1943, it spanned an array of colonial territories: mainly FEA (encompassing Chad, Ubangi-Shari, French Congo, and Gabon) and Cameroon, a country largely under French mandate. It was the gold from Gabon and Congo that contributed to financing the cause, just as it was soldiers from Chad, Cameroon, and Ubangi (today's Central African Republic) who made possible early military operations in Libya and the Horn of Africa. Lastly, it was the rubber from the FEA and Cameroon that boosted Free France's importance for the overall Allied cause from 1942 forward. In Africa, Free France raised armies, levied taxes, and extracted large quantities of raw materials. Above all, as of August 28, 1940, Brazzaville, the present-day capital of the Republic of Congo, became the capital of Free France, its diplomatic hub, its center of authority, and the basis of its legitimacy.

This altogether peculiar Free France colonial bloc, comprising central Africa and a part of the Pacific, soon took its place among the other Allied empires. Neither the Dutch nor the Belgian colonies followed the example set by the majority of French colonies, which remained "faithful" to Vichy. Instead, they rallied behind the United Kingdom's war effort as soon as their mother countries were defeated. Grasping the global context, de Gaulle and his commissioner for the colonies, René Pleven, put forward their portion of France's colonial empire as a sizable asset. In time, Free France's colonial empire would grow as Vichy lost its own; by 1944, only Indochina remained outside the Free French fold.

The term "rallying" does not adequately describe the way in which FEA and Cameroon took the Free French side in August 1940. Africans were not consulted on the issue at the time, nor was the European population living in those territories. In effect, the key decisions were made by a handful of leaders. In Chad, governor Félix Éboué, a Guianan man of color, opted to align with General de Gaulle and the British authorities of neighboring Nigeria. Besides his opposition to the discriminatory policies issued by Vichy, Éboué was responding to rumors of an Italian armistice commission that would be crossing into Chad from Libya. He was aware of his position on the front line against the Italian enemy. In the other territories, it was military officials mandated by de Gaulle — the white men Edgard de Larminat and Philippe Leclerc — who managed to tilt the colonies from the outside. Capitalizing on British connections and financing as well as on a Belgian foothold (Leopoldville), Larminat stole power away from the Vichy authorities in Brazzaville on August 28, 1940, the day after Cameroon tipped and two days after Chad came over.

How does one explain the success of these Gaullist offensives? The regions in question were undeniably vulnerable, since Vichy had made it a priority to defend Algiers and Dakar instead. Leclerc was thus able to capture Douala with a couple dozen men in a canoe crossing over from British mandate Cameroon. The Calabar paddlers were not convinced this clandestine operation would succeed; some witnesses report that they were threatened and beaten into submission. This does not mean, however, that Africans were not willing participants in operations elsewhere. African war veterans from FEA and African units stationed in Brazzaville played a crucial role in the August 1940 changeovers. Power relations were flipped in the process: in Brazzaville an African infantryman, won over by the Gaullist cause, trained his gun on Commander Sacquet, who had remained loyal to Vichy. Thereafter, on the day after the switchover, Leclerc solemnly proclaimed Cameroon "independent." By that, he meant independence from the Vichy regime rather than national sovereignty, but the phrase resonated nonetheless.

Still, Vichy did not admit defeat. An internecine war raged in Gabon until November 14, 1940. Soon, the only land border between Free France and Vichy France emerged between Chad and Niger. Despite what could be appropriately termed a pan-imperial civil war, the Free French authorities managed to construct a state, or rather, a Free French colonial federation. They also put forward the astonishing notion that legitimate France had been transferred in 1940 from the banks of the Seine to the shores of the Congo.

In constitutional terms, the entity termed Free French Africa was established by decree in Brazzaville, where the institutions of Free France were laid down. Éboué, Larminat, and military physician Adolphe Sicé endeavored to turn Brazzaville into a proper capital city. It was not long before there was a local radio station broadcasting the voice of Free France, an officer's training school, an official newspaper,

foreign legations and consulates, even command posts
and a military hospital. A new French currency replaced
the prevailing West African Bank franc. Yet this nascent
state was rife with internal squabbles: high commissioners
(Larminat, Sicé) and the governor (Éboué) engaged in a
ruthless power struggle. When it came to policy toward the
indigenous population, patterns of abuse were once again
widespread. The war effort was used to justify the harshest
practices in mines, for example.

Militarily, General de Gaulle's priority was attacking
Axis forces at the first opportunity. This choice arose from
several considerations: to prove that Free France was not
fighting against Vichy alone (as in Dakar and Gabon), to
persuade Vichy North and West Africa to rally to the cause,
and especially to demonstrate that France had never ceased
to engage the enemy, countering its defeatist image. More
than seventeen thousand soldiers were recruited from these
regions between 1940 and 1943, over and above the African
troops already in place in 1940. Some of the new recruits were
volunteers, others were enlisted in questionable conditions.
Recruiters often subcontracted, and distributed bonuses to
people who did not understand the documents they were
signing. Consequently, some recruits deserted within days of
enlisting.

Still, Free France was victorious thanks to these African
soldiers, the *tirailleurs*. In total, FEA and Cameroon

soldiers accounted for around a third of the first Free France combatants. Leclerc's column, which against huge odds captured the Italian fortress of Kufra, Libya, in 1941, comprised 295 Africans and 101 Europeans; likewise, the 1942–1943 campaign in the Fezzan rested on a force of 2,700 Africans and 550 Europeans. The cliché of the first Gaullist combatant as a Breton fishermen therefore needs updating: the archetypal 1940 Free French fighter was just as likely to be Chadian. Indeed, one of Free France's most distinctive features was its rich diversity, its cosmopolitan character. At the Battle of Bir Hakeim in 1942, for example, the Free French forces that held the line against Rommel included the Second March Battalion (BM2) out of Ubangi-Shari, a battalion from the Pacific (New Caledonia, Tahiti, etc.), as well as the Thirteenth Half-Brigade of the Foreign Legion, which was in part comprised of German Jews and Spanish republicans.

Rethinking France from an African perspective is hardly a recent historical trend: it was already General de Gaulle's absolute priority in 1940. During the most precarious phase of its fledgling existence, Free France relied on FEA and Cameroon. These territories provided fighters, resources, legitimacy, and a capital city, transforming Free France from a landless movement into an actual government.

Eric Jennings

REFERENCES

Crémieux-Brilhac, Jean-Louis. *La France libre*. Paris: Gallimard, 1996.

Jennings, Eric. *Free French Africa in World War II: The African Resistance*. Cambridge: Cambridge University Press, 2015.

Munholland, Kim. *Rock of Contention: Free French and Americans at War in New Caledonia, 1940–1945*. New York: Berghahn Books, 2005.

Muracciole, Jean-François. *Les Français libres: L'autre résistance*. Paris: Éditions Tallandier, 2009.

Saurat, Denis. *Watch over Africa*. London: J.M. Dent and Sons, 1941.

Weinstein, Brian. *Eboué*. Oxford: Oxford University Press, 1972.

RELATED ARTICLES
1446, 1914, 1917, 1931, 1960

1940

Lascaux: World Art and National Humiliation

The wondrous cave of Lascaux was uncovered by chance
in September 1940. Coming only weeks after the Fall
of France, its discovery was viewed by a demoralized
nation as something approaching a mystical portent. The
state of preservation of the Lascaux paintings was so
remarkable that the site quickly became a mass symbol of
the worldwide origins of human art. It also drew a flood of
visitors who damaged the frescoes beyond repair.

Montignac sur Vézère, in the Périgord, in the second week
of September 1940.

The collapse of the mighty French Army before Hitler's
Wehrmacht having delayed the reopening of the local
school, a group of teenagers used the time to explore the
surrounding woods. The oldest of them, Marcel Ravidat,
was eighteen; already out of school, this apprentice
mechanic had managed to avoid conscription during the
eight-month "phony war" of September 1939–April 1940.
He was something of a leader. In the woodlands flanking the

hill of Lascaux, which overlooked the valley and the small town, he had found the narrow entrance to a cave. This limestone area had been a spelunkers' paradise ever since the 1860s, and it naturally offered a rich promise of adventure. Marcel speculated that a secret passage there might lead to the manor house nearby, a property of the ancient ducal family of La Rochefoucauld.

What the teenagers stumbled upon after worming through the cave entrance defied their expectations: a vast gallery of prehistoric frescoes, with lines so graceful and colors so vivid they seemed to have been preserved by a miracle. Taken soon after the discovery, the first color photographs attest to the frescoes' gorgeous pristine quality. Quite alone with all this for several days, the boys camped beside the narrow crack in the stone that had led them to a prehistoric masterpiece, utterly forgotten in human memory.

The official account of the discovery of Lascaux contains the names and key attributes of the boys: in addition to Marcel Ravidat, there were Jacques Marsal, fourteen, also a native of Montignac; and two others, Georges Agniel, seventeen, and Simon Coëncas, thirteen, from Paris, both of whom would soon return to the occupied capital to reenter school. When he arrived home on October 3, 1940, Simon learned that he was no longer a French boy like any other; from that day on he would be categorized as a Jew. A few days earlier, the national press of France, controlled as it was by German occupying forces in the northern zone and by heavy Vichy censorship in the south, had formally announced his discovery of "the most beautiful decorated cavern in the world." The conclusion was unanimous. "We should rejoice in this news, despite our present distress," wrote the editorialist of the venerable conservative newspaper *Le Journal des débats* on the 29th of September. Thereafter, the discovery gradually mutated into a scientific and technical epiphany, becoming a kind of moral vaccine against France's present misery.

Of course the boys had been unable to keep their secret to themselves. Léon Laval, the Montignac schoolteacher and an amateur archaeologist, was one of the first to hear about it. He quickly understood that this was something special. Among many others marooned south of the Loire by France's military disaster was the priest Henri Breuil, an international specialist in Paleolithic art who had been a refugee in the area between Brive and Les Eyzies ever since the month of May. Alerted by Laval, the Abbé Breuil hurried to Montignac on September 23, instantly recognized the cave frescoes as unique in the world, and pronounced them to be more than twenty thousand years old, from the Aurignacian or Périgordian period. On September 29, in a report addressed to the Académie des Inscriptions et Belles-Lettres in Paris, Breuil anointed Lascaux the "Sistine

Chapel" of Perigordian art, placing it above the Spanish cave of Altamira, which he had described in exactly the same terms forty years earlier, at the beginning of his career. Ever since the discovery of Altamira, France and Spain had fought over the leading role in the preservation, if not the origination, of European Paleolithic cave art.

With Lascaux, the Périgord achieved undisputed primacy in the artistic heritage of all humanity.

In the wake of the military, political, and moral disaster that had befallen France, a reawakened scientific quest for the universal origins of mankind was balm to a nation brought low by its acceptance of defeat. Published in *Le Temps* of November 7, 1940, an article by the prehistorian Count Henri Bégouën made an academic plea for the international dissemination of his country's cultural prowess. "Amid the sad events of the present, [the discovery at Lascaux] is not only a distraction but also a source of comfort, an invitation to French savants to give more attention than ever before to the eminently French sciences of anthropology and prehistory." Ever since the "invention" of prehistory at Abbeville in the Somme department in 1859, scholars interested in the origins of man had been largely focused on French territory. After the discoveries of Cro-Magnon Man in 1868 and the Neanderthals of La Chapelle-aux-Saints in 1908, signs and vestiges of human origins had become sources of ever-deepening interest.

Did Lascaux-mania mark a revival of Reason, for the nation that had consecreated the rights of man and now found itself defeated? Or was it just a craze for a branch of science still in its infancy? On all the continents of the old world — from China to South Africa — the Abbé Breuil was known as the tireless missionary of a discipline that he had brought into the prestigious Collège de France in 1929. To maintain the "Catholicism" of prehistoric times, there had to be a pope, and Breuil gladly played the role. Might this renewal of Rome not combine with eternal France in microcosm, a France whose spirit alone was invincible?

Let us return to the moment of discovery: It all fit perfectly into a narrative of national unity, with a priest and a secular teacher brought together on the property of an ancient aristocratic family by intrepid young men, the youngest of whom was Jewish, though all were educated equally between the provinces and Paris. By chance and narrative necessity, this story condensed a version of France that could be seen not only as eternal, but also as the seed of a new origin myth. Years later, postwar France would tap this story about adolescents and adolescent humankind to establish the caves as both vectors of profitable tourism and sources of patrimonial reverence. The prospects was alluring even if the former might, it is true, devour the latter.

It was possible that Lascaux was nothing but an updated version of the apparitions of the Virgin Mary in the nineteenth century, transcendent but national in character, with caves as a ubiquitous background. The anthropologist Daniel Fabre has shown how the "providential" narrative of Lascaux's discovery, which has spawned numerous television films and comic strips, gives force to the idea of an immanent, universal apparition from an absolute past. It suggests, in particular, that our origins are literally endless and lacking any point of departure, supplying a symmetrical (and spurious) remedy to the crisis of progress and the future of what Paul Valéry called "mortal civilizations." This postmodern cult of revelation was put into poetry by Georges Bataille, who in 1955 associated "the birth of art" with the name of Lascaux. In doing so, he linked the aesthetic of prehistory to the summit of modern art, from Picasso to the neo-expressionist Miquel Barceló.

With the discovery of Lascaux began the scientific globalization of French prehistory. From its 1940 wartime discovery to the conditions of its massive exploitation as a tourist venue after 1948 and finally to Culture Minister André Malraux's abrupt decision to close it to the public in 1963, the caves had all the elements of an epic drama. In effect, Lascaux enabled France to endow its national heritage with a new form of sacrality. With these caves, France conferred upon the world the power to behold what will inexorably become invisible. Of this power, heads of state and their ministers of culture remain the supreme guarantors.

A photo essay in several pages in *L'Illustration* offered the public on January 4, 1941, a chance to contemplate a "revelation" that had the power to banish the darkness of a gloomy new year. The British press took up the story a year later; in 1947, *Life* magazine spread the Lascaux images around the world. Sometimes dubbed "the prehistoric Versailles," these secular and regal caves attracted over a million visitors over a period of fifteen years. After 1963, this magnetic thrill of real contact gave way to the authority to grant or refuse entry. With a ritual daily visit limited to five rigorously selected visitors, the cavern was now restricted to an elite of enthusiasts who clearly had the means to wait a long time to make the pilgrimage. After the *maladie verte* of the 1960s (a green mold introduced by artificial air circulation), the cave walls continued to deteriorate steadily, so much so that in 2000 the historic monuments administration closed the cave definitively. Access to the supreme sanctuary of France's cultural heritage has been confined ever since to the ministers and presidents of the Republic, who alone have the privilege to consume and celebrate firsthand an apparition that was once hailed universal and national.

In his speech marking the fiftieth anniversary of the discovery in September 1990, François Mitterrand pronounced the word "France" only once, but mentioned "the world" no fewer than five times, concluding that the art of Lascaux "demonstrates with great force something that should make us think long and hard: namely, the bond that unites mankind, everywhere and at all times." Twenty years later, after a similar visit to Lascaux in September 2010, Nicolas Sarkozy proposed the creation of a new historical institution devoted to French history, the Maison de l'Histoire de France. His project was abandoned in 2012.

After the transformation of an element of man's universal heritage into a national and quasi-royal asset, a substitute was put in place, testing the limits to which those in charge of France's cultural heritage were prepared to go in "virtualizing" Lascaux. The division of roles between the protective, overarching state and the local authorities, who used the site to generate revenue, preserved a status quo that earlier had been seen as destructive and contradictory. Although dethroned in 1995 by the Chauvet Cave in the Ardèche, whose frescoes predated those of Lascaux by some 15,000 years, the Dordogne region, grappling as it was with industrial and agricultural crises, did manage to claw back control of an asset it viewed as a valuable tourist attraction. The classification of the Vézère Valley and its prehistoric locations as a world heritage site in 1979 allowed the department to proclaim itself a Pays de l'Homme (literally, A Land of Mankind) using as its symbol the iconic bull of Lascaux. In 1978, elected officials in the region took the (considerable) economic risk of commissioning a partial facsimile of the cave frescoes, which very few people at the time believed would be successful. Erected a few hundred meters from the original site, Lascaux II has since 1983 attracted between two and four hundred thousand people a year.

Then came another idea. If a mere copy was capable of bringing the world to Lascaux, why not bring Lascaux to the world? One virtual path led to another. In December 2016, François Hollande came to Montignac to inaugurate a new International Center for Cave Art: Lascaux IV, the "complete" version, situated at the base of the hill, which, to all intents and purposes, was now a full-blown sanctuary financed by the Pays de l'Homme. While awaiting this fresh flood of tourist money, the elected leaders of the Périgord had secured their rearguard: their Lascaux III reproduction, packed into nine shipping containers, had been released in 2012 to tour the planet. After Chicago and Houston in 2013, Montreal in 2014, and Paris and Brussels in 2015, this portable but strictly inauthentic reproduction of Lascaux arrived in July 2016 at Seoul before moving to Japan in 2017.

In the few months it toured the shores of the Pacific, more than a million people paid to see it. The same number had paid, over fifteen years, to view — and almost destroy — the primitive marvel in the quiet valley of the Vézère.

Yann Potin

REFERENCES

Demoule, Jean-Paul. "Lascaux." In *Realms of Memory: The Construction of the French Past*, edited by Pierre Nora and Lawrence D. Kritzman, 162–90. New York: Columbia University Press, 1998.

Fabre, Daniel. *Bataille à Lascaux: Comment l'art préhistorique apparut aux enfants*. Paris: L'Échoppe, 2014.

Fauvelle, François-Xavier, and Yann Potin. "Le pèlerin, le missionnaire, l'ambassadeur: Figures du voyageur Henri Breuil." In *Sur les chemins de la préhistoire: L'abbé Breuil, du Périgord à l'Afrique du Sud*, edited by Noël Coye, 183–196. Paris: Somogy éditions d'Art, 2006.

Félix, Thierry, and Philippe Bigotto. *Le Secret des bois de Lascaux*. Sarlat: Dolmen, 1990.

Geneste, Jean-Michel, Chantal Tanet, and Tristan Hordé. *Lascaux, une œuvre de mémoire*. Périgueux: Fanlac, 2003.

RELATED ARTICLES

34,000 BCE, 52 BCE, 1420, 1763, 1815, 1871, 1907

1942

Vél' d'Hiv'–Drancy–Auschwitz

On July 16 and 17, 1942, thirteen thousand men, women, and children were arrested during the massive Vél' d'Hiv' round-up. The persecution of Jews in France was a French matter, implemented by the Vichy government; their extermination, however, was a German and European enterprise.

On July 21, 1942, the boxcars that had left the Bourget-Drancy station two days earlier at 9:05 a.m. came to a stop at the earthen platform of a sidetrack located about a half mile south of the Auschwitz station, some five hundred yards from the Birkenau camp. The place would be called the *Judenrampe*, the Jews' platform. The thousand or so men, women, and children, exhausted from their cramped three-day journey in overcrowded wagons without food or water, overwhelmed by the stench, jumped out of the cars amid incomprehensible mayhem. For most of them, everything had happened so fast. Arrested on July 16 or 17 at their place of residence in Paris, loaded onto buses and driven to the

Drancy internment camp, then herded back onto the same buses the next day and packed off in cattle cars headed for an unknown destination, they arrived, stunned beyond words, into an utterly alien, unnameable world. All 121 women and 504 of the men were marched into the camp and assigned registration numbers that were tattooed onto their forearms. 375 other men were walked over to one of two peasant cottages that had been repurposed as gas chambers, known from then on as Bunker One and Bunker Two.

This was the seventh convoy to leave France, but the deportees were the first to be murdered upon arrival at Auschwitz. By late September 1942, thirty-four trains coming from France had stopped at the *Judenrampe*, one every two or three days. On July 16, the first train to arrive from the Netherlands had preceded theirs, the very same day the Reichsführer-SS Heinrich Himmler started his inspection tour of the Auschwitz-Birkenau camps. The architect of the Final Solution was present at the gassing of the Dutch Jews. 38,500 Jews would be deported from the Netherlands that year, 1942, while 42,000 French Jews were deported during the same period. Belgian Jews would follow, a total of 16,500, a trainload every four days. Meanwhile, the Warsaw ghetto was being emptied out: between July and September, trains operating like clockwork delivered 300,000 Jews to the gas chambers of Treblinka.

The Vél' d'Hiv' raid of July 16 and 17, 1942, which

ended with this passage to Auschwitz, exemplifies the tragic
fate of Jews in France during the war. It does so through
the sheer number of arrests: thirteen thousand. It does so
because, for the first time, arrests involved not only men
of working age, but also women and children (over four
thousand). It does so, moreover, because, though ordered
by the Germans, this roundup was carried out by the French.
Most of all, it does so because, unlike previous raids, this one
was a clear component of the Nazis' "Final Solution of the
Jewish Question."

Nazi leadership was hoping to accelerate the pace of
deportations out of France. On June 11, 1942, Theodor
Dannecker, the SS officer in charge of persecuting the Jews
of France, was in Berlin to attend a conference convened
by Adolf Eichmann. As a follow-up to the Wannsee
Conference that on January 20, 1942, broadly outlined the
organizational plans for the Final Solution, this conference
addressed the operational breakdown among the occupied
western European countries of the Netherlands, Belgium,
and France. If over one million Jews had been murdered by
the *Einsatzgruppen*, Germany's paramilitary death squads,
after the Wehrmacht entered the Soviet Union on June 22,
1941, the year 1942 was even more terrible, with 2,700,000
murders, mainly at the "killing centers" of Chełmno, Bełzec,
Sobibór, and Treblinka. Nazi anti-Semitism was, in the
words of Saul Friedländer, a "redemptive anti-Semitism":

the Jews who dominated the world, whether the Bolsheviks in the USSR or the capitalists in the United States, had to be eradicated so that the "Aryan" thousand-year Reich might reign.

History refers to the roundup of July 16 and 17 as the "Vél' d'Hiv' raid" because the families caught in its net were first taken to the Vélodrome d'Hiver, a venue for political conventions and indoor cycling races (destroyed in 1959), while bachelors and childless couples were conveyed directly to Drancy. It has also become one of France's commemorative sites in remembrance of the deportation of its Jews.

On July 16, 1995, after a heated controversy over outgoing President François Mitterrand's collaborationist past, newly elected President Jacques Chirac acknowledged France's responsibilities in one of the most famous speeches of the Fifth Republic. "On July 16, 1942," he recalled, "4,500 police and gendarmes, officially authorized by their superiors, complied with Nazi orders" and conducted early-morning raids in Paris and the surrounding region, arresting some 13,000 Jewish men, women, and children at their places of residence and herding them into police stations before "loading them unceremoniously onto Paris buses and police vans." The victims were taken to the Vélodrome d'Hiver, where they waited "in wretched conditions" to be directed to "one of the transit camps — Pithiviers or Beaune-la-Rolande — opened by the Vichy officials." Jacques Chirac mentioned other such raids in Paris and the provinces, the seventy-four trains in all that left for Auschwitz, the 76,000 French deportees who would never return. And commenting further: "France, nation of Enlightenment and human rights, land of welcome and asylum, France, on that day, committed an act beyond repair. In a breach of faith, it turned over to their executioners those it should have protected." The "criminal madness of the occupier" had been "backed by Frenchmen, by the French State."

The Jews in France suffered persecution from the earliest days of German occupation and the creation of the Vichy state. It followed the same basic model, with a few local variants, that was implemented by Nazi Germany and exported to the countries it had conquered: definition of who was Jewish, ban of Jews from certain professions, expropriation of their personal assets, detention, and deportation.

Whether foreign, naturalized, or French, all were caught in the crosshairs of Vichy French and Nazi German legislation. During the first two years, German injunctions that only applied to the occupied zone and Vichy became decrees enforced nationwide, gradually but inexorably isolating them from the rest of the population, depriving them of their means of subsistence. It was "the time of

decrees," as French statesman Edgar Faure put it: revision
of pre-1927 naturalizations — around fifteen thousand
denaturalization decisions were handed down; abolition
of the 1939 decree, called the Marchandeau law, which had
made racial slurs a criminal offence, reopening the way for
a surge of anti-Semitism; the September 27 order by the
German military command that defined who was Jewish
("those who belong or have belonged to the Jewish faith,
or who have more than two Jewish grandparents," meaning
"grandparents who belong or have belonged to the Jewish
faith") and required that Jews declare themselves to the
census-takers (which the overwhelming majority actually
did) and display on the storefront of every Jewish-owned
shop a sign reading "Jewish business."

On June 2, 1941, the French picked up where the
Germans left off and conducted a census of their own. These
surveys, in defiance of French republican tradition, brought
to light an unlikely, erratically defined Jewish population.
Whether the definition leaned more on religion, as did the
German order, or on race, as did the October 1940 French
decree on the status of Jews ("is considered Jewish any
person descending from three Jewish grandparents, or two
grandparents of the same race if that person's spouse is him
or herself Jewish"), whether narrowly or broadly construed,
it always defined Jews by the standard of their lineage. The
freedom of choice afforded by France's emancipatory

republican values were thus annulled. This census-taking provided the basis for a larger system of personal records. The prefectural administration of the Seine department compiled a central catalog, which was then broken down into four subcatalogs by name, address, profession, and nationality. These records proved useful during various mass arrests, notably the raid on July 16 and 17, 1942.

The Vichy government issued the October 3, 1940 law "regarding the status of Jews," enforced in both the occupied and free zones. It consisted mainly of the long list of professions that Jews were henceforward banned from practicing. They could no longer hold any political office and were banned from jobs in the press, communications, the movie industry, and, with few exceptions, civil service. Further measures were planned to limit their numbers in the liberal professions. A law was adopted on October 4 pertaining to foreign nationals on record as ethnically Jewish: "They can be detained in special camps by decision of the prefect of their département of residence." In addition, they could "at all times be placed under house arrest" by the same prefect. More than fifty thousand foreign Jews were deported, comprising three-quarters of all Jews deported from France.

The German occupiers were just as quick to impound property. Their second decree, on October 18, 1940, laid the foundations for what would come to be called "economic

Aryanization," a neologism that Gallicized a term coined by the Third Reich, *Arisierung*, or the transfer of Jewish assets to non-Jews. These gradually enforced measures sought to prevent Jews from "putting down material roots," according to French historian Joseph Billig. Consistent with its own logic — extending its authority over the entire country and preventing stolen goods from finding their way to Germany — the Vichy government decided it would also gain a stake in the Aryanization of Jewish property. Where the Germans, in the first phase, required every Jewish enterprise to acquire a temporary "Aryan" administrator, the French initiated a second phase with the March 29, 1941, creation of what was basically the ministry of anti-Semitism, officially entitled the General Commission for Jewish Questions.

The situation of Jews was clearly worsening. Tracked, dispossessed, and excluded from many professions, they could also be detained, if they were foreigners, at the whim of some administrator. They were now living on the fringe of the nation.

May 1941 marked the start of the roundups: 3,700 men, mostly foreigners, were arrested on May 14. On August 20 and the days that followed, over 4,000 Jews would be taken to the Cité de la Muette, an unfinished housing project in Drancy, outside Paris, recently converted into a detention camp for Jews.

To those in France, three places symbolize the Shoah (as the Holocaust is called in France, among other countries). There is the Vél' d'Hiv', where commemorations have taken place since the end of the war, officially so since 1993; Drancy, where a memorial was erected in 2012; and Auschwitz, where the victims of the Vél' d'Hiv' roundups were murdered along with one million other children, women, and men from all over Nazi Europe. For if the persecution of the Jews in France was a French affair, their extermination is a matter for the European historical record.

Annette Wieviorka

REFERENCES

Friedländer, Saul. *The Years of Extermination: Nazi Germany and the Jews, 1939–1945.* New York: HarperCollins, 2007.

Hilberg, Raul. *The Destruction of the European Jews.* 3rd ed. New Haven: Yale University Press, 2003.

Klarsfeld, Serge. *La Shoah en France.* 4 vols. Paris: Fayard, 2001.

Wieviorka, Annette. *Auschwitz: La mémoire d'un lieu.* Paris: Hachette Pluriel, 2005.

———, and Michel Laffitte. *À l'intérieur du camp de Drancy.* Paris: Perrin Tempus, 2012.

RELATED ARTICLES
1347, 1572, 1683, 1894, 1927, 1962

1946

The Yalta of Film

The first Cannes International Film Festival was launched
on September 19, 1946. This fertile blend of world cinema
and nonstop party-going had an important diplomatic
dimension: the world's great powers, now at peace, would
divvy up their respective attributions — and artistic
awards, too.

The first International Film Festival opened on the evening
of September 19, 1946, with a ceremony on the Cannes
Croisette. It featured a procession of flower-covered
floats — peaceful ones, as an editorialist for *Le Monde*
wryly put it — representing the various nations taking
part. As they rumbled past, the Mexican float was seen to
be "high in both color and form," and the one from the
USSR "multihued like a jug of Bohemian glass, releasing
into the air a steady stream of doves." The American float
was adorned with great amphorae of carnations made out of
strips of film bearing the familiar logos of MGM, RKO, and
Paramount, while the Swedish contribution was "laden with

nymphs whose legs were long and beautiful" (*Le Monde*, September 21, 1946).

This was followed after nightfall by a torchlit parade of swaggering, bugle-playing Senegalese infantry in full ceremonial uniform, which "was much admired." Then came the mandatory fireworks display to inaugurate an all-night ball. This commenced with several songs and a spirited rendering of the "Marseillaise" by the American star Grace Moore, gorgeous "in a cream-colored gown that shimmered with gold spangles." There were crowds of onlookers, kitsch galore, spangles, beautiful people dancing all night.

The actual film projections only started next day with *Berlin*, a socialist-realist documentary presented by the Soviet contingent. This opened a program of forty-eight other films. Over the next sixteen days, each one was watched by hundreds of officials, international representatives of the profession, critics, and "young optical gluttons," as *Le Monde* somewhat oddly described the fans.

Thus the Cannes Film Festival was based from the start on an unnatural but fertile alliance between the art of glitz and the skills of artifice; of trivial party-going and cinema at its most prestigious. The blend of wordly sociability, cinematic myth, and pure vulgarity won the festival an enduring reputation. Whatever qualms the world of cinema may have felt about Cannes, it gravitated toward the venue.

In 1946, the occasion was highly diplomatic in tone. Its embodiment was the first delegate of the festival, Philippe Erlanger, who was also the head of the "artistic exchange" department at the Ministry of Foreign Affairs in Paris, so it was clear to everyone that the underlying purpose of the festival was to celebrate the triumph of the victorious Allies. The films that were shown, all of them chosen by national selection committees, reflected this balance just as much as the intricate maneuvers of the diplomatic corps, "which was better represented than the cinema itself" (*Le Monde*, September 21, 1946), or the parade of flower-covered floats. The USSR, the United States, Great Britain, Sweden, Denmark, India, Czechoslovakia, Switzerland, Mexico, and Italy had all sent films and film directors to compete against the French selection. For France, the priority was to succeed not only as the host but also as a significant participant, patriotically and culturally, in the concert of nations that was just then beginning to emerge from the unspeakable misery of war.

In this sense, the first Cannes Film Festival of 1946 mirrored Cannes 1939 — the founding festival which almost took place but didn't. The aborted event of 1939 — organized as it was by Minister of National Education and Fine Arts Jean Zay — began on August 6 with the arrival of a train at the town railway station carrying the inventor of the cinematograph, Louis Lumière himself. Appointed honorary president of the festival, Lumière had traveled from the neighboring town of La Ciotat, where he lived, to inspect the site where it was to take place. The Grand Hotel, the Palm Beach Hotel, and the municipal casino had been mobilized to receive an array of international guests; the poster by Jean-Gabriel Domergue, an adopted Cannes resident, was finished and ready; Gary Cooper, Tyrone Power, Annabella, Norma Shearer, George Raft, Cary Grant, James Cagney, David Niven, Spencer Tracy, and Barbara Stanwyck were already present on the Croisette, having arrived aboard a liner chartered by MGM. Hollywood itself had sent no fewer than twelve films, among them Howard Hawks's *Only Angels Have Wings*, Frank Capra's *Mr. Smith Goes to Washington*, Victor Fleming's *Wizard of Oz*, Cecil B. DeMille's *Union Pacific*, and Leo McCarey's sublime *Love Affair*.

Jean Zay had embraced the idea of a prestigious event that could rival the Mostra of Venice. That festival was entirely controlled by Mussolini and Goebbels, to the point where, in 1938, its awards had all been won by fascist and Nazi propaganda films, the whole affair having been boycotted by the British and the Americans. The "Free World" had thus planned to mount its own film festival and present its own awards, at Cannes...until the German Wehrmacht brutally interrupted their final preparations by invading Poland on September 1, 1939.

But in 1939 as in 1946, the same question arose: why was it that an event like this simply had to take place in France? And more precisely, why in Cannes? France still strongly affirmed that it was — and had been ever since Louis XIV and Napoleon and the Universal Exhibitions of the nineteenth century — the homeland of world art. In the twentieth century it also saw itself as the homeland of cinema: after all, Lumière, a Frenchman, had invented the art form — a fact beyond all doubt in the French mind, ignoring the first moving pictures of the American Thomas Edison. French cinematography was not only powerful, but also of very high quality; it had produced masterpieces and filmmakers capable of impressing the entire world, if not yet a mass audience enthralled by Hollywood. In the eyes of the world brought together to admire "French beauty," it was only in Cannes that a synthetic form of magic could blend art and fun, cinema and tourism, great actors and beautiful people. "No other country was more qualified than France to preside over an event of this kind, in a spirit of artistic creation, absolute freedom and guaranteed impartiality," wrote the historian Olivier Loubes in his study of Jean Zay. And indeed this was the specific boast of the managing committee of the International Film Festival in its inaugural circular, published on July 17, 1939.

The spirit of 1939 was resurrected in 1946. *Le Monde* announced that at Cannes people were expressing themselves in all the world's languages. Special trains, with blue carriages hailing from distant capitals, offered glimpses of a succession of beauty spots to hundreds of film professionals as they converged on Cannes. The very occasion which made it possible for them to see these marvels, the International Film Festival, invited them to compare the sapphire eyes of Gene Tierney to the color of the Mediterranean, the sky overhead to the canted horizons of John Ford, and the honey-skinned swimmers on the beaches of the Côte d'Azur to the water-ballerina Esther Williams.

Thus it was that the Cannes festival offered a double discourse, which was nevertheless perfectly coherent: it celebrated and welcomed the victorious unity of the Allied nations, but it also magnified France. Better still: French grandeur — which in cinematic terms was completely illusory in the year of 1946 — was never more striking than when seen from abroad and consecrated by international scrutiny. "The festival must be a victory for France. For that we need the cooperation of all other countries," declared the festival committee in 1939. Seven years later, the same idea was still prevalent: the cultural victory of France could only be endorsed by international admiration. France would never triumph alone in a corner, its glory could only be affirmed before the eyes of a united world and by its own endeavor.

Thus the 1946 event was set in the logic of shared roles; it was a kind of cinematic Yalta Conference. The festival was not merely a carefully calibrated dose of film and tinsel, directors and starlets. It also looked for a balance between, first, the industrial muscle Hollywood could provide by coming to the Croisette in force (and after 1946 to movie theaters, following the Blum–Byrnes trade agreements); second, the affirmation of an art whose legitimacy was based on awards given to the best of its own; and third, a cultural diplomacy aimed at satisfying each of the film genres that were present. Three assumptions — or principles — guided this approach, which were to settle the place of French cinema in the world for the duration. They were these: the most powerful, widely-distributed and impressive cinema in the world was American; the cinema that "had things to say about the world" was international; and French films were more elegant, more original, and more artistically framed than any others.

The first Cannes Film Festival closed on Saturday, October 5, 1946, with a triple program of screenings, an idea destined for a great international future as cinematography grew more specialized. This program included a Hollywood movie (Walt Disney's *Make Mine Music*), an official Soviet film (*Glinka*, a romanticized film of the composer's life and work); and an incomparable French film (Jean Cocteau's *Beauty and the Beast*). The first sought to impose a

1101

commercial standard on the rest of the world, as advocated by Eric Allan Johnson, the new president of the American Motion Picture Association. The second glorified Russian patriotism. The third, finally, offered a demonstration of French eccentricity that was as stylish and dandified as it was fantastical.

The final awards, announced by the president of the jury, George Huisman, director of the École des Beaux-Arts in Paris, confirmed that diplomacy had been hard at work behind the scenes. Every country won a prize: *The Red Meadows* (Denmark), *Lowly City* (India), *The Last Chance* (Switzerland), *Men without Wings* (Czechoslovakia), *The Turning Point* (USSR), *Symphonie Pastorale* (France), *Brief Encounter* (UK), *The Lost Weekend* (US), *Maria Candelaria* (Mexico), *The Ordeal* (Sweden), and *Rome, Open City* (Italy) were all given a Grand Prix. The Palme d'Or award would not appear until 1955, when it was given to Delbert Mann's *Marty*.

The overall winner, as was proper, was a French film. René Clément's *Battle of the Rails*, a tribute to the heroic resistance put up by French railway men in Occupied France, received the Prix du Jury, the only supranational award. As has frequently occurred in the history of the festival, this film reflected current political circumstances, offering a soothing paean, welcomed by the jury and critics alike, to the glorious resistance of French railroad workers.

Meanwhile, filmmakers from all over the world continued to sample the other pleasures afforded by the festival.

Finally, in what is now an established Cannes tradition, an authentic masterpiece — Alfred Hitchcock's *Notorious*, starring Ingrid Bergman — was completely ignored. It took a decade before a completely different set of critics, the young Turks of the cult film magazine *Cahiers du Cinéma*, consecrated Hitchcock as the "greatest formal genius in the history of the cinema." But this belongs to a whole other episode in the story of France's cultural interaction with the wider world.

Antoine de Baecque

REFERENCES

Erlanger, Philippe. *La France sans étoile: Souvenirs de l'avant-guerre et du temps de l'Occupation*. Paris: Plon, 1974.

Fléchet, Anaïs, Pascale Gœtschel, Patricia Hidiroglou, Sophie Jacotot, Caroline Moine, and Julie Verlaine, eds. *Une histoire des Festivals (XXe–XXIe siècle)*. Paris: Publications de la Sorbonne, 2013.

Latil, Loredana. *Le Festival de Cannes sur la scène internationale*. Paris: Nouveau Monde, 2005.

Loubes, Olivier. *Cannes 1939: Le Festival qui n'a pas eu lieu*. Paris: Armand Colin, 2016.

Piniau, Bernard, and Ramon Tio Bellido. *L'Action artistique de la France dans le monde*. Paris: L'Harmattan, 1998.

Schwartz, Vanessa R. *It's So French!: Hollywood, Paris, and the Making of Cosmopolitan Film Culture*. Chicago: University of Chicago Press, 2007.

RELATED ARTICLES
1771, 1900

1948
Universal Human Rights

France — birthplace of a museum of human rights? The 1948 Universal Declaration of Human Rights, promulgated in Paris's Palais de Chaillot, was a milestone in international law. But the story behind its genesis is one of vying interests and powers. Still, the Declaration provided a narrow legal path to freedom for colonized nations.

On December 10, 1948, the General Assembly of the United Nations convened at the Palais de Chaillot to adopt what would become a seminal text for the modern human rights movements — the Universal Declaration of Human Rights. Although the scope of this didactic and moral manifesto was symbolic rather than legal, its impact on regional and international human rights has been undeniable. The text itself was the culmination of a long history, beginning with the French Declaration of the Rights of Man and of the Citizen and the American Bill of Rights. Unlike those first documents, the United Nations' Declaration of Human Rights was not the product of a single nation's legal system, but a truly universal document.

To be sure, an earlier document, the Declaration of the International Rights of Man, had been adopted in 1929 by a closed circle of international legal scholars — the Institute of International Law. That earlier declaration was then spread internationally by organizations committed to the rights of man. It had been initially proposed by a Russian legal scholar exiled in France, André N. Mandelstam, who sharply criticized the genocide of Ottoman Armenians and fought to extend the protections for minorities that the major Allied powers had promulgated after World War I. Mandelstam believed that laws protecting minorities did not go far enough. In light of expanding dictatorships, he argued for the creation of protections for all men, wherever they lived. Together with an international network of liberal legal experts, speaking out against state sovereignty, Mandelstam sought to place the individual at the center of international law and advocated equal rights between men and women.

Historians have long debated who initiated and thus best embodies the 1948 Declaration. French delegate to the League of Nations and Nobel Laureate René Cassin? Eleanor Roosevelt? Drafter John Humphrey? President of the Commission on Human Rights Charles Malik? Human rights activist Peng Chun Chang? This quest has overemphasized the role of a few personalities to the detriment of a serious analysis of documentation submitted by the Secretariat of the United Nations and sufficient attention to ideological power relationships, national and/or religious political issues, and NGO initiatives. All had an impact on the drafting process.

The 1948 Declaration goes well beyond the purview of Western powers. Indeed, the postwar period was marked by uprisings from peoples under imperial domination, an undermining of state sovereignty protected under article 2(7) of the Charter of the United Nations, and the Nuremberg and Tokyo trials, which showcased the tragic consequences of unbridled state sovereignty. In the spring of 1946, the United Nations Economic and Social Council (ECOSOC) created a Commission for the Rights of Man tasked with drafting proposals on freedom of information, the protection of minorities, women's rights, and discrimination based on race, gender, language, and religion. It also drafted the International Declaration of the Rights of Man.

That was the wide-ranging, multifaceted impetus behind the 1948 text. Although international events such as decolonization and the Cold War reshaped the postwar geopolitical sphere, the Commission of the Rights of Man was primarily made up of scientists and intellectuals. Many Commission members had diplomatic experience and represented different religious, political, and ideological systems. The Commission met three times, alternating with a drafting committee that presented its report to the ECOSOC in August 1948. In turn, the ECOSOC examined the document at its General Assembly of 1948 in Paris. Several forces impelled a change in the scope of the project over this long development phase: the bracketing of minority rights and of people's rights to self-government; a shift in the makeup of the Commission, from a panel of independent experts to an assembly of government officials; and a status downgrade, from a convention with legal implications to a simple declaration.

A vast intellectual movement, with wide-ranging philosophical and ethical viewpoints, surrounded this process. UNESCO convened a summit of one hundred and fifty experts and intellectuals from across the globe to reflect on the philosophical issues raised by international human rights. Intellectuals from different continents made suggestions as a means of rounding out and amending Western perspectives. For instance, Mahatma Gandhi wrote the following in a letter addressed to Julian Huxley, UNESCO's director at the time:

> I learnt from my illiterate but wise mother that the sole rights that warrant protection come from duty well done. Thus the very right to live accrues to us only when we perform our duties as citizens of the world. From this one fundamental statement, it is perhaps easier to define the duties of

men and women and to correlate every right to a
corresponding duty. Every other right can be shown
to be a usurpation hardly worth fighting for.

The adoption of this text cannot be understood without
taking into account the United States' role. Two main
concerns characterized the country's position during the
three years of negotiation. The first had to do with the
relationship between the American constitutional system
and international law. At issue for legal advisers in the
State Department was how to protect US sovereignty
and help create international human rights. The second
concern related to mounting Cold War tensions between
1945 and 1948. Two political and legal frameworks, both
driven by universalist aims, now faced one another. To
be sure, the Cold War did not thwart the adoption of the
Declaration, but it did limit the document's impact on US
human rights policy. France also made proposals, through
a subcommission created in 1947, whose ideas were voiced
by René Cassin to the UN's Commission for the Rights
of Man. Nevertheless, there was some reticence when it
came to France's colonies. In the 1950s, Cassin's proposals
to the UN were stalled due to wars of decolonization
and particularly the Algerian War. As legal expert René
Degni-Ségui has pointed out, although the Declaration
ignored decolonization, it was adopted and appropriated by

decolonization movements. Thus, the Declaration became a constitutional common denominator among states that had recently won their independence from the former French empire. The document even played a central role in the final communiqué of the Asian–African Bandung Conference of 1955. Elsewhere across the globe, the legal implications of the 1948 text engendered debate and arguments over its scope and even legitimacy.

On December 12, 1948, having recently adopted the Convention on the Prevention and Punishment of the Crime of Genocide, the General Assembly of the United Nations voted for the Declaration after eighty-five grueling debates within its Third Commission. In the end, the document had been transformed from an "international declaration" to a "universal declaration." For René Cassin, the declaration was founded on an expanded conception of international society, one comprised of human beings as well as states. The declaration included thirty articles and a preamble acknowledging the need for all states and governments to respect fundamental human rights. The text lays out basic human rights, including their social, economic, and cultural dimensions.

The Declaration was unanimously adopted, with eight abstentions (the USSR and five other Communist states, along with Saudi Arabia and the Union of South Africa). This took place without much public fanfare, even in

France. In 1948, headlines were instead dominated by the Berlin Blockade and the question of Palestine. Still, French diplomacy saw it as a win, a wonderful achievement on the hundredth anniversary of the 1848 Revolution and the abolition of slavery in France. But would this be a new age for the people? In the immediate aftermath, France and the United Kingdom were equally loath to publish the Declaration beyond their respective mainlands and even have it translated into the languages their imperial subjects could understand.

Dzovinar Kévonian

REFERENCES

Barsalou, Olivier. *La Diplomatie de l'universel: La guerre froide, les États-Unis et la genèse de la Déclaration universelle des droits de l'homme (1945–1948)*. Bruxelles: Bruylant, 2012.

Lauren, Paul Gordon. *The Evolution of International Human Rights: Visions Seen*. 2nd ed. Philadelphia: University of Pennsylvania Press, 2011.

Pateyron, Éric. *La Contribution française à la rédaction de la Déclaration universelle des droits de l'homme: René Cassin et la Commission consultative des droits de l'homme*. Paris: La Documentation française, 1998.

Slotte, Pamela, and Miia Halme-Tuomisaari, eds. *Revisiting the Origins of Human Rights*. Cambridge: Cambridge University Press, 2015.

Winter, Jay, and Antoine Prost. *René Cassin and Human Rights: From the Great War to the Universal Declaration*. Cambridge: Cambridge University Press, 2013.

RELATED ARTICLES

212, 1790, 1804, 1919, 1920

1949

Reinventing Feminism

Published in May 1949, Simone de Beauvoir's *The Second Sex* caused an uproar among intellectuals and writers, who clamored for or against the scandalous work. Feminist and women's organizations remained silent, however. Still, the book was an immediate international success and inspired a new wave of feminism.

The polemics surrounding *The Second Sex* upon its publication in France may come as a surprise. Books written by women about the female condition tend not to draw much interest. But when this two-volume work came out in Gallimard's prestigious Blanche imprint in May and October 1949, it created a scandal.

The controversy started when the novelist François Mauriac asked, in *Le Figaro*'s literary supplement: "Does women's sex ed belong in a literary and philosophy review?" Targeting what he viewed as the "abject" mores of the Saint-Germain-des-Prés literary scene, Mauriac used his piece to call the country's Christian youth to react. In response, forty letters were published in the supplement's subsequent issues.

But the debate went beyond the pages of one newspaper. In less than a year, most of France's dailies and intellectual periodicals weighed in: the right-wing media (*Le Figaro, Aurore, Liberté de l'esprit*), the left (communist periodicals *Les Lettres françaises* and *La Nouvelle Critique*; more moderate left-wing journals like *Esprit, Combat, Les Temps modernes,* and *Franc-Tireur*), the Protestant press (*Réforme, Les Cahiers protestants, Bulletin jeunes femmes*), the mainstream media (*Le Monde, Samedi-Soir, Paris-Match*), and literary journals (*Les Nouvelles littéraires, Noir et blanc, Empédocle, La Revue du Caire, La Revue de Paris, Hommes et mondes, La Table ronde, La Nef*).

Leading intellectuals and lettered people of all stripes penned pieces for or against Beauvoir's work. In addition to Mauriac, who was a major Catholic writer, a former Resistance fighter, an editorialist at *Le Figaro*, and a member of the Académie Française, other figures who responded included Jean Kanapa, a former student of Jean-Paul Sartre and a philosopher who founded and edited *La Nouvelle Critique*; Julien Gracq, a professor of history and geography, novelist, and literary critic who opposed *littérature engagée*; Roger Nimier, a novelist and contributor to the literary journals *Carrefour* and *La Nef*; Emmanuel Mounier, the founder of personalism and the journal *Esprit*; Jean-Marie Domenach, a future editor for *Esprit*; and Francis Jeanson, a contributor to *Les Temps modernes* and *Esprit* and a member of the reading committee for the French publishing house Le Seuil. Lesser-known figures also weighed in.

Men dominated this critical response, but a number of women had their say, including Colette Audry, a literature professor, screenwriter, playwright, and good friend of Beauvoir and her partner, Jean-Paul Sartre; Françoise d'Eaubonne, a young novelist and essayist; Jeannette Prenant, a philosopher and communist; Dominique Aury, an editor, translator, and editorialist for *Les Lettres françaises*; as well as Claudine Chonez, a television journalist who gave Simone de Beauvoir the opportunity to respond to her critics.

Feminist organizations, which had faced strong marginalization and increasing irrelevance since the late 1930s, did not comment on the matter. Even more robust women's organizations kept quiet, such as the Union of French Women, a communist group. The only exception was the Movement of Young Women (similar in persuasion to Karl Barth's Protestant reformers), which had previously showed interest in parallel questions on relationships and love. Born after the war, this movement represented young people and was less reticent to discuss sex.

Why did this work stir up such a media frenzy? Jean-Paul Sartre's hegemony over the postwar cultural scene, thanks to his position as founder and editor of *Les Temps modernes*, provides a first clue to understanding the impact of Beauvoir's work. A graduate of the École Normale Supérieure with a degree in philosophy, Sartre proved a highly successful playwright, novelist, and philosopher. *Les Temps modernes*, founded in 1945, quickly became a mainstay of intellectual life. In just one year, between May 1948 and July 1949, eight issues published excerpts of forthcoming books, drawing the attention of the literary world. In sum, Sartre was at once the main voice of postwar French existentialism and the embodiment of the committed intellectual, intervening in countless public debates, never hesitating to criticize his intellectual opponents.

Beauvoir was also known as a critic with a diverse body of work: at that time, three novels, a play, two philosophical essays, and a travel narrative. Still, she remained in Sartre's shadow, commonly described in the press as "a disciple of the existentialist," "Our Lady of Sartre," or "the great *Sartreuse*." To a large extent, attacks against Beauvoir were actually critiques of Sartre's all-encompassing intellectual presence.

A second explanation for the response to Beauvoir's book can be traced to Cold War polemics, which proved so vigorous in France, with its robust and influential Communist Party. The trial of Soviet defector Victor Kravchenko, the clarion calls from André Malraux and Laurent Casanova to intellectuals, and the "book battles" of communist activists all testified to deep divisions within French cultural circles.

Neutrality was not an option; one had to choose one's camp. Yet Sartre and *Les Temps modernes* championed free choice, offering a sharp critique of both sides and acting as a third, intermediate political and cultural option. Unsurprisingly, then, the right (led by Mauriac) and the communists (guided by Jean Kanapa) were the harshest in their condemnation of *The Second Sex*. Interestingly, their arguments against the work tended to converge. Conversely, Christian progressives and the noncommunist left supported Beauvoir's ideas, or at the least, they did not distort her arguments. As could be expected, contributors to *Les Temps modernes* heaped the most praise on her work.

To be sure, there were exceptions to this neat political and cultural division. Some right-wing writers acknowledged the merits of Beauvoir's thinking, including the novelists Thierry Maulnier and François Nourissier; one of Nourissier's first publications was a response to Mauriac's question. Some communists, such as Dominique Desanti, spurned the party line. As for Albert Camus, for all his progressiveness he accused Beauvoir of "making a mockery of French masculinity."

In parallel, another surreptitious war was being fought, this one against the transformation of gender relations. Criticism was particularly sharp with respect to three chapters in which Beauvoir takes on the sexual order, published in the May, June, and July 1949 issues of *Les Temps modernes*:

"Women's Sexual Initiation," "The Lesbian," and "The Mother." Provoked by these sections, critics denounced *The Second Sex* as a "primer in erotic selfishness," a manifesto for "sexual egotism," and even "base pornography."

Beauvoir begins "The Mother" with a fifteen-page defense of contraception and abortion, rejects the idea of maternal instinct, and undermines the value of motherhood, which she calls a source of alienation for women. Daycare centers and nurseries would, she writes, prove more beneficial to children than a mother's care. Such arguments must be placed in their historical contexts. Since the 1930s, France had sought to increase birth rates by promoting family policies that kept women in the home. Natalism had reigned across the political spectrum ever since neo-Malthusians were quashed by a law in 1920 that prohibited importing, manufacturing, selling, and advertising contraceptives. Although the baby boom was robust in postwar France, it did little to soothe demographic fears; on the contrary, the ideal of the stay-at-home mother kept finding new proponents.

In "The Lesbian," Beauvoir uses an existentialist interpretive lens to equate homosexuality and heterosexuality, challenging sexological and psychoanalytical dogma by deeming both "situational choices." Critics denounced this chapter as a "defense of homosexuality." "Women's Sexual Initiation," finally, argues that heterosexual relations are inherently unequal, shaped as they are by imbalances of power. The topics Beauvoir addresses in these chapters (abortion, lesbianism, sexual violence) would be at the heart of second-wave feminism more than twenty years later.

The work's nefarious reputation intrigued readers, who rushed out to buy the two volumes — one thousand pages in all. Twenty-two thousand copies of *The Second Sex* were sold in France within weeks of its publication. Other editions followed, and a million copies were sold in forty years.

The Second Sex also became an international literary phenomenon. In the beginning, it was passed around in Francophile circles whose members followed existentialism. Interestingly, the critical divide played out in similar ways abroad. Catholic dictatorships in southern Europe banned the book; Spanish and Portuguese translations were therefore made in Argentina (1954) and Brazil (1960). In 1968, following two failures, a Catalan edition was authorized in Barcelona. In the Eastern Bloc, the book wasn't published until after the fall of the Berlin Wall, with the exception of a Serbo-Croatian translation in 1982.

The Second Sex faced fewer barriers to publication in Western Europe, with an edition in West Germany in 1951, an English translation in the United States in 1953 (thanks to editor Blanche Knopf and retired zoology professor Howard Parshley), and an Italian translation of *Il Secondo Sesso* published by Il Saggiatore in 1961. A new generation of intellectuals emerged and sought to revitalize feminism by drawing from Beauvoir's ideas. Let us name a few: Françoise d'Eaubonne, Colette Audry, and Andrée Michel in France; Betty Friedan and Kate Millett in the US; María Campo Alange and Maria Aurèlia Capmany, the "Catalan Beauvoir," in Spain; Alice Schwarzer in West Germany; Irene Selle in East Germany, and so on.

Beginning in the 1990s, as women's studies and feminism were incorporated into university curricula, the work continued to have an impact in eastern and northern Europe. It was translated in Bulgaria (1996), Russia (1997), Romania (1998), and Sweden (2002) and also made its way to Francophone and Anglophone Africa, and to Asia by way of Japan (where a first translation came out in 1953), Taiwan (1972), and then China (1988). While the first translations of *The Second Sex* have been criticized for their lack of precision or what they have left out, new, more faithful translations have been made in German (1992), Japanese (1997), Castilian (1998), English (2009), and Chinese (2012), to name but a few.

As a sign of her enduring influence, since 1983 the Simone de Beauvoir Society and its journal *Beauvoir Studies* have tracked the rich output of Beauvoirian studies.

Sylvie Chaperon

REFERENCES

Beauvoir, Simone de. *Feminist Writings*. Edited by Margaret A. Simons and Marybeth Timmermann. Chicago: University of Illinois Press, 2015.

Chaperon, Sylvie. *Les Années Beauvoir (1945–1970)*. Paris: Fayard, 2000.

Delphy, Christine, and Sylvie Chaperon, eds. *Cinquantenaire du "Deuxième Sexe."* Paris: Syllepse, 2002.

Galster, Ingrid, ed. *"Le Deuxième Sexe" de Simone de Beauvoir*. Paris: Presses de l'université Paris-Sorbonne, 2004.

Lecarme-Tabone, Éliane. *"Le Deuxième Sexe" de Simone de Beauvoir*. Paris: Gallimard, 2008.

Mann, Bonnie, and Martina Ferrari, eds. *On ne naît pas femme: on le devient...: The Life of a Sentence*. Oxford: Oxford University Press, 2017.

Simone de Beauvoir Society. "The International Simone de Beauvoir Society Website." http://beauvoir.weebly.com

RELATED ARTICLES
23,000 BCE, 1840, 1842, 1903, 1984, 2011

1953

"Our Comrade Stalin Is Dead"

The news broke on March 5, 1953: Stalin was dead.
French communists were in mourning, the true believers
overwhelmed with sorrow. Worship of the USSR and its
leader peaked with the momentous passing of the man who
had fascinated intellectuals, workers, and farmers alike.
Moscow's star would start to wane only later, in the 1970s.

Word of the death came on the morning of March 5, 1953,
in a meeting hall in the north Paris suburb of Genevilliers
during the national convention of the French Communist
Party (PCF). Choked up and teary-eyed, even the most
seasoned delegates were overcome with emotion. Finally,
veteran PCF leader Jacques Duclos summoned the strength
to utter these few words: "Our comrade Stalin is dead." He
then recited a first homage to the deceased. Others would
follow in the party's various media outlets — national,
regional, and local newspapers and a range of magazines.
Tributes included declarations by leaders, articles by
prestigious intellectuals, and testimonies from simple

party loyalists. Party headquarters in both Paris and the provinces displayed portraits of Stalin draped in black as a sign of mourning, while a memorial was set up at the Seine Federation headquarters.

On the day of the funeral in Moscow, several tributes were organized throughout France, often with a minute of silence observed in the workplace in large companies in Paris, Normandy, and the Lorraine region. On March 10, a solemn remembrance ceremony was held at the Vel' d'Hiv', the Paris velodrome. Four days later, a long text made the front page of *France nouvelle*, the main PCF weekly, aptly summarizing the message the party intended, right down to the overblown rhetoric:

> The heart of Stalin, our illustrious comrade-in-arms and brilliant pursuer of the path of Lenin, enlightened leader, friend, and brother to the working people of all nations, has stopped beating. But Stalinism is alive and well. It is immortal. The sublime name of the genius of world Communism will shine forth through the centuries with blazing brightness, and shall be forever uttered with love by an eternally grateful humankind. To Stalin we shall remain forever faithful. By their undying devotion to the sacred cause of the working class, of the people, of democracy and socialism, of national sovereignty and independence, and of peace, Communists will strive to earn the righteous title

of Stalinist. Everlasting glory to our great Stalin,
whose enduring scientific masterworks will further
our effort to unite the people and become the leading
force of the nation. Under the invincible banner of
Stalin, with his glorious Communist Party as our
model, we shall march ahead toward victory, and
forge a free, strong, and flourishing France.

Stalin worship began in the 1930s, reached its first peak
in 1939 with the sixtieth birthday of "the little father of the
peoples," celebrated with great fanfare by the PCF, and
attained its Cold War zenith with the entire communist
"counter-society" united in its devotion to the deceased
leader. This social subculture of sorts, comprised of a
mosaic of various entities, never cut itself off entirely
from the rest of society. The party's internal organization,
which gave it 26 percent of the vote in 1951 (even though
its membership of 220,000 had dropped by 60 percent since
December 1947), labor unions like the CGT, and other
mass organizations sought to standardize values, rules, and
regulations so as to project the impression of a monolithic
whole. French communism displayed an essentially united
front, especially when facing its adversaries, but it was also
internally diverse due to its presence in the furthest reaches
of society and to the multiple ways its adherents defined and
practiced communism.

Its powerful bond with the USSR and its *Vojd* (leader)

for nearly a quarter century distinguished the PCF from other French political parties. This bond was forged at the outset of the party's creation. France was politically, ideologically, and geo-strategically crucial for Moscow. The land of the Great Revolution of 1789 and the 1871 Paris Commune, two important events in Bolshevik mythology, France also figured as a major colonial and global power, and then after World War II, a significant force within Europe. In addition, following Hitler's destruction of the German Communist Party in 1933, the PCF stood as the most important such party in the West.

For good reason, then, the Soviets focused special attention on the French party during the interwar period, dispatching special Comintern envoys, including the famous Czech Communist Eugen Fried, who reorganized the party in disarray. These envoys forged and financed the PCF apparatus, selecting and training its leaders and cadres and eliminating outright opponents and the halfhearted rank and file. Although it largely functioned to serve Soviet interests, the PCF did leave some latitude to French party leaders. The USSR would continue to weigh heavily in the PCF's strategy, even into the 1960s and beyond, when the French party was gaining more autonomy. There were only two serious disagreements with the Soviet Communist Party, which stirred some internal controversy: in 1956, when PCF leader Maurice Thorez opposed the de-Stalinization policy initiated by the Khrushchev report presented at the Twentieth Soviet Party Congress, and in 1968, with the Soviet invasion of Czechoslovakia.

The unwavering loyalty of most PCF leaders and cadres, the overwhelming majority of whom came from rural and working-class backgrounds, reflects in part the multifaceted debt they felt they owed the USSR: an education, a culture, a profession, a status, material and symbolic advantages within the communist world. But let us not underestimate how strongly the Soviet Union acted on the world's imagination, among militants and fellow travelers alike. Throughout its history, the USSR projected a positive image with an ever-changing and wide-ranging set of traits, which formed a mythology that remained effective until the irreparable split caused by de-Stalinization in the mid-1950s. This mythology, first and foremost, was of the USSR as the land of revolution and the new man, the so-called dictatorship of the proletariat, the workingman's paradise, the utopian promise of universal brotherhood, and the alternative to soulless capitalism. As of the 1930s, it held itself up as the model of democracy, the vanguard of anti-Fascist and anti-Nazi struggles, dazzlingly illustrated by Red Army victories at Stalingrad and elsewhere. The USSR also claimed to exemplify rational economic organization by virtue of its planned economy, capable of outstanding industrial and agricultural performance; of its excellence in science and technology; and of its harmonious, egalitarian society, with guaranteed health and education. Finally, the USSR extolled its role as peacekeeper and supporter of Third World struggles against colonization and oppression.

These themes were relayed to party militants, voters, and more broadly French public opinion by the PCF and subsidiary organizations such as the Friends of the Soviet Union, which became France–USSR in 1945. But the propaganda was not one-size-fits-all. While the messaging aimed at workers praised the Soviet Union as a kind of workers' paradise, it refrained from mentioning collectivization to farmers.

Likewise, reception and assimilation of this propaganda could vary considerably. Party leaders might embrace it out of deep conviction, or else out of self-interest, imagining that one day, like their Soviet counterparts, they could occupy governmental positions of power. The wide-ranging reasons for the French communist intellectuals' infatuation for the USSR are well known, for the latter have written profusely on the subject. There was a fascination for regenerative violence, a yearning for a radical break, a quest for a form of secular humanism, a quasi-religious need to believe in something, the call to brotherhood, and the appeal of this rationalist, scientific way of thinking. Not to mention that the USSR and its allies could prove highly generous when it came to material favors, symbolic rewards, and flattery. It is more difficult, however, to ascertain the draw for regular working-class communists. In most cases, their party adherence could be explained by their own living conditions, their situation at the workplace or place of residence, or their degree of engagement in collective struggles. The USSR was perhaps a source of hope, a dream, but also a rhetorical weapon to use against the boss, a way of differentiating oneself from socialists. In other words, this adherence constituted one component among others of their identity, albeit not the fundamental motive for their commitment. Still, the French communists' love for the USSR did set them apart from their fellow countrymen, as evidenced by a number of surveys conducted during the 1950s, in which the USSR was shown to be broadly unpopular in France.

There is a French specificity to this story. However indifferent or even hostile many people were toward communism as an ideology, this feeling was tempered by a sense of respect and empathy toward the USSR. The Soviet Union impressed them as an impressive experiment in economic and industrial modernization, lauded by numerous experts and educators. The USSR also gave expression to eternal Mother Russia. Some were faithful to the Soviet ally who had fought Hitler's Germany and the Fascists; others drew from a knee-jerk anti-Americanism; and yet others felt, consciously or not, deep historical and political connections between the French and Bolshevik revolutions, both of which rested on a strong state as a decisive force of change.

Be that as it may, from the 1970s onward, French public opinion turned further against the Soviet Union. French communist sympathy for the USSR also abated somewhat, except among the leading cadres. Disappointment gave way to disenchantment, and contributed, along with other factors, to the gradual erosion of its influence and to its political decline, which accelerated sharply with the rise of the French Socialist Party in 1981.

Marc Lazar

REFERENCES

Bulaitis, John. *Maurice Thorez: A Biography*. New York: I.B. Tauris, 2018.

Courtois, Stéphane, and Marc Lazar. *Histoire du Parti communiste français*. Paris: Presses universitaires de France, 2000.

Goulemot, Jean-Marie. *Pour l'amour de Staline: La face oubliée du communisme français*. Paris: CNRS Éditions, 2009.

Lazar, Marc. "The French Communist Party." In *The Socialist Camp and World Power 1941–1960s*. Vol. 2 of *The Cambridge History of Communism*, edited by Norman Naimark, Silvio Pons, and Sophie Quinn-Judge, 619–41. Cambridge: Cambridge University Press, 2017.

———. *Le Communisme, une passion française*. Paris: Perrin Tempus, 2005.

Martelli, Roger. *L'Empreinte communiste: PCF et société française (1920–2010)*. Paris: Éditions sociales, 2010.

Montebello, Fabrice. "Joseph Staline et Humphrey Bogart: l'hommage des ouvriers. Essai sur la construction sociale de la figure du 'héros' en milieu ouvrier." *Politix* 6, no. 24 (1993): 115–133.

RELATED ARTICLES

1051, 1789, 1907, 1936, 1968, 1989

1954

Toward a New Humanitarianism

January 1954: homeless people were freezing to death in the streets of France. In February, Abbé Pierre made a radio broadcast calling people to help. Within days, the country banded together in support of the homeless. As the movement gained international traction, Abbé Pierre became a media icon and a prophet for a new form of political activism.

In 1953–1954, as France grappled with an unprecedented housing crisis — the culmination of wartime destruction, the baby boom, and a rural exodus — the country was seized by a freezing winter. Temperatures dropped to five degrees Fahrenheit in Paris and minus twenty-two degrees in Alsace. Thousands of homeless people, whether single or married, searched desperately for impromptu lodgings. Shocked by these bleak conditions, a priest and former deputy of France's Popular Republican Movement, Henri Grouès, filed an amendment proposal to build emergency housing. This former monk, who had founded a small charity organization called Emmaus in 1949, is better known by his Resistance alias, Abbé Pierre. A decision on his proposal was indefinitely postponed by the National Assembly in early January 1954. That same night, an infant froze to death in one of the Emmaus housing projects. Calling for political action, Abbé Pierre published an open letter to the minister of reconstruction and housing on the front page of *Le Figaro*.

His missive fell on deaf ears. And so he spent the month of January raising awareness among journalists, launching a donation campaign, and handing out soup, coffee, bread, and blankets at nightfall. On January 31, thanks to the support of Georges Verpraet, a journalist friend of his, Abbé Pierre opened the first Emergency Committee to Help the Homeless, together with a Fraternal Temporary Relief Center, in Courbevoie (outside Paris). The following morning, news came of the death by hypothermia, outside of the Châtelet Theater in Paris, of a sixty-six-year-old woman who had been evicted for missing rent payments. That same night, eight adults and three infants died of cold in France. In response, Verpraet invited Abbé Pierre to cowrite a text that the two of them would read on Radio Luxembourg.

"My friends, the time has come to help!" The priest's spontaneous and poignant call for assistance was, in the words of French sociologist Luc Boltanksi, not a "rebuke" but an appeal to "pity." Abbé Pierre sought to revive "France's collective soul" and rally his fellow countrymen to act and donate "blankets, tents, and gas stoves." The response was immediate. Phone operators were overwhelmed. Hundreds of "fraternal relief centers" were created across France; subway stations and the Orsay train station were requisitioned. On February 4, the French Parliament voted to fund a 10-billion-franc program to build emergency housing. This "charity uprising" raised 1 billion francs (22 million euros today) and launched a movement that transcended religious and political differences.

At the time, Emmaus was a small organization made up of Parisian builders and ragmen. In just a few days, it gained national prominence and Abbé Pierre became a media icon. He certainly looked the part. As the critic Roland Barthes famously put it, "his face shows all the signs of an apostle: his caring gaze, Franciscan hairdo, missionary beard, fur-lined jacket, and pilgrim's cane. He ticks off all the requirements of a modern legend." His activism reached beyond France: *L'Osservatore Romano*, the Vatican's newspaper, sang his praises, and he became a sought-after celebrity, with appearances in London, Brussels, Tournai, Zurich, Geneva, Fribourg, and Lausanne. In 1955, he met President Eisenhower in the United States, was invited to Canada by the cardinal of Montreal, and received a call from the future king of Morocco to help with the slums. He spoke at the Katholikentag festival in Cologne before an audience of 800,000; in 1957, he traveled to Holland and Portugal; in 1958, to Austria, Belgium, and Scandinavia; in 1959 to India, where he met Vinoba Bhave, Jawaharlal Nehru, Indira Gandhi, and Mother Teresa. He was then hosted by the president of Lebanon, before flying off on a tour of South America — where he mingled with Dom Hélder Câmara and Josué de Castro, then chairman of the Food and Agriculture Organization of the United Nations. In 1960, he visited Nobel Peace Prize winner Albert Schweitzer in Gabon.

In most of these places, Abbé Pierre left behind disciples who would grow into a vast network, known since 1969 as Emmaus International. He also attracted many young foreigners who, after a stay in France, would go on to establish groups in their home countries. The Emmaus experiment in the winter of 1954 also gave birth to ATD Fourth World, an organization founded in Noisy-le-Grand, a shantytown outside Paris where homeless people were sent that infamous winter.

This sequence of events, often repeated since then, marks an important stage in the broader history of national and international humanitarianism.

National chapters of the Red Cross, the International Committee of the Red Cross (ICRC), and American evangelical organizations had organized massive charity campaigns since the mid-nineteenth century. In 1876–1878, for instance, Florence Nightingale, a network of missionaries, and the press rallied to raise 700,000 pounds sterling for famine relief efforts in India. In the interwar period, the Near East Relief, an American Protestant NGO, succeeded in raising more than $100 million ($1.3 billion today) for victims of the Armenian genocide. International charity campaigns for famine victims in Russia and Spanish refugees during the Spanish Civil War were similarly immense.

In France, Secours Catholique had recently launched more modest campaigns during Lent to fight disease (1947), to help infants (1948), "the elderly and those with hidden burdens" (1949), and suffering children (1950–1951), and then, with the famous actor Bourvil, to provide housing (1952–1954). The organization also invited Christians to participate in one-time humanitarian response campaigns — for disaster victims in Avignon (1951), Agen and Montauban (1952), Holland and Cephalonia (1953). The 1954 charity effort, however, was different for three reasons. First, mass media (the radio) expanded the scale and responsiveness of outreach efforts; second, a prophet for solidarity came of age; and third, all this generated a new form of political activism.

The charitable excitement created by the "Winter of '54" died down as the housing crisis faded and the economy picked up during France's Thirty Glorious Years. Yet if we look closely at this event, it becomes clear that people were still signing on to such campaigns. The growing internationalism of French charity organizations from the 1950s on further increased their renown and financial strength. There was a growing awareness that poverty was a more pressing issue in the southern than in the northern hemisphere. Many factors contributed to this understanding: improved quality of life in France, the development of international organizations, decolonization, and also the Christian desire to keep the Third World out of the hands of communists. Humanitarian *development* accordingly became a hallmark of the 1955–1980 era. The French Catholic think tank Economie et Humanisme refocused its mission to help the Third World, Emmaus founded the Institute of Research and Action against Misery in the World, the Vatican created the Catholic Committee against Hunger and for Development in 1961, Secours Catholique launched its "micro projects," dedicated to local development, and the founder of the Little Brothers of the Poor established Frères des Hommes in 1966.

This humanitarian movement took on a new, media-friendly form in the late 1960s: charity without borders. The Red Cross's traditional emergency aid missions were joined by increasingly political aid campaigns and cyclical, event-based campaigns, for instance in Biafra, where a secessionist province of Nigeria was threatened by genocide

(1967–1971). Televised images coming out of that crisis, together with bold interventionist rhetoric (as opposed to the neutrality and silence of the Red Cross), forged a new figure in humanitarian aid: Bernard Kouchner, a French doctor and politician. After Biafra, Kouchner went on to create Doctors Without Borders in 1971. Ten years later, a splinter organization, Doctors of the World, was formed. The new ethical stance altered the entire humanitarian field, in its national as well as global manifestations.

The social and economic crisis of the 1980s, with its rising unemployment and growing proportion of insecure jobs (part-time, unskilled, lacking job security, benefits, or possibilities for advancement), drew renewed attention to poverty in domestic France. Abbé Pierre again took up his crusade for the "new poor" and the "homeless," gaining an enduring reputation as "France's most beloved personality." He began with stopgap measures: emergency housing, food and clothing distribution, as well as the creation in 1984 of food banks by Secours Catholique, Emmaus, Entraide Protestante, the Salvation Army, and the Restaurants du Coeur, an organization set up in 1985 by the famous French comic Coluche.

The persistence of this crisis led to a search for more preventive and curative solutions, and also for more effective political positions. Beginning in 1987, Abbé Pierre took up the cause of Alter-globalization, a movement for a kind of "third way" that encouraged international cooperation without the pitfalls of free trade. From 1990–1994, he worked to support the homeless and the undocumented who were being helped by the association Droit au Logement (Right to Housing). Since the mid-1990s, media-savvy charity organizations have exploited these multiple registers, navigating between avoidance of politics (witness the Secours Populaire's "holiday campaign," which each year subsidizes trips for tens of thousands of people), subversiveness (as when Les Enfants de Don Quichotte spoke out for the homeless in 2006 by occupying the banks of the Canal Saint-Martin with tents), science (the Abbé Pierre Foundation's annual reports on poor housing conditions since 1996), and institutional participation in decision-making centers.

Yet despite these permutations, such French charity organizations have remained faithful to the spirit of aid that grew out of the winter of 1954, implicitly adhering to a dictum from Secours Catholique: "May charity today [become] policy tomorrow."

Axelle Brodiez-Dolino

REFERENCES

Barthes, Roland. "Iconography of Abbé Pierre." In *Mythologies*, translated by Annette Lavers, 47–49. New York: Farrar, Straus & Giroux, 1972 [1957].

Boltanski, Luc. *Distant Suffering: Morality, Media and Politics*. Translated by Graham D. Burchell. Cambridge: Cambridge University Press, 1999.

Brodiez-Dolino, Axelle. "1er février 1954: L'appel de l'abbé Pierre." *Historia* 794 (February 2013): 26–30.

———. *Emmaüs and the Abbé Pierre: An Alternative Model of Enterprise, Charity and Society*. Translated by Alexandra Harwood. Paris: Presses de Sciences Po, 2013.

Fehrenbach, Heide, and Davide Rodogno, eds. *Humanitarian Photography: A History*. Cambridge: Cambridge University Press, 2015.

RELATED ARTICLES

177, 1790, 1825, 1920

1958

Algiers and the Collapse of the Fourth Republic

On May 13, 1958, the day the newly appointed prime minister was to appear before the French National Assembly, a coup d'état was staged in Algiers, precipitating the fall of the Fourth Republic. While the authors of the coup were calling upon General de Gaulle to guarantee that Algeria would remain French, Algerian independence fighters were taking their war for independence to the international arena.

By 1958, the war for Algerian independence, sparked four years earlier by the National Liberation Front (FLN), was not alone in exposing the inadequacy of the Fourth Republic. The constitution itself carried the seeds of its own demise: it forced the parties into circumstantial alliances based purely on electoral calculations aimed at eking out the majority required to form a government, however fragile. Once out in the open, disagreements among allies triggered the downfall of one short-lived ministerial team after another. Furthermore, these postwar boom years were accompanied by high inflation. Thus, the government of Félix Gaillard, whose overthrow would eventually bring down the regime, spent its electoral capital on constitutional reform and financial matters. Still, the war for Algerian independence was central to the 1958 crisis and the unfolding of its key event: May 13. As a symbol of regime change, the date is powerfully evocative in France.

The outbreak of the Algerian war in 1954 was a response to two major developments: first, that the French authorities had proven incapable of meeting the demands of Algerians, who had long denounced the blatant inequalities of colonial society; and second, a growing urge to initiate an armed struggle that had been building ever since the 1945 massacres of Algerians by imperial troops and settlers at Sétif. It was increasingly apparent that any attempt at popular mobilization would be met with fierce repression.

By 1958, the conflict had become international. Félix Gaillard would confront this reality after the February 8 bombing of the Tunisian village of Sakiet Sidi Youssef by French warplanes that were pursuing Algerian enemy combatants who had slipped over the border. Casualties were heavy, with dozens dead and some one hundred wounded. Habib Bourguiba, president of the newly independent Tunisian republic, whose relations with France were still strained, fired back with the blockade of a French military base in the Tunisian coastal town of Bizerte, the closure of consular offices, and a call for the withdrawal of all French troops still stationed in the ex-protectorate. More importantly, he appealed to the United Nations. Fearing that hostilities might spread across the Maghreb, the British offered to broker a settlement to the conflict, bringing their "good offices" to bear. However, on the grounds that "Algeria is France," any kind of foreign intervention had always been denounced by the French as unwelcome meddling in their domestic affairs.

Since the outset of the war, international entanglements were hindering the French cause. In 1956 in particular, the Suez debacle and the hijacking by the French Secret Service of a Moroccan plane transporting the leaders of the FLN — denounced as a veritable act of "air piracy" — put France in a tight spot. Meanwhile, the FLN and the independence cause were pleading their legitimacy to a world audience. The FLN turned this appeal into a workable strategy, from the delegation they sent to the Bandung Conference in April 1955 to the high-profile declaration of the young Senator John F. Kennedy, who, on July 2, 1957, took a position in favor of "shaping a course toward political independence for Algeria." Arab and Asian nations made sure that the Algerian question was a regular item on the United Nations agenda, taken up for debate by the General Assembly. Having failed to convince enough parliamentarians that France should maintain sovereignty over its domain, Félix Gaillard was unseated on April 15, 1958, a few days after he met with Harold Beeley of the British Foreign Office and Robert Murphy of the US State Department.

Yet again, the Fourth Republic awaited a new government. President René Coty sought counsel, trawling the political parties and their leaders for a coalition able to cobble together a majority for the umpteenth prime minister. On May 9, he believed he had found a solution in the shape of centrist politician Pierre Pflimlin. The May 10 edition of *Le Monde* summed up the potential prime minister's positions: "Intensify if necessary the military effort where required; seize every opportunity to engage in talks; do not let the war spread to the rest of North Africa." The second option raised serious issues for the partisans of French Algeria, entrenched as they were in their defense of the status quo. And like every other time Paris seemed to show signs of weakness, Algiers rumbled: 1958 was hardly a first.

While the history of the city's popular mobilization has yet to be written, historians have drawn attention to one important moment: the winter of 1955–1956, and in particular what came to be known as "the day of the tomatoes," February 6, 1956. That day, a crowd reportedly lobbed tomatoes at Prime Minister Guy Mollet, who had come to Algiers to induct new resident minister General

Georges Catroux, but the settlers of Algiers were having none of it. As it happened, this day marked the culmination of a series of street protests begun three months earlier, expressing anger over a sequence of recent events: FLN cofounder Mostefa Ben Boulaïd's escape from prison; the lifting of the state of emergency brought about when the National Assembly was dissolved; the Republican Front's victory in the legislative elections, spearheaded by Guy Mollet and his vow to bring peace to Algeria; and the removal of Jacques Soustelle, the governor of Algeria, whom settlers worshiped for his enduring support for a French Algeria.

Veterans' organizations emerged as the most effective leverage for group action. By choosing the Algiers war memorial as their rallying point, they reminded the authorities of their duty toward all those who, in the not so distant past, had proven their loyalty by shedding blood for the homeland. The monument was enshrined at the center of a vast graded esplanade that rose from the port all the way up to the Place du Forum, the location of the governor general's offices. Demonstrating in front of the war memorial was a symbol unto itself, but the location was also strategic, a few hundred meters below the center of power.

On May 13, 1958, the day on which newly appointed Pierre Pflimlin was supposed to appear before the National Assembly, general strike notwithstanding, a wreath-laying ceremony was scheduled at the war memorial, with veterans in attendance. This was an obvious reprise of the 1955–1956 precedent, even though new actors were involved this time around: the Gaullist faithful, metropolitan activists, and senior military commanders. This event, too, must be situated in its international context, for another crisis was unfolding simultaneously with France's regime debacle, and its stakes involved nothing less than the application of international wartime law on behalf of Algerian prisoners. On May 9, the day René Coty turned matters over to Pflimlin, the FLN broke the news that it had executed three French soldiers it had been detaining. It was in their honor that the wreath was to be laid at the Algiers war memorial. The FLN announcement was a boon for those seeking to bring down the Fourth Republic, since it stoked popular fury in Algiers. The FLN was operating on a different logic, however. Even though the announcement appears to have been timed to coincide with the regime crisis, the actual execution is believed to have taken place on April 30 (it is still impossible to establish the exact date and circumstances of the act).

At any rate, the FLN communiqué presented the executions as a rejoinder to the statement made on April 24 by Taleb Abderrahmane, a twenty-six-year-old chemist, designer of the "Battle of Algiers" bombs that had bloodied the city the previous year and had led to the deployment of French paratroopers in the city, the widespread use of torture, and a rash of summary executions. Abderrahmane was sentenced to death three times by the military tribunal of Algiers. In a statement that sent shock waves through the media, he said he was ready to make the "sublime sacrifice" that his execution would represent, just as his "already martyred brothers" had done before him: "Rest assured that the guillotine is for us what the cross represents in your churches." Taleb was no mere "militant," as is often written, if mentioned at all, in French history manuals, but rather, an important officer of the FLN in Algiers. This important detail is frequently overlooked in books that tend more often to start the May 13 narrative with the announcement of the execution of the three soldiers.

In essence, the FLN pursued its legitimization strategy by internationalizing the conflict and arguing for equal treatment for Algerian and French prisoners. Its communiqué asserted that the three soldiers had been executed subsequent to a "sentence" handed down by a "special tribunal of the National Liberation Army" for the crimes of "torture, rape, and assassination." I quote an FLN leader: "We shall not respect the law of war unless our adversary does the same. Let it be known to the families of French soldiers in Algeria. It is up to them to demand that the massacre of Algerian combat prisoners cease." Responding to this line of argument proved complicated for the French. *France-Soir*, for instance, dared to posit in its May 12 edition that, according to international conventions, "a detaining power may not convict prisoners of common-law crimes without informing the Red Cross beforehand and granting it permission to ensure the fairness of the trial." Once the principle of international oversight was admitted, however, was it possible to argue that it should apply to one belligerent but not the other? How could one insist that the Algerians comply when France refused to do so?

The announcement of the execution of the three soldiers proved ill-timed for the FLN. The regime crisis swamped its attempt to open the debate on reciprocity of prisoner treatment and the recognition of international law by both parties. The communiqué primarily had the effect of galvanizing the Algiers crowds which, on May 13, 1958, bristling at the choice of Pierre Pflimlin and outraged by the execution of three young Frenchmen, were in a fiercely oppositional mood. The leaders of the demonstration had no trouble steering it up to the General Government offices, which they took by storm. A Public Safety Committee, bringing together military officials, activists, and Gaullists, appealed to de Gaulle, who made his return to power conditional upon a change of regime.

Thus, René Coty appointed de Gaulle prime minister, giving him the green light to start drafting a new Constitution, submitted by referendum to the French people on September 28, 1958, and ratified on January 1, 1959. The Fifth Republic was born. The impact of this major break has made May 13 a powerful point of entry into the political history of the French Army, Gaullism, republican institutions, and national rifts. Thus was set in stone, and for a while to come, a national vision — albeit truncated — of May 13, erasing the FLN's strategy of appealing to international auspices.

Sylvie Thénault

REFERENCES

Branche, Raphaëlle. *Prisonniers du FLN*. Paris: Payot, 2014.

Byrne, Jeffrey James. *Mecca of Revolution: Algeria, Decolonization, and the Third World Order*. New York: Oxford University Press, 2016.

MacDougall, James. *A History of Algeria*. Cambridge: Cambridge University Press, 2017.

Meynier, Gilbert. *Histoire intérieure du FLN (1954–1962)*. Paris: Fayard, 2002.

Thénault, Sylvie. *Histoire de la guerre d'indépendance algérienne*. Paris: Champs Flammarion, 2012.

———. *Une drôle de justice: Les magistrats dans la guerre d'Algérie*. Paris: La Découverte, 2001.

Zancarini-Fournel, Michelle, and Christian Delacroix. *La France du temps présent (1945–2005)*. Paris: Belin, 2014.

RELATED ARTICLES
1683, 1848, 1863, 1940, 1961

1960

The End of the Federalist Dream and the Invention of
Françafrique

The year west and central African countries gained their independence was also the year of missed opportunities for political alternatives. These failures set the stage for a new policy of French influence in the country's former colonial empire.

The experiment was short-lived, if not dead on arrival: on June 20, 1960, Senegal and French Sudan merged to accede to independence under the name Fédération du Mali. This federation was seen to inaugurate an authentic alternative political project in West Africa. Besides harkening back to the storied Mali Empire, it represented the end product of a battle waged by Senegalese politician Mamadou Dia and Sudanese activist Modibo Keïta to radically reform West African geopolitics. This Malian marriage would not survive the summer of 1960, however. By the end of a political crisis that divided Senegalese and Sudanese political officials over four August days, the divorce was final. Senegal unilaterally proclaimed its independence on September 5, and Dia stepped aside in favor of Léopold Sédar Senghor, who became head of the new Senegalese state. Sudan, which lost the most in this failed union, declared independence on September 22 under the name of the Republic of Mali, the last vestige of that squandered union.

This failure sealed the balkanization of Francophone Africa; in other words, the colonies of French West Africa (AOF) and French Equatorial Africa (AEF) declared independence within the borders of their former colonial divisions rather than as larger federated territories. Félix Houphouët-Boigny, president of the Ivory Coast, and Jacques Foccart, President de Gaulle's mastermind on African affairs, could not have been more satisfied.

The Federation of Mali emerged after fifteen years of political misunderstandings between France and Africa. With the advent of the Fourth Republic in 1946, the French Union was created in the hopes of reforming the colonial empire. In reality, much of the empire had already undergone major transformations, leaving Africa as the heart of the new French Union: a specific ministry was now devoted to Indochina, protectorates depended on the Ministry of Foreign Affairs, four former colonies — Martinique, Guadeloupe, Guiana, and Réunion — were now full-fledged departments, and the three departments that made up Algeria were overseen by the Ministry of the Interior. But what was the Union's purpose? To settle the issue of civic equality for their "nationals," or to provide more effective window dressing for the colonial regime? It was now four decades since Blaise Diagne, the first African deputy in the French Chamber of Deputies, had invoked a 1916 law to force the colonial republic to own up to its contradictions by granting French citizenship to the residents of Senegal's four communes (Dakar, Saint-Louis, Rufisque, and Gorée) as a compensatory measure for the African blood shed on the battlefields of World War I. This kind of concession had become a legitimate prospect for colonial Africa, which was, after all, the cradle of Free France during World War II, having provided manpower and economic resources as early as 1940.

In this context, the French Union's inaugural law in 1946 banning the use of bonded labor raised hopes for many Africans. But over the following decade, despite efforts by African political elites, colonial reform did not come about. A boundary continued to separate citizens of the Union from French citizens, or in African terms, the colonized from the colonizers. Civic segregation was established with the creation of a double electoral college in which whites were overrepresented and thus wielded all political clout. It took the 1956 Reform Act, finally enforced a full year later, for a semblance of equality to emerge with the dismantling of the double college system. African governing councils were now elected on the basis of universal suffrage and obtained greater authority, even if the colonial governor of each territory still presided over them. The spirit of the laws that should have prevailed with the French Union was fulfilled after a ten-year delay.

These half-baked reforms were taking place during the race against time between anticolonial agitation and (in French eyes) a more controlled process of decolonization. Political and social protest had indeed been on the rise since 1945. By 1955, unbeknownst to the French public, France was carrying out acts of colonial repression that were turning into all-out war in southern Cameroon — Bassa and Bamileke country — against the Union of Cameroon Populations, a nationalist politico-military organization. This conflict was connected to the ongoing Algerian war, as witnessed by the shuttling of French military personnel trained in counterinsurgency techniques from one theater of operations to the other.

After Indochina and the Maghreb, Africa became, in the late 1950s, the third front in the political decolonization of the former French empire. With his return to power in 1958, Charles de Gaulle decided to speed up the time frame. In the Fifth Republic, the old French Union was replaced by the Franco-African Community, which was to function as a "vehicle from one historical era to another," in the words of de Gaulle himself. According to this vision, Africa was to be the international showcase of Gaullist decolonization and the cornerstone of national power in the midst of the Cold War. This was a paradoxical project, to say the least, since it endorsed decolonization while maintaining French influence in its "private preserve" in Africa. For the latter, de Gaulle turned to Jacques Foccart.

In Africa, the unfulfilled dream of the French Union made room for the renewed possibility of federation. According to this rationale, and based on the legacy of the 1956 Reform Act, African governments could initiate a process toward independence by taking steps laid out by the AOF (the Mali Federation) and the AEF (the Centrafrique project). New prospects were opening up as the possibility of a negotiated decolonization with France became more tangible.

The Ivory Coast's Houphouët-Boigny, who was hostile to a project driven by Mali and Senegal, had an excellent grasp of the positions and concerns of the Franco-African political class, with which he had become familiar since the end of World War II. On the French side, he was a savvy crossover with a foot in both the Fourth and Fifth Republics; a deputy at the National Assembly in Paris, he was promoted to several ministerial positions between 1956 and 1961. On the African side, he had since its inception in 1946 headed the African Democratic Rally (RDA), the most important Francophone African political organization, which had expanded its presence within both the AOF and the AEF. In 1946, he was one of the chief architects of the law abolishing bonded labor. Finally, he was Ivory Coast's strongman. Since the Reform Act went into force, he took the opportunistic path and pushed the RDA to take power through the ballot box.

Things came to a head in May 1958, with the political crisis over Algeria and de Gaulle's return to power. By July, a federal quarrel had broken out. During the drafting of the Fifth Republic's constitution, Houphouët-Boigny came out in favor of balkanization and a gradual process of transition to independence by stages, in opposition to proposals for immediate independence and/or the formation of larger federated arrangements. The high point of Gaullist propaganda was reached in August 1958 when de Gaulle toured Africa as the mythic "Brazzaville leader" of 1940 Free France and presented a stark choice: either join the new Franco-African Community as a quasi-autonomous republic or go down the path of immediate independence alone. But in the AOF, especially after the Guinean politician Ahmed Sékou Touré's memorable speech ("We prefer freedom in poverty to wealth in slavery") and widespread street demonstrations in Dakar, signs of protest were increasingly apparent.

Thus, the September 28, 1958, referendum addressed a precise political issue that, in Africa, differed slightly from the question presented to the French. The overwhelming victory of the "yes" vote in favor of the Community concealed what was in fact a heavily regulated electoral process. Foccart's intent was to play into the hands of Houphouët-Boigny. Behind the scenes, he was quick to lean on his loyalists, such as Don Jean Colombani, who was sent to Niger to neutralize the "no" campaign. In the end, only Guinea-Conakry would vote against. France broke ties with the Sékou Touré regime, which became the target of destabilization operations by the French secret service (SDECE) in 1959 and 1960. France could not afford to see Guinea, already turned toward the Eastern Bloc, become the backdoor to communist subversion in West Africa. The Cold War had already made its way to the banks of the Belgian Congo, at the gates of Brazzaville.

In this tense atmosphere, behind the Community's calm facade, a real showdown was underway inside the RDA between the Houphouët-Boigny clan and his adversaries. On the eve of the 1958 referendum, a consensus was taking shape around Sékou Touré and Modibo Keïta to call for immediate independence and the formation of a grand federation. Between 1958 and 1960, Houphouët-Boigny did whatever it took to seal his own West Africa policy and sideline his rivals inside the RDA, over which he wielded exclusive control. He first formed a security buffer around Ivory Coast by entering into an entente with Niger, Upper

Volta, and Dahomey, deterring them one by one from the federation project. By early 1960, there remained only Senegal (which had never bought into the RDA network) and Sudan, still pushing for the Mali Federation, which, by the time it declared its independence on June 20, 1960, was already politically exhausted.

Between 1958 and 1960, the RDA became the African backbone of French policy on the continent. Ivory Coast asserted itself as the cradle of this new geopolitical strategy, with Houphouët-Boigny and Foccart emerging as the genuine founders of *Françafrique*. Working behind the scenes, out of the limelight of officialdom, Foccart managed to secure independence for African countries on France's terms. In May 1960, the dismantling of a "communist plot" in Brazzaville enabled the abbot-president Fulbert Youlou, the RDA's man in the Congo, to consolidate his power. In the fall of 1960, the SDECE proceeded to physically eliminate the anticolonialist Cameroonian leader Félix Moumié by thallium poisoning. Thanks to secret agreements included in the 1960 decolonization agenda, a postcolonial pact was concluded in which France provided military protection in exchange for exclusive rights to certain raw materials.

In December 1960, it was the former colonies' turn to come to France's rescue. During the Algerian debate at the fifteenth session of the United Nations General Assembly, the founding act of this Franco-African diplomacy played

1157

out on the international stage. The African countries "friendly to France," newly elected to the UN just weeks before the opening of the session, voted, as instructed by Houphouët-Boigny, against the Kennedy plan for Algeria. They thereby safeguarded Gaullist sovereignty in the settlement of the Algeria crisis.

Jean-Pierre Bat

REFERENCES

Bat, Jean-Pierre. *La Fabrique des "barbouzes": Histoire des réseaux Foccart en Afrique*. Paris: Nouveau Monde, 2015.

Cooper, Frederick. *Citizenship Between Empire and Nation: Remaking France and French Africa, 1945–1960*. Princeton: Princeton University Press, 2015.

Gérard, Claude. *Les Pionniers de l'indépendance*. Paris: Inter-Continents, 1975.

Hecht, Gabrielle. *Uranium africain, une histoire globale*. Translated by Charlotte Nordmann. Paris: Le Seuil, 2016.

Mel, Frédéric Grah. *Félix Houphouët-Boigny: Biographie*. 3 vols. Paris: Karthala/CERAP, 2010 [2003].

RELATED ARTICLES

LEAVING THE
COLONIAL EMPIRE,
ENTERING EUROPE

How to sustain dreams of national grandeur after the loss of a colonial empire? Such was the question facing France at the outset of the sixties, following General de Gaulle's return to power amidst intense turmoil in 1958 and the swift approval, by referendum, of the Constitution that founded the Fifth Republic.

As Indochina, Morocco, and Tunisia secured independence (in 1954 and 1956), a "war" that dared not speak its name — the French euphemistically spoke of "events" — raged in Algeria between 1954 and 1962. The massive deployment of conscripts, the unrelenting struggle of the Algerian independence fighters (the National Liberation Front, or FLN), and the widespread use of torture by the French army set off a world-scale crisis that eventually led to the downfall of the Fourth Republic. Numerous intellectuals, including Frantz Fanon, championed Algeria as symbol of the new Third World vanguard. The atmosphere was highly charged in metropolitan France, with ever-present threats of a military coup and string of attacks by the OAS (Secret Army Organization), an armed right-wing group that sought to maintain French rule in Algeria. De Gaulle boldly opted for peace, signing the Évian Accords that on March 18, 1962, made Algeria independent. Decolonization soon reached all French colonies in Africa, and by the early 1960s little remained of France's once far-flung empire.

The imperial past was far from over, nonetheless.

Countless human, economic, cultural, and memorial ties would continue to bind the metropole to its former colonies. With the end of the Algerian war came a massive repatriation of some five hundred thousand pieds-noirs, a term designating European settlers and their descendants, many of whom had lived in Algeria over multiple generations. Likewise, the Harkis, Muslim soldiers who had chosen to serve France instead of the Algerian independence cause, were forced into exile by the new Algerian power holders, and housed in miserable conditions in southern French towns, abandoned and forgotten. The war was indeed over, but tens of thousands of Maghrebi workers continued to pour into France to take part in its economic modernization. And they were not alone: Spaniards and Portuguese flowed in as well, for both economic and political reasons, along with many French citizens from overseas territories in the Caribbean and elsewhere.

With its old legacy as a land of asylum, France remained a haven for victims of poverty and repression, exemplified during this period by the Chilean émigrés fleeing the Pinochet dictatorship after 1973, or the Vietnamese and Cambodian boat people in 1979. Humanitarian action gained new impetus in the 1970s with the creation of Doctors Without Borders, who came to world attention for their commitment to the civilian populations in Biafra. French hospitality stalled, however, once the economy began to slump. In 1974, the government imposed a temporary halt to labor-related immigration, allowing only family reunification. Two years earlier, a right-wing populist legislator who had fervently defended French Algeria, Jean-Marie Le Pen, founded the National Front. His openly xenophobic, far-right party experienced a meteoric rise in the 1980s and 1990s. Immigration, once considered a purely administrative matter, became a national obsession in French political debates.

Though bereft of its empire, France was not giving up on its quest for power at the international level. De Gaulle and his successors challenged the country to recover from this setback and reassert its sovereignty. Wedged between the two superpower blocs, France strived to make its voice heard in the UN Security Council and to escape American oversight within NATO (it withdrew from the integrated command in 1966). It also claimed a special role on the African continent, where, under foreign policy adviser Jacques Foccart, exponent of the notion of Françafrique, it maintained close but opaque and sometimes dubious ties to its former colonies through the mid-1970s.

France's development of nuclear weapons, tested in the Sahara in the early 1960s, was part of this move toward geopolitical and energy-related independence. This was an era of large-scale, state-funded projects such as the space program: the Astérix satellite, France's first and only the sixth in the world, was sent into orbit in 1965; the Ariane rocket was launched from Kourou in French Guiana in 1979. The development of a supersonic aircraft, the Concorde, and the creation, in partnership with other European countries, of the aircraft manufacturer Airbus fit this pattern of high-profile prestige projects.

Metropolitan France itself underwent major improvements, all part of the drive toward technological modernity that engineers, urban planners, and ambitious civil administrators deemed paramount. The proactive overhaul of France's coastal towns and the upgrading of ski resorts and transportation networks (highways and high-speed trains, or TGV) during the sixties and seventies turned France into one of the leading tourism destinations in the world. Likewise, promoting the country's rich culture and heritage became a top priority at the highest levels of government. Officials spoke of a French "cultural exception" (if not preeminence), as witnessed by New Wave cinema, the bold paradigm shifts of the nouveau roman, a literary genre that abandoned the conventions of traditional novels, and the prestige of major summer music and theater festivals, backed by generous subsidies from the Ministry of Culture and local governments by the 1980s.

France's longing for sovereignty did not come at the

expense of Europe. The country was one of the founding members of the European Economic Community, signed into being with the 1957 Treaty of Rome. Despite de Gaulle's early reluctance, France carried out its modernization within this vast economic and commercial framework in the seventies and eighties. Its agriculture was the first to benefit: the Common Agricultural Policy, introduced in 1962, fostered a production-driven model that for decades gave priority to mechanization, chemical inputs, and large-scale farming. Most significant was the rapprochement between France and West Germany, with the signing of the Élysée Treaty in 1963, and then the friendly relations that President Valéry Giscard d'Estaing maintained with Chancellor Helmut Schmidt in the 1970s; the same was true of François Mitterrand and Helmut Kohl throughout the eighties. The Franco-German "couple" became one of the engines of European construction, with senior French officials like Jacques Delors, president of the European Commission from 1985 to 1995, laying the groundwork for economic and monetary union.

When Socialist candidate Mitterrand allied with the Communists and won the 1981 presidential election, his country stood in stark contrast to Margaret Thatcher's Britain and Ronald Reagan's America, where neoliberal economic reforms were the order of the day. Unthinkable since the creation of the Fifth Republic, the return to power of Socialists revived the fears that had accompanied the Popular Front's election victory in 1936. Some imagined Soviet tanks rolling down the Champs-Élysées. Such unfounded fears aside, Mitterrand's agenda was indeed radical for a country that had been struggling to curb unemployment and inflation since the two oil crises of 1970s. His government abolished the death penalty, imposed a tax on the wealthy, nationalized banks and insurance companies, and provided a fifth week of paid vacation. But by 1983, upon the advice of Jacques Delors, Mitterrand opted for an "austerity turn": reforms were postponed to prevent further slipping of the franc or soaring deficits. By anchoring themselves to Europe, the Socialists had to jettison some electoral promises. Still, Mitterrand won reelection in 1988, a year before the splashy bicentenary celebrations of the French Revolution.

Several years before the economic and social crisis of the seventies and eighties had fully erupted, de Gaulle's dreams of national and technological grandeur were already being contested. By the 1960s, many voices were protesting the rampant conservatism of Gaullist France. An increasingly well-educated youth demographic was curious about the world and excited by the countercultures thriving on both sides of the Atlantic. People were denouncing the Vietnam War and discarding their illusions regarding the Soviet Union, which only fed their hunger for alternative models. They looked to Mao's China, to the Cuban experiment of Fidel Castro and Che Guevara, or to Salvador Allende's Chile. In a deceptively serene France, protests broke out in May 1968: barricades sprung up across Paris, Situationist slogans covered every available public wall space, and across France, workers went on strike to demand more autonomy and respect. Though short-lived, the revolt left an enduring mark on French society. Feminists were quick to rally for women's right to control their own bodies (leading to the legalization of abortion in 1975); ecologists contested the production and technology-driven model by occupying the Larzac plateau in 1973; and associations were created to defend the rights of various groups, including gays, prisoners, and political refugees.

This surge of new social movements paralleled the emergence of critical currents of thought that soon gained international notoriety. After Jean-Paul Sartre and Raymond Aron, American campuses avidly adopted the ideas of Michel Foucault, Jacques Derrida, and Pierre Bourdieu, a new generation of intellectuals who, despite the differences separating them, were soon labelled "French Theory."

With the economic downturn, mass unemployment, and a new ecological consciousness, globalization took on a more sinister aspect in France during the 1970s and 1980s.

Internationalist hopes were fading, Soviet and Communist Chinese models no longer seemed appealing, and liberal capitalism could see no further obstacle to its inevitable triumph.

1961

"The Wretched of the Earth" Mourn Frantz Fanon

Frantz Fanon passed away a few months short of Algerian
independence. Against a vision of popular liberation
limited to identity politics and nationalism, Fanon, the
philosopher and anti-colonial psychiatrist became, from
Fort-de-France to Tunis by way of Saint-Alban, the
vanguard spokesperson of the Third World cause before it
turned "postcolonial."

A name that resonates like a clarion call to revolution:
Fanon in Algiers, Fanon in Tunis, icon of a "Third
World" that is now outdated both in the lexicon and on
the world agenda. Of course, we all know *The Wretched of
the Earth*, his seminal analysis of the damaging effects of
colonialism, whose landmark preface by Jean-Paul Sartre
continues to resonate with its sweeping statements in a
style that rivals even the author's feverish prose. Fanon,
only thirty-six, was dying of sudden onset leukemia when
the book was published in December 1961 (by the young
publisher François Maspero) and immediately censored by

the Gaullist authorities, as were his previous publications. Since 1954, France had been mired in the so-called events in Algeria. The French authorities' euphemism for war was the inverse reflection of Fanon's own glorification of violence, which he deemed necessary, empowering, and redemptive. Given the recent terrorist attacks in Paris, this leaves a sour taste today.

These stock images of Fanon and his book tend to eclipse a rich personal trajectory and a prolific mind. We too often forget that before he became friend and ally to the leadership of Algeria's freedom fighters, Fanon was an Antilles native and also a Gaullist in his youth. But he was first of all a psychiatrist, at the forefront of parallel revolutions, both political and psychiatric. It was while working in an asylum in Blida, Algeria, and later in a Tunis facility, that he began to reflect upon what ethnologist Georges Balandier had dubbed "the colonial situation." Just as Michel Foucault was writing his dissertation on the history of madness (defended and published in 1961), Fanon was engaging with another "great confinement." Like the insane, the colonized were excluded from Western rationality.

Fanon was a French citizen from the country's West Indies territories. Born in 1925 in the heyday of France's colonial empire, he was a native of the island of Martinique, with parents in the civil service. His mother, a "mulatto," had Alsatian ancestors, though Fanon was a black

1170

"Afro-Caribbean," as he put it. As a person of mixed race, he was familiar with the pigmentary hierarchy that, for two centuries, had structured a complex Antillean society that, obsessed as it was with fine-tuned racial classification, had practically invented racial prejudice. Like all Antillean children, he was taken to pay homage to the abolitionist Victor Schœlcher at the monument in Fort-de-France. Schœlcher had been the glory of the French Caribbean since April 27, 1848, when he managed to wrest France's second decree abolishing slavery from the ephemeral Republican government. Schœlcher is also the name of the French lycée Fanon attended, the very lycée in which the Caribbean poet and essayist Aimé Césaire began teaching in 1939.

The mood in Martinique was tense during the Vichy years, notably after Admiral Georges Robert's fleet had disembarked, bringing gold from France's national reserve for safekeeping from the Nazis. Since June 1940, Martinique was under the authority of Pétain's Vichy regime. The prevailing racism of the local society had no trouble accommodating the values of a new regime that found in its far-flung empire (the Caribbean, Réunion, Indochina) support for its flagging legitimacy and a kind of laboratory for the policies it intended to implement back home.

The young Fanon chose the path of dissent. At eighteen, he left the island for neighboring Dominica (under British control at the time). He joined a battalion that landed first in Morocco, then Algeria, and finally in southern France, where it staged a northward ascent into Alsace. These young Martinicans who had come to deliver France from Hitler's armies suffered from the cold and the country's simmering racism, in contrast to the black American GIs, who were greeted with open arms by the French. At twenty, with his medals and war wounds, Fanon was a seasoned veteran of Free France — like General Raoul Salan, he would later joke. Fanon was a clear-eyed but brooding war hero. Back in the Antilles in 1945, he met up with his teacher Aimé Césaire, who, with the support of the Communist Party, had recently been elected mayor of Fort-de-France as well as deputy to the French National Assembly, elected in Martinique. But Fanon did not share the integrationist convictions of Césaire, a key drafter of the 1946 law that turned Martinique, like other former colonies, into a *département*, i.e., a component of the French administrative framework. The same thing had happened in Algeria in 1848.

So Fanon left his island home and headed for mainland France, where he enrolled in medical school in Lyon in 1946, eventually graduating with a degree in psychiatry. His professional turning point came with a crucial fifteen-month residency at the Saint-Alban hospital, a hotbed of therapeutic innovation, known for its "institutional psychotherapy," whereby medical staff and patients lived together in an experimental arrangement, a revolutionary idea for its time. The institution was headed by François Tosquelles, an anti-Franco émigré psychiatrist from Spain who, during the bleakest years of Francoism, had welcomed outlaws and refugees to his isolated clinic in the remote Lozère region. This experience in asylum psychiatry left a lasting mark on Fanon's emerging theory of colonial domination, as expressed in his *Black Skin, White Masks* (1952), a work whose form and content broke with the prevailing anticolonialism of the French left. Fanon's emphasis on wounded subjectivity rather than the more standard socio-economic considerations came to many as a shock. He also opposed the so-called dependency complex put forward by psychologist Octave Mannoni as the matrix of a colonized person's psychological make-up. Mannoni had already been singled out for criticism in another landmark text from the early 1950s, Aimé Césaire's *Discourse on Colonialism*. It is certainly no coincidence that two writers from the Antilles produced the groundbreaking texts that would provide the foundation of postcolonial studies several decades later.

In the meantime, Fanon's intellectual path coincided with the major currents of the day, whose philosophical language he made his own: existentialism and phenomenology. His articles appeared in the literary journals *Les Temps modernes* and *Esprit*, while the philosopher and Algerian independence activist Francis Jeanson prefaced his *Black Skin* before Jean-Paul Sartre did the same for *The Wretched of the Earth*. It was somewhat ironic that this theorist of the marginalized should find himself at the very heart of the Parisian left's intellectual elite, albeit not one of its active participants. Though he never fully embraced it, he was also associated with the social scene of the city's black intellectuals, a French version of the Black Atlantic that had been taking shape since 1947 around the literary journal *Présence africaine* and reached its zenith in 1956 with the first Congress of Black Writers and Artists at the Sorbonne. Attendees at this historic event included Malian ethnologist Amadou Hampâté Bâ, Richard Wright, James Baldwin, and of course, Césaire and Léopold Sédar Senghor, the elder statesmen of the Negritude movement. Compared to these latter two — renowned men of letters, poets of the French language, and political officials of the Fourth Republic — the Antillean psychiatrist was seeing things from a decidedly subversive perspective. By that date, it should be recalled, Fanon had already been in Algeria for three years, engaging in the field of operations that would lead to the outbreak of war with France. Not surprisingly then, he was shifting his reflections on colonialism into an environment of open conflict.

Like the Antilles, Algeria was France...and not France. In a French Algeria populated by nine million disenfranchised Muslims (until 1947), one million French citizens, and one hundred and thirty thousand Jews who were declared citizens by dint of the 1870 Crémieux Decree, citizenship status was fraught with problems. Likewise, universal voting rights were flouted by the two-tiered electoral system established in 1947. Colonial society was fragmented, and although there existed no official segregation policy, the separate-and-unequal status quo was there for all to see. Like Antilleans, the Algerian Jews who worked with Fanon at the psychiatric hospital in Blida were citizens, but second class. Fanon had before him a colonial society at its purest, reflected in microcosmic form at the Blida-Joinville psychiatric facility where he worked: two thousand patients and a corps of caregivers, in the heart of a political conflict, considered by the political authorities as a "nest of *fellaghas*," or freedom fighters.

In Blida, from 1953 to 1956, and again in Tunis, from 1957 to 1961, head physician Fanon endeavored to promote a "social therapy" that diverged from the prevailing penitentiary model of asylums. Isolated in a war-torn country, the insane asylum was a tragic sounding board for colonial Algeria's many fractures. By way of the asylum, Fanon actively engaged in the cause of Algerian independence. It was in his capacity as physician, in fact, that he was first approached by the Algerian Revolution, to address the psychiatric disorders of its fighters. Only later would he assume the role of theorist and quasi-official ambassador to Black Africa for the provisional government of the Republic of Algeria, which he backed from his post in Tunis from 1957 to 1961.

Though French intellectuals did protest the army's use of torture in Algeria — activist historian Pierre Vidal-Naquet was particularly vocal — this was not enough for Fanon. By opting to leave metropolitan France in 1957, he was hitching his fate to the Algerian struggle while clearly distancing himself from the National Liberation Front (FLN) leadership, whose Arab nationalism and underlying religiosity he underestimated. In his view, the Algerian cause would tip the balance in favor of independence for all of Africa (Fanon proved right in this regard). But in Accra in 1959 and Tunis in 1960, Fanon was already warning the first generation of African leaders, already speaking from the other side, in the name of the masses, alerting a still unified Third World against a corrupt bourgeoisie, the cult of heroes, and the clannish infighting that could lead the decolonization struggle astray. Since colonialism played on ethnic difference to divide and conquer, independent nations had to overcome this legacy, he proclaimed in his final book. With urgency in his voice as his own death loomed, Fanon now addressed the new "wretched of the earth," no longer the proletariat of industrialized countries, but the poor of newly independent nations. He was painting a dark and, alas, visionary picture of things to come. Fanon, the archangel of independence, made his exit a beat too early.

Fanon's readership was considerably increased thanks to the almost immediate translation into English of *Les damnés de la terre* (*The Wretched of the Earth*). By 1963, a first translator had made the text available to Black Power movements in the United States and to English-speaking Africa. Malcolm X and Eldridge Cleaver were reading him, as were Amílcar Cabral in Guinea and Kwame Nkrumah in Ghana. If the revolutionary violence of the 1960s laid claim to the Fanon oeuvre, his work became an even more central reference for the postcolonial studies that flourished in the eighties and nineties. These new readers, students and academics for the most part, found tools in his works for critiquing the bodies of knowledge imported from the colonial context. They were also introduced to the notions of ambivalence, hybridity, and negotiation that underpin this theoretical current. Fanon's thought extends well beyond his purported justification of violence, into a reconfiguration of intellectual concepts that had been "polluted" by colonialism. Purging as it does the time-worn methodologies and epistemologies surrounding the colonial question, his work represents a genuine paradigm shift, with incalculable ramifications.

A second English translation of *The Wretched of the Earth*, published in 2004 with a foreword by critic Homi

Bhabha, provides further proof of the book's perennial relevance for an ever-growing and diverse readership, among which a sizable contingent of postcolonial thinkers. From universities in Europe and India back to Africa (thanks to the Cameroonian intellectual Achille Mbembe), a new generation of thinkers is grappling with this mid-century revolutionary, this icon of the wars for independence, this visionary critic whose book is seen today as a touchstone of postcolonial critique. Fanon continues to inspire what the Caribbean writer Édouard Glissant called the One-World, *le Tout-Monde*.

Emmanuelle Loyer

REFERENCES

Césaire, Aimé. *Discourse on Colonialism*. Translated by Joan Pinkham. New York: Monthly Review Press, 2000.

Cherki, Alice. *Frantz Fanon: A Portrait*. Translated by Nadia Benabid. Ithaca, NY: Cornell University Press, 2006.

Fanon, Frantz. "Antillais et Africains." *Esprit* (February 1955): 261–69.

———. *Œuvres*. Paris: La Découverte, 2011.

———. *The Wretched of the Earth*. Translated by Richard Philcox. New York: Grove Atlantic, 2004.

Renault, Matthieu. *Frantz Fanon: De l'anticolonialisme à la critique postcoloniale*. Paris: Éditions Amsterdam, 2011.

RELATED ARTICLES

1863, 1940, 1949, 1968, 1984, 2008

1962

Jerusalem and the Twilight of French Algeria

The end of the French mandates in Syria and Lebanon
did not mean the end of the policy of French imperial
"protection" of Christian and Muslim holy places in
the Middle East. By a curious anomaly, until 1962 the
sovereignty that France claimed over Algeria allowed it to
control the Maghrebi (or Moroccan) Quarter of Jerusalem.

In the evening of February 12, 1962, a short meeting was
held in the office of France's minister for foreign affairs,
Maurice Couve de Murville. The topic under discussion was
the fate of an Algerian Muslim foundation, the Waqf Abu
Madyan, strategically located in a residential quarter that
commanded access to the Western Wall (known to Muslims
as al-Buraq Wall) in Jerusalem.

Outside the office, Paris was in an uproar. Four days
earlier, there had been a shocking police massacre of pro-
Algerian demonstrators at the Charonne Métro station in
Paris; the following day, half a million people were expected
to follow the victims' funeral procession to Père Lachaise

Cemetery. A month later, France and Algeria would sign the Évian Accords, providing for a cease-fire and sovereignty for Algeria. Still, the heads of French diplomacy took the time to settle the fate of the Maghrebi Quarter of Jerusalem, which for a few weeks longer would remain a tiny French colonial outpost in the Middle East, a sort of French mandate, or rather a Franco-Algerian mandate in Palestine, at the heart of the Holy City. The fact that such an outpost even existed is now largely forgotten.

On that gloomy evening in Paris, a decision was made in the central control tower of the French diplomatic service to forsake Jerusalem's Maghrebi Quarter and withdraw from legal proceedings then underway in Israel to seal the ownership of the Waqf's buildings. For many months, the government in Algiers had been complaining bitterly that France was continuing to support — albeit at arm's length — a "community that speaks of breaking every link with France and even of waging war on us." The Algerians of Jerusalem, for as long as they were called "French-Algerian Muslims," had for a while been utilized to support the French policy of protecting holy sites in the Middle East. They had now lost their usefulness as French Algeria faded into the past.

We must go back to Jerusalem in the 1950s to understand the origins of this important but little-known episode in the history of France's relations with Arabs and Muslims, and its influence on later French relations with Israel and the Jewish diaspora. Seen from Palestine, which was then part of Jordan, it was clear that France had uncontested rights over this small area of the Holy City: "Status of Jerusalem North African Colony: France Appoints Algerian to Head Local Inquiry" was the headline in the daily newspaper *Falastin* on August 12, 1955, followed by a long report on Hadj Lunis Mahfud, professor of Arabic at the Sétif College, then visiting Jerusalem, who had "come from Saudi Arabia after the hadj" to prepare a report on the management of the Franco-Algerian foundation. In effect, the purpose of the Waqf had always been to help, lodge, and generally take care of North African residents or visitors to the Holy City.

If France effectively found herself in the position of managing this highly strategic quarter of Jerusalem, it was because of the sovereignty that it exercised at the time over Algeria. The original Muslim religious foundation and its quarter were created at the end of the twelfth century by a descendant of an Andalusian mystic and Sufi master, Abu Madyan or Sidi Bou-Médiène, a comrade of Saladin when the city was wrested back from the Crusaders in 1187. In 1949, the French consul in Jerusalem seized an unexpected geopolitical opportunity that appeared just after the first Arab–Israeli war. At that time, the Waqf Abu Madyan found itself abruptly deprived of the income source on which it had always depended — a result of Israel's annexation of the village of Ein Karem, which was a few miles to the west of the walls of the Old City and thus within Israel's new, internationally recognized frontiers. France, then the sovereign power in Algeria, was legitimately entitled to take under its protective wing this portion of the holy site, which was on Jordanian territory, thereby gaining a solid diplomatic advantage within the covert struggle between Israel and Jordan over the demarcation line that had split Jerusalem in two.

The French consul, reporting back to his minister in Paris on July 6, 1949, wrote: "Can we hope to gain any profit from the Abu Madyan situation? The government must decide. Nevertheless, seen from my humble vantage point, it is entirely possible that our special position beside the Wailing Wall may turn out to be of great use." Copies of this letter were carefully forwarded to Algiers, Tunis, Rabat, and Amman...as well as to a mysterious "Professor Massignon."

Louis Massignon was effectively France's linchpin figure in the Middle East during the brief interval (1949 to 1962) in which France administered the Waqf Abu Madyan. Massignon was an eminent French scholar of Islam, a member of the Arab Language Academy in Cairo, a professor at the Collège de France, an ardent Christian, a fierce advocate of "Franco-Muslim friendship," and the founder of the Christian Committee for Franco-Islamic

Understanding as well as, in 1954, the Islamic–Christian Pilgrimage of the Seven Sleepers of Ephesus. He had also been an "honorable correspondent" of the French intelligence services in the Middle East, ever since the day he entered Jerusalem on December 11, 1917, with the British General Allenby. Over the years, in correspondence addressed to every level of the French diplomatic service, he had defended the "sacred mandate" of France vis-à-vis the North Africans of Jerusalem. This was in his view a decisive element of a foreign policy that needed to be not only "Arab," but also "Muslim"-oriented. Massignon firmly believed that this would prove to many Algerians tempted by national independence that France was actively taking care of their interests, not only inside but also outside Algerian territory.

In 1951, Massignon published a long article in the *Revue des études islamiques* about the Waqf Abu Madyan, distributing five hundred independently printed copies across France and the Arab world. Later, in May 1952, he went to Tlemcen in Algeria, the shrine of the saint Abu Madyan Bou-Médiène, where he founded a committee for the protection of the Waqf. Immediately afterward, on June 17, he maneuvered the Algerian assembly into passing a resolution to "safeguard the Algerian Waqfs in Palestine, for the benefit of North African Muslim pilgrims." Finally, on November 13, 1955, he solemnly announced on

Algerian radio — in Arabic — that France would finance the restoration of the Koranic School of the North African quarter in Jerusalem. Tunisia and Morocco, which both had citizens residing in Jerusalem under French protection, would provide financial support as well.

The crucial fact underlying all this — as Massignon told anyone who was willing to listen — was that the Waqf Abu Madyan physically commanded the gateway to the al-Aqsa Mosque and encompassed the very foundations of the Wailing Wall. Moreover, according to him, "the interest of Algerian Islam for this Waqf, which is viewed as a stepping stone on the way to a reestablishment of the qibla (direction of prayer) of Islam in Jerusalem, was its enduring association with the memory of the Saint of Tlemcen" (to whom, by the way, the Algerian revolutionary leader and later president Houari Boumédiène owed his nom de guerre). In 1954, a collection was organized at the gates of the Tlemcen Mosque, which raised 78,000 French francs; these funds were sent by Massignon himself to the French consul in Jerusalem, who redistributed them on the spot to needy North Africans.

Thus for some years the idea of a French "Algerian and Muslim" policy in the Holy Land produced concrete and resonant results.

The story came to an abrupt end in 1962, when — overnight — France lost all legitimate right in international law to intervene on behalf of any Algerian foundation anywhere. In reality, after a few years of fighting, the effects of the Algerian war of independence began to be felt even in Jerusalem. In the aftermath of the Suez crisis, in September 1956, tracts distributed by the Jordanian branch of the FLN (Algerian National Liberation Front) had denounced "the massacres perpetrated by France in North Africa and its barbarous campaign against the Algerian people," declaring that "North Africans have cured themselves of the deadly disease of French colonial protection." Louis Massignon nevertheless continued to champion the free distribution of bread to the North African poor of Jerusalem during the feast of Ramadan in 1957, "at the risk of breaking up the 'Franco-Muslim community' proclaimed by the president of the Council — and even at the risk of destroying my own France-Islam committee."

The deep current of history had turned against Massignon and Franco-Muslim friendship. In May 1961, a few weeks after the abortive coup d'état of France's generals in Algeria, the Algerian government began to harbor serious suspicions about the position the French were taking in Jerusalem to "counterbalance the influence of the FLN on the Algerian community in Palestine." This was confirmed in the fall of 1961. Although the French ministry of foreign affairs was still declaring in July that the abandonment of Jerusalem's North African quarter would cause "irreparable moral damage to French interests in the Arab world and especially in North Africa…to the point where we may be suspected of conniving with Israel," the massacre of Algerian demonstrators in Paris on the night of October 17, 1961, created an unbridgeable chasm between French and Algerian intentions. In February 1962, a few days after the Charonne massacre, France bowed to the inevitable and abandoned its defense of Algerian interests in Jerusalem. Despite the efforts of Jean-Marcel Jeanneney, the first high representative of France in Algeria, during the winter of 1962–1963, the new independent Algerian state renounced all responsibility for the Waqf and refused to involve itself in the defense of its citizens in Jerusalem. The Waqf Abu Madyan was henceforth bereft of all international legal protection.

Four years later, in June 1967, after the Six Day War and the Israeli annexation of Jerusalem, the marooned Maghrebi quarter was evacuated and bulldozed by the Israeli army. This opened up what is today the Western Wall esplanade, the most sacred of all Jewish religious sites.

Six months later, during a press conference on November 27, General de Gaulle famously described the Jews as "an elite people, self-confident and dominant." Perhaps this may be interpreted in the light of what happened to the Waqf Abu Madyan — especially if we read the full text of de Gaulle's remarks. "Now that the Algerian affair has been concluded," he went on to say, "we have readopted the same policy of friendship and cooperation toward the Arab peoples of the East that was maintained by France in earlier centuries." Referring to French relations with Israel, the general declared, somewhat strangely, that "we did not give our backing to Israel's establishment in a quarter of Jerusalem it had overrun."

De Gaulle's way of speaking was at once prodigiously powerful and deeply exasperating, for, in its convoluted manner, it managed to enunciate, without ever clearly expressing, a certain idea of France in the world.

Vincent Lemire

REFERENCES

Liskenne, Anne. *L'Algérie indépendante: L'ambassade de Jean-Marcel Jeanneney (juillet 1962–janvier 1963)*. Paris: Armand Colin, 2015.

Massignon, Louis. "Documents sur certains waqfs des lieux saints de l'Islam: Principalement sur le waqf Tamimi à Hébron et sur le waqf tlemcénien Abu Madyan à Jérusalem." *Revue des études islamiques* 19 (1951): 73–120.

Ryad, Umar. *The Hajj and Europe in the Age of Empire*. Leiden: Brill, 2016.

Segev, Tom. *1967: Israel, the War, and the Year that Transformed the Middle East*. New York: Metropolitan Books, 2007.

RELATED ARTICLES
1095, 1798, 1869, 1958, 2003

1962

Farming: A New Global Order

The Common Agricultural Policy of the budding
European Union responded to conflicting interests and
coincided with rapid de-ruralization in France. De Gaulle's
government used the CAP as a tool to modernize national
farming and consolidate farms. Paradoxically, in so doing,
it reduced the political power of traditional farming.

In 1962, *Encyclopédie française* published an article, "From
Peasants to Farmers," that redefined the agricultural elite.
The image it portrayed of this new class of farmers was
one of "free men" and "company executives." Indeed,
unlike salaried workers in "ant colonies," farmers displayed
expansionist energy and contributed to technical progress.
They were agents of modernity.

That same year, French farming began turning toward
new horizons. A new Common Agricultural Policy (CAP),
first proposed in 1950 by France and included in the Treaty
of Rome that instituted the European Economic Community
in 1957, broke down trade barriers when it was adopted by

the European Council on January 14, 1962. The Council's decision created a common market for grain, pork, eggs, poultry, fruits and vegetables, and wine. Meanwhile, the European Agricultural Guarantee Fund ensured farmers would receive a minimum price for goods and subsidized exports. The Fund covered any discrepancies between the guaranteed price and going world rates. With large surpluses in wine and grain, France in particular benefited from this scheme. That August, a French law rounded out an earlier 1960 agricultural law on farming cooperatives. This new law granted the Land-Use and Rural Settlement Corporation (SAFER) a preemptive right to acquire property for productive use; it also created a retirement annuity (IVD) for elderly farmers who ceded their land for use by younger people. The CAP and these French farming laws contributed to large-scale changes to French farming between 1946 and 1974. Agricultural production almost doubled during that time, while the workers in this industry fell from seven million to fewer than three million.

For the Third Republic, rural life had provided a cultural, social, and political bulwark against the "dangers" of the working class. Now urban planners, young farmers, industrialists, managers, and agronomy experts sought to integrate rural life into the nation's industrial economy. It was imperative for France to turn toward external markets, free up currency through exportation, and increase production as a means of feeding growing urban centers. The other priority was to free up rural labor, needed in industrial plants and the service industry. In this radical shift in farming practices, dubbed the "end of small farmers" by sociologist Henri Mendras, aspects of production that had once been overseen by farmers — energy, soil fertilizers, seeds, plant protection, husbandry, and livestock health — were now purchased from industry (tractors, gas, fertilizers, certified seeds and varieties, pesticides, and so forth). Land was no longer a question of tradition or a source of annuities. It had become a tool of commercial production.

The name often given to this period, "The Silent Revolution," is misleading. It obscures the loud tensions engendered by such change, including the July 1962 occupation of actor Jean Gabin's large property in Normandy by farmers protesting the difficulties they faced acquiring farmland, or the dumping of hundreds of tons of artichokes onto the streets of Saint-Pol-de-Léon in Brittany on June 23 to protest a collapse in prices. The first years of the Fifth Republic were marked by unrest in the agricultural sector, and especially within the main farming union, the FNSEA, which, led by former executives of the Vichy regime's Peasant Corporation, had gained significant influence over the Fourth Republic's parliamentary system in the 1950s. In 1957, it successfully lobbied for agricultural price indexation.

Yet the modernizing liberals and technocrats who came to power with de Gaulle in 1958 believed that agricultural price indexing slowed down industrial expansion. The administration of Michel Debré accordingly did away with it in December 1958. That provoked violent protests in 1959 and 1960. The working class having been tamed by consumption after the war, the rural class was now perceived as the main threat by French elites.

The laws of 1960 and 1962, like the 1962 CAP, were a means of accelerating the economic overhaul of French farming and avoiding a rural backlash. This transformation was made possible by a partnership between de Gaulle's government, which sought to modernize farming to install the Fifth Republic, and a movement of "young farmers," most of them trained by the JAC Movement (Jeunesse Agricole Catholique, or Catholic Rural Youth). They formed a union in 1957, which competed with the FNSEA. They were younger, less influenced by the General Association of Wheat Producers, more persuaded by entrepreneurial values, more enthused by the modernizing impulse of the postwar economic boom. These young farmer did not limit their demands to agricultural pricing, which in any case tended to benefit large-scale grain producers more than small- and mid-size farms. No, their requests were daring: annuities for the smallest farms and for old farmworkers who would leave the land to others, and production reforms that would yield mid-size family farms capable of selling their goods on the market.

Gaullist modernizers would coopt these "young farmers," forming alliances and bringing them into negotiations on the 1960 and 1962 laws. The aim was to dampen "agrarian" outcry against change by giving a voice to modern "young farmers." These modernizers also hoped to replace the Fourth Republic's "agro-parliamentarism" with co-management by the state and the agricultural sector. However, the death of millions of farms was not openly discussed in the new farming laws or in public speeches by the young farmers. Instead, partisans let the public believe that anyone who invested to make their farm commercially "viable" would grow and prosper. Only bit by bit would a minimum farm size become decisive for public aid.

Despite considerable conflict, this alliance did achieve its goals. Once the "young farmers" had taken control of the FNSEA in 1963, their vision of farming gained a hegemonic status within the agricultural world. This new FNSEA agreed to co-manage the agricultural sector with the Fifth Republic since, as its secretary general declared in 1963, "power... is now held...by technocrats." This partnership between farmers and the state led others to welcome profound economic and social changes: the disappearance of millions of farmers, mounting debt among those who became agricultural entrepreneurs, the declining political and symbolic influence of the agricultural world, which only generated 5 percent of France's gross domestic product in 1974 (compared with 17 percent in 1946). French society was now decidedly urban, and its economy was dominated by the industrial and service sectors.

Together, an economic shift (France became the world's second largest agro-food exporter in the 1970s), social change (the end of rural society and the inclusion of agriculture into the expansion of French capitalism), and electoral upheaval (the rural world became an electoral bastion for Gaullism in the late 1960s) formed the basis of the orderly revolution the Gaullists had in mind. The latter would have been impossible without the CAP. Beginning in 1962, European outlets absorbed French grain surpluses (which dated back to 1951, but at a higher global rate) and limited the wine crisis. Moreover, Europe's coffers financed an "agricultural welfare state," with the least profitable operations receiving aid and the most profitable farms obtaining subsidies. Without European intervention in pricing, the French model supporting small family farms could not have existed, and rural indignation could not have been overcome.

However, the shift in the French agricultural sector went beyond national and even European borders. It was also part of a global change in agricultural and food production, consumption, and accumulation. Between the

1870s and the 1930s, the backdrop for world farming can be characterized as an internationalization of markets tempered by border protections and colored by imperial relationships. Grains (and meats) were exported from North America and other European settlements toward Western Europe, which in turn exported labor, capital, and industrial goods back to the colonies. A new order emerged after 1945, and prevailed until the 1970s. Its main features were the following: agriculture as a major field of public intervention; increasing industrialization of agriculture and livestock in Europe; growth in food industries and services, overtaking domestic preparation of raw ingredients; and, finally, population growth across the globe, with Western Europe becoming a major wheat exporter thanks to CAP subsidies.

France's rise to dominance as a grain exporter was part of the new agricultural and food order that spread across the globe after 1945. It was also the result of greater flows of materials, energy, and natural resources around the world. French agricultural performance was therefore inextricably linked to production on a global scale, including the billion tons of Moroccan phosphates and Algerian and Middle Eastern gas (a third of French consumption in 1962). From 1959 to 1973, farms produced twice as much per acre, but consumed three times more fossil fuel. The nation's energy performance plummeted while gas emissions sky rocketed. Regrettably, the impact of this shift in agricultural practices on the planet has become increasingly apparent.

Far from constituting a purely French achievement, the "modernization" of the country's farming practices was therefore the product of new European farming policies, a shift in the world economy, and global environmental mutation.

Armel Campagne, Léna Humbert, and
Christoph Bonneuil

REFERENCES

Bruneteau, Bernard. *Les paysans dans l'État: Le gaullisme et le syndicalisme agricole sous la Cinquième République*. Paris: L'Harmattan, 1994.

Friedmann, Harriet. "From Colonialism to Green Capitalism: Social Movements and Emergence of Food Regimes." In *New Directions in the Sociology of Global Development*, edited by Frederick H. Buttel and Philip David McMichael, 229–67. Vol. 11 of *Research in Rural Sociology and Development*. Bingley, UK: Emerald, 2005.

Knudsen, Ann-Christina L. *Farmers on Welfare: The Making of Europe's Common Agricultural Policy*. Ithaca, NY: Cornell University Press, 2009.

Lynch, Édouard. "Le 'moment Debré' et la genèse d'une nouvelle politique agricole." In *Michel Debré, Premier ministre (1959–1962)*, edited by Serge Berstein, Pierre Milza, and Jean-François Sirinelli, 335–63. Paris: Presses Universitaires de France, 2005.

Patel, Kiran Klaus, ed. *Fertile Ground for Europe?: The History of European Integration and the Common Agricultural Policy since 1945*. Baden Baden: Nomos, 2009.

RELATED ARTICLES

5800 BCE, 1247, 1860

1965

Astérix among the Stars

In 1965, the cartoon hero Astérix accomplished his fictional
tour of Gaul and gave his name to the first French satellite
to orbit the earth. The French press was ecstatic. Was the
nation's global power about to be relaunched too? Amid
the fanfare surrounding the launch, it was sometimes
forgotten that the nation's space autonomy owed much to
earlier international cooperation.

On November 26, 1965, France officially joined the elite
of space powers. With the launch of *Astérix*, the first
French satellite, from the military base of Hammaguir in
Algeria, France became the third country after the Soviet
Union (1957) and the United States (1958) to possess its
own space agency, the National Center for Space Studies
(CNES, created in 1962) and its own access to space beyond
the world's atmosphere. This exploit was all the more
astonishing in that, prior to the late 1950s, the country had
barely engaged in space research at all.

   Astérix showed that French technology was capable

of tackling a completely new domain with a rapidity that beggared belief, pioneering new methods of organizing scientific research and institutions that would coordinate that research. In purely technical terms, success was sealed by the development of a rocket capable of carrying payload into orbit. The launcher, called *Diamant-A*, was part of a program known as Pierres Précieuses (Precious Stones); it carried a satellite, *A-1*, which the public later came to know under the more telling name *Astérix*. This small capsule weighing about ninety pounds would communicate back to Earth a variety of data concerning the launch itself. Even though this capsule soon stopped functioning, it turned France into a serious European competitor in the race for independent access to outer space.

For many years — and this is particularly true of human activity in space — historians have favored a binary interpretative approach that reduced the Cold War to a confrontation between the United States and the USSR. Yet despite the undeniable importance of both world powers, the *Astérix* satellite and French space activity in general make clear that it would be wrong to discount the European nations in the field of space exploration. Viewed transnationally, and thus more globally, an intense circulation of techniques and individuals had existed for some time, along with extensive sharing and transmission of knowledge about space. The historian Asif Siddiqi, a specialist in space activities, has noted that, just as in the nuclear domain, "every nation involved [in the development of ballistic missiles and space technology] has been a proliferator and has taken advantage of proliferation."

Informal international space-research networks first took shape in Europe and the United States in the 1920s, while the development of ballistic missiles in Germany shortly afterward benefited greatly from exchanges of technology and knowledge with other countries. In the 1950s, German engineers and scientists who had participated in the construction of wartime V-2 missiles contributed to the space programs of the two superpowers, with France and the United Kingdom also gaining from their knowledge. Later, China and Japan took advantage of the new technologies flowing out of the USSR and United States. Thus only ten years after *Astérix* reached orbit, all these countries had become members of the exclusive club of space powers. They were joined in the 1980s by India and Israel, who also relied on the support offered by Western Europe, the United States, and the Soviet Union.

Even so, the scale of transnational exchange should not blind us to the relevance of the nation itself as a basis for analysis. Technologies developed through space research played a vital role in the construction of a new national identity for postwar France. Indeed, the burgeoning space research sector in the late 1950s contributed to a broader venture: the modernization and reinvention of France as a dynamic, diplomatically and militarily autonomous technological power. There was an overriding military imperative to this impetus, embraced by de Gaulle after his election as president in 1958, as demonstrated by the production, in parallel with the development of space technologies, of new nuclear weapons as a means to project French power. France's participation in both the arms and the space races added political and symbolic clout to the country's advances in the postwar decades.

The *Diamant* launcher was the product of this uneasy relationship between military goals and civil applications. Although *Diamant* was a civil project, much of its technology came from the military domain, and more specifically the Pierres Précieuses program that France had put in place in the early 1960s. Persuaded that in the event of a new war it could not depend on the United States or the United Kingdom, de Gaulle's France sought to attain its strategic objectives by developing its own nuclear deterrent and its own independent capability to deliver nuclear warheads. When in 1961 de Gaulle gave the SEREB ballistic missile research consortium the green light to continue developing a launcher, French engineers had already successfully tested powder-propelled missiles using trial vehicles. By combining powder-propelled and liquid-propelled stages, they came up with the Saphir guided missile — which became the blueprint for the *Diamant* launcher that blasted *Astérix* into orbit.

Predictably, the French press celebrated *Astérix* as a feat of huge national importance. Yet France had been quietly engaged in a variety of cooperative scientific endeavors from the time of its earliest space forays, beginning with a research program known as the International Geophysical Year (1957–1958). One early French satellite rode on a NASA launcher. Ever since its own creation in 1958, NASA had routinely invited other nations to participate in the conquest of space; France (like several other European nations) had welcomed the opportunity to send engineers and scientists to the United States, where they acquired new knowledge and learned to orchestrate complex technical projects. All this contributed to the establishment of a common language for the field of space activities on both sides of the Atlantic.

Within Europe, too, thanks to the initiatives of influential scientists like Edoardo Amaldi and Pierre Auger, efforts in the domain of space research and exploration began to be coordinated in the early 1960s. France took part in the creation of the European Space Research Organization (ESRO), which was founded in 1962 — in the spirit of the European Organization for Nuclear Research (CERN) in Geneva — to pool European resources dedicated to the development of scientific experiments and satellites for space. The much more sensitive question of a European launcher, explicitly excluded from ESRO, was entrusted to another European consortium set up in March 1962 under the name of European Launcher Development Organization (ELDO). France pledged to build one of the three stages of this launcher, which was named *Europa*. Even though ESRO had many difficulties and ELDO was ultimately a failure, this dual approach made it possible for France to take the lead in European space research, notably by militating in favor of a European space agency in the mid-1970s. This brought innovation and research — launchers and satellites — together under a single umbrella organization.

All this stemmed from the original *Astérix*, a modest technological advance that remains to this day the historic symbol of France's entry into space politics and activities, a vast sector to which it has made significant contributions since the 1950s.

Sebastian Grevsmühl

REFERENCES

Carlier, Claude, and Marcel Gilli, eds. *Les trente premières années du CNES, l'agence française de l'espace (1962–1992)*. Paris: La Documentation française/CNES, 1994.

Gaillard, Florence. "La construction symbolique de l'espace européen." *Hermès* 34 (2002): 105–19.

Krige, John. "Embedding the National in the Global: US–French Relationships in Space Science and Rocketry in the 1960s." In *Science and Technology in the Global Cold War*, edited by Naomi Oreskes and John Krige, 227–50. Cambridge, MA: MIT Press, 2014.

Siddiqi, Asif. "Competing Technologies, National(ist) Narratives, and Universal Claims: Towards a Global History of Space Exploration." *Technology and Culture* 51 (2010): 425–443.

Sourbès-Verger, Isabelle. "Sur la notion d'indépendance." In *Interdépendance: Un projet d'art contemporain*, edited by Gérard Azoulay, 13–16. Paris: Édition de l'Observatoire de l'Espace, 2015.

RELATED ARTICLES

1968

"A Specter Haunts the Planet"

The young revolutionaries of May 1968 were obsessed
with Cuba, Vietnam, and China's Cultural Revolution.
They were not alone. In Berkeley, Berlin, the Italian city
of Trento, Prague, and Warsaw, hundreds of thousands of
student protesters denounced the political status quo and
the hegemony of the world's two superpowers. In the end,
however, these protesters failed to trouble either one.

On May 13, 1968, a series of gigantic rallies took place all
over France. Protesters chanted "Ten years / enough! Ten
years / enough!" in an explicit attack on President Charles
de Gaulle. Next, workers at the Sud-Aviation aircraft
factory in Bouguenais, near Nantes in western France,
broadened their industrial action and occupied their factory.
A comic strip began to circulate, imbued with the spirit of
the Situationist movement: a James Bond figure declaring,
"A specter haunts the planet: the specter of the workers of
Sud-Aviation. Every traditional power on earth has joined
the hunt for this specter: the Pope, the President of the

Supreme Soviet, Harold Wilson, François Mitterrand, the radicals of France, the American police." This was a parody of the Communist manifesto published 120 years earlier by Karl Marx and Friedrich Engels. Nevertheless, above and beyond a playful, offbeat humor tinged with seriousness, a new form of internationalism was taking shape. It was based on a new interpretation of world history by people who were convinced that they would end the status quo.

The events in France in 1968 are only readable through the prism of the larger world. Their international dimension was more than mere context; it was a serious call to arms for anyone ready to take part in a transnational mass movement that was completely indifferent to the traditional frontiers of nations. It is true of course that not all of those involved had the same internationalist outlook. The students were the quickest to embrace this fact; they were also the most determined to take advantage of these new possibilities for international action by using their own networks for moving people and information from place to place. The time students had available, new modes of transporation making it possible to travel freely, and the political turmoil affecting universities everywhere gave them a clear edge in this regard.

The same was broadly true of established revolutionary organizations like those of international anarchism, Trotskyism, or Maoism. However, in the case of the workers' movement, governed by the French Communist Party, internationalism had lost its gloss. The Popular Front had after all signaled a turn inward between the wars, with France's Communists reconciling themselves with the "Marseillaise," the *tricolore*, and the 14th of July Bastille Day. Nevertheless, other forms of transnational solidarity were already in place, maintaining multiple contacts between militant French workers and their comrades abroad.

The ongoing revolutions in China and Cuba and the Vietnam War were viewed as potential breaches in the established order. The world's hegemonies were showing themselves to be vulnerable. Both systems of domination, eastern and western, looked to be weakened; even the relative harmony of their coexistence was under threat. Both camps faced destabilizing challenges. Cuba had touched a nerve — not only because of the charisma of Che Guevara, whose recent death had intensified his aura, but also thanks to its brand of internationalism. Between 1967 and 1968, the regime of Fidel Castro had shown itself willing to criticize the Soviet Union or take a leading role in fomenting revolution in other countries. In May 1968, the Centre d'Information pour la Révolution, an action committee in Paris, described the Cuban revolutionaries as "poets of action." Vietnam was more than a mere backdrop. A whole generation had already identified the fighting there as the next stage of the battle against colonialism, following the

Algerian war of independence. Opposition to the American military intervention was one of the most virulent points of protest: at the university of Nanterre, just outside Paris, the March 22 Movement was created in protest against the arrest of a militant belonging to the Vietnam National Committee. Two days before, the windows of the American Express office in Paris had been smashed, an action justified in a tract that defined the international support coalescing behind the American students who were burning their draft cards for enrollment in the US Army. On June 10, in the midst of a strike that had spread across France, the *Tribune du 22 Mars* published a communiqué issued by an anti-imperialist organization of American deserters and conscientious objectors.

Within the French student movement, what was happening day by day in Berkeley, Berlin, Trento, and Leuven (Belgium) was instantly circulated; the same was true of events in Prague and Warsaw. Interest in the news from abroad was sharpened by practical experience, daily student meetings, and the rapid circulation of information. On February 17 and 18, around five hundred French militants traveled to Berlin to join a protest march against the war in Vietnam. Participants made and strengthened contacts. Alain Krivine of the French JCR (Jeunesse Communiste Révolutionnaire) stayed at the house of Rudi Dutschke of the German SDS (Sozialistische Deutsche Studentenbund).

Karl Dietrich Wolff, another leader of the SDS, went to Nanterre to speak on the West German student movement. At the end of March, Belgian militants from Leuven arrived in the French capital to describe what was happening in their own student-occupied university. After the horrific, near-fatal shooting of Rudi Dutschke in Berlin on April 11, there were huge protest marches in Paris and Strasbourg. New revolutionary texts were feverishly translated, among them the "Manifesto for a Negative University" devised by the students of the University of Trento, which rejected official control and proposed counter-courses (i.e., courses held without officially appointed lecturers). These were subversive, to say the least.

Meanwhile, as the international press relayed news of this contestation, students poured into Paris from every corner of Europe to join the insurrection, among them a group of British students who joined the march on the Renault factory in Boulogne-Billancourt. The original goal of this march was to make common cause with the workers. However, the factory gates were slammed in the students' faces — a graphic demonstration of the deep suspicion toward leftist radicals among some French union militants. The students who later arrived from the University of Gothenburg in Sweden, bringing money they had collected for the French strikers, were given a similarly hostile reception. On May 21, the militant broadsheet *Action* headlined the extra-parliamentary opposition movement in Berlin. Conversely, this strike by seven million French workers and the wave of factory occupations began to change the West German radical movement's view of the workers. The latter had clearly shown themselves to be less "integrated" into the system than Dutschke and his friends had imagined.

Finally, on June 12, the student leaders Daniel Cohn-Bendit and Alain Geismar went to London to take part in a BBC program about the student movement in Europe. Cohn-Bendit, twenty-three, was then based at Nanterre. He had experience of student politics in several different countries, and was able to use this experience to build a cross-border revolutionary project. Summoned before a university disciplinary panel for insubordination, he began by declaring a false identity as Kurón-Modzelewski, naming himself after two Polish students then in prison for criticizing the Warsaw regime. Denounced as a "German anarchist" by French Communist leader Georges Marchais on May 3, Cohn-Bendit (nicknamed *Danny le Rouge*) was flatly denied entry to France on May 24. This led to mass rallies and burning barricades in Paris, whereupon Cohn-Bendit entered France secretly (albeit with the French police hot on his trail, as their records clearly show).

On May 30, anti-student counterdemonstrations brought a million people out on the Champs-Élysées. Among slogans like *"Renault au boulot!"* ("Back to work, Renault!") and

"*Les cocos à Dachau!*" ("Send the Reds to Dachau!"), the crowd chanted "*Le rouquin à Pékin!*" ("Send the redhead to Peking!"). Cohn-Bendit was famously red-haired; conservative France was convinced he was an agent of the Chinese Republic, even though as a militant anarchist he had rejected the Maoist regime as sectarian and authoritarian.

The student movement set out to show its solidarity with the workers and break the social divide between intellectuals and manual laborers. Students thus helped strikers by standing on the picket lines shoulder to shoulder with them. The Billancourt divide between workers and young radicals should not obscure the effective forms of solidarity that took form elsewhere. French police archives show that from the earliest days of student action in May 1968 to the final extinction of the movement at the end of June, students and young workers fought side by side in the same pitched battles, on the same barricades, in the same confrontations with riot police. From May 3 onward, police arrest records show that sheet metal workers, fitters and lathe operators, ordinary employees from the national electricity company and postal services, café waiters, hawkers, delivery men, and salesmen all took part in the movement.

We also know that many nationalities were represented because the police drew up special dossiers on the foreigners they arrested. On May 24 in Paris, there were numerous Algerians and Tunisians (musicians, mechanics, and laborers), as well as Italians and Portuguese (specialized workers, restaurant waiters, and site foremen) and more generally young people from Brazil, the United States, Germany, Britain, Switzerland, Yugoslavia, Cameroon, Senegal, Japan, and Vietnam. Self-organization was the order of the day, with spontaneous committees for foreigners, anti-imperialist "committees of the three continents," and action committees for the slums put into operation. Word went out from the Sorbonne that for the first time in history, foreigners could be at home in France. Some of the action committees and local committees even demanded the abolition of the status of "foreigner," claiming that they deserved the same rights and freedoms as the French. These committees drew inspiration from the Paris Commune of 1871 — which also lasted only two months — whose labor minister was the Hungarian worker Leó Frankel and whose military head was the Polish worker Jarosław Dąbrowski.

From this revolutionary perspective, the very concept of nationality seemed reactionary, especially since foreigners quickly became special targets for the police. The targeting grew much worse after June 10–12, when eleven far-left organizations were dissolved and opposition rallies were formally forbidden. Once again, the archives of the police and intelligence services reveal mass expulsions from France and large numbers of people refused entry to

French territory. In short, it became dangerous, especially for foreigners, to take part in protests.

Thereafter things gradually returned to normal. June saw a slow and frequently bitter decline of the movement, with the death of the student Gilles Tautin and the workers Pierre Beylot and Henri Blanchet in final confrontations with riot squads and mobile police units. Elections were promised, which protesters considered bogus and even treasonous. Militant students at the Sorbonne had dreamed that the newfound power of France's democratic workers would quickly crush Franco's regime in Spain and that of the Colonels in Greece. They also hoped that the workers and students of Italy would follow the lead of their French comrades. History quickly proved them wrong. Yet action committees all over the world continued to mobilize as 1968 wore to a close, protesting against the invasion of Czechoslovakia by Warsaw Pact troops in August and against the savage repression of workers and students in Mexico in October.

Ominously enough, in the fall of 1968, during the Italian demonstrations that foreshadowed the Red Brigades era, a song could sometimes be heard in Italian streets: "*Ce n'est qu'un début / continuons le combat*" ("Don't give up the fight / It's only just begun").

Ludivine Bantigny

REFERENCES

Artières, Philippe, and Michelle Zancarini-Fournel, eds. *68, une histoire collective (1962–1981)*. Paris: La Découverte, 2008.

Bantigny, Ludivine, Boris Gobille, and Eugénia Palieraki, eds. "'Les années 1968': Circulations révolutionnaires." Special issue of *Monde(s): Histoire, espaces, relations* 11 (2017).

Gilcher-Holtey, Ingrid. *A Revolution of Perception?: Consequences and Echoes of 1968*. New York/Oxford: Berghahn Books, 2014.

Horn, Gerd-Rainer. *The Spirit of '68: Rebellion in Western Europe and North America (1956–1976)*. Oxford: Oxford University Press, 2007.

Klimke, Martin, Jacco Pekelder, and Joachim Scharloth, eds. *Between Prague Spring and French May: Opposition and Revolt in Europe, 1960–1980*. New York/Oxford: Berghahn Books, 2011.

RELATED ARTICLES
1357, 1789, 1840, 1848, 1871, 1892, 1936

1973

The Scramble for Oil in a Floating World

With the 1973 oil crisis, the postwar economic growth
model unraveled. A new form of globalization loomed,
one more financialized and less regulated. France was
gripped by nostalgia for its postwar boom years, as the
country grew increasingly aware of the ecological cost of
industrialization.

On October 17, 1973, in response to Western support
for Israel in the Yom Kippur War, the Organization of
Petroleum Exporting Countries (OPEC) imposed an
embargo, a production slowdown, and a stunning price hike.
Within a few months, the price of the world's chief energy
resource quadrupled, rising from three to twelve dollars a
barrel. (The barrel would reach nearly forty dollars in 1980,
during the second oil crisis.) It was a geopolitical turning
point and a breach in the unfair exchange that Western
industrialized countries, the United States in particular, had
been imposing since the end of World War II on nations
possessing coveted raw materials. Though the terms of

exchange for countries exporting ore and agricultural commodities would steadily worsen until 1989, this "oil shock" still represented what may be called the second act of decolonization. Given the clout wielded by OPEC and the rise of Asian industrialization, globalization was looking less and less like a process set in motion by the industrialized West through some imperial urge or by means of new international institutions that fell under its helm. Rather, it seemed to have taken on a life of its own.

The year 1973 thus dealt the first blow of "globalization shock," lasting until 1985. There was a genuine shift away from the economic status quo that had prevailed since 1945. In 1973 developing countries came before the United Nations to call for a more balanced "new world economic order," at a time when the power and confidence of the industrialized West seemed to falter. The US was withdrawing from Vietnam; terrorism was undermining Italy and threatening Germany; France was having to face its Vichy past thanks to the 1973 French translation of Robert O. Paxton's groundbreaking *Vichy France: Old Guard and New Order, 1940–1944*. This coincided with the rise of xenophobia and the extreme right. The National Front party was created in 1972; a year later, the neo-fascist group New Order organized a grand meeting under the slogan "Stop Illegal Immigration." Violent attacks against ethnic minorities were not uncommon (depicted and denounced in filmmaker Yves Boisset's *The Common Man*).

For a French economy that depended on petroleum for two-thirds of its energy consumption, the oil crisis represented a tipping point. Rising energy costs, which corresponded to a 3 percent drain on the GDP in 1975, pushed France's trade balance into the red in 1974 and sparked inflation. The government embraced "energy saving," launching catchy campaigns against electricity waste, but also promoting a vast nuclear energy program that it claimed would ensure "energy independence" and bring France back from the brink of economic hardship.

People often fall into the somewhat lazy habit of blaming the oil crisis for all the era's economic turmoil: the slowdown in growth, the 1974–1975 recession, the rise in unemployment, and the fiscal deficit. The crisis, supposedly, ended a sunny period of modernization and abundance, France's glory years of rapid economic growth, from 1946 to 1975, which economist Jean Fourastié called the Thirty Glorious Years. This account, however, is largely called into question by historians nowadays. The facts tell a more complex story, for the mass production model of growth and capital accumulation was already losing momentum in the late sixties and early seventies. Consumption of household appliances and other manufactured goods, an important engine of growth, had peaked; trade union activity was on the rise, French youth were openly rebelling, and industrial profits were slumping. By the late sixties the models of Fordism and embedded liberalism were on their way out, based as they were on fixed exchange rates and a mix of multilateral free trade and strong state intervention to ensure growth and full employment.

First came increased tax exemption for money moving through the City of London (the offshore market for Eurodollars) in the 1960s. Next, in 1971, President Nixon unilaterally revoked the gold standard — the direct international convertibility of US dollars into gold — effectively ending the Bretton Woods system. The move ushered in an era of floating exchange rates and fostered a powerful resurgence of financial speculation. Third, with the January 3, 1973, Bank of France legislation intended to regulate state finance through the central bank (ostensibly to curb inflation), the French government began to favor the development of the interbank market and increased the share of private over public monetary creation.

Admittedly, not until 1984 did the state begin to borrow primarily from commercial banks, and even though the high growth years were ending, the purchasing power of salaried workers remained strong until around 1983, early in the Mitterrand years. But we can conclude that, with these private interbank and financial markets in Eurodollars, in exchanges, and in public debt, the three key elements of a reemergent rentier capitalism — in which a reconstituted mass of capital seeks to enhance its value as loan capital — were already in place on the eve of the oil crisis, at a time when the cost-effectiveness of industrial capital had been waning since the late 1960s.

The glut of petrodollars after October 1973 further accelerated the transfer of wealth to loan capital (including in Third World countries, where the financing of industrial imports and exported raw materials led many nations into severe debt crises, starting in the early 1980s). At the same time, France was experiencing an increasing imbalance of loan capital as a percentage of GDP, a phenomenon that economist Thomas Piketty has discussed in his work. This gap would widen throughout the eighties, with capital outpacing labor in the share of value added. Rising petroleum costs therefore should not mask the more broad-based reshaping of social relations at the national scale and beyond, as the world transitioned into a new phase of capitalism, that of global finance and neoliberalism.

In France, this transition resulted in a period of stagflation, lasting roughly from 1973 to 1982, with its litany of factory closures (textile plants, steelworks, etc.), and a postwar record high unemployment rate, surpassing one million in 1977. Urged forward by the radical movements of the late sixties, the trade unions fought back, as witnessed by the heroic but short-lived experiment in worker-managed industry at the failing Lip clock factory between June 1973 and early 1974. But the government was determined to punish this kind of mobilization: "Let them be jobless and stay jobless." Their struggle could not be allowed to succeed at the risk of "unraveling the social fabric," in the words of then minister of economy and finance and future president Valéry Giscard d'Estaing. And indeed, social activism began to stall by the mid-1970s.

The oil crisis also had the more positive effect of pushing people to think more seriously about the material constraints and ecological limits of the growth model that shaped the postwar years. Even Jean Fourastié, the champion of the productivity model he had been depicting for three decades as the result of a skillful blend of investment, science, and rationalized workplaces, had to concede that this system relied heavily on "the use of mechanical energy." He noted that, thanks to fossil fuels, every French worker had one hundred twenty-four "mechanical slaves at his disposal" in 1973, compared to forty in 1938. This observation supports what today's economists are concluding, namely, that two-thirds of the French growth over the three postwar decades can be explained by the simple influx of fossil fuels. This purely material, thermodynamic explanation must have been disappointing for those who liked to believe that these changes had been manmade.

In 1973, the militant agronomist René Dumont published *Utopia or Else...*, a layman's version of the Club of Rome reports on resource depletion and social justice issues inherent to growing concerns about ecology, notably its 1972 *The Limits to Growth*. Dumont claimed that all world citizens should have equal access to resources and an equal right to pollute, within the bounds of the Earth's carrying capacity. Politicians and world officials were taking the environmental crisis seriously, creating national and international institutions to address the issue (e.g., the creation of a Ministry of the Environment in France in 1971, the 1972 Stockholm Summit). In 1974, Dumont was the first green candidate in a French presidential election. The candidates addressed environmental challenges and the notion of unsustainable growth head on. On August 25–26, 1973, a civil disobedience movement bringing together environmentalists, Christians, pacifists, farmers, and leftists, some eighty thousand people in all, had protested the extension of a military base on the Larzac plateau in southwestern France, a battle they eventually won. Out of this victory emerged a new rural left that would play an active role in environmental and anti-globalization movements in the decades to come.

Rather than criticize progress and growth, some preferred to invest their hopes in new technologies that claimed to solve the ecological, economic, and sociological conundrums of the time. There was biotech, with the first laboratory-produced GMOs in 1973, as well as space exploration, computerization, and robotics. The idea of a technologically driven revolution, popularized by Daniel Bell and Alvin Toffler in the United States, was picked up in France by the "Group of Ten," a transdisciplinary discussion group comprised of scientists such as Henri Atlan, Joël de Rosnay, and Henri Laborit, political figures including Robert Buron and Michel Rocard, and thinkers like Jacques Attali, Edgar Morin, and René Passet. This group urged societies to move beyond a civilization based on mineral resource extraction, toward one founded on knowledge and optimization of the living world. They envisioned an ecologically minded modernization of capitalism, whereby wealthy nations would transition toward a postindustrial economy, with emphasis on tertiary sectors rooted in information technologies, unbound by either ecological limits or state regulations. Although Western economies did manage to stabilize the proportion of fossil fuels in each dollar of GDP, their production of greenhouse gasses would continue to increase, leading to the changes in climate that are now witnessed the world over.

Christophe Bonneuil

REFERENCES

Chassaigne, Philippe. *Les Années 1970: Fin d'un monde et origine de notre modernité*. Paris: Armand Colin, 2012.

Chesnais, François, ed. *La Finance mondialisée*. Paris: La Découverte, 2004.

Ferguson, Niall, Charles S. Maier, Erez Manela, and Daniel J. Sargent, eds. *The Shock of the Global: The 1970s in Perspective*. Cambridge, MA: Harvard University Press, 2011.

Pessis, Céline, Sezin Topçu, and Christophe Bonneuil. *Une autre histoire des "Trente Glorieuses": Modernisation, contestations et pollutions dans la France d'après guerre*. Paris: La Découverte, 2013.

Vigreux, Jean. *Croissance et contestations (1958–1981)*. Paris: Le Seuil, 2014.

RELATED ARTICLES

1720, 1816, 1860, 1875, 1962, 1983, 1992

1973

The Other 9/11

The coup d'état mounted by the Chilean military on
September 11, 1973, gave the French an uncomfortable
reminder of their own thwarted hopes for reform and
revolution. Perhaps as a result, political refugees from
Chile were warmly welcomed by a nation that once again
embraced its duty to offer hospitality.

Well before the attacks on the Twin Towers, the date
of September 11 was associated with an event of global
importance: the 1973 overthrow of the Chilean Socialist
Government of Popular Unity by Chile's armed forces,
with the covert backing of or at least a prior understanding
by the CIA. For the socialist left in Latin America and both
Eastern and Western Europe, this coup came as a major
emotional and political shock, not to mention a moment of
profound sadness shared by an entire generation. The first
news from Chile was quickly followed by shattering images:
the fascist soldiers, in their breathtaking certainty that their
cause was just, had allowed photographers and cameramen

from all over the world to work with absolute freedom. The intention was to spread an atmosphere of terror, to stifle any will to resist among the Chilean people, and to make their triumph crystal clear to the world.

Photographs of La Moneda Palace, the Chilean president's official residence, under attack by the Chilean air force, were taken from the top of a neighboring building by a young reporter, Dagoberto Quijada; within a few days they had been viewed all over the world. The same was true of the photograph of a white-faced, helmeted President Allende, armed with a machine gun and surrounded by bodyguards, a few hours before he was driven to suicide. Dozens of photographers were on hand to record the repression that followed the coup: the nameless corpses in the streets, bloodied and beaten; the mass arrests; the hundreds of men herded into the national stadium. All appear in the television documentary *Septembre chilien* by Bruno Muel and Théo Robichet. Finally, there was the sinister face of the army's commander in chief, General Pinochet, caught by Dutch photographer Chas Gerretsen during a celebration of Catholic mass, in what was to become the best-known image of the South American dictator. And everywhere in the background: the radiant smiles of ordinary soldiers.

For several weeks — that is, before the Yom Kippur War and the worsening oil crisis took over the world's news headlines later that fall — the major French newspapers

Libération, *L'Humanité*, and *Le Monde* led with the news from Chile, "the daily terror and persecution," the heavy responsibility of the CIA, the plight of political prisoners, and the martyrdom of President Allende. The initial shock grew and persisted across the world: indeed in several European countries, including France, it led to a political mobilization that extended well beyond socialist intellectuals and the militant left. Along with feelings of dejection, the horror of the coup generated a powerful movement of solidarity with Chile's helpless political prisoners, the families of the "disappeared," and above all the refugees. The lasting impact of this shared generational experience on France's public, associative, and political life cannot be overstated.

Why did the fate of a nation of barely nine million inhabitants, stretched between the Pacific and the Andean mountain chain some six thousand miles from Paris, matter so much to the relatively placid France of Georges Pompidou?

The first reason had to do with the French left, whose awareness of the continent had been on the rise for some years. Socialism in Latin America appeared to have found a way to build itself within the rules of democracy. Che Guevara was dead (1967); 1968 had seen the "failed revolution in Paris that almost changed human history" (French singer Renaud, "Hexagone," 1975); China no longer held much inspiration for the young, whose political weapons of choice were now polemical and rooted in small collectives. Yet in Chile, in a subcontinent that the United States had turned into their own jealously guarded hunting ground, a sixty-two-year-old Marxist doctor and his Socialist/Communist coalition had triumphed in a presidential election by advocating a gradual transition toward socialism. For the French left, which had been searching for a unifying cause, the voice of Chile — officially supported by Cuba — offered a source of inspiration.

In November 1971, two exploratory French delegations went separately to Santiago, the Chilean capital. One of them was led by François Mitterrand, who had recently been appointed leader of the French Socialist Party at the Epinay Congress; the other was headed by two Communists, Jacques Duclos and Étienne Fajon. The parallels between the Chilean and French situations were obvious and strongly emphasized in France, to the point where some of the statements in the preamble of the "common program" of the French Socialist/Communist union (June 1972) parroted word-for-word those of the December 1969 election platform of the Chilean Popular Unity. Thus the French media's projection of a comradeship and shared destiny between socialists on either side of the Atlantic fueled growing anxiety in France about the fate of the Chilean government. This became acute in the summer of

1973, when Chilean conservatives and influential capitalists declared open war on Allende's government. In France, a powerful surge of sympathy and solidarity followed the coup d'état, sparking street demonstrations by political parties, youth organizations, and trade unions from September 12 onward.

The Popular Unity government and the coup that destroyed it were brandished as symbols and chosen as a field of struggle by the French left. "Chile is very close to us," said the militant and former student leader Maurice Najman in 1974, "not only because, like us, it is trying to find a new way between the two traditional political extremes, but also because it revives our memory of the civil war in Spain. And that memory is alive in every European." The journalist Maurice Clavel added on October 3: "We are seeing the same helmets, the same faces, the same bleeding men and weeping women." One might add: the same language, the same slogans ("*No pasarán!*"). This association of images and ideas powerfully influenced the way people viewed the political refugees, to whom, from the first hours of the coup, France — along with other European and Latin American nations — offered asylum. Without a doubt, a sense of guilt about France's failure to intervene in Spain in 1936 had something to do with this generosity.

Chile was also the symbol of sacrificed hopes. Jacques Fauvet, editor of *Le Monde*, wrote angrily on September 13 that "the fact of a president elected by universal suffrage, who has paid with his life for a few generals' breach of that trust, constitutes an uncommon drama that is not limited to one man or one people. It represents a universal crisis for the ideas of 'revolution within the law' and 'legally organized Socialism.'"

The cause of Chile rapidly distinguished itself from the international struggle for the victory of socialism. French critics of Pinochet embraced his Chilean opponents as victims rather than as revolutionaries; as civilians rather than as fighters; as torture victims, prisoners, and citizens deprived of their rights rather than as militants. This reading of Chile's plight had real relevance in a decade when the idea of a universal and necessary defense of human rights acquired widespread relevance. President Pompidou responded to this public emotion with a delicate balancing act, paying lip service to the government of Pinochet (along with the other Western countries that were unable to deviate from the American official line) but allowing his ambassador Pierre de Menthon to give asylum to hundreds of persecuted Chileans.

As Renaud pointed out in another couplet of his song: "When in September / people and liberty are murdered / in the heart of Latin America / few voices are raised. / An ambassador arrives / he is welcomed with open arms. / Fascism is a gangrene / infecting Santiago and Paris." In addition to the new ambassadors, refugees from Chile were also welcomed by a heavily mobilized, independent network of organizations, supported by the French state. The flood of exiles brought the Chilean political situation home to French society. It was not so much their numbers that imprinted on the collective imagination; there were about ten thousand refugees, the overwhelming majority having requested and obtained the status of political refugees. Most striking of all was the collective enthusiasm and the public consensus that allowed these men and women to settle in France, the quality of their reception, and the involvement of the French state.

A powerful associative network began acting on behalf of the refugees as soon as news of the coup broke, so that by October 2 there was close coordination involving several ministries and the United Nations High Commission for Refugees (UNHCR). The French government allowed all political refugees to remain in France for as long as necessary. Numerous associations worked together, from secular and religious groups with long histories of defending human rights and helping migrants (among them the Human Rights League, the Service Social d'Aide aux Émigrants, Cimade, Secours Populaire Français, and Secours Catholique) to more recent organizations founded in the wake of the Algerian War and in response to humanitarian and legal problems arising from postcolonial immigration (France Terre d'Asile, founded in 1971; and GISTI, the Groupe d'Information et de Soutien des Travailleurs Émigrés, founded in 1972). The refugees were given six months of benefits, including access to social services, lodgings, food, and language courses; they were housed all over France, including in the countryside; and the vast majority encountered deep sympathy and solidarity from their hosts.

This warm welcome reflected a key moment in the history of political asylum in France. In one respect, it was a new beginning given that France was for the first time offering refuge to non-Europeans, following a procedure that had only recently been made possible by the New York protocol (also known as the "Bellagio Protocol") of 1967, building upon the Geneva Convention of 1951. The political class's unanimous, heartfelt response to this political repression facilitated the reception of other refugees from Latin America and elsewhere in the years that followed — notably Argentinians after the 1976 military putsch, and Asian "boat people." It also allowed France to position itself (for a while) as a country of asylum on a global scale, quite independent of the logic of political blocs. This position proved short-lived, however. France may have opened its doors to Chileans — undeniable and sympathetic victims — but it did not prove as generous when it came to migrants who sought better economic opportunities or, years later, to African and Asian asylum seekers. During the "right-to-asylum crisis," levels of asylum attribution dropped from eighty percent to less than twenty percent within a few years while the number of applications soared and would-be immigrants found themselves accused of hiding their true economic motivations.

For a moment, French society (and not just its leftist elements) had come together in recognition of the Chilean drama. The nation was only too aware of the Spanish Civil War's echoes in the Chilean situation, of the clear political and humanitarian issues at stake, and of France's obvious moral responsibility. Alas, it all proved to be a parenthesis. All too quickly, France's moment of fraternity sadly gave way to an era of closure and suspicion.

Maud Chirio

REFERENCES

Guzmán, Patrício. *La Batalla de Chile, la lucha de un pueblo sin armas*. Directed by Patricio Guzmán. New York: Icarus Films, 1975–78.

Moine, Caroline, and Olivier Compagnon, eds. "Chili 1973: un événement global." Special issue of *Monde(s): Histoire, Espaces, Relations* 8 (November 2015).

Poinsot, Marie, and Bernardo Toro, eds. "L'exil chilien en France." Special issue of *Hommes et migrations* 1305 (January–March 2014).

Prognon, Nicolas. "France: Welcoming Chilean Exiles, a Mark of the Resonance of the Unidad Popular in French Society?" In *European Solidarity with Chile 1970s–1980s*, edited by Kim Christiaens, Idesbald Goddeeris, and Magaly Rodríguez García, 187–207. New York: Peter Lang, 2014.

RELATED ARTICLES
1808, 1825, 1889, 1923, 1936, 1948, 1968

1974

Curbing Migration

July 1974: Faced with a sagging economy, the French
government issued a temporary ban on labor-based
immigration. Like West Germany and the United
Kingdom, France made it clear that it would rein in
migration during difficult economic and political times.
The ban turned immigration into a central topic of political
debate in France, which it has remained ever since.

On July 3, 1974, at a meeting presided over by newly
elected French president Valéry Giscard d'Estaing, the
Cabinet of Ministers decided after much deliberation
to enact a temporary ban — until October — on work-
related immigration. Viewed today as the first in a series
of restrictive policies to combat an economic crisis, this
decision was but one of many measures enacted to protect
foreigners living in France. The man behind the ban was
André Postel-Vinay, a former Resistance fighter turned
senior government official responsible for population and
migration questions at the Ministry of Labor. Known as the

1233

first "minister for immigrants," Postel-Vinay also advocated for measures to resolve housing problems for foreigners living in France.

The justification for regulating migratory flow reflected to an extent prevalent attitudes across Europe. Among others, a West German decision had curbed labor immigration in November 1973. British leaders had likewise voted to prevent arrivals of new workers to the Commonwealth in 1971. But the change in Europe's economic fortunes after the first oil crisis was by no means the only reason for this shift in immigration policy. In France, high-level government officials took advantage of the international situation to make a political statement on immigration. Indeed, it is worth remembering that in the three decades preceding this decision, immigration was not a national issue; the only people who gave it any thought were department heads in charge of doling out residency papers and work permits.

Procedurally speaking, the decision of July 3, 1974, differed little from policies enacted over the preceding three decades. As a means of avoiding parliamentary debate, legislators enacted policy changes through government circulars rather than amendments to the law. In 1946, 1.7 million foreigners lived in France. By 1975, that number had doubled to 3.4 million. But despite that growth, the legal framework had not changed. In contrast with the interwar period and its hodgepodge of laws and decrees, ordinances adopted in 1945 were a coherent and conscious reflection of the state's needs. After the war, the team surrounding General de Gaulle actively sought to break with policies set by Marshal Pétain. However, their aim had not been to overhaul the legacy of the prewar Third Republic. Within the Ministry of the Interior, former members of the Resistance, including Cabinet leader Pierre Tissier, set the foundations for the new immigration policy. On the one hand, they were eager to distinguish themselves from demographer Georges Mauco, who since the 1930s had pushed for the selection of foreigners based on country of origin and capacity to assimilate; on the other hand, they opposed communist immigrant organizations that fought to expand immigrant rights beyond a tacit renewal of interwar provisions.

In order to avoid an unwieldy parliamentary debate, government officials drafted broad and purposely vague ordinances: the ordinance on French nationality of October 19, 1945, made naturalization contingent on demographic need (this marked a return to the spirit of the law of 1927). The ordinance of November 2, 1945, on conditions for entering and staying on French soil, revived 1938 legislation, but added a new National Bureau of Immigration (ONI). Taking over from the Société Générale d'Immigration, which had performed this function for private companies since 1924, the ONI would oversee the recruitment and organization of foreign labor.

After the liberation at the end of World War II, the French government therefore appeared to endorse an immigration policy that did not serve the interests of big business. In reality, the institutional framework imagined by a coalition of high-level Gaullist and Socialist officials quickly went awry. Beginning in the 1950s, economic renewal and the need for manual labor led business leaders to pressure the government to end the ONI's monopoly on immigration. That wish was granted by the circular of April 18, 1956, which provided papers to foreigners who agreed to work in sectors where labor was in short supply. This did not mean, however, that the state had ceded control of migration. Since the issue was not subject to public debate, immigration policy was guided by anonymous bureaucrats who used confidential circulars to adjust the law to the economic and political climate.

So, while the signing of the Geneva Convention in 1951 appeared to imply new rules for refugees, in reality, the government still had the last word. Indeed, beginning in the late 1950s, a distinction was made between "real Hungarian refugees" and "fake asylum-seeking Yugoslavians." On the one hand, Hungarian refugees fleeing Soviet tanks in Budapest in 1956 benefited from streamlined procedures and a quick turnaround for their three-year residency cards. On the other, Yugoslavian exiles arriving in France at the same time were deemed ill-suited to labor needs and denied residency.

More broadly speaking, immigration officials were given discretionary power to favor some nationalities over others. After decolonization and the signing of the Évian Accords between France and Algeria in 1962, two types of migration met the needs of the labor force: foreigners from Spain and Portugal, whose residency was still covered by the ordinance of 1945; and migrants from Algeria (and to a lesser degree from sub-Saharan Africa), who were free to circulate and reside within French borders as part of the agreement reached after Independence. Beginning in 1963, migration from the Iberian Peninsula was encouraged as a way of compensating for the freedom of circulation policies benefiting Algerians and Africans. It was during this period of robust economic growth that high-level officials seized control of immigration policy and migratory flow to further their political agendas.

The first measures adopted to stanch the flow of immigration targeted Algerians. Since French officials were unable to reach an agreement with their Algerian counterparts, limitations placed on Algerian immigration were decided unilaterally in Paris in October 1964, at first as a means of countering "fake tourists." The following year, restrictions were extended to the arrival of Algerian families. Other nationalities were not yet targeted, but in the summer of 1971 officials from the Ministry of the Interior extended these measures to migrants from Francophone African states. Meanwhile, family-based immigration continued to be encouraged among Italian, Spanish, and Portuguese migrants. This was the first phase in a long process to control migrations flows. The result was a renewal of racially based demographic engineering reminiscent of the interwar period.

The second phase, which targeted labor-based immigration, began just a few months later. Faced with a slowing economy, the government adopted two circulars (known as "Marcellin-Fontanet") in early 1972. They prevented foreigners from obtaining residency cards without having work authorizations, marking a shift from individual, permanent papers to collective authorizations granted at the government's discretion. But again, these hardening immigration policies were enforced for some types of foreigners and not others. Migrants from the European Economic Community received special treatment. Portuguese migrants, for instance, continued to receive working and residency papers. By 1975, Portuguese and Algerians had become the largest foreign groups living in France.

The decision to enact a temporary ban on foreign workers and their families hence capped a process that had begun years earlier. The notion of a need to "control the flow of migration" now permeated the highest levels of government. Still, international law imposed important exceptions. Asylum seekers, refugees, and foreigners from some southeast Asian nations, spouses of French nationals, citizens of the European Economic Community, and skilled workers were not affected by the ban. Beyond such legal distinctions, it was left to bureaucrats alone to interpret laws overseeing the entry and residency of foreigners in France.

Since 1974, no French government has questioned the need to control the flow of migration. Still, protests from migrant groups and others have occasionally had an impact. A law enacted on July 17, 1984, marked an important moment in immigrant rights: it created a ten-year residency card giving recipients the right to practice the profession of their choosing, without prior authorization. Yet, despite such gains, the climate has hardened, with the rise of the National Front and public debates on national identity and the place of Islam in the French Republic. Meanwhile, European directives on visas, asylum seekers, and posted workers (embodied in the French imagination by the "Polish plumber," a phrase which has come to symbolize cheap immigrant labor from Central and Eastern Europe) have injected energy into current debates on whether to control France's borders or expand European norms. France and Germany have provided different responses to this influx of refugees. Their divergent approaches show that immigration policy remains a national issue, revived with every election.

Alexis Spire

REFERENCES

Bruno, Anne-Sophie, Philippe Rygiel, Alexis Spire, and Claire Zalc. "Judged on Their Paperwork." *Population* 61, no. 5 (2006): 621–643.

Laurens, Sylvain. *Une politisation feutrée: Les hauts fonctionnaires et l'immigration en France.* Paris: Belin, 2009.

Lyons, Amelia. *The Civilizing Mission in the Metropole: Algerian Families and the French Welfare State during Decolonization.* Stanford: Stanford University Press, 2013.

Rosenberg, Clifford. *Policing Paris: The Origins of Modern Immigration Control Between the Wars.* Ithaca, NY: Cornell University Press, 2006.

Weil, Patrick. *How to Be French: Nationality in the Making since 1789.* Translated by Catherine Porter. Durham: Duke University Press, 2008.

RELATED ARTICLES

719, 1923, 1927, 1998

1983

Socialism and Globalization

In March 1983, François Mitterrand made his decision:
from now on his government's political priority would be
the battle against inflation and France's economic deficit.
This was the outcome of two years of debate that had
divided the country's Socialists since 1981. Yet at the same
time — in a singular paradox — the French left became
the instigator of a globalization it sought to contain.

On December 19, 1983, François Mitterrand told Jacques
Attali, one of his closest advisers, that he felt "torn between
two ambitions: building Europe and building social justice
in France." Less than two years after his arrival in the
presidency, Mitterrand was right to be hesitant. Despite
pursuing a determined policy of reflation, he now faced
a serious deficit, soaring inflation, and also growing
unemployment. In contrast, his European partners,
beginning with Margaret Thatcher's United Kingdom and
Helmut Kohl's Germany, had made opposite economic
policy choices. Was France, a founding member of the

European Monetary System (EMS) since 1979, still capable of controlling its economy? The upcoming municipal elections made it necessary to pass over this subject in silence, but the results proved disastrous for the government. The conservative RPR and UDF opposition parties won handily, while the far-right National Front made historic inroads.

Mitterrand's prompt response was to reshuffle Prime Minister Pierre Mauroy's administration for the second time since 1981. His (reappointed) minister of economy and finance, Jacques Delors, went to Brussels and negotiated a 2.5 percent devaluation of the franc against a 5.5 percent reevaluation of the deutschmark. On March 23, 1983, the president made his new direction clear with a televised broadcast to the nation: "We have not wanted and we do not want to isolate France from the European Community of which we are an integral part.... What I expect (of the prime minister) is not that he should put in place some kind of new form of austerity, but that he should continue what he has begun in a way that is adapted to the current time of rigor." Mitterrand thus preferred "rigor" to "austerity," a word that had been far too closely associated with the policies of the Valéry Giscard d'Estaing/Raymond Barre government of 1976–1981. Two days later, at an emergency meeting of the council of ministers, his administration announced an income tax rise, a bond issue, a tax on gasoline, a levy on sales of alcohol and tobacco, an increase in the cost of public services, and a strict spending limit for French tourists traveling abroad.

Thus, on March 25, 1983, priority was abruptly given to the struggle against deficit and inflation. This squeeze was described as an "embrace of rigor." At the time, the French right viewed these measures with a certain circumspection, and even irony: nationalizations, the thirty-nine-hour week, and retirement at age sixty remained untouched. Instead of doing an honest U-turn, the government was "dancing on the spot." On the left, the remedies prescribed proved divisive. For some, common sense had won the day, while for others — especially Mitterrand's political rivals — this decision constituted a rank betrayal.

This episode gave birth to a myth, that of the brutal conversion of an inexperienced French left to the market economy. In reality, the extent of the change of course was in many ways exaggerated. Contrary to the conventional wisdom, French Socialists were fully prepared to govern in the field of economics. Throughout the 1970s, the party had integrated into its working committees a series of leading experts who were familiar with the statistical models used by the high administration and the government. This was the case of Jacques Attali himself, a graduate of the École Polytechnique and the École Nationale d'Administration (ENA) and a member of the council of state, and of Michel

Rocard, a politician and ENA graduate who had worked at the Ministry of Finance. Still, while they agreed on the basics, the economists of the Socialist Party had a number of disagreements among themselves.

On the one hand, the members of the CERES (the Centre d'Études, de Recherches et d'Education Socialistes), directed by Jean-Pierre Chevènement, intended to impose a Marxist reading of French problems. On the other, Rocard's supporters were more concerned with preserving the market as a tool for allocating resources. Between these poles, the *Mitterrandistes* advocated a reconquest of the domestic market as a priority, along with the promotion of cutting-edge technologies. During the election campaign of 1981, Mitterrand decided — despite his Marxist-sounding rhetoric — to place Jacques Delors in the vanguard of the battle. This Christian trade unionist, who had worked not only at the general planning committee and the Bank of France but also for right-wing politician Jacques Chaban-Delmas when he was prime minister under Georges Pompidou, was expected to reassure both France's civil service mandarins and European bureaucrats in Brussels. The Socialists were well aware of the pressures that economic interdependence exerted on their program, which insisted on the "measures required so that a growth in demand could be satisfied by domestic production," thereby circumventing foreign constraints that might stymie the policy of reflation. In fact, the Socialists were hoping to convince their European partners by relying on the favorable opinion that the arrival of a left-leaning government might inspire across the rest of Europe.

The policy of rigor is best judged in the light of the choices that were made after May 1981. Economic policy underwent progressive change. When he arrived in power, Mitterrand had refused to devalue the franc. Against the advice of some of his ministers (notably Chevènement and Rocard, who were for once in agreement), he wanted to keep France in the European Monetary System despite the destructive attacks being made on European currencies and the drastic hike in interest rates imposed by the American Federal Reserve. But the situation deteriorated rapidly. Despite keeping Renaud de la Genière as governor of the Bank of France until 1984 and despite the nomination of Michel Camdessus at the head of the Treasury in the spring of 1982 (both men were conservative ENA graduates who had served in previous administrations), the government failed to win the confidence of the financial markets. A first devaluation took place on October 4, 1981 (the franc lost 8.5 percent of its value against the mark); a second one followed on June 12, 1982 (5.75 percent this time). These devaluations were accompanied by a freeze of prices and salaries between June and November 1982. Objectives for the budget deficit were set at 3 percent of the GNP. Though completely arbitrary, this criterion was nevertheless passed on to posterity through a series of European treaties, from Maastricht (1992) to Lisbon (2007).

Delors, who was calling as early as November 1981 for a "pause" in the implementation of social reforms, appeared to have gained the ascendancy by 1982. Yet Mitterrand continued to seek counsel from people across the political spectrum, for instance Jean Riboud, managing director of the multinational Schlumberger corporation, who advocated leaving the European Monetary System and lowering interest rates. Still, those to whom Socialist politician Pierre Mauroy picturesquely referred as the "*visiteurs du soir*" (night visitors) — i.e., Mitterrand's private interlocutors — failed to impose their solution. Indeed, some ministers who had initially been favorable to allowing the franc to float on the currency markets changed their position. This was the case of Laurent Fabius and Pierre Bérégovoy, influential Socialists belonging to Mitterrand's inner circle who were convinced by the arguments of Michel Camdessus. The events of March 1983 were more a "termination point than the breaking point," in the words of social historian Matthieu Tracol. On the one hand, the government encountered difficulties that had been foreseen; on the other, the decisions it announced were broadly in line with those that had come before.

March 1983 turned out to be a key month. The symbolic

parenthesis opened in May 1981 had closed. As it had under Giscard d'Estaing, the struggle against inflation once again became the principal concern of French economic policy, taking the place of full employment as an overriding goal for the government. Keynesian solutions were not suited to an economy that was deliberately kept open, and the neoliberal tide that had broken over Germany, the United Kingdom, the United States, and France during the experiment led by Raymond Barre as prime minister returned to the fore. The backlash was all the more violent because the left had created the conditions for it. In January 1984, the government passed a law to initiate the liberalization of the banking sector. When the right regained power in 1986, it privatized, liberalized, and deregulated. The left took its revenge in 1988, when Mitterrand won reelection, but in the sphere of economic policy the strategy known as competitive deflation remained in place. Its aim was to contain inflation and increase the margins of businesses. In the name of Europe, France had finally opted to align itself with Germany and in doing so forfeited its monetary sovereignty.

The architect of austerity policies in France, Delors, was appointed head of the European commission in January 1985. During his ten-year tenure, the European Economic Community transformed itself into the European Union, and the Single European Act (1986) and Maastricht Treaty (1992) gave birth to the single European market and a single currency. In January 1987, Michel Camdessus became director-general of the International Monetary Fund (IMF). During his term, a number of member nations from the southern hemisphere were forced to make structural political adjustments, and IMF loans began to be granted progressively, and only to those who moved toward free markets.

We are thus left with the singular paradox of a French left that, in the words of economist Rawi Abdelal, did more than succumb to "the realities of globalization." In the final analysis, this left was one of the main instigators of globalization.

François Denord

REFERENCES

Abdelal, Rawi. *Capital Rules: The Construction of Global Finance*. Cambridge, MA: Harvard University Press, 2007.

Fulla, Mathieu. *Les socialistes français et l'économie (1944–1981): Une histoire économique du politique*. Paris: Les Presses de Sciences Po, 2016.

Hall, Peter A. "The Evolution of Economic Policy Under Mitterrand." In *The Mitterrand Experiment: Continuity and Change in Modern France*, edited by George Ross, Stanley Hoffmann, and Sylvia Malzacher. New York: Oxford University Press, 1987.

Lee, Jae-Seung. "Between Ideology and Europe: The French Socialists and the EMS Crisis, 1981–1983." *International Area Review* 7, no. 2 (2004): 109–133.

Saunier, Georges. "Le gouvernement français et les enjeux économiques européens à l'heure de la rigueur, 1981–1984." In *Milieux économiques et intégration européenne au XXe siècle,* edited by Eric Bussière, Michel Dumoulin, and Sylvain Schirmann. Paris: P.I.E. Peter Lang, 2007.

RELATED ARTICLES
1720, 1860, 1936, 1992, 2011

1984

"Michel Foucault Is Dead"

Michel Foucault died of AIDS in 1984, when the epidemic barely had a name. The great French philosopher was only fifty-eight, and yet already he was the intellectual personification of a new analysis of political power, based on the way it is exercised upon the human body. Today, Foucault's universal dissection of power is viewed as one of the cornerstones of intellectual globalization.

Michel Foucault est mort. Rarely can the present tense have been so correctly applied than in the headline of the French daily *Libération* on June 26, 1984. The announcement of the death of Foucault, professor of philosophy at the Collège de France, was a significant event. Since then, critics have taken the great scholar, historian, and social theorist to task for failing to declare he had AIDS. This is unfair for, in 1984, next to nothing was known about the coming pandemic. People were still explaining it *sotto voce* as "gay cancer," a scourge of "the Four H's" (homosexuals, hemophiliacs, Haitians, and heroin addicts), and the consequence of bestial sex with green monkeys in the jungles of the Congo.

Foucault died within weeks of contracting AIDS, and

"the real scandal that is death" abruptly put an end to his unparalleled intellectual journey, just as the second and third volumes of his landmark *The History of Sexuality*, *The Use of Pleasure* and *The Care of the Self*, were arriving in bookshops. Foucault's death led Daniel Defert, his lover, to found an association called AIDES to fight the disease in the fall of 1984. Indeed the struggle against AIDS was beginning even as the philosopher himself lay dying; and this in itself was thoroughly Foucauldian. Never had his signature concept of biopower, defined in the first volume of *The History of Sexuality*, as "the explosion of numerous and diverse techniques for achieving the subjugation of bodies and the domination of populations...by modern nation-states," seemed so relevant.

With Foucault's sudden passing came the realization that nothing would ever be the same again. After teaching at the University of Tunis for two years, he had returned to Paris in 1968, after student protests led to the founding of a new teaching institution, the Centre Universitaire Expérimental de Vincennes. As head of its philosophy department, and later as a fellow at the Collège de France, Foucault radically — and sensationally — altered the idea of the role of the intellectual in France. Instead of speaking on behalf of others — the downtrodden, the defeated, the silent — he presented himself as their heir and successor and spent the 1970s forging a new philosophical relationship between theory and practice. Within the Groupe d'Information sur les Prisons, which he cofounded in 1971 to examine the state of French prisons, he took a step sideways — away from the Maoists who surrounded him. Far from seeing rioting prisoners as revolutionaries, he took them seriously as subjects for study; he listened to and transmitted their demands; he did not see them as some kind of novel political movement but a "site" of gagged speech, a space of silence. In doing so, he denounced the intolerable condition of France's common-law prisoners in the Pompidou years, enabling the prison psychiatrist Edith Rose to reveal the general use of straitjackets, among other horrors, in the *Nouvel Observateur* on December 27, 1971.

Foucault had been to Madrid with actor Yves Montand to denounce the execution of anti-Franco militants, and he had spoken — along with his fellow intellectuals Gilles Deleuze, Roland Barthes, Jean-Paul Sartre, Simone de Beauvoir, and André Glucksmann — at the Théâtre Récamier in support of the Soviet dissidents Vladimir Bukovsky and Leonid Plyushch, on the evening when Leonid Brezhnev was received at the Élysée Palace. He had also supported the cause of Dr. Mikhail Stern, a Soviet Jew who had an anti-Semitic court case brought against him. On May 11–12, 1979, he wrote in *Le Monde*: "My moral stance is *anti-strategic*, meaning that I am respectful when something singular arises, and intransigent when power subverts the universal.

The choice is simple but the work is uneasy. One always has to keep an eye on what is going on beneath the surface of history, on what is shaking and stirring it; one must also pay attention to what is happening in the background of politics and know where unconditional boundaries must be set. That's my job: I'm neither the first nor the only person to have tackled it. On the other hand, I clearly chose it."

In 1978, his conclusions from two spells in Iran prompted a series of articles in the Italian daily *Corriere della Sera*. These signaled a momentous break with the past; indeed they echoed Voltaire's reaction to the 1755 Lisbon earthquake, often referred to as the first disaster of the modern era, with political, religious, and philosophical consequences that reached far beyond the physical damage. Foucault opened his first report, dated September 28, with the following words: "In the two great salt deserts at the heart of Iran, the earth has just quaked. Tabass and forty villages have been annihilated." Foucault had deliberately chosen to ignore the other political events that were taking place before his own eyes: the fall of the shah, Mohammad Reza Pahlavi, amid the protests mounted by Shi'ite students. In so doing, he set forth a radically different conception of the intellectual and a new historical paradigm. For him, there was no longer any question of describing what happened in Iran (and later in Poland, with the Solidarity movement and the strikes in the naval shipyards of Gdańsk) as "revolutions." He called these events "uprisings," meaning the Nietzschean rising of an individual or collective force, of a subjective entity previously unknown.

This was an important change. What the philosopher was suggesting — and coldly analyzing — was nothing less than the demise of "revolution" as a notion relevant to modern times.

It is difficult to avoid the link between this diagnosis and the worldwide explosion of dismay at Foucault's death. People may have thought that his influence was largely restricted to France, but it was from Tunisia, California, Brazil, and Eastern Europe — most notably Poland — that the most heartfelt tributes came. Foucault was known as a philosopher who published books, but in fact it was his way of reading current events through an analysis of power that focused not on the individual but on myriad other factors, some of them microscopic, which made him a dazzling diagnostician of the present. Above all, Foucault found an escape route from Marxism — another way of reading contemporary human societies that, instead of denying domination, squarely confronted it, unaffected by outside influences.

Foucault's reputation has soared since his death; he is now acknowledged as the first thinker of globalization. After the fall of the Berlin Wall, his books and teachings spread like wildfire in former democratic republics but also in many

Latin American countries (notably Argentina, Brazil, and Chile) where Marxism was the dominant reference. In 2004, the twentieth anniversary of his death, conferences in Rio de Janeiro and Bogotá brought together not only researchers but also many other social actors: trade union leaders, activists, and artists.

Unlike Jean-Paul Sartre's approach (among others), Foucault's method of thinking had no universal design or aim, and there was no need to import it from somewhere else. The idea was to use his approach to knowledge as a set of tools (he himself described his work as a "toolkit"). This method is rooted in specific historical moments — the societies of postwar Western Europe — but there is nothing superior or biased about it. It strives perpetually to detach itself from its point of departure, to escape the thought patterns of past teachings. In some respects, it allows certain topics to come into being for the first time. The discourse of the Foucauldian intellectual is specific; it may be likened to that of a physician working in a coal mine, who is able to pinpoint health threats to miners from his own firsthand knowledge and observation.

Here is Foucault:

> Intellectuals used to be in the habit of working in terms of what was universal, exemplary, true, and right for everyone. Now they concentrate on specific sectors, precise points where they

happen to be located due to the conditions of their existence — the hospitals, asylums, laboratories, and universities where they work, their homes, their family lives and their sexual relationships. They have certainly acquired a clearer, more immediate awareness of social struggles, and face problems that are specific, not universal, worlds apart from those of the 'proletarian masses.' Still, they are closer to those masses, I think, for two reasons: because they witness real, material, day-to-day struggles, and because they often confront — though perhaps in other forms — the same enemies as the peasantry or the masses (in our time, these enemies are the multinationals, the police and justice systems, and real estate speculators).

In 1984, Foucault died in what he sometimes called the "space of the world" (*l'espace du monde*). He had traveled much around the globe, to Sweden, Poland, and West Germany for the cultural services of the French Ministry of Foreign Affairs during de Gaulle's presidency, and later to newly independent Tunisia, before teaching in Brazil and the United States in the 1970s.

The worldwide dimension of Foucault's thought is among the earliest and most spectacular manifestations of the globalization of academia in the last decades of the twentieth century. His ideas have spread because of their capacity to be used, transformed, and twisted. This applies not only to Foucault but also to all those who, since the beginning of the twenty-first century, have fallen under the umbrella of "French Theory." What might the writings of Jacques Derrida, Michel Foucault, Gilles Deleuze, Félix Guattari, and Jean-François Lyotard have in common? There have been plenty of suggestions, including a razor-sharp rapport with the French language that makes them well-nigh untranslatable or changes their ideas, when they are in fact translated, into something completely different. There was something quintessentially French about "French Theory" that can only be rendered by a gesture not of betrayal (*trahison*) but of *translation*. In French, this means a "shift" or a "displacement," as opposed to *traduction*, which means translation. This displacement so modifies the work that an American version of Foucault — to take but one example — stands out like a sore thumb. And yet, his work encapsulated — in French — a vital moment in the history of France's intellectual life. Identity emerged out of distortion.

And so, on June 25, 1984, Michel Foucault died, dispossessed of his own work, just as he had dreamed he would be and just as he had forecast in 1972, in the preface to the first Gallimard edition of his *Madness and Civilization*. As a toolkit or an intellectual weapon, this book now belongs to his readers.

Philippe Artières

REFERENCES

Defert, Daniel. *Une vie politique*. Paris: Le Seuil, 2014.

Grmek, Mirko D. *Histoire du sida: Début et origine d'une pandémie actuelle*. Paris: Payot, 1989.

Macey, David. *The Lives of Michel Foucault*. New York: Vintage, 1995.

Mangeot, Philippe. "Foucault sans le savoir." In *L'Infréquentable Michel Foucault*, edited by Didier Eribon, 89–100. Paris: EPEL, 2001.

Roman, Laba. "'Solidarité' et les luttes ouvrières en Pologne (1970–1980)." *Actes de la recherche en sciences sociales* 61 (March 1986): 7–33.

RELATED ARTICLES

1633, 1852, 1889, 1948, 1949, 1961, 1968, 2008

TODAY IN FRANCE

The end of history was a bust. Loudly proclaimed by the political scientist Francis Fukuyama in the summer of 1989, it was meant to celebrate the victory of liberal democracies throughout the world. But this victory never happened — despite the demonstrations in Tiananmen Square in the spring of 1989, and despite the fall of the Berlin Wall in November of that same year, which would signal the reunification of Germany, the fall of the communist regimes in Eastern Europe, and the breakup of the Soviet Union. Unbridled financial innovation and deregulation of the economy plunged the capitalist world (which is to say the whole world) into a profound social, moral, and political crisis, marked by unprecedented market failures (starting in 2007 with the subprime mortgage crisis), an economic recession whose widespread effect on employment was devastating, and a general trend toward authoritarian governments and xenophobic policies. Feeding into the crisis was a new breakdown in the world order, marked by an increase in terrorism, from September 11 and the ensuing wars in the Middle East to the conflicting outcomes of the Arab Spring of 2011.

Was France's role simply to endure this crisis? To view things this way is to accept the notion that France is a country under siege. Incessantly questioning their place in the world, some of the French became during these decades carefree advocates of globalization while others joined the camp of its resolute and highly energized opponents. The narrow victory of the "yes" in the 1992 referendum on the Maastricht Treaty, which ratified the closer integration of European nations into the European Community, prefigured a resounding "no" vote in 2005, when French voters were asked to ratify a treaty establishing a constitution for the European Union. The enchanted moment when France, undergoing renewed economic growth, celebrated the 1998 World Cup victory of its *black-blanc-beur* (black, white, and Arab) national soccer team was over.

But had France ever wiped the slate clean of its colonial past? There was every reason to doubt it, with nationalist, anti-immigration candidates finding growing electoral success from 1983 onward. In 2002, Jean-Marie Le Pen, the head of the extreme-right National Front party, made it to the second round of the presidential election. The death of Martinican poet Aimé Césaire, the great literary and political voice for Negritude, in 2008 and the ambivalent reactions that followed revived memories of France as a colonial power. These memories had already resurfaced in 2005, when rioters in Paris protested police brutality against residents of poor, increasingly ethnic suburbs. Images of burning cars and schools were broadcast across the world.

For a moment, though, it seemed that France might raise its voice again in the old, vaunted style: pro-

Arab, anti-American, and gloriously insubordinate. Addressing the UN General Assembly in New York in 2003, Dominique de Villepin, minister of foreign affairs for President Jacques Chirac, explained France's refusal to join the American-led coalition against Iraq. But it was also in New York that, in 2011, other hopes faded, those of Dominique Strauss-Kahn, managing director of the International Monetary Fund and undeclared candidate in the upcoming French presidential elections. This signaled the end of the end of history, and the return of the event. What happened in New York would have important repercussions in France. In 2015, the dynamic was different. When jihadists attacked Paris on January 7, 8, and 9, and then again on November 13, the emotional outpouring began in France before traveling the world over.

On January 11, 2015, at the Paris rally held to commemorate the victims of the attacks on Charlie Hebdo's offices, the entire world seemed to reach out in sympathy, suggesting that what happened in France could affect every part of the globe. As it wended its way from the Place de la République to the Bastille, by way of the Quai Voltaire, the sorrowful procession was accompanied by a planetary wave of emotion that brought France back to its revolutionary era. For in most countries, the French Revolution is a fixture in history curricula. This explains why the world at large came together in Paris for the bicentennial celebration of the Revolution in 1989. Swathed in a dress that evoked the French flag, the American opera singer Jessye Norman sang "La Marseillaise" — a solemn moment during a festive parade that, marching to the drums of Tiananmen Square and stepping out to the sounds of world music, joyously celebrated the planet's tribes. A brotherly call for the melding of cultures, the popular ceremony of July 14, 1989, showed a revival of confidence in the political values that underlay the French Republic. The French melting pot was still working; with a model that combined tolerance with stability and prosperity, French society could integrate immigrant populations and countercultural or religious isolationism. This consensus view was, however, presented in a depoliticized framework.

Was that consensus delusional even then? In 1989, and again in 1998, and then again in 2015, the French flag was carried by crowds. But was it always emblematic of the same France? And, conversely, was France still facing the same world?

1989

The Revolution Is Over

France's universalist commemoration of the two-hundred-year anniversary of the storming of the Bastille resonated with the worldwide democratic movements of 1989, from Beijing to Berlin. Divergent memories of that epochal moment marked a resurgence of the historical event, which did not limit itself to revolution alone.

The first chapter of historian François Furet's 1978 book *Interpreting the French Revolution* is entitled "The French Revolution is over." His argument brings two complementary fields to bear. The first is scientific: Furet posited that once the French Revolution was finally declared over and done, political passions could cool and historians could break with the sacrosanct Jacobin-Bolshevik interpretation of the event. Not only did the latter group substitute commemoration for honest scrutiny, but it also kept alive the illusion that politics alone could change society or even mankind itself. By the same token, it refused to read revolutionary violence as the expression of a system, of an ideology, even as "the Gulag [was] leading to a rethinking of the Terror" due to the apparent similarities between the French Terror and Stalinism. The second field at work in Furet's book was more pointedly political: accepting that the Revolution was over put an end to the culture of conflict inherited from this period, and laid the groundwork for the consensus and tradeoffs that define modern liberal democracies. This theme was developed in 1988 by Furet and two other historians, Pierre Rosanvallon and Jacques Julliard, in a book, *La République du centre*, which would provide second-wave leftists the historical perspective they were lacking.

Furet's verdict may have sparked outrage in 1978, but by the eve of the Bicentennial it was glaringly obvious that the idea of revolution was in crisis. For in the interim, the Union of the Left had dissolved, the French Communist Party could muster a mere fifteen percent of the vote, and the austerity measures introduced by the Socialists opened once again the gap between the left's rhetoric and its governmental practices. Meanwhile, Mikhail Gorbachev's USSR was engaged in a massive reform program, the first effect of which was to expose the incongruities of Soviet-style management, while access to Soviet archives now made it possible to document the regime's history, including its grimmest chapters.

France's far right and more moderate right-wingers

took to popularizing the image of the French Revolution as the template of totalitarianism, spinning the quashing of the 1793 anti-revolutionary uprisings in the Vendée region as the first modern-day genocide. More generally, people had grown disenchanted with politics altogether, and in the summer of 1989, Francis Fukuyama took the world by storm when he announced the "end of history." The postmodernists, for their part, diagnosed a crisis in the world's "grand narratives," whether that meant notions of nation, progress, or, of course, socialism. For some, a retreat into the private sphere had to take precedence over collective action. In *L'ère du vide* (The Age of Emptiness, 1983), a reflection on modern individualism, philosopher Gilles Lipovetsky claimed that postmodernism, "the second individualist revolution, characterized by broad-based privatization, the erosion of social identities, waning interest in politics and ideology, and the destabilization of personality," ushered in the era of games, humor, and true hedonism, unbound by the constraints of historical thought and holist societies.

Against this background, it made little sense to commemorate the Revolution when the very idea no longer held out any promise or prospects. It was understood by a broad spectrum of the media that the Bicentennial could only strike people as a cheesy anachronism.

Not surprisingly, then, the public responded positively

to Furet's insistence that France had to choose between deeper understanding or splashy commemoration. Michel Baroin and Edgar Faure, the first two presidents of the Bicentennial Mission, both of whom died before July 14, 1989, opted for a forward-looking commemoration with an emphasis on human rights and "the extra-genetic mutation [that would yield] a humankind for the third millennium." This commemoration would, Faure hoped, "approach unanimity." He was proposing to celebrate "this extraordinary consensual movement that emerged in France between July 13, 1789, in the evening and July 15 in the morning." But it would be Furet, oracle of the notion that the French Revolution — and revolution per se — had run its course, whom the media would crown "king of the Bicentenary."

Furet's notorious phrase, "The Revolution is over," also marks a kind of closure of France's role in the world. From the standpoint of the state, this sentence could not possibly become the focal point of a commemoration, that all-important form of political messaging.

Reelected in 1988, François Mitterrand entrusted the Bicentennial Mission to historian Jean-Noël Jeanneney, who announced his intention to celebrate "the luminous side of the Revolution." As with previous commemorations, the events calendar would be limited to remembrances of what took place in the single year of 1789. Jeanneney also relied heavily on an economic and social history of the Revolution (now open to cultural perspectives as well) and its most prominent scholar, Michel Vovelle, director of the Sorbonne's Institute of the History of the French Revolution

As if to prove that the Revolution was not a lifeless object of academic study, Vovelle carried out seventy trips abroad in two years in order to support the 320 commemorative colloquia that took place across the globe. For his part, Jeanneney, to demonstrate that his team was keeping its ear to the ground, capitalized on the commemoration fever that had taken hold in the regions beyond Paris, where the Bicentennial featured prominently in newly developing regional cultural scenes. He was equally attuned to the anniversary's celebrations throughout the world, where no fewer than fifty national committees had been formed.

In short, the Bicentennial Mission sought to demonstrate that, although some in France felt the Revolution had run its course, it remained a relevant, universal reference point. The Mission financed a film for French television, Serge Moati's *Journal d'un bicentenaire* (Diary of a Bicentenary), which insisted that the bicentenary had been warmly received in numerous countries, especially in Chile, where intellectuals and artists fervently recited the Declaration of the Rights of Man and of the Citizen.

The Mission also hired star graphic artist and advertising

filmmaker Jean-Paul Goude to design the July 14th parade extravaganza in Paris. Avoiding the typical reenactment clichés associated with historical commemorations, Goude chose to represent all the peoples of the world in a universal, though affectionately stereotyped, federation that heralded a "planetary melting pot" — already underway via world music. When it was all over and Goude's spectacular was declared a success, Margaret Thatcher, one of the leaders he had invited to Paris for a summit of wealthy and poor countries, remarked that the English Revolution had taken place first. Mitterrand quipped bemusedly that it was not his fault if the peoples of the world identified with the French Revolution, and no other.

But the march of history has a way of reactivating the web of analogies between the French Revolution and unfolding world events, and the year 1989 was replete with examples. From April 15 to June 4, Chinese students occupied Tiananmen Square and raised a makeshift statue to the goddess Liberty, their symbol of democracy, before tanks crushed the demonstration. In Eastern Europe, where Gorbachev had opted for non-intervention in the domestic affairs of satellite countries, events took a different turn. One by one, the socialist states imploded under popular pressure. The political geography inherited from World War II was swept aside. For once, the winds of history blew softly. With the exception of Romania, the former leaders put up little resistance, and the revolutions were truly velvet this time around. If 1789 took the world by surprise, so did 1989. And the storming of the Bastille seemed to have predicted the fall of the Wall, two centuries on. But were these revolutions, strictly speaking, or devolutions? Or even counterrevolutions? How were all these events to be defined?

For François Furet, the events of 1989 sounded like a validation of his basic premise: "Like history having the last laugh on the twentieth century's waning years, everything conspired to locate the bicentenary of the French Revolution at the crossroads, between a celebration of 1789 and the last gasp of revolutionary political culture." Still, the "enigma" remained as to why this political culture had endured at all beyond the founding of the Third Republic in 1870.

For philosopher Edgar Morin, 1989 simply represented the closure of a cycle begun in 1917: "On a planetary scale, the 1789 tortoise caught up with and surpassed the 1917 hare. More than France, it is the rest of the world that most fittingly celebrated the Revolution. Or better still: in 1989, we clearly saw that 1789 was catapulted out of the past and into the future, while 1917 fell apart before our disbelieving eyes." It was around this forward-looking interpretation that the French government could rally, the only one that could stir up emotions and restore hope — if only temporarily — in a political future. On July 14, following the June massacre in Tiananmen Square, Goude's spectacular parade down the Champs-Élysées opened with a huge Chinese drum draped in black, accompanied by silent marchers bearing ideograms expressing "Liberty, Equality, Fraternity" instead of the originally scheduled choreography.

Cut now to late December 1989, when the mortal remains of three heroes of the Revolution, the philosopher Condorcet, the abolitionist Abbé Grégoire, and the mathematician Gaspard Monge, were transferred to the Panthéon, where France commemorates its glorious citizens. Minister of Culture Jack Lang drove home the Bicentennial's final message:

> When an order breaks down, when people have risen up and act at the speed of thought, and think to the rhythm of their hope, when everything rushes forward and radicalizes. 1789 was reborn in Prague in 1989, in Berlin in 1989, in Moscow in 1989, in Budapest, Sofia, Santiago, Chile, in Beijing in 1989. Who could have imagined, back in January of this year, when the celebrations of the Bicentenary were officially opened, that 1989 would witness revolution on the march all across the globe? A year unlike any other. Let us pause and take it all in, and remember how fortunate we are to experience this amazing moment! This evening does not mark the end of the Bicentenary, but rather a prelude: a kind of overture to the third century of our freedoms in the making.

If Jack Lang's high-flown rhetoric was prompted mainly by the deeply historical setting of the event, and also the will to conserve the considerable symbolic capital that the Revolution represents for France, the fact is that the French Revolution remains an invaluable resource for thinking about history as it unfolds. Its inexhaustible substance can be refreshed, no matter how it has been previously appropriated or retooled over the course of the twentieth century. No historian has had the last word on the Revolution, no social use of this historical event precludes any other in the future.

Patrick Garcia

REFERENCES

Ducange, Jean-Numa. *La Révolution française et l'histoire du monde: Deux siècles de débats historiques et politiques (1815–1991)*. Paris: Armand Colin, 2014.

Engel, Ulf, Frank Hadler, and Matthias Middell, eds. *1989 in a Global Perspective*. Leipzig: Leipziger Universitätsverlag, 2015.

Garcia, Patrick. "The Bicentennial of the French Revolution and the Human Rights Declaration, 1989." In *Encyclopedia of Europe: 1914–2004*, edited by John Merriman and Jay Winter. New York: Scribner, 2006.

—. *Le Bicentenaire de la Révolution française: Pratiques sociales d'une commémoration*. Paris: CNRS Éditions, 2000.

Hobsbawm, Eric. *Echoes of the Marseillaise: Two Centuries Look Back on the French Revolution*. New Brunswick: Rutgers University Press, 1990.

Judt, Tony. *Postwar: A History of Europe since 1945*. New York: Penguin, 2005.

Kaplan, Steven Laurence. *Farewell, Revolution: Disputed Legacies, France, 1789/1989*. Ithaca, NY/London: Cornell University Press, 1995.

—. *Farewell, Revolution: The Historian's Feud, France, 1789/1989*. Ithaca, NY/London: Cornell University Press, 1995.

RELATED ARTICLES

1789, 1794, 1848, 1871, 1953, 1968

1992

A Very Muted "Yes"

Beyond its technicalities, the Maastricht Treaty sought
to take advantage of a new multipolar world order to
strengthen the financial power of a Europe that was bound
to expand. But the principle of economic globalization that
lay behind the treaty brought about a profound and lasting
split within the French electorate over the very idea of
Europe.

The controversy around the Maastricht Treaty began
as a linguistic one: should it be pronounced "Mastrikt,"
with consonants brusque and brutal in the image of a cold
European technocracy, or enunciated more languidly as
"Maaastrirt," rolling the r's to evoke the peaceful Dutch
town on the banks of the River Meuse that was open to
cross-border exchanges with its close Belgian and German
neighbors? Philippe de Villiers, standard-bearer of those
opposed to the ratification of the treaty, used the first version,
while the Belgian journalist Christine Ockrent, undisputed
queen of French television news, preferred the second.

When the Treaty of European Union (as it was more formally known) was signed on February 7, 1992, by the twelve member states of the European Economic Community (EEC), everyone expected a smooth ratification process — except perhaps in the United Kingdom. The French National Assembly did indeed validate it with dispatch. Nevertheless, the referendum held in Denmark on June 2, 1992, changed all that when the Danes rejected the treaty by a slim majority of 50.7 percent. The following day, President Mitterrand decided to submit it for direct ratification by the French people.

Held on September 20, 1992, France's Maastricht referendum ended with a muted "yes" vote: 51 percent in favor, with a high rate of voter participation (70 percent). This was a surprise, because the preceding referendum on the European question, held by President Pompidou on the enlargement of the EEC to include new countries like the United Kingdom, had resulted in a 60 percent "yes" vote and a hefty rate of abstention. This time around, the French were passionately engaged, coming within a whisker of rejecting the treaty in spite of initial polls predicting a comfortable victory. How is this to be explained?

In European terms, the Maastricht Treaty represented a considerable deepening of the institutional foundations of a united Europe. The European Union (EU) replaced the EEC, and the adoption of a single currency was promised, at relatively short notice, as the conclusion of a three-stage process. Under the treaty's provisions, European decision-making would become substantially more federal, the domains of competence of European institutions would grow, and a European citizenship status would be created. The latter, added to national citizenship status, would confer European diplomatic protection abroad, the right to study and work in other EU countries, and the right to vote in local and European elections.

On the other hand, the economic orientation of this new agreement was ambiguous. From the point of view of the French government, the treaty was a victory because it allowed for a monetary union with Germany, and this was expected to be an indispensable tool for lowering French interest rates. Monetary union would make it less expensive for the French state and the country's companies and families to borrow money. Obviously, on matters such as inflation, deficit, and debt, there would have to be conformity with what were termed the "Euro convergence criteria," but these had been favored by French decision-makers since 1983. Social Europe also appeared to be strengthened by Maastricht's social charter and the EU's extended competence in areas such as the environment. The presence of Jacques Delors, a French Socialist, as president of the commission seemed to guarantee this direction. German attitudes toward the Maastricht Treaty also seemed to coincide with French opinion: east of the Rhine, the treaty was criticized for insisting too much on industrial policy and offering no guarantee of monetary orthodoxy.

At the same time, neoliberal Europe had left its mark on the treaty, with the exceptions obtained by the Conservative government of the UK in the application of the social charter, and by the convergence criteria toward policies of austerity on which the proposed monetary union was based. Meanwhile, the European competition policy was expected to grow stronger, threatening national industrial priorities. Everything would thus depend on how the treaty was interpreted.

Beyond Europe, Maastricht clearly reflected the uncertainties of a new world order in which France was struggling to find a place. The treaty was concluded as a direct result of the end of the Cold War. If, despite its hesitations, the Federal Republic of Germany agreed to the monetary union demanded by France, it was in order to alleviate the fears aroused by the rapid reunification of Germany, which had taken place in October 1990, less than a year after the fall of the Berlin Wall. In parallel, the other countries of the former communist bloc became liberal democracies aspiring to enter the future European Union. The collapse of the USSR around Christmas 1991 left a world dominated by the Americans. With the new world order proclaimed by George Bush on September 11, 1990, and the "end of history" — the inevitable victory of liberal democracy prophesied by Francis Fukuyama — France appeared to be reduced to the rank of middling power. During the Cold War, in contrast, Paris had been able to make its voice heard. As a former imperial country that had become deeply anti-imperialist, France could denounce the United States while taking advantage of its nuclear umbrella and facing little contradiction in Europe, where Germany was still theoretically an occupied power.

Geographically, France lay at the center of the various European institutions, confined at the time to the Western political bloc. Everything changed with the upheavals of 1989–1991, which brought Germany back into the heart of European affairs. Moreover, the war in the former Yugoslavia exposed not only the geopolitical powerlessness of the EEC (despite the promise in the Maastricht Treaty of a "common foreign and security policy"), but also its divisions: while Germany quickly recognized Croatia's independence, France hesitated in view of its traditional alliance with Serbia.

All this took place against a backdrop of accelerating economic globalization. Maastricht coincided with the end of the Uruguay round of the General Agreement on Tariffs and Trade (GATT), an extensive international negotiation to liberalize exchanges, which for the first time encompassed the circulation of agricultural products. This aroused deep anxiety in France, for the massive subsidies of the EEC's common agricultural policy were called into question. Ever since its beginnings in 1948, French leaders had understood the construction of Europe as a means of galvanizing and regulating economic globalization, which itself was viewed as both a stimulant and a destabilizing factor. But in 1992, the conjunction of Maastricht, the end of the Uruguay round of GATT, and an economic crisis that hit the entire continent called this dynamic into question.

These economic and geopolitical uncertainties fed an increasingly passionate referendum campaign. On May 6, 1992, before the referendum was even announced, the principal themes of the "no" campaign were announced by Jacques Calvet, CEO of Peugeot Citröen. Writing in *Le Figaro*, he denounced a Europe in thrall to what he called "Anglo-Saxon ultra-liberalism," to a bureaucracy that imposed far too restrictive norms, and to German domination. The "no" camp quickly broadened beyond the traditional extremes, the National Front and the French Communist Party, both of which had always been opposed to the construction of a Europe based on the values of liberal democracy. The novelty here was that many influential figures claimed to be pro-European but opposed to Maastricht, denouncing the treaty as economically too liberal and politically too federal. This was the case on the right with Philippe de Villiers — a revelation of the campaign — and future president of the National Assembly Philippe Séguin. On the left, Jean-Pierre Chevènement distanced himself from the Socialist Party's official position and appealed to his supporters to vote no. The Green party, too, was divided. Meanwhile the principal parties in power — Mitterrand's own Socialists, former president Valéry Giscard d'Estaing's Union for French Democracy (UDF), and even the Gaullist Rally for the Republic (RPR), which completed its pro-European mutation under the leadership of Jacques Chirac — came out in favor of ratification.

This did not prevent the "yes" vote from collapsing in the opinion polls prior to the vote — from 70 percent to around 50 percent. The calm determination and analytical power of Minister of European Affairs Élisabeth Guigou, a key figure on the pro-Maastricht side, suddenly seemed insufficient to win the day. At this crucial moment Mitterrand decided to enter the fray. On September 3, he confronted Séguin, the leader of the "no" campaign among French moderates who had made a powerful speech during the National Assembly's ratification debate on May 5. Mitterrand won the upper hand during the televised debate between the two men, leading the "yes" camp to a scrappy victory.

Many saw the referendum's result as an effect of the times, and especially of the economic crisis — with unemployment soaring above 10 percent, a Europe demonstrably powerless to end the civil war in the former Yugoslavia, and a deeply unpopular Socialist government. Beyond this short-term analysis, the referendum appeared as a structural watershed, with the "permissive consensus" on European integration being replaced by "democratic deficit." The construction of Europe was no longer a distant prospect that would (perhaps) contribute to world peace. It now looked like an increasingly menacing technocratic enterprise over which people and their elected representatives had little or no control. There was also the worrying prospect of the EU's enlargement to a dozen or more Eastern European countries, further diluting French influence on the European project. Economically, the union symbolized a liberal globalization that seemed threatening to a French nation-state that was still Colbertist and Keynesian to the bone. Finally, postreferendum analyses confirmed that a shared characteristic of "yes" voters was their education level. French people who voted "no" tended to feel threatened by globalization, and this was especially true of farmers and laborers. Still, the democratic deficit critique extended beyond these social groups, and even beyond the borders of France itself. Germany was the last country to ratify the treaty on account of a raft of objections lodged with the constitutional court at Karlsruhe, some of which were based on the notion that European institutions lacked legitimacy.

In the end, the French controversy had few short-term consequences. Denmark obtained concessions from its European partners at the end of 1992. A new referendum was organized there in 1993 and yielded a clear "yes." The reforms that were expected to bring greater legitimacy to European institutions were consigned to a future treaty, to be decided upon. Nevertheless, in the long term the shadow of Maastricht has lingered over the relationships between France, Europe, and globalization. The same debates and divisions were to resurface in 2005 during the referendum on the European Constitution. This time, the outcome was a resounding "no."

Laurent Warlouzet

REFERENCES

Duhamel, Olivier, and Gérard Grunberg. "Référendum: les dix France." In *L'État de l'opinion 1983*, 79–85. Paris: Le Seuil, 1993.

Dulphy, Anne, and Christine Manigand. *La France au risque de l'Europe*. Paris: Armand Colin, 2006.

Moravcsik, Andrew. *The Choice for Europe: Social Purpose and State Power from Messina to Maastricht*. Ithaca, NY: Cornell University Press, 1998.

Virtual Centre for Knowledge on Europe, 2018, www.cvce.eu

RELATED ARTICLES

Lothar Wahlheiser

1998

France and Multiculturalism: *"Black-Blanc-Beur"*

July 12, 1998: France's national soccer team won the World Cup, sending French people from all walks of life out into the streets to celebrate. This show of unity was as striking as it was short-lived. Soon, social divisions splintered the energizing myth of an ethnically integrated France.

When the French national soccer team won the World Cup in the summer of 1998, all of France seemed to come together in a singular moment of social and ethnic unity under a tripartite slogan, *"La France black-blanc-beur"* — "France is black, white, and Arab." In a country still deeply shaken by the terrorist attacks of 2015–2016, this sentiment may seem outdated. Young "Muslims" on a quest for jihad have since carried out deadly attacks that seem to undermine the possibility of a "French melting pot." It is as if this celebration of a multicultural team were nothing but a heat-of-the-moment "invention" by media commentators. But let's not fall into the trap of looking at the past — this historic moment for France's soccer team — through the lens of the present day. To give the 1998 victory its due and appreciate its multiple dimensions, we must situate it in its historical contexts, in terms of sports, social relations, and politics.

We must remember, first, that France's 1998 soccer team was more black and white than it was *beur* (of North African origin). Zinédine Zidane was the only player of Maghrebi descent on the team. But what a player! With two thrilling headers, he became a hero in the World Cup final against Brazil. "Blacks," on the other hand, were more numerous and diverse: a majority could trace their ancestry to the West Indies (Lilian Thuram, Thierry Henry, Bernard Diomède), French Guiana (Bernard Lama), and New Caledonia (Christian Karembeu); a single player had parents from Sub-Saharan Africa (Patrick Vieira, from Senegal); and Marcel Desailly was an altogether different case, having been born in Ghana and adopted in France by a French consul. The rest of the team, the "whites," mostly came from working-class native French families rooted in local territories.

The 1998 team was a far cry from today's generation of soccer players, whose salaries have been inflated thanks to fierce competition between professional clubs. Many of these earlier players did not grow up in the "bubble" soccer training centers now provide. Some faced racism or financial hardship early on and developed a kind of social and political consciousness. Such was the case for Thuram, who first encountered racism when he moved from his birthplace of Guadeloupe to the French mainland at the age of nine. He obtained his high school degree (the bac), married a West Indian nurse from the projects where he grew up, involved himself in black causes, and even named his eldest son Marcus, after Jamaican-American Black Nationalist Marcus Garvey. He also wore a T-shirt in commemoration of the 150th anniversary of the abolition of slavery in France and liked to "talk politics" to the press.

In short, one could trace all of recent French history just by looking at the backgrounds of these players. France's 1998 team represented the diverse facets of French society: not just working-class or rural segments, but also people from the suburban projects and descendants of France's colonial past (overseas departments and territories, African immigration). To the extent that soccer has become a part of a nation's identity, on par with the national anthem, folklore, and food, the 1998 team presented the new face of France.

News articles and televised reports give a sense of the story spun about this sports team: it was seen as proof of national unity. The victory on July 12 unleashed a level of mainstream jubilation rarely seen in France since the Liberation in 1944. One million people crowded onto the Champs-Élysées; impromptu festive gatherings dotted city centers throughout the nation. Though they received less coverage, rural towns participated in the exuberance too. This was clearly a moment of true collective joy, which went hand in hand with a feeling of national unity running through all walks of life in France: men and women, the middle class and the working class, whites and blacks, Parisians and provincials. It was as if the upper classes (the "bourgeoisie") felt they owed this success to the French working classes, and as if the country's white natives wanted to show their appreciation to the children of postcolonial immigration.

Let us not forget how much this victory owed to the French *banlieue* — the suburban projects. Zidane was a child of Castellane, a rough neighborhood at the base of Marseille's northern districts. During the World Cup, each national victory, together with the incredible shows of skill by the *banlieue* heroes (Thuram's two goals in the semifinal, Zidane's headers), captured the imagination of young people from these hard neighborhoods. The national team became "their" team.

Consider Leïla, born in 1973 to Algerian immigrants: "During the World Cup, I was working in my city's youth division, managing the Youth IT Bureau (YITB). Our offices were in a rough neighborhood. With the help of YITB staff, young people set up a TV in the middle of the projects, running an extension cord from our offices. Somehow, they had managed to find a TV and an antenna, and in less than ten minutes, fifty people came out to barbecue and watch the game. It was a festive atmosphere....The excitement grew with each new game....I remember it was a really standout summer in the neighborhood....The mood shifted in late August [after the World Cup], when it came time to return the rented equipment and vehicles (a minibus). The kids and even the staff had been careful not to tell us that they were using the minibus as a party van every night the national team won. And on the night of the finals, they'd all ended up on its roof. Needless to say, we lost our deposit...."

1998 was also the year in which soccer stopped being a purely male, provincial, poor, and working-class pastime in France. Before then, talking about the sport in intellectual circles or at dinner parties in Paris was almost a faux pas. The World Cup changed that, and a growing number of women began to follow a sport that had until then been a largely male preserve.

Moments of national excitement and shared joy always yield images and symbols that leave a lasting impression on our collective memory. In this case, I am reminded of the photographs of Zidane and the slogan "Zidane for President" that were projected onto the Arc de Triomphe. "A son of Algerian immigrants won us the World Cup!" Fifteen years after the March for Equality and Against Racism (in which a group of French citizens of North African descent marched from Marseille to Paris to protest racism), the presence of these second-generation immigrants was finally perceived as an asset for athletic competitions and the economy. Zidane had a tremendous impact on society following the July 12 victory, embodied by "Zizoumania."

Consider then-president Jacques Chirac and his change of heart on "cultural mixing" in France. The same president who in 1991 had given an unfortunate speech on the "noise and stench" of immigrants living in public housing projects, now declared, on July 14, 1998, "this multicolored French team projects a positive image of France's strength and humanism." Charles Pasqua, firm-handed minister of the interior under former president François Mitterrand, got even more caught up in the fervor. In an interview with *Le Monde*, he used the soccer victory to advocate for a massive push to grant papers to undocumented foreigners: "The World Cup has proven that integration has had a ninety percent success rate in this country. It's also reinforced the idea among French people that France is a self-sufficient nation. In such moments of national strength, France can be generous, and we should do something concrete. De Gaulle likely would have done so." Meanwhile, the National Front celebrated what it saw as a symbolic victory, warmly congratulated Zidane, then turned around to recast him as a "child of French Algeria."

The summer of 1998 was very much a singular moment

of social and ethnic cohesion, as reflected in the slogan *La France black-blanc-beur*. This event did not happen in a social and political vacuum. On the one hand, if this victory can be understood as a French model for integration and society, it is because the national team was an expression of the nation's founding ideals of secularism and social cohesion. On the other hand, this moment of national fellowship also happened to coincide with a burst of economic growth in 1997–1998 that translated into lower rates of unemployment, particularly among young people. For a fleeting moment, this conjunction of economic "happiness" and national pride made integrating the disenfranchised youth of France's *banlieues* seem possible.

Sadly, that did not last. But things could have turned out differently. The dramatic shift in geopolitics (9/11, the war in Iraq, perpetual unrest in the Middle East), internal social strife in French society (the 2005 riots), and the stunning policy weaknesses of back-to-back administrations all stifled this inspirational myth. In its stead, to cite Benjamin Disraeli speaking of nineteenth-century England, our deeply divided society now seems to house "two nations."

Stéphane Beaud

REFERENCES

Beaud, Stéphane, and Philippe Guimard. *Traîtres à la nation? Un autre regard sur la grève des Bleus en Afrique du Sud*. Paris: La Découverte, 2011.

Gastaut, Yvan. *Le Métissage par le foot: L'intégration, mais jusqu'où?* Paris: Autrement, 2008.

Jablonka, Ivan. "Le nom des jeunes sans nom." In *Jeunesse oblige*, edited by Ludivine Bantigny and Ivan Jablonka, 227–94. Paris: Presses Universitaires de France, 2009.

Noiriel, Gérard, Geoffroy Laforcade, and Charles Tilly. *The French Melting Pot: Immigration, Citizenship, and National Identity*. Minneapolis: University of Minnesota Press, 1996.

Thiesse, Anne-Marie. *La création des identités nationales (Europe XVIIIe–XIXe siècle)*. Paris: Point-Seuil, 2001 [1999].

Thuram, Lilian. *8 juillet 1998*. Paris: Anne Carrière, 2004.

RELATED ARTICLES
1927, 1931, 1974, 2008, 2015

2003

"This Message Comes to You from an Old Country..."

How much has the memory of Dominique de Villepin's skillfully framed speech opposing the Iraq invasion at the United Nations on February 14, 2003, given his compatriots the courage to believe that their "old country" was not done yet? On that day, striking a delicate if passionate balance between France's last will and its rebirth, the French foreign minister breathed new life into the nation's once-independent policy toward the Arab world.

There are some speeches that stand like monuments to the glory of the French nation. One man speaks out in splendid solitude and suddenly he is "the voice of France," expressing the deepest essence of its people's pride and becoming the man of the moment, a messenger of truth and standard bearer of the nation's identity. With just such a speech, Dominique de Villepin, an unelected scion of France's political aristocracy who had been appointed minister of foreign affairs by President Jacques Chirac, made himself comparable to André Malraux accompanying Jean Moulin to his grave at the Panthéon in 1964, de Gaulle broadcasting from London on June 18, 1940, or Jean Jaurès intoning against the shooting of strikers at Fourmies in 1891. All of them uttered words of such power that everyone else seemed to have fallen silent. On February 14, 2003, Villepin brought to the United Nations in New York the image of a just France with a noble vision of international politics. Responding to Donald Rumsfeld's mockery of a feeble "old Europe," he dealt a sharp lesson — and a sharp correction, albeit all too vain — to the warmongers of America.

What did Villepin say? To begin, he followed the traditional French foreign policy line against war in the Middle East on the grounds that normal procedures should be fully respected and all peaceful solutions explored before the UN could resort to hostilities. He reminded his audience that France had been instrumental in formulating this policy, thus avoiding a repeat of the first Gulf crisis scenario, whereby France's participation in the coalition against Saddam Hussein had created major splits within the French government. He then evoked the right of an "old" European nation to say no to a fresh invasion of Iraq. In this, he was reading strictly from the Gaullist playbook of French independence from the United Nations and more particularly from the NATO alliance. With this reference, clearly embedded in his conclusion, the speech became the voice of France. It also met with thunderous applause.

This message comes to you today from an old country, France; from a continent of Europe that has known war, occupation, and barbarity. France is an old country and she does not forget; she is well aware of what she owes to the defenders of freedom who came from America and elsewhere. And yet France has always stood upright before mankind, in the face of history. Faithful to her values, she will act resolutely, together with all other members of the international community. She believes in our ability to build a better world — together.

Beyond its immediate implications, this speech expressed a different loyalty, one which bound France to its own Arab policy. This policy has a complex and changing history. It prints upon the history of the Arab world, as seen from France, a special idea that linked the Middle East to Bonaparte's extraordinary expedition to Egypt, and to the agreements made following the Ottoman capitulation whereby eastern Christians would be protected within the Ottoman Empire. This wide-ranging policy encompasses Christianity, revolutionary Enlightenment, European colonization, and even Third Worldism. It thus offers an approach through which France could — and still can be — reconciled with itself. For example, the country's kinship, or, rather, its special relationship with the East had led

France to intervene in 1860 to save the Christians of Mount Lebanon, and more than a century later to intervene in the Lebanese civil conflict.

Yet this policy was not immediately linked to the French Empire in Algeria. The fact is that over the years, behind the screen of its all-accommodating Arab policy, France carefully contrived to avoid any association of its Arabic-speaking colonies in the Maghreb with the wider Arab world.

Since the mid-nineteenth century, the left and right in France felt obliged to agree upon a common Arab policy, which they aligned with a shared conception of the East, often making it the scene of exceptions to the rule of universal values. Secularism (*laïcité*) was obviously a case in point, being scarcely applicable in a region where the stated French priority was to "defend Christianity." Paradoxically, the Algerian chieftain Abd el-Kader bridged the gap between the policy of colonial conquest and a "French Arab policy" in 1860. Long deemed public enemy number one, he morphed into the "best enemy," a French protégé and valiant citizen representing French values, after defending Christians from persecution in Damascus (to which he had been exiled by the French).

Nevertheless, "French Arab policy" also marked a turning point in French colonialism. At the outset, everything possible was done to keep the Middle East and its "protected" peoples as separate as possible from the French Maghreb.

The period between the two world wars and the installation of French mandates in the Levant forced a change in this position. In the French colonial view, the Maghreb was first and foremost a region of Africa, perceived as part of France's African Empire. But the work of French Arabist scholars, notably those who accompanied Marshal Hubert Lyautey to Morocco in the early years of the twentieth century, radically altered this perspective. Louis Massignon and his successor Jacques Berque moved unhindered from one territory to another, establishing connections between the Middle East and the Western Arabian regions, and demonstrating how much these regions had in common. In view of the growing autonomy of the Arab peoples placed under French protection, little by little their recommendations became the Arab policy of France. This transformed the country's colonial policy.

Culture was the key element. In 1928, a committee of Arabists came together at the instigation of Philippe Berthelot, a key diplomat in the ministry of foreign affairs. Influenced by Massignon, who had just come back from a mission to Syria, Berthelot laid the groundwork for a strategy that would combine a strong French presence, top-down stewardship, and careful appreciation of local conditions.

> We must make overtures — especially in Damascus — to those educated Muslims who are strongly opposed to us since they are the most

resolute and bitter adversaries of our mandate. We are lucky enough to have among our compatriots a certain number of men like MM. Massignon, William and Georges Marçais, Godefroy-Demombynes, Wiet, Massé, Colin, and Lévi-Provençal, all of whom are in the first rank of European Arabists.… By sending one or two of these scholars to Syria for a few months every year to collaborate with local academics and writers, a contact may be established between French science and Arab culture.

From that moment, France set about forging a specific link with the Arab world: one of reciprocal knowledge, founded in science and mutual esteem and centered upon language and modernity.

Dominique de Villepin, as we have seen, was reading from the score established by de Gaulle's famous utterance: "I flew to the complicated Orient with simple ideas. I knew that amid the tangle of issues there, an essential contest was taking place. So I had to be essential too." De Gaulle's maxim of French Oriental policy did not come from nowhere; it is sometimes forgotten that he spent two years of his life in the Levant, between 1929 and 1931, observing the French at work. He understood the politics of pressure and influence; he had witnessed the consequences of the nationalist uprisings of 1925–1927 as well as the development of a French Arab policy that sought to bypass religious patronage and make common cause with the region's modernist elites. As a participant in the military pacification of the region, he strongly opposed the liberal approach; a similar distrust of French Republican parliamentarians made him critical of Syrian and Lebanese public life in the late 1920s, as the protagonists staggered from crisis to crisis. Still, despite his suspicions, de Gaulle was well aware that the Middle East had reached a turning point. France's new Arab policy was fundamentally pro-Muslim — and it meant the end of the privileges enjoyed by the Christian elites under French protection.

Decolonization, as we know, soon became a bloody affair that scarred this policy, but also a domestic matter and a vehicle for promoting French commercial and strategic interests. Georges Pompidou, Valéry Giscard d'Estaing, and Jacques Chirac all followed the same line, fostering links with their Arab counterparts and managing to keep France in the game because it "had to be essential too." France won huge weapons contracts — from Iraq during the Iran–Iraq War and right up to the eve of the 1991 invasion — and these came with generous agreements to protect France's clients. More than any speech to the UN, Chirac's Arab policy guaranteed him immense popularity throughout the region. It consisted of a series of gestures, from the comic-heroic fracas in the Old City of Jerusalem in 1996, where he publicly berated his overbearing Israeli minders, to "family" holidays with the King of Morocco, a personal friendship with the Lebanese Rafik Hariri, and treatment for the dying Yasir Arafat in a Paris hospital.

Chirac's dealings with — and on behalf of — the Arabs showed bravado, a light touch, and a certain arrogance in his manner of siding with the weak. He stood shoulder to shoulder with Arab dictators, indulging them more often than they deserved. France drew the benefits from this long history of accommodation, which Villepin claimed to reject in his speech. At the same time, France showed itself to be in tune with the Arab street, advocating a foreign policy based on fraternity between peoples and a form of geostrategic populism that included the use of English. Chirac's famous question on his arrival in Palestine — "You want me to go back to my plane?" — exemplified the delight he took in making himself popular with the Palestinian population, but also in highlighting the difference of approach with his Socialist prime minister, Lionel Jospin, who was pelted with stones when he visited Ramallah three years later.

In reality, the French Arab policy has in its different incarnations functioned as a cynical trompe l'oeil to preserve markets and commercial advantages for France. The Arab world France has preferred has invariably been one that could be relied upon to stay exactly as it had been, with pristine beaches, slow archaeological digs, and endless conflicts. Who cared if this stability was tightly controlled by a dictatorship as long as the dictatorship in question did not threaten France? Working on this principle, France gave its solid support to military governments in Algeria, Muammar Gaddafi's Libya, Saddam Hussein's Iraq, Bashar al-Assad's Syria, Zine al-Abidine Ben Ali's Tunisia, and the Makhzen's Morocco. Yet, certain French politicians continue to wear this long history like a badge of honor, declaring themselves to be friends, even connoisseurs of the Arab world. Such was the case of Jean-Pierre Chevènement, who resigned his post rather than go to war against Saddam's corrupt regime. For the record, Chevènement was appointed head of the Fondation d'Islam de la France, the Islamic Foundation of France, immediately after the Paris atrocities of 2015. He secured the position on the basis of his long friendship with the Muslim community.

Leyla Dakhli

REFERENCES

Aeschimann, Éric, and Christophe Boltanski. *Chirac d'Arabie: Les mirages d'une politique française*. Paris: Grasset, 2006.

Dakhli, Leyla. "L'expertise en terrain colonial: Les orientalistes et le mandat français en Syrie et au Liban." *Matériaux pour l'histoire de notre temps* 3, no. 99 (2010): 20–27.

Khoury, Gérard. *La France et l'Orient arabe. Naissance du Liban moderne (1914–1920)*. Paris: Armand Colin, 1993.

Laurens, Henry. *Le Royaume impossible: La France et la genèse du monde arabe*. Paris: Armand Colin, 1990.

Nouschi, André. *La France et le monde arabe depuis 1962: Mythes et réalités d'une ambition*. Paris: Vuibert, 1994.

RELATED ARTICLES

1095, 1715, 1790, 1798, 1825, 1863, 1883, 1960, 1962

2008

The Native Land in Mourning

On April 17, 2008, Aimé Césaire, founder of the Negritude
movement, died at Fort-de-France in Martinique.
Paradoxically, the national consensus and avalanche
of official tributes that followed his death were at odds
with his poetic and political engagements and his radical
anticolonialism.

An emblematic figure of black Francophone literature, on a
par with Léopold Sédar Senghor and Léon-Gontran Damas,
Aimé Césaire was a poet ahead of his time, a debunker of
racial clichés, and a tireless enemy of colonialism. His credo
is best expressed in his famous play *Et les chiens se taisaient*
(*And the Dogs Were Silent*), first performed in 1958: "My
name: insulted. My first name: humiliated. My state: in
rebellion. My age: the stone age. My race: the human race.
My religion: brotherhood."

Born in Martinique in 1913, Césaire was educated at the
Lycée Schoelcher on his native island. He reached Paris in
1931 with a scholarship and entered the preparatory class

for advanced studies in literature at the prestigious Lycée Louis-le-Grand. There he met Senghor, from Senegal, and Damas, from French Guiana, with whom he was later to launch the Negritude movement. In 1935, now a student at the École Normale Supérieure, he encountered the Harlem Renaissance, which had reached Paris along with a group of exiled black American writers. This movement was later to have a direct influence on the emancipation of black students in France, who would cite the work of Langston Hughes during their protests in 1968.

The word *négritude*, which appeared for the first time in Césaire's 1939 poem *Cahier d'un retour au pays natal* (*Notebook of a Return to the Native Land*), was destined to become central to the process of black self-affirmation, through pride in African roots and rejection of the aesthetic canons imposed by the West. From 1931 onward, most black intellectuals in France had laid out their views and experiences in the *Revue du monde noir* (Review of the Black World), but money being in short supply, the magazine had folded after six issues. The more radical and political publication that replaced it, *Légitime défense*, was confined to a single issue by pressure from the French authorities.

Aimé Césaire, who was by then the president of the Antillean students' association, saw the opening and started another periodical, *L'Étudiant noir* (The Black Student), whose purpose he explained as follows: "A small student newspaper called *L'Étudiant martiniquais* was already in existence; so I decided to broaden it and call it *L'Étudiant noir*, with a view to working with black people from all over the world, not just Martinicans...which is to say that to some extent Negritude was replacing assimilationist ideology." Thus *L'Étudiant noir* played a significant role in the expression of a Negritude whose definition varied according to the temperament and personal history of its initiators. Césaire's own Negritude was not necessarily the same as Senghor's, which was more ideological in tone. The Martinican poet himself outlined the differences: "Senghor is an African. He has behind him a continent, a history, and the wisdom of the ages. I am Caribbean, a man uprooted and torn away from Africa."

In 1939, Césaire returned to Martinique and became a teacher at his old lycée. Two years later, he, his wife Suzanne, and their friends founded yet another periodical, *Tropiques.* With the publication of *Notebook of a Return to the Native Land,* Negritude became a formal idea, written and carried by poetry. It also attracted the attention of the leading philosophers of the time, especially Jean-Paul Sartre, whose 1948 preface to Senghor's *Anthologie de la nouvelle poésie nègre et malgache de langue française* (Anthology of the New Negro and Malagasy Poetry in the French Language) carried the title of "Black Orpheus." He defined the new Black African movement as follows:

"Negritude is neither a state nor a collection of vices and virtues nor a set of intellectual and moral qualities. It is a certain emotional attitude to the world...a kind of tension of the soul, a choice made by oneself and others, a way of rising above the soul's raw data, in short a project and a willful act. Negritude, to use the jargon of Heidegger, is *being-in-the-world-of-the-Negro*."

Negritude, as Césaire himself defined it, came into existence because of — or thanks to — the white man, original coiner of the term "negro." "The whites invented Negritude....This word *negro* that people throw at us, we've taken it for our own. It's a defiance word, transformed into a foundation word. But Negritude must be seen as a humanism. By reaching beyond particularism, we arrive at the universal. The point of departure is the black man, but the point of arrival is man — no more and no less."

As a politician, Césaire was criticized for promoting the vote to make his island — and certain other French colonies — departments of France rather than opting for full independence. His *Discourse on Colonialism* suffices in his defense because this short work is one of the most virulent charges against a political system that the poet himself deemed iniquitous and toxic: "Between the colonizer and the colonized, there's only room for hard labor, intimidation, pressure, police, theft, rape, compulsory cultures, suspicion, distrust, arrogance, self-importance, boorishness, mindless elitism, debased masses."

In his 1956 "Letter to Maurice Thorez," Césaire thunderously quit the French Communist Party because of his opposition to its handling of the post-Stalinist period. "What? All the other Communist parties are changing. Italy. Poland. Hungary. China. Yet the French Communist Party, in the middle of it all, looks smugly at itself and says it is satisfied....Personally, I think that the black peoples are now primed with energy and passion; they lack neither vigor nor imagination. But these forces can only wither away in organizations that are not their own, that are not created for and by them and adapted to ends that only they can determine." In the same way, Césaire castigated the Eurocentric vision of French Communists, which he called "unconscious chauvinism." In its place, he proposed what he called "fraternalism" among French Communists. With this in mind, he created the Martinican Progressive Party together with the autonomist physician Pierre Aliker and other allies. According to its founding statutes, the party was "nationalist, democratic and anti-colonialist, inspired by the socialist ideal."

But the people of the French Caribbean could no more escape the mirages of consumerism and internal political strife than anyone else. Poetry once again became Césaire's priority. He began a life's work that raised him more and more to the position of "guardian of the damned," as the Martinican psychiatrist and essayist Frantz Fanon phrased it, or "voice of the mute," as he described himself in his own *Notebook*. Reading between the lines, it is clear that he planned to continue with his political and social activities under the cloak of art, in such a way that nobody would be able to distinguish the politician from the poet. After *Les Armes miraculeuses* (Miraculous Weapons, 1946), *Soleil cou-coupé* (Cut-off Sun, 1948), and *Corps perdu* (Lost Body, 1950), Césaire published *Ferrements* in 1960 and *Cadastre* in 1961. Literary critic Jean-Louis Joubert has described Césaire's increasingly messianic body of work as follows: "It is probable that the fascination of the work of Césaire is down to the coherence of his poetic project. In poem after poem he repeats the same dramatic framework, namely the destruction of an old world and the birth of a new one, developed amid a web of key images such as sunshine, natural disasters, wild animals, and the flowers of the Antilles. He describes the manner and the time (imperative and future) of the longed-for revolution. Each of his poems sets up and magnifies a verbal disaster in which colonial disorder plunges to its destruction, amid a cataclysm that liberates the promise of the future. Although Césaire clings to his apocalyptic vision till the end, his final collection (*Moi, laminaire*, 1982) is troubled by the ache of failure: in these last poems his volcanoes are extinct and the roots he has developed in his native land are withered."

Aimé Césaire died, aged ninety-four, on April 17, 2008. President Nicolas Sarkozy paid tribute to him: "He was a great humanist, in whom all those who fought for the emancipation of peoples in the twentieth century might see themselves reflected." France saluted one of its greatest French-language poets, whose theatrical work was crowned in 1991 by the adoption of his play *La tragédie du roi Christophe* into the repertoire of the Comédie Française.

But Césaire also made a significant contribution to what is nowadays called world literature. When, with his colleagues Senghor and Damas, he introduced the word *Négritude* into black African literature, he opened new pathways for study, envisioning an alternative interpretation of the world in which the African imagination and the African diaspora constitute the missing link to a world redefined around a culture of exchange and mutual comprehension.

In the twilight of his life, Césaire remained resolute in his views. In 2005, for example, he refused to meet Sarkozy — then France's interior minister — who was contemplating a trip to the Caribbean. The visit was canceled. By his refusal, Césaire showed his opposition to the law of February 23, 2005, that required schools to teach the "positive aspects" of colonization. These principles were diametrically opposed to the cause that

Césaire had championed throughout his life and above all to the substance of his *Discourse on Colonialism*. Two years after being snubbed, Sarkozy (now president of the French Republic) made a controversial speech in Dakar in which he claimed that "the drama of Africa is that Africans have not sufficiently permeated the history of mankind."

In 2008, Sarkozy finally visited Martinique. He did so to attend Césaire's funeral, though the family refused to allow him to make a speech from which he might have drawn some kind of political advantage. A number of voices later demanded that the poet be admitted to the Panthéon, but the people of Martinique insisted that his ashes remain on the island of his birth. Nevertheless, on April 6, 2011 — in the presence of Sarkozy — Césaire did enter the Panthéon, albeit in a symbolic fashion: he is represented in a fresco in the nave of this monument to the individuals in whom the French nation takes such pride.

Alain Mabanckou

REFERENCES

Bouvier, Pierre. *Aimé Césaire, Frantz Fanon: Portraits de décolonisés.* Paris: Les Belles Lettres, 2010.

Césaire, Aimé. *Discours sur le colonialisme,* suivi de *Discours sur la négritude.* 1955. Paris: Présence Africaine, 2000.

————. *Notebook of a Return to the Native Land*. Translated and edited by Clayton Eshleman and Annette Smith. Middletown, CT: Wesleyan University Press, 2001.

————. *A Season in the Congo*. Translated by Gayatri Chakravorty Spivak; with an introduction by Souleymane Bachir Diagne. London/New York: Seagull Books, 2010.

Confiant, Raphaël. *Aimé Césaire: Une traversée paradoxale du siècle*. Paris: Stock, 1993.

Fonkoua, Romuald. *Aimé Césaire*. Paris: Perrin, 2010.

RELATED ARTICLES

1842, 1907, 1931, 1953, 1960, 1961

2011

Power Stripped Bare

On May 14, 2011, Dominique Strauss-Kahn, chairman of the International Monetary Fund and a likely frontrunner in the French presidential election of 2012, was arrested in a New York hotel for sexual assault. The news went global, but the fallout affected France first and foremost.

The script seemed done and dusted. Once again, France was awaiting the return of a savior, a providential leader. This time he was expected to come from the other side of the Atlantic. Dominique Strauss-Kahn was the head of the International Monetary Fund, an institution sprung from the ruins of World War II. The French political media was fixated on him: when would he declare his candidacy for the French presidency?

Nicolas Sarkozy's term, which had begun with such high self-confidence, was moribund. The debt crisis of 2008 was partly responsible, as was the impatience of the French with the futile gesticulations of their government and its perpetual confusion between public and private life. Luckily a light glittered in Washington. A trained economist, a member of the Socialist party in the 1970s, twice a minister in the 1990s, Strauss-Kahn personified a form of modern social democracy that could be reconciled with globalization. Though Ségolène Royal had edged him out for the Socialist nomination in 2007, the polls now predicted he would win handsomely. The party's nomination was open to all leftist voters in the fall of 2011. With a view to renovating France's rusty democratic process, a major political party was for the first time holding an American-style primary.

And then, in the middle of the night of May 14 (Paris time), the news broke. It was broadcast first on Twitter, still little-known at the time, and then relayed worldwide by traditional media. The savior, the professor of economics, the IMF chairman who hopped from capital to capital to help sovereign states on the verge of bankruptcy, had just been arrested in New York. He was charged with sexual assault and attempted rape on the person of Nafissatou Diallo, a hotel chambermaid who had arrived in the United States from Guinea in 2004.

The scene of this drama was room 2806 of the Sofitel New York, a brand belonging to the French-owned AccorHotels, the world's sixth-largest luxury hotel group. Sofitel's website proudly indicated that its establishments offered "comfort, modernity, and French *art de vivre*." What happened next is common knowledge — perhaps too common: a suspect in handcuffs, unshaven and rumpled; the perp walk; Rikers Island; incomprehension and indignation; communiqués from Euro RSCG, Europe's largest PR agency; hotshot Manhattan lawyers; the total, unflinching support of Strauss-Kahn's wife, journalist Anne Sinclair.

Despite the supposed omnipotence of spin doctors, nothing took place as expected. May 14, 2011, was a turning point, a moment when the probable gave way to the unpredictable. There was an avalanche of images, revelations, and counter-inquiries, of conspiracy theories and deep psychoanalysis about an encounter between the world's most powerful dispenser of money and an African immigrant worker. All this combined, day after day, to hatch a modern fable of power, sex, and money at the dawn of globalization and social networks — a fable that the most fanciful novelist wouldn't have dared to imagine. Most astonishing was the realization that mundane events had retained their ability to upend both reality and the lenses through which we perceive this reality. Mired in legal difficulties, grappling with the 24/7 exposure of his private life, Strauss-Kahn was finished — all the more so when the scandal broadened to include bevies of prostitutes at orgies in the Lille Carlton hotel. French political history departed abruptly from the predicted course. François Hollande won the Socialist primary that October and then the French presidency in May 2012.

The main consequence of this world event was, in the end, strictly national. Precisely because it took place in New York, financial capital of the world and endless source of fascination, governed by a judicial system and an ethical framework so different from their French counterparts, it caused a massive upheaval in the order of things and proved deeply revealing. For, beyond the sequence of events it set into motion, this scandal allowed the French public to grasp deeper trends and dynamics that governed their country's mores and social structures. Basically, during these long weeks, France's elites and their attitudes to globalization were called into question.

Emblematic of a confident nation at ease with globalization, Strauss-Kahn's competence, networks, and civility were praised by all. This image of openness and modernity, this capacity to reassure the great powers and the business community went back to the 1990s, when Strauss-Kahn — then a Socialist deputy — had occupied the post of minister of the economy, finance, and industry in the government of Prime Minister Lionel Jospin. At that time, the French left, buoyed by the return of economic growth, overhauled the thirty-five-hour week, same-sex unions (known in France as PACS), and universal health coverage while launching privatizations and tapping its minister's reputation to sell its debt to foreign investors (some of these French treasury bonds were nicknamed "DSK bonds").

Strauss-Kahn's career symbolized an outward-looking, cosmopolitan, and polyglot France. Indeed, he seemed as much in his element at Davos as he was in the Paris suburb of Sarcelles — until, that is, his first legal difficulties just before the turn of the century, when he was accused of financial corruption and resigned from the International Monetary Fund.

He did not fully recover until 2007. Defeated in the Socialist primary, the former minister was propelled to the leadership of the IMF by the support of several European leaders — including France's new president, Nicolas Sarkozy, who was only too happy to ship off this powerful rival. The challenge Strauss-Kahn had to face was on a par with his ambition. At that time, the IMF's location and goals remained undefined, and its system of internal governance required reform to take account of emerging nations and their demands. Globalization lacked a human face, one compatible with the hope of the just and stable growth that it was expected to generate. Strauss-Kahn was the fourth Frenchman to occupy the post of IMF chairman and managing director, after Pierre-Paul Schweitzer (1963–1973), Jacques de Larosière (1978–1987), and Michel Camdessus (1987–2000), all of whom had earlier been directors of the French Treasury. At the same time, two former French government inspectors of finances, Jean-Claude Trichet and Pascal Lamy, were presiding over the destinies of the European Central Bank and the World Trade Organization. Thus between 2005 and 2010, France was the breeding ground not only of globalization's architects and regulators, such as maverick WTO director Lamy, but also of its most famous adversaries, including the anti-globalist environmental campaigner José Bové.

Then came the subprime mortgage crisis, a perfect opportunity for the new IMF chairman to impose himself as the leading interlocutor of governments and financial markets. The IMF's clear-sightedness was much praised at the time. Instead of aping the inertia of public authorities in the 1930s, the fund urged massive intervention by governments to avert the collapse of the international banking system. Two years later, the private debt crisis was transformed into a crisis of sovereign debt, and the IMF, under the direction of Strauss-Kahn and his chief economist Olivier Blanchard (also French), set up multiple loans and credits for the likes of Iceland, Ireland, and Portugal — countries in grave difficulty that promised to enact painful structural reforms and austerity policies. In 2010–2011, the Greek financial crisis brought Europe even closer to the abyss.

The sordid humiliation of the IMF chairman therefore took place against a background of extreme financial vulnerability, at a moment when all eyes were fixed on the institution he was leading. In the end, the shock was less severe than expected for everyone but the IMF and the

French Socialist Party. Strauss-Kahn resigned, and, a few weeks later, another French minister, Christine Lagarde, took his place. What a startling contrast between the sluggish reputation of the French economy, downgraded by the financial rating agencies at the beginning of 2012, and the dazzling ability of its elites to raise themselves to the highest posts in global governance.

The Sofitel affair took its place in a series of scandals that, around 2010, placed the spotlight on the practices of French economic and political leaders and exposed a complex interweaving between networks, investments, and private and public sector leaders. Sandwiched between the Bettencourt affair and the Cahuzac scandal, both of which revealed the scale of tax evasion among French citizens with high incomes and enormous fortunes, the Strauss-Kahn case showed how closely official globalization and the world of finance and international organizations were linked to an underground, unsavory form of globalization, that of prostitution networks and high society debauchery. From luxury hotels to strip clubs on the French–Belgian border, the DSK sequence of events shed a pitiless light on the social and geographical frontiers of globalization at the beginning of the twenty-first century.

The fall of Dominique Strauss-Kahn took down another figure, a mythical one: the French seducer, the gallant male intoxicated by beautiful women and grand ambitions, the irresistible French lover. This imposture collapsed forever in the eyes of the world — and of France itself. In the wake of these revelations, proponents of the code of seduction à la française, with its sophisticated love games and flirtatious exchanges, took aim at the puritanism and hypocrisy of an Anglo-Saxon society that could not conceive sexual relations outside of law and marriage.

But the truth was now out in the open, too patent to deny. Behavior like DSK's had been widespread but tolerated in years past. Now, another French "exception" was dissolving in the face of globalization — namely the age-old barrier between public and private life and the stubborn refusal to see sexual harassment for what it is: an outrage upon women. Thus the Sofitel affair, like the new technologies and the new cultural norms spreading around the world, played its part in making transparency an imperative of democracy.

Nicolas Delalande

REFERENCES

Abdelal, Rawi. *Capital Rules: The Construction of Global Finance.* Cambridge, MA: Harvard University Press, 2007.

Bacqué, Raphaëlle, and Ariane Chemin. *Les Strauss-Kahn.* Paris: Albin Michel, 2012.

Jaunait, Alexandre, and Frédérique Matonti, eds. "Consentement sexuel." Special issue of *Raisons politiques* 46 (2012).

Lemoine, Benjamin. *L'Ordre de la dette: Enquête sur les infortunes de l'État et la prospérité du marché*. Paris: La Découverte, 2016.

Solomon, John. *DSK: The Scandal That Brought Down Dominique Strauss-Kahn*. New York: Thomas Dunne, 2012.

Wagner, Anne-Catherine, ed. "Le pouvoir économique: Classes sociales et modes de domination." Special issue of *Actes de la recherche en sciences sociales* 190 (2011).

RELATED ARTICLES

1720, 1784, 1860, 1983

2015

The Return of the Flag

The shock waves from the terrorist attacks that struck
Paris in January and November 2015 were felt all over the
world. In their wake, the tricolored flag of France suddenly
appeared in the windows of ordinary people everywhere.
Its last mass showing had been on a joyous Champs-
Élysées in 1989. The latest, in 2015, took place in a much
more somber world.

Was 2015 the year of the return of the tricolor flag? All over
France, in January and again in November, the banner of
the Republic appeared overnight in the windows of millions
of homes and offices. Soon thereafter, it vaulted across the
planet to adorn the central monuments of Australia, Great
Britain, Germany, and the United States. The day after the
November terrorist attacks in Paris, it was flown on the
Sydney Opera House and atop the Empire State Building,
beside the statue of Christ on Rio's Corcovado and above the
Brandenburg Gate in Berlin. This was a wordless statement:
by raising the tricolor, country after country declared
their support for a beleaguered France and promised their
engagement (up to a point) on France's behalf.

In a year that saw almost monthly terrorist attacks — Paris in January, Copenhagen in February, Tunis in March, Garissa, Kenya, in April, Sousse, Tunisia, in June, Ankara in October, and then on November 13 Paris again, leaving a total of 130 dead on the café terraces of the 10th and 11th arrondissements, in the Bataclan concert venue and in Saint-Denis, on the edge of the city — people all over the world awaited the appearance of their own national flag on the Eiffel Tower or the Sydney Opera House.

Why did some nationalities (say, the French) have a right to these silent signs of solidarity while others did not? Were some victims of terrorist atrocities less important than others? Did the beflagged locations abroad obey the same half-mast protocol as official French government buildings? And whose decision was it that, after the appalling Islamic State group attack on its Bardo Museum (twenty-four dead, forty-five wounded, nearly all of them Western visitors), Tunisia should have its flag flown on the Eiffel Tower?

In addition to colors, there were words and above all slogans — notably *"Je suis Charlie."* It first appeared the evening of the January 7 attack on the editorial board of the weekly satirical newspaper *Charlie Hebdo*, an attack that killed eleven journalists and staff members and one policeman guarding the paper's offices. *Charlie Hebdo* had been under serious threat for years on account of its mocking attitude to religion, especially Islam. Another attack took place the next day, killing a municipal policewoman, followed the day after by an assault on a kosher supermarket at the Porte de Vincennes in Paris, in which four people died. The simple *"Je suis Charlie"* slogan summed up all this horror, to such effect that when news of the attacks on the Bardo Museum came through on March 18, the cry was instantly *"Je suis Bardo."* Nevertheless, when other murderous attacks were claimed by Islamists, *"Je suis Mali"* and *"Je suis Kenya"* found a diminished echo.

Red, white, and blue are colors everyone can understand, especially when accompanied by words so simple that they make sense even to those who do not speak French. And figures too — no fewer than four million people assembled in silence at various rallies in tribute to the victims of January 11. This made it possible to tabulate collective emotion.

The legacy of 2015 is that of a media culture that can summarize any event, however complex and dramatic, in a matter of seconds. Politicians grasped this only too well. From the static gathering of chiefs of state, arm in arm, in Paris on January 11, right through to November 13, when a request was made by President François Hollande for citizens to display the tricolor in their windows, the French government sought to transform the commemorative aftermath of the terrorist attacks into images that could be exported in different forms.

With what success, though? Social networks and

impromptu happenings do not follow commands issued from on high. Who decided, on the afternoon of January 7, to call a rally on the Place de la République, only a few hundred meters from the site of the attack on *Charlie Hebdo*? Who determined that the base of the huge statue in the Place de la République, so recently renovated, should become an altar to the victims of the atrocity? Who predicted that simple messages of condolence, children's drawings, and flickering candles would attract thousands of people to pay homage to the murdered cartoonists? Who mobilized the "*Je n'ai pas peur*" torches for the spontaneous demonstration on January 7? Who came up with the idea of parading a giant Marianne puppet from the avant-garde ensemble Théâtre du Soleil through the streets on the 11th arrondissement?

Nobody. Or rather everybody. The creativity that was unleashed, aware of its place within a world of global images and media, reminded French men and women that their streets and public spaces still belonged to them.

Yet these events took place in a country that had sustained violent terrorist attacks for several decades. France had been hit numerous times since the 1980s. Apart from the continual threat of domestic terrorism — from Corsican extremists, for instance — most of these attacks were linked to French foreign policy. The attacks of 1985–1986 were a response to France's position in Lebanon, while those of 1995–1996 (committed by Khaled Kelkal, a child of the

Lyon suburbs who became the first French Islamist terrorist) originated in the Algerian Civil War. They echoed, within France, the attacks against the headquarters of the French United Nations contingent in Beirut in 1983, or the murder of the French Trappist monks of Tibhirine, Algeria, in 1996. Placed in the Métro or in railway carriages, in stations or by the windows of department stores, bombs had long taught the French — and especially the Parisians — to beware of unattended luggage and pay attention to the slogan "*Attentifs, ensemble*" ("Watchful, together"), repeated on Métro loudspeakers. For years, there had been a military presence in France's streets and railway stations, part of an anti-terrorist strategy known as *Vigipirate renforcé*, which was put in place after the attack on the Saint-Michel station in 1995. *Vigipirate*, which was originally expected to be temporary, has remained in place ever since. To this day French infantrymen armed with submachine guns are a common sight in Paris, a surprise to no one but foreign tourists. They draw attention to a diffuse but real threat, but, in March 2012, they could not prevent Mohammed Merah from shooting soldiers and then slaughtering children and their teachers in a Jewish school in Toulouse.

Despite these government measures, the recurrence of terrorist acts in France doesn't mean that the population has gotten used to them. Which is why, in January and November 2015 nobody could say they weren't afraid — for themselves or their families. Indeed, there was another source of fear: that the hopes aroused on the Champs-Élysées on July 14, 1989, by a Parisian parade — relayed by all media and considerably more festive than that of the Place de la République on January 11, 2015 — would be shown to have come to naught. Orchestrated by a figure from the world of advertising and show business, Jean-Paul Goude, the 1989 parade had assembled thousands of traditional musicians — who played every instrument from the bagpipes to the hurdy-gurdy — and scores of musical and dance groups from all over the world. July 14, 1989, was a powerful manifesto for a France that was open to the world, in which the drums of Doudou N'Diaye Rose, American marching bands, and Arab dancers performed side by side with the "tribes of the French provinces," as Goude called them. His intention, symptomatic of an era marked by the birth of the anti-racist movement SOS Racisme, was to "unite French and African tribal music" at a single event. The huge parade was preceded by a group of people tossing red, white, and blue flags to the crowd; it concluded with the "La Marseillaise," sung by Jessye Norman, the opera diva, draped in a voluminous tricolored gown.

The topic of the moment was *métissage*, or multicultural blending, and the exaltation of a diverse France, which many hoped to see reborn as *black-blanc-beur* (black, white, Arab) on the same Avenue des Champs-Élysées that witnessed the 1998 victory parade of the World Cup–winning French soccer team.

So what had been lost, between the patriotic but globalized élan of 1989 and the solemn gatherings of 2015? Hostility to immigration and immigrants had strengthened. With every election, French voters opted in greater numbers for the National Front of Jean-Marie Le Pen and his daughter and successor Marine Le Pen. Closures of French factories and their relocation to Eastern Europe, Asia, and North Africa raised deep reservations about the value of the open borders imposed by an increasingly unpopular European Union. Finally, the acrimonious 2007–2008 debates on secularism (*laïcité*) and national identity eroded the idea of an open country, inclusive of all colors.

Nevertheless, in 2015 the red, white, and blue banner returned to the balconies of France. The many nuances these hues represented in 1989 had faded, but not altogether vanished. Who will revive them, and to what end?

Emmanuel Laurentin

REFERENCES

Boucheron, Patrick, and Mathieu Riboulet. *Prendre dates (Paris, 6 janvier–14 janvier 2015)*. Paris: Verdier, 2015.

Girardet, Raoul. "The Three Colors: Neither White nor Red." In *Realms of Memory: The Construction of the French Past*, edited by Pierre Nora and Lawrence D. Kritzman. Translated by Arthur Goldhammer, 3–26. New York: Columbia University Press, 1998.

Ory, Pascal. *Ce que dit Charlie: Treize leçons d'histoire*. Paris: Gallimard, 2015.

RELATED ARTICLES

1789, 1892, 1894, 1927, 1968, 1974, 1989, 1998, 2003

INDEX

INDEX

censorship: of *Encyclopedia,* 619–620, 624; freedom of expression *vs.,* 650–652; increasing, 523–525; of University of Paris scholars, 316–317

Césaire, Aimé, 1171–1174, 1262, 1303

Chalcolithic, 94–96

Champagne, Rashi in, 266–272

Champagne fairs, 299–306

Chanel, Gabrielle "Coco," 1022–1030

Chanel No. 5, 1021–1025, 1028–1030

charity, by Emmaus International, 1131–1134, 1137

Charlemagne (*aka* Carolus Magnus, Karl der Grosse), 127–129, 333, 749–750; crowned Emperor, 186–187, 193–194; division of empire of, 132, 371; grandsons of, 207, 371

Charles, dauphin of John II, 387

Charles, Duke of Lower Lotharingia, 232–233

Charles, Holy Roman Emperor, 449–450

Charles I of Anjou, 295

Charles II of the English Commonwealth, 536–537

Charles IX, King, 492; massacre of Protestants and, 494–501

Charles of Anjou, 342–346

Charles of Navarre, as pretender to throne, 385

Charles the Bald, 132, 197–198; Oaths of Strasbourg by, 208–209, 213; Vikings and, 220–221

Charles the Bold, 451

Charles the Fat, 215–217

Charles the Simple, 221–222, 235

Charles V, Holy Roman emperor, 455

Charles V, King, 400–402, 481

Charles VII, King, 424; consolidation of realm by, 280, 409, 449; economy and, 427–428; illegitimacy of reign of, 409–410

Charles VIII, King, 348, 433–434; credited with starting Renaissance, 446; death of, 439; Italy and, 438–446, 448–449; territory of, 441–442

Charles X, King, 688, 711

Charlie Hebdo, attacks on offices of, 1263–1264, 1323–1324

Chauvet Cave, 62, 65–72, 81, 1083

Chevènement, Jean-Pierre, 1244, 1281, 1301

Childeric, funeral of, 170–172

Chile, 1223–1231

Chimalpahin, 507

China, 339, 635–636, 775, 990; rebellions in, 948, 1206

Chirac, Jacques, 1090, 1290, 1299–1300

chivalry, 260, 264, 347–348, 442

cholera: epidemics of, 711, 775, 796–797; lack of understanding of, 794; pathology discovered, 796–797, 915; responses to, 796–798; vaccine against, 915–916

Christendom, 282, 305; schisms in, 373–374, 411

Christianity, 133–134, 215. *See also* Catholic Church; Protestants; Arianism, 164, 174; of Clovis, 169, 171–176; Council of Nicaea in, 173; Gaul martyrs for, 143, 145–150; influence of Rashi on, 266–272; Islam *vs.,* 283, 285–289, 416; Latin, 263, 282; in Lyon, 144–146; missionaries of, 219–220, 351; St. Martin and, 163–165

Christians: French protecting, 863, 1295–1296; Jews' relations with, 271–272; persecution of, 186, 258, 863

church, 224–225, 366, 619. *See also* Catholic Church; Christianity; religion; opposition to Enlightenment, 624, 629; power of, 198–

INDEX

INDEX

Normans, 354, 440;
England and, 251–
255; as Franks, 250,
254–257; Tupi natives
and, 486–492
North Africa, French
conquest of, 340
North America, 459–463,
503. *See also* United
States
Notre-Dame Cathedral,
298; influence of, 351,
356–357; Napoleon's
coronation at, 742–
743, 746; scholars
freed from oversight
by, 316–317
nuclear energy, 1216
nuclear weapons, 1163,
1200

O

Oaths of Strasbourg,
206–212
oceans, in *Catalan Atlas*,
398
Odo, 224, 227
Odo, King (*aka* Eudes),
217, 234
Odo, Marquis of
Neustria, 234
Odo (of Bayeux), 250
oil, 1221; crisis of, 1216,
1234; prices of, 1214,
1218
Old World, definition
of, 378
One Hundred Days,
Napoleon's return
from exile in, 768
Order of Saint John,
holding Cem, 430–432
Ordinance of Villers-
Cotterêts, 476–485,

492
Organization of Petro-
leum Exporting Coun-
tries, 1214–1215
orientalism, 582–589,
874
Orléans, Duke of, 793;
Philippe, 595, 600, 618
Orléans line, 792
Otto I (king of Germany
and Italy), 235, 242
Otto II, Emperor, 244
Otto IV, Holy Roman
Emperor, 308–312
Ottoman Empire, 444;
brothers' fight for con-
trol of, 430–431; refu-
gees from, 1032–1034;
siege of Vienna by, 433,
554, 566
Ottomans, 435–436;
Armenian genocide by,
1033–1034, 1106;
Egypt and, 725–728;
Greeks *vs.*, 710, 783–
785, 789–790
Ottonians, and
Capetians, 242–243

P

Pacific region, 837
pacifism, 964, 1019
Paleolithic, 60, 75–76
Pamiers, freedom for all
in, 413–414
Pan-African Congress,
1005, 1009–1010
Panthéon, 938, 958,
1272, 1310
papacy, 428. *See also*
popes; in Avignon,
360–367; French influ-
ence on, 364–365, 367;
homes of, 361–363;

negotiating Napoleon's
coronation, 746; oppo-
sition to, 363, 713; pol-
itics and, 343–347,
364–365, 433, 451; on
Protestants massacred
by Catholics, 498; uni-
versalism of, 372, 440
Papal States, creation of,
192
Paris, 301, 353–354, 646,
680, 803, 1005–1006,
1051–1052; bourgeois
of, 386; as capital,
175–176, 217; causes
of tension in, 495,
1131–1132; delegation
from Persia in, 591–
594; epidemics in,
381–382, 793, 795–
796; foreigners in, 615,
711, 805, 905, 1062–
1063; growth of, 297;
image of, 321, 323,
614, 682, 717, 840,
942, 963; intellectual
life in, 618–619, 717,
1174; occupiers seiz-
ing art, 768–769; pro-
tests in, 711, 803, 821,
880–882, 1208; public
health movement cen-
tered in, 799; religion
and, 466, 494–497,
1086–1090; support
for Greeks in, 782–
786, 789; terrorist
attacks in, 1263, 1285,
1321–1323, 1326; uni-
versal expositions in,
690, 941–948; Univer-
sity of Paris, 316–323
Paris, Treaty of, 622,
625–627, 766

1348

INDEX

Pompadour, Madame de, 617

Pompidou, Georges, 1276, 1299

popes, 293, 372. *See also* papacy; *specific popes*; on Charles I's expansion of territory, 295–296; emperors and, 186, 312; independence of, 191–192; on Sicilian rebellion, 342–345

Popular Front, 966, 1059–1066, 1206

popular sovereignty, 660–661, 667, 759, 889

population, 372, 840; decimated by plague, 377, 391; effects of climate on, 378; efforts to increase, 1043, 1118; growth of, 90, 614, 968; non-natives in, 1042–1043, 1234

Portugal, 459, 529, 555, 710, 753–754; imperialism of, 439–440, 460, 488, 530–531

positivism, Comte's, 908–909

postal service, 506, 889

postcolonial studies, 1177–1178

postmodernism, 1267

Pothinus (saint), 145–146, 149

pottery, 91; Bell Beaker, 95; of Cardial culture, 91; Corded Ware, 95; Linear Band, 92–93

poverty, 966, 1016, 1136–1137

prehistory, 86–87. *See also* cave art; French leadership in field of, 1079–1080; globalization of, 1081

prisons: Foucault on, 1252; penal colonies as, 826–832

property law, 805; slavery and, 413–414, 419

protectorates, establishment of, 838

Protestant Reformation, 373, 467

Protestants, 268; Calvin and, 466–474; emigration of, 469, 498, 565; German rulers as, 564, 567; as immigrants, 568–569; Louis XIV's suppression of, 554–555, 562; massacre of, 494–501; persecution of, 565–566, 569–570; pressured to convert, 564–565; reactions to Descartes, 525; renouncing faith, 497, 500; repression of, 472–473, 566; rights given in Edict of Nantes, 506, 562–563

protesters, 1220, 1263, 1289–1290; 1968, 1204, 1212; massacre of, 1179, 1186

Protis, 98–100

Provençals, 204–205, 342

Provence, 132, 175, 183, 313, 362, 378, 417–418

Provence, kingdom of, 224–225, 364–365

Prussia, 568, 709, 768, 889. *See also* Franco-Prussian War; French wars with, 857, 941–942; peace with, 880–881

psychiatry, 1170–1175

public health: Pasteur's lack of influence on, 913–914; responses to cholera and, 795, 798–799

public order, 697–699, 707, 759–760

public sphere, development of, 617–619

Pyrenees, Treaty of the, 514–515, 527, 529

Q

Quran, translations of, 282, 284–285, 288–289

R

race, 679–681, 1238; fear of war, 759; hierarchies of, 489–491, 558–560; World Cup victory and, 1262, 1285–1287

racism, 1011; in colonial societies, 678–679, 1055, 1152, 1170–1171, 1175; Du Bois fighting against, 1005, 1010; opposition to, 1289–1290, 1326

radioactivity, discovery of, 952–957

radiocarbon dating, 81

railroads, 712, 889

Rashi (*aka* Rabbi Shlomo Yitzchaki), 266–272

reason, 609–611

OFF THE BEATEN TRACK

ABSOLUTISM AND POWER: 1610, 1659, 1682, 1683, 1686, 1715, 1763.

THE ARAB POLICY (OF FRANCE): 1798, 1863, 1962, 2003, 2015.

BELGIANS AND THE FLEMISH: 511, 1095, 1202, 1214, 1357, 1662, 1789, 1804, 1815, 1832, 1936.

THE CARIBBEAN: 1791, 1961, 1998, 2008.

CATHOLICISM ("ELDEST DAUGHTER OF THE CHURCH"): 177, 397, 511, 800, 910, 1270, 1336, 1420, 1572, 1685, 1858.

CHINA: 1270, 1347, 1380, 1534, 1662, 1683, 1686, 1769, 1795, 1816, 1832, 1871, 1900, 1919, 1965, 1968, 1989.

COLONIES: 52 BCE, 212, 1066, 1095, 1270, 1534, 1763, 1791, 1798, 1852, 1863, 1883, 1891, 1900, 1917, 1940, 1958, 1960, 1961.

COUNTRYSIDES, REGIONS, AND LANDSCAPES: 5800 BCE, 397, 1247, 1683, 1793, 1816, 1965.

CRUSADES: 1095, 1202, 1270, 1456, 1494, 1798, 1863, 2003.

"CULTURAL EXCEPTION": 1287, 1380, 1494, 1539, 1712, 1751, 1769, 1784, 1793, 1795, 1815, 1842, 1875, 1900, 1921, 1946, 1989.

DECLINISM AND SELF-HATRED ("NEVER CALL ME FRANCE AGAIN"): 1137, 1357, 1763, 1940, 1973, 1983.

DEFEAT: 52 BCE, 1357, 1420, 1763, 1815, 1871, 1940, 1958, 1962.

DIVERSITY ("FRANCE IS"): 34,000 BCE, 23,000 BCE, 600 BCE, 52 BCE, 1105, 1446, 1790, 1791, 1923, 1927, 1974, 1998.

DOUCE FRANCE (TEMPERATE CLIMATE): 12,000 BCE, 5800 BCE, 1610, 1793, 1816, 1973.

ENGLAND: 1066, 1137, 1357, 1420, 1662, 1720, 1763, 1769, 1784, 1798, 1816, 1860, 1869, 1913.

EUROPEAN (THE IDEA): 1420, 1795, 1804, 1815, 1848, 1894, 1914, 1920, 1962, 1965, 1992.

FLAIR ("THE FRENCH TOUCH"): 52 BCE, 177, 1066, 1137, 1214, 1610, 1683, 1763, 1825, 1832, 1869, 1962, 1998, 2003.

A FONDNESS FOR OTHERS: 52 BCE, 1270, 1420, 1686, 1715, 1769, 1815, 1825, 1863, 1900, 1948.

FOREIGNERS ("THE") AND XENOPHOBIA: 52 BCE, 1143, 1446, 1484, 1686, 1715, 1720, 1790, 1815, 1848, 1892, 1894, 1900, 1927, 1973, 1974, 2015.

FRANCOPHOBIA ("FRENCH BASHING"): 882, 1282, 1494, 1686, 1763, 1794, 1815, 1871.

LATIN AMERICA: 34,000 BCE, 1270, 1534, 1550, 1610, 1659, 1808, 1852, 1889, 1973.

LIBERTÉ, ÉGALITÉ, FRATERNITÉ: 1789, 1790, 1791, 1793, 1794, 1795, 1848, 1871, 1875, 1900, 1954, 1974.

LUXE, CALME ET VOLUPTÉ: 500 BCE, 1682, 1715, 1815, 1900, 1913, 1921.

MAGHREB AND ALGERIA: 719, 1066, 1270, 1683, 1863, 1958, 1962.

MYTHS, HEROES, AND NATIONAL MYTHOLOGY: 52 BCE, 511, 800, 842–43, 987, 1214, 1270, 1380, 1420, 1515, 1572, 1633, 1789, 1804, 1989, 2003.

"NATIONAL IDENTITY": 52 BCE, 719, 1214, 1270, 1336, 1420, 1515, 1572, 1682, 1789, 1808, 1825, 1914, 1940, 1958, 1992, 1998, 2008.

NEAR EAST: 5800 BCE, 1095, 1270, 1494, 1683, 1712, 1798, 1863, 1962, 2003, 2015.

ORIENTALISM: 1712, 1863, 1962, 2003.

OVERSEAS (OUTRE-MER): 1270, 1534, 1763, 1791, 1852, 1863, 1883, 1891, 1919, 1960, 2008.

PARIS ("CENTER OF THE WORLD"): 511, 1051, 1137, 1215, 1270, 1357, 1380, 1539, 1769, 1789, 1793, 1815, 1848, 1900, 1907, 1989, 2015.

PEOPLES: 52 BCE, 1270, 1420, 1515, 1610, 1682, 1771, 1789, 1815, 1842, 1871, 1900, 1920, 1940, 1953, 1954, 1960, 1968, 1998, 2011, 2015.

POPES AND PAPACY: 800, 1095, 1214, 1215, 1282, 1336, 1804.

PORTUGAL AND BRAZIL: 1214, 1380, 1494, 1683, 1808, 1889, 1974.

PROTESTANTISM: 1536, 1572, 1685.

PROVIDENTIAL MEN (AND WOMEN): 52 BCE, 1420, 1494, 1515, 1610, 1798, 1804, 1848, 1940, 1958, 2011.

"QUAI D'ORSAY" (FRENCH FOREIGN MINISTRY): 1962, 2003.

THE REPUBLIC: 1794, 1795, 1848, 1871, 1889, 1900, 1920, 1989, 2015.

REVOLUTIONS AND UTOPIAS: 1357, 1789, 1832, 1840, 1848, 1871, 1968, 1989, 2011.

RIGHT / LEFT: 1789, 1794, 1840, 1860, 1892, 1894, 1914, 1936, 1953, 1983, 1992, 2011, 2015.

SCIENCE AND THE CULT OF PROGRESS: 1751, 1793, 1875, 1889, 1891, 1903, 1965.

SEA(S): 600 BCE, 1270, 1347, 1662, 1763, 1804, 1869.

SETTLEMENT AND MIGRATIONS: 34,000 BCE, 12,000 BCE, 5800 BCE, 600 BCE, 52 BCE, 212, 719, 882, 1066, 1095, 1247, 1446, 1534, 1763, 1852, 1927, 1974.

SLAVERY: 177, 212, 1446, 1763, 1791, 1848, 1961, 2008.

SPAIN AND SPANISH FRANCE: 719, 1282, 1515, 1534, 1659, 1808, 1936.

SUB-SAHARAN AFRICA AND *FRANÇAFRIQUE*: 34,000 BCE, 5800 BCE, 719, 1270, 1380, 1446, 1659, 1791, 1891, 1919, 1940, 1960, 1961, 1998.

SUBORDINATION AND INSUBORDINATION: 1357, 1789, 1832, 1848, 1871, 1892, 1940, 1968.

SWITZERLAND: 1515, 1536, 1789, 1804, 1848, 1883, 1892, 1900, 1913.

"THESE ELITES WHO GOVERN US": 500 BCE, 48, 719, 1066, 1095, 1215, 1484, 1682, 1789, 1892, 1913, 2011.

UNITED STATES OF AMERICA: 1763, 1789, 1907, 1919, 1936, 1946, 1973, 1984, 2003, 2011.

UNIVERSAL: 212, 910, 1215, 1494, 1751, 1789, 1790, 1794, 1795, 1815, 1848, 1875, 1900, 1920, 1948.

WOMEN: 23,000 BCE, 500 BCE, 177, 882, 1051, 1137, 1420, 1771, 1784, 1903, 1921, 1949.

WORLDLINESS, FRIVOLITIES, AND APPEARANCES: 1550, 1682, 1769, 1804, 1900, 1913, 1921, 2011.

For a full list of contributors, please visit gallicbooks.com